THE INTERNATIONAL MARINE BOOK OF
SAILING

THE INTERNATIONAL MARINE BOOK OF

SAILING

Robby Robinson

INTERNATIONAL MARINE / McGRAW-HILL

Camden, Maine • New York • Chicago • San Francisco • Lisbon • London • Madrid •
Mexico City • Milan • New Delhi • San Juan • Seoul • Singapore • Sydney • Toronto

The McGraw·Hill Companies

1 2 3 4 5 6 7 8 9 10   RRDSHEN   0 9 8

Library of Congress Cataloging-in-Publication Data

Robinson, Robby.
 The international marine book of sailing / William "Robby" Robinson.
     p. cm.
   Includes index.
   ISBN: 978-0-07-053225-0 (hardcover : alk. paper)
   1. Sailing. 2. Seamanship. I. Title.
   GV811.R5825 2008
   797.124—dc22

                    2008002166

ISBN 978-0-07-053225-0
MHID 0-07-053225-7

Questions regarding the content of this book should be addressed to
www.internationalmarine.com

International Marine/McGraw-Hill books are available at special quantity discounts to use as premiums or for use in corporate training programs. For more information please visit the Contact Us pages at www.internationalmarine.com.

Questions regarding the ordering of this book should be addressed to
The McGraw-Hill Companies
Customer Service Department
P.O. Box 547
Blacklick, OH 43004
Retail customers: 1-800-262-4729
Bookstores: 1-800-722-4726

For Carol, the best of shipmates

CONTENTS

Preface

Take a walk down a dock. Maybe you're content just to look, to survey the boats, the gear, the people from a solid grounding. But if you feel the pull, if the challenge of going out on the water quickens with each step, this book was written for you.

Sailing isn't the only way to leave the dock, but to me and to countless others, it's far and away the most rewarding. Start with the obvious—the wind is free—but there's much more to it than that. Using the wind to get where you want to go and do what

you'd like to do is a skill worth learning. Right from the outset, whether trimming a sail or making a tack, you'll feel the satisfaction that comes from making progress, from building mastery. The elements of seafaring are centuries old, yet modern sailors still learn something every time they cast off. Practical, intriguing, involving, enlightening, a sailor's lot is indeed a happy one.

Experience will always remain the best teacher. I began (and ended) this book firm in that belief. Having spent "time in the boat" with hundreds of students, I know that most beginners have problems accessing their own experience. Whether imprisoned by a set of "do this" commands, frightened by imagined perils, or too confused to sort out priorities, they isolate themselves from cause and effect. An instructor's hand on the tiller or the sheet often makes it easy to get past this stage, but explanations and principles rarely help.

That's how we (the publisher and I) came up with the format for this book. The last thing I wanted was to make you think too much. The worst thing I could imagine was a book that stood between the learner and the experience of sailing. Paring it down to essentials, I tried to script a blueprint, a passport onto the water, a gateway to experience. I aimed to put you where you belong at the beginning: at the helm, with the sheet in your hand.

From there the book does its best to mirror the learning process. I concentrate on walking you through added sails, drills, maneuvers, and concepts at a measured pace (aided immensely by the publisher's clear, complete, intelligent diagrams and focused, detailed, and annotated photos). When I introduce a new term, it's defined. Each new subject builds on one you've already mastered.

When I was a lad I crewed aboard the America's Cup 12-meter *Weatherly*. Though a junior champion with a Bermuda Race under my belt, I was still awed. Sailing a 12-meter with skipper Arthur Knapp was as close to the big time as I could imagine. It wasn't the America's Cup, just the Stamford-Vineyard Race, a 200-miler that was the traditional closer for the Long Island Sound summer season, but just being on the boat was great. When I came aboard, one of the first things pointed out to me was a small glass case on the bulkhead to starboard of the companionway. In red letters on the outside I read: "IN CASE OF EMERGENCY BREAK GLASS." Inside was Knapp's classic book *Race Your Boat Right,* a 400-page hardcover bible of advanced sailboat racing wisdom.

Years later, when I cowrote *Sailors' Secrets,* I felt a debt to Knapp. In compiling that volume of tips, suggestions, and favorite solutions my method was, "if it's of use, it's in the book." This book follows the same tradition. I'm not suggesting that you need to know everything in these pages to be a good sailor, but a good sailor likes to know where to look for the essentials.

A world under sail awaits. Happy sailing!

Robby Robinson
Marshfield, Massachusetts

First Sail

Sailing may begin as a sport, but it soon becomes a passion and a way of life. It will pay back everything you put into it with a lifetime of pleasure. There's a lot to learn, but that's part of its fascination—sailors can keep learning all their lives and still not know it all. On the other hand, you can learn enough to sail a boat in a single afternoon—less time than it might take to learn how to hit a golf ball or cast a fly. No other pursuit offers such a deeply satisfying combination of short-term accomplishment and long-term discovery.

Still, when you walk down the dock for the first time, you enter a world that can seem foreign and confusing. Skills, terms, traditions, gear—how do you start?

Begin at the beginning. Go sailing. Experience is the best teacher, and it makes the best sailors. It sounds offhand to say "Learn to sail by sailing," but that's how to get started. Time under sail will show you what it is you need to know.

But experience without interpretation can be baffling and frustrating. You can eventually learn to speak Russian by walking the streets of Moscow, but without an interpreter it won't be easy, and you'll make a lot of mistakes along the way. This book is your interpreter.

Take sailing terms, for instance. In the beginning, the words sailors use may sound foreign and arcane. Why does "right" need to be "starboard" and "back" become "stern?" Cadets aboard the U.S. Coast Guard barque *Eagle* must learn the names of 150 different lines (a line being a rope in use aboard a boat) and where each of them belays, or is made fast (see page 30), in order to be promoted. Terms are valuable—they enable precise and concise communication between crew and captain—but going sailing puts them in their place. They are tools to be picked up from this book and mastered as you progress, not unyielding masters to serve as a barrier to progress.

The essence of sailing is moving with the wind over the water. Sitting on the dock, you might notice pronounced changes in the wind, but you won't get a true feel for what the wind's up to until you go sailing. Once you cast off you'll find that the wind is never constant for long. You'll *feel* your boat respond to each puff or lull—faster, slower, flatter, more deeply heeled (tipped). The boat seems alive, and through the wheel or tiller in your hand, you'll feel and respond to its hum, vibration, and pulse. You'll admire the purposeful beauty of its silent sails, and you'll begin to contemplate their subtle alchemy with rudder and keel or centerboard, the fundamental magic through which a boat transforms moving air into forward motion.

That's what you should study—your boat's resonance with the breeze, the life that comes to it from the wind. Go sailing!

May this book help you along that challenging, rewarding, and enriching way.

A Boat to Learn In

You can learn to sail in virtually any boat. Choose one that's sturdy, stable, and simple if you can, but almost any boat that's available and functional will do.

Boats that are responsive—answering each change in wind, helm, or sail trim with a clear and proportional change in performance—are the best to learn on. A sluggish boat is hard to read. If there is a lag time in her reactions to the wind, she can easily hide many of the things you need to know. If she is slow to **answer the helm**, or respond, she can be misleading (not to mention boring) to sail. In order to learn, you need to be able to make sense of your experience under sail, but that's hard to do if it's difficult to sense what is happening in the first place.

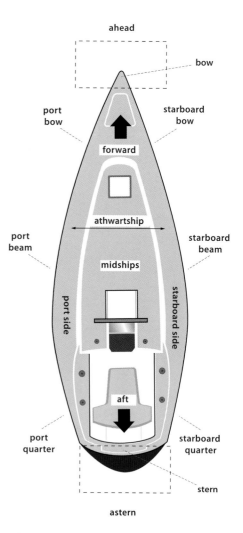

Directions and locations on a sailboat. The front and back ends are the bow and stern, respectively.

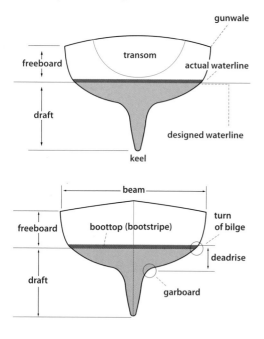

A sailboat's hull as seen from astern and ahead. Fixed keels like this one prevail on boats over 25 feet long, but many smaller boats substitute a retractable centerboard or daggerboard (see illustration on page 5) and thus have two drafts—one with the board down and one with the board up. With its board up a boat is easy to trailer, to sail in shallow water, or to land on a beach.

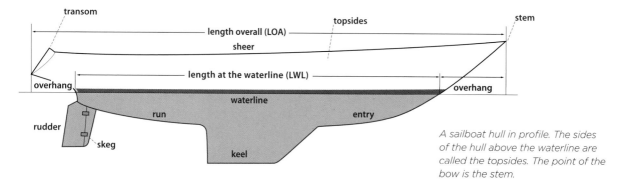

A sailboat hull in profile. The sides of the hull above the waterline are called the topsides. The point of the bow is the stem.

Small boats tend to be more responsive than large ones, light boats more responsive than heavy, and slender boats more responsive than beamy. Boats with **centerboards** or **daggerboards**—retractable fins that you lower into the water beneath the hull in order to help convert the sideways push of wind on sails into the forward motion of boat through water—tend to be more responsive than boats with **keels**, which are fixed fins that do the same thing. (Centerboards pivot around a pin when retracted, whereas daggerboards are pulled straight up.) These general guidelines are marked by plenty of exceptions.

Although a responsive boat will speed your learning and build your skills more quickly, a boat that's *too* responsive can be distracting, confusing, or even too much to handle, throwing changes at

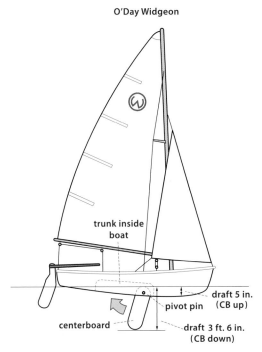

O'Day Widgeon

trunk inside boat

draft 5 in. (CB up)
pivot pin
centerboard
draft 3 ft. 6 in. (CB down)

The O'Day Widgeon, 12 feet 4 inches long, is designed for a two-person crew but is easy to solo as well. The draft is just 5 inches with the centerboard up. Light (just 340 pounds), responsive, but stable, it's great for teaching young sailors but can also be enjoyed by reasonably nimble adults. It can even fly a small spinnaker (see Chapter 4)—and it makes a lot of sense to learn spinnaker handling on a small boat like this before wrestling with the behemoth spinnaker of a 35-footer.

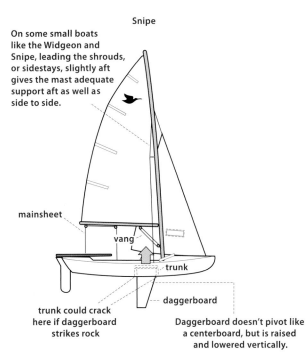

Snipe

On some small boats like the Widgeon and Snipe, leading the shrouds, or sidestays, slightly aft gives the mast adequate support aft as well as side to side.

mainsheet
vang
trunk
trunk could crack here if daggerboard strikes rock
daggerboard
Daggerboard doesn't pivot like a centerboard, but is raised and lowered vertically.

The 15-foot, 6-inch Snipe was designed for plywood construction in 1931, during the Great Depression. Today the boats are built of fiberglass but retain the chine (the near-right angle between the hull sides and bottom) that plywood construction required. The flat bottom enables the boat to plane in the right conditions. Draft with the daggerboard up is 6 inches, and the boat weighs 400 pounds. This is one of the world's most popular and enduring one-designs.

Optimist

With more than 150,000 of these square-bowed, square-sided little daggerboard dinghies sailing worldwide, the Optimist—"Opti" for short—may just be the most popular sail trainer ever designed. Young sailors start in Optis at age 6, then graduate to something more exciting between ages 12 and 14. The **cat-rigged** (single-sailed) 7-foot, 9-inch boat weighs just 77 pounds. The mast is 7 feet 5 inches tall—easily handled by a young sailor—while a **sprit** supports the head of the mainsail above the masttop. The boat is equipped by its builder, Vanguard Sailboats, with three nylon flotation bags that will keep it afloat if it capsizes or **swamps** (fills with water). The Optimist is sanctioned for solo and two-person worldwide competition by the International Sailing Federation (ISAF), but Optis are too small for most adults.

The simple, inexpensive Optimist pram is billed by its class association as the boat the youth of the world learn to sail in, and they may be right.

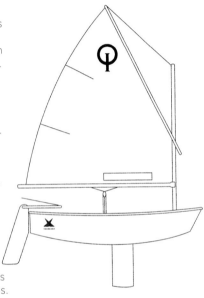

Other Junior Trainers

These include the Y-Flyer, the Sabot, and many others with good reputations as starter boats. Some are too small for most adults, but by no means all. Then there are regional favorites like the Beetle Cat. This cat-rigged 12-foot centerboarder has been hand-built of wood (cedar planking on oak frames) in Wareham, Massachusetts, for more than 75 years. It is heavier (450 pounds) and pricier than a fiberglass sailing dinghy of similar size, but Beetle Cat owners never seem to tire of their boats.

The Beetle Cat is handsome, salty, and roomy. Locally built favorites like this are sailed in all parts of the world.

Sunfish

Since its introduction in 1962, the Sunfish has ushered thousands of new sailors into the sport. Easy, affordable, and fun, this 14-foot "board boat" with its small footwell does everything a real sailboat does, and does it well. Sailing this ISAF-sanctioned boat is a wet experience, so wear a bathing suit. You will find the inevitable capsizing more refreshing than terrifying. The boat is so easy to right, "even a child can do it." Rivaling the Optimist as the most popular sailboat on the planet, the Sunfish is one of the best to start in. Two kids or one adult can fit in one comfortably, though you might get tired of ducking the boom each time you tack. A new one costs about $2,700.

Like the Snipe, the 120-pound fiber-glass Sunfish retains the hard chines of its plywood predecessors. These simple boats provide as much fun per pound as any.

Laser

This 13-foot, 10-inch Olympic-class boat was introduced in 1970. Like a Sunfish, a Laser has a dagger-board and is ideal for sailing off the beach. Both boats provide a wet, fun ride, but a Laser is faster than a Sunfish, fast enough to get up on the surface of the water and **plane** over it rather than plowing through it. Though simple in concept, the boat is demanding to sail. In a gust of wind you must hook your feet under the **hiking straps** in the cockpit and **hike out** (lean out over the water) to counter the boat's heeling. When the puff passes, however, you'll need to get back inboard quickly or the

Like the Opti and Sunfish, the 130-pound Laser is cat-rigged (with no jib) and has no stays (wires that help support the mast). This boat is exhilarating when it takes off on a screaming plane.

boat might capsize **to windward** (toward the wind). Planing in a Laser is an exhilarating experience for adults as well as kids. The boat is raced solo but can be sailed by two. More than 180,000 have been built, and new ones cost about $4,800.

Escape

Modern, lightweight, and tough, the Escape 11.5 ($2,200) is easy to rig and handle yet lively enough to exhilarate and extend you. The Escape can be sailed solo or with crew. Her sail rolls around the mast, which makes it easy to lessen sail area if the wind pipes up. Cat-rigged boats like the Escape, Sunfish, Optimist, and a raft of others allow you to concentrate on how a sail works. Adding a jib adds horsepower but divides your attention.

Soling

Solings are an Olympic racing class, but the 27-foot sloops are also very popular with sailing schools. With a big sail plan and optimized lines, they are lively. With a heavy keel, they are also pleasingly stable. They provide good features of both big boats and small—students can "feel" what's happening, yet they are not perched constantly on the distracting edge of capsize in a fresh breeze. With a jib to tend, there are controls enough to involve three students. Many instructors find the boat's long afterdeck an ideal out-of-the-way perch to teach from.

Capri 14.2

Versatility, durability, and good sailing manners make this centerboarder a good trainer. She is **sloop-rigged** (with a jib as well as a mainsail) but has a forward position for the mast so she can be sailed under just her mainsail and remain well balanced. She accommodates up to four sailors without losing her zip. She is affordable ($3,275). Responsive without being finicky, and simple to sail without being rudimentary, this is a fine all-around boat.

The Capri 14.2

Sonar

This 23-foot ISAF-sanctioned keelboat provides lively racing and pleasurable daysailing. Fast and nimble, the boat has an uncomplicated rig—good for learners—and an $11\frac{1}{2}$-foot cockpit with room for eight people. New Sonars cost $27,000, but they can be purchased used for as little as $5,000.

The 23-foot Sonar was designed by Bruce Kirby, designer of the Laser, in 1980 and has been providing spirited racing and fast, comfortable daysailing worldwide ever since.

the learner faster than he or she can handle them. Just as neither a Mack truck nor a Corvette seems the ideal vehicle for learning to drive, neither a big, ponderous sailboat nor a fidgety rocket ship will make as satisfactory a starter boat as a wholesome, reasonably sprightly boat.

Comfort, too, is important. Few small sailboats are couch potato comfy, but you'll learn best when you don't have to dodge waves or duck the boom. Big boats, while not usually as responsive as small ones, can provide more comfort.

In the wet world of small boats you must often counterbalance the tipping effect of the wind with your own weight. Big boats with weighted keels free you from that responsibility so that you can concentrate on other things. Small centerboard boats will also **capsize**, or tip over, more readily than keelboats. This isn't always a bad thing. If you're young—or young at heart—capsizing a Sunfish on a summer's day can be exhilarating, and learning how to right and bail out a capsized boat can be useful, as can the knowledge you gain of how a boat behaves when you're pushing it too hard. But most adults, given a choice, would rather not capsize and might therefore prefer to learn in a keelboat.

If you understand why some boats make better teaching platforms than others, it may help you get the most from whatever boat you learn in. Sailing is partly conceptual, partly intuitive. You need

Colgate 26

This 25-foot, 8-inch keelboat is big enough to seat several adults comfortably and to prepare a learner for handling larger boats, yet small and responsive enough to make a great learning platform. Its small cabin has sitting headroom and weekend cruising accommodations. It is well mannered and includes enough sail controls for high-performance sailing without being overly complicated. An outboard motor on a stern bracket gets the boat back to the dock when the wind dies. With positive foam flotation, the boat is virtually unsinkable. At 2,600 pounds it is less easily trailered than the other boats on these pages, but with a maximum **beam** (width) of 8 feet 6 inches, it is nevertheless legal for highway towing. Conceived by Steve Colgate of the Colgate Offshore Sailing School after 40 years of teaching sailing, the Colgate 26 is a fine vessel especially for adults who are uncomfortable on a smaller boat. It's also more expensive than the other boats here—as much as $25,000 used.

Exciting sailing on a Colgate 26 in use at Steve and Doris Colgate's Offshore Sailing School. The fin keel and spade rudder are clearly visible.

J/22

Descended from the popular J/24, this "little sister" keelboat provides an equally impressive sailing performance. Her fine stability and extra-large cockpit make her a good boat for full-sized people to learn in. Not only do students have room to sail without falling over one another, but they can sit comfortably to trim and steer. That helps concentration. A full-blown international racing class, the J/22 lets learners progress from main-alone starter sessions to advanced spinnaker work.

to master concepts, but it's also important to interpret sensations and respond to physical changes. Small, responsive boats may dampen your face and shoes, but they activate the seat of your pants. They are ideal for developing a "feel" for sailing.

Big, stiff boats may have faint pulses, but they afford time and opportunity to think. The best boats to learn in are responsive enough to offer a good, immediate feel for what's happening and well-mannered enough to keep learning focused and fun.

Other Good Boats to Learn In

The variety of sailing dinghies and small keelboats for the new sailor to choose from is little short of amazing. There isn't room here to offer more than a small sampling, but the accompanying photos show a few more.

Designed in 1962, the Ensign features a traditional full keel with attached rudder (see Chapter 7) and weighs 3,000 pounds. It is thus not as fast as the Sonar, which—though 6 inches longer—has a fin keel and separated spade rudder and weighs 900 pounds less. Still, the boat makes a lively daysailer with a huge cockpit that can fit six comfortably, and it is still actively raced (usually with a crew of three, although four are shown here) in the Northeastern U.S.

Or how about learning on a multihull? This Hobie Wave is rotomolded of polyethylene, making it ideal for beaching and rough use (though heavy at 245 pounds). The twin hulls are molded into shallow keels, eliminating the need for daggerboards, and the masthead float prevents the boat from turning turtle should it capsize. It's easy to singlehand, or you can carry six adults.

The 420 is a two-person centerboarder that young sailors race worldwide.

If you're not bent on one-design racing, you can find other keelboats in the size range of the J/24 that perform almost as well, cost less to purchase and maintain, and offer more comfortable weekend cruising accommodations. These include the Tanzer 22 and the C&C 24, among others. The owner of this Tanzer 22 paid just $2,500 for it. Boats like this are ideal for adult learners: comfortable, stable, forgiving, easy to singlehand, and inexpensive on the used-boat market.

The J/24 has earned a reputation as the world's most popular one-design keelboat. Easy to handle and forgiving over a wide range of wind speeds, the boat provides spirited racing, fun daysailing, and even cramped weekend cruising (provided you're content not being able to sit up straight in the cabin).

Getting Aboard

Boarding a sailboat is usually straightforward, but sometimes it can be tricky. Sooner or later, in fact, it may offer an embarrassing lesson on stability or an unplanned swim. Getting aboard may not be the biggest problem in sailing, but it's undeniably the first.

Big boats and little boats demand different approaches. With small boats (say, under 20 feet long), balance is key. When you step aboard, the boat will "give" underfoot, and light boats with no keel underneath them will give a lot. Keelboats give less. Balance yourself and keep low. Be alert to the motions of the boat and the best places to sit down. If you're as careful to keep your weight low and centered as a canoeist or kayaker has to be, you'll have no problem. No sudden lurches, no heavy steps! It's tempting to grab the mast or **stays** (the wires that support the mast) to steady yourself, but that will tip most small boats. The higher up you grab, the more you unbalance the boat. Step into the middle of a small boat, not on its rail or the edge of its deck.

Big boats are more stable and less tippy, but they can present other obstacles to the would-be boarder. High sides are one, and

At anchor with the swim ladder down, a transom step really comes into its own. On this boat the helm seat folds down to give access between cockpit and transom.

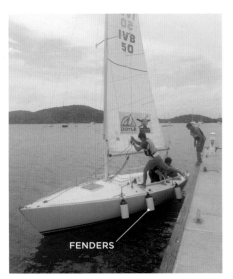

The crew should fend off whenever two boats come alongside. Note that the fenders on the launch on the right are hanging too low to cushion it effectively from the sailboat on the left.

FENDERS

BIMINI

LIFELINE GATE

TRANSOM STEP

SWIM LADDER

When you have a shroud to grab, a low lifeline to clear, a stable keelboat deck to land on, and the chance to step down instead of climbing up, boarding a boat can be a casual affair. This boat is an IC-24, a J/24 modified for Caribbean use with low-hung lifelines, a huge cockpit, and a much-reduced cabin.

Boarding a cruising sailboat with standard thigh-high lifelines can present a gymnastic challenge, especially when you're trying to climb over that high side from a low-lying dinghy. The gate in the lifeline helps, as does the fact that the deck you're landing on will hardly notice your weight. Like many modern cruising designs, this Oceanis 323 has a transom step aft, making the stern an easier place to board when it's accessible. A canvas bimini to shade the cockpit is almost universal on cruising boats in tropical and subtropical climates.

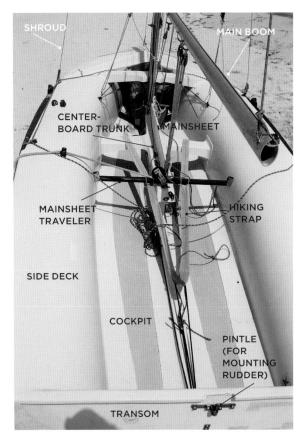

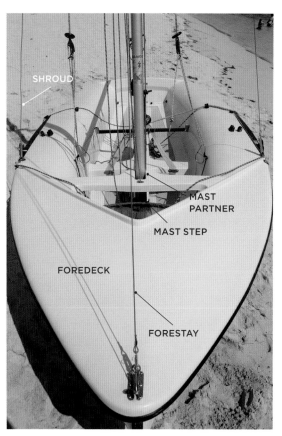

A sailing dinghy like this 420 is more sensitive than a keelboat to crew weight distribution, but if you keep your weight low on boarding, you'll have no trouble. The 420 contains a lot of positive buoyancy in its side decks (which the manufacturer, Vanguard, calls seat tanks), and this makes the boat virtually unsinkable. These two views give a good sense for what you find in the cockpit of a sailing dinghy.

LANGUAGE OF THE SEA
LEE

From the Old English hleo—meaning "shelter" or "warmth"—lee has long meant "a place sheltered from the wind." The late Alf Loomis, revered *Yachting* magazine writer, called his column "Under the Lee of the Longboat," referring to that pocket of shelter to leeward of the dinghy where wind is deflected and spray turned away. A lee is a good thing indeed.

"Windward" and "leeward" are opposite directions. The windward side of an island or boat is the side facing the wind, while the leeward side is the side away from it. Windward and leeward are mortar and brick, yin and yang. Because everything in sailing has to do with the wind, windward and leeward have a lot to do with everything.

On the windward side of an island you'll find a rough coast beaten straight; on the leeward side there are coves and bays. On the lee side of the pier you'll hang free; on the windward side you'll beat against the dock. On the windward side of a boat in a "rail-down breeze" you'll feel the full force of the wind and maybe the spray. On the leeward side—the low side of the heeling boat—you'll be sheltered from the wind and spray (but your weight may be needed to windward to counter the heeling forces). To windward of the longboat, you're exposed and damp. Under the lee, you're cozy.

On the other hand, when your boat is to windward of the nearest land, the shore to leeward of you is a lee shore, and in heavy weather a lee shore is a dangerous place. If your boat were to be tossed on a lee shore by wind and waves, it could be pounded to pieces by the elements.

Stability at Rest

Big boats tend to weigh more than little boats, and weight adds to stability at rest. That's why the littlest boats are the tippiest. But it's weight in the keel that makes the most difference to stability. Sailboat keels exist both to enhance stability and to resist leeway, and the former purpose is the reason why the bottom of a keel is **ballasted**, or weighted, with iron or lead. Boats that don't have fixed keels resist **leeway**—being pushed sideways instead of forward by the wind—by means of a movable foil, usually a centerboard or daggerboard. These foils, however, aren't ballasted and therefore don't enhance stability. That's why a centerboarder tips more when you step aboard, while a keelboat is more docile. Even if both boats are about the same size and shape, the weight hanging underneath the keelboat will make it harder to tip. Contrary to widely held belief, lowering a centerboard does little or nothing to increase a boat's stability. Add **inside ballast** (weight in the **bilge**, or lower portion of the hull's interior) to a centerboarder, however, and you make her stiffer.

In general, weight down low adds stability. Weight up high takes it away. Stability under sail involves many of these same elements.

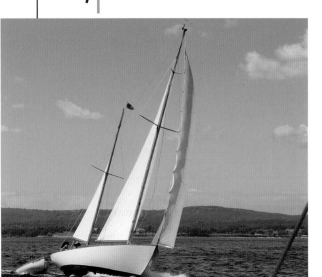

Leeway affects all boats but is most noticeable on a centerboard or dagger-board boat when the board is not all the way down.

Both the centerboard and the rudder of this 420, which are clearly visible beneath the water, help prevent leeway, but they don't add stability. Instead, stability has to come from the hull's width and fairly flat bottom. This solo sailor counterbalances heeling by hooking his feet under the hiking straps and leaning out to windward.

Although we can't see the keel of this traditional-looking yawl, it is probably a full keel with attached rudder (see Chapter 7). A keel not only prevents excessive leeway but limits heeling. A little more jib halyard tension would remove the scalloping in the jib's leading edge, or luff.

Form Stability

In order to float, a boat needs to displace a volume of water equal in weight to its own weight. The boat makes a hole in the water. When the water displaced from that hole weighs as much as the boat does, an equilibrium is reached, and the boat floats. It is a simple yet wondrous phenomenon, like so much to do with boats. The same principle that floats a glass bottle filled with air will float a huge aircraft carrier built of steel and bearing many planes and the equivalent of a city.

But floating objects have varying degrees of stability (resistance to sideways tipping), depending in part on their shape. A bottle, for instance, is stable floating neck-up, but turn it neck-down and it becomes unstable and exhibits a tendency to flip over.

When the hull of a boat presses into the water, the buoyant force of the water pushes back. That is the source of **form stability**. A wide-beamed boat will be more stable than a narrow boat because beam provides increased leverage for the buoyant forces. A flat-bottomed boat is more stable at rest than a round-bottomed hull, because almost all of the buoyant force is pushing up. The shape of the hull "organizes" and directs the buoyant forces. The more they are arrayed to buoy up the hull, the more the hull resists tipping.

That is why a centerboard sailboat is likely to be beamier than a keelboat of the same length. Lacking the stability provided by keel ballast, the centerboarder needs more form stability.

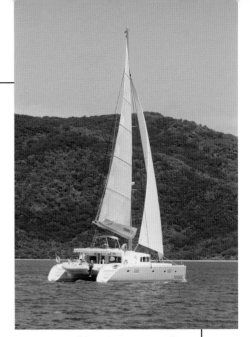

Even a small beach catamaran like the one pictured on page 9 derives high stability from the width between its two hulls, but a big cruising catamaran like this one is the ultimate in form stability. A dinghy or keelboat would be heeling in this breeze, but not this boat. Note how the dinghy is out of the water on davits for offshore sailing.

lifelines (the wire "railings" along the deck edge) are another. Steps, ladders, or gates are sometimes available but don't always simplify matters. Throw away any illusions of a graceful arrival and just climb aboard.

When boarding from a rowboat or launch, be careful not to pinch your fingers, nick the yacht, or gouge the dinghy or launch. (Whenever two boats come together it's normal to fend off—hold them apart by hand.) Often the boat you're boarding provides a bit of a lee—protection from wind and waves—along one side. That's the best side to approach, all other things being equal. Boarding over the transom, or back of the boat, is sometimes encouraged by transom steps but makes for a difficult piece of boathandling in your dinghy. Coming alongside is more seamanlike.

Don't underestimate people's pride in their boats. "Permission to come aboard?" is a good formality to observe. Black-soled shoes that leave marks on decks are rarely welcome. Taking off your shoes

LANGUAGE OF THE SEA
DINGHY

A dinghy is a little boat, usually 8 to 12 feet long, that shuttles crew, passengers, and supplies between a sailboat or powerboat and the shore. It might be propelled by oars, in which case it is also called a rowboat or pulling boat. It might be propelled by a small outboard motor, in which case it might be an inflatable rubber boat rather than the more traditional wood or fiberglass construction. In either case the dinghy is also called a tender. When the boat it tends puts to sea, the humble dinghy is left on the mooring, towed behind, or hoisted on deck.

When you sail a small boat from a dock or beach, you won't need a dinghy to get to it. If you're sailing an Optimist, Laser, or other small open boat with a centerboard or daggerboard, however, the boat itself is referred to as a sailing dinghy. When preparing a sailing dinghy to sail away from a dock or mooring, the first thing to do is to lower the centerboard or daggerboard. Only then are you ready to rig and hoist the sails. When you're sailing off a beach, you may need to raise either the mainsail or jib first, wade the boat into water deep enough to allow you to lower the centerboard or daggerboard partway, then heave yourself aboard and sail into deeper water from there. Beach boats should have kick-up rudders, in which the lower half of the blade pivots around a pin to rotate out of harm's way when it contacts the shore.

A rigid dinghy like this fiberglass one (left) rows well, whereas an inflatable dinghy (right) rows poorly but has great carrying capacity and is fast and maneuverable with a small outboard.

A lovely wooden sailboat with dinghy in tow. When venturing offshore it is better to carry the dinghy on deck.

to assure that you track no grit or sand aboard is polite, even if not always expected. Pay attention to what you grab. A radio aerial may look handy, but it could prove expensive. Lines aren't usually good handholds because you don't know what they're attached to.

Boarding a boat, like sailing itself, is about progress, not perfection. Welcome aboard.

Rigging the Boat

Rigging an unfamiliar boat can be confusing even to an experienced sailor, because there is a variety of hardware, systems, and devices for **bending on** (attaching) sails. When you are new, you are constantly confronted with questions: "How does that work?" "What is that?" "Did I do that right?"

Don't worry about mastering every detail about rigging. You'll develop a big picture and begin to know what you need to know before long. Some boats sit at the dock or on a mooring with their mainsails stowed along the boom, and possibly with their jibs rolled up on furlers. They're already "rigged." Others, though, need their sails attached every time they go out.

Rigging the Mainsail

It's almost always best to hoist the mainsail first. If the mainsail is not **furled** (gathered in a roll) or **flaked** (gathered in stacked folds) on the boom, take it out of its bag. Unless your boat has a "character" rig from a bygone era, its mainsail, like its jib, is triangular. All three corners have reinforced holes, called **grommets**, sewn into them. Identify the **head**, or top corner. If there

is nothing written on the sail, the head of the mainsail will almost always have a stiff board in it. The **tack**, or forward lower corner, is where the bottom of the sail is "nailed" to the boat. That's where sailmakers usually put their logos. The bottom corners of a square sail on the sailing ships of yore were called clews, and to this day the after lower corner of a triangular sail is also its **clew**. These names—head, tack, and clew—apply to virtually every sail.

The edge of a sail between the head and tack is known as the **luff**, and the edge between the tack and the clew is the **foot**. Most mainsails attach to the mast along the full length of the luff, and to the boom along the full length of the foot. One way to achieve this is with sliding cars that are sewn at intervals into the sail edges and run along mast and boom tracks. Another is via **boltropes** sewn along the sail's luff and foot, which fit into corresponding grooves in mast and boom. In lieu of a continuous boltrope, still other sails have cylindrically shaped plastic or

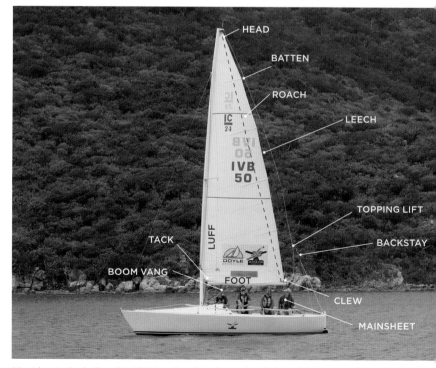

Most boats, including this IC-24, sail well under mainsail alone. The extra sail area behind the straight dashed line from the clew to the head is called the roach, and it's supported by wood or fiberglass battens that are inserted into pockets in the leech.

① MAST STEP

② GOOSENECK PIN
BOOM

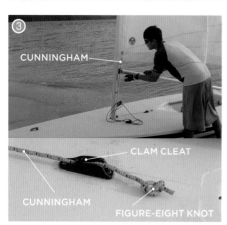

③ CUNNINGHAM
CLAM CLEAT
CUNNINGHAM
FIGURE-EIGHT KNOT

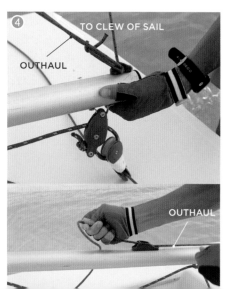

④ TO CLEW OF SAIL
OUTHAUL
OUTHAUL

⑤ CLEW TIE-DOWN
SQUARE KNOT

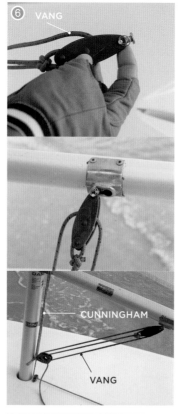

⑥ VANG
CUNNINGHAM
VANG

⑦ MAINSHEET
STOPPER KNOT
TRAVELER

Rigging the sail on a Laser *is about as quick and easy as it gets. Once you've done it a couple of times, it will take you no more than 5 minutes.* **1.** *A sleeve in the luff of the sail slides over the mast, and it is common practice to roll the sail around the mast for storage. If this is the case, begin by stepping the mast in the boat.* **2.** *Slide the boom onto the gooseneck pin.* **3.** *Unroll the sail (this is easier if the boat is pointing into the wind), slip the battens into their pockets, and reeve the cunningham through the deck fairlead or turning block to the clam cleat as shown, finishing with a figure-eight knot (see page 168) or a loop with a bowline (see page 167).* **4.** *Tie the outhaul to the boom-end fairlead with a bowline, then lead it through the clew of the sail, back through the fairlead, and forward along the boom to the designated clam cleat, finishing with a figure-eight or a bowline loop.* **5.** *Wrap the clew tie-down line once or twice around the boom and finish with a square knot (see page 113). This line should be underneath the outhaul and not so tight as to prevent the clew from sliding along the boom.* **6.** *Insert the pin on the upper vang block into the keyhole slot on the boom fitting.* **7.** *One end of the mainsheet is retained in the becket of the boom-end block with a stopper knot (such as a figure-eight, page 168). Reeve the other end through the traveler block, back through the boom-end block, forward through the boom bail and the forward boom block, then down through the ratchet block on deck. (You should hear the ratchet clicking when you haul in the sheet. If you don't, you've gone through the ratchet block the wrong way.)* **8.** *When you're ready to install the rudder, you will pass the tiller underneath the traveler but over the traveler bridle as shown.*

⑧ BAIL
RATCHET BLOCK
TILLER EXTENSION
TRAVELER BRIDLE
TILLER
TRAVELER

Lazyjacks

Lines strung between mast and boom to control a sail as it is lowered are known as **lazyjacks**. Not only are they handy, but they are also evidence that at some ancient time, nautical terms made sense: "Lazy," to sailors even today, means "in place but not in action." Thus, a line run through the proper blocks but without load on it is known as a "lazy guy." "Jack" has a number of meanings, but the one that fits best is "any device or contrivance that replaces human labor." *The American Heritage Dictionary* uses "bootjack" as an example. Thus, this system of lines, a contrivance just waiting there to help control the main when lowered, is aptly named. Or you could say, "Any man jack who needs such help is lazy."

① MAST · GOOSENECK · BOOM

② BATTEN

③

④ CLEW GROMMET · FOOTBOLT ROPE · CLEW SLUG

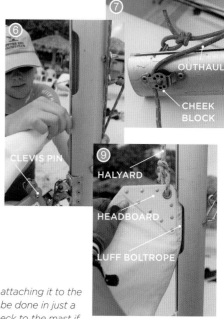

⑤

⑥ CLEVIS PIN

⑦ OUTHAUL · CHEEK BLOCK

⑧ CLAM CLEAT · OUTHAUL

⑨ HALYARD · HEADBOARD · LUFF BOLTROPE

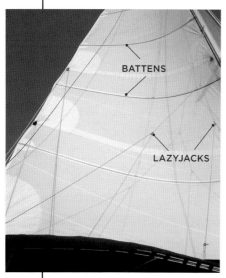

BATTENS

LAZYJACKS

This Lagoon 38 catamaran is rigged with windward and leeward lazyjacks and a fully battened mainsail. When lowered, the mainsail is guided by the lazyjacks into the integral sail cover—sometimes called a lazybag—for stowing. Just zip the bag closed and you're done. Hoisting the sail can be a bit more difficult. The helmsman must hold the boat directly into the wind, and the crew, while hoisting, have to be careful that the batten ends don't snag the lazyjacks.

Rigging the mainsail on a 420 *requires attaching it to the mast as well as the boom, but still it can be done in just a few minutes.* **1.** *Attach the boom gooseneck to the mast if it is not already in place, and make sure the mainsheet and boom vang are rigged.* **2.** *Unroll the mainsail and install the upper batten, thin end first (the other battens are shorter and should already be installed) . . .* **3.** *then secure it with the Velcro flap.* **4.** *Feed the mainsail's clew slug and foot boltrope into the opening at the forward end of the groove on the top face of boom.* **5.** *Pull the foot of the mainsail aft along the boom.* **6.** *Secure the tack of the sail either by inserting the boom fitting's clevis pin through the tack grommet or, as here, by sliding a slug at the foot of the luff into the mast groove.* **7.** *Returning to the clew, rig the outhaul through the clew grommet and the block at the end of the boom . . .* **8.** *then tension the outhaul and cleat it in the clam cleat on the boom.* **9.** *Tie the main halyard to the headboard with a bowline (page 167), then feed the first few inches of the luff boltrope into the mast groove. Stop there unless you're ready to hoist sail and get underway immediately.*

metal slugs sewn at intervals into the luff and foot.

Regardless of which arrangement your mainsail employs, start with its clew and run the sail aft along the boom, attaching it as you go. When you've attached the foot of the main to the boom, fix the tack in place with the fitting provided. Then go back to the clew, draw it aft until it's taut, and fasten it. On some boats you do this by inserting the clew into a movable car; on others, you use a short length of line, called an **outhaul**, that is tied to the clew. The outhaul may or may not run through a **block**, or pulley, be-

LUFF
BOLTROPE

fore being **made off** or **belayed** (tied) to a **cleat** that is mounted for this purpose on the boom. Puffy, lazy wrinkles along the foot of a mainsail mean it's too loose. Knife-edge creases mean it's stretched too tight.

Does the sail have **battens**—strips of wood or fiberglass to keep its aft edge, or **leech**, from fluttering? If so, match each batten with a pocket of corresponding length and insert them.

If the breeze is fresh, the sail may thrash around at this point. To tame it, you can roll up the sail temporarily along the boom and tie it there. To ready the sail for hoisting, fit the luff cars over the mast track or the boltrope or slugs into the mast groove, starting at the head of the sail and working down. As you go, check that all slides are on straight. It's ridiculously easy to put a slide on backward. On some boats it's best to attach the **halyard** only when you're ready to hoist. Otherwise the sail may "hoist itself" in the breeze.

Your mainsail's rigging may very well include a **boom vang**, which flattens the sail by applying downward pull on the boom, and a **cunningham**, which stretches the luff of the sail. If you encounter these, rig

A keelboat mainsail *is usually furled (or flaked) and covered on the boom when not in use, as on this IC-24. Preparing it for sailing is a quick job.* **1.** *Remove the sail cover.* **2.** *Remove the gaskets (also known as sail ties or sail stops) that secure the flaked sail on the boom.* **3.** *Uncleat the main halyard and attach its shackle to the head of the sail.* **4.** *Feed the luff boltrope into the mast groove, remove the slack from the halyard, and the sail is ready to hoist.*

Battens

Originally a batten was any thin strip of wood. Old-time sailors "battened down" for bad weather by covering hatches and ports with canvas tarpaulins nailed down with battens. Sailmakers use **battens** (slats of wood or fiberglass) along the free-flying leech of a sail to dampen flutter there and to support the edge. On most mainsails the leech describes a convex curve when viewed in profile. That extra sail area outside the imaginary straight line drawn from head to clew, called the **roach**, makes the sail more powerful, but it must be stiffened with battens to be effective. Modern battens are tapered—thick end outermost—to do these jobs better.

Some boats have full-length battens running from the luff to the leech of the mainsail. These decrease flogging and help a sail maintain a uniform shape, and they are also popular because they stack when the sail is lowered to simplify furling, especially when used with lazyjacks. Full-length battens are rare on small boats, however.

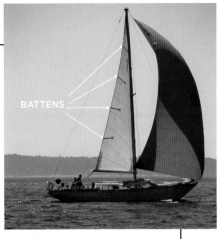

Partial battens in the mainsail of a lovely, traditional-looking sloop.

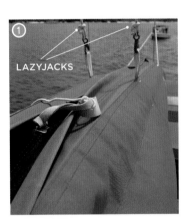

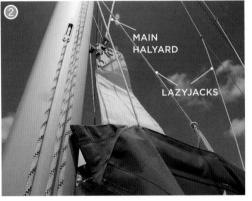

On an Oceanis 323 rigged for charter cruising, *preparing the mainsail for hoisting is the soul of simplicity. **1.** Unzip the sail cover, which is integral with the lazyjacks and remains on the boom. **2.** Attach the main halyard. The luff of the sail is already attached to the mast via slugs that ride in the mast groove, so . . . **3.** the sail is ready to hoist.*

Without much wind pressure on this mainsail, the inner ends of its full battens are curving to windward rather than leeward. If the boat heads up or the wind picks up, the battens will assume their normal shape.

them as described and then forget them for now. We'll talk about their use in Chapters 2 and 4, but in the meantime you can sail perfectly well without adjusting them at all.

The accompanying photos show the steps for rigging the mainsail on two sailing dinghies, a small keelboat, and a cruising sailboat. Together these examples cover most of the broad variations you might encounter on sailboats. Other boats may differ in details, but if you can rig these boats you can rig any boat.

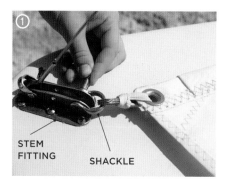

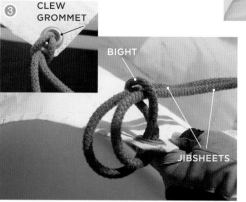

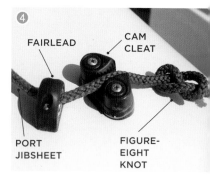

HEAD

LUFF

LEECH

TACK

FOOT

CLEW

DOYLE

An IC-24 under mainsail and jib.

STEM FITTING

SHACKLE

CLEW GROMMET

BIGHT

JIBSHEETS

FAIRLEAD

CAM CLEAT

PORT JIBSHEET

FIGURE-EIGHT KNOT

Rigging the jib on a 420. 1. *Attach the tack to the stem fitting with the shackle or clevis pin provided. (Unlike many boats, the luff of the jib does not attach to the forestay on this boat.)* **2.** *Shackle the jib halyard to the head of the sail.* **3.** *An easy way to rig the jibsheets is to double your jibsheet line, poke the resultant bight through the clew grommet, then lead the two tails (each of which becomes a jibsheet) through the bight.* **4.** *Lead each jibsheet through its fairlead and cam cleat, then tie a figure-eight or other stopper knot in the end. Now the jib is ready to be hoisted.*

Rigging the Jib

Attach a jib first at the tack. That keeps the sail from sliding off the foredeck and makes it easier to attach the luff. The best way to avoid head-versus-tack confusion is to label the corners, but if you're forced to figure it out without labels, a jib is skinny at the head and fat at the tack. You only have to experience the embarrassment of hoisting the jib upside down once to imprint in your memory which is which. Shackle the tack to the fitting on the deck at the base of the **headstay**—the wire running from high on the mast down to the front end, or stem, of the boat.

If the jib has snaphooks—called **hanks**—attach them to the headstay, working upward from the lowermost one and making sure they're all oriented the same way. Each hank has a spring-loaded piston like the one in the snaphook at the end of a dog leash. The **jibsheets** (the lines by means of which the jib is trimmed in or eased out according to the direction of the wind relative to the boat) are attached to the clew—usually with knots (often bowlines, see page 167) rather than shackles. A whack in the head from a knotted jibsheet might hurt, but not as much as a whack from a piece of metal hardware. Take a turn around the sail with a jibsheet or another line to secure it on the foredeck until you are ready to hoist it. Depending on

FORESTAY

PISTON HANK

SNAPSHACKLE

①

② JIB HALYARD

③ FIGURE-EIGHT KNOT

SHEET BLOCK

④

ROLLER-FURLING DRUM

FURLING LINE

①

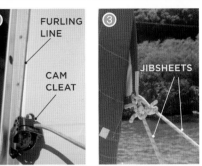

② FURLING LINE

CAM CLEAT

③ JIBSHEETS

④

STARBOARD JIBSHEET

PORT JIBSHEET

Rigging the jib on an IC-24. 1. *Attach the tack to the snapshackle on the stemhead fitting, then attach the piston hanks to the forestay, starting at the bottom of the luff and working up. The hanks should lie fair, not twisted, and all face the same way.* **2.** *Make sure the jib halyard isn't wrapped around the forestay or other rigging aloft, then attach its snapshackle to the head of the jib.* **3.** *Lead each jibsheet through its track-mounted sheet lead block, then tie a stopper knot in the end.* **4.** *The jib is ready to hoist.*

Halyards

Another term that says what it does is **halyard**. That's what lines used to "haul" "yards" aloft on square riggers were called. The triangular sails of a modern boat are a lot easier to raise than the huge square sails of old with their heavy wooden yards, but the lines (or wires) used to raise them are still known as halyards.

A masthead configuration like this likely belongs to a keelboat at least 22 to 24 feet long. A smaller sailboat does not normally require a masthead crane.

Windex (wind indicator)

VHF antenna

masthead crane

masthead

block

grommet

forestay

backstay

jib halyard

headboard

halyard falls inside mast

main halyard

On the Oceanis 323, *as on many cruising boats, the jib (or genoa) stows and sets on a roller-furling luff-foil extrusion that is fitted to the headstay. From the roller-furling drum at the foot of the headstay* **(1)**, *a furling line leads aft to a cam cleat on the side deck by the cockpit* **(2)**. *The jibsheets remain rigged to the furled sail* **(3, 4)**, *the leech area of which is covered with a UV-resistant cloth. To unfurl the headsail, you release the furling line and haul in the port or starboard sheet, all from the comfort of the cockpit.*

Sheets

Halyards hoist the sails, but we need sheets to control the sails once hoisted. The **mainsheet** trims the mainsail in to allow the boat to sail closer to the wind, or eases the sail out when the wind blows from farther aft. There is only one mainsheet, but for reasons that will become clear soon enough, a jib usually requires two **jibsheets**, only one of which—the one on the leeward side of the boat—will be in use at any given time. The other sheet is the lazy sheet.

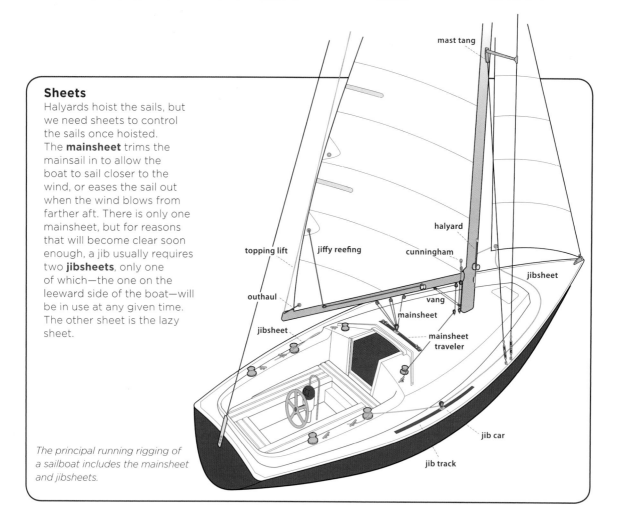

The principal running rigging of a sailboat includes the mainsheet and jibsheets.

Shackles

Shackles are generally U-shaped, made of metal, and used to join things. More secure and quicker to work than a knot, shackles are used on most boats to join control lines to sails. Whether a halyard is rope or wire, you'll probably find a shackle at the end of it. To connect the sail, open the shackle, place the grommet inside the U, and then screw the pin tight to close the shackle. A **screw shackle** works well on the main halyard, which must be secure and which will not be undone while sailing. For jibs, which may be changed from time to time, a **twist shackle** is the usual solution. The pin twists to allow a quick release, and you twist it again to close it. **Snapshackles**, which can be opened under load (just pull the pin) are ideal for spinnaker sheets and guys (see page 223) and are sometimes used on spinnaker and jib halyards as well. Shackles that close with a nut and bolt, cotter pin, or split ring are too finicky and slow for running rigging but work well enough for other connections.

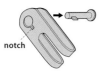

pin with flange in end;
to withdraw pin,
rotate to align
flange with notch

notch

threaded pin

*Mainsail tack and halyard shackles are frequently either the flanged-pin twist or screw-pin variety **(left)**. Jib tack, jib and spinnaker halyard, and spinnaker sheet shackles are frequently snapshackles, which you can open under load by pulling on the pin's lanyard **(right)**.*

SNAPSHACKLE PIN

SNAPSHACKLE LANYARD

the boat and the wind strength, you might decide not to attach the halyard yet.

Some racing sailors dislike hanks because they disturb the flow of air over the jib and permit a slight scalloping along the leading edge of the sail. The alternative is to install an extrusion of aluminum or plastic over the headstay. This **luff foil** contains one or more grooves through which a boltrope sewn into the luff of the jib passes, just as the boltrope in a mainsail slides through a groove in the mast. This makes the leading edge of the jib more aerodynamically efficient, but it also means that the jib will be free to blow all over the foredeck when it exits the foil upon lowering. Hanks are more convenient, especially for shorthanded crews.

Some cruising sailboats feature a variation of a luff foil that has bearings at the top and bottom ends. With this **roller-furling** arrangement, you can stow the jib by rolling it up around the headstay and luff foil rather than lowering it to the deck each time you finish sailing. A control (furling) line leads aft to the cockpit from a drum that rides on the lower bearing. Easing the control line while you trim in the sheet unrolls the jib. Releasing the jibsheet while you pull on the control line rolls it up again. You can even roll up the jib partway to reduce sail when the wind strengthens.

The accompanying photos show three variations on headsail rigging. It takes less time to attach the sails than it does to describe the options. Your boat is rigged and ready.

Frapping and Gasketing

Loose halyards banging against hollow aluminum masts make a racket that can annoy your crew and neighboring boats. Stringing the halyards away from the mast to muffle the noise is known in some circles as **frapping**. Whatever you call it, it's a good habit. A similar practice is to use little strips of cloth or line to tie sails up when they're not flying. Called **gaskets**, **sail ties**, or **sail stops**, they're essential—don't throw them overboard when you untie them.

Names for things proliferate around boats. When sail ties are used to tie halyards away from the mast, they're sometimes called gilguys.

Hoisting the Sail

Where is the wind coming from? Before you hoist sail, you need to answer this critical question.

You can feel the breeze on your face or moistened finger. You can see it fluttering flags ashore and on other boats, and stirring ripples on the water. Your boat might have a **masthead fly**—an arrow atop the mast—that points into the wind like a weather vane. But why does the wind arrow in a book's instructional diagram point *with* the wind, while the arrow at the masthead points *into* it? That's a fair question, but soon enough all these indicators will become the soul of simplicity. In the meantime, to clear up the confusion, point your finger into the wind. *That's* where it's coming from! That's what you need to know. You'll learn more about reading the wind later in this chapter.

Your boat should be pointing into the wind when you hoist sails. Later you will discover circumstances—light breeze, open water, well-mannered boat—in which you can bend this rule, but you have to know a rule before you can bend it. If you're swinging to a mooring or hanging from the lee side of a dock by only a bow line (see page 30), your boat is already **head to wind**. If there is adequate room around you, you will be able to hoist sail and sail away.

Things get more complicated, but not impossible, when your boat is lying against the windward face of a dock. If you have current as well as wind to deal with, you've chosen challenging circumstances for a first sail!

If you are setting sail under engine power—having powered away from a dock or mooring according to common and sensible practice—choose an open spot and head slowly upwind.

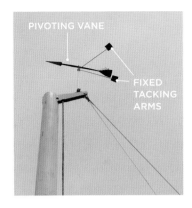

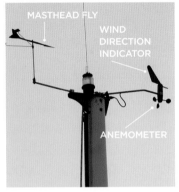

Top: As this masthead fly indicates, a moored or anchored boat heads into the wind absent a strong current. **Middle:** This masthead carries wind instruments as well as a fly, and cockpit readouts on this boat will show wind direction and strength. **Bottom:** This boat's fly vane is aligned with the starboard-tack arm, indicating that the boat is sailing about as close to the apparent wind as it can.

Hoisting the Mainsail

Despite being your biggest sail, the mainsail is easiest to control. Raise it first and set the jib later, most likely while underway. Attach the main halyard, making certain that it leads straight from the top of the mast to the sail and isn't caught in the rigging. Keep some tension on it to keep it led properly. Now **loose** the mainsheet—the sailor's admonition to put plenty of slack in the sheet and leave it uncleated and **free to run**. All other mainsail controls—including the downhaul, boom vang (if rigged), cunningham (if rigged), and reefing lines—should also be loose.

Now unfurl the sail and hoist away. It should run up freely and smoothly. If it binds, don't force it—check for a snag, a wrap in the sail or halyard, or an unloosened sail tie or reefing line. If your boat has lazyjacks, perhaps the leech of the sail has snagged one of them. The point is, the main should go up easily.

Heading the boat into the wind with the boom free lets the sail **weather vane**, and that keeps it from catching wind. Air passes on both sides, so the sail flutters without pulling. This prevents side loads that hamper hoisting, tip your boat prematurely, or both. It also keeps the boat from sailing on her own. Let the sail **luff** completely (flap powerlessly). Keep the mainsheet loose.

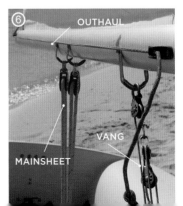

Hoisting the mainsail of a 420.
1. *These two sailors are preparing for a beach launching. One hauls on the halyard while the other feeds the luff boltrope into the mast groove to prevent it from jamming.* **2.** *When the sail is nearly all the way up you should find a loop or a stainless steel ring spliced into the halyard. Run the tail of the halyard around the cleat then back up through the loop as shown, then use this additional purchase to haul the mainsail to full hoist. (Note that the head of the stowed spinnaker in the background of this photo is helpfully labeled. We'll look at spinnakers in Chapter 4.)* **3.** *Cleat the halyard, then coil the halyard tail and tuck it out of the way between the cleated halyard fall and the mast.* **4.** *Pass the cunningham through the grommet provided . . .* **5.** *then down through the clam cleat on the starboard side of the mast before finishing with a stopper knot.* **6.** *The mainsail is now ready to go. Keep the mainsheet loose so the sail can luff in the breeze.*

25

TOPPING LIFT

CLEW GROMMET

OUTHAUL

CUNNINGHAM

Hoisting the mainsail of an IC-24. 1. *As with the 420, it is necessary to feed the luff boltrope into the mast groove.* **2.** *The higher the sail gets, the more it will tend to fill with wind, making further hoisting more difficult, a tendency you can minimize by leaving the mainsheet loose and free to run.* **3.** *This mainsail is loose footed—i.e., the foot is not attached to the boom—a configuration that is common on dinghies but unusual on keelboats like this one.* **4, 5.** *Even more unusual, the mainsail is not attached to the boom at the tack, but depends on cunningham tension to pull the tack toward the boom. Once that's done, the sail is ready.*

Check the **set** of the sail. The luff—the edge from head to tack—should be smooth and tight. If your boom is fixed to the mast—that is, if it cannot be adjusted up and down by means of a downhaul—tension the luff of the sail by means of the halyard or cunningham. If your boat has a downhaul, however, leave it loose, hoist the main to the top, cleat the halyard, then haul down on the downhaul to tighten the luff.

Now you're ready to cast off from the mooring or dock, or to stop the engine if you've been under power.

LANGUAGE OF THE SEA
LUFF

A useful but confusing term, "luff" has three related meanings:

- When a sail "lifts" and flutters, it is luffing. The more pronounced the luff, the bigger the loss of power. A sail luffing completely (also called flogging) is not pulling at all.
- The forward edge of a sail is called its luff—as we've already seen—and that's where luffing first occurs.
- To steer into the wind is to luff up.

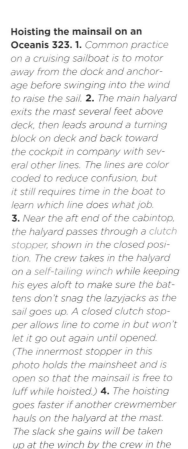

Hoisting the mainsail on an Oceanis 323. 1. *Common practice on a cruising sailboat is to motor away from the dock and anchorage before swinging into the wind to raise the sail.* **2.** *The main halyard exits the mast several feet above deck, then leads around a turning block on deck and back toward the cockpit in company with several other lines. The lines are color coded to reduce confusion, but it still requires time in the boat to learn which line does what job.* **3.** *Near the aft end of the cabintop, the halyard passes through a* clutch stopper, *shown in the closed position. The crew takes in the halyard on a* self-tailing winch *while keeping his eyes aloft to make sure the battens don't snag the lazyjacks as the sail goes up. A closed clutch stopper allows line to come in but won't let it go out again until opened. (The innermost stopper in this photo holds the mainsheet and is open so that the mainsail is free to luff while hoisted.)* **4.** *The hoisting goes faster if another crewmember hauls on the halyard at the mast. The slack she gains will be taken up at the winch by the crew in the cockpit.*

5. *The last inches come harder. The mast crew can help by* swaying, *or* swigging, *on the halyard as shown. As she eases off on her purchase, the winch grinder will take up the slack she gained.* **6.** *When the sail is up, the helmsman* bears away *from the wind, turns off the engine, and starts to sail.*

SECOND REEF

VANG

FIRST REEF

TURNING BLOCK

MAIN HALYARD   MAINSHEET

MAINSHEET

MAIN HALYARD

CLUTCH STOPPERS

Mainsail Controls

Mainsheet: This is the primary control for the mainsail. By **trimming** (pulling in) or **easing** (letting out) the sheet, you control the sail's angle with the wind, and that controls both how hard the sail pulls and in what direction.

Other lines or systems regulate the size and shape of the sail. Most boats have them, and you may have to deal with them, if only to make sure that they are loose. While you should master the sheets first, be aware of:

Downhaul: If your boat has this line, it pulls down on the boom at the mast, stretching the luff of the mainsail. You want enough luff tension to create a vertical wrinkle in the luff when the sail isn't full of wind, but not so much that the wrinkle persists when the sail is full and **drawing**.

Boom vang: On a small boat this is a line led through a system of blocks, but on a bigger boat—one over 30 feet long or so—it is often a hydraulic ram. Tensioning the vang pulls down on the boom at a point about one-third of the boom length aft of the mast. This flattens the sail and straightens the leech, and is of greatest use when sailing **off the wind** (as opposed to sailing to windward), as we shall see later.

Cunningham: This control, when present, stretches the luff and makes the sail flatter for upwind sailing. It can be adjusted while the sail is drawing, at which point the halyard and downhaul are under too much tension to be readily adjustable. As mentioned, you can safely ignore the cunningham and vang while you get comfortable with the more critical controls.

Outhaul: This line or fitting controls how tightly and how far the foot of the sail is pulled along the boom. Tightening the outhaul as the wind increases flattens the lower portion of the mainsail, reducing its power.

Reefing lines: To **reef** the mainsail—reduce its size—when the wind is overpowering the boat, you take up on these lines. For more on reefing, see page 111.

Topping lift: This line or wire holds up the free end of the boom when the sail isn't set.

Traveler: Often, on keelboats, the mainsheet leads through a block that rides on a traveler, a device that permits it to slide from side to side of the boat. Except when the wind is overpowering your boat, adjust the traveler to windward to keep the boom nearly over the boat's centerline. In a strong wind or a sudden puff, ease the traveler to leeward to reduce power.

Again, you need not be overly concerned with these controls now. None of them is necessary to make the boat sail, and there will be plenty of time later to play with them.

When you sail a Laser, the cunningham, vang, mainsheet, and outhaul are all within easy reach, but you have to learn how to multitask.

The 420 controls are equally as convenient. The outhaul is on the starboard side of the boom.

TRAVELER CAR

TRAVELER

MAINSHEET

VANG

*Most keelboat mainsheets ride from side to side on a traveler, but the IC-24 mainsheet is mounted on a swivel in the middle of the cockpit sole **(above)**, handy to the helmsman **(top)**. This is just one of the modifications made to the J/24 class in its transformation to an IC-24.*

*The Oceanis 323 mainsheet rides on a traveler car **(top)**, allowing the mainsheet lead to be adjusted from side to side across the cabintop. From the forward boom block the mainsheet leads forward (arrow, middle photo) to a turning block*

*at the mast base, then runs aft through a clutch stopper to the winch **(above)**. This roundabout configuration enables the boat to carry a bimini (to shade the cockpit) without interfering with the mainsheet.*

Hoisting the Jib

Most sailboats have jibs, and if yours does, you're probably eager to hoist it. For the balance of this chapter, however, let's leave it down. Learning with a single sail helps you focus on how a sail works with the wind. When you add the jib, you split your focus. Mainsail-only sailing is also best for tight quarters—leaving a dock or mooring, weaving through an anchorage, or negotiating a narrow channel. It gives you good visibility, keeps your speed manageable, and gives you good control for maneuvering. We'll add the jib to the mix in Chapter 2.

Casting Off

Now that you've hoisted the main, the sail will tell you the wind direction, pointing into the wind like a weather vane as long as you have the mainsheet properly loosened. Even though this causes noisy flogging and a swinging boom if the breeze is at all fresh, don't trim the sail tight just yet. You don't want the sail to fill with wind and start the boat heeling or moving before you actually **cast off** (untie) from the dock or mooring. Keep the sail "in neutral" by letting it weather vane until you're ready to go.

Plan your exit. Perhaps you are hemmed in by other boats. Maybe (because of obstacles, shallow water, etc.) there is only one direction to depart in. Docks present problems of their own. Current may be a factor; if at all possible, you want to exit *with* the current, not against it. Casting off is a beginning step, but that doesn't keep it from being tricky.

For now, let's assume you are leaving a mooring and have open water all around. Because you are not moving through the water, if you turn the rudder nothing much will happen. No rudder is effective unless it's deflecting a stream of water—a stream that is provided by the boat's forward motion, by an inboard engine's propeller discharge, or both. If you simply cast off, you will drift backward, unable to control where your boat goes. It's possible to back

The Cleat Hitch

To fix, or **belay**, one end of a line, **cleat** it. The term comes from the traditional horned cleat (derived from the even more ancient belaying pin). Modern boats use a variety of cleats, many of which secure a rope mechanically instead of with a knot. You'll learn how they work as we go along, but the old-fashioned belay for a horned cleat is still an excellent knot to know. Wrap a full turn around the base, lay on a figure eight, and lock it with a half hitch as shown. There's your cleat hitch. When cleating a mainsheet, however—especially in a small centerboard boat—leave off the half hitch. You want to be able to uncleat the sheet and let it out in a hurry should you wish to dump wind from the sail.

Tying a cleat hitch. **1.** *Approach the base of the cleat at an angle if possible, so as to prevent jamming.* **2.** *Take a full turn around the base, then wrap over the top.* **3.** *Continue in a figure-eight fashion . . .* **4.** *and complete the figure-eight with a half hitch, with the end underneath.* **5.** *The finished knot.*

away from a mooring by drifting astern, steering in reverse until you bring the wind over one side, then trimming the sheet and sailing away, but that takes practice (see the In Irons section, page 45).

The simplest way to get going, if the situation permits, is to go forward, and the easiest way to move the boat forward without engine power is to pull her along the mooring line. If you want to sail off to your right, untie the mooring line but keep it in your grasp. Now pull on the line while you walk aft along the port side of your boat. The boat will spin off to starboard—especially if the rudder is turned to starboard (tiller to port)—and start to move ahead. The more momentum you provide by pulling, the easier it becomes to steer. Steer to starboard, toss the mooring line into the water, trim your sail to catch the wind, and you're underway.

You get the best sail power, control, and flexibility of heading with the wind **on your beam**—that is, perpendicular to the boat's heading, blowing directly over its side. Head to your right (away from the wind) until the wind blows squarely across your course, and trim sail. If the sail doesn't fill, head farther away from the wind while you still have enough momentum to do so.

You're sailing!

Sailing off a beach or motoring away from a dock are other ways to get started.

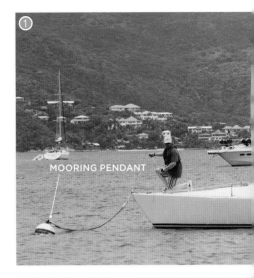

MOORING PENDANT

One way to cast off a mooring.
1. *The foredeck crew unties the mooring pendant . . .* **2.** *then walks it aft, which imparts forward motion and steerageway to the boat. Here the helmsman wants to turn to starboard, so the crew walks the pendant aft along the port side.* **3.** *Reaching the stern, the crew tosses the pendant overboard, clear of the boat.*

Launching a 420 from the beach. 1. *In this case the pintles are transom mounted, and you slide the rudder-mounted gudgeons down over them.* **2.** *A tang on the lower pintle locks the rudder in place.* **3.** *Both of these sailors are boarding together, demonstrating that the 420 offers plenty of stability. The centerboard is partway down and visible beneath the boat.*

Launching a Laser from the beach. 1. *Install the rudder by inserting its* pintles *into the transom-mounted* gudgeons, *or sockets. The blade pivots up to rest on the sand.* **2.** *Now push off, in this case with the daggerboard already down . . .* **3.** *and climb aboard, getting your weight inboard as quickly as possible. This cockpit is half full of water, but once the boat is planing the self-bailer will empty it.*

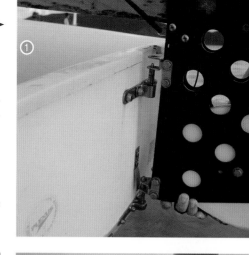

PINTLE

GUDGEON

5

Leaving a dock under power. 1. *It's customary in a cruising sailboat to leave a dock under power, then hoist sails outside the confines of the anchorage area. Here most of the docklines have already been handed aboard.* **2.** *Because the wind is blowing the boat against the dock, however (as you can see by the orientation of the anchored boats in the distance), a crewmember keeps a turn of the after spring line around the dock cleat. By powering gently ahead against this spring line with the rudder turned toward the dock, the helmsman can kick the stern away from the dock.* **3, 4.** *Once the stern is clear of the dock, the crewmember brings the after spring line aboard and the helmsman backs out.*

Pintles and Gudgeons

The traditional method of hanging a rudder on a wooden ship was with pins (**pintles**) fitted to sockets (**gudgeons**), which were mounted either on the **sternpost** (a vertical timber) or the after end of the wooden keel. Though the wooden sailing ships of yesteryear have all but disappeared, the terminology persists in connection with sailing dinghies. When you board a sailing dinghy, before hoisting the mainsail, you may need to mount the rudder. Once you find the rudder (the tiller will be attached to it), carry it to the stern and look at the outside of the **transom** (the flat, vertical, after end of the boat). You should see two gudgeons in vertical alignment on the transom, into which the rudder's pintles will fit.

The Eye of the Wind

To sailors, the **eye of the wind** is the precise direction from which it's blowing. No boat can sail in that direction. If the wind is coming from the north, the closest you can come to sailing north is either northeast or northwest—that is, 45 degrees to one side or the other of the wind. An especially **close-winded** boat may be able to improve that to about 40 degrees off the wind, but that's about as good as it gets.

Face the wind and hold both arms out at 45 degrees from the direction you're facing. If you head your boat anywhere outside the 90-degree arc in front of you, the sailing is good. Head anywhere between your arms, though, and the wind angle will be too small for a sail to work. Think of that zone between your outstretched hands as a desert—you may pass through, but you'll get no sustenance while you're there.

The true-wind circle.

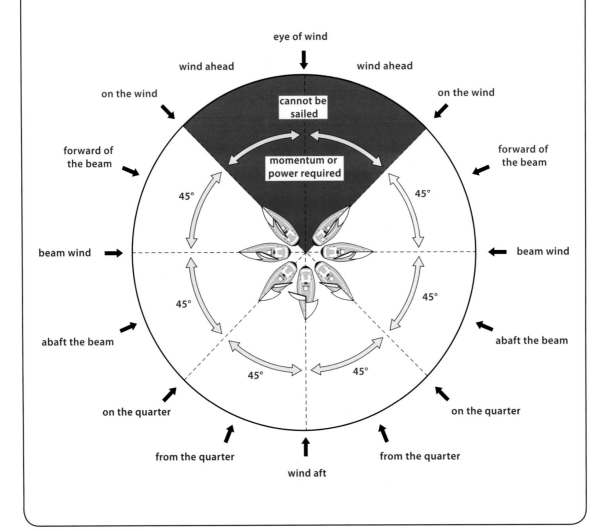

Steering

Steering a sailboat is simple. If your boat has a wheel, it's just like steering a car—turn the wheel right to go right. A tiller, on the other hand, works like an outboard motor—push the tiller left to make the boat turn right. In either case it's the rudder that does the turning. Moving the rudder to starboard sends the bow to starboard, but only if the boat is moving. When a boat is stopped, it's like a car in a parking lot—turn the wheel and nothing happens.

Steering is like riding a bicycle—once you learn it, you'll never forget. Learn by sailing in the same direction for a while. It's easiest across the wind rather than with it or into it. Pick a target—a buoy or a distant landmark—then point the boat directly at it.

Your first reaction will probably be relief. Steering really isn't all that hard. But your boat may not want to stay pointed at the target for long. Bringing her back on course, you may overcorrect and swing past the target. Settle in and try to get the feel of it. The boat will instruct you. Does she turn into the wind consistently, and does that tendency—called **weather helm**—increase with each puff of wind? Does she stray more upwind of your target than downwind?

Wind and water forces make a sailboat go, but not necessarily straight. Most boats are designed to have a tendency to turn into the wind. This weather helm is a desirable safety factor as long as it is not too pronounced, but it takes getting used to. Instead of thinking "left" and "right," try **up**—into the wind—and **down**—away from the wind. Boats should head up on their own, but they need to be turned down. The pull to one side may remind you of driving a car with mismatched tires, but the resultant feel is normal and a key to steering well.

Try steering by slightly increasing or decreasing the rudder's resistance to the boat's tendency to turn. See if you can keep the boat straight by alternately increasing and easing up on the helm. Your course may resemble something of an S-curve, but that shouldn't worry you. Steering straight isn't always fastest, as long as your S-curves are gentle. Fix on your target, and test your anticipation and concentration. Sailors learn to **meet the course**, which simply means slowing a turn before the target heading is reached.

Hold the boat on course for 5 minutes, and you've passed the test. Good helmsmanship includes maneuvering and responding to wind and waves as well as steering straight, but it begins, as you just did, with developing a feel for the boat.

EXTENSION

TILLER

The Laser tiller is equipped with an extension so the sailor can hike out.

Wheel steering is easy—turn the wheel to starboard to turn the boat to starboard. The binnacle houses the chain that transmits the wheel's torque to cables, which in turn transmit the force via turning blocks to the rudder. The binnacle also supports the compass for convenient viewing from the helm. Note how the canvas bimini shades the cockpit.

BINNACLE

Steering to a Compass

Sooner or later you'll find yourself sailing a compass course—perhaps because of fog or darkness, or perhaps while crossing a featureless expanse of open water. In preparation for that day, have a look at the compass that should be easily visible from the helm of your boat. There should be a fixed mark on the compass casing that's aligned with the bow of the boat. The compass card moves, but this **lubber line** stays fixed, indicating the boat's heading. ("Lubber" comes from "land lover," because true salts at one time considered steering by this mark a form of cheating.) Even with the line, it takes practice to steer by a compass. We'll cover this in the Navigation chapter.

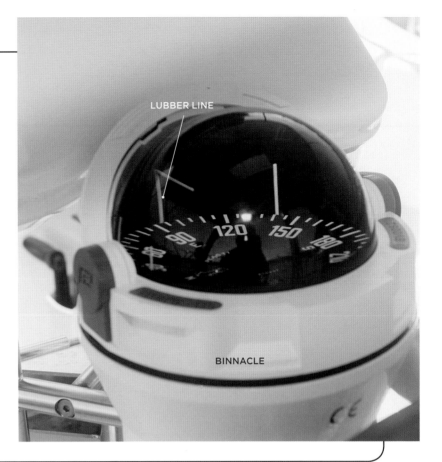

A binnacle-mounted compass on a wheel-steered boat.

Weather Helm

Most boats want to turn into the wind, the tendency called **weather helm**. Weather helm gives boats their "feel," and a modest degree of it is desirable. Those few boats with an urge to head downwind have **lee helm**, which is undesirable and should be corrected if possible. To explain "helm," think of a ship weather vane. It points its bow into the wind because it has more sail aft of the pivot point than ahead of it. A boat pivots (around a **center of lateral resistance**) the way a vane does. Greater push from the sails behind the pivot point (mainsails are bigger than jibs) creates weather helm. Too much weather helm is undesirable—it makes the boat hard to steer, and the rudder resistance you have to apply to stop the boat from turning into the wind slows you down. A boat with too much weather helm may just need sail-shape adjustment or reefing, as we'll discuss in a later chapter, or it may need to be retuned to cure its tendency. Sometimes in a centerboard boat you can relieve weather helm by pivoting the centerboard farther aft.

Sculling

Sculling is one way to get a stalled boat moving. Simply wag the rudder from side to side. This form of paddling is a last resort when there is no wind. It is illegal when racing, is bad for your steering gear if continued for long, and is impossible with a wheel-steered boat, but if your tiller-steered boat comes to a stop 6 feet short of the mooring, it's a good thing to know.

Sculling also lets you steer when your boat is stopped or unresponsive. Wag the rudder hard one way and it sends the bow that way by propelling the stern in the opposite direction. When your boat doesn't answer its helm, it may respond to sculling.

Trimming the Sails

My father taught me to trim a sail with this advice: "Let it out until it luffs, then trim it in until it stops." I didn't know anything then about how lift develops perpendicular to a foil, or about attached flow or the Bernoulli effect. I didn't know why his advice worked, but it did. The farther you ease your sails, the better they work—but only to the point where they begin to luff. Trim commandment #1 is "ease thy sails."

As you ease the sheet, watch the sail. When you see it beginning to flutter, to break, to lift along its leading edge, or luff, it is just beginning to lose power, and the wind is beginning to lift the back of the sail as well as flow smoothly across the front. That's when you should trim the sail. Pull it in with your eye on the flutter, and stop trimming as soon as the luff stops. At that point you have found the optimal trim, the razor edge between too loose and too tight that puts the sail at its best. But wind speed and wind direction change all the time, and the razor edge changes with them. To stay well trimmed you have to periodically readjust the sails. Ease out the sheet a little at a time, watching

the sail. When it begins to flutter or lift, trim back in until it is once again firm and drawing. Relax. Repeat.

When you pull a sail all the way in but can't stop it from luffing, your boat is headed too close to the wind. You've wandered into that 80- to 90-degree no-go zone we mentioned, and you'll have to **bear off** or **head down** in order to fill the sail. When you do, note how the boat comes to life and picks up speed. Note how the sail fills into a solid, powerful curve. After a while you'll be able to tell just by feel—without looking—when your boat is sailing **full and by**, properly trimmed and properly steered.

The sheet harnesses a sail's power. To **depower** a sail, ease the sheet until the sail luffs. That spills wind from the sail and slows the boat. To slow the boat further, keep easing until a good part of the sail is luffing. To counteract a puff that threatens to heel the boat too far, ease the sail until the boat starts to straighten up. Luff your sails to slow down or straighten up your boat.

You can also use the jib and main to turn and brake the boat. **Back the jib**—let's say to

starboard—by holding the clew of the sail so far out to starboard that it cups the wind on its back side. This will push the bow to port. You can use a backed jib to spin away from a mooring, to help you out of irons (see the In Irons section, page 45), or to accelerate the boat's turn through a tack. To brake the boat during an approach to a landing (or at any other time), **back the mainsail**. Push the boom out to windward (as in the photo on page 45) so the wind hits the back of the sail. Push harder to brake harder.

Sail Shape

How hard and efficiently a sail lifts a boat along its course depends not just on the strength of the wind and on sail trim, but also on the shape of the sail. Trim controls a sail's angle to the wind and has much to do with how much of the wind's force is converted to forward motion versus heeling, but sail shape plays a role as well. By changing a sail's shape, you change its ability to pull. Sail trim is like a car's accelerator, while shaping a sail properly is like changing from four cylinders to six.

The deeper the curve of a sail, the greater its potential power. Giving a sail more **belly** (or **draft**) lets it pull harder. Flattening a sail decreases its pull but makes it harder to luff, more "close winded." Sail shape and sail trim are related, but while the sheet adjusts trim, controls such as the halyard, boom vang, traveler, backstay, cunningham, leech line, and others are involved in shaping a sail. For more on shaping a sail, see page 96. To work with a sail, first learn to trim.

Unless you're steering too nearly into the wind, pulling in the mainsheet will cure a luffing mainsail (page 38). When only a partial luff (below) remains, you have only a little more trimming to do until the sail is full of wind, with no luffing at all (right).

Points of Sail

Where is the wind coming from, and where do you want to go? Once you hoist sail and clear the anchorage, these two questions are foremost. If your chosen destination lies in the no-go zone we discussed above—in other words, if it lies upwind or to windward—you won't be able to point directly at it and will have to zig and zag to get there. One perfectly logical—even laudable—response to that eventuality is to change your destination. After all, it's not the destination you care about while sailing—if it were,

you'd be in a powerboat. No, it's the journey that matters, so why not go wherever the wind takes you?

That's all well and good, but sometimes you have no choice. Maybe the only open water lies upwind. Maybe you're meeting someone at an upwind destination. Maybe you have it on good authority that the wind will blow from this direction all day, and you'd rather sail to windward now so you can coast home in the afternoon. To make these decisions,

you have to think about the **points of sail**.

Imagine a clock face with your boat in the center and the wind blowing from 12 o'clock. The no-go zone lies in the 90-degree pie wedge between 10:30 and 1:30. When you sail as close to that no-go zone as you can, with your sails trimmed in as far as they can come, you are **close hauled**. When you sail toward 6 o'clock, with the wind directly behind you, you are **running**. Everything between close hauled and running is **reaching**.

Sail Force and Sail Trim

The aerodynamic principles by which a sail powers a boat through the water are even more complex than those that enable an airplane to fly, and remain difficult to summarize. An airplane wing has a rigid sectional shape, while a sail is a flexible, changing membrane. Imagine a mainsail viewed in cross section as in the accompanying illustration. The dashed line shows the so-called **chord length** from luff to leech, and the sail "pulls" across this entire length. At all points this pull, or **lift**, is perpendicular to the sail surface. In the illustration, lift vectors pointing off to the boat's side won't help propel it forward; rather, they will only increase the boat's angle of heel. Only those vectors with a forward component will help propel the boat, and the object of sail trim

is to maximize the overall forward component of the vectors. As you ease a sail, you accomplish just that—until the point at which the sail begins to luff.

"The tighter I trim, the faster I'll go," is a common misconception. The opposite

is true. Remember: "Ease thy sails." In summary:

- Luffing means a sail is too far out, not pulling with its full force.
- For maximum forward propulsion, let a sail out as far as it can go without luffing.
- When in doubt, let it out.

Only the trim from the forward one-quarter of the sail generates a useful forward component. The goal of sail trim and sail design is to maximize that forward component near the sail's luff.

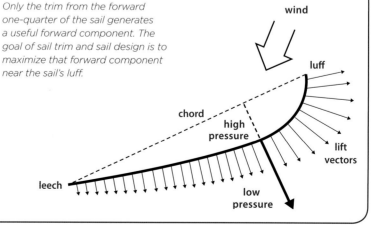

The points of sail.

⑥ no-go
zone

wind

① close hauled
(beating)

close
reach ②

45° to 50°
close-hauled

50° to 80°
close reach

80° to 100°
beam
reach

③

100° to 165°
broad reach

165° to
180° run

broad
reach

run ⑤   ④

What the points of sail look like on and off the boat:
1. *close hauled;* **2.** *close reach;* **3.** *beam reach;* **4.** *broad reach;* **5.** *running;* **6.** *the no-go zone.*

Let's take a closer look at what this means in practice.

With the wind coming over your stern—with your boat heading between roughly 5 o'clock and 7 o'clock—you are running. Your boat will be relatively flat in the water. You'll need to ease your sails out all the way to get the most from them, and in fact the mainsail will probably start to bear against your boat's spreaders or shrouds—forcing you to stop easing—before it begins to luff. Because your boat's forward motion reduces the apparent speed of the wind coming from behind, the conditions aboard will feel relatively warm and mild. The boat may develop something of a side-to-side rolling motion.

Running sounds like the speediest point of sail, and in square-rigger times it was. Triangular sails, though, work best with the wind blowing along them—so that they can develop lift—rather than against them. Eased way out for running, the sails are pushed by the wind, which is much less efficient than sailing upwind or on a reach. That's one reason why sailing dead downwind can be slow.

Now round up toward the wind so that it blows across the boat. You'll pick up speed, your angle of heel will increase noticeably, and you'll feel cooler. If you round up only a little, so that your heading is roughly between 5 o'clock and 3 o'clock on **port tack** (with the wind coming over your port side) or between 7 o'clock and 9 o'clock on **starboard tack**, you're on a **broad reach**. When you're heading is either 3 o'clock or 9 o'clock, you're on a **beam reach**. With the

A 420 running on port tack, with the sail to starboard (above) and on starboard tack with the sail to port (below). The boat is level and the sailing is easy.

wind on the beam, a well-trimmed sail will be about halfway out. If you head up still further, but not all the way to close hauled, you're on a **close reach**.

To mariners of old, a "reach" was a stretch of open water. Sailing with the wind on the beam is definitely "open" relative to close hauled, and it's the point of sail on which you're most likely to "reach" your destination quickly and easily.

Now head even farther toward the eye of the wind. If you enter the no-go zone, your sails will luff no matter how tightly you trim them. Fall away enough to fill your sails when they're trimmed all the way in. The breeze will be angling in over the bow. You'll notice the waves more, and the wind will feel stronger and colder. You'll be heeling more, too. You'll think you're going fast until you look at the waves, the knotmeter, or a windward mark, at which point you'll realize that reaching is faster than **beating**.

It isn't hard to imagine how sailors came up with this name for upwind sailing. It might have been from beating their heads against a wall in frustration over having to zig one way and zag the other in order to make a little progress into the wind, or maybe the pounding that happens in a breeze felt a lot like the beatings the old ship captains doled out to lazy sailors. "Beat" is how you'll feel after you do it for a while. **Tacking** is another name for this point of sail.

A close-reaching boat becomes close hauled like this one when, with the sail or sails trimmed all the way in, the helmsman has headed as high as he can without causing the sails to luff.

A Laser on a fairly tight reach—i.e., somewhere between a close reach and a beam reach.

If the helmsman tries to sail above close hauled, he enters the no-go zone. The sails luff and the boat stops.

Just as an Eskimo has numerous words for snow, a sailor has a seemingly endless assortment of terms that strike at the core questions of sailing: Where is the wind coming from and where do we want to go?

When we are beating, or tacking, or sailing close hauled, we might also say we are sailing upwind, on the wind, or against the wind, or we might say we are working to windward or to weather.

When we turn from a beat to a close reach, we might say we're cracking off or easing off or bearing off a little, or that we've freed our wind. If we keep turning until we're on a broad reach or even a run, we might say we're sailing off the wind, downwind, or with the wind. Life is easy when you're sailing with the wind instead of against it.

An Optimist (top) and a Laser beating. Both boats have their sails close hauled, and their daggerboards are down to minimize leeway while crew weight counters the wind's heeling force. Small boats teach a great deal about sailing that you can carry into bigger boats when and if you choose.

In Irons

When you're stopped with your bow pointing into the wind, your sails flogging, and your boat not answering its rudder, you're **in irons**. Drifting powerless this way is like being shackled hand and foot. Who hasn't found themselves in irons—unable to go, unable to steer?

You may be in irons, but chances are you're moving, either drifting backward or skating sideways. Use that motion. If you're drifting backward, steer in reverse. To turn the bow to starboard, put the rudder to port (tiller to starboard). If you're sliding sideways, center the rudder and then steer gradually. A rudder clamped hard over provides no control.

Use what steerage you've got. When your boat is pointing across the wind instead of into it, trim your sails and go.

That's actually the hardest part. As you trim it, the sail spins you back into the wind. Try to trim it just enough to get you going, then ease it to relieve the helm. Trim and ease until you get going well enough to steer in forward. Now you're out!

The crew on this 420 is backing the mainsail, which is causing the boat to back up. If the helmsman turns the rudder to port, the bow will fall off to starboard—and vice versa. This is a good way to get out of irons.

Beating

Ah, what a zigzag wake we weave.
1. These sailors want to reach the yellow marker, but it lies in the no-go zone to windward, so they can't sail directly toward it. Instead they trim their sails to close hauled and prepare to beat to get there. 2. First they zig on port tack. 3. Then they tack over to starboard and start adding a zag to the zig. At first, from our perspective, it appears they will be able to reach the marker on this tack. 4. But appearances have deceived us, and it is now clear that they will have to tack at least once more. 5. So they tack back over to port . . . 6. for another zig. 7. Now another tack. 8. Will they make it on this starboard tack? 9. No. Back over to port they go. 10. Time for another tack to starboard. 11. We'll be astounded if they don't make it this time. 12. Success at last! Lesson: No matter how big or high-tech your sailboat, the only way to reach an upwind destination is by indirection.

You are at the south end of the lake. You want to get to the north end. Where's the wind coming from? If it's from the east, west, or south, just point your boat and go. You can reach or run directly there. If the wind is from the north, though, you will have to beat.

The eye of the wind provides no power—point your boat north and your sails will luff no matter how you trim them. Therefore, sail **close hauled** (with your sails trimmed as tightly as the breeze will allow) and point as close to north as you can. Fill your sails by heading off, away from the eye of the wind. Now work back toward your target. Focus on the forward edge of your sail. It will begin to luff at approximately the same point each time you head up to windward, and you will feel the boat slow and flatten out when this happens. Head off slightly. You will see the sail fill, feel the boat heel, and hear

slip instead of moving forward. Keels are always in position, but in a centerboard or daggerboard boat you will have to be sure the board is all the way down when you are beating. If the board is down and you're still sliding sideways, ease the sails to let them generate more forward power.

Even sailing close hauled, if you head in only one direction you'll ground out on the east or west shore long before you get to the top of the lake. To get there, you'll need to crisscross the lake, sailing first along one side of the eye of the wind, then along the other. When the wind is coming in over your starboard bow, you're on starboard tack. When the wind comes in over your port bow, you're on port tack. When you turn from one tack to the other through the eye of the wind, you're **tacking** (see photos and page 54).

Beating is challenging. You can't sail directly into the wind, but by sailing the edges of the no-go zone, first on one side and then the other, you can, sooner or later, get there from here.

the water move faster past the hull. You are going faster, but you are heading farther from your destination. If you were to carry this to its extreme, you would find yourself zooming back and forth across the lake on a beam reach, going fast but never getting any closer to the north end.

The trick is finding the optimum balance between reducing the distance sailed—which you do by pointing as high (as close to the wind) as possible—and increasing your speed—which you do by heading off. At first you're likely to stray from one extreme to the other. Work to find the edge and stay on it. When you do, you're sailing in the groove.

When close hauled, your sails will generate their maximum side force. Unless you have a keel or centerboard in place, you will side-

Reaching

Sailing across the wind puts a sailboat at her best. The sails have a strong forward component in their pull, yet enjoy maximum airflow. The side forces are manageable, and in a centerboard boat you can pull the board halfway up to reduce your boat's underwater resistance. The payoff is maximum efficiency and maximum velocity. With the wind on the beam, sailing is easy and fun.

Technically speaking, every point of sail between close hauled and running downwind is a reach. You're on a **close reach** when the wind is forward of the beam and a **broad reach** when it's aft of the beam. On any reach you can alter course with no fear of wandering into the no-go zone or of tacking or jibing unintentionally. Reaching is uncomplicated, and that makes it the best point of sail for learning the basics. You can concentrate on one aspect of sailing at a time, and you are free to focus on the essentials: steering, trimming the sails, and balancing the boat.

On a reach you can see that a well-trimmed sail pulls harder than a sail that's luffing and pulls straighter than an overtrimmed sail. With the wind on the beam, the turning force of the sails is most evident. Learn to control that helm and steer *through* it instead of *against* it.

When a boat heels in the wind, it loses power and becomes harder to steer. If you counterbalance the wind's force and keep the boat flat, however, you gain both speed and control. This is true for any point of sail, but it is easiest to see on a reach.

Reaching also spotlights how the **apparent wind** (see page 53) works. If you head closer into the wind, its force increases. Head away and the apparent wind diminishes. The classic wisdom for sailing fast on a reach is to head up in the lulls and off in the puffs. By altering course in rhythm with the wind, you can add apparent wind in the dead spots, then ride the gusts downwind to get where you need to go.

Lateral Resistance

Sails, especially when close hauled, produce at least as much sideways thrust as forward pull. Keels, centerboards, and daggerboards are there to resist sideslipping, or leeway, and help boats turn sail power into straight-ahead progress. A bigger underwater appendage provides greater lateral resistance. But most modern keels and boards also generate a hydrodynamic lift. Produced by the flow of water over the keel or board, this lift pulls the boat to windward even as the sails push it to leeward. Lift amplifies lateral resistance, and the more lift a keel or board generates, the less it must depend on sheer size. But underwater foils generate lift only when a boat is moving. You'll make more leeway when you're stopped or going slow than when you speed up.

Wind Shifts

Wind blowing from offshore tends to be fairly steady, while wind sweeping over the water from nearby land is likely to be shifty. Virtually every wind, though, changes direction on a minute-by-minute basis. In a steady breeze these variations may be less than 10 degrees, while in a shifty wind they can exceed 30 degrees or more. Shifts affect sailing on all points of sail, but at no time are they more critical than when beating.

When the wind shifts so that you can head closer to where you want to go, we call that a **lift**. When the wind swings toward the bow so that you have to head farther from your target, that's a **header**. If you can see why a lift on one tack is a header to a boat on the opposite tack, you're already seeing the big picture.

Reaching. *If a boat is sailing neither close hauled (40 to 50 degrees off the wind) nor on a run (165 to 180 degrees off the wind), it must be reaching. Thus, fully 115 degrees of the 180-degree sailing semicircle is reaching.* **1.** *A close reach is almost but not quite close hauled.* **2.** *A beam reach puts the boat at right angles to the wind and waves.* **3.** *Bearing off from a beam reach puts the boat first on a broad reach . . .* **4.** *then a very broad reach . . .* **5.** *and finally a run.*

Reaching is so much simpler than beating. You just point at your destination, trim your sails to catch wind, and go. No wonder cruising sailors often avoid upwind destinations.

Heeling

Hieldan means "to tilt" in Old English. Sailing vessels have always tended to tilt. Heeling means tipping under wind pressure. All sailboats heel. Even catamarans, with their ultrawide stability bases, heel a little. Most monohulls heel a lot, given enough wind.

Heeling is not all bad. It relieves wind force so masts don't break or sails rip. Still, it's inefficient; it spills power from sails, adds weather helm, and can even make your rudder stop steering. It's uncomfortable—life on a slant is nobody's ideal. And it can be unsettling. Capsizing is a legitimate concern—especially in a centerboard or daggerboard boat.

In a small boat you can resist heeling by moving your weight to the windward side of the boat. The farther to windward you move, the more resistance you provide. All crew in a small boat should think of themselves as movable ballast, available if needed to resist heeling. In racing sailboats you'll frequently see crewmembers lining the windward rail, sitting with their legs dangling overboard. In a small boat you might even see one or more crewmembers **hiking to windward**—leaning out over the water with their feet secured beneath a hiking strap. In some high-performance sailing dinghies, this leverage can be enhanced even further with a **trapeze**—a rope or wire tether that leads from high on the mast and clips to a crewmember's harness. The crew then plants his or her feet on the windward rail and leans out over the water, supported by the trapeze. But this brand of athletic competitive sailing is not for everyone.

Even on a keelboat like this J/24, crew weight on the rail (what racers call "rail meat") can help counter the wind's heeling force and make the boat faster. Weight to windward isn't necessary to prevent capsize of a keelboat, however, as it can be in a dinghy. If this boat weren't racing, her crew wouldn't be riding the rail.

A graceful wooden sailboat participating in the Eggemoggin Reach Regatta, on the coast of Maine, hosted by WoodenBoat *magazine.*

In larger boats, crew weight alone is not enough to counterbalance the force of the sails. Keelboats use **fixed ballast**—weight suspended below the water—to accomplish the same task with greater leverage and efficiency. **Internal ballast**—weight placed as low as possible inside the boat—is another option, but is less efficient than keel ballast. The auxiliary engine of a keel

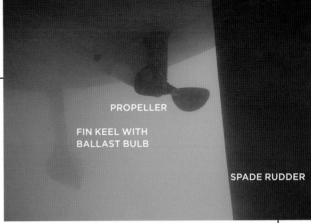

PROPELLER

FIN KEEL WITH
BALLAST BULB

SPADE RUDDER

On this 420 the helmsman hikes out while the crewmember goes one step further, riding the trapeze to place his body weight at the end of a lever arm from the mast. You're unlikely ever to see a trapeze on a keelboat, and they're rare on solo dinghies too.

Looking forward at the hull bottom of an Oceanis 323 cruising sailboat, we see, right to left, the spade rudder, the propeller, and, in the distance, the fin keel with its ballast bulb that gives the boat much of its stability.

sailboat is a form of internal ballast. A boat's ballast, it is hoped, exerts enough righting force so that the boat will pop back upright no matter how far it is heeled. The evidence shows that no boat is immune to capsizing when the conditions are severe enough, but take heart—under ordinary conditions, no keelboat is likely to capsize.

For the wind to push you over, it must have something to push against. Releasing the sheet will dump the wind from the sail and thereby release the heeling force. **Feathering** your course—heading up until the sails luff—accomplishes the same thing. **Flattening** your sails, as discussed starting on page 96, will also depower them, but **reefing** a sail (making it smaller; see page 111) or replacing it with a smaller sail is even more effective. Resist heeling, control it, and accept it.

Running

What could be better than a tailwind? You might imagine a breeze from astern as the ideal and think that running must be the best point of sail. It is definitely nice to be traveling with the waves rather than bashing into them; there are no jarring impacts of wave on hull, no spray flying over the deck. The air feels warmer, the breeze lighter, and the freedom to point the boat toward your target and let her go is also nice.

With the wind from astern, the sail can go all the way out without luffing. Ease the mainsheet until the mainsail grazes the rigging or the spreaders, and stop there to prevent the sail from chafing. This swings the imaginary sail force arrow well forward, so that the sail is pulling almost dead ahead.

The bad news, though, is that it isn't pulling very hard. For one thing, the boat's forward speed detracts from the force of the wind. If your boat is sailing downwind at 6 knots in 16 knots of breeze, the sail feels only 10 knots of **apparent wind**. (The actual breeze

An Optimist pram running. This sailor has pulled his daggerboard up for additional speed downwind.

A Laser sailing downwind with daggerboard up.

of 16 knots is called the **true wind**.) Second, because the sail is perpendicular to the wind, it generates little or no lift; the force it generates comes solely from the wind's push against it. Because the sail feels less breeze and works less efficiently, a boat is not as fast downwind as it is when reaching or, sometimes, even beating.

To get from one tack to the other when sailing upwind, as already mentioned, you turn your bow through the eye of the wind in the maneuver known as tacking. The sail or sails will luff as you turn through the no-go zone, weather-vaning from one side of the deck to the other as the boat turns. Eventually you wind up on the other tack, with the wind blowing on the other side of the sails. When you're sailing downwind, you can get from one tack to the other by turning your stern through the eye of the wind in a maneuver

A cruising sailboat on a smooth and level run. This is a good time for lunch in the cockpit. The drinks won't spill, the dishes won't slide, and with the apparent wind reduced by the boat's speed, even the napkins will stay put.

known as **jibing**. The big difference is that the sails do not luff when jibing. Rather, when the boat turns sufficiently to bring the wind to bear on the backside of the mainsail, the sail can swing across the deck from well out on one side to well out on the other with startling force, possibly damaging the rig or even knocking someone overboard. That is why a jibe must be controlled, as discussed shortly. It is also why, even when running, you need to be acutely aware of where the wind is coming from. Steer alertly to avoid unintentional, uncontrolled jibes.

Centerboard Up
With the wind from astern, the sail pulls mostly ahead. You don't need much lateral resistance, because the sideways forces are very small. That lets you pull up your centerboard or daggerboard and eliminate its drag. There's not much you can do about a fixed keel, though.

True Wind
Not to be confused with true versus magnetic compass directions, the **true wind** is simply the actual wind speed and direction—the wind you would experience if your boat were not moving.

Boom Vang On
When you're running, you want as much sail in front of the wind as you can get. Tensioning the boom vang holds the boom down, which keeps a flat expanse of sail presented to the wind. Allowing the boom to climb skyward with the waves or puffs makes the sail smaller and less effective. As mentioned earlier, however, you can ignore the boom vang if your hands are full elsewhere.

Apparent Wind

The wind that a sail feels is the **apparent wind**—a vector combination of the true wind and the boat's forward motion. Let's say that you're underway at 5 knots (1 knot is 1.15 statute miles per hour) under engine power in a flat calm—that is, a complete absence of wind. You will feel 5 knots of apparent wind from dead ahead. Or let's say you're sailing at 5 knots on a beam reach in a true wind of 10 knots. The apparent wind you feel will be 12 knots, and it will be slightly forward of your beam due to your boat's forward motion.

When the true wind is forward of the beam, the motion of your boat adds strength to it. The apparent wind is then stronger than the true wind. With the wind astern, the apparent wind is less than the true wind. Added speed (wind from ahead) makes the apparent wind come more on the nose. When you slow down, the apparent wind direction moves farther aft.

By the same token, a puff in a true wind that is blowing from forward of the beam will cause the apparent wind to move farther aft (sailors call that an **apparent lift**), and a lull will swing the apparent wind farther forward (an **apparent header**). A puff in a true wind that is blowing from aft of the beam will cause the apparent wind to move farther forward, and a lull will swing it farther aft. That is why, when reaching, you get the fastest overall speed by heading down during the puffs and up during the lulls.

Theoretically, you could construct a vector diagram to derive apparent wind from true as shown here, but the apparent wind is what your masthead fly and your telltales point to, and it's what you feel and trim your sails to. You don't

need to calculate it. You do, however, need to appreciate that if you're sailing downwind but will soon be turning upwind, the apparent wind will get stronger when you do.

The important thing to remember is that the apparent wind—not the true wind—is what a sail feels, and we therefore trim to the apparent wind, not the true wind.

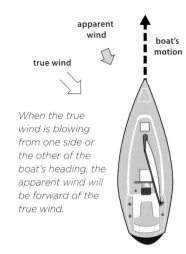

When the true wind is blowing from one side or the other of the boat's heading, the apparent wind will be forward of the true wind.

When a boat is traveling directly into the wind, the apparent wind speed is the sum of the true wind and boat speeds. When the boat is traveling with the wind, its forward motion reduces the apparent wind speed.

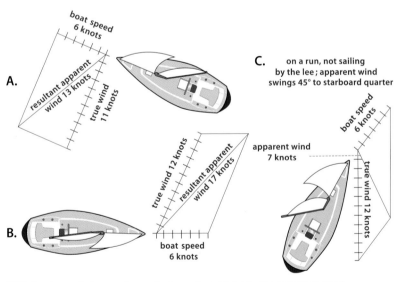

*With the true wind on or forward of your beam (**A, B**), the apparent wind will be stronger and farther forward. If the true wind is aft of your beam (**C**), the apparent wind will be forward of the true wind but weaker.*

Tacking and Jibing

The legendary Buddy Melges, Olympic and world champion racer, calls tacking and jibing "the blocking and tackling of sailing," and there's little doubt that they are sailing's most fundamental maneuvers. And yet an around-the-world sailor once told me that it took him an entire summer to learn the difference between the two. Tacking and jibing are very different. The boat handling and sail trim involved are different. Still, they are joined at the hip because both take you from one side of the eye of the wind to the other. But why do you need them and what are they for?

Point one hand into the wind. Now hold your other arm behind you and point the way the wind is blowing. Your hands create a line, and that line divides the circle of your horizon (or the 360 degrees of a compass) in half. There is a 180-degree semicircle to your right and an equal arc to your left. On any course that you steer to your left, the wind will hit your sail on its starboard side. On any course that you steer to your right, the air will hit the left side of your sail. When the wind is blowing over your starboard side, you're on starboard tack, and vice versa. Either tack, though, gives you access to only one half of the circle of possible directions and possible destinations. You need both tacks to get around.

Whenever a desired course change takes you from one side of the eye of the wind to the other, you must either tack or jibe. Let's say that you are reaching west across a lake with the wind from the north. To turn and go east, you could head into the wind and tack or you could steer away from the wind and jibe. Which is better? It depends on your present and future courses, the wind strength, and the waves.

Both tacking and jibing let you change tacks. Whether you're heading into the wind or away from the wind, tacking and jibing let you bring the wind from one side of your boat to the other. They open up the entire circle. They let you sail anywhere.

Tacking

To tack, you turn your bow into and through the eye of the wind, crossing the no-go zone in which sails have no power and can only luff and flog. Use your boat's momentum to complete your turn through the dead zone and out the other side. This is easiest in light winds, because the lighter the wind, the less its stopping power. A good breeze, however, can stop your boat's turn, especially if it's accompanied by a steep chop. Tacking, in fact, is one way of many that sailors can find themselves in irons (see page 45). So pick your spot to tack—a lull in the breeze, a flat spot in the waves— and steer smoothly (too sharp a turn will brake you) from one side of the wind to the other.

"Ready about?" is the traditional warning from the helmsman that you want to tack.

"Yes, ready," is the ideal response from your crew. "Ready about" is not so much a command as a question. You shouldn't tack until all hands are set. Get that acknowledgment, then tack the boat.

"Hard alee" is the helmsman's traditional signal that the rudder has been turned hard over to begin the tack. Head

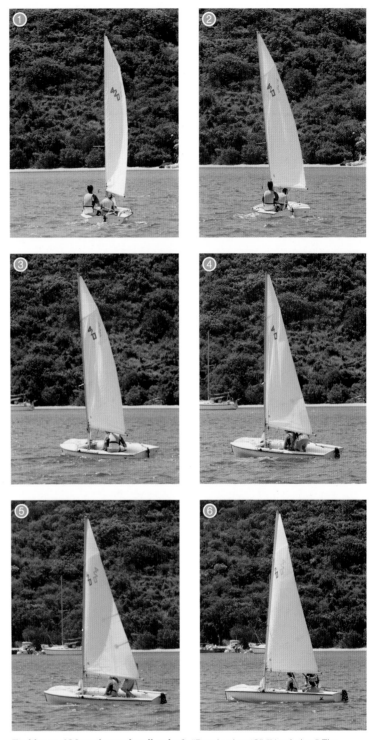

Tacking a 420 under mainsail only. 1. *"Ready about?" "Hard alee."* The helmsman puts the tiller to leeward. With no jib to worry about, all the crew has to do is duck. **2.** *As the boat turns through the eye of the wind—the no-go zone—the sail luffs across.* **3.** *Now it's the helmsman's turn to duck.* **4.** *The helmsman begins to shift his weight to the new windward side.* **5.** *The sail fills on the new side and the boat begins to gather way.* **6.** *The helmsman is again seated to windward. In this light breeze the crew remains centered to keep the boat level.*

Tacking a keelboat under mainsail only. 1. *With the boat close hauled on port tack, the helmsman initiates the tack.* **2.** *As the boat swings into the wind, a crewmember takes advantage of this opportunity to loosen the boom vang, which need not be tight for upwind sailing.* **3.** *With the tack completed, the boat leans into the wind and begins to gather way on starboard tack. Daysailing under main alone is a pretty casual affair.*

the boat into and through the wind, but don't use any more rudder than you need to carve your turn. If you are going from close hauled on one tack to close hauled on the other, keep turning until the wind angle on the new tack is about the same as it was on the old. You may

Starboard Tack

Whenever your sails are set to port, you are on starboard tack. This is because the wind is blowing over the starboard side of your boat. Your boat should sail equally well on either tack—if it doesn't, the rig needs to be tuned. Port-tack vessels give way to any starboard-tack vessels they "cross tracks" with. Maybe this goes back to the ancient belief that right was the lucky hand and left unlucky, but whatever the source, sailboats on opposite tacks still follow this.

want to head a bit farther away from the wind at first to build back speed, then work your way toward the close-hauled "edge" as your speed increases. Easing the main will help while you bear off, but within a minute or two of tacking, your sail trim should be the same as it was on the old tack.

In this chapter we are sailing under mainsail alone, but if you were flying a jib, it would of course need to be tacked when the mainsail is. Tacking a jib involves freeing the old sheet and trimming in the new one (the one that was unused, or lazy, when you were on the previous tack). The old sheet should be held until the jib has just a bit of wind on its back. That acceler-

"Ready About?"

In the days of fighting sail, this was a command, not a question, and it meant, "Get ready to come about." To **come about** means to head through the wind, and that was tough to do in those days. Today, sharp commands bringing instant obedience may look good in the movies, but sailing works better along friendlier lines. Don't expect your crew to leap to the rigging when you say "ready about." Rather, it's a question, albeit one that the crew should acknowledge. When they're ready, tack the boat. Approach even the simplest of maneuvers by assuring that your crew is together and ready. It's a good way to sail.

ates the sail onto the other side without prolonged flogging. Trim on the new side as fast as possible before the jib fills.

Jibing

While tacking heads you into the wind, jibing turns you away from it. To jibe, you could simply bear away until your stern passes through the eye of the wind, at which point the wind will pass from one side of the sail to the other and will swing the sail to the opposite side of the boat. The challenge is that your sails are still full when they change sides, and that makes jibing more difficult and—if done in an uncontrolled fashion—more exciting than coming about, and in the worst case a little frightening. An uncontrolled or accidental jibe can involve a crashing boom and

Jibing a 420 under mainsail only.
1. *The boat is sailing nearly dead downwind, so to steer more to the right these sailors will have to jibe. The helmsman says, "Ready to jibe?" Then, saying "Jibe ho," he begins the turn while trimming the mainsail.* **2.** *Now he has turned far enough to let the wind reach the back of the sail, and you can tell it's close to swinging across the boat. The crew is ducking, and the helmsman continues to haul in the mainsheet so the sail can't pick up too much momentum when it swings.* **3.** *There goes the sail, but he has it trimmed and under control.* **4.** *Now he must let the sail out promptly on the other side, or else it might force the boat to round up into the wind—or, in a stiff breeze, even to capsize. Meanwhile both sailors use their weight to counter the jibe-induced heel.* **5.** *The boat settles into the new tack. They're still sailing more or less downwind, but now on starboard tack instead of port.*

TELLTALE

VANG
BRACKET

TELLTALE

VANG

An up-close look at an uncontrolled jibe. 1. *The sail is out against the shrouds for downwind sailing and appears normal, but the telltale on the port shroud, which is streaming ahead and to port instead of starboard, should tell the helmsman that he's sailing by the lee, with the wind coming in over the starboard quarter. He needs to either turn left or shift the mainsail to port to prevent an accidental jibe.* **2.** *Instead he turns even farther to the right. Now the wind is getting behind the sail, causing the sail to bubble and act uneasy. The boom may rise or make feints to the centerline, too. If you're paying any kind of attention, you'll know something's wrong, and a look at the telltale or the masthead fly should tell you what it is.* **3.** *The helmsman has ignored the warnings,*

and now the boom is preparing to swing across the boat, uncontrolled by the mainsheet. There is still time to avert the jibe with a sharp swing to port, but only barely. **4.** *Now it's too late to prevent the uncontrolled jibe. The good news is that no one's head is in the way of the boom.* **5.** *Completing its violent swing, the boom fetches up against the shrouds, the mainsheet, and the boom vang. The starboard shroud telltale indicates just how badly the boat was by the lee before the jibe. And that suddenly slack boom vang tells us that something may have broken.* **6.** *Yup. The bracket that held the vang to the base of the mast has torn loose, shearing the rivets that were holding it. This will soon be fixed with a rivet gun. The damage could have been worse.*

whipping sheets, both of which are best avoided.

If you want to avoid jibing altogether, you can simply choose to tack instead. Though tacking is a less direct way of getting from a broad reach on port tack to a broad reach on starboard tack, almost all sailors use this maneuver from time to time.

Most of the time, however, a controlled jibe is perfectly safe and nothing to fear. All you have to do to control the jibe is to control the swing of the sails—most particularly the mainsail.

Begin by calling to your crew, "Ready to jibe?" When your crew answers affirmatively, signal that you're initiating the jibe

---

By the Lee
When your stern has passed through the eye of the wind but your sail has yet to swing across, you are sailing **by the lee**. The boom will lift unless it's vanged down. The mainsail may bubble or flutter (like luffing, but less consistent or distinct) along the mast. You are sailing on a razor's edge, as close to jibing as you can be without the mainsail slamming across the boat. You might sail by the lee for a short while on purpose (to save having to jibe twice to round a mark, for instance). Generally, though, it's a dangerous practice. You should either complete a jibe or head back up on your current tack.

Jibing the Jib
Jibing the jib is much simpler than jibing the main. The process is the same as tacking—you cast off the old sheet and trim in the new. The jib is easy to jibe because the main steals much of its breeze when you're sailing downwind. Still, keep control of it by easing the old sheet gradually as you pull in the new. If you let the old sheet **fly** (cast it off completely), the jib can balloon forward of the boat and wrap itself around the headstay.

---

with the time-honored "Jibe ho." Then begin bearing off.

As you head down, trim in the mainsail to keep it under control. If the breeze is strong, you'll have to be heading almost directly downwind before you can trim the sail without heeling the boat excessively or upsetting the helm. With a little experience, you'll find that spot where the main is "trimmable" and be able to remain on that course long enough for the trimmer to pull in the mainsail before you continue the turn. This is a good maneuver to practice in a moderate breeze before you execute it in a fresh one.

Trim the boom as close to the center of the boat as you can, then resume your turn, steering the stern through the wind. When the boom swings

---

across the boat's centerline, duck if and as necessary, then *let the sheet run free!* This last part is crucial, because it allows the force of the boom coming across to dissipate. *Don't* hold tight to the sheet, because that causes the boom to slam to a destructive halt. It can also cause excessive heeling and will cause the mainsail to fight the rudder, possibly forcing a continuation of the turn far past the point at which the helmsman attempts to stop it. Let the sheet run.

You'll need both hands to trim, so steer with knees and elbows if you're sailing alone. Use consistent, incremental, moderate course changes through your turn; if you turn too sharply, the sail will slam over untrimmed.

Goosewing Jibe
This picturesque term describes an unpicturesque jibe. If the top half of the sail catches on a spreader (not likely but possible) or is pinned against the rigging by a strong breeze, the top part of the sail may stay on the old side when the boom swings across the boat. It's alarming. The boat becomes hard to control; damage to sails or rig threatens. The solution is to jibe right back again to get the entire sail back on one side. Then you can figure out what went wrong and try your jibe again.

Reading the Wind

More than any maneuver or technique, reading the wind is the key to learning how to sail. You may know that if you put the wind on your beam you'll be reaching, but that doesn't do much good if you can't find the wind.

Your primary wind indicators are the ones on your boat. They show you the **apparent wind**—which, you'll remember, is the sum of the true wind and the wind your boat makes by moving. The apparent wind is what hits your sails and drives your boat. It's the wind you're sailing in and the wind you must trim to. Apparent wind is the wind to watch.

To read the apparent wind angle, you can use your masthead fly as already mentioned, your telltales (see below), or electronics. Every change in wind angle requires an answering change in sail trim or course in order to maintain your boat's optimum speed. Like most rules in sailing, this is one you'll start to bend as soon as you learn it—neglecting constant adjustments for the sake of relaxation, for example—but again, you have to know a rule before you can know when it's OK to bend it.

Your reading of the strength of the wind need not be as precise as your reading of its direction. Anemometers are common on bigger boats, but on most small boats a rough guess will serve you well enough. In contrast with wind direction, it is the strength of the **true wind** that you care most about. After all, if your boatspeed were so great as to create a 40-knot apparent wind from a 15-knot true wind (which would be possible only in a high-performance multihull or sailboard), you could always slow down. To choose a more common situation, suppose you are sailing downwind at 9 knots in an apparent wind of 11 knots. Eleven knots isn't much, but the true wind is 20 knots, which means you'll probably need to reef your sails when you start back upwind.

The Beaufort scale (page 60) is a famous compilation of observable signs (rising smoke, sea state, behavior of flags, etc.) that give an indication of wind strength. Knowing in broad strokes how hard the wind is blowing is crucial to speed, safety, and comfort.

Using Telltales

We've already snuck a peek at the use of telltales. Now let's take a closer look. Broadly speaking, any wind indicator is a telltale, telling the story of the wind. Flags on shore, birds in flight, smoke streaming, ripples crossing the water, and the crests of waves are all telltales of a sort, and as time goes by you'll use them all. But **telltales** in the particular sense of the word are short lengths of ribbon, yarn, or even audiotape. They make accurate, precise, convenient, economical wind indicators. You'll find them on most sailboats, and they let you see the wind in several ways.

I count myself among those sailors who prefer to read the wind from "woollies" tied to the boat's shrouds than from a masthead fly. A 6-inch length of yarn (or polyester, which lasts better than wool and is just as sensitive) can tell you where the wind is coming from just as clearly as an arrow, and you don't have to divert your attention to the masthead in order to consult it. (A masthead fly is still valuable, however, because the wind changes **aloft**—at the masthead—before it does **alow**—on deck.) You have to unsnarl telltales occasionally, and you have to tie them far enough outboard for clear air and high enough for visibility, but they're more sensitive and convenient than any arrow.

You can also put telltales on sails. A piece of yarn (any color but white) attached to a sail lets you see the airflow over

UPPER JIB TELLTALES

WINDWARD SHROUD TELLTALE

LEEWARD SHROUD TELLTALE

LOWER JIB TELLTALES

The telltale on the starboard shroud tells this sailor that she's on a close reach. Both pairs of telltales on the luff of the jib are also visible, and the fact that these are streaming aft suggests that the jib is optimally trimmed for the wind.

it. Yarns on both sides of the jib luff create a "stall warning" system. In smooth air, the yarns stream smoothly along the sail. In turbulent air, they twitch and flick and rise. In dead air they droop. Watch the yarns! When the windward and leeward woollies are streaming straight aft and in parallel, in laminar bliss, the sail is pulling to its maximum. When the leeward telltale lifts and flutters, either you're sailing too far off the wind or the sail is too tight. When the windward telltale rises and flutters, either you're sailing too close to the wind or the sail is too loose. It's common to array three pairs of telltales along the jib luff: one about a quarter of the way up, one at mid-luff, and one three-quarters of the way up. Together, these comprise a priceless guidance system constructed from pennies' worth of yarn.

Telltales are also great on the leech of the mainsail. Most people affix them roughly halfway between the battens. A drooping woolly means that section of the sail is experiencing anemic airflow off its after edge. A jerking, jiving streamer, on the other hand, means that part of the sail is overdosed with air. Adjust your sail controls until all the telltales are pointing merrily straight aft. Then your sail will be looking and drawing its best.

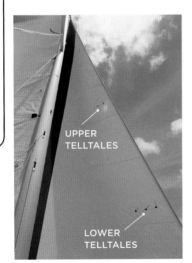

UPPER TELLTALES

LOWER TELLTALES

Telltales on the roller-furling jib of a cruising sailboat. The windward telltales are lifting both high and low, which tells us that either the jib needs to be trimmed or the boat needs to head down slightly. Since the jib looks close hauled, probably the helmsman is pinching and needs to bear off.

The masthead fly on this cruising sailboat tells us that the boat is close hauled on starboard tack. The leech telltales are streaming, indicating that there is at least some flow over the mainsail, and the topping lift is slack, as it should be when the sail is up. The reefing lines are improperly under tension, however, which is cupping the leech of the sail to windward and introducing a bubble near the clew. A slab-reefing system like the one on this boat is convenient for shorthanded cruisers, as we'll see in Chapter 2, but suffers from a lot of friction. When you shake out a reef you often have to forcibly recover slack in the reefing lines before the mainsail will set properly.

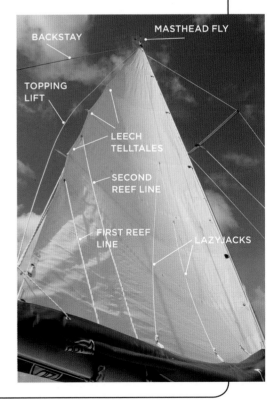

BACKSTAY

MASTHEAD FLY

TOPPING LIFT

LEECH TELLTALES

SECOND REEF LINE

FIRST REEF LINE

LAZYJACKS

The Beaufort Scale

Sir Francis Beaufort, an admiral in the British Navy, first published his table in 1805. Today it is included in virtually every marine almanac, sailing manual, and seamanship text because two centuries of use have proved it both accurate and useful. By resolving the continuous curve of increasing wind speed into twelve distinct **forces** and describing how to recognize each of these, it gives you a handy yet objective way to estimate wind strength. Couple that with the knowledge of how your boat responds to any given wind force, and you have what you need to adapt to the wind.

Beaufort Force 0. *Wind: 0 knots. Sea state: Sea like a mirror.*

Beaufort Force 1. *Wind: 1–3 knots. Sea state: Ripples like scales, no crests.*

Beaufort Force 2. *Wind: 4–6 knots. Sea state: Small wavelets, crests glassy and do not break.*

Beaufort Force 3. *Wind: 7–10 knots. Sea state: Large wavelets, crests break, whitecaps begin.*

Beaufort Force 4. *Wind: 11–16 knots. Sea state: Small waves, numerous whitecaps.*

Beaufort Force 5. *Wind: 17–21 knots. Sea state: Moderate and longer waves; whitecaps and spray.*

Beaufort Force 6. *Wind: 22–27 knots. Sea state: Larger waves, numerous whitecaps, much spray.*

Beaufort Force 7. *Wind: 28–33 knots. Sea state: Sea heaps up, waves break, foam blows in streaks.*

Beaufort Force 8. *Wind: 34–40 knots. Sea state: Moderate waves of greater length, foam blows in long streaks.*

Beaufort Force 9. *Wind: 41–47 knots. Sea state: High waves, rolling sea, dense streaks of foam, spray reduces visibility.*

Beaufort Force 10. *Wind: 48–55 knots. Sea state: Very high waves, overhanging crests, sea white with foam, visibility reduced.*

Beaufort Force 11. *Wind: 56–63 knots. Sea state: Exceptionally high waves, sea covered with foam, visibility poor.*

Returning to a Mooring

You've probably heard the story—everything about the first sail went beautifully until the skipper tried to get back to the mooring or dock.

Sailing downwind is easier than sailing upwind. Keep that in mind. Try to stay upwind of home base if you can. When you hike down into the Grand Canyon, you're told that getting back up to the rim takes three times as long as going down. If possible, manage your sail so as to make the way home short and direct—a run or a reach rather than a long, uphill beat. Remember, too, that the tide can rise or fall 4 feet in as little as 2 hours in many areas. The tidal current that you were counting on to carry you home may reverse itself and work against you. The breeze can pipe up or die or change direction. The fog can roll in. Sailing puts you in touch with the elements. Keep track of what Mother Nature is up to as you sail.

Picking up a mooring is harder than leaving it. The object when you return is to control your boat's course and speed so that you "park" her bow-to your mooring. That makes it relatively simple to grab the mooring line and lower your sails in a relaxed and orderly way. Given ideal conditions, you can succeed on your first try.

Face the wind and hold your arms out sideways. Everything in front of you is upwind, and everything behind is down-

Making a mooring. 1. *Approach on a reach, aiming for a spot two or three boat lengths to leeward of the mooring buoy.* **2.** *When directly to leeward of the mooring, round up toward it, letting the sail luff.* **3, 4.** *The foredeck crew picks up the mooring pendant and secures it to the foredeck cleat.* **5.** *Get the mainsail down promptly so the boat doesn't sail back and forth around its mooring.*

wind. Sail upwind until, while you're facing into the wind, your mooring is directly to your left or right side, then head toward the buoy. As you head for the mooring the apparent wind will be just forward of your beam. If you're flying a jib as well as the mainsail, get the jib down now. Let the mainsail luff completely, and let the boat slow almost to a stop. In a centerboard boat, your board should be down for maximum steering control and minimum leeway. Now add a little speed by trimming. Trim and ease as needed to control your speed. Easy does it. When you get within three or four

boat lengths of the buoy, head toward a spot two boat lengths downwind of the target. Controlling your speed, round up to the buoy so that when you get there the boat is heading directly into the wind and stops within an arm's length of it.

Whenever you pick up a mooring or make a landing, control your speed so that you arrive at your target with as little forward momentum as possible. Wind strength and direction, current strength and direction, sea state, maneuvering room, and the weight and carrying power of your boat will vary enough to make virtually

every pick-up or landing different. Still, a course that allows you to speed up or slow down by trimming or easing sail is the ideal approach no matter what the situation. If at first you don't succeed, simply abandon the effort, then make a new approach and another try. Don't try to rescue a bad effort with heroics. Each approach offers lessons to be learned. And don't worry—you're not conning the *Queen Elizabeth II* or a 747. The sheet and tiller are all the controls you need. Try again. (For returning to a dock rather than a mooring, see page 170.)

Securing the Boat

There's more to leaving a boat than locking doors and rolling up windows, but it's the same idea. When you're leaving your boat on a mooring, be certain you secure the mooring line, known also as the **mooring pendant** (pronounced "pennant"). Check and double-check how it's fastened. If there is a **fairlead**, or **chock**, on the bow, lead the line through it. This assures that the line is channeled through a polished, low-friction metal fitting rather than sawing

back and forth across the foredeck as it would if led directly overboard from the foredeck cleat. Make sure you have **chafing gear** on the mooring line at any possible point of friction, such as a chock, deck edge, or shroud. You might also wish to attach a safety lashing as a backup for the mooring line if you'll be leaving the boat for any length of time.

Stowing the sails involves either taking them off and bagging them or furling them in

place. To assure that a sail will fit in its bag, and to minimize creased and cracked sail fabric, flake or fold the sail before you bag it. You can usually manage this on board. Roller furlers are handy for headsails. Make sure, though, that the sail is rolled in tight with no loose flaps to catch wind, and that the control line is cleated securely to keep the sail from unrolling while you're away. A rolled headsail should have a strip of UV-resistant fabric sewed over its leech to

Furling or Flaking the Mainsail

Headsails can be thrown below or lashed on deck, but when the main comes down it needs taming. It can lie over the companionway or an open hatch or fill the cockpit with battens and cloth. Safety is a prime consideration. Sheet in the swinging main boom, close the companionway hatch of a cruising sailboat, and leave enough open water around you so that you can manage a few minutes of diminished visibility.

The traditional **furl** is descended from the furling done aloft on square-riggers. Gather the mainsail on one side of the boom, stretch it aft, point the battens aft, and roll fold over fold of the mainsail toward the boom, gathering each fold into the belly of remaining canvas, until you've made it a neat tube that you can then cinch tightly in place atop the boom with **stops**, **ties**, or **gaskets**, which are simply short lengths of line or bungee cord or strips of canvas.

To roll a mainsail instead of furling it, detach the head of the sail from the mast track and halyard and, starting from the head and working along the luff, roll the sail around the headboard until you reach the foot, which is still attached to the boom. You will have created a sausage of sail. Tie the tube to the boom. Rolling is neat, but it buries the head, is harder to do at sea, and requires detaching the luff of the sail from the mast.

Flaking the main is best done as it is being lowered. Make a loose fold along the boom with the first section of sail to come down. From there, build a stack of folds accordion-style. Flaking is the only way some bulletproof racing mains can be furled. It takes crew, coordination, and patience.

Whether you furl, roll, or flake, you'll want to cover the mainsail with a canvas sail cover before you leave it. Protecting it from sun, wind, and rain will keep it in good shape much longer.

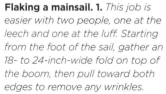

Flaking a mainsail. 1. *This job is easier with two people, one at the leech and one at the luff. Starting from the foot of the sail, gather an 18- to 24-inch-wide fold on top of the boom, then pull toward both edges to remove any wrinkles.*
2. *Repeat, stacking the folds.*
3. *Some sailors like to finish by wrapping the head around the boom to secure the stacked sail.*
4. *Secure with sail ties, or gaskets. Cover with a canvas sail cover to protect the sail from the sun and weather.*

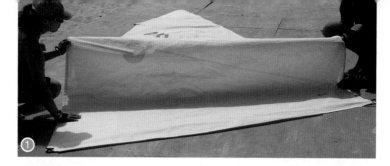

prevent the exposed leech from rotting in the sunlight while you're away.

A mainsail can be flaked, rolled, or furled atop the boom in the traditional fashion. There's no "right" way, but it is unseamanlike to leave a baggy sail draped as an afterthought over the boom. A ship may distinguish herself by "the cut of her jib," but "the furl of her main" is another visible signature of her skipper's habits. Do a careful, tidy job of furling. To protect the furled or flaked mainsail from sunlight, cover it with a fitted canvas sail cover before you leave.

Movement means chafe, and chafe leads to damage. Everything should be stowed in its most immobile position. Avoid slack in the mainsheet, slap in the halyards, play in the helm, and unsecured items, locker doors, drawers, and hatches. Check around.

Finally, set **running rigging** so that it is ready to run when you are next ready to use it. Coil and hang the tails of halyards, sheets, and control lines to make them ready to go. Give some thought to how things might change while you're away. Is your boat properly secured

Folding a dinghy mainsail. 1, 2, 3. *Starting at the foot, flake toward the head. Partial battens can remain in the sail.* **4.** *The topmost batten in a 420 mainsail is full length and has to come out for folding.* **5.** *Fold the flaked sail to fit its bag.*

against heavy weather? Rain? Sun? Petty thievery?

Inspect the mooring line one last time, and you're done.

Flaking a Jib

Harder, smoother cloth—such as Mylar, Kevlar, or heavily coated Dacron—is most susceptible to creases and cracks, but crinkling lessens the efficiency and shortens the life of any sail. So don't just stuff a jib or other headsail into its bag—flake it instead. Flaking applies to rope as well as cloth and means simply to coil in loose folds. You can't really coil a sail, but you can lay it up in pleats so that it will unfold easily. Stretch an edge of the sail taut, then gather the body of the sail toward that edge in regular, medium-sized (about two hands' width) folds. Accumulate the folds in a pile, roll the pile to fit the bag, and you're done.

It makes sense to give some thought to how you want a sail to come out of its bag before you put it in. If you want it to come out head first, bag the sail with the head on top. And if you want instant access to the luff of the sail upon opening the bag, flake it to order.

You can fold a jib similar to a main-sail. If the jibsheets stay on the sail for storage, fold them inside.

Dressing to Sail

"What to wear?" It's often the first question asked, even though it's the last one I'm tackling in this chapter. If you've never been sailing or are just getting started, your concern makes perfect sense. Protection is much more important than fashion. Safety, comfort, and utility are the style at sea.

The traditional watch-words have long included a loose fit, tough fabrics, and double seams. When it comes to warmth, however, modern clothing technology has elaborated on this elemental wisdom. Synthetic/wool blends for socks, breathable shells for jackets, and the wondrous fleeces that insulate superbly and wick water away while resisting moisture and remaining light and comfortable are all options the sailors of yesteryear didn't have. Khaki and denim still do well for a summer's afternoon, but there are other options now when you're expecting wet and cold conditions.

Wear soft-soled shoes for protection and traction. Barefoot sailing is dangerous; stubbed toes are merely painful, but slips can be fatal. Most sneakers are good, but running shoes are prone to twist, cross-trainers can be slippery, and basketball soles are often clumsy. Soft-soled sandals and flip-flops are comfortable but useless for working or walking around on deck. For dedicated boat use, the proven boat shoe is still a great bet. Athletic shoes made with a boating sole have also become popular. They provide good comfort and support along with a grip on slippery decks. Whatever you wear, your soles should be white (black soles leave marks), and rippled treads are notorious for picking up grit and tar that can savage decks.

Your chances of keeping dry are good on some sailboats, remote on others. The threat of getting wet, however, is always there. That makes foul-weather gear something that most sailors own. Many also buy sea-boots of some sort. Once you

Socks

In wintertime wear light cotton socks under heavy wool socks and try like hell to keep your feet dry. Even in summer it's nice to have a sock (just about any sock) inside a clammy boot. Wool/synthetic blends retain heat better than synthetic socks, especially when wet, Still, wet socks are no fun to ship with, and many sailors go without when they can.

go sailing you'll appreciate the need for wet-weather clothes, but until you have some idea of the kind of sailing you'll do, don't run out and buy a suit that may not suit you.

At any rate, anticipate some contact with water. If your watch won't take it, don't wear

Shorts and a jersey made of quick-drying synthetic fabrics are ideal for fair-weather dinghy sailing, as are lightweight, high-grip shoes meant for use in and around the water. Lacking these, however, shorts, a T-shirt, and nonscuff sneakers will get you by in warm weather. You'll want a sleek and unobtrusive PFD like this one, and good sunglasses. Open-fingered sailing gloves protect your hands. Add layers of clothing on cool days.

Caps and Hats

The knitted watch cap is a wonder. It hugs your head, dries in a flash, stows in your pocket, and warms your blood. Remember a watch cap for sailing at night or offshore. You see baseball-style caps everywhere. Most are adjustable and can be snugged down so neither a typhoon or the boom can knock them off. Wear them under a foul-weather gear hood to help you see and anytime to shade your eyes. Baseball caps work well at sea. "Spinnaker hats," straw hats, "camel drivers," and a variety of other lids protect well from sun. Some are even nice for scooping water over your head in the doldrums. Hats that stay on in a breeze are a plus.

it. Beyond that, choose clothes that dry quickly or that can be worn with at least minimal comfort when wet. Whether you're cruising, racing, or day-sailing, it's a good idea to make sure that you're prepared for the extremes you might meet. Take a bathing suit to keep cool, rain gear to keep dry, and a wind-breaker to keep warm. Then build from there.

Gloves

Time was sails were made of canvas, and you could tell real sailors by their callused hands. Today it's smart to protect your hands and improve your grip with sailing gloves. Gloves for warmth are harder to find: lobsterman's gloves are clumsy; ski gloves are slippery when wet; driving gloves aren't tough enough. Wear mittens and take them off to work the lines? Most frostbite sailors, I've noted, sail bare-handed. Still, even in summer it gets cold enough to warrant gloves at sea.

Layering works well at sea. A fleece to don under the jacket, a workshirt to put under that, a T-shirt under that, and you're ready to follow the thermometer up and down. Long trousers or jeans—cut as loosely as your fashion sense allows—will block the sun if need be. Shorts, long-sleeved shirts, and pullover tops complete the basics. In cold weather, long underwear made of silk dries fast, can be worn to sleep in, and affords lots of warmth for little weight.

Take what you need and leave the rest. There's never enough room on a boat. Pare down when you pack. Spread everything out and go through it twice. Take something out on each pass, and you're on the right track. Leave room for a heavy sweater or fleece vest, sunscreen, sunglasses, and a hat. Now you're set to sail just about anywhere out of a stowable duffel.

Sunscreen

The only problem with a watch cap is that it won't protect your face and neck from sun, and protection from sun is vital. Wear sunscreen lotion with a high SPF (sun protection factor) to hold skin cancers at bay.

And don't forget to renew your sunscreen periodically throughout the day.

Tress Control

A scarf may be too dowdy, a hat too hot, a hairband too prissy, a rubber band too crass, but how to tame your hair? The sailors sporting bandannas in those old movies were doing just that. How can you swashbuckle if you can't see? If you've got hair, you need to deal with it when you sail.

Harnesses and PFDs

These necessities work only when worn, so choose comfortable gear. The Coast Guard mandates that boats carry personal flotation devices (PFDs) for all on board. Safety harnesses are not required by law, but they are a must for those on deck at night, offshore, or in bad weather. Some skippers ask every sailor bring to bring both PFD and harness aboard, but most supply PFDs at least. If you own your own, though, you'll know that it fits and works. See Appendix 4 for more on PFDs and Chapter 7 for more on harnesses.

Foul-Weather Gear

Huddling under an army poncho doesn't cut it for long. If you've got suitable wet-weather gear, though, wet weather is simply an annoyance instead of a catastrophe. Foul-weather gear, like sneakers, has gotten more specialized (and more expensive). Wet suits are what lots of people use on dinghies and sailboards (where they're always wet). Dry suits are geared to seal body heat in. Survival suits go a step further; flotation suits keep you up. Most sailors, though, still wear garden-variety storm gear. It, too, comes in different varieties—light and flexible for inshore, astronautical for offshore. Medium-priced, medium-weight neoprene-coated "fisherman's" foul-weather gear is still very serviceable.

CHAPTER TWO

Controlling Your Boat

You've completed your first sail. You boarded your boat, rigged its sail, and cast off. You worked with the wind to sail where you wanted to go, and then you sailed home and put the boat to bed. You can honestly say now that you know how to sail. The purpose of the rest of this book is to build on that knowledge until you become a sailor in the fullest sense of the word—a go-anywhere, all-weather sailor, at ease and in tune with your boat, the wind, and the waves, and ready to anticipate and cope with whatever comes along. So what does it take to reach that mastery?

Patience. There's a lot to learn. Even the masters are still learning, and the real ones acknowledge that.

Energy. Going after it helps you "get it."

Good sense. Know what you know and what you still need to learn.

And, as the New York cabbie told the tourist who asked him how to get to Carnegie Hall, "Practice, practice, practice."

But the one quality above all others that will make you a complete sailor is a state of deep engagement. If the powerful curve of a sail—the way it can harness wind to pull you across the water—incites in you a sense of wonder; if, each time you learn some new thing about the nuances of sailing, you want to learn more; if you lose track of time while sailing; if even a windless afternoon under a hot sun or a cold, wet homeward slog seems redolent with promise and adventure, then you're already well on your way.

Becoming a sailor takes time. Simply spending time on the water and getting familiar with what once seemed strange is part of the process. Revisiting concepts and information that may have swamped you in the beginning lets you get a grip on them. After a while you'll feel different on a boat. Those first halting moves will become more fluid and instinctive.

In this chapter it's time to add a jib, sail through a few new situations, and add new techniques. As the pieces fall into place, give a thought to the blind men describing the elephant: whether you have the tail, the trunk, or the tusk, chances are that what you have in your hands is not (yet) the whole behemoth. But take your time. Every hour you commit to this new passion will add another detail to the emerging picture, and that progress is itself the goal. After all, you are in a boat and sailing—isn't that enough?

Chapter 1 dealt with the essentials. This chapter helps you cement that foundation and move ahead, gaining control.

Setting the Jib

In Chapter 1 you learned how to sail under mainsail alone. On some small boats, as we saw, that's the only sail you have. But if the boat you're sailing has a **jib**, or sail in front of the mast, before long you'll want to set it. Doing so is likely to transform your boat from a draft horse to a thoroughbred.

Because it is usually boomless and smaller than the mainsail, the jib is typically much easier to hoist. When the breeze is light you can conveniently hoist it at the dock or mooring before getting underway, but when the wind is fresher you will soon discover the downside of this convenience. Unrestrained by a boom, and trailing a faceful of rope from its clew, a jib will whip and slap in the wind. You would need to trim it to stop it from flogging, but you don't want to do that until you're ready to leave the mooring or dock. Set a small jib at the dock or mooring on a calm day or if you have to, but it's usually easier to set a jib underway.

Assuming that you've gotten underway under mainsail alone, the easiest way to raise the jib is to turn to a broad reach—almost a run—with the wind approaching from well aft

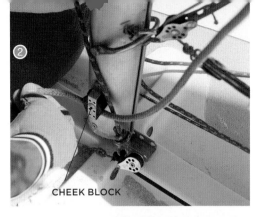

Hoisting the jib on a 420. **1.** *After rigging the jib (see Chapter 1), these sailors choose to hoist it prior to launching from a beach.* **2.** *The 420 jib halyard is part wire (for low stretch) and part rope (for better grip). When the sail is most of the way up you will come to the transition from rope to wire, with a becket block separating the two. At this point, reeve the rope tail through the cheek block at the base of the mast . . .* **3.** *then back up and through the becket block, forming a three-part tackle with which to tension the halyard.* **4.** *And here's an advantage of hoisting the jib on the beach: while one crewmember tensions the halyard, the other sways on the forestay, which bends the mast forward and allows more halyard tension.* **5.** *With the jib luff fully tensioned, the halyard is fastened with a cleat hitch.* **6.** *Coil the halyard tail and tuck it between the halyard and the mast, out of the way.*

TELLTALE

of the beam. Now raise the jib in the blanketed area, or **lee**, that you've created forward of the mainsail. The sail can fill without thrashing, while your off-the-wind course reduces heeling and gives you a stable platform on which to work. When it comes to **dousing** a jib, pulling it down in the lee of the main is again the easiest way.

Though hoisting the jib is relatively light work, tensioning the halyard takes some muscle. The luff of the sail should be straight, a bit better than tight. Make sure your jib hasn't sagged. If the luff (leading edge) of the jib is scalloped, ease the jib out until it luffs (flutters), then hoist it tight. Then trim the sheet and resume sailing.

Jibs on roller furlers offer more flexibility. They're a breeze (so to speak) to roll out. Just make sure the control line for the furler drum doesn't snag or kink as the sail fills with wind, because that's a hard snafu to

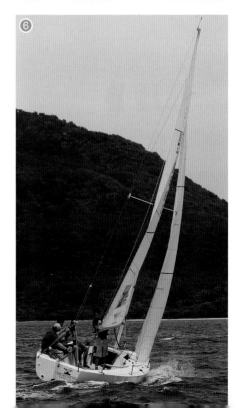

Hoisting the jib on a small keelboat. 1. *The jib on this IC-24 is fully rigged (see Chapter 1) and ready to hoist. Having cleared the anchorage under mainsail alone, the helmsman bears off to a broad reach (as indicated by the shroud telltale) to put the jib in the lee of the mainsail, and the crew starts hauling up the jib.* **2.** *The halyard leads back to the cockpit. When the crew has gained as much as possible hand over hand, he wraps two or three turns clockwise around the winch, then inserts the winch handle to gain a mechanical advantage for those last inches.* **3.** *A scalloped jib luff indicates that the halyard is not yet tight enough.* **4.** *Still not quite tight enough. (Note that this jibsheet leads inside the shrouds.)* **5.** *When properly tensioned and trimmed . . .* **6.** *the jib shifts the boat into a higher gear.*

① LAZY JIBSHEET

ACTIVE JIBSHEET

FURLING LINE

②

③

④ SELF-TAILER

FURLING LINE

⑤ TURNING BLOCK

CHEEK BLOCK

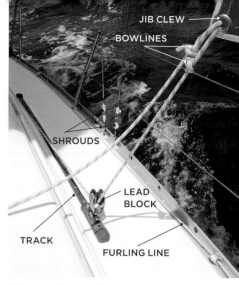

This view aft along the leeward deck of the Oceanis 323 shows the jib-sheets tied to the jib's clew cringle with bowlines.

Setting a roller-furled jib.

1, 2. With the boat on a broad reach, release the furling line and haul in the active jibsheet, in this case the port sheet, while maintaining a light tension on the furling line to keep the sail under control and prevent snags on the furling drum. *3.* As the jib begins to fill, the crew throws a couple of turns around the sheet winch for control . . . *4.* then uses the winch handle to trim the last few feet of sheet. Note that this winch is self-tailing; when the line is jammed into the self-tailer as shown, it can continue to come in but won't slip out. Note too that the turns always go around a winch clockwise. The furling line is visible under the crew's left foot. *5.* The jib is full and drawing, and the boat leans into its increased sail area and leaps ahead. The jib on this Oceanis 323, like that on the IC-24, is small enough to trim inside the shrouds. The sheet runs through a track-mounted lead block, back to a cheek block mounted on the cabinside aft, then up to the winch.

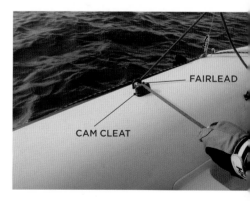

Any genoa big enough to overlap the shrouds, as this one does, will have to sheet outside them.

On a 420 the jibsheet trims through a simple fairlead and is cleated in the cam cleat shown. No winches or turning blocks are needed for a jib this small.

undo. Rolling in the jib? Head off until it's blanketed by the main. Wait until the sail starts to collapse or hang, then roll it up by pulling in the furling line. Keep a light tension on the leeward sheet to help the sail roll up evenly. **Roller-reef** the jib—i.e., roll it up partway—if the wind freshens and starts to overpower your boat. Cleat the furling line when you have the sail area where you want it.

Handling jibsheets is a little like handling the reins of a horse; you trim the sheet on the leeward side and leave the windward sheet **lazy**—i.e., loose and free. When you change tacks, change sheets. The jibsheets sometimes comprise a single length of line that is spliced or knotted at its midpoint to the clew of the jib. (See, for example, the 420 jibsheets on page 20.) Usually, though, the two sheets are two separate lines, one end of each being fastened to the clew, often with a bowline (see page 167). Most jibsheets travel through a **fairlead** of one sort or another en route from the jib to the trimmer's hands. On a sailing dinghy the fairlead might simply be a smooth-bored bronze or stainless steel

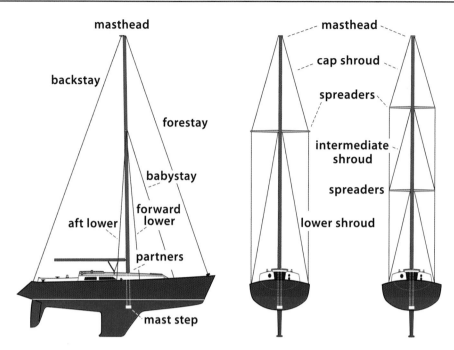

masthead

backstay

forestay

babystay

forward lower

aft lower

partners

mast step

masthead

cap shroud

spreaders

intermediate shroud

spreaders

lower shroud

Shrouds

A sailboat's mast is kept upright by guy wires, much like a radio tower. Chapter 1 mentioned the headstay (or forestay), which leads from the mast to the front of the boat and from which the jib is flown. The **backstay** is the opposing wire from the masthead to the stern. **Shrouds** support the mast from side to side. The shroud leading from the masthead to either side of the boat is the **upper shroud**, or simply the **upper**, or sometimes the **cap shroud**. The upper may be augmented with one or two **lower shrouds** per side, which attach to the mast about one-half to two-thirds of the way up; an **after lower** lands on the side deck aft of the upper shroud, while a **forward lower** lands forward of the upper shroud. Lower shrouds prevent the mast from buckling at mid-height.

Most boats over 15 or so feet long have at least one set of **spreaders**—struts standing out from either side of the mast at an angle slightly above the horizontal. The upper shrouds run over the ends of the spreaders, and the result is

On a masthead-rigged boat the mast may be stepped in the bilge of the boat or on deck. There may be two or more sets of spreaders, though a boat less than 32 to 35 feet long is more likely to have only a single set. A small, heavy-weather staysail can be flown from a babystay, staysail stay (not shown), or inner forestay, though this feature is more common on boats intended for offshore work than on coastal sailers.

a larger, more advantageous angle between the shrouds and the masthead. Lower shrouds land on the mast at the base of the lowest set of spreaders.

A boat whose headstay runs to the top of her mast has a **masthead rig**. Conversely, when the headstay extends only partway up the mast, the boat has a **fractional rig**. Jibs on masthead boats are proportionally larger than those on fractionally rigged boats. Some masthead boats, in fact, have jibs larger than their mainsails.

The great clipper ships had manila shrouds and stays. Then galvanized steel wire replaced manila, and currently most boats have stays and shrouds of stainless steel. Each of these materials has been stronger and more resistant to stretching than its predecessor. On some high-performance sailboats, stainless

steel wires have been replaced by carbon fiber rod rigging, which has almost no stretch. Rod rigging is twice as expensive as stainless steel, however, and more difficult to repair and replace, so most boats still use stainless steel wire.

HEADSTAY LANDS AT MASTHEAD

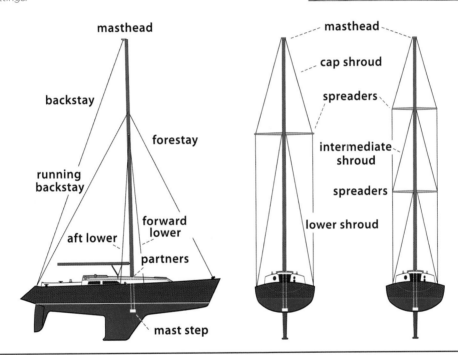

BACKSTAY
ADJUSTER

On a fractionally rigged boat the headstay lands well below the masthead. On a large boat the headstay tension is opposed by a pair of running backstays—the windward of which is always cinched tight—but a smaller fractionally rigged boat like a J/24 or IC-24 does not need the runners. The backstay in a fractional rig is adjustable, and tightening it will bend the masthead aft and flatten the mainsail to depower it in heavy weather. The backstay in the photo is about midway between its light-air and heavy-air settings.

masthead

backstay

forestay

running
backstay

aft lower

forward
lower

partners

mast step

masthead

cap shroud

spreaders

intermediate
shroud

spreaders

lower shroud

LANGUAGE OF THE SEA
FAIR

When a halyard, sheet, or other line runs smoothly and without impediment from its load to its working end—when any directional changes are accomplished with minimal friction and without chafing points—it is said to have a fair lead. "Fair" is always good at sea. A navigation channel with no hairpin twists is a fairway. The curves of a boat's lines are said to be fair if they are without abrupt kinks, knuckles, or hollows. A delightful breeze from a blue sky marks a fair day.

Any piece of hardware that intervenes between the loaded end and the working end of a line to keep its pull straight and true is a fairlead. Wherever a line has to make an abrupt turn in order to lead fair into a cleat or winch, it will pass through a fairlead, which will take the form of a turning block if the line is carrying a significant load. The bearing-mounted sheave of the turning block enables the line to alter direction with a minimum of friction.

Headsails

There must have been overlapping jibs before 1927, but when a nameless experimenter that year set a bigger jib that extended aft past the mast on his 6-meter class boat, he won the regatta. The race was a light-air affair off Genoa, Italy, and jibs that overlap the mast, shrouds, and mainsail have been called **genoa jibs** or simply **genoas** ever since.

Jibs—including genoas—are **headsails**, but so too is a **staysail** (also known as a **forestaysail**), which sets from an **inner headstay** (also known as a forestay or **staysail stay**—another area of confusing terminology, as mentioned in Chapter 1) on some cruising sailboats. The inner stay runs from partway down the mast to a point on the foredeck partway between the stem and mast, so a staysail is substantially smaller than a nonoverlapping jib, much less a genoa. A staysail is a heavy-weather sail, reducing the headsail area and moving it back from the front of the boat when the wind is strong and the seas are boisterous, and thus it is often called a **storm jib**, though a storm jib can also be flown from the headstay. Sometimes all you can do when confronted by sailing terminology is sigh. Fortunately these sails are a lot easier to trim than to name.

Since roller-furled genoas are almost universal these days on cruising sailboats over 30 feet long, and since a roller-furled sail can be roller-reefed to smaller sizes, the typical headsail inventory for a coastal cruising sailboat is limited to its roller-furled genoa and possibly a storm jib. But a roller-furled headsail is less aerodynamically efficient than a sail that sets from hanks or a luff-foil groove, which is why racing keelboats don't have roller furlers. Instead they carry an assortment of headsails of graded sizes, and as the wind increases the foredeck crew must take down a big sail and hoist a smaller one in its place. These sails might range from a #1 genoa that overlaps the mainsail by 50% or more to a #3 genoa that only slightly overlaps the mast, or to a working jib or (on a fractionally rigged boat like the J/24) a **blade jib** that doesn't overlap at all and trims inside the shrouds.

A boat might carry, in addition, a lightweight **drifter** or **reacher** for sailing off the wind in a gentle breeze and a **spinnaker** for downwind sailing, but such specialized sails need not concern us now. For our present purposes, a headsail is a jib, and if it overlaps the mast we'll call it a genoa, and that's that.

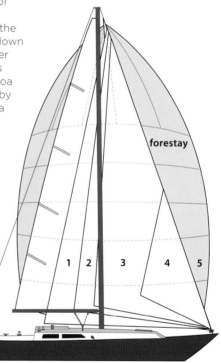

Headsail choices for a masthead-rigged boat: **1.** *#1 genoa;* **2.** *#2 genoa;* **3.** *#3 genoa;* **4.** *storm jib;* **5.** *cruising spinnaker. Most modern cruising boats substitute a single roller-furled genoa for the #1, #2, and #3 genoas.*

eyelet that is bolted to the deck; more typically, however, it will be a block with a turning sheave to relieve friction while trimming. Before you hoist, make sure the sheets are led properly. Look at how they are laid out. Trace the sheet from the sail back to you. The sheets from a small jib may lead aft inside the shroud or shrouds. The sheets from a bigger jib are likely to lead outside the shrouds. You may not know exactly what's right, but loops, twists, and "unfair" leads are wrong.

Trimming the Jib

Jibs with fixed sheeting positions trim pretty much like mainsails. When you're reaching, let out the jib until it luffs, then trim it in until it stops. When you're sailing close hauled, trim it all the way in, head up until the jib barely begins to luff, then head off slightly until it is once again full and drawing. The first signs of luffing in the jib are subtle. Watch for the merest hint of a flutter or backwind.

When sailing close hauled, you'll find that the luff of the jib flutters before the main does. There's nothing between the jib and the breeze, so it makes a better "barometer" for finding the edge of the wind. Even so, especially in a light breeze, the jib begins to lose efficiency well before it exhibits obvious fluttering. Jib telltales are your best guide. Sew or tape a pair of telltales one-third to one-half of the way up the jib's luff, or leading edge, with one telltale on either side of the sail. When the windward telltale lifts toward the vertical, you should trim in the jib slightly if reaching or bear off slightly if sailing close hauled. When both telltales stream aft in unison, with the windward telltale lifting just slightly, you are in perfect trim. When the

JIB TELLTALES

By the time your jib's luffing is this obvious, your boat's performance has tanked. Use your jib telltales to correct your sail trim before it reaches this point. Note that the windward telltale of each pair shown here is pointing almost straight up.

leeward telltale lifts, droops, or flutters—in other words, when it **stalls**—you should ease the jib if reaching or head up slightly if sailing close hauled.

Many sailors attach a second pair of telltales higher on the luff and sometimes a third pair lower. Perfect sail trim is attained when all the pairs stream aft in unbroken unison. Jib luff telltales cease to be effective trim indicators when a boat bears off below a beam reach, however.

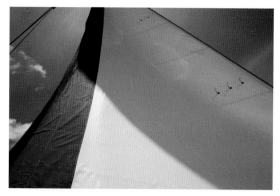

This jib has multiple pairs of luff telltales for redundancy. At left we see that the windward telltale of each pair is lifting, while the leeward telltale (just visible through the sail) is streaming aft. This means the jib is about to luff, and indeed, in the next instant (right) it begins to do so. If sailing a reach, the jib must be trimmed in; if sailing close hauled, the helmsman must bear away from the wind until both telltales of each pair stream aft.

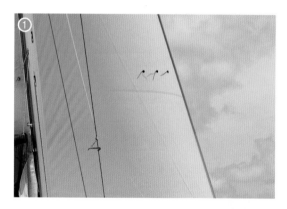

Jib trim by luff telltales.

1. *The leeward telltales are stalling. The helmsman is steering too low for the existing jib trim, which is fine when regaining boatspeed after a tack but suboptimal at other times. Either the jibsheet should be eased or, if close hauled, the helmsman should steer closer to the wind.*

2. *Now the windward telltales are lifting, which suggests that the helmsman has overcompensated and, if close hauled, is pinching— i.e., heading slightly too high.*

3. *This view from the helm shows the ideal balance for a boat sailing close hauled—the windward telltales are barely lifting, while the leeward telltales stream aft, which means this boat is at its most efficient.*

The flow of air off the jib when you're close hauled will cause the apparent wind to approach the mainsail at a narrower angle than it approaches the jib. Put another way, the main is headed slightly relative to the jib. To counter this, the jib should be eased slightly relative to the mainsail, which is trimmed in moderate conditions almost to the boat's centerline. Even so, the mainsail is likely to experience a **backwind**—a flow of air from the jib that impinges on the main's leeward side and makes it appear to be luffing. A backwind bubble in the luff of your mainsail is often unavoidable and generally not that harmful. If you can't eliminate it without either trimming the mainsail too tightly or easing the jib too far for efficient close-hauled sailing, you must learn to live with it.

The good side of the jib-mainsail interaction is the so-called **slot effect**—air accelerated through the slot between the main and jib energizes the mainsail, turbocharging it with more power.

But sails also steal from one another. No matter how tightly you trim it, a jib won't pull when you're sailing so far

Sailing upwind in a fresh breeze, this IC-24 is carrying a pronounced backwind in its mainsail. The jib telltales are streaming aft as they should be, and the masthead fly tells us that the boat is sailing its tacking angle and is not too close to the wind, but the mainsail leech telltales are fluttering and drooping. Mainsail backwind is usually more subtle than this.

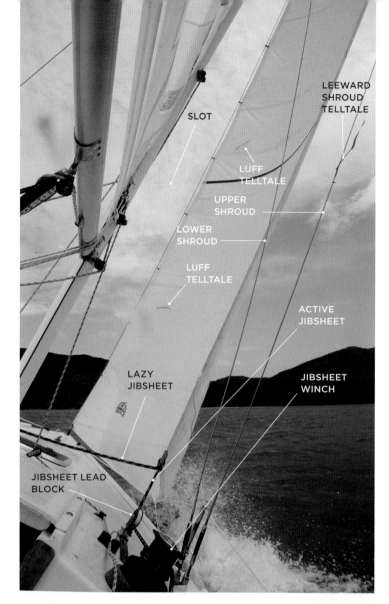

LEEWARD
SHROUD
TELLTALE

SLOT

LUFF
TELLTALE

UPPER
SHROUD

LOWER
SHROUD

LUFF
TELLTALE

ACTIVE
JIBSHEET

LAZY
JIBSHEET

JIBSHEET
WINCH

JIBSHEET LEAD
BLOCK

When a boat is close hauled, the slot between the jib and mainsail accelerates the flow of air over the main. Both pairs of luff telltales are streaming aft, with the upper windward telltale lifting slightly, a sign that the jib is well trimmed. The slight scallop in the jib's luff and the wrinkles emanating from its hanks, however, indicate that the halyard isn't quite tight enough for this fresh breeze. The loose foot of the mainsail on the IC-24 is clearly visible.

The mainsail on this broad-reaching 420 (left) is pulling strongly, but the jib is listless, a sure sign that it's being blanketed by the main. In order to keep the jib pulling while bearing off farther, the crew can wing out the jib on the opposite side (right). A whisker pole could extend the jib clew farther out, making it even more efficient.

CONTROLLING YOUR BOAT

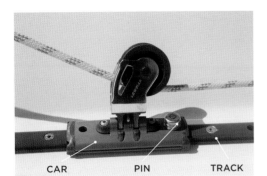

CAR   PIN   TRACK

A jibsheet lead block. To move the block forward or aft, lift the spring-loaded pin and slide the car along the track—easy when the jibsheet is slack but difficult or impossible when it's loaded.

When the mainsail and jib leech curves match like this, it's a good sign that your sails are set up well.

Whisker Pole

When boats are running or reaching broad off the wind, their jibs are blanketed by the mainsail. To hold the jib out and away to the opposite side so that it will fill and pull, you can use a **whisker pole**.

Lighter and shorter than a spinnaker pole, this specialized spar lets the jib perform efficiently **wing and wing** instead of drooping behind the main. A boathook might work in a pinch.

Backwind

Backwind

The exhaust released from the leech of a sail is called **backwind**, and it resembles the vortices that spin off airplane wings or the wake that shudders your car when a truck passes on the highway. Remember that air flows on either side of a sail, and when this divided flow recombines at the leech it creates choppy turbulence. Backwind is considered bad air because sails can't get as much power from it as from smooth, laminar flow. Bad air spins off the leech of a sail, spirals to windward (which is why jibs backwind mainsails), and trails astern. When you're sailing upwind you leave a cone of turbulent air extending at least seven boat lengths in back of you, even as you throw a wind shadow seven boat lengths to leeward. When you're racing, you can use both your wind shadow and your bad air to attack and defend against other boats.

off the wind that it's blanketed by the main. Once the mainsail comes between the jib and the wind, the headsail will flap listlessly—a fact you take advantage of whenever you bear off to a broad reach in order to hoist or unfurl a jib. Some-times that listless flapping will look like luffing, and the trimmer's instinct is to trim the jib in, but that's the wrong response in this case. The correct cure is either to steer a little closer to the wind so that the jib isn't blanketed or to **wing** the jib out to windward and into clear air, supporting it there with a **whisker pole** if necessary.

Most keelboats have adjustable jibsheet lead blocks. Moving them changes the shape of the jib to suit conditions, but for all-around sailing the foot and leech should be tensioned about equally. Moving the lead block aft will tighten the foot and loosen the leech. Moving it forward does the reverse. Look to create smooth curves, about equal in depth, along both edges. If the jibsheet bisects the angle between the jib's foot and leech, that's a good start. You want the curve of the jib leech to match the curve of the mainsail leech. For now, however, position the port and starboard lead blocks near the midpoints of their respective tracks and leave them there. That should be fine for our present purposes.

Jibsheet Loads

Even a small jib pulls hard. Mainsheets are multipart tackles that provide some mechanical advantage, but tackles are impractical on jibsheets, which need to flop across the foredeck and trim quickly on each new tack. Many dinghies and other small sailboats mount quick-release cam cleats for the jibsheets, as we've already seen; these take a fresh grip on each increment of sheet the trimmer pulls in, and will not release it unless the trimmer yanks upward. On a small sailboat a cleat is all you need to tame the jibsheet, but most boats longer than, say, 18 to 20 feet are equipped with jibsheet winches to provide a mechanical advantage to the trimmer. Learn to use the gear you've got, but don't tie off the jibsheet so it can't be eased quickly. Depowering the mainsail is a boat's first response to a heeling gust, but sometimes you'll need to ease the jib too.

Sailing under Full Sail

Tacking and jibing, sailing upwind and downwind, trimming and easing: these are the foundation elements of sailing, and taken one by one, they are easy enough to learn. By this time you've already learned them! Now let's set out under both mainsail and jib as you assemble those elements into the fluid ensemble called sailing.

Tacking with two sails is only slightly more complicated than tacking under main alone, as the accompanying photos illustrate, and jibing with two sails is really no more difficult. When you jibe from one broad reach to the other, it is the mainsail you must keep under control, as described in Chapter 1, whereas the jib is docile and will flop across the foredeck without force or protest. If the crew keeps the jib on a short enough sheet so that it can't wrap itself around the headstay, there is little that can go wrong.

Tacking with two sails.

Tacking a dinghy under mainsail and jib is the work of an instant. This is just like the mainsail-only tack described in Chapter 1 except that the crew casts off one jibsheet and trims the other as the tack progresses.

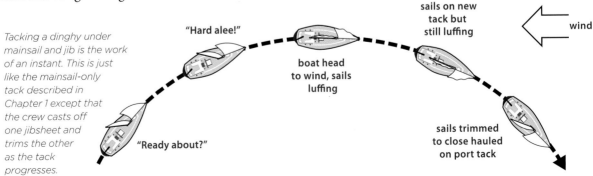

"Hard alee!"

"Ready about?"

boat head to wind, sails luffing

sails on new tack but still luffing

wind

sails trimmed to close hauled on port tack

Tacking a small keelboat. *This is no more complicated than tacking a dinghy except that the jib loads are higher and the jib must therefore be trimmed on a winch in all except the lightest breezes.* **1.** *When the crew is ready, the helmsman pushes the tiller to leeward.* **2.** *The starboard-side jibsheet has been released, and the jib is luffing across the foredeck.* **3.** *The port-side jibsheet is trimmed, while the starboard-side crew clears any snags or tangles in the lazy sheet so that it's free to run.* **4.** *Fully trimmed, the boat takes off on its new tack. The mainsheet on this IC-24 is unusual for a keelboat in that it does not ride on a traveler and therefore needs no adjustment when the boat tacks. Note the darker streaks in the water, which denote oncoming puffs of wind.*

Tacking a cruising keelboat under mainsail and jib.
1. *The helmsman asks "Ready about?"* **2.** *When the crew is ready, the helmsman says "Hard alee" and starts the turn through the wind.* **3.** *The port-side jibsheet has been released, and the starboard-side crew is ready to trim the new jibsheet as the jib luffs across the foredeck.* **4.** *The boat has turned past head to wind, and the jib has traveled across the foredeck and is now being trimmed. The reefing lines, which stay permanently rove, can just be seen flopping at the leech of the mainsail.* **5.** *With the jib fully trimmed, the boat sails its new tack in a fresh breeze. The mainsheet traveler car will need to be moved to windward, as we'll see later in the chapter.*

Sailing in Circles

This one is simple. Find a mark (a channel buoy or lobster pot or mooring) surrounded by open water, then sail circles around it.

It doesn't matter whether you approach the mark from upwind or down. Make a full circle around it, 360 degrees. You'll have to tack in order to do this, and unless your initial approach is dead downwind, you're also going to have to jibe. Go around again, then circle the other way. See how tight you can make the circle, or time the turn to see how fast you can get back to your starting point.

Sailing around a mark gives you a single point of reference. You can tell easily and instantly how you're doing, which helps you appreciate acceleration, leeway, and the effects of the helm. It becomes crystal clear how tacking and jibing grant you access to all the points of the compass, and the best way to perfect your tacking and jibing is to practice, practice, practice while the lessons of experience are still fresh. Think of what's happening in terms of cause and effect. As you do your laps you're covering all the basics

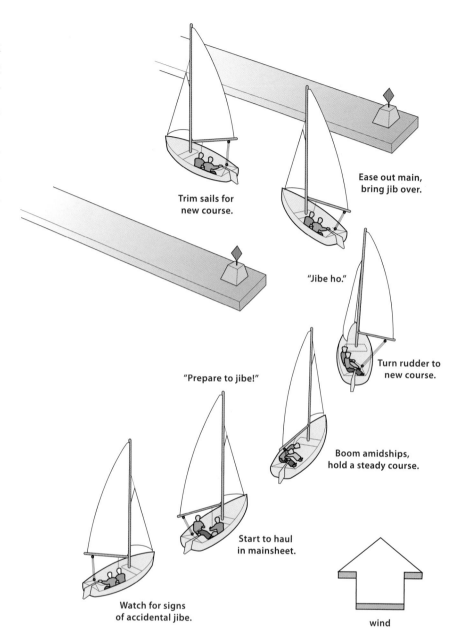

Trim sails for new course.

Ease out main, bring jib over.

"Jibe ho."

Turn rudder to new course.

"Prepare to jibe!"

Boom amidships, hold a steady course.

Start to haul in mainsheet.

Watch for signs of accidental jibe.

wind

Jibing with two sails. *Once you can tack and jibe in circles as in the exercise described on this page, jibing into a channel as shown will be easy.*

of sail handling and steering. If you want to get to Carnegie Hall, think of this as practicing your scales.

Sailing to Windward

Sailing close hauled is simple enough, but it is the toughest element to master because it most rewards nuances of sail trim and steering. Minor changes in sail trim or heading make comparatively little difference to boat speed when you're reaching, but they can make your boat accelerate a notch when you're close hauled.

Sail 3 minutes downwind from your mark, 4 at the most, then turn upwind and sail back, timing yourself. You should have to tack at least once to get back; if you can point directly at the mark when you turn upwind, you weren't sailing dead downwind when you left it.

Now repeat the process, sailing downwind for the same amount of time as before. See if you can improve on your time back to the mark. Do as many of these short beats as you can stand, adjusting sail trim, headings, and the speed of your tacks as you search for the optimum settings.

Sailing a Triangle

Find a nearby target and sail to it. From there find another target. Then sail back to your original mark. Take another lap around the triangle you have made, tacking and jibing as necessary, then reverse your direction and sail around it the other way. Time your laps, practicing sail trim. Try rapid tacks and gentle ones, gradual course changes and abrupt ones. Find out what works best for your boat. Try it again when the conditions are different—a little more or less wind, a little more or less chop—and see what changes.

Maneuvers, points of sail, sail-trimming techniques, commands . . . these are all tools. When you practice using the tools, even if it's only to sail in circles, you get a better grip on them. If you are open to it, this sort of controlled, intense sailing provides clear and immediate feedback and will teach you a lot in a short time. Sailing circles, windward-leewards, and triangles will accelerate your learning.

Now go for a sail. You've earned it. Pick your weather (your safe weather window will expand as you get deeper into this book) and don't wander too far from home waters quite yet (we'll learn navigation in Chapter 5), but go sailing.

Handling Lines

Lines, lines, and more lines— they snake around a sailboat's deck, willing servants if you understand their uses, mysterious impediments if you don't. The most common include sheets, halyards, mooring pendants, anchor rodes, and docklines, but on the typical sailboat you'll find at least a half-dozen others—often more—each there to do a particular job with unmatched efficiency. It's cordage that harnesses the wind, moors the boat, and gives you the reins.

"Worm, parcel, and serve" was what they taught sailors in the old days. Today no one knows that worming means filling the lay (the spiraling groove) in a twisted rope with twine, **parceling** involves wrapping the wormed line in tarry canvas, and **serving** means cinching the parceled mess up tight with twine. Modern line is made from synthetic fibers. It doesn't deteriorate the way old-time hemp did. Chafe is its major enemy, and some types—polypropylene in particular—can't tolerate sun, but lines today are virtually maintenance free.

So the job now is keeping lines straight, both by learning which one does what and by keeping them free of kinks, knots, and tangles. Color coding makes figuring out the lines easier, but you must still study each one, tracing its course to determine what it does. Zero in first on sheets, halyards, and primary control lines. You may see a cat's cradle of additional lines, but get the essential ones straight first.

Good seamanship dictates that all lines be ready to use at all times. A knot in the mainsheet might prevent you from easing it to spill a puff of wind; a kink in a halyard might cause the sail to stick aloft. The same is true of control lines and dock-

TURNING BLOCKS

CLUTCH STOPPERS
(IN CLOSED POSITION)

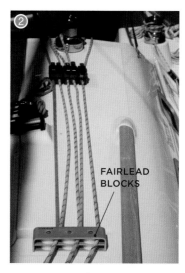

FAIRLEAD BLOCKS

SELF-TAILER

FEEDER ARM

Another look at the clutch of lines leading to the cockpit in the Oceanis 323 cruising sailboat. *(Page 27 shows the main halyard in use.) The lines turn through blocks at the mast base* **(1)***, head aft through fairlead blocks and a bank of clutch stoppers at the cockpit end of the cabintop* **(2, 3)***, and are stowed in coils in the cockpit* **(4)***. The lines are color coded, and the clutch stoppers are labeled to help with identification, but you still need to know where the other end of each line is, and any new boat takes a little time to learn. The clutch stoppers here are all in the closed position—see the opened stopper on page 27. Note the line wrapped clockwise around the self-tailing winch* **(4)***. To use the winch, wrap at least two more turns of the line around the drum, then lead the line up over the feeder arm and jam it into the self-tailer* **(5)***. Insert the handle into the top of the winch and turn!*

lines. They need to be ready to run smoothly and freely. That's why you coil them.

Working with line is a high, fine art, and line handling has always been a big part of the sailor's trade. Knowing how to sweat a line or pay it out under strain, how to heave a coil, set a sail, or work a winch was once what marked a sailor as a "salt." Times have changed, but handling lines is still at the center of sailing. It's a necessity and, you'll find, a pleasure.

Three-Strand and Braided Line

From Egyptian times forward, rope has been made by winding fibers together. **Three-strand** or **cable-laid rope**, made by twisting three strands into one, became the most common construction, with manila and cotton the most-used fibers.

Ropes today are made of synthetic fibers such as Dacron (polyester) and nylon. Dacron stretches only modestly and is popular for halyards and sheets. Nylon stretches more generously and is popular for anchor rodes and docklines, where its elasticity absorbs shock loads. And today a host of high-tech fibers—including Kevlar (an aramid fiber), Spectra (a polyethylene), Technora (a copolymer), and others—are available (at a price) to high-performance sailors who want superb strength with an absolute minimum of stretch, windage, and weight.

Most daysailors and cruisers, however, are perfectly happy with Dacron and nylon, both of which are available in a variety of constructions. Because three-strand rope stretches significantly under load, it is used principally for those rare applications in which stretching is an advantage. Anchor rodes, for example, are often three-stranded nylon for the greatest possible shock-absorbing elasticity. Most other lines aboard today's sailboats have a braided construction of one sort or another, in which the strands of the rope are interwoven rather than twisted together. **Single-braid rope** is uniform in cross section, whereas **double-braid rope** consists of a braided core surrounded by a braided cover. In **parallel-core rope** a core of straight yarns is enclosed by a braided cover. Braided line stretches less than three-strand line, has no natural twist, and is easier on your hands. As can be seen in Appendix 3, however, splicing braided line is harder than using it.

Three-strand nylon line. Fibers are twisted to make yarns, which are twisted the opposite way to make the three strands, which are twisted the original way to make the line.

A single-braid line has a solid braid throughout its cross section, with no core.

A double-braid line consists of a braided core inside a braided cover, or sheath. Here the cover is pulled back to expose the core.

Parallel-core rope has a core of parallel, unwoven fibers inside a braided cover.

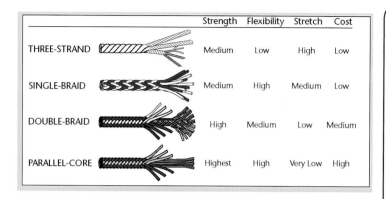

	Strength	Flexibility	Stretch	Cost
THREE-STRAND	Medium	Low	High	Low
SINGLE-BRAID	Medium	High	Medium	Low
DOUBLE-BRAID	High	Medium	Low	Medium
PARALLEL-CORE	Highest	High	Very Low	High

LINE GUIDE FOR THE CRUISER AND CASUAL RACER

Application	Polyester Single-Braid (e.g., Regatta)	Polyester Double-Braid (e.g., Sta-Set)	Polyester Braid/ Parallel Core (e.g., Sta-Set X)	Polyester Braid/ Vectran Core (e.g., Sta-Set X+)
Main/Genoa Halyard	Not Rec.	Good	Excellent	Excellent
Main Sheet	Excellent	Excellent	Fair	Good
Genoa/Jib Sheets	Very Good	Excellent	Very Good	Very Good
Reefing Lines	Good	Excellent	Excellent	Good
Spinnaker Halyard	Not Rec.	Very Good	Excellent	Excellent
Spinnaker Sheets	Good	Very Good	Excellent	Good
Spinnaker Guys	Not Rec.	Good	Excellent	Excellent
Foreguy/Topping Lift	Good	Excellent	Very Good	Good
Vang	Good	Excellent	Good	Fair
Control Lines	Very Good	Excellent	Good	Fair
Runner Tails	Not Rec.	Good	Very Good	Very Good
Furling Lines	Excellent	Very Good	Fair	Fair

RUNNING RIGGING SIZE GUIDE (Based on polyester double braid)

Application	to 20'	20–25'	26–30'	31–35'	36–40'	41–45'	46–50'	51–60'
Main Halyard	1/4"	5/16"	3/8"	7/16"	1/2"	9/16"	5/8"	3/4"
Genoa Halyard	1/4"	5/16"	3/8"	7/16"	1/2"	9/16"	5/8"	3/4"
Main Sheet	5/16"	5/16"	3/8"	7/16"	1/2"	1/2"	9/16"	9/16"
Genoa Sheets	5/16"	5/16"	3/8"	7/16"	1/2"	9/16"	5/8"	5/8"
Reefing Lines	1/4"	5/16"	3/8"	7/16"	7/16"	1/2"	1/2"	9/16"
Spinnaker Halyard	1/4"	5/16"	3/8"	7/16"	1/2"	9/16"	5/8"	3/4"
Spinnaker Sheets	1/4"	1/4"	5/16"	3/8"	7/16"	1/2"	9/16"	5/8"
Spinnaker Guy	5/16"	5/16"	3/8"	7/16"	1/2"	5/8"	3/4"	3/4"
Foreguy/Topping Lift	1/4"	1/4"	5/16"	3/8"	7/16"	1/2"	9/16"	9/16"
Vang	1/4"	1/4"	5/16"	3/8"	7/16"	1/2"	9/16"	9/16"
Control Lines	3/16"	1/4"	5/16"	3/8"	7/16"	1/2"	9/16"	9/16"

Check the Load

Before you untie any line, you should know what's on the other end and how hard it's pulling. Some lines, such as jibsheets, are under no strain at some times and a monstrous load at others. Other lines, like the topping lift that holds up the end of the main boom on many boats when the mainsail isn't up, are defying gravity; the strain might not be huge, but if the line gets away from you the boom might fall on your head. The boat herself will place almost no strain on her mooring or anchor line in a flat calm, but in a 20-knot breeze the same boat will want to take off on her own, especially when she's tossed by an incoming wave. Before you grab a line, know whether you're grabbing a tiger by its tail. A bar-taut rope that hums when you pluck it is easy to tell from a lightly tensioned line. Whenever you need to ease out a line under strain, the best practice is to retain a wrap or two around the winch drum or a turn around the base of the cleat. Ease up on the tail of the line that you're holding, and the load at the other end will take the slack from the winch or cleat while you remain in control of the situation. This technique is called **surging** the line, and it works. If the easing starts to get away from you, clamp a stop to it. Surging a line under load is much better than trying to outmuscle the load.

Easing a jib-sheet under load. The turns around the winch take most of the strain, enabling the trimmer to control how much line is eased with light hand pressure on the winch.

Rope vs. Line

What's the difference? According to the *American Merchant Seaman's Manual*, rope is "any cord more than 1³/₄ inches in circumference." But the same source drops the size requirement when talking about **line**, which it defines as "a piece of rope that is used for a specific purpose." The general rule is that when it comes from the store, it's rope, but when you put it to use or tie it to something, it becomes a line.

Coiling and Faking

You should stow any unused line aboard so that it's free of kinks and tangles and ready to use when needed. The usual solution is to **coil** the line. Put one end on deck or drape it from one hand. Working away from the end with the other hand, make a loop of line and drop it on top of the end. Make another loop of the same size, and keep piling them one atop the other to build the coil.

Most three-strand line is **right-laid**, which means that the strands spiral upward to the right no matter which end of the rope you hold up. You should therefore coil three-strand line clockwise in order to coil **with the lay** and thus prevent the rope from kinking and twisting. To further help the loops lie fair (that word again!), try rolling the line between your fingers slightly as you coil it.

Braided line, by contrast, has no built-in twist, so making all the loops coil the same way will cause it to kink and twist. As a result, some rope manufacturers suggest not coiling braided line at all, but coiling is such a convenient way to store unused line that giving up on it would be a shame. Instead, make clockwise loops as with three-strand line,

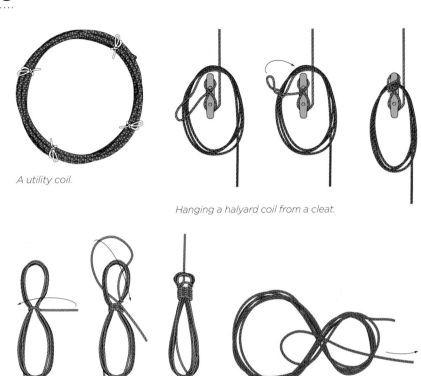

A utility coil.

Hanging a halyard coil from a cleat.

A gasket coil.

Faking a line into a figure-eight coil.

but configure every other loop so that the end toward which you're coiling is underneath (if coiling on deck) or inside (if coiling over one hand). This so-called **alternate hitch coiling** takes some getting used to but will keep the loops from twisting. You can coil rigging wire, a garden hose, or an extension cord the same way.

Line will often dictate the diameter of the coil that suits it best. To avoid kinks and thick coils, make the loops as large as you conveniently can, but not so large as to snag moving parts

or drag on deck. When coiling the tail of a belayed halyard, coil away from the belay and toward the free end, so that the twists you introduce by coiling can work their way out through the end.

One easy way to secure a coil is to unlay the last loop and wrap the longer end thus created several times around the girth of the coil. Next form a **bight** (a tight loop) in the remaining end, tuck that bight through the eye of the coil above the wraps you just made, then wrap the bight up over the top of the coil. Pull on the end to cinch the bight tightly around the coil, and you've created a **gasket coil** that you can store flat or hang by its free end in a locker.

To coil a halyard tail—or the end of any cleated line—so

that it will release quickly when you need it, start 12 to 18 inches from the cleat and coil toward the free end, spinning out the twist as you coil. When the coil is completed, you can pass that initial uncoiled 12 to 18 inches through the body of the coil to form a bight, then hook the bight over the cleat—twisting it once or twice if you wish—to hang the coil.

To ensure that a coiled line pays out smoothly, make sure the line feeds from the top of the coil rather than its bottom. For instance, coil jibsheets between tacks if you wish, but be sure to place your coil's bitter end down so the sheet will release cleanly.

If you'll be storing a coiled line for days or weeks, use three or four pieces of string to tie it up. The result is a **utility coil**.

This approach takes a little longer, but it's the only one to use for garden hose or rigging wire. No matter where or for how long you stow it, that line is ready for instant use.

Faking (sometimes called **flaking**) means arranging a line so it will run out without snagging. It's one step more foolproof than coiling because one loop of a coil will sometimes grab another when the line is paying out. Faking arranges bights or figure eights of line so they can run out smoothly. It is not self-tending or permanent, however. You can't fake a line and then walk away and leave it. Stow lines coiled, but fake a line that needs to run freely and soon.

Rope Terminology

Rope is amazing stuff—simple in appearance, versatile in use. To work lines quickly and efficiently, however, sailors must be able to identify and communicate not only which line but also which portion of a line needs to be handled. The **standing part** of a line is the part that either is or will be under tension between the load and the inboard cleat or line handler. For purposes of knot tying, the standing part is the part of the line leading away from the knot you are tying, toward the load. If you

A bight of line.

grab that standing part at any point and double it in your fist, you have created a bight. A bight in which the rope crosses itself is a **loop**.

A loop of line.

Taking a Strain

We've talked about easing a line under tension by surging it— i.e., feeding it slack little by little while retaining a turn around the cleat or bitt or a wrap or two around the winch. Conversely, if the formerly slack line you're holding starts pulling hard, transfer the strain from your hand to something stronger. Take a turn around a cleat and let *it* take the strain. With a dockline, take a turn around a piling. With a sheet, take a wrap or two around a winch. Whenever the strain is serious, **snub** the line in this fashion.

Snubbing a line takes the strain off you and can also make it easier for you to pull on the line. Say, for example, you've raised the jib almost all the way. Let's say that the jib halyard on your boat **makes off to** (is tied to) a cleat on the mast, and there is no halyard winch for the jib. The best way to get the halyard truly tight is to sweat it up that last inch or two. Wrap the halyard once around the cleat. Holding the tail tight with one hand, lean out on the halyard's standing part with the other, pulling it away from the mast. Now ease up on the standing part, meanwhile transferring the resulting slack around the cleat and into the tail. Repeat. This is called **sweating**, **swaying**, or sometimes **swigging** the line (see the photo on page 27).

Wrapping a line around your hand for extra purchase can be a temptation but is best avoided.

Gauging a Strain
Whenever you have mechanical advantage on your side—when you're working a winch, a windlass, a multipart tackle, or even an engine—keep close tabs on the strains you're creating. You won't feel resistance in many cases. You have to look for it. The anchor may be hooked on a rock, or the sail may be snagged on a spreader. If you don't want to bend the anchor or tear the sail, be wary how you apply mechanical advantage. Any unusual resistance from a halyard or other line you handle frequently is a good sign that something is tangled, jammed, or hung up.

Heaving a Line
On occasion you may have to throw a line ashore, to another boat, or even to someone overboard. Those occasions are rare, however. Usually, when docking or tying up to another boat, you have the luxury of either stepping from boat to dock with line in hand or passing (as opposed to throwing) the line to a helper. Passing is better than throwing, because it eliminates the risk of a loose line in the water that could foul a propeller. So rare is the need to heave a line, in fact, that most of us are hazy on how best to do it.

For maximum distance and accuracy, start by breaking the coil in half. Grasp one half in your throwing hand, holding the rest in your other hand. You want the thrown coil to carry and then spill in the direction of your target, and you want the remaining part to pay out smoothly and not hang up. I often drop the end I want to hold onto the deck and step on it or even tie it off.

Throwing underhand is most accurate, but a sidearm delivery provides greater range. Compromise with a slinging motion halfway between underhand and sidearm. Drop the foot on your throwing side a bit behind you, point your shoulders and hips at the target, then uncoil and let the throwing part fly. Probably the hardest part is paying out the balance of the coil from your nonthrowing hand. Open your palm toward the target, and drop the coil on the deck if you must to get it to run out freely. Follow through to a point well above the target—overthrowing is fine, as the line will fall in place. Underthrowing, however, would mean having to try again.

And don't lose touch with your end of the line. That would make a bitter end!

Sweating works just as well with docklines. If a heavy boat has stretched her lines taut and you want to bring her in to the dock, don't pull the line—sweat it. You'll get a much better response. When you're breaking out an anchor or stretching a sail along the boom, try the same technique.

Wrapping a sheet or dockline around your hand to get a better grip is a natural response to an increasing load, but it's not good practice. Strain on the line might take you with it or cut into your hand. If there's no winch or cleat within reach on which to snub the line, try leading it across your shoulders—let your back be the belay.

Shaping a Sail

Though sails lie flat on a floor, there is curvature built into them. When filled with wind they look like wings, not boards, and that's because sailmakers build them with **draft**, or **camber**. Some sails are cut fuller—i.e., with more **belly**—and some flatter.

The curve of a sail bends the air that flows over it. The flow over the leeward, convex surface of the sail is faster than the flow over the windward, concave surface—just as the flow is faster over an airplane wing's curved upper surface than its flat lower surface—and the re-

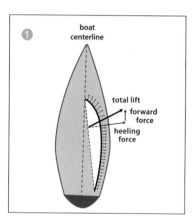

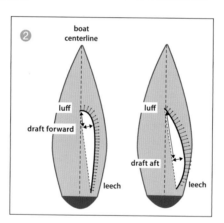

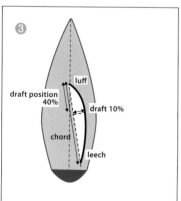

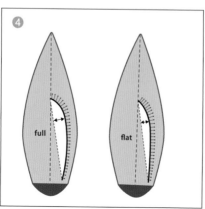

Sail shape and lift. 1. *The force, or lift, generated by a sail includes a large heeling component that we must counteract with crew weight, hull shape, keel ballast, and sail trim, and a small forward component that we must maximize with sail trim.* **2.** *Moving the sail's maximum draft forward will increase the forward component of lift. If the draft is allowed to move toward the leech, the sail will generate a lot of heeling but not a lot of forward speed.* **3.** *The best compromise in practice is to carry the maximum draft about 40% of the chord length aft of the luff— or perhaps as much 45% for the mainsail and as little as 35% for the jib.* **4.** *A fuller, deeper sail generates more power. A draft of 10% to 15% is typical of a mainsail, while a jib can be slightly deeper—say, 12% to 20%.*

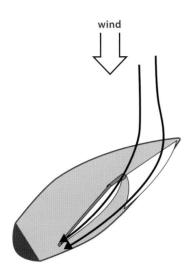

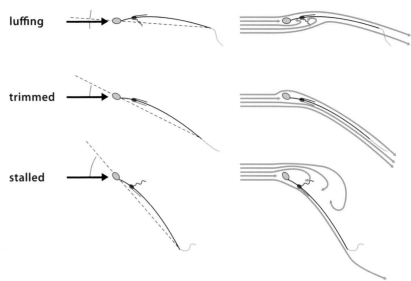

As wind approaches the sails, it bends, putting the jib in an apparent lift relative to the mainsail. This permits the jib to be slightly fuller and also permits it to be eased slightly relative to the main, generating a greater forward component of lift.

Efficient sailing, especially when close hauled, depends upon a smooth, laminar flow on both sides of the sail. Overtrimming creates turbulence on a sail's leeward surface, and the sail stalls, slowing the boat.

sult is **lift**, which can be represented by vectors perpendicular to the sail's leeward surface. The deeper the draft, or curve, of a sail, the greater the lift it can generate. Since lift is power, a fuller, deeper sail is a more powerful sail. Sail area also affects power, but when two sails have the same area, the one with the deeper draft pulls harder.

A sail is not a rigid foil like an airplane wing. Instead it's a flexible, adjustable membrane. You can't give a sail any more fullness, or draft, than the sailmaker built into it, but you can make it flatter when conditions warrant. A deeper sail provides more power for punching through waves or for making progress in a light breeze. A flatter sail generates less power, which is exactly what you want when the wind starts to overpower your boat, and it also creates a wider angle of attack with the wind and therefore enables you to sail a little closer to the wind.

You can also adjust the position (as opposed to the depth) of a sail's maximum draft, and the accompanying drawing of a sail cross section shows why this can be worth the effort. The vectors represent the forces generated by the wind flowing over the sail of a close-hauled boat. Much of this generated power is useless, serving only to heel the boat. It is only the forward com-

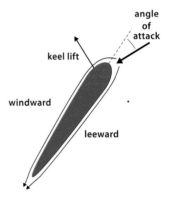

And here's something else to chew on while we're looking at the forces involved in sailing. The preceding illustrations make it easy to imagine why the sails' forces push a boat to leeward. Were it not for the counteracting influence of the boat's underwater foil—its keel or centerboard—we'd find it impossible to make progress to windward. The foil functions partly by resisting the sideways push through the water, but that doesn't explain why its effectiveness increases as the boat speeds up. When the boat is sailing fast and making a few degrees of leeway, the water approaching the foil must travel farther and therefore faster to get around the windward face than around the leeward face. That creates low pressure to windward and lifts the boat in that direction. And there you have it—the secret of sailing!

Effects of halyard tension. 1. *With no vertical wrinkles near the luff of this luffing sail, this is not full halyard tension.* **2.** *It proves perfectly fine when the boat is sailing off the wind, when a full sail is desirable.* **3.** *But when the boat hardens up to close hauled, scallops appear in the luff of the main, a sign that more halyard tension is needed, and the wind has blown the mainsail's draft position—its point of deepest draft, or belly—more than halfway back from luff to leech.* **4.** *Now the crew has tightened the main halyard, and the sail looks a lot better. The luff is smooth, and the draft position is forward of the halfway point between luff and leech. What remains is to work some slack into those reefing lines, which at the moment are distorting the leech. (We'll discuss the use of the reefing lines shortly.)*

DRAFT POSITION

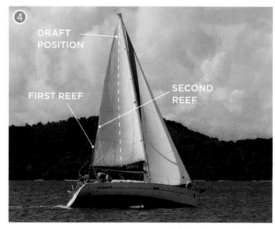

DRAFT POSITION

FIRST REEF

SECOND REEF

ponents of the vectors in the illustration that propel the boat through the water. The deepest point in a sail's curve is where the greater part of its power is generated. You want the maximum draft of your sail forward (especially when you are close hauled) in order to maximize the forward components of the force vectors. The deepest draft in a mainsail usually wants to be about 40% to 45% of the way back from the leading edge; in a jib it should be about 30% to 40% of the way back.

So how can you accomplish this? Here we'll cover the basic sail-shape adjustments, while saving the further nuances for Chapter 4.

Mainsail

When you hoist the mainsail you tension its luff with the halyard or downhaul (or both) until a vertical wrinkle appears

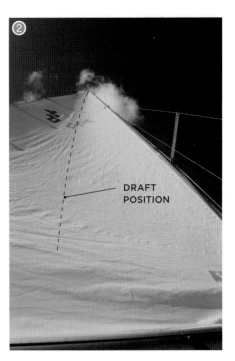

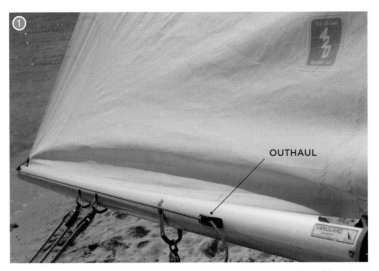

Mainsail shape on a sailing dinghy. 1. *The outhaul tension on this 420 mainsail looks good. When the boat is launched and the sail trimmed, the wind will smooth out that horizontal wrinkle along the foot, and if it doesn't it will be easy to release some outhaul tension.* **2.** *With the sail trimmed, the luff tension also looks good. It is only as tight as it needs to be to prevent horizontal wrinkles or scalloping along the luff, but no tighter. The top batten runs the full length from leech to luff (which is why it must be taken out when the sail is folded for storage) and shows the position of maximum draft. Here it is a little forward of the midway point, which is what you want.* **3.** *When close hauled, trim the mainsail until the top batten is parallel with the boom. When it's about right, as here, the leech telltales should be streaming most of the time.* **4.** *Here the sail is overtrimmed, the top batten is hooked to windward, and the leech telltale has stalled.*

there. When the sail fills with wind, the wrinkle should disappear; if it doesn't, you've made the luff too tight, so you should slightly ease the halyard or downhaul. This degree of luff tension should place the maximum draft where you want it—forward of the sail's midpoint. A strengthening wind will move the draft aft and at the same time deepen it. More luff tension will counter this, moving the draft forward again and flattening the sail, which depowers it.

Similarly, you want to tighten the outhaul until a wrinkle appears along the foot of the luffing sail. When the sail fills with wind, the wrinkle should disappear. If the wind increases, add more outhaul tension to flatten the sail.

In a light breeze—and when you're sailing a broad reach or

run—easing the outhaul and luff tension will make the sail fuller and more powerful.

As you trim the mainsheet for close-hauled sailing, you pull the boom in toward the boat's fore-and-aft centerline. When the boom is almost to the centerline, further trimming pulls it down more than in, reducing the sail's twist and tensioning the leech, both of which (up to a point) add power and pointing ability. If you overtrim, however, the boat will slow down and feel sluggish. (We'll come back to this in Chapter 4.) In a puff, you can spill wind from the sail by easing the sheet a little to let the leech twist. If you still feel overpowered, ease the sheet some more to let the sail luff.

Jib

As mentioned earlier, you want the jib halyard tight enough so that the luff of the sail isn't scalloped and doesn't show horizontal wrinkles. If you tighten it to the point that the sail develops a vertical wrinkle even when full of wind, however, you've made it too tight and therefore less powerful. In light air you want less halyard tension for a fuller sail.

Mainsail trim on a keelboat. 1. *This IC-24 mainsail is slightly undertrimmed for close-hauled sailing. The top batten is leaning to leeward relative to the boom, and the leech is twisting open aloft, which will allow too much wind to spill ineffectively off the top of the sail.* **2.** *Now the sail is overtrimmed. The battens are hooked to windward and the leech telltales have stalled.* **3.** *Here the trim is about right, with the top batten paralleling the boom and the leech tight but not cupped. A little more halyard or cunningham tension might remove the horizontal wrinkles from the luff, and the persistence of a horizontal wrinkle along the foot when the sail is full suggests that a little less outhaul tension is in order.*

As with the mainsail, the last bit of jibsheet trim for close-hauled sailing pulls the clew down more than in, which reduces leech twist and adds power and pointing ability. When further trim fails to improve pointing, you've trimmed

Sail Shaping

Sailmakers use several techniques to build flat panels of cloth into sails with a curved shape. Most often they cut the **luff**—the leading edge of the sail—in a convex curve that bulges outside the straight line between the sail's tack and head. When this curved luff is forced to take the shape of the straight mast (or headstay), that extra material is displaced inside the triangle. The more extra material there is, the fuller the sail. With some variation the same technique is used along the bottom the sail and even where panels of cloth are sewn together.

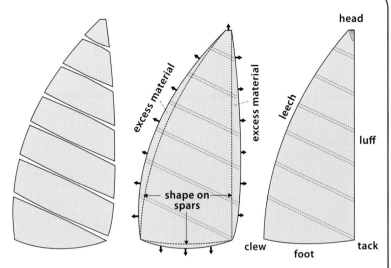

The cloth panels for a sail are cut with convex edges (left), and when these are stitched together, a process known as broadseaming, *they build shape into the sail (middle). When this mainsail's luff is forced to conform to a straight mast, the camber of the sail becomes more pronounced (right).*

---

the jib or genoa too far and should ease it out a couple of inches.

As previously mentioned, if your boat is longer than 20 feet or so, each of your two jibsheets may very well pass through a lead block that is mounted on a length of track on the boat's side deck. If this is the case, moving the block forward will tighten the leech of the jib and make the sail fuller and more powerful. Moving the block aft will allow more twist in the leech and make the sail flatter and less powerful. Note: Unless the wind is light, you won't be able to move the lead block that is currently in use and under tension. Adjust the lazy jibsheet block, then wait until you tack to adjust the opposite one.

Putting It Together

When the wind freshens and your boat starts heeling more than is comfortable, you can tighten the halyards and mainsail outhaul to flatten the sails; move the jibsheet leads farther aft; and ease the main- and jibsheets enough to induce leech twist and spill a little wind. If you're still overpowered, you

Draft

None of the fifteen definitions of **draft** in the *American Heritage Dictionary* fits what sailmakers mean by the word. However, the dictionary does tell us that draft can mean "the depth of a hull in the water," and that the root of the word is *dragan*, which is Old English for "to draw," or pull. Depth and pull—both of these are clues to the sailmaker's meaning.

The draft of a sail is its depth of curvature, or camber, and it is draft that gives sails their pull. A flat sail has less curvature and therefore less pull than a full one.

The point where a sail's maximum depth occurs determines the direction in which it will pull. When the draft is forward, the sail pulls forward more effectively.

So draft can refer both to the depth and the position of a sail's maximum curvature, not to mention a race car drafting at the Indianapolis 500, the draft of a fire in the fireplace, a military draft board, a yacht designer's drafting board, or beer from the tap.

can ease the sheets more until the sails start to carry a partial luff at all times—although this is neither efficient nor good for the sails. At this point it's time to consider reducing your sail area, which we'll discuss next.

You don't *have* to adjust a sail's shape in order to sail, but shape adjustment will help you sail better. In Chapter 4 we'll look at the additional controls—the mainsheet traveler, boom vang, cunningham, and backstay—that enable you to optimize sail shape on some boats, but you can get along fine without any of these. Here are the basics: deepen the draft for power, keep it positioned forward of the sail's midpoint for maximum forward thrust, and flatten the sails to depower them or make them more close-winded. And when you're feeling lazy, forget these finer points and just enjoy the sailing.

TOP BATTEN

LEECH TELLTALE

SHROUD TELLTALE

LUFF TELLTALES

This is good close-hauled trim. The leech curves of main and jib are in harmony. The main's top batten (just visible) is paralleling the main boom, and the leech telltales are streaming. The windward luff telltales on the jib are lifting just slightly, indicating that the boat is sailing "in the groove," and the windward shroud telltale confirms that the boat is as close to the apparent wind as it can get. Now, if only that jib halyard were a little tighter!

Controlling Heel

Your boat will **heel**, or lean, in all but the lightest breezes. Heeling makes many new sailors nervous, but it is in fact perfectly natural, and even healthy to a point. Think of a bough yielding to a gust of wind rather than trying to stand stiff and motionless. The more a sailboat heels, the more wind it spills from its sails and the more lightly the wind pushes against it. That is one reason heeling is a self-correcting process; another is that a boat's hull is designed to resist deep heeling. Further, in a keelboat, the weight of the ballast at the bottom of the keel works like a force at the end of a lever to return the boat to its upright position. As you become accustomed to your boat, moderate heeling no longer feels strange or dangerous.

When the wind is barely a breath, small-boat sailors often move crew weight to the leeward side to induce heeling. This helps the sails swing into position to harness what little breeze there is.

Under other conditions, however, heeling is inefficient. It changes the hull's shape in the water, which adds resistance, and it accentuates **weather helm**—a boat's tendency to turn into the wind—which makes steering harder. To counteract weather helm you have to apply more rudder angle through the tiller or wheel, which means even more resistance in the water, which makes your boat slower.

Your point of sail governs heel. Heeling will increase as you head up from a beam reach to close hauled, but then it will decrease again when your sails begin to luff. When you're close hauled you can feather into the puffs to lessen their power, and you can bear off in the lulls to add wind flow.

Conversely, the boat will flatten out as you bear off from a beam reach to a broad reach, and it will be nearly level when you're sailing dead downwind. With the wind on or aft of the beam, therefore, you can head down in a gust to decrease the apparent wind by hauling it farther aft. Turn into the wind in a lull—sailors call this **heading up**—to increase the apparent wind by moving it farther ahead. Your ability to adjust course gives you control over the flow of wind into your sails.

> ## Hiking Straps
>
> To hike effectively you need to hook your feet under something. It's possible to hold a jib or mainsheet and hike, or to rig a hiking line, but most small centerboard boats have straps, as we saw in Chapter 1. Running fore and aft on either side of the cockpit, they can normally be adjusted to a height that lets you sit with your butt over the water and lean into the puffs, as the sailors are doing in the photos on pages 12 and 36. Stomach and thigh muscles feel the strain. Hiking takes not only straps, but also conditioning and commitment.

A jib's leech line, when present, emerges from the leech a short way above the clew. It should be no tighter than necessary to stop the leech from fluttering.

Other Sail Controls

On many sailboats the mainsheet rides on a **traveler**. When you're close hauled in a light to moderate breeze, adjusting the traveler car to windward keeps the boom nearly over the centerline. When your boat is overpowered, however, easing the traveler car to the leeward end of the traveler depowers the mainsail and reduces weather helm. Some racing sailors prefer to play the traveler rather than the mainsheet in upwind puffs.

The **boom vang**—on a boat that has one—likewise exercises some control over mainsail shape, but vang tension is more useful off the wind (to keep the leech from twisting) than close hauled. Many boats, too, have adjustable backstays and can bend the mast aft underway, which flattens the main. So does increased outhaul and halyard tension, as we've already seen. We'll look more at how these various controls are used in conjunction with one another to optimize sail shape in Chapter 4.

Trapezes

The ultimate in hiking, trapezing lets you lean your whole body out over the water. Like hiking, it forces you to be attuned to the lulls and puffs and adjust your position often. The strain on your body is surprisingly small. Tacking takes training, though, and if you miss the hookup of your harness to the new windward stay, you might miss the boat!

A 420 crewmember wearing a trapeze harness. A trapeze wire leads from high up on the mast on either side of the boat, and once he clips the other end to his harness, he can plant his feet on the boat's gunwale and lean way out over the water.

Sailors on the C-cat Alpha, designed by Canadian naval architect Steve Killing, ride trapezes to victory. This is extreme sailing. The C-cats have sails that resemble airplane wings and reach speeds in excess of 30 knots.

Dumping the air from your sails altogether by letting out the sheets will always stop heeling, but this tactic leaves you dead in the water with no wind in your sails. There are better ways to deal with heeling.

Particularly in a small boat, you can counteract tipping with crew weight. It's a question of leverage: the farther out your weight is to windward, the more effective it will be. **Hiking** involves extending your head and torso beyond the windward side of the boat so as to leverage your body weight. That is why most small-boat tillers are fitted with tiller extensions; these **hiking sticks**, as mentioned in Chapter 1, let the helmsman hike out to windward, beyond arm's length from the tiller. **Hiking straps** in the cockpits of sailing dinghies help the crew do the same thing. Hooking their feet under a strap enables them to lean farther out to windward. Some high-performance dinghies go one step further with a harness attached by means of a wire or rope to a point well up on the mast. A crew wearing the harness of this so-called **trapeze** can plant his

or her feet on the windward rail and lean way out over the water for a bit of athletic, high-performance sailing.

Big boats are less influenced by crew weight, but still, when racing, their crews will seat themselves in a line along the windward rail. In general, the farther you get out on the seesaw, the better you balance the sails.

Leech control is another weapon. A tight leech cups the breeze and transmits maximum heeling force, but if the air slides along the sail and escapes, wind force is diminished. By easing the leech of a sail you help the wind skate off the trailing edge, and as we saw in the previous section, letting the jib or mainsheet out a few inches will accomplish this. In addition, however, most jibs have **leech lines**. Loosen yours until the leech flutters, then tighten them so the leech just quivers but is not cupped. Some mainsails have leech lines, too. Because most sail power comes from the forward half of the sail, easing the back part reduces heel without significantly diminishing drive.

A boat that heels easily is called **tender**, whereas a resistant one is considered **stiff**. The factors that determine your boat's inherent stability—its hull shape, the height of its center of gravity, and the location and weight of its ballast—are mostly beyond your control, but you can certainly stow gear low and toward the center of the boat, sail her on her lines (neither bow down nor stern heavy), and keep her upright enough (less than 25 degrees of heel) so that her natural stability remains effective.

> ### Racks and Wings
>
> Performance boats of many types, most particularly the Sydney Eighteens ("Eye-deens," as they say in Australia, where these flat-out racing dinghies originated) and Hobie Turbo catamarans, control heel with **racks** (cantilevered pipework extensions on either side of the hull) that allow sailors a wider platform to hike or trapeze from. Some racing keelboats have **wings**—solid flare-outs above the waterline—for the same reason. Flatter truly is faster.

Controlling Helm Balance

New sailors often sense that a boat "has a mind of her own." If you want to read that mind, you'll need to understand your boat's helm balance, often called simply **helm**. Once you fathom what it is, helm is relatively easy to control.

Think of your boat's mast extending through her and into the ground, leaving the boat to spin like a giant weather vane. If you (mentally) raise the jib, the boat will spin until her bow is pointed directly downwind. Try this on the water if you like. Lash the wheel or tiller, raise the jib, sheet it tight, and watch her head downwind.

Now drop the jib and raise and trim the main. The boat will pivot until her bow points *into* the wind, and there she will stay.

What's the lesson?

Sails set forward of the mast push the bow away from the wind. Sail area flown aft of the mast pushes the bow into the wind.

A boat's true pivot point is not her mast, but the **center of lateral resistance** (CLR) of her hull. You can find that center for any boat by drawing her underwater profile on a piece of cardboard. Cut out the shape, including the keel but not the rudder, and balance it on a knife edge. It will balance along the axis that leaves equal areas of underwater profile forward and aft. This is the boat's pivot point—her CLR—and a vertical axis through this point will be near (though usually slightly aft of) the mast.

When equal force is applied forward and aft of the CLR, the boat will travel straight ahead. With more sail force behind

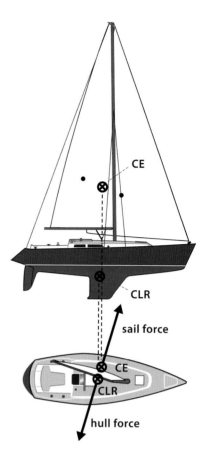

**Balanced helm:
no rudder needed**

The black dots show the geometric centers of the mainsail and jib, respectively. The combined effect of those two centers is the sail plan's overall CE, denoted here by the open circle. When the CE has a slight lead over the CLR, the two will be in balance (above), and the boat will sail, ideally, with a light weather helm. If the CE is aft of the CLR (page 107, left), the boat will carry excessive weather helm, and if the CE is too far ahead of the CLR (page 107, right), the boat will have lee helm and will head off the wind if left untended, which can be dangerous.

Balancing Sail Forces

If you balance the sail area ahead of the mast with the area behind, you're on your way toward a balanced helm. To reduce weather helm, flatten the mainsail and ease off on the sheet or traveler. Then try overtrimming the jib or moving the jibsheet lead forward. When no amount of sail shaping or sheet adjustment can relieve weather helm, it's probably time to reef the mainsail.

On the other hand, what if your boat has **lee helm**—the tendency to bear away from the wind when left unattended? Lee helm is undesirable and fortunately rare, but if you encounter it, try easing the jib a bit and trimming the mainsail. If that doesn't work, try tightening the backstay (if it's adjustable), and if that doesn't work, try roller-reefing a jib set from a roller furler. If your jib is hanked to the headstay rather than roller furled, try taking it down and setting a smaller jib in its place. With work you can persuade your boat to sail straight.

CE

CE

CLR

sail force

CE

CLR

hull force

**Weather helm:
boat wants to
turn into the wind**

CLR

sail force

CE

CLR

hull force

**Lee helm: boat
wants to turn
downwind**

the pivot point than in front of it, though, she wants to turn **to weather**—i.e., into the wind, and she is said to be carrying weather helm. Controlling helm is a question of adjusting the sail forces forward and aft of the pivot point.

A moderate weather helm is desirable. It provides a consistent "feel" to the tiller or wheel, without which the steering would feel mushy and unreliable. It also provides a safety margin, ensuring that a boat left to her own devices will round up harmlessly into the wind instead of sailing off on her own. Most designers build weather helm into their boats by locating the sail plan's **center of effort** (CE; the focal point of the sail forces) behind the CLR.

Centerboards

You don't have much control over a keelboat's pivot point, although it may move a little as the boat heels or when weight is shifted. In a centerboarder, however, raising or lowering the board moves the CLR a lot. The pivot point is at its forwardmost when the board is fully lowered. Raising the board—which involves swinging it aft and up—will move the pivot point aft, decreasing weather helm. You can try raising the board partway if your boat carries too much weather helm, but the negative effects of less centerboard on stability and resistance to leeway may cancel out the benefits of

reduced weather helm. More often than not, the better way to reduce weather helm is with the sails and rig.

A 420 centerboard fully raised (top) and pivoted partway down (bottom).

Reducing Sail

We have already considered a variety of tools you can use to depower your boat in a freshening breeze. You can flatten your sails, ease your sheets a little, ease the mainsheet traveler, or move the jibsheet blocks farther aft. You can feather up into a gust when close hauled or bear away from it when reaching. And when none of these suffice, you can ease the sheets

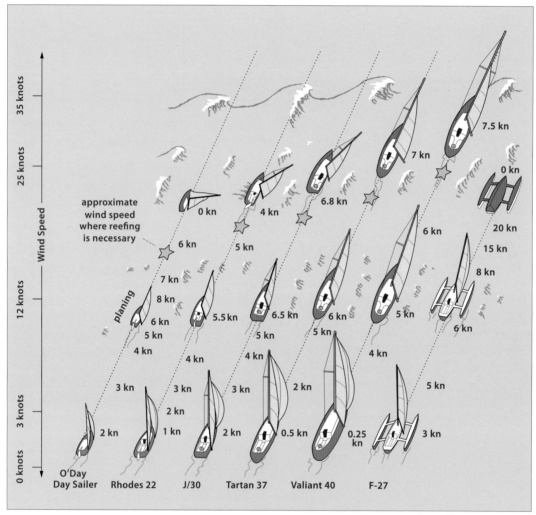

Here's a comparative look at how a few representative boats respond to an increasing wind. The O'Day Day Sailer, a centerboarder, ghosts along nicely in a faint breeze and offers fast planing performance with a wind speed in the low teens, but it should be reefed in a wind of 15 knots or so and should be back at the dock in anything more than 20 knots. The Rhodes 22, a keel-centerboarder, requires a bit more wind to get moving and will not plane, so its top speed is less than that of the smaller Day Sailer. But it can carry full sail up to, say, 18 knots of wind before it requires a reef to maintain helm and sail balance, and it will keep staggering along in 20 or 22 knots. The J/30 has a light hull and lots of sail area for racing, so it will sail well in a light breeze and attain speeds of nearly 7 knots when the wind is in the high teens. By that time, though, it requires crew weight to help control heel, and its flat bottom pounds uncomfortably in a chop. The Tartan 37 and Valiant 40 are progressively more powerful keelboats, with lesser light-air performance but more ability to stand up to a strong wind. The F-27 trimaran offers great light-air performance and speeds in the 20-knot range in a fresh breeze, but the boat requires careful and skillful handling in a strong wind to avoid trouble.

a lot to dump the wind from your sails.

Most of the time these tools will be all you need. But there will be days when the wind is consistently strong enough to overpower your boat despite these tactics. Then your choice is either to head for home or to reduce sail. The true wind strength that forces you to this choice depends on the size and design of your boat but is typically 14 to 18 knots for a small centerboarder, 16 to 20 knots for a small keelboat, and perhaps the mid-20s for a bigger keelboat. Once the procedures for reducing sail feel familiar and comfortable, you'll find sailing in these conditions rewarding and exhilarating.

There are three common ways to reduce sail. If your headsails are hanked on rather than roller furled, you can replace a genoa with a smaller jib. You can take down either the mainsail or the jib altogether and continue under just one sail. Or you can reef the mainsail and perhaps roller-reef the jib.

The simplest of these is to reduce the number of sails you have up. Drop the main? A boat handles differently under jib alone, but it's a solution that

LANGUAGE OF THE SEA
REEF
Reef comes from the Old Norse *rif*, meaning "ridge or reef." Maybe the Vikings recognized that shortening sail was a good way of staying off the rocks.

Wind Force

The force of the wind varies with its velocity squared. Thus a 4-knot breeze packs four times the force of a 2-knot breeze (2 x 2 = 4, while 4 x 4 = 16), and an increase from 10 knots (10 x 10 = 100) to 14 knots (14 x 14 = 196) can effectively double sail loads. You don't need to sail with your calculator, but keep in mind that seemingly small changes in wind speed can produce significant changes in wind force.

Wind force also varies (to a much smaller degree) with temperature. Because cold air packs molecules more tightly than hot air, it is denser. As the temperature drops, wind force goes up, but only as much as about 5%.

The pressure of the wind in the sails as a function of wind speed. When the wind speed goes from 10 to 20 miles per hour, its pressure rises from 0.4 to 1.6 pounds per square foot.

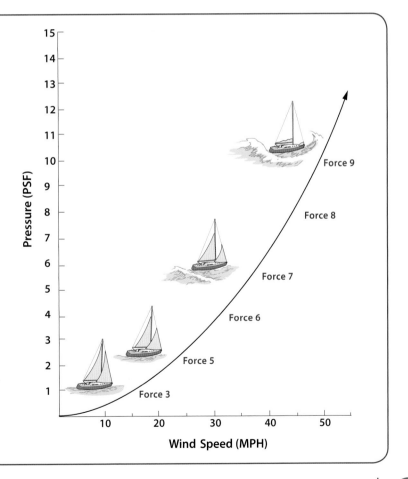

many people adopt. Sail area is reduced by more than half. Jib-alone sailing works best on a beam or broad reach. Upwind, most boats develop unruly lee helm under jib alone, and jibs flop around a lot dead downwind. I prefer getting rid of the jib.

Most boats, even boats with relatively small mainsails, sail acceptably well under main alone, as we saw in Chapter 1. Maneuvering with just the main is much easier. A mainsail can be stabilized in waves via the sheet, traveler, and boom vang (see Chapter 4), and it's easy to trim. Most sloop-rigged sailing dinghies—such as the O'Day Widgeon, the 420, and others—have no provision for reefing the mainsail but handle well under mainsail alone. When the wind comes up, simply drop the jib.

But suppose your boat has a reefable mainsail and a selection of jibs of different sizes, and suppose you need a one-third reduction of sail area to cope with a 20-knot breeze. Let's further suppose that you can achieve that by dropping the jib and sailing under mainsail alone, or by reefing the mainsail and replacing your jib

with a smaller one. You know by now that the jib and mainsail work together to produce an aerodynamic whole that is greater than the sum of its parts. And you know that helm balance is achieved with equal sail areas ahead of and behind the boat's CLR. So you can well imagine that your boat will sail better under reefed main and reduced jib than it will under mainsail alone.

Dropping a sail will bring your boat back under control but will not make it faster—at least not when you're sailing upwind. Reefing is another story.

The keel or centerboard of a deeply heeled boat is so far from vertical that it no longer resists leeway and generates lift effectively. With her sail plan leaned way out to leeward, the boat also develops excessive weather helm, which you can combat only by forcing the rudder way down to leeward, which further slows the boat. A dramatic angle of heel may *feel* fast, but your boat is in fact staggering along at reduced speed. By reefing and letting your boat "stand on her feet," you often enable her to perform better—even with a smaller sail—than she did when "standing on her ear."

So reefing, when possible, is the best response to a freshening breeze. On sloop-rigged small boats with unreefable mainsails, you can drop one sail—usually the jib. But what about cat-rigged small boats like the Sunfish and Laser? You can't reef them, and you can't drop the sail, so you'll probably have to head for home when the breeze gets stiff. Wear a PFD on a boat like this, and prepare to get wet. Fortunately, recovery from a capsize is simple on a Sunfish or Laser, as we'll see below.

Reefing the Mainsail

Reefing used to involve sending men aloft on a square rigger, but gear and techniques have evolved to let the modern sailor reef from the cockpit. Still, some sailors shy away from reefing, thinking it easier or somehow more macho to brave the elements and put up with an overburdened boat. But reefing is actually straightforward, if not always easy, and it's better than the alternatives (including staying home).

Perhaps the easiest way to tie in a reef is before you hoist the sail and leave the dock or mooring. If your mainsail is reefable, you will find reefing cringles—metal-rimmed grommets pressed into reinforced sailcloth—about one-quarter of the way up the luff and leech of the sail. The luff cringle will become the sail's new tack. Hook it over the tack hook (on the gooseneck where mast and boom join) if you have one; otherwise tie it into place.

The leech cringle will be the sail's new clew. Tie it into place with a reefing line. Most reefing lines lead from inside the boom and are meant to be passed through the grommet and back to the boom on the opposite side of the sail, tensioned from

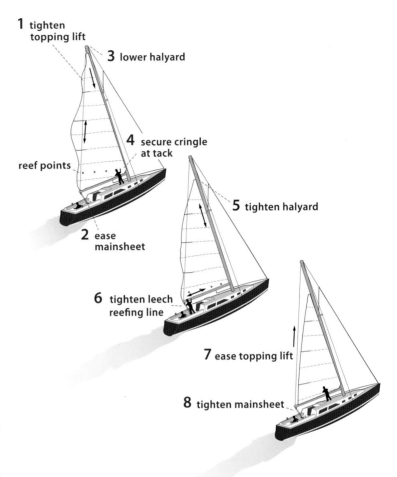

1 tighten topping lift

3 lower halyard

4 secure cringle at tack

reef points

5 tighten halyard

2 ease mainsheet

6 tighten leech reefing line

7 ease topping lift

8 tighten mainsheet

Reefing a mainsail under sail using single-line reefing. 1. *Support the main boom either by tightening the topping lift or adjusting a rigid hydraulic boom vang until it will hold the boom up when the halyard is eased.* **2.** *Ease the mainsheet until the sail carries a full luff.* **3.** *Lower the halyard enough so that . . .* **4.** *someone can secure the reefed tack cringle at the gooseneck.* **5.** *Retighten the halyard.* **6.** *Pull on the leech reefing line until the reefed clew cringle is pulled down to the boom. You will need to run the reefing line to a winch in order to accomplish this.* **7.** *Ease the topping lift or release the rigid vang.* **8.** *Trim the mainsheet and resume sailing.*

Reefing Cringle

A grommet is a reinforced eyelet or hole in cloth or leather. A **cringle** is created when a grommet is given extra reinforcement or layers of cloth to make it not just a hole, but a strong point. Tack and clew cringles are standard. Reefing cringles are added at either end of each "reef" or chunk of reduced sail.

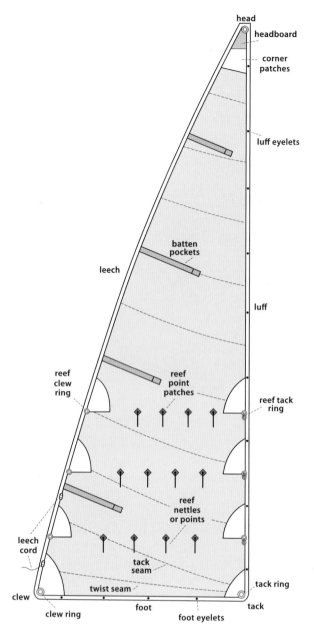

A mainsail with three reefing positions, showing the reef points (also called nettles), the reefed tack cringles (or rings), and the reefed clew cringles.

boom). Fair leads with good tension in both directions are needed to make the reef set right.

Sometimes you will see a row of small grommets known as **reef points** between the reefed tack and clew. Until recently a reef wasn't complete until each reef point was cinched to the boom—either by spiraling a continuous length of line through the grommets or by tying paired, short lengths of line dangling from each reef point around the bottom of the boom—thus containing and securing the unused portion of the sail. Today's sail fabrics are strong enough, however, to render the reef points optional rather than mandatory. Even if your sail has them, you can tie them at your convenience or not at all. Now hoist away.

the boom end, and made fast to a cleat on the end of the boom.

If you find no permanently rigged reefing line on the boom, you can tie down the clew using any suitably sized spare length of line. The important point is to pull the sail both aft (along the boom) and down (onto the

Reef Knot

We know it better as the square knot, but the **reef knot** was the traditional way of cinching up the unused portion of a sail at a reef point. Left over right/right over left, it produces a knot that won't jam. Insert a **slip** (bow-like loop), and you can untie it with a single pull.

Tying a square or reef knot. 1. *Cross the left end over the right one.* **2.** *Make a turn.* **3.** *Now cross the right end over the left one.* **4.** *Make another turn.* **5.** *Cinch tight. The knot should look symmetrical, like this.*

If you cross left over right, then left over right again, you'll end up with a granny knot like this. Note the lack of symmetry. This is not a secure knot.

Reefing under Sail

You don't have to tie in your reef before you hoist sail. In fact, one of the virtues of reefing is that it enables you to adjust to the wind as you go. On a long passage or a short daysail, you can reduce sail underway.

First make sure there's a reefing line led through the reefing cringle in the leech of your sail. Most sailors leave a line there permanently—with plenty of slack so as not to interfere with the sail under normal conditions. That way it's available for quick and convenient use if needed. If you don't have one rove (to **reeve** a line is simply to lead it through a block, eyelet,

or cringle), you can do it while you reef, but threading the needle when the boom is thrashing and the sail is flapping isn't easy. It's better to be prepared.

With the boom vang (if you have one) loose, take the weight of the boom onto the topping lift. Make sure you make it fast because it will be the only thing

REEFED TACK CRINGLE

To reef this cruising sailboat, *the crew has furled the jib and is using engine power to hold the boat about 40 degrees off the wind.* **1.** *Now the halyard is eased until the crew at the mast can get the reefed tack cringle down to the boom. The cringle on this sail has a stainless steel ring sewn into it to make this job easier.* **2.** *The crew slips the tack ring over the metal hook on the gooseneck that is provided for this very purpose. If your boat has no such hook, secure the reefed tack with a lashing of line.* **3.** *Now the halyard goes back up. The crew at the mast sways on the halyard to help the cockpit crew, who is using a winch. Then the reefing line will be tightened to pull the reefed clew down to the boom.* **4.** *The reefed mainsail has been trimmed, the jib has been partially unfurled to a reefed position, and the boat is sailing happily under reduced sail.*

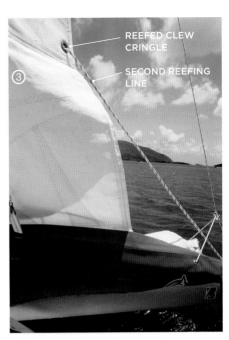

REEFED CLEW
CRINGLE

SECOND REEFING
LINE

REEFED CLEW
CRINGLE

Double and Triple Reefs

Unless you head offshore or intentionally challenge gale-force winds, you're unlikely ever to need more than a single reef in the mainsail. But voyaging mainsails provide a second and sometimes even a third reefing position, each one leaving a progressively smaller sail.

If you need a double reef (say, for 27 to 30 knots or so of wind), the second reef proceeds just like the first. **1.** Secure the new tack cringle at the gooseneck. **2.** Once the halyard is retightened, pull down the new clew cringle to the boom with the second reefing line. Here the main halyard is still on the winch but will need to removed so that the crew can get some mechanical advantage on the reefing line. **3, 4.** As he winches in the reefing line, the new clew comes down to the boom. Note that the unused bunt of the reefed sail is captured by the lazy bag on this boat, so there are no reef points to tie. **5.** Here the mainsail is double-reefed. The next step if the boat is still overpowered would be to roller-reef the jib more deeply.

Roller Reefing

Roller reefing once referred to rolling up the mainsail around the boom. Rolled in that way, the reef can be any size you want it. The gear was cumbersome, however; rolling underway was sometimes difficult, battens had to be removed, and the reefed sail seldom set well on both tacks. Roller reefing of this variety is not often installed on boats anymore. It has been replaced by in-boom furlers. The idea is the same as a jib furler, except that the main is wound around a mandrel inside the boom. The systems aren't foolproof, but they offer infinite range and efficient shapes. They also accommodate full-length battens, remove the fear that a jam will leave you with an uncontrollable sail, and provide a convenient way to furl the mainsail when your sailing is done.

Single-Line Reefing

Tying a reef into the main has been called **jiffy reefing** or **slab reefing** because it shortens a sail quickly and in preset chunks, or slabs. A variation that is particularly popular on shorthanded cruising boats (because there is no need to go to the mast and attach the tack) is **single-line reefing**, in which a single line is led through the tack and clew cringles. You reef simply by lowering sail and tightening that line. The system isn't perfect—it develops a lot of friction and makes for some tough cranking—but it works.

holding up the boom when the sail is lowered. A rigid hydraulic vang will do that, too, if your boat has one, but a topping lift is still a good precaution. The weight of people leaning on the boom could overcome a vang.

Next ease as much wind out of the sail as possible. Heading straight into the wind will do that, but it's better to minimize loss of way, flogging of the headsail, and the pitching motion of the boat by coming just close enough to the wind to enable you to relieve pressure by easing the mainsheet.

Lower the halyard until the tack grommet on the luff of the mainsail comes down to the tack hook. Fix the tack on the hook. It's important to fix the tack before you tighten the clew. You can't do it the other way around.

Now take up the reefing line as tight as you can get it. You want the clew as far aft and as close to the boom as possible. On a big boat you may have to take the reefing line to a winch to muscle it in. Do what you must to get it tight. Any play in it adds strain and deforms the set of the sail.

Once the clew is snugged down, hoist the main again.

In-Mast Reefing

Mainsail furlers that operate on the same principle as roller furlers for jibs have been around for a while. Making them strong enough to reef the sail (as opposed to furling it entirely) was the first hurdle. Fears of jamming and the need for smaller, battenless sails remain a problem, and in-mast furling has not proven any faster than tying in a reef. On the other hand, you have infinite possibilities for sizing the reefed main rather than the two or three sizes you can choose with tie-in reefing.

Storm Trysail

A small, jib-like, heavy-duty sail set in place of the mainsail, the **storm trysail** is flown when even a double-reefed mainsail would be too much sail for the conditions. Most often the trysail sets from a separate track on the mast so that the main can be furled on its boom and stowed amidships. It usually trims by means of a pair of sheets, like jibsheets, that lead to turning blocks at the stern. A boat with a third reefing position in its mainsail probably doesn't need a trysail, and unless you embark on long-distance voyaging (and perhaps not even then) you're unlikely ever to have to fly one. See Chapter 7.

Luff tension should be at least as great as it was before. Ease the topping lift so that it's slack, and trim the newly reefed sail. While you're sailing, complete the job by cinching up the unused portion of the sail with the reef points if desired.

Reefing the Jib

Jibs that reef like mainsails exist only as a rare anachronism. The standard practice with hanked-on headsails is instead to **change down** when it blows, which means replacing the jib with a smaller one. There are still a lot of boats sailing with hanked-on headsails, but on newer performance-oriented boats grooved headfoils have largely supplanted hanks. Nonetheless, reducing headsail size on these boats still involves changing down.

For shorthanded daysailing and cruising boats, however, changing headsails is too much work. Instead, the majority of such boats are fitted with roller-furling headsails, and the

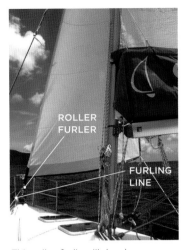

ROLLER FURLER

FURLING LINE

This roller-furling jib has been reduced in size by about 25% by roller reefing.

Roller Furlers

Developed originally just to furl or stow the jib, most rollers now make it possible to roll the sail partway in to reef it. Most modern systems use a luff extrusion. The sail fits into it, and the tube rotates around the headstay, rolling the sail onto it. Foil-shaped extrusions are for higher performance, while round tubes (sturdier and perhaps more reliable) are fine for general-purpose sailing. Furling drums may be open (good for access) or closed (good for protection of the innards). If the top swivel becomes jammed or the halyard winds around the extrusion, however, you may have a jib you can neither reef nor douse.

Changing Jibs

Changing jibs underway gets harder as wind and waves increase. By heading downwind you can blanket the jib, flatten the boat, and ride with the waves to enjoy an orderly and relatively stress-free reduction in sail size. A **racing change**, however, minimizes loss of speed and distance by switching jibs without changing course. Shortening sail this way puts a premium on preparation, crew coordination, and expertise.

furling mechanisms are robust enough to use for reefing. With a rig like this, a smaller headsail is only a few rolls away.

Roller-reefing a headsail is easier if you head downwind. Shortening sail under a load places great strains on the swivels (top and bottom) in the system, and even with improved bearings and hardware it pays to relieve the strain as much as possible. If you let the sail run free, however, the sheets can whip about and cause an uneven roll or break something. The best compromise is to bear off until you have a moderate hand tension on the sheet, just enough to stabilize the clew but not so much that you can't roll against it. Now take up on the furling line while you ease the sheet. When you have the headsail area where you want it,

cleat the furling line and you're done.

There are various systems, but most work best if the furling line comes off the drum to a fairlead that is on the same level. Angling the line up or down is asking for overrides. A common problem is kinks in the furling line that can jam in a block or lead as the sail is unrolling. Fake down the furling line so that it runs free.

When you make a sail smaller you raise its clew. That means that the old lead position for the headsail sheet is probably too far aft. When you reduce sail, change lead positions.

Reefing a jib on a furler rarely produces a flat sail, because the roller leaves the sail's built-in camber underrolled. To compensate for this many sailmakers build foam inserts into the headsail's mid-luff. Still, most roller-reefed jibs remain less than ideal for windward work in heavy weather. Also, rolling the sail toward the bow moves its force forward. What you really want in heavy weather is not only to lessen sail area but also to lower your sail plan's CE and to compress the sail forces around the hull's CLR. For this reason many offshore boats set a small staysail from an inner forestay in truly heavy weather.

Recovering from a Knockdown or Capsize

Can your boat tip over? The short answer is "Yes, but . . ."

A keelboat—unless being driven too hard—will tip over only in the most extreme conditions, which usually means a major storm or hurricane. You'll always have advance warning of these conditions if you're paying attention to the weather forecasts. Unless you're far offshore, there is no reason to be caught at sea by a storm.

And although a small centerboard or daggerboard daysailer will tip over in a stiff breeze, tipping over in a boat like this is no big deal if you know how to right it. In fact, your sailing instruction should include a capsizing or two in a Sunfish, 420, Optimist, or other small boat just to conquer the fear of the unknown.

Before we go further, let's get the terms straight. If a big gust of wind should ever heel your boat until its mast is in or near the water, you will have suffered a **knockdown**. If your boat at that point keeps rolling until its mast points straight toward the bottom, it will have **capsized**, or **turned turtle**. The term capsize is often used as a synonym for knockdown as well as turning turtle, especially when the boat being knocked down is a centerboard boat and therefore unlikely to right itself.

Prevent knockdowns and capsizes before they start. Anticipate puffs and offset them by spilling wind from your sails as needed. Feather up into gusts when you're close hauled, and bear away from gusts when

San Francisco Bay is justly famous for its afternoon sea breeze, and this boat has broached while carrying a spinnaker in what might be 30 knots of wind. Sixty degrees of heel is not a knockdown, though it probably feels like one to the crew. The rudder is stalled and useless, and the crew is going to have to dump wind from the sail plan in order to regain control.

COMPANIONWAY OPENING

VENTILATION LOUVER IN DROPBOARD

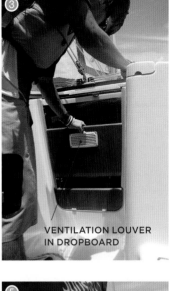

HATCH

Until you venture offshore—*and quite likely even then—you should never have to face heavy weather at sea. If you ever do, however, reducing sail is just one of the steps to prepare a cruising sailboat for what's coming. You should also get loose gear off the deck, lash down anything (including your dinghy, an anchor, etc.) that could get loose and either be lost or cause damage if a wave washes over the boat, stow items in the cabin securely, dress warmly, wear a safety harness, and secure the hatches against boarding seas.* Battening down *is what sailors call this last measure, because the sailors of 150 years ago would cover cargo hatches in a storm with heavy canvas held down around the perimeter by through-bolted wooden battens. You can secure the companionway of a cruising sailboat with* dropboards, *as here* **(1, 2, 3, 4)**, *then pull the hatch shut* **(5)** *to fend off spray and solid water.*

you're reaching. Reef the sails on a big boat, or drop a sail altogether on a small sloop-rigged boat.

As mentioned above, keelboats can take knockdowns and might even put their sails in the water. But they're designed to right themselves. If sufficient water enters the boat, however, a ballasted boat might sink after righting itself. If you must sail in heavy weather, sail with ports and hatches closed, and wear a safety harness so that a knockdown won't separate you from your boat. If your keelboat goes on her side, ease your sheets. It may be too late to spill wind, but slack sheets will keep the water in the sails from pinning you down.

A knockdown can occur in an ordinary strong breeze if you carry way more sail than you should. Suppose you are competing in a race with other J/24s. The final leg is a 2-mile reach to the finish in 24 knots of wind, and if you pass two boats you can win the race

Above: *The tether attaching this safety harness to a strong point on deck is visible behind the steering wheel.* **Right:** *A racing crew wears harnesses in an Irish Sea gale in the Fastnet Race.*

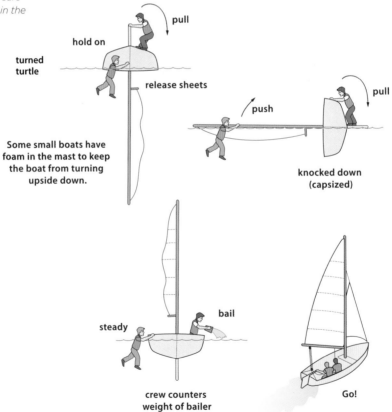

turned turtle

hold on

pull

release sheets

Some small boats have foam in the mast to keep the boat from turning upside down.

push

pull

knocked down (capsized)

steady

bail

crew counters weight of bailer

Go!

Righting a capsized daysailer.

The sailor of this capsized Laser will have to use his weight on the daggerboard as leverage to right the boat.

and the season series. So you throw caution to the winds, so to speak, and tell your crew to set the spinnaker (see Chapter 4), praying that your boat can carry it and that it will give you just enough additional speed to win. In this scenario there may be a knockdown in your immediate future.

That knockdown, if it happens, may begin with a broach. To **broach** is to round up broadside to the wind and waves, suddenly and involuntarily. Boats broach when too much heeling makes their rudders ineffective or when they bury their bows in a wave and pivot on the bow. To avoid broaching, avoid running dead before the wind and seas in heavy air. Counteract weather helm by easing the mainsail. Put the wind on your quarter (which gives room for easing) instead of directly over the stern. Reduce sail and keep the boat as flat as possible.

As indicated above, a centerboarder can capsize. The usual reason is that something prevents you from easing the sheets —maybe the sheet jams in a block, or someone is tangled in it, or the boom hits the backstay, or the sheet is wrapped around

Sailors of Lasers and other single-person dinghies *can often recover from a capsize without even getting wet.* **1, 2.** *As the boat capsizes, the sailor releases the mainsheet and scrambles over the weather rail and onto the daggerboard.* **3, 4.** *He leans back against the rail and prepares to reboard as the boat starts to come back upright.* **5, 6.** *Once back aboard he gets his controls back in hand and resumes sailing. The progress of the powerboat in the background gives some idea of how quick this process is.*

RECOVERING FROM A KNOCKDOWN OR CAPSIZE

the tiller. Once a boat without a ballasted keel gets over on her side, your odds of staying upright diminish. Some dinghies are so weight sensitive you can flip them with a careless move. As the weight of the wind increases, keep an increasingly sharp eye out for excessive tipping. Keep the boat as flat as you can, and make sure the main- and jibsheets are free to run.

Jibing is another cause of capsizes. The swing of the boom from one side to the other can roll the boat. If you're handling the sheet during a jibe, handle it correctly—trim in fast as you prepare to jibe, then let the sheet run when the boom swings across. In heavy air, tack instead of jibing. Tacking is much more controlled and less abrupt.

The good news is that most centerboarders, unlike most ballasted keelboats, will float when full of water. Although your overturned boat may seem crippled, don't try to swim for shore. Stay with the boat. Count heads, make sure everyone is OK and calm, then set about setting things right.

If your boat has turned turtle, she will be harder to right than if she's still on her side. Before you exert too much force on a turtled boat, make sure her mast isn't stuck in the bottom. If it is, try to swim her so she is broadside to the wind and waves. Their force may help withdraw the mast from the mud. Try to free the mast with gentle coaxing. Prying violently can bend or break it. Upside-down boats want to stay that way. Once the boat is on her side, ease sheets if you can. You may even have to free halyards and pull sails down. First, though, tip the boat enough to grab her centerboard. Most are strong enough for you to hang on, but be careful. If your weight on the centerboard won't bring the boat upright, try taking off sail. Now ease your boat upright; she won't come all at once, but stay at it.

Swim her bow into the wind before you right her completely. That will keep the wind from filling her sails when she pops up and capsizing her again (or sailing her away).

Getting aboard can be hard. The transom is a low spot, good for getting on most boats, and it keeps your weight centered. Boarding over the side might tip

Bailers

"The best bailer is a frightened sailor with a bucket," or so the saying goes. True as that may be, there are any number of bailers. A bucket is the biggest, a hand pump may be the fastest, but even with an oar, board, or your cupped hand you can splash an amazing volume of water from a small boat. Bailing is not rocket science, but bailing a swamped boat is hard work. The water can flow in as fast as you can bail it out, so first you have to get her to float high enough to be bailable. Shoving cushions, coolers, life jackets, or any other bulky objects under a deck where they will displace water can sometimes make the difference. Also you might be able to arrange a "big wave out, little wave in" exchange by rocking the boat hard one way and gently the other. The headway that you make by slopping water out in this fashion is small, but sometimes it's enough to let you begin conventional bailing. Obviously, you can't get aboard until the boat can support your weight. Bail from outside at first if you have to. Many small sailboats have **self-bailers**, which are holes in their bottoms set up so that suction draws out the water from the inside when the boat is moving. When the boat is stopped, most such bailers will let water in. When you're bailing a swamped boat, make sure to close the bailer!

The suction self-bailer on a 420.

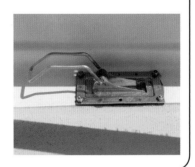

Personal Flotation

On a sunny day in August, capsizing might be fun. Most other times it isn't. Consider how much less than fun it would be, however, without the support and security of your life vest, otherwise known as a **personal flotation device** (PFD). See Appendix 4.

Modern PFDs, including this inflatable Type III, are so comfortable and unobtrusive that there really is no reason not to wear one when you're offshore, or in unsettled conditions, or even all the time.

INFLATION PULL CHORD

her over again unless another swimmer balances your weight from the other side. If you need it, make a foothold by tying a loop in a line, or use the jib (tied tight) as a boarding sling.

If you're left with a swamped boat that you can't bail, you can drift downwind to shallow water or, in the worst case, "swim" her (under jib alone) across the breeze to safety. Remember, though, to stay with the boat.

Practice capsizing. It sounds drastic, but good sailing schools and courses include a capsize drill to give learners the experience of going over and then righting the boat.

CHAPTER THREE

Sailing Seamanship

A lifetime of sailing begins with your first step down the dock, and you took that step and a few more besides in Chapters 1 and 2. Now it's time to expand your focus from your boat's helm and sails to consider such things as coping with tide and current, interacting with the boats around you, and docking or anchoring when the day's sailing is done. It's time to learn more about seamanship.

Few are they who can walk on water. No matter how strong a swimmer you may be, the sea is not home, as sailors since before Noah have sometimes learned to their dismay. To thrive on the water, sailors must salt their adventures with caution. The seafaring guidance and lore passed down through generations of sailors can seem vaster than the oceans themselves. There's wisdom in the yarns, help and hands-on instruction from books like this one, and experience wherever you seek it. There are online forums, articles, and postings, some even specific to the type of boat you sail. But how can you know what you need to know?

There is no foolproof agenda or curriculum for seafaring, but here are a few bearings to help you plot your course:

1. **Experience is the best teacher**, and this book will serve you best if you alternate your reading with time on the water. You can't walk down the dock while you're sitting on the couch. But gain your experience incrementally. When you're comfortable sailing in a moderate breeze, try a fresh one, but not yet a gale. Practice anchoring and docking in settled conditions with ample elbow room before you try these maneuvers in roiled waters crowded in on every side by expensive floating real estate. The organization of this book is incremental because the best experience is incremental.

2. **Safety comes first**, both on the water and in this chapter.

3. **Trust yourself.** Consider, for example, the internationally recognized nautical Rules of the Road, which are introduced in this chapter. These prescribe the actions to be taken by each vessel whenever two come together. One of the two is advised to give way and the other to maintain its course and speed. Despite a common misconception to the contrary, however, neither has the right-of-way. When a collision seems imminent, the Rules require you to do whatever is necessary to avoid it, and more often than not when a collision leads to a legal judgment, both skippers are considered at fault. Once you have learned the basic Rules, look beyond them to your own experience, intelligence, and common sense. The Rules require it.

As Pericles told the Athenian assembly in 432 BC, "Seamanship, just like anything else, is an art. It is not something that can be picked up in one's spare time; indeed, it allows one no spare time for anything else." This, he told the assembly, was why Athens ruled the waves. Therefore, he concluded, "we have nothing to fear from Sparta. Spartans are farmers, not sailors."

When war between Athens and Sparta broke out it lasted nearly 30 years, so perhaps the great statesman was not so great a military strategist. Still, for more than 2,000 years, Pericles' words have constituted fair warning that gaining nautical knowledge is a serious pursuit, one that can be habit forming.

Sailing Safely

Sailing is a pleasure and a relaxation, but it also entails genuine challenges. No matter how peaceful your time on the water, you are never that far from being in the water. No matter how well you learn to control your boat, you and she are "out there" with forces bigger than both of you. After all, part of the attraction of going out on the water in the first place is the element of risk.

Acknowledge the risks. In order to meet them, even though you can't anticipate them all, you need to accept that they're real.

Meet the risks. Put safety first and do your utmost to ensure it. The Coast Guard is hard working and vigilant, but you can't always depend on being rescued. Instructors can be wonderful, but they can't stand forever between you and the sport. Look out for yourself. Sailing is about freedom and individuality and challenge, but they're all tied together by our willingness to take care of ourselves. Scratch a sailor, and he or she bleeds self-sufficiency.

The Coast Guard teaches well the attitude of safety: "Overshadowing the individual safety rules is forehandedness. All hands must anticipate potential problems and take action to avoid them. Safety-consciousness, imparted in some measure by the ship herself and in some measure by shipboard evolutions, will grow as an attitude in every member of the crew."

Your boat is not a ship, nor do we who sail for pleasure call our boat-handling maneuvers "evolutions," but the Coast Guard's blueprint is a good one: Think ahead, and think safety. Experience is the best safety teacher. Deepen your own experience, look to others, anticipate problems, examine answers. Take care of yourself.

Keep the Water Out
The first priorities of seamanship are to keep the water out of your boat, your boat on the water (as opposed to the rocks!), and yourself and your crew out of the water. As long as you keep water, boat, and people in their respective places, any mishaps you suffer are unlikely to be emergencies.

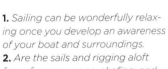

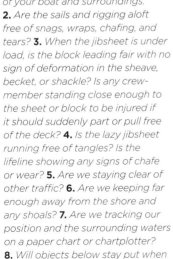

1. Sailing can be wonderfully relaxing once you develop an awareness of your boat and surroundings. **2.** Are the sails and rigging aloft free of snags, wraps, chafing, and tears? **3.** When the jibsheet is under load, is the block leading fair with no sign of deformation in the sheave, becket, or shackle? Is any crewmember standing close enough to the sheet or block to be injured if it should suddenly part or pull free of the deck? **4.** Is the lazy jibsheet running free of tangles? Is the lifeline showing any signs of chafe or wear? **5.** Are we staying clear of other traffic? **6.** Are we keeping far enough away from the shore and any shoals? **7.** Are we tracking our position and the surrounding waters on a paper chart or chartplotter? **8.** Will objects below stay put when the boat heels, rolls, or pitches?

Take Care of Yourself and Your Crew

Seasickness, sunburn, and hypothermia are genuine discomforts when they occur, and even potential dangers. Prevention is the best cure.

Just about anything that moves on a boat can deliver a wallop. The prime culprit, though, is the boom. Keep it in mind—and away from your head. When you're sailing downwind, imagine what would happen in a sudden, uncontrolled jibe. Is the boom high enough above the deck to pass harmlessly over the heads of anyone in the cockpit? What about that crewmember standing on the side deck—could he be knocked overboard in a jibe? Could the mainsheet conceivably wrap itself around some unlucky crewmember's neck as it sweeps across the cockpit?

Keep your fingers clear of a sheet-loaded winch drum, and avoid wrapping a loaded genoa sheet around your hand for extra purchase. Suppose a genoa sheet or spinnaker guy under great tension leads aft to a turning block, then forward to a winch. Before you plant your feet just forward of that turning block, imagine what would happen if the loaded block were suddenly to tear loose from the deck. When you lower an anchor, make sure the anchor rode is free to run and isn't looped around your ankle. And understand that a good-sized spinnaker filled with a fresh breeze will generate a lot more force than you can control without a lot of mechanical advantage. If the spinnaker fills (see Chapters 4 and 6) before you can wrap the guy around a winch drum or cleat, know when to let go—or you'll suffer rope burns.

Most shrouds and stays and many halyards are made of stranded stainless steel wire. When one of the strands breaks it protrudes from the wire, creating a **meathook** in the halyard or stay that's bad for hands. Cockpit lockers and cabin drawers, doors, and hatches have a fiendish propensity for pinching fingers. Splinters, stove burns, sprains from breaking a fall . . . all hands are vulnerable. Forewarned is forehanded.

What Is Seamanship?

When you trim your sails and steer your boat to coax its last tenth of a knot of performance, you are sailing well. When you do these things and simultaneously keep constant mental track of your position, observe boats that might be on a converging course with yours, attend to your boat's needs, keep the decks clear and the sheets ready to run, note weather trends, and stay ready for anything, you are also exercising good seamanship.

Seamanship is the whole tortilla. It includes but is not limited to boat handling, docking, anchoring, navigating, and boatkeeping. It comprises equal parts experience and vigilance. The former tells you how to respond to events, but the latter keeps your brain out ahead of your boat to anticipate those events before they occur. Good seamanship is characterized by a constant game of "what if": What will you do if the wind is much lighter and the current stronger out in the channel? What could happen if you get too close to that lee shore and the wind dies and the engine won't work? What is your escape route if, just as you approach the crowded dock, that small outboard operated by kids suddenly veers into your path?

Experience improves and informs your seamanship, and awareness lets you accumulate experience without serious mishap. It isn't nearly as hard as it sounds. When you learned to drive a car, things at first seemed to come at you randomly and out of nowhere, but road awareness came quickly with practice. Seamanship is similar. There are no lane markers or traffic signs to guide you, but on the other hand you're typically traveling only one-tenth as fast as an automobile.

Anchoring

There's little mystery in anchoring—at least on the surface. Just drop the anchor in, tie it on, and you're done. The deeper you delve into this topic, though, the more you'll find there is to know.

The first anchors were stone—the bigger the better, since they held solely because of their weight. More than two millennia ago, however, seafarers discovered that hooking an anchor into the bottom provided more holding power than resting it on the bottom, and stone anchors with protruding sticks or shaped protrusions came into use.

Heavier is still better for holding power, but when it comes to handling, stowage, and cost, the lighter the anchor the better. Lighter? Heavier? That's why there are so many types. Modern anchors come in a variety of shapes, mostly designed to provide added holding power with less weight.

To further complicate the subject, different shapes are optimal for different bottom types. Hard sand is easy for most anchors to bury in, but some anchors hold well in mud while others don't. Rocks, seaweed, and thin sand over a hard bottom are troublesome no matter what sort of anchor you put down, but some anchors are better at penetrating weed or gripping a rock than others.

Some sailors rarely anchor, while others find it an every-day necessity. No matter where and how you sail, though, take at least one anchor with you. A cruising sailor should carry two:

Kedge

Suppose your boat runs aground on a sandy bottom. You might load an anchor and rode into your dinghy, row the anchor into deeper water, drop it there, then pull the boat toward the anchor with the rode to break free from the sand and get back afloat. If you aren't towing a dinghy, you might even wade with the anchor into deeper water. Either way, you've just **kedged** your boat free, and the anchor you deployed could therefore be called a **kedge**. Pivoting-fluke anchors such as the Danforth (see below) make the best kedges because they are easy to carry (or even throw) yet pack good holding power. They also make good stern anchors and lunch hooks for similar reasons. In short, pivoting-fluke anchors are multipurpose utility anchors.

Anchor Anatomy

The pointed blades by which anchors bury into the bottom are called **flukes**, and the shape of the flukes and their setting angle are important variables. Some of the anchors that grab best are hard to stow because their flukes are so spiky. The **shank** of an anchor is the shaft that connects the flukes to the anchor rode. Its length and its angle with the flukes help bury them. The **stock**, on an anchor that has one, is a crossbar or rod oriented at right angles to the shank; its function is to force the lowered anchor into the proper attitude for digging in. Stockless anchors are mostly dead weight. The junction between flukes and shank is the anchor's **crown**. One of the neatest ways of retrieving an anchor is to lift it out via a light line attached to the crown rather than having to break it out by pulling on the stock.

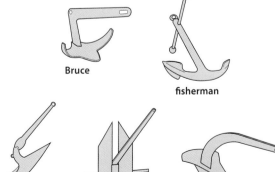

Common anchor types.

Bruce

fisherman

plow

Danforth

Spade

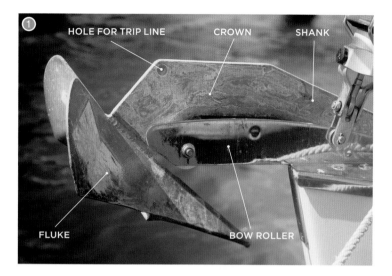

1

HOLE FOR TRIP LINE   CROWN   SHANK

FLUKE   BOW ROLLER

1, 2. *Many cruising sailboats over 30 to 33 feet long carry their primary anchor on a bow roller, where it is rigged and ready to lower. The anchor on this Beneteau Oceanis 323 is a galvanized steel Delta, a type of plow anchor that sets quickly and reliably and holds well in firm sand and mud.*
3. *The anchor chain leads back to an electric windlass that is recessed into a foredeck anchor locker. A setup like this makes anchoring easy and quick. When anchoring among rocks, you can attach a buoyed line through the hole in the crown. If a fluke should jam under a rock, pulling on this trip line will usually free it.*

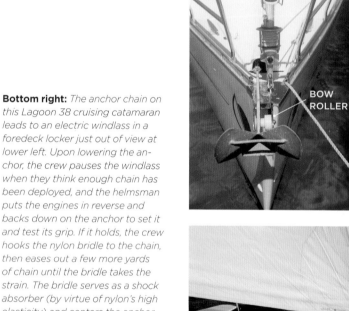

2

BOW ROLLER

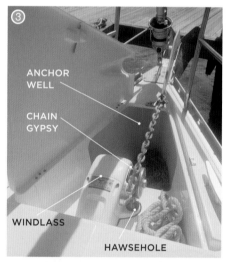

3

ANCHOR WELL

CHAIN GYPSY

WINDLASS

HAWSEHOLE

Bottom right: *The anchor chain on this Lagoon 38 cruising catamaran leads to an electric windlass in a foredeck locker just out of view at lower left. Upon lowering the anchor, the crew pauses the windlass when they think enough chain has been deployed, and the helmsman puts the engines in reverse and backs down on the anchor to set it and test its grip. If it holds, the crew hooks the nylon bridle to the chain, then eases out a few more yards of chain until the bridle takes the strain. The bridle serves as a shock absorber (by virtue of nylon's high elasticity) and centers the anchor rode between the catamaran's two hulls to keep the boat facing into the wind. The anchor shown is a CQR, an immensely popular type among cruising sailors, yet the crew of this boat could rarely coax theirs to set quickly and firmly during a week of sailing among Croatia's Adriatic islands—whereas the backup anchor, a Danforth, always set properly the first time. No one ever figured out why.*

BRIDLE

ANCHOR CHAIN

a **primary anchor** that will hold the boat in a wide range of bottom types and weather and sea conditions, and a **secondary anchor** to deploy as a supplement in those rare times when the primary alone isn't enough. Some boats carry a third, light anchor—sometimes called a **lunch hook**—to use for midday stops when the crew remains on board or close at hand.

No matter what your boat is, the "right" anchor is the one that works best to meet your priorities and solve your problems.

Choosing an Anchor

The two most popular anchors on sailboats are the **plow** and the **pivoting-fluke anchor** (which is also known as the **lightweight**). Most boats carry one or the other, or both. Other types appeal for various reasons, and some modern designs may even be superior overall, but the lightweight and the plow work well and have earned worldwide loyalty.

In terms of straight-line holding power, the lightweight (once it sets) is the champ. On the other hand, it will some-

There's a lot riding on your choice of anchor.

ANCHOR TYPES

Anchor Type	Brand-Name Examples	Best In:	Not So Good In:	Stowability	Comments
Plow	CQR, Spade, Delta, Rocna, Manson, etc.	Sand, thick mud, rock, coral, weed	Silt, sloppy mud, gravel	Usually stows well in a bow roller; hard to stow belowdecks	Excellent all-around anchor; CQR needs to be heavier for size of boat than other plows
Pivoting-fluke	Danforth, Fortress, West Marine	Sand, mud	Rock, grass, clay, weed	Stows well on deck or in a locker	Ideal for kedges; can be reluctant to reset after dragging
Claw	Bruce, Claw	Rock, weed, coral, sand	Mud, soft sand	Awkward to stow except in bow roller	The heavier the better; good all-around anchor
Fisherman		Rock, coral, weed	Any other bottom	Cannot stow in bow roller; needs to be dismantled	Needs to be very heavy to be effective

Northill Anchor

Distinguished by its "convertible" crossbar, the Northill was used in seaplanes and combines flat stowage, light weight, and good holding. It buries only a single fluke and so may snag the rode, but it is better in rocks than more popular types.

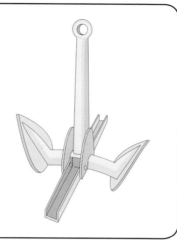

Northill anchor.

Yachtsman Anchor

Also called the **fisherman** or **Herreshoff**, this is the traditional anchor of sailors' tattoos and nautical gewgaws. It excels at gripping rocks or penetrating a weedy seafloor, but its fluke area is so small that it needs to be much heavier than other anchors to provide equivalent holding power in sand or mud. Its demountable stock lets it stow flat on deck or in the bilge. Heavy and unwieldy, it is still valued by some sailors as a storm hook.

Pivoting-Fluke Anchors

The pivoting-fluke anchor, or lightweight, was developed for maximum holding power. Its sharp, flat flukes are quick to grab most bottoms and depend very little on weight to make them bury. It makes a superb small-boat anchor, holding extremely well for its weight, but the anchor can be slow to bury itself or to reset if it's **tripped**—i.e., if it's snatched out of the bottom when the boat swings. It sets best in sand and soft mud but less well in clay, weed, or rocks. It is easy to stow in a locker when the flukes are pivoted to align with the shank, and this makes it the typical choice for a boat without bow-roller stowage, as well as a popular secondary anchor on larger boats. The original pivoting-fluke anchor is the **Danforth**, still widely available and universally popular. Similar anchors include the **West Marine Performance** and the **Fortress**, which is built of lightweight aluminum and disassembles for easy storage. You can get the holding of a traditional 8-pound Danforth in a 4-pound Fortress. Some versions have adjustable fluke angles. Fortress anchors have proven bendable in use, however, and can "swim" when you want them to sink.

RING

SHANK

STOCK

FLUKE

CROWN

The wide, flat flukes of a Danforth pivot around the shank so as to penetrate the bottom no matter which side up the anchor lands. The long stock prevents it from landing on edge.

The ultralightweight Fortress anchor assembled and disassembled for stowage.

Plow and Scoop Anchors

Plows make excellent primary anchors on sailboats with bow rollers on which to stow them. Like claw anchors, they hold best in firm sand or mud, can penetrate weed, and may grip among rocks. Although effective on a wide variety of bottoms, they hold less well in soft silt, sloppy mud, and gravel. The original plow—the **CQR**, characterized by its hinged shank—is still a favorite of cruising sailors, but some report that it doesn't always set reliably. The **Delta**, a fixed-shank plow, is considered by many to be more reliable than the CQR. Both types depend more on weight than a pivoting-fluke anchor does but don't break out easily if the wind shifts and the pull comes from a different direction. Another plow, the **HydroBubble**, has a plastic float to keep the fluke properly oriented for digging into the bottom.

Scoop anchors, the flukes of which have concave upper surfaces, have evolved from plows. The **Spade** has a weighted fluke tip to enhance its setting ability. The **Rocna** and **Manson Supreme** feature roll bars meant to orient them properly for digging into the bottom and to prevent them from capsizing under strain.

The CQR (1) and HydroBubble (2) are plow anchors. The Spade (3), Rocna (4), and Manson Supreme (5) are scoops. The CQR resembles a Delta with a hinged shank, the purpose of which is to allow a boat to swing to wind and current shifts without breaking out the anchor's flukes.

times skate over a compact surface without setting, and its stock is prone to fouling the anchor rode. Plows (the best known of which is the CQR) are designed to literally plow into the bottom when pulled by the rode, and this makes a plow a bit easier to set when the anchor needs to cut through a layer of weed, grass, or mud to find solid ground. For the security that comes from quick re-setting, the plow is likewise the better bet.

Stowage and handling are almost as important as holding power. A pivoting-fluke anchor may be small and light, but its corners, points, and angles make it a hazard to stow. Plows stow beautifully on bow rollers, but if you have to handle your anchor to set it, weight becomes an obvious drawback—a plow needs to be as much as 30% to 40% heavier to equal the holding power of a lightweight. Neither anchor is a dream to handle, but the plow is less apt to catch or snag objects (or people) on deck.

Most daysailers and racers carry pivoting-fluke anchors, while most cruising boats carry a plow on a bow roller as the primary anchor. A combination that makes excellent use of both is to complement the plow

Claw Anchors

A claw anchor can penetrate weed to find the underlying sediment and may even find something to grip on a rock bottom. On the other hand, although it holds well in firm sand, it may fail to hold in soft sand or mud. Still, it's a good all-around choice for primary anchor on a boat that's big enough to stow it on a bow roller. Stowing it any other way is awkward at best. The **Bruce** anchor is among the most popular choices of cruising sailors because it grabs the bottom so readily. Its holding power may be matched or surpassed by other types, but the ease of getting it down on many types of bottom and its rapid resetting when inadvertently broken out are its selling points. Note that inferior copies have appeared since the Bruce patents expired; the Bruce is made from high-tensile steel.

The Bruce, a claw anchor, rivals the CQR in popularity as a primary anchor on boats longer than 30 to 33 feet.

with a pivoting-fluke anchor stowed close to the helm. As an "anchor at the ready," a pivoting-fluke anchor's high holding and light weight make it a good stern anchor, emergency hook, or kedge.

One tack taken to improve the lightweight and the plow has been to make them from lighter, stronger metal, which yields bigger anchors at comparable weights. The 8-pound Danforth Hi-Tensile, for example, has twice the holding power of a traditional 8-pounder. A tapered shank and L-shaped fluke have been added to resist breaking out and to encourage faster resetting.

One-piece plow-shaped anchors (like the Delta) are now made from manganese steel. Ballast added to the fluke tip makes the Delta "self-launching" and helps it set quickly. A 14-pound Delta is rated the equal of a 25-pound CQR.

High-performing anchors may cost more (up to twice the price of those they replace), but good ground tackle is good insurance. Other anchor types have strengths that may make them an interesting alternative or good backup.

An attempt to break this down by sailboat size and sailing style might look like this:

- **Sailing dinghy or small daysailer:** One anchor will do, most likely a 4- to 6-pound Danforth or other pivoting-fluke anchor that will be easy to stow in the boat.
- **Cruising sailboat less than 28 feet long:** Your primary anchor will probably be a pivoting-fluke type that might fit into an anchor well on the foredeck. If it won't fit there, you might be able to stow it on a stainless steel bracket that attaches to the bow pulpit, and if that won't work you'll probably have to store it in a cockpit locker and carry it forward each time you need it. Your secondary anchor may well be another pivoting-fluke anchor. If you don't find a plow or claw anchor too inconvenient to stow, however, there is something to be said for carrying two anchors of different varieties. When one doesn't set, perhaps the other will.
- **Cruising sailboat longer than 33 feet:** Your primary anchor may well be a plow or claw type that stows on a bow roller. If so, your secondary can be a pivoting-fluke variety.

- **Cruising sailboat between roughly 28 and 33 feet long:** You may or may not have a bow roller, and even if you do, your boat may or may not trim well with the weight of an anchor and chain stowed way up on the bow. Choose from the two foregoing options according to your circumstances and preferences.

Assembling Your Anchor Rode

Maybe because it's the line the boat "rides" to, the anchor line (and everything else between boat and anchor) is called the **rode**. Your anchor, your rode, and various connectors between components together constitute your **ground tackle**.

The rode may be rope, chain, or a combination of the two. If it is rope, the material of choice is nylon, which combines high strength with reasonably light weight and great elasticity. Indeed, the shock-absorbing capacity of a nylon rode is its greatest advantage. A nylon rode is also comparatively inexpensive and easy to stow, but it's susceptible to chafing and will allow a boat to sail around its anchor.

A chain rode is enormously strong and resistant to chafe, but it is also much heavier, more expensive, and harder to stow. Its weight is an advantage in one sense: the sag (called **catenary**) it induces in the an-

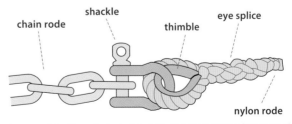

In a combination chain-nylon rode, the connection between the two is often made with a shackle through a thimbled eye splice in the nylon. The thimble protects the nylon from chafe.

RECOMMENDED RODE SIZES

Boat LOA (ft.)	Nylon Rode Diameter	Chain Diameter by Type	Weight (lbs. per 100 ft.) (all-nylon/all-chain/all-HT chain)
up to 25	3/8"/9 mm	3/16" proof-coil	3.5/50
26–31	7/16"/11 mm	1/4" proof-coil/BBB	5/76–81
32–36	1/2"/12 mm	5/16" proof-coil/BBB, 1/4"/HT	6.5/115–120/70
37–44	9/16"/14 mm	3/8" proof-coil/BBB, 5/16"HT	8.2/166–173/106
45–50	5/8"/16 mm	3/8" proof-coil/BBB/HT	10.5/166–173/154
51–62	3/4"/18 mm	3/8" proof-coil/BBB/HT	14.5/166–173/154

chor line causes the angle of pull at the anchor to be more nearly horizontal, which maximizes the anchor's holding power. In the accompanying table, **proof-coil chain** is the most economical, **BBB** has shorter links and works well on windlasses, and **high-test (HT) chain** is stronger and more expensive than either of the other two.

Voyagers debate the virtues of an all-chain rode versus nylon line, but most cruising and smaller boats compromise with a combination. Chain at the anchor end of the rode guards against chafe on the bottom and provides a more nearly horizontal angle of pull, while nylon at the boat end handles easily, lessens weight, and serves as a shock absorber to keep the boat from jerking the anchor free. Cruising sailors using an all-chain rode will frequently hook a nylon **snubber** (see pages 138–139) to the chain in order to introduce some elasticity to the rode.

If you choose a chain-nylon combination, you should have at least 6 inches of chain for every foot of boat length, and twice that is better. The more chain you use, the shorter the **scope**, or length of anchor rode, you will typically have to deploy.

Anchor Rode Connectors

Chain should be connected to the anchor with a sturdy shackle that is one size larger than the chain. For example, use a 5/16-inch shackle with a 1/4-inch chain. A galvanized steel shackle will be stronger after repeated use or prolonged immersion than one of stainless steel. At its other end, the chain is joined to the nylon rode either with a rope-to-chain splice or by means of a shackle through an eye splice in the nylon. The splice should be made around a galvanized thimble to prevent chafe. The rope-to-chain splice is preferable for use with a windlass.

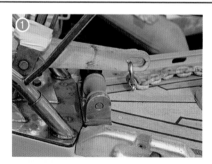

Anchor rode connections. **1.** Connect the chain to the anchor with a shackle, the pin of which should be wired so that it can't unscrew itself. **2.** Connect chain to nylon with a rope-to-chain splice . . . **3.** or, again, with a shackle through a thimbled eye splice.

Setting an Anchor

"Lower the anchor, don't throw it." I can still hear my father instructing me, and it's still the best anchoring advice I know. Setting the anchor means getting it to grab the bottom. Throwing the anchor lessens your chances. It may snag on its rode, and even if it doesn't, you can't control its descent. Wait, instead, until your boat is motionless or has a bit of sternway—i.e., until it's drifting slowly backward. Lower the anchor (even 100-pounders get lighter underwater; even chain can be paid out under control) to the bottom. When you feel it hit, give line gradually.

And how do you kill your boat's motion so that you can anchor? That part is usually easy. Whether you're moving under sail or engine power, you round up into the wind or current, whichever is the stronger factor (usually it's the wind), let your sails luff, and simply wait for the boat to stop. It will then balance there momentarily before beginning to drift backward, and that momentary pause is the ideal time to lower your anchor.

Don't, whether by heaving your hook or letting 50 feet of chain pile atop it, lose touch with your anchor. Place it. Then set it.

To set it, keep a light but consistent strain on the rode as you drift backward. You can go too fast if you use reverse engine power. Gradually insinuate the anchor into the ground. Don't slack the line completely. Don't drag the anchor backward. Just maintain strain enough to help the anchor "drift" across the bottom and bury itself. If you feel a "nibble," snub the line momentarily to deepen it, but trying to set the hook too soon will leave you with nothing.

Placing the anchor on the bottom gives you a pretty good idea how deep the water is. Let out line equal to three or four times that depth, then test the anchor by taking a strain. Take a turn around a cleat and stop paying out line. Let the rode stretch taut. If the boat keeps drifting, the anchor has not bitten in. If you swing into the wind and stop drifting backward, you've got a grip.

To get a dragging anchor to bite, pay out more line, this time keeping slightly more tension on the rode. The more scope you let out, the more nearly horizontal the pull from the boat becomes—at least up to a scope of roughly ten times the water depth—which helps the anchor dig in. You can see this. If the rode is coming out of the water close to the boat, you are pulling mostly up and lifting the anchor. The farther from your bow the rode enters the water— the flatter the angle between rode and water—the flatter the pull.

Once the anchor is holding, set it more firmly by reversing under power or backing the mainsail. The object is to back hard enough against the anchor to see if it's really holding. The time to find that out is now, not in the middle of the night when a storm descends. If it's holding, bury it deeper. If it isn't, you can sometimes coax the flukes to bite by easing and then snubbing as you reverse. Setting the anchor deep will also make it harder to break out should the wind swing into a new direction. And if it does break out, the more scope you have out the greater the likelihood that it will reset itself with minimal dragging.

Is the anchor firmly set? If you've judged distances, wind direction, and the influence of any current correctly, you're anchored in sufficiently deep

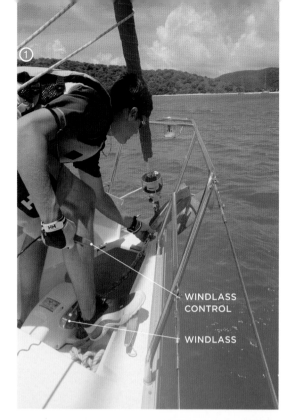

① WINDLASS
CONTROL

WINDLASS

②

⑤ CHAIN
GYPSY

NYLON
SNUBBER

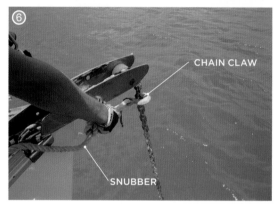

⑥ CHAIN CLAW

SNUBBER

Anchoring with an electric windlass. 1. *As the boat approaches the selected anchoring location, the foredeck crew opens the anchor locker and makes sure the anchor is free to run. This cruising sailboat carries its primary anchor, a Delta, on a bow roller and uses an all-chain rode. If the anchor is lashed or clipped to the bow roller, it should be freed at this time.* **2, 3.** *While the boat maneuvers, the crew lowers the anchor off the roller to hang from the chain.* **4.** *When signaled from the helm, and when the boat's forward motion has stopped, the crew lowers away. You want the boat to fall back on its rode, as here, not overrun it.* **5, 6.** *When nearly enough rode has been paid out, the helmsman either backs down gently under engine power or lets the boat drift back in the wind or current to set the anchor and ensure that it is holding. If it is, the crew may decide to place a nylon snubber as a shock absorber on an all-chain rode, as here.* **7.** *With the snubber cleated on the foredeck, the crew eases out more chain until the snubber takes the strain. This snubber will have to be eased another 15 or 20 feet before it is long enough to be an effective shock absorber. And here's a review question for you: Should the crew simply take the loaded snubber off the cleat and into his hand in order to ease it? No way. He should retain one or two turns around the cleat, then surge the line around the cleat to ease it rather than trying to assume the entire load himself.* **8, 9, 10.** *And here's how the completed setup looks above and below the water. When anchoring a boat less than 30 feet long you probably won't have the convenience of a windlass, but your anchor will be smaller, your rode will be either all-nylon or a combination of chain and nylon, and the forces involved will be smaller.*

water with good protection and sufficient room between you and other boats to allow them all to swing without mishap.

Where to Anchor?

"Anywhere your line is long enough," is the simplest answer. Even out of sight of land the water is often less than 50 feet deep, and in an emergency you might be able to anchor in that depth by stringing together 200 feet of line. Most of the time, though, the problem is too little depth, not too much. When the tide goes out and the wind swings 180 degrees (they will!), will you still be floating?

Anchoring in a channel is prohibited. Even if you anchor near one you may be disturbed by passersby. Anchor well clear of channels.

Boats anchored together make an area an anchorage. If they are about your size and type, that's a good sign. Moored boats swing in tighter circles than anchored boats, and that makes anchoring among them tricky, but boats at anchor will have about the same amount of scope out. If the wind changes, the theory goes, they should swing clear of one another.

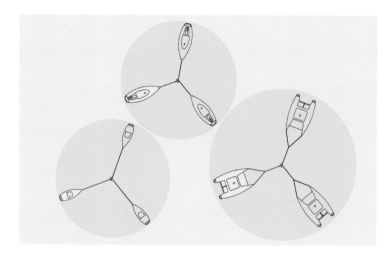

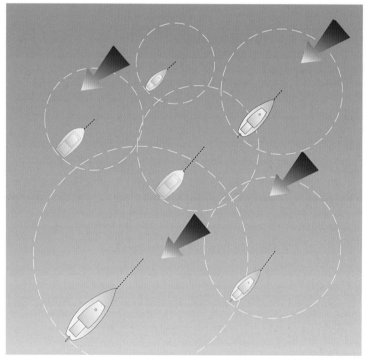

The ideal spot for anchoring is sheltered from wind and waves (not just those of the moment but those expected during the night), out of the nearest navigation channels, and in water deep enough at low tide to float your boat but not impractically deep. Having satisfied these requirements, you'd like a spot that will allow you to swing 360 degrees without contacting your nearest neighbor (top), but in a crowded anchorage that can be difficult or impossible to achieve. Short of that, if you anchor among similar boats, you can expect that all will swing in unison to wind or tide (above). If a problem develops, however, remember the #1 rule of anchoring etiquette: first arrivals have primary rights; late arrivals should be ready to weigh anchor and move if they threaten to foul their neighbors.

Scope

Meaning literally "the length of an anchor cable," **scope** is the ratio of rode length to water depth plus freeboard. If the water depth is 12 feet, your bow is 3 feet above the water, and you've let out 60 feet of rode, your scope is 4:1.

Scope is critical in setting an anchor. It determines your boat's radius of swing as well as the anchor's holding power. The angle of the anchor rode—its "slope" from boat to anchor—varies with scope. It's like the grade of a hill—the steeper the gradient, the more slippery the slope. Making the slope flatter makes the hook more secure. Remember the adage: "When in doubt, pay scope out."

On the other hand, hauling line back is work, and swinging room is almost as vital as holding power, so there are limits on scope. If you're the only boat around, unlimited scope may be fine, but when you need to control your swing (as you almost always do), you have to rein in. In general, make your rode long enough to help the anchor dig in but short enough to swing comfortably.

A scope of 3:1 is the least you'll need to get the anchor to grab at all. Under normal circumstances a scope of 4:1 is about right for an all-chain rode, while a chain-rope combination might require 6:1 and an all-rope rode might need 10:1. In a crowded anchorage in calm conditions, you can get by with less, but when the wind or seas get up you'll need

more. (Anything greater than 10:1 puts you into the realm of diminishing returns, however, as the table makes clear.)

If you are anchoring in waters with significant tides, be sure to factor the tide into your calculations of scope. Suppose you anchor at low tide in 10 feet of water, and the tidal range is 10 feet. Your bow is 2 feet above the water, so at low tide you let out 48 feet of rode in order to achieve a scope of 4:1. At high tide your scope will be just 2.2:1 unless you let out more scope as the tide comes in. Mark your rode (24-foot or 4-fathom lengths are convenient) so that you'll know how much scope you have out. Let the chart, depth sounder, or your own soundings tell you the depth.

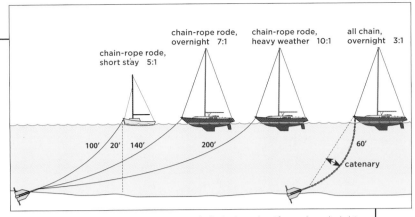

Recommended scope for chain-rope and all-chain rodes. If your bow height is 4 feet, the charted low-water depth where you're anchoring is 17 feet, and the expected rise of tide is 4 feet, then the maximum depth you expect is 25 feet. For an overnight stay in settled conditions on a combination chain-nylon rode, a 7:1 scope or 175 feet of rode should be about right. In calm conditions and a crowded anchorage a shorter scope may be better, but in heavy weather you want more. The catenary introduced by an all-chain rode puts a more horizontal pull on the anchor, enabling a shorter scope.

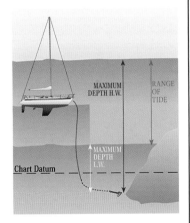

If you anchor at mid- or high tide, how will you know if you'll have sufficient depth of water under the keel at low tide? Both the depths marked on your chart and the heights of tide predicted in tide tables (see later in this chapter) are referenced to an average depth at low tide. Suppose the charted depth where you'd like to anchor is 8 feet and the predicted height of tide at low water is 0.5 feet. You can expect 8.5 feet of water at low tide, and if your boat draws 5 feet or less you should be fine. If your boat draws 7 feet, on the other hand, you'll be cutting things too close for comfort—the trough of one good powerboat wave might drop your keel on a rock beneath.

ESTIMATED PERCENT OF MAXIMUM HOLDING POWER AS A FUNCTION OF SCOPE

Scope Ratio*	2:1	4:1	6:1	8:1	10:1	> 10:1
Percentage of Maximum Holding Power	10	55	70	80	85	> 85

*(length of rode) ÷ (vertical distance from bow chock or bow roller to seafloor)

Anchoring among Other Boats

When you have a choice, anchor near boats that are similar to yours. Powerboats swing differently from sailboats, and light, fin-keeled sailboats range about their anchors much more actively than heavy, long-keeled sailboats do. When you're the last boat into a crowded anchorage, you have to respect the early arrivals. Don't anchor too close, and don't drop your anchor on top of someone else's.

The Bitter End

Over the years I've seen anchors go over the side without a rode shackled to them, and I've also watched the **bitter end** of more than one anchor rode slither over the bow because no one thought to fasten it to the boat. Come to think of it, perhaps that's why the inboard end of an anchor rode is called the bitter end. It's a good idea to check the rode-anchor connection whenever you drop anchor, and to firmly affix the bitter end of the rode to the boat. Don't make the fix too permanent, though. I heard one story of a frightened sailor with a hacksaw having to cut through a chain rode attached with a rusty shackle in order to escape his anchor and sail away from a stormy lee shore. Lash—don't shackle—the bitter end of a chain rode to the boat. You can always cut the lashing or untie it if you need to extend your rode.

Ranges

Use a **range** to tell when your anchor is holding and to check against dragging while you're at anchor. Sighting across a fixed object on your boat (such as a lifeline stanchion), line up two permanent objects one behind the other. The closer they are to abeam the more helpful. Now check your heading. As long as the objects are in line when you are pointed the same way, you're stationary. If you drag (or swing), the alignment will change. You can get the same reference by taking a bearing on a single landmark. If you are on the same heading and sight from the same spot, it should stay constant.

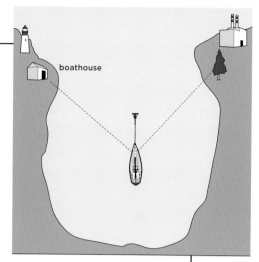

When you anchor, establish a range or two ashore so that you'll know if you're dragging. As long as the boathouse stays aligned with the lighthouse on one shore and the tree remains in front of the power plant stack on the other, this boat's anchor is holding.

Wherever you anchor, estimate your distance from your anchor and swing it 360 degrees. Anything inside this mentally calculated swinging circle might be a problem. Other anchored boats will swing, too. That makes them less of a concern than docks, rocks, moored boats, or even mooring buoys. If any of the above are inside your circle, you have a point of potential contact.

You will anchor in a variety of places, at different stages of tide, and for differing reasons. Anchoring is rarely the same twice, but the object always remains the same—to get the anchor to grab the ground. Place it; pull gently; let out scope; test the anchor; get it to grab; then set it! Nothing about anchoring matters more than getting the hook into the ground.

Retrieving an Anchor

Normally the biggest concerns when you **weigh**, or recover, your anchor are maneuvering clear of other boats and cleaning up the mess on deck. If you're the lone boat, maneuvering may not be a problem, but when you come "unstuck" with boats anchored close around you, it can be. Plan your exit before you break free.

Come up slowly on the rode, bringing the scope angle closer and closer to the vertical. Any boat with an electric windlass also has an engine, and you will almost certainly have the engine running for this maneuver, powering slowly ahead toward the anchor as you recover the rode with the windlass. On a boat less than 30 or so feet long you may well be recovering the rode hand over hand—possibly under sail rather than power—but the procedure remains essentially the same. Shorten scope as much as possible without disturbing the hook. Orient the boat to give yourself maximum control and freedom of movement, then break the anchor loose. It should come up easily and leave you on the departure course you want.

If your boat is head to wind when the anchor breaks out, use a burst of forward engine power to get your bow pointed in the right direction, but give the foredeck crew time to get the anchor to the surface and secure it before you start powering out of the anchorage. If you're under sail, you can back the jib to the side opposite the direction in which you wish to sail away, or you can let the boat

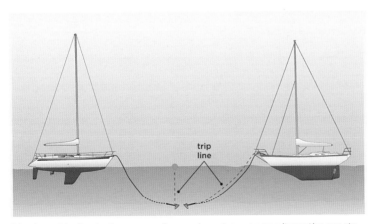

Rigging a trip line to the crown of an anchor gives you an alternative way to hoist it if the flukes get jammed under a rock or a neighbor's chain. You can buoy the trip line (left), but in a crowded anchorage it might be better to bring it back aboard (right) so as not to foul your neighbors.

drift backward with the rudder hard over to the side opposite your desired departure course.

Breaking out an anchor can take 50% of its holding power. If your anchor doesn't break out easily, let the boat do the work. Pull the rode in tight, bringing the boat directly over the anchor. Take as much strain as you comfortably can, then cleat the rode, using the boat's buoyancy to pull. To add oomph, put all hands on the bow. Cinch the rode tighter. Now move everyone all the way aft. Sometimes you can lever the hook free that simply.

Waves, or even the wake from a circling dinghy, can help too. The next escalation is to forge slowly ahead under engine power with the rode strapped tight. (Sailing off a fouled hook is possible but reckless.) You will have good steam up when you break free. Mind the throttle.

If power doesn't work, chances are the anchor has hooked something bigger than it is. Old-timers were prepared for what they called **foul ground**. Many would attach their anchor rode to the crown of the anchor, then run the rode to the free end of the shank (the usual attachment point) and seize it there with a lashing. An anchor rigged this way works normally under ordinary loads, but when it fouls, a strong upward pull will break the lashing and allow the hook to be backed out via its crown. Leaving a bit of slack between crown and seizing helps break the lashing.

A more cumbersome alternative is to set the anchor with its rode attached in the usual place at the free end of the shank but with a secondary **trip line** tied to the crown and buoyed at its other end. If the anchor fouls, pick up the buoyed trip line and pull on the crown. Do not set a trip line with much slack, however, or it may find a way to foul your keel, rudder, or propeller.

If your anchor fouls and all attempts to break it free from the surface fail, you or someone you hire may have to dive on the mess. Finally, it's not uncommon to buoy the end of the rode with a cushion or fender and leave the anchor behind. Unfortunately, it is uncommon to get your abandoned anchor back later.

Relieving the Strain

If your anchor is hooked on a cable, another anchor line, or some other mystery cordage, the solution is simple, in theory: pass another line beneath the cable, lift on the new line until it takes the cable's weight, then pull your own anchor free.

If your rode fouls your propeller, you'll have to relieve the strain on the prop before you can set it free. Tie a line (a rolling hitch—see page 169—is good) onto the anchor rode below the prop, then winch or pull in the line until it takes the strain off the prop. Now unwind the rode from around the prop.

Minimizing the Mess

Whatever sand, silt, mud, or weed is on the bottom may come aboard with your anchor. Swirl and splash as much of the crud off the hook as you can while it hangs at water level. Deck wash hoses are made for this, but a long-handled mop (perhaps in combination with a bucket on a line) is a fine, low-tech way to clean an anchor before you stow it.

From the Cockpit

Singlehanded sailors thought it up, but any sailor can do it. Setting and retrieving your anchor from the cockpit can be a real convenience. To set, take anchor and rode aft from the bow chock, outside lifelines and shrouds. Lower when ready over the side, then tend the line as usual either by walking forward or by leading the inboard end of the rode aft.

To pick up the anchor, use a **lizard**—the picturesque designation for any line tied around a rode. Shorten scope in the conventional way, then repair to the cockpit. Take a strain on the lizard as shown in the illustration. The loop will bring the rode to you and break the hook free.

Using a lizard. 1. Tie the lizard to the anchor rode with a rolling hitch (see page 169), and lead it aft to the cockpit. 2. Shorten scope. 3. Haul on the lizard to bring the rode to the cockpit, enabling you to recover the anchor from there.

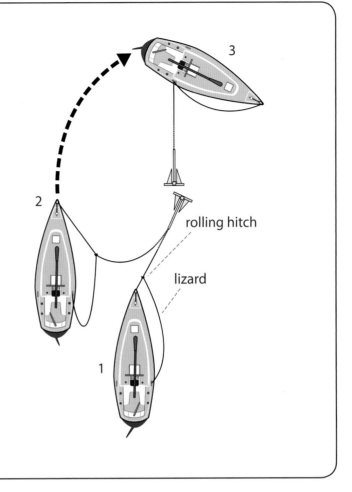

rolling hitch

lizard

Fathoming the Tide

Tide is the seawater's up-and-down movement. **Tidal current** is the horizontal flow of water that gets it done. The two are intimately connected, but they are not the same. Imagine a sheltered bay that communicates with the open ocean through a single narrow channel between headlands. The bay at **high tide** contains twice as much water as it does at **low tide**. That additional volume must flow in through the narrow channel over the course of a little more than 6 hours, which means there will be a substantial **flood current** during that time. After a brief interval of **slack water** called the high-water stand, there will then follow a substantial **ebb current** as the bay empties out over the next 6 hours prior to another period of slack water called the **low-water stand**, following which the cycle repeats itself. (In this example we're assuming a **semidiurnal tide**—with two high waters and two low waters in each 24-hour period—which is the norm in most parts of the world. Some coastlines depart from this norm, however, as we'll see.)

With their usual drive toward economy of speech, seafarers call the flood current a **flood tide** and the ebb current an **ebb tide**—or simply the **flood** and the **ebb**—but a tidal current is not the tide itself. The two concepts are as different as horizontal and vertical.

Suppose you wish to sail your boat from the ocean into our hypothetical bay. The chart shows low-tide depths as shallow as 4 feet in the entrance channel, and your boat draws 5 feet, so you risk running aground if you attempt the channel at low tide. But the local range of tide is 6 feet, so at midtide there should be at least 7 feet of water everywhere in the channel. Is it safe to proceed? Here are the considerations:

- **Is the tide rising or falling?** "A rising tide floats all boats," the saying goes. If you run aground on a rising tide, you'll soon float free. If you run aground on a falling tide, you may be stuck several hours until the next

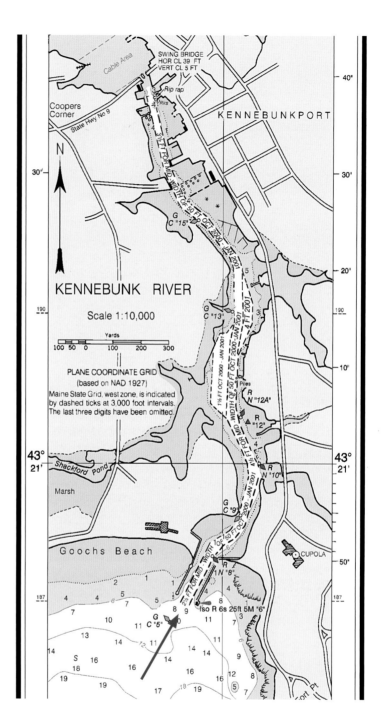

KENNEBUNKPORT

GOOCHS BEACH

Suppose you'd like to visit the pretty seaside village of Kennebunkport, Maine—about a half mile up the Kennebunk River—and your boat draws 6 feet. The chart tells you that the river channel is dredged to a controlling depth of 4.5 feet. (Note: The red arrow superimposed on this segment of Chart #13286 shows where the accompanying aerial photo was shot from.) You've heard that the actual low-water depth is 6 feet, but that information is a couple of years old, and you've also heard that the river shoals with time. The channel is narrow, and the tidal current, though usually less than 2 knots, is nevertheless significant. The average range between high and low tide is about 9 feet. A narrow, shoal entrance like this shouldn't be attempted in rough seas without local knowledge, but let's say the seas are calm, the breeze gentle. High tide on the day of your visit will be 3 p.m. The best time to head upriver will be after mid-tide on the flood—say, between noon and 1 p.m. By that time the depths in the channel should be at least 7.5 feet, and with the tide still rising, even if you run aground you'll float off quickly. The flood tide will boost you upriver. In town you may find a marina with more than 6 feet of water dockside at low tide, in which case you may decide to stop overnight. If not, however, you should exit the river on the ebbing tide by 5 p.m. Stay much longer, and you'll run the risk of being stranded aground.

rise. In the meantime, what will happen to your boat as the tide drains further? How badly will she pound if the wind and seas rise before you're free? It's better to navigate tricky waters on a rising tide than a falling one.

- **What are the sea conditions?** Suppose the waves around you seem to be averaging about 3 feet high. Wave height is measured from trough to crest, and the trough of a 3-foot wave will be approximately 1.5 feet below the level of still water, while the crest will be 1.5 feet above still water. The trough of a 3-foot wave in water that is nominally 7 feet deep, therefore, will in fact put your boat in 5.5 feet of water. When you consider that there are always a few waves that are significantly higher than average (and therefore a few troughs that are lower than average), and that the waves are likely to steepen in the shallow water of the entrance channel, you will have to conclude that you need more than 7 feet of water in the entrance if a sea is running. Imagine having your boat "dropped" onto

a shoal in the trough of a wave—that's not something you want to experience.

- **How much current is there in the channel?** Suppose your speed under sail in the prevailing light breeze is 3 knots. You won't be able to negotiate the channel against an ebb current of 3 knots, whereas a flood current of 3 knots would whisk you into the bay at a speed over ground of 6 knots. Then too, a strong ebb tide will cause incoming seas to steepen dramatically; 4-foot waves could easily become 9-foot waves with their crests much closer together. This is what makes many inlets dangerous.
- **How long do you want to remain in the bay?** If you're entering at mid-flood, and you only want to remain a few hours, you'll have to leave before mid-ebb—i.e., within approximately 6 hours (assuming a semidiurnal tide). Failure to do so will confine you in the bay for an additional tidal cycle.

This hypothetical example suggests some of the ways tidal rise and fall and tidal currents can affect navigation.

What Causes Tides?

The gravitational pulls of the moon and sun both attract earth's waters, but the sun's influence is only 46% as large as the moon's because, though the moon is much smaller than the sun, it is also only one-quarter of 1% as distant. The moon's pull is strongest at points on earth directly beneath it. That produces a high-tide bulge beneath the moon and a corresponding though complicated-to-explain bulge on the opposite side of the earth. As your location on earth spins away from the moon, the tide ebbs. Some 6 hours later the earth's rotation has "moved" the moon a quarter of the way around the globe, and you experience low tide. Six hours after that the moon is directly overhead on the opposite side of the world, and you get a second high tide.

Ebb and flood, 6 hours each, day in, night out, the semidiurnal tide cycle is a fact of saltwater sailing in most places. Because the moon orbits the earth even as the earth spins beneath the moon, it actually takes a bit longer than 24 hours for a particular spot on earth to "catch up" with the moon on each rotation. Thus the tides "advance," with high tide occurring about 50 minutes later each day of the sidereal month, which is the 27.5 days required for the moon to complete a full orbit around the earth.

When the moon and sun line up with the earth (at the new moon and full moon), their combined pull produces the maximum tides of the month— the highest high tides and the lowest low tides—and these are known as spring tides. When the moon and sun as seen from the earth are at right angles (the moon's first and third quarters), the sun's pull partially counters the moon's, and we experience the smallest tides of the month (the lowest highs and the highest lows), the neap tides. The cycle from one full moon to the next takes 29.5 days, which is called the synodic month. Tide patterns vary across the globe, but all are predictable.

In the absence of geographic effects, every coastline around the world would experience modest semidiurnal tides, with two high and two low waters in each 24 hours 50 minutes. But ocean basins, gulfs, bays, sounds, and rivers modify the basic pattern in ways that are often dramatic. The Atlantic coasts of Europe, Africa, and North America all experience a semidiurnal pattern, but the mean range between high and low tides is as little as 0.5 to 3 feet in parts of Florida, North Carolina, Virginia, and the Chesapeake Bay, and as much as 30 feet or more near the head of the funnel-shaped Bay of Fundy, where the flood tide comes in

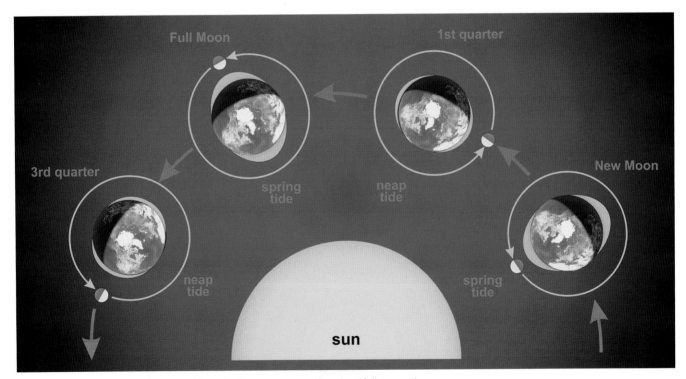

The spring tide—neap tide cycle. At new moon and again at full moon, the gravitational forces of the moon and sun are additive, and we experience spring tides. During the first and third quarters of the moon, the effects of the moon and sun partially cancel each other, and we experience neap tides.

like thunder. Along the Atlantic coast of France, too, the tide can rise as much as 36 feet, while at some equatorial latitudes there is hardly any rise and fall. The northern Gulf of Mexico experiences only one high and one low water daily—a **diurnal tide**—while the Pacific Coast of the United States and parts of the Caribbean basin have two high waters of greatly unequal height daily, a phenomenon known as a **mixed tide**.

Factor the Tide

Consult a tide almanac to learn the times and heights of high and low water where you sail. There will often be one in your local newspaper, and the information is readily available online. In the absence of a tide almanac, note the time of high tide one day and

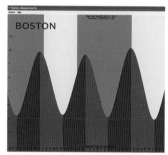
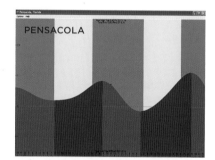

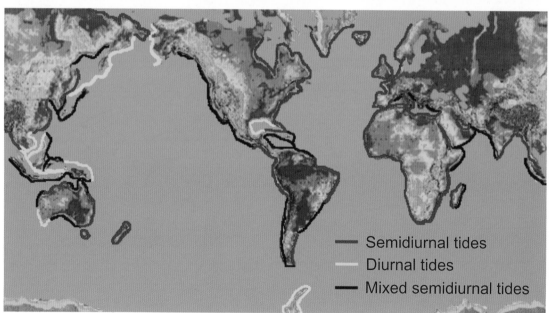

Areas of the world with semidiurnal, mixed, and diurnal tides.

add 50 minutes (in an area of semidiurnal tides) to estimate its time the next day. To estimate the height of the tide, look at a piling or the water along a beach at low tide. You'll be able to tell by algae, barnacles, and water and weed lines how much higher the water will rise at high tide.

Launching your boat, tying it up, sailing it, beaching it, rescuing it from a grounding, or taking it under a bridge, you should know the state of the tide. No plan, in fact, is really a plan until you factor in the tide.

Tide Tables

You can find local times and heights of high and low tides in government publications, almanacs, beachgoers' calendars, newspapers, fishing reports, marina bulletin boards, and online sources, to name a few. Such tables are compiled annually; a 2009 tide table will do you no good in 2010. The predicted times may be standard or daylight saving time; if the former, you'll have to add an hour during the summer. The predicted heights will be referenced to the same **datum** as the local navigation charts, which in North America is **mean lower low water** (MLLW; see below).

For example, the predicted height of the midday high tide in Boston Harbor for August 2, 2008, is 10.5 feet, while the following low tide has a predicted height of −0.3 feet (i.e., 0.3 feet below MLLW; a **minus tide** like this one is a sure indication of a spring tide). Suppose on that day you want to cross a shoal in Boston Harbor that has a charted depth of 4 feet, and your boat draws 5 feet. At high tide there will be 4 + 10.5 = 14.5 feet of water over the shoal, and you can cross without problem. At low tide there will be 4 − 0.3 = 3.7 feet of water on the shoal, and you will run aground. But let's say

you want to cross the shoal at 5:15 p.m. Your tide table tells you that low tide will be at 1736 hours, which translates to 5:36 p.m. But the tide table gives eastern standard times, so you add an hour to make the prediction correspond with clock time. Low tide will therefore be at 6:36 daylight saving time—a little over an hour from when you want to cross. Can you cross the shoal safely? Intuitively you realize you are too close to low tide to attempt it. If you're unsure in such a situation, however, try using the Rule of Twelfths (see page 153).

Boston, Massachusetts, 2008

Times and Heights of High and Low Waters

DATE   NEW MOON   TIME OF TIDE   HEIGHT OF TIDE

	July				July				August				August				September				September		
	Time	Height			Time	Height			Time	Height			Time	Height			Time	Height			Time	Height	
	h m	ft	cm		h m	ft	cm		h m	ft	cm		h m	ft	cm		h m	ft	cm		h m	ft	cm
1 Tu	0256 0907 1506 2120	−0.8 9.6 0.3 11.7	−24 293 9 357	**16** W	0345 0959 1544 2201	0.9 8.4 1.8 9.9	27 256 55 302	**1** F	0432 1047 1643 2300	−1.0 10.0 0.1 11.5	−30 305 −3 351	**16** Sa	0435 1049 1643 2257	0.3 9.2 0.9 10.3	9 280 27 314	**1** M	0546 1200 1806	−0.5 10.5 −0.3	−15 320 −9	**16** Tu	0519 1129 1742 2352	−0.3 10.7 −0.5 10.6	−9 326 −15 323
2 W	0353 1006 1602 2217	−1.1 9.8 0.0 11.9	−34 299 0 363	**17** Th	0427 1042 1627 2243	0.6 8.6 1.6 10.1	18 262 49 308	**2** Sa	0523 1139 1736 2352	−1.1 10.2 −0.3 11.4	−34 311 −9 347	**17** Su	0514 1127 1725 2337	0.1 9.5 0.5 10.5	3 290 15 320	**2** Tu	0020 0628 1242 1851	10.6 −0.2 10.5 −0.2	323 −6 320 −6	**17** W	0601 1210 1827	−0.3 11.0 −0.8	−9 335 −24
3 Th	0448 1102 1658 2313	−1.3 10.0 −0.1 11.9	−40 305 −3 363	**18** F	0506 1122 1709 2323	0.4 8.8 1.3 10.2	12 268 40 311	**3** Su	0611 1227 1827	−1.0 10.4 −0.3	−30 317 −9	**18** M	0552 1204 1807	−0.1 9.9 0.2	−3 302 6	**3** W	0105 0710 1323 1937	10.1 0.2 10.3 0.1	308 6 314 3	**18** Th	0037 0644 1253 1915	10.5 −0.2 11.2 −0.8	320 −6 341 −24

A portion of a 2008 tide table for Boston. The table provides the time of each high and low tide for each day of the year and also the height of each tide relative to mean lower low water (MLLW), which is the vertical datum used by NOAA's National Ocean Service in its tide tables (and in the soundings printed on nautical charts). In the 24-hour clock, 0000 is midnight and 1200 is noon. Thus the time of low water on the afternoon of August 2 is 5:36 eastern standard time or 6:36 daylight saving time, which is the time showing on your watch. The fact that this is a minus tide (−0.3 feet) suggests that it is a spring tide, and indeed we see that the new moon was on August 1, so a run of spring tides can be expected.

Mean Lower Low Water

In the past, the datum used by charts and tide tables for the East Coast of North America was **mean low water** (MLW), the average height of all low tides at a given place. About half of all low tides are below this height, and half are above. On the Pacific Coast, however, where mixed tides produce one low tide each day that is substantially lower than the other, the datum is **mean lower low water** (MLLW), the average height of the lower of the two daily low tides. To avoid confusion, MLLW has been adopted as the datum throughout North America, and all U.S. charts are incorporating it in their new editions. On the East and Gulf coasts and in the Great Lakes, however, MLLW will mean the same as MLW—the average height of all low tides—and charted water depths will remain the same.

The average height of low water is a logical yardstick, but on a lower than average low tide there is less depth than the chart says there is, as we saw in the example above. Extreme low tides in Boston Harbor are as much as 1.8 feet below charted datum—truly a **drain tide**—so beware. Conversely, the highest high tide in Boston Harbor is 12.3 feet above MLLW, while the smallest high tide is just 8.5 and the average is 9.5.

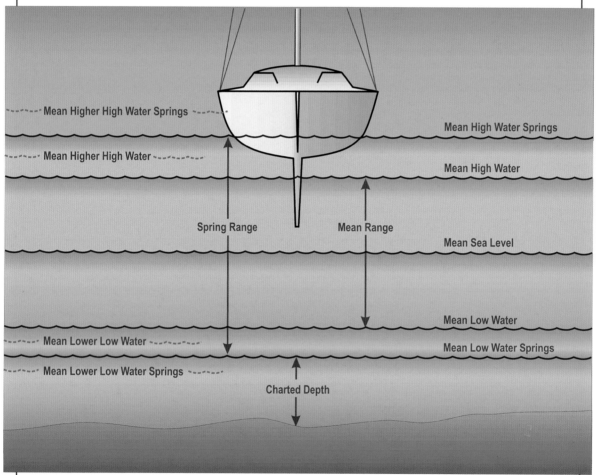

A graphic representation of vertical datums. Depths, or soundings, on U.S. charts are usually referenced to mean lower low water (MLLW), whereas bridge clearances and heights of lights are referenced to mean high water (MHW). In the UK, depths are usually referenced to the lowest astronomical tide (LAT), which is lower than MLLW, and heights of terrestrial objects are referenced to mean high water springs (MHWS), which is higher than MHW.

The Rule of Twelfths

You shouldn't cut things so close that you ever need to figure tide heights to the inch. A good guess is what you are more likely to need, and for that we have the **Rule of Twelfths**. The rule states simply that the tide rises or falls in increments of 1-2-3-3-2-1. That is, in the first one-sixth of its rise (or fall) duration, it rises (or falls) one-twelfth of its range. In the next sixth it rises two-twelfths of its range; then three-twelfths; then another three-twelfths; then two-twelfths; then one-twelfth. In an area of semidiurnal tides, that will be one-twelfth of the range in the first hour, two-twelfths in the second hour, three-twelfths in the second hour, three-twelfths

in the third hour, and so on. Thus, if you know the time and height of high or low tide, you can predict the height at any time, then add that height to charted soundings.

Let's return to our Boston Harbor example to see how this works. You know that the low tide will be at 6:36 p.m. and its height will be –0.3 feet. You also know that the previous high was 10.2 feet, so the range was 10.2 + 0.3 = 10.5 feet. You want to cross that shoal about an hour before low tide, so the tide will be about one-twelfth of its range above the low-tide height. One-twelfth of 10.5 is a little less than 1 foot, and –0.3 + 1.0 = 0.7. The tide height over the shoal when you want to cross

it is thus about 0.7, which means the depth of water on the shoal is 4.7. Since your boat draws 5 feet, you are well advised not to attempt this!

As another example, on a 12-foot semidiurnal tide, how deep will the water be 3 hours and 20 minutes after low tide? In the first hour one-twelfth of the tide—i.e., 1 foot—is added to the low-tide depth. In the second hour, two-twelfths (2 feet) is added, and in the third hour three-twelfths (3 feet). In the final 20 minutes the water deepens an additional foot. Since 1 + 2 + 3 + 1 = 7, we can estimate with reasonable confidence that 3 hours and 20 minutes after low tide, the water will be 7 feet deeper than it was at low tide.

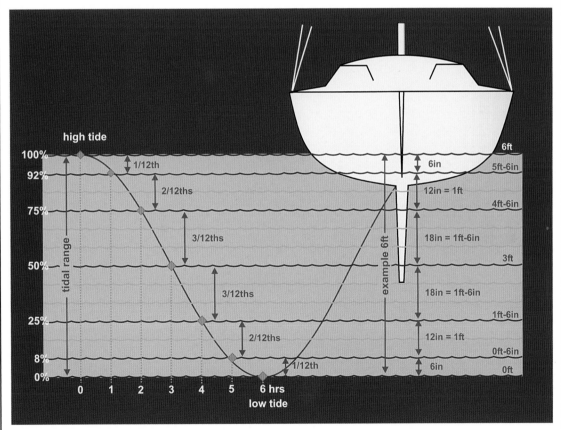

A graphic representation of the Rule of Twelfths. Once you obtain the local height of tide at the time of interest, apply it to the charted depth to obtain a working estimate of actual depth.

Reference Stations and Tidal Differences

The U.S. government and other national governments tabulate annual tide predictions for principal harbors (called reference stations in the United States and standard ports in the United Kingdom). Times and heights of tides at other locations can be found via a table of differences that is referenced to the principal harbors and published in the back of the annual government-compiled tide tables. Suppose, for example, that you want to know the time and height of the midday high tide at Neponset, Massachusetts, on August 2, 2008. Neponset is referenced to Boston in the table of differences compiled by the National Ocean Service, or NOS (a division of the National Oceanic and Atmospheric Administration, or NOAA); the table tells you that the high water at Neponset is always 2 minutes earlier than at Boston, and its height is always the same. All you need to do, therefore, is look up the time and height of the midday high tide in Boston for August 2, 2008, then apply the 2-minute time correction for Neponset. Newspapers, websites, and locally produced tide tables do this work for you in many popular boating waters, and you may sail all your life without ever having to use a table of differences.

TABLE 2 – TIDAL DIFFERENCES AND OTHER CONSTANTS

No.	PLACE	POSITION		DIFFERENCES				RANGES		Mean Tide Level
		Latitude	Longitude	Time		Height				
				High Water	Low Water	High Water	Low Water	Mean	Spring	
	MASSACHUSETTS, outer coast Time meridian, 75° W	**North**	**West**	h m	h m	ft	ft	ft	ft	ft
		REFERENCE STATION —			on Portland, p.36					
	Merrimack River									
821	Plum Island, Merrimack River Entrance	42° 49.0'	70° 49.2'	+0 06	+0 29	*0.88	*0.88	8.00	9.12	4.30
823	Newburyport	42° 48.7'	70° 51.9'	+0 31	+1 11	*0.86	*0.86	7.8	9.0	4.2
825	Salisbury Point	42° 50.3'	70° 54.5'	+0 55	+1 18	*0.83	*0.56	7.64	8.71	4.01
827	Merrimacport	42° 49.5'	70° 59.3'	+1 26	+2 08	*0.76	*0.50	7.05	8.04	3.70
829	Riverside	42° 45.8'	71° 04.6'	+1 56	+3 30	*0.62	*0.35	5.72	6.52	2.80
831	Plum Island Sound (south end)	42° 42.6'	70° 47.3'	+0 12	+0 37	*0.94	*0.94	8.6	9.9	4.6
833	Essex	42° 37.9'	70° 46.6'	+0 22	+0 31	*1.00	*0.94	9.18	10.47	4.90
835	Annisquam, Lobster Cove	42° 39.3'	70° 40.6'	+0 11	+0 03	*0.97	*0.97	8.81	10.04	4.74
837	Rockport	42° 39.5'	70° 36.9'	+0 06	+0 06	*0.95	*0.97	8.70	9.92	4.71
					on Boston, p.40					
839	Gloucester Harbor	42° 36.6'	70° 39.6'	+0 00	−0 04	*0.93	*0.97	8.80	10.03	4.73
841	Salem, Salem Harbor	42° 31.4'	70° 52.6'	−0 02	−0 05	*0.94	*0.97	8.93	10.18	4.79
843	Lynn, Lynn Harbor	42° 27.5'	70° 56.6'	+0 01	−0 03	*0.97	*1.00	9.16	10.44	4.92
	Boston Harbor									
845	Boston Light	42° 19.7'	70° 53.5'	−0 01	−0 02	*0.95	*0.97	9.05	10.03	4.85
847	Deer Island (south end) . . . . LOCATION	42° 20.7'	70° 57.5'	+0 01	+0 00	*0.97	*0.97	9.3	10.8	4.9
849	BOSTON	42° 21.3'	71° 03.1'		Daily predictions			9.49	11.07	5.09
851	Charlestown, Charles River entrance	42° 22.5'	71° 03.0'	+0 00	+0 01	*1.00	*1.00	9.5	11.0	5.0
853	Amelia Earhart Dam, Mystic River	42° 23.7'	71° 04.6'	+0 01	+0 02	*1.01	*0.97	5.72	6.52	5.11
855	Chelsea St. Bridge, Chelsea River	42° 23.2'	71° 01.4'	+0 01	+0 06	*1.01	*1.01	9.6	11.1	5.1
857	Neponset, Neponset River	42° 17.1'	71° 02.4'	−0 02	+0 03	*1.00	*1.00	9.5	11.0	5.0
859	Moon Head	42° 18.5'	70° 59.3'	+0 01	+0 04	*0.99	*0.99	9.4	10.9	5.0

TIME DIFFERENCES, HIGH AND LOW

HEIGHT RATIOS, HIGH AND LOW

RANGES

This table of differences from the National Ocean Service's 2008 tide tables for the eastern coasts of North and South America references Neponset, Massachusetts (a subordinate station), to Boston (a principal station). Times of high and low tides at Neponset are 2 minutes earlier and 3 minutes later, respectively, than at Boston, and their heights are 1.0 times the corresponding heights in Boston—in other words, they're the same.

Figuring the Current

As your boat moves through the water there's a fair chance the water is moving, too. That's current. Sailors see tidal currents most often, but a wind-generated current, a river current, or even an ocean current could also affect you.

Tidal currents, as we've already seen, are the horizontal movements of water required by the tide's rise and fall. The overall flow in bays and estuaries is toward shore (flood) on a rising tide and away from shore (ebb) on a falling tide. This basic in-and-out movement fills and empties bodies of water so varied, however, that tidal currents can run in virtually any direction.

The accompanying tidal current charts for northern Puget Sound are representative. At maximum flood the incoming tide races south down the west shore of Whidbey Island at up to 3.4 knots, but then a portion of it swings east and then north around the south end of Whidbey. If you were 1 mile south of Whidbey at maximum flood,

Maximum flood (above right) and ebb (right) currents off Bush Point in Puget Sound.

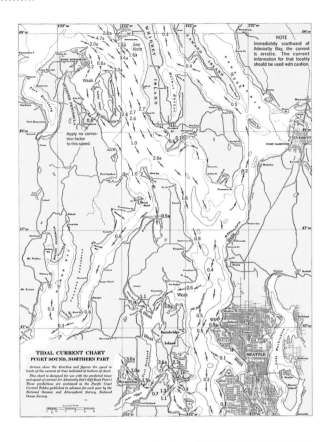

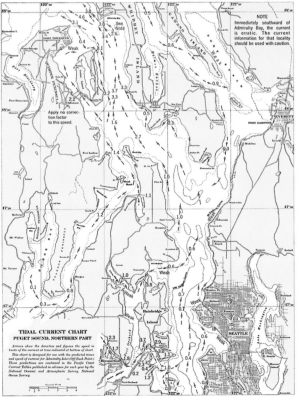

Boston Harbor (Deer Island Light), Massachusetts, 2008

F–Flood, Dir. 254° True   E–Ebb, Dir. 111° True

	July				August				September			
	Slack	Maximum	Slack	Maximum	Slack	Maximum	Slack	Maximum	Slack	Maximum	Slack	Maximum
	h m	h m knots	h m	h m knots	h m	h m knots	h m	h m knots	h m	h m knots	h m	h m knots
1 Tu	0250	0532 1.3F	**16** W	0123 1.3E	**1** F	0150 1.5E	**16** Sa	0213 1.2E	**1** M	0313 1.5E	**16** Tu	0209 1.3E
	0835	1229 1.2E	0341	0658 1.0F			0419 0733 1.3F		0431	0748 1.2F	0538	0855 1.4F	0519	0805 1.5F
	1508	1745 1.4F	0937	1346 1.1E	● 1011	1419 1.4E	○ 1022	1435 1.1E	1132	1540 1.5E	1111	1430 1.3E
	2057		1551	1913 1.1F	1640	1953 1.3F	1650	2001 1.2F	1805	2119 1.3F	1747	2021 1.4F
			2142		2229		2234		2352		2329	
2 W		0101 1.4E	**17** Th	0206 1.2E	**2** Sa	0242 1.5E	**17** Su	0245 1.2E	**2** Tu	0402 1.4E	**17** W	0238 1.3E
	0344	0641 1.3F	0423	0741 1.1F	0510	0827 1.3F	0512	0823 1.3F	0624	0941 1.3F	0601	0835 1.5F
	0932	1334 1.3E	1015	1429 1.1E	1104	1511 1.4E	1101	1504 1.2E	1218	1629 1.4E	1152	1502 1.4E
●	1601	1852 1.3F	1636	1955 1.1F	1734	2047 1.3F	1732	2031 1.2F	1853	2207 1.2F	1831	2057 1.4F

We've previously learned that the afternoon low tide on August 2, 2008, at Neponset, Massachusetts, will be at 6:39 p.m. Now let's find something about the tidal currents at Neponset on that day. From the National Ocean Service's 2008 tidal current tables for the Atlantic Coast of North America, we learn that the maximum ebb current in Boston Harbor will be at 3:11 p.m. standard time on August 2, which is 4:11 DST, and that current speed is 1.4 knots. The low-water slack comes at 6:34 p.m., and the previous high-water slack came at 12:04 p.m. The maximum flood current of 1.3 knots occurs at 9:47 p.m.

LOW-WATER SLACK   MAXIMUM FLOOD   HIGH-WATER SLACK   MAXIMUM EBB

TABLE 2 – CURRENT DIFFERENCES AND OTHER CONSTANTS

No.	PLACE	Meter Depth	POSITION		TIME DIFFERENCES				SPEED RATIOS		AVERAGE SPEEDS AND DIRECTIONS						
			Latitude	Longitude	Min. before Flood	Flood	Min. before Ebb	Ebb	Flood	Ebb	Minimum before Flood		Maximum Flood		Minimum before Ebb		Maximum Ebb	
		ft	North	West	h m	h m	h m	h m	knots	knots	knots	Dir.	knots	Dir.	knots	Dir.	knots	Dir.
	BOSTON HARBOR–PRESIDENT ROADS–cont. Time meridian, 75° W				on Boston Harbor, p.16													
1321	Charles River	10	42° 22.18'	71° 03.38'	Current weak and variable													
1326	East Boston, Pier 10, southeast of	10	42° 22.55'	71° 02.80'	+1 35	+0 50	+0 28	+0 16	0.2	0.3	--	--	0.2	017°	--	--	0.4	194°
	.... do.	25	42° 22.55'	71° 02.80'	+0 01	+1 05	+1 23	+0 51	0.3	0.2	--	--	0.3	030°	--	--	0.2	193°
1331	Chelsea River, west of bascule bridge	10	42° 23.07'	71° 02.53'	+0 02	-0 26	+0 43	-0 46	0.2	0.2	--	--	0.2	048°	--	--	0.2	240°
1336	Chelsea River, below bascule bridge	10	42° 23.03'	71° 01.70'	+0 29	+0 37	+0 37	-0 04	0.2	0.2	--	--	0.2	088°	--	--	0.3	272°
1341	Mystic River Bridge, 0.1 n.mi. west of	10	42° 23.15'	71° 03.02'	+0 31	-0 10	-0 46	-0 16	0.1	0.1	--	--	0.1	267°	--	--	0.1	093°
1346	Mystic River Bridge, northwest of	10	42° 23.15'	71° 02.95'	-0 20	+1 04	+0 22	-0 44	0.1	0.1	--	--	0.1	300°	--	--	0.1	098°
1351	City Point, 0.8 n.mi. SSE of	10	42° 19.22'	71° 00.88'	+0 13	+0 34	+1 19	+1 03	0.5	0.5	--	--	0.6	248°	0.1	170°	0.6	069°
1356	Squantum Point, 0.8 n.mi. northeast of	10	42° 18.63'	71° 01.70'	+0 18	+0 35	+1 16	+0 51	0.4	0.4	--	--	0.4	216°	--	--	0.5	036°
1361	Squantum Point, 0.4 n.mi. NNE of	10	42° 18.38'	71° 02.23'	+0 14	-0 06	+0 41	+0 52	0.4	0.4	--	--	0.4	266°	--	--	0.5	091°
1366	Neponset River	10	42° 18.25'	71° 02.58'	-0 25	-0 32	+0 45	+0 35	0.4	0.4	--	--	0.4	218°	--	--	0.4	025°

In the table of differences in the back pages of the tidal current tables, we find that low-water slack at Neponset is 25 minutes earlier than in Boston Harbor, which would make it 6:09 p.m. on August 2, 2008—30 minutes prior to Neponset's low tide. High-water slack is 45 minutes later than in Boston Harbor, making it 12:49 p.m., or just 7 minutes after Neponset's high tide. And the maximum ebb and flood currents are about 0.4 times as strong as in Boston Harbor, making them both about 0.5 to 0.6 knot. In general the times of high and low tide and the times of high-water slack and low-water slack are causally related, but they are not the same.

therefore, you would be set northeast by the tide, not south as you might expect. In the same location at maximum ebb, you would be set southwest, not north.

Offshore and in wider bays and gulfs, the general in-and-out pattern of flood and ebb is replaced by rotary tidal currents, which change direction continually throughout the tidal cycle without a slack-water pause.

In many coastal waters the tidal currents are gentle enough to ignore, but where they're not, you need local knowledge or tidal current charts or tables in order to predict them. Tidal current charts like the ones shown for Puget Sound are rare, unfortunately (these were published in 1973!), but the NOS compiles annual tidal current tables for the East and West coasts of North America. These give the times of slack water along with the times, velocities, and di-

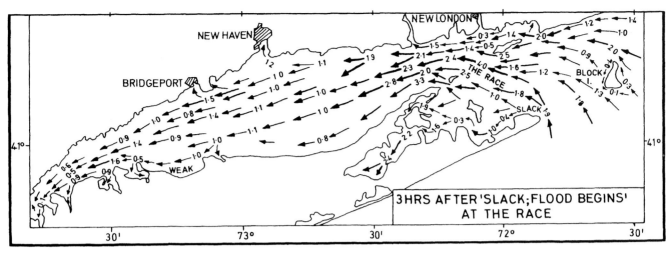

A tidal current chart depicting the maximum flood from the Atlantic into Long Island Sound through The Race.

rections of maximum ebb and flood currents for key locations (of which there are 27 between New Brunswick and Texas, for example), along with a table of differences covering hundreds of secondary stations. These tables are somewhat harder to use than the tide tables. If you're using electronic charts on board, your software may very well superimpose a current arrow on the chart to show you in what direction and at what speed the local tidal current is running.

You must also be aware that times of slack water do not always correspond with times of high and low water in bays and estuaries, nor is the maximum flood or ebb always or even often at mid-tide. The horizontal transport of water represented by the currents is certainly connected with the tide's rise and fall, but the relationship is complex.

The water level on an ocean beach rises without much current to be seen. Where a large body of water fills through a narrow entrance, however, the current can be dramatic. All of Long Island Sound fills and empties through The Race, and

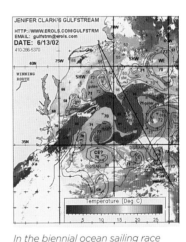

In the biennial ocean sailing race from Newport, Rhode Island, to Bermuda, choosing a route across the Gulf Stream is a key strategic component. This chart created by oceanographer Jenifer Clark shows a pronounced southward-turning meander in the normally north-flowing stream in June 2002, and the winning boat that year, whose route is shown, took full advantage, enjoying a southward boost to the west of the rhumb-line (straight-line) course. Clark sells routing information like this to cruisers, racers, and offshore fishermen.

the maximum flood there is 4 knots. Tidal currents vary, but they're strongest where large volumes of water pass through narrow channels.

A wind-generated current sets in after surface water has been pushed in the same direction for half a day or more by the wind. Its speed may be only 5% or less of the wind velocity, and it will set you farther to the right than the wind does, but it's there.

There are a number of ocean currents, but probably the best known is the Gulf Stream. A "river running in the sea," it wheels clockwise around the North Atlantic basin and affects climate, ecology, and weather as well as navigation. Its main stream is powerful (over 2 knots), and it spawns both clockwise and counterclockwise eddies of similar force. The "Stream" shows that current doesn't disappear out of sight of land.

Rivers run to the sea. River currents run strongest in the deepest channels. Shallow spots have less current. Current accelerates on the outside curve of a bend and slows on the inside.

To maximize a fair current (no matter what kind), stick with the channel. To duck a foul current, get out of the channel, hugging the shore or crossing the shallows (where friction slows the water) if you can. Points, docks, and breakwaters can block the current, even setting up favorable countereddies.

Tidal currents first change direction inshore.

Because wind can ruffle the current, "wind against the tide" signals a rough, wet ride. A 1-knot contrary tide can double the heights of waves and shorten them at the same time, making them dramatically steeper.

A favorable current boosts your speed over the bottom but not the flow of water past your rudder. The boat speeds up, but your steering may seem sluggish because of the current behind you.

Correcting for Current

If you know the current's set and drift, you can determine how it will affect your course and distance traveled. Assume you're headed north at 4 knots. Bucking a southerly current of 0.5 knot will not affect your **course made good** (i.e., your course over ground or over the sea bottom, as opposed to the course you're steering) but will reduce your distance traveled after 1 hour to 3.5 nautical miles. Riding a northerly 0.5-knot current will increase your distance traveled after 1 hour to 4.5 nautical miles but again will not affect your course made good.

An easterly current of 0.5 knot will **sweep**, or deflect, you 0.5 nautical mile east of your intended track after 1 hour. To correct for this current **on the beam**, plot a point 4 miles ahead and 0.5 mile west of your intended track, then steer toward that point. The drift of the current will bring you back to your desired course made good, and if your speed through the water is 4 knots, your actual distance traveled after 1 hour will be somewhat less than 4 miles.

If the current is approaching obliquely from your port or starboard bow, it will slow you down, but not as much as if it

Much of the time the current you encounter is small enough to ignore or to compensate for in eyeball fashion. There is unmistakably a tidal current flowing past this lobster pot buoy, but it appears to be less than half a knot. Let's assume the worst case and say that it's setting you at right angles to your course at 0.5 knot, and let's say your speed is 4 knots. In 1 hour the current would set you no more than 0.5 mile to the left or right of your desired course, which is a deflection of 7° or less. So if you're steering 270° and the current is setting you to the north, adjust your course to 263° and call it good. If you're steering toward a visible destination, not by the compass, just steer a bit "upstream" of it.

were directly on your bow, and it will push you off course, but not as much as if it were directly on your beam. If it is approaching from your port or starboard quarter, it will speed you up, but not as much as if it were directly astern, and it will push you off course, but not as much as if it were directly on your beam.

Correcting for current set and drift is rarely as precise or as complicated in practice as it sounds on paper. In most coastal waters on most tides, the current drift will be less than 0.5 knot, and you can either ignore it or make an educated guess as to its effect on your course and speed made good and compensate accordingly. If the current is stronger, you'll be able to see its direction and guess its speed by observing the "wake" it leaves around navigation buoys, lobster pot buoys, mooring buoys, etc. Again, correct your course steered and your mental calculations of speed made good accordingly, then make further adjustments on the fly if your actual progress through charted

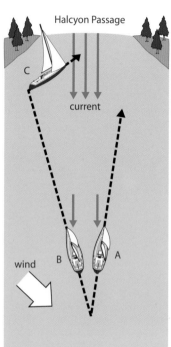

The lee-bow effect. *Suppose you're sailing close hauled toward Halcyon Passage but find yourself bucking a tidal current on the approach. You could bear off a little for more boat speed (A), but if you do the current will be on your windward bow, making the approach more difficult. This might instead be a time to pinch higher into the wind than you normally would, if by so doing you can put the current on your lee bow (B). This lee-bow effect will then help you to windward so that ultimately you may be able to bear off to a beam reach and blast through the passage with plenty of room between you and the lee shore (C).*

Suppose you're sailing across Vineyard Sound at mid-ebb. You lay a course (as described in Chapter 5) from your point of departure, the bell buoy off Vineyard Haven, to your destination, the bell off Falmouth's inner harbor. That course, you find from the chart, is 342° magnetic, and the distance you'll be covering is 3.2 nautical miles. You find from the tidal current tables that the ebb current is angling across your course toward 297° True (current directions are always given in degrees true) at 2 knots. the current will thus be boosting you toward your destination, but it will also be setting you to the west. In a light southwesterly breeze your speed through the water, according to your knotmeter, is fluctuating between 3.6 and 4 knots. With the boost from the current, you guesstimate your speed over ground at 5 knots. (A GPS receiver would tell you this speed precisely, as we'll see in Chapter 5.) At that speed you'll travel 3.2 miles in 0.64 hour, or just under 40 minutes, during which time the current will set you about 1.25 nautical miles to the west and north. To compensate, measure a vector from your destination bell buoy 1.25 miles upcurrent, then steer toward the end of the vector in order to proceed crabwise to your desired destination. In other words, steering a course of 007° magnetic should make your course made good 342° magnetic. If any of this sounds obscure now, Chapter 5 will clear it up.

waters differs from what you thought it would be. We'll return to this subject in Chapter 5, where we'll see, among other things, how much easier and more precise these calculations are made by global positioning system (GPS) navigation.

Observing the Rules of the Road

When boats meet on the water, there are no stop signs, traffic lights, yield signs, or lane markers to govern their movements. Instead, all mariners on coastal and ocean waters are expected to follow the 35 rules of the nautical road that have been codified by international agreement in the COLREGS (the International Regulations for Preventing Collisions at Sea). A very similar set of rules applies in the United States on the Great Lakes, on rivers and inland waterways, and on coastal bays and estuaries inland of the magenta COLREGS demarcation line that you will find printed on navigation charts that straddle the line. These U.S. Inland Rules differ only in occasional details—never in intent or substance—from the COLREGS. The Coast Guard requires all powered boats over 39 feet long—including all sailboats of that length with auxiliary engines—to carry a complete copy of the Rules on board. Still, the gap between the Rules and sailors is wide.

To earn a third mate's license in the old days you needed to write both the International and Inland Rules verbatim. Some day we may all be forced to do the same thing. Until then, however, the problem with the Rules is that not enough of us know them. And even if you know them, does the other guy? What's the good of knowing the proper signal if only you know what it means?

But things on the water tend to work out. Common sense and common courtesy keep sailors safe and apart most of the time. You won't need to know all 35 rules verbatim if you pay attention, stay clear of potentially bad situations, and bear in mind the Rules' working essence, which is as follows:

- The first rule, the one that supersedes all others, is **AVOID** COLLISION! More often than not when a collision occurs, both boats are deemed to be at fault.

- There is no right-of-way vessel. When two boats meet, one is advised by the Rules to **stand on** and the other is advised to **give way**, but the stand-on boat does not have right-of-way. In other words, if a collision occurs, the stand-on vessel cannot expect to be held faultless.

- The more able vessel is required to give way to the less able. Thus, a power-driven vessel (including a sailboat under engine power, even if its sails are also set) gives way

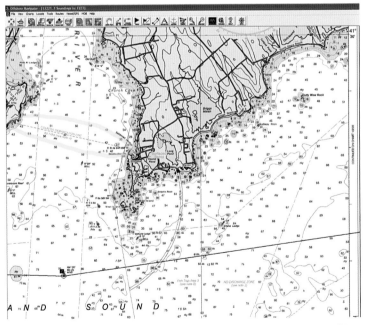

Seaward of the dashed magenta demarcation line (circled in yellow) on this chart, the International Rules apply. Upriver of the line, the Inland Rules apply.

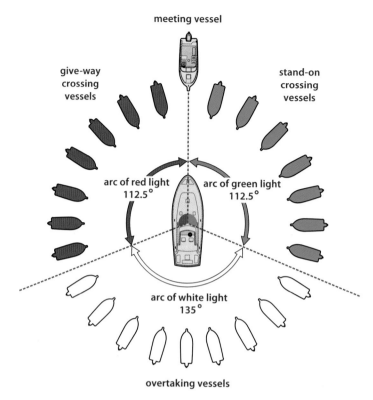

meeting vessel

give-way
crossing
vessels

stand-on
crossing
vessels

arc of red light
112.5°

arc of green light
112.5°

arc of white light
135°

overtaking vessels

When boats under power (including a sailboat with its engine in gear, even if its sails are also up) meet head on, both should alter course to starboard. When their courses cross, the boat that has the other on its starboard bow is the give-way boat. And an overtaking boat, even if under sail, should keep clear of the boat it is overtaking.

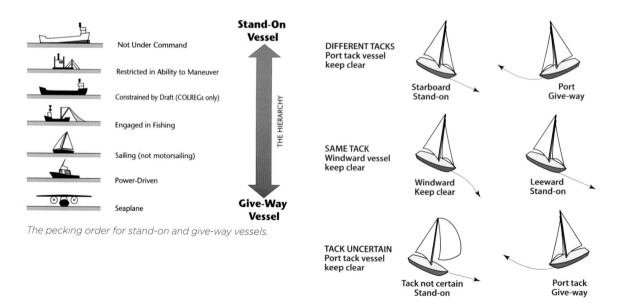

Not Under Command

Restricted in Ability to Maneuver

Constrained by Draft (COLREGs only)

Engaged in Fishing

Sailing (not motorsailing)

Power-Driven

Seaplane

Stand-On Vessel

THE HIERARCHY

Give-Way Vessel

The pecking order for stand-on and give-way vessels.

DIFFERENT TACKS
Port tack vessel keep clear

Starboard
Stand-on

Port
Give-way

SAME TACK
Windward vessel keep clear

Windward
Keep clear

Leeward
Stand-on

TACK UNCERTAIN
Port tack vessel keep clear

Tack not certain
Stand-on

Port tack
Give-way

The International and Inland Rules for sailing vessels.

Big over Little

Part of COLREGS, Rule 9, states: "A vessel of less than 20 meters in length or a sailing vessel shall not impede the passage of a vessel which can safely navigate only within a narrow channel or fairway."

Give this directive the broadest possible interpretation. Avoid ships! The bigger the ship, the more severe her "blind spots" and the less her ability to stop or maneuver. Avoid having to say "I didn't think anything that big could move that fast." Rights on real-life waters are proportional to gross tonnage.

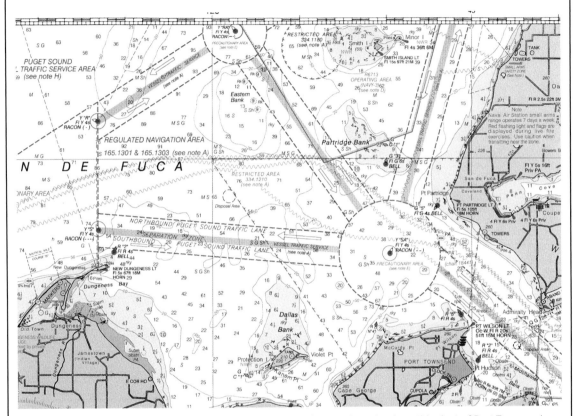

The lanes of the Vessel Traffic Service, or VTS—i.e., the shipping lanes—show clearly on this chart of Port Townsend, Washington. Sailboats should stay out of these lanes when possible and cross them perpendicularly and expeditiously when necessary. Big ships travel faster than you might suspect.

to a vessel under sail alone, which in turn gives way to a boat being rowed. A moving boat gives way to one that is anchored. A boat that is unrestricted by draft or circumstance gives way to one that is confined to a channel by reason of its draft or size or to a vessel that is encumbered (towing, fishing, etc.). And a seaward vessel gives way to a vessel that is maneuvering to avoid an obstruction.

- An overtaking boat gives way to the one it is overtaking.

Lights

The **steaming**, or **running**, **lights** that must be shown by a boat operating between sunset and sunrise extend beyond the standard red (port) and green (starboard) sidelights that all power- and sailboats must display. A power-driven vessel of 50 meters long or longer must also exhibit a white masthead light forward, a second white light higher and abaft the first, and a white stern light. This display provides a nighttime picture of size and heading along with indications of course change. Rules 23 through 29 of the COLREGS spell out the various light combinations to be displayed by a dredge, a vessel dragging a net, a tug with a tow, and so forth, and the best way to keep these straight is to carry a quick-reference guide with you if you sail at night. But do learn to recognize and interpret the basic configuration of a large power-driven vessel on sight.

Power-driven vessels of less than 50 meters need not display the second masthead light aft, and those of less than 12 meters can combine the masthead light with the stern light to form a single white light visible through the full 360 degrees. They can also combine the red and green sidelights in a single light at the bow.

When your boat is under sail alone you should display the sidelights and a white stern light. If your boat is under 20 meters you can combine these into a single tricolor masthead light.

POWER-DRIVEN VESSELS UNDERWAY (Rule 23)

VESSEL/RULE	GROUPS	SHAPES	VIEW FROM STARBOARD SIDE	BOW	STERN
INLAND—GREAT LAKES ONLY Rule 23(a) Power-driven ≥50 m	Masthead Sidelights All-around for 2nd masthead + stern	None			
BOTH COLREGS AND INLAND Rule 23(a) Power-driven ≥50 m	2 Mastheads Sidelights Sternlight	None			
Rule 23(a) Power-driven <50 m	Masthead Sidelights Sternlight	None			
Rule 23(c) Power-driven optional <12 m	Sidelights All-around in lieu of masthead and stern	None			
COLREGS ONLY Rule 23(c)(ii) Power-driven <7 m & <7 kn max.	Sidelights if practical All-around	None			

TOWING & PUSHING (Rule 24)

RULE/VESSEL	GROUPS	SHAPES	VIEW FROM STARBOARD SIDE	BOW	STERN
BOTH COLREGS AND INLAND 24(a)/Towing astern (Tow ≤ 200 m) If vessel ≥50m, add	2 vert. Mastheads Sidelights Sternlight Towlight Masthead aft ●	None			
24(a)/Towing astern (Tow > 200 m) If vessel ≥50m, add	3 vert. Mastheads Sidelights Sternlight Towlight Masthead aft ●	♦			
24(b)/Composite (treated as single power vessel) If composite ≥50m, add	Masthead Sidelights Sternlight Masthead aft ●	None			
COLREGS ONLY 24(c)/Pushing ahead or towing alongside (not composite) If vessel ≥50m, add	2 vert. Mastheads Sidelights Sternlight Masthead aft ●	None			
INLAND ONLY 24(c)/Pushing ahead or towing alongside (not composite) If vessel ≥50m, add	2 vert. Mastheads Sidelights 2 towing lights Masthead aft ●	None			

The more common running light combinations required on power-driven vessels. Other combinations apply in specific circumstances. When you sail at night it is a good idea to carry a cheat sheet aboard.

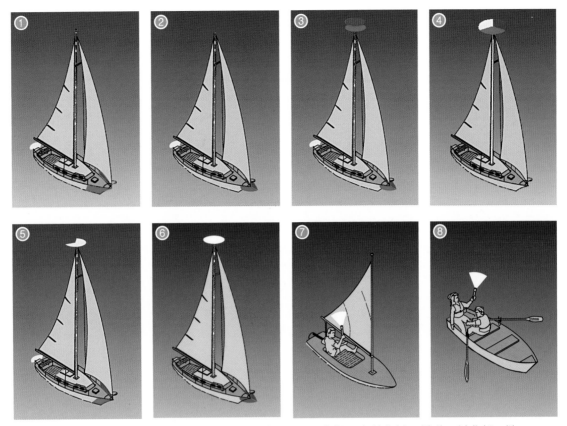

When you're sailing at night, the Rules require you to show a stern light and sidelights with the sidelights either sepa-rate (1) or combined (2). You can, if you wish, augment these with all-around red and green lights at the masthead (3) so that anyone approaching from astern will know you are under sail. If your boat is less than 20 meters (65 feet) long, you can combine the stern light and sidelights into a single masthead tricolor (4), thus potentially increasing your range of visibility and saving battery power. If your boat is less than 20 meters long but using power as well as sail, you need to augment the stern light and sidelights with a masthead light visible to crossing vessels (5), but if your boat is less than 12 meters (39 feet) long you can combine the stern light with the masthead (6). A boat of less than 7 meters (23 feet) under sail alone can simply shine a flashlight on the sails (7), and a rowboat likewise just needs a flashlight (8).

- Every boat must always maintain a lookout. You must always be alert to the risk of collision, and if you're in doubt whether such risk exists, you should assume that it does. A give-way boat should make early and obvious course and speed changes so that the stand-on boat knows his intentions.
- A boat should at all times proceed at a safe speed. Sailboats rarely go faster than a fast walk, of course, but in dense fog a safe speed might be as little as 2 knots. Though the Rules do not specify what constitutes a safe speed, admiralty courts have repeatedly defined it as a speed that will permit a boat to come to a stop within one-half of its range of visibility.

Power over Sail
Even with sails up, a sailboat is a powerboat under the Rules when her engine is in gear. And even when she is under sail alone, a sailboat overtaking a powerboat is bound to give way.

Collision Course

"Constant bearing, decreasing range" is the classic indicator of an impending collision. When the **bearing** of an approaching boat (its angle off your bow) remains the same while it closes with your boat, the two boats are on a **collision course**. Actual compass bearings help in a crossing situation, but don't let a change of a few degrees dissuade you from taking action to avoid impact.

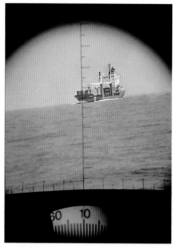  

When the bearing to an approaching vessel remains constant while its distance off decreases, you are on a collision course.

Sound

Though underused, sound signals are useful when underway in the fog, leaving a marina berth, approaching a blind turn, and in other situations. One short blast means you're altering course to starboard. Use two short blasts to signal your intent to alter course to port, three short blasts for operating astern propulsion, and five short blasts to signal that you don't understand the intentions of an approaching boat.

- When two power-driven boats meet head-on, both should alter course to starboard so as to pass port-to-port whenever possible. When two power-driven boats are on crossing courses, the one that has the other on her starboard side should give way.

- Do not anchor in channels or traffic lanes. A small boat underway in a crowded fairway or channel should stick to the periphery of the channel, leaving the deepest water for the big ships that need it most. When crossing a channel, do so as expeditiously as possible and without blocking ship traffic.

- When sailboats meet, the one on port tack should give way to the one on starboard tack. If both boats are on the same tack, a windward boat should give way to the leeward one, and one that is sailing free should give way to one that is close hauled.

You won't go wrong if you follow this guidance.

Tying Knots

One of the first things you learn on the water is that knots are not only convenient but necessary. A good knot is quick to tie, holds securely, and is ideally suited to the job it is asked to do. It will not come untied inadvertently, yet it will not jam or resist untying when its job is complete. The rewards of good knots accrue every day on the water.

And there aren't many knots you'll need every day. You've already learned about cleating, and the square knot was explained in Chapter 2 (page 113). Review that pair, then learn the following four new knots, and you'll be ready for anything.

Bowline

The bowline (pronounced "bō-lin") allows you to fashion a loop in the end of a line or fix a line through ring. Once you know the knot, you'll find endless uses for it. Drop a bowline over a piling. Join two lines with interlocking bowlines. Tie a jibsheet into the clew of a jib or a halyard into a mainsail headboard with a bowline. The bowline is the king of knots and the gift that keeps on giving. It's the hardest of the basic

*To tie a **bowline**, pass the end of the line over its own standing part to create a loop **(1)**, then poke the end up through that loop **(2)**, leaving an eye of the desired size. Next pass the end behind the standing part of the line **(3)**, then push the end down through the original loop **(4)**. Tighten the knot by pulling carefully on the end and the standing part **(5)**, and you're done.*

knots to learn, but you'll use it every time out.

The photos show the static method of tying a bowline, but despite well-meaning efforts by various mentors to couch it in terms of rabbits and trees ("the rabbit pops out of his hole, runs around the tree, then dives back down his hole"), the static method always confused me. Then I ran across the dynamic method: Take the bitter end in one hand and the standing part in the other. "Flip-flop" your hands so you loop the standing part around the hand with the bitter end. From there it's simple to complete the knot by passing the end behind the standing part and down through the loop. The flip-flop is hard to describe, but once you get the feel of it you can tie the knot without looking, and that's useful and ultimately easier than chasing a rabbit around a tree.

Figure-Eight Knot

To keep any line that's led through a block or sheave or fairlead from running out and getting loose when you don't want it to, use a **stopper knot**. An **overhand knot**—a loop with the end poked through—is a primitive stopper, but it lacks bulk and will grab and compress itself under strain until you need a marlinespike or maybe even a knife to get it undone. The **figure-eight knot** is a bulkier stopper knot that will jam as intended in a block or fairlead but not on itself. It unlocks easily no matter how much strain it's been under, and it's about the simplest knot you'll encounter.

Clove Hitch

Fixing a line to stay fast (rather than slide back and forth) is the talent of the **clove hitch**. It lets you moor your boat to a post,

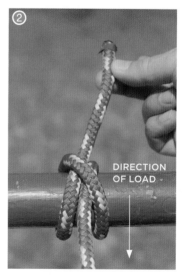

*To tie a **figure-eight knot**, pass the end of a line over its standing part to form a small loop near the end **(1)**. Next wrap the end behind the standing part **(2)**, then over and finally down through the original loop **(3)**. Tighten the knot **(4)** and you're done. To break the knot, slide the "inboard" loop up the standing part.*

DIRECTION OF LOAD

*If you're tying a **clove hitch** around a horizontal rail rather than a vertical post and you pass the bitter end to the right of the standing part for the first loop **(1)**, make your second loop to the left of the first and once again pass the end to the right of the standing part **(2)**. Do not reverse directions around the post or rail—keep "wrapping" in the same direction.*

piling, or tree and come back to find it there. Its two loops tighten in opposite directions and grab each other. You can tie it by passing the line around a post or rail (or any strongpoint) or dropping it over the top. The key is to build identical loops and to cross over the standing part of the first loop as you make the second loop. If you pass the bitter end beneath the standing part for the first loop, then make your second loop above the first. If you pass the bitter end over the standing part for the first loop, make your second (identical) loop below the first.

Clove hitches may slip under uneven strain. I always finish the knot with a half hitch around the standing part to lock it.

Rolling Hitch

The rolling hitch is my favorite knot. Though I probably overuse it, it's always stood me in excellent stead. It lets you attach a line to another that's under strain, and you can use it to belay a line under strain. (It's next to impossible to tie a bowline in a line under strain.) You can also use it to tie a line back onto itself after it passes through a ring or around an anchor point; this is handy when you're lashing an object (say a dinghy) on deck or to the top of your car, because you can tension the lashing by sliding the hitch up the standing part.

If you are cinching or sweating a line taut—as when lashing—belay it with a rolling hitch. This lets you fix it at just the right length.

These few knots give you a solution for every line-handling scenario. There are many others, of course, the most useful of which include the cleat hitch (page 30), and the selection in Appendix 3—among them the sheet bend, the round turn and two half hitches, and the anchor bend. Add those to your starting quartet, and you'll have not just an answer but an elegant answer for every job.

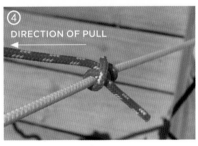

*To tie a **rolling hitch**, pass the end of your line around the line, wire, or post you're tying to **(1)**. Whether you make the turn toward or away from the planned direction of pull is up to you. Most experts recommend making the turn toward the eventual direction of pull, but the photos show the opposite. Now pass the end a second time around the cable or post, still working either toward or away from the direction you will be pulling from **(2)**. Consistency is the key: If your first turn was away from the strain, your second turn must continue away. If your first turn was toward the strain, your second turn must continue toward. Complete the knot by passing the end over the two hitches you've just made and adding a third hitch on the opposite side of the first **(3)**. The direction of travel is the same for all three turns. Pull on your line **(4)**, and the rolling hitch grips without sliding.*

Docking

You learned how to pick up a mooring in Chapter 1, but we postponed docking. A dock is fixed. Not only may the wind not be blowing across it from exactly the right direction, but a fixed dock doesn't yield if you hit it. Making a landing is challenging whether you're using the engine or the sails to do it. Still, the steps toward successful docking are the same as for mooring—prepare, plan, command, and secure:

1. **Prepare the boat.** Get your docklines in place, alert the crew, and have fenders at the ready.

2. **Plan the approach.** Figure wind, current, space, maneuverability, and available help on the dock. It's crucial to have a clear idea of what you're trying to do before you do it. Adapting a plan as you go is fine, but proceeding without one is asking for trouble.

3. **Command the situation.** Act and speak firmly and clearly to get the job done.

4. **Secure the boat in place.** You may "park" the boat perfectly, but a failure to tie her up quickly can turn your command performance into a fire drill.

Whether you plan to dock under sail or power, answer these questions before you make your approach:

- Where exactly are you going to dock? You may not have any choice, but if you do, consider the water depth at the pier and in the approach, the height of the dock (Can you and your crew step onto it safely? Is it too high or too low?), its condition (Is it fendered? Are there cleats or posts to tie to?), and its accessibility (Am I allowed to tie up here? Is there enough room to land without endangering other boats?).

- How should you approach? Do your utmost to land heading upwind and upcurrent. Approaching against both is the ideal unless one or the other is negligible enough to be ignored. Either one coming from behind you with any strength makes your speed difficult to control and creates genuine stopping problems. It also complicates tying up. You always want an escape route open, giving you the option of bailing out and circling around for another attempt if things aren't working out. Riding a current or a tailwind makes it extremely tough to change your mind.

Fending Off

Not many landings are so eggshell perfect that they don't require a little human intervention to keep the boat from either bumping the dock or missing it altogether. Cushioning or **fending off** is normal—it's best to step onto the dock and push back from there, and even when a boat is approaching faster than she should be you can sometimes deflect her along—but no one should even think about getting between an immovable dock and an unstoppable boat. Neither is it unusual to have to throw or carry a line across a foot or two of water to save what would otherwise be a missed landing, but no crewmember should attempt to launch himself across a wide expanse of water to reach the dock. A missed landing is just a missed landing—you circle around and try again—but a crewmember injured or in the water is something else again.

Fenders

You can use cushions or life jackets to protect your boat in a pinch (no pun intended), but **fenders** made for the purpose of absorbing the blow of boat against dock are more effective and convenient. Tie them so they hang at water level, bottoms just kissing the waves. You may have to adjust them upward once you're docked, but hanging them low initially assures that nothing will sneak beneath them to get at your hull.

Deploy your fenders along the midlength portion of the boat, where the beam is greatest. Fenders deployed too far forward or aft will hang uselessly, not bearing against the dock. When you're entering a tight slip with obstacles on either side, place a fender both port and starboard where the boat is widest. To lie against a wall or the dock, however, hang fenders just forward and aft of the hull's widest point.

Fenderboard.

That way she will ride evenly instead of pivoting around her midship "bulge."

Hanging fenders from lifelines is common but not the best practice—when you open the lifeline gate to step ashore the lifelines may droop, dropping your fenders into the water. It's better when possible to tie fenders to fixed objects such as cleats, lifeline stanchion bases, or slotted toe rails. A **fenderboard** allows you to localize protection (against a piling, for instance).

- What if the wind and current are both factors, but the wind is against or across the current? You'll want to make your final approach against the stronger of the two. Rarely is this neat or easy.

- Which side of the boat will you be docking on? Deploy your fenders on that side, and get your docklines ready to run. Tie their inboard ends on deck and lead them out through and then back over the lifelines (if present), so they can be tossed or carried to the dock with maximum speed and efficiency when the time comes.

Sending a Line Ashore

To make the most of a helping hand on the dock, get your helper a line—most often the first line ashore is the bow line, and most often you can hand it across rather than heave it—and ask him to make it fast. Whether your helper is a sailor or a farmer, have him belay his end. Now you can tend and adjust the dockline from the boat while your helper helps with other lines.

Docklines

A bow line and a stern line might be all you need to immobilize a boat if there is room to lead them well forward and well aft, respectively. With a boat of any size, though, it's almost always best to add **spring lines**.

Run an **after spring** aft from amidships or just forward of amidships. The **forward spring** should run forward from amidships or just aft of amidships. Tension all four lines against each other to prevent the boat from wracking or twisting at the dock.

In a bow-first landing, the bow line is commonly the first one ashore. With a turn or two around a dock cleat or piling it can be used to help snub the boat's forward progress, but doing so may also pivot the bow toward the dock, so make sure you have a fender deployed forward of amidships. Snubbing the boat with an after spring line is somewhat more elegant and also more convenient when you're sailing alone or shorthanded. Imagine, as you come alongside a dock, that you're able to step away from the helm, loop your carefully prepared after spring line around a passing cleat or piling, then bring the end back aboard, snubbing it around an amidships cleat to stop the boat. Then you step calmly to the dock, from where you can easily reach your prepared bow and stern lines to make them fast before the bow or stern has a chance to swing away from the dock. Now that's elegant seamanship!

To land in a space that's not much longer than your boat, come in at a sharper than normal approach angle and

① STERN LINE

AFTER SPRING

FORWARD SPRING

X BOW LINE SHOULD IDEALLY BE TIED HERE

BOW LINE

② AFTER SPRING

FORWARD SPRING

③

1. *This bow line would be more effective if led more directly to the dock where indicated, but you have to work with the cleats you're given!* **2.** *A closer look at the forward and after spring lines and the stern line. Note that the end of the forward spring line is flemished, which is a neat way to leave a line that will be there awhile.* **3.** *The fenders should be concentrated near amidships, where they'll bear most effectively between boat and dock. Their height should be properly adjusted, too. It's common practice to hang them from the lifeline, as here, but a stanchion, cleat, or slotted toe rail provides a more secure fastening point when available.*

get the after spring line made fast to the dock. Then power forward against the spring with your rudder turned away from the dock, and your stern will swing in while the spring line prevents you from hitting the boat ahead.

Whenever you're short-handed or when the wind or current is particularly strong, decide which dockline will be most critical. Make sure that it is led correctly and laid out ready to go ashore before you start your approach.

Docking under Sail

The idea is simple: let the wind stop you just as you reach the dock. The execution, however, can be a little less simple. Too fast—you crash. Too slow—you wallow in irons.

To carry out even the simplest docking plan takes judgment and precision. And docking plans can quickly get complex thanks to a fickle wind, a foul current, limited maneuvering space, or unforeseen developments. Docking under sail is anything but simple in practice, yet, it's a necessity in an engineless sailboat and a very good thing to know even in a boat with auxiliary outboard or inboard engine power. If you're going out, you have to get back. Here are some pointers:

- **Start by studying the big picture.** Given a choice, your best option is to land on a face of the dock from which the wind will be blowing toward you. Provided you have open water for the approach, your landing should then be straightforward. Approach your spot on a close reach, keeping the apparent wind 50 to 60 degrees off your bow. Slow your boat to a crawl by luffing sails. (I prefer landing under main alone—single sail, single focus, single "throttle.") Adjust speed and course (trim for speed, luff to slow) until you're there. If you need to brake, back the main.

  You can control your progress down to the last inch with sails and rudder on a close reach, but if you sail close hauled toward the dock you lose something: there is no way you can accelerate except by heading off—away from your target. Don't sail too close into the wind on your approach.

  If you approach on a beam reach, your course will take you past the dock rather than to it. A close reach gives you maximum control.

- **Know your boat.** There will be times when you don't have enough space to make a controlled approach. Often that forces you to "shoot" into the wind and let it kill your momentum before you reach the dock. A light dinghy will go from full speed to full stop in two boat lengths, while in the same breeze a boat that weighs over 1,000 pounds may coast five or six boat lengths.

  If you've never put the helm down and watched your boat glide head to wind, how reliable will your glide estimate be when you're charging into a pier? How will you judge how round a turn you

WIND

Docking under sail *is simple with no current and the wind blowing parallel to a wide-open dock.* **1.** *Having dropped their jib, this crew approaches on a reach under mainsail alone.* **2.** *They round into the wind to kill speed. The fenders are in place, and the crew have bow and stern lines ready.* **3, 4.** *When they can step to the dock without leaping, the crew take the lines ashore and secure the boat. Next they'll get the mainsail down and add spring lines if necessary.*

must make to maintain momentum, or how sharp a turn you'll need to kill it? As the wind lightens, its stopping power decreases. How far does your boat glide in 5 knots of wind or in 25? Shooting the breeze and gliding to a stop with the stem plate 6 inches from the wharf takes not only luck but also a hard-won knowledge of how your boat behaves.

- **Use all your controls.** The less speed you have on your final approach, the less way you will have to kill. Take speed off before your final turn. Spill wind from the sails. Fishtail. Trim the main amidships if you're dead downwind (then let it run free when you turn across the breeze). Remember always that the rudder is a superb brake. Tricky and desperate-sounding measures though these may sound, they are better than plowing into a piling. Falling short may bruise your ego, but it's far and away the better side to err on. Whatever it takes, approach as slowly as you can.

- When the wind is blowing along rather than from the face of the dock on which you must land, your preferred approach will of course be the one that enables you to round up into the wind for your landing.

- If you must approach or even land with the wind behind you, use what you've got. I once saw an expert skipper land the 12-meter

Lionheart under mainsail alone in an onshore breeze in Brighton Marina. He approached on a run, circled into the wind off the pier, dropped the mainsail, continued turning through a second full circle, and coasted to a stop alongside the pier. That's one way to get in from the windward side. Another way is to use the jib alone. It works nicely because you can weather vane a jib to depower it through a full 360 degrees. In most cases drifting in slowly from upwind, even under bare poles, can bring you close enough to manage a wind-on-the-dock landing.

- Don't leave the sails up any longer than you have to once you're docked.
- The current runs about 2 knots past my dock. Landing under sail has proven awkward and embarrassing more often than not, but one thing I've learned is that when the current complicates a landing, you should invent the easiest plan you can.

Current against the wind is difficult. When the wind is stronger than the current I land into the wind, using its stopping force (even backing sail as necessary) to hold against the flow. I make the stern line fast first. If the current is the stronger force (which at my dock means the wind is less than 10 knots), I sail downwind to the dock, then slow beside it, trimming the mainsail amidships. I get the bow line fast first, then scurry to douse sail before the boat takes off on her own.

Docking under Power

There's no denying that an engine adds control, and it's nice to have reverse. Still, a single-screw inboard- or outboard-driven, deep-keeled, high-sided, tall-rigged sailboat doesn't exactly jump through hoops the moment you fire up the "iron genny." Docking under power is simpler than docking under sail, but it's basically the same.

The best approach is still upwind when you have a choice. Glide in neutral and let the wind slow you down.

Docking under power *is easy when there's no current, the wind is blowing toward the dock, and you can land port-side-to with room to windward.* **1.** *This boat approaches comfortably to windward of its berth, then lets the wind push it toward the dock as it sidles in.* **2.** *When the boat is alongside, the helmsman applies a touch of reverse to remove the boat's remaining way and to pull the stern toward the dock via prop walk. The fenders are deployed, and the docklines are ready.* **3.** *All that remains is for the crew to step ashore with the lines and fend off as necessary. No worries about a missed landing in these conditions.*

WIND

No matter the conditions, you want to maintain just enough for-ward momentum to steer. When you're about a boat length from the dock (less if a strong wind, current, or both are against you—you be the judge), engage reverse. You will continue forward. Proceed ac-cording to circumstances following these general guidelines:

- If your port side is to the dock and you have an inboard engine with a right-handed propeller, steer your bow close against the dock. (Your propeller is right-handed if its blades turn from left to right at the top of their swing—i.e., if they spin clockwise when viewed from astern with the engine in forward gear. Most mod-ern engines are right-handed.) The paddle effect of your prop in reverse will pull your stern to port and lay you straight along-side.

- If you are landing starboard-side-to with an inboard engine and a right-handed propeller, the action of the propeller in reverse will tend to thrust your stern away from the dock. Usually you can overcome this tendency with port rudder while you're still mov-ing forward, with starboard rudder if your boat starts moving sternward, or simply by getting a stern line to the dock. Should a further correction be needed, however, you can apply a brief burst of forward engine power against port rudder. The prop wash across the rudder blade will walk your stern toward the dock before the boat acquires much forward momentum, and you can then shift back into reverse. It's better to make gradual corrections and keep the rpms as low as possible, but sometimes you have to use hard rudder and a shot of power to make mid-course corrections.

- If your boat's auxiliary power is an outboard engine, port-side and starboard-side landings are essentially the same. Unlike the fixed prop of an inboard engine, an outboard engine lower unit is steerable in forward or reverse, and this can be a real help when landing. It takes a bit of mental and physical gymnastics to co-ordinate your rudder steering with your outboard steering, but once you get used to it you'll find your boat nimble and the results satisfying.

Prop Walk

A propeller blade grips the water more solidly at the bottom of its swing than the top, and this difference generates a side thrust on the stern. If the propeller is right-handed, as most are, its blades will travel right to left at the bottom of their swing in forward gear, and the resulting side thrust will tend to pull the stern to starboard. In reverse gear the side thrust will pull the stern to port. You can turn this so-called **prop walk**, or **paddle effect**, to advantage in a port-side-to landing. In a starboard-side landing you'll simply have to factor it in and counteract it.

Headreaching

A boat that's moving makes **headway**. When she is moving upwind under momentum alone, she is said to be **headreaching**. Weight has the most to do with how far a boat will **carry its way** from a given speed. It takes longer to slow down the heavier you are. Freedom from drag also increases a boat's reach for a given speed. The more wind and water resistance she presents, the less well she will headreach.

Pivot Point

A boat turns around her **pivot point**, which is forward of amidships when the boat is moving ahead. That means her stern swings in a wider arc than her bow. Be sure your stern doesn't swing wide enough to hit the very object you turned your bow away from.

Most modern boats tend to fall off the wind when under power in a crosswind, because their shallow hulls pivot around deep, central keels. Rather than holding course in such conditions, they tend to turn downwind. Watch for this and correct it early to stay on course. It's rarely a problem when the boat is under sail.

Backing In

To get into a tight slip or set a bow anchor, sometimes it's best to back into a dock. The tendency of a right-handed prop to pull the stern to port in reverse is just one of the disconcerting aspects of backing an auxiliary sailboat. On the other hand, backing stern-first into a stiff headwind makes a virtue of the bow's tendency to point downwind, and that can sometimes make things easier. Deal with the prop by applying enough reverse to get the boat moving backward, then shifting to neutral. That stops the portward pull but leaves you with steerageway. Alternate reverse and neutral as needed to back straight, even applying a brief burst of forward with port rudder if necessary to correct course. The prop's slipstream in forward deflects off the rudder to provide powerful turning. In reverse the stream goes the other way, giving the rudder much less oomph.

CHAPTER FOUR

Sailing Farther, Sailing Better

Since your first sail, as you've progressed through the fundamentals of sail trim, boat handling, and seamanship, every step along the way has expanded your sailing horizon. Now is a great time—anytime is a great time—to polish your sailing skills simply by sailing alone. There is nothing quite so good for blowing away the cobwebs and solidifying the basics, nor is any other leisure activity quite as satisfying as sailing by yourself. When you can complete a triangular course solo in a light to moderate breeze, go looking for heavier air. Don't put the rest of your sailing on hold while you wait for a blustery day, but don't shy away from it either. When you sail solo, every challenge is yours to meet, every consequence yours to answer, every success yours to celebrate, every moment yours to experi-ence. In this crowded, cluttered, hyperconnected world, few activities return you to your elemental self as effectively as sailing alone.

Only you can guarantee that you'll sail flawlessly. I don't think I've ever seen a perfect solo sail. But I have seen, almost without exception, people come back from their solo sailing more confident, solid, enthusiastic, and capable than they were when they cast off. Sailing solo gives you a heightened involvement. You're not only more aware of where you're going, you're solely responsible for what it takes to get there.

What it might take, in addition to what you already know, is navigation skills and a bit more boat- and sail-handling know-how, all of which are in this chapter.

Using Aids to Navigation

Just as automobile drivers need lights and stop signs, mariners need aids to navigation. In the United States the U.S. Coast Guard maintains a comprehensive deployment of buoys, lights, beacons, and markers without which safety at sea would be only a distant dream. These **aids to navigation** (ATONs) are all shown on nautical charts (which we'll cover later in this chapter), but they are also designed to work on their own, telling any sailor who can read them how to pass safely.

Two buoyage systems are in use worldwide. North and South America, the Caribbean basin, Japan, Korea, and the Philippines use the Region B system of the International Association of Lighthouse Authorities (IALA), whereas Europe, Africa, Australia, and most of Asia use the IALA's Region A standards, which are the same in concept but differ in a few details. Both systems use **lateral marks** to delineate channel edges; **safe water marks** to guide mariners into midchannels and landfall approaches surrounded by deep water; and **isolated danger marks** to warn mariners away from rocks or wrecks of limited extent that have safe water on all sides.

In the IALA-B system, red lateral marks should be kept to the right by vessels returning to port, while green marks are kept to the left—thus the rubric well known throughout the Western Hemisphere, "red, right, returning." The system is elegantly redundant. All red marks are given even numbers. Red **daymarks** (also called **dayboards**) are triangular, and the most common red **buoys**, called **nuns**, are conical and thus look triangular from a distance. All green marks are given odd numbers, green daymarks are square, and the most common green buoys, called **cans**, are cylindrical and thus look square from a distance. When returning from sea, leave any green, odd-numbered, square, or cylindrical buoy to port and you will be in the channel. When you're heading out, of course, leave green marks to starboard.

The colors are reversed in regions of the world governed by the IALA-A system. Leave red, even-numbered marks to port and green, odd-numbered marks to starboard when re-turning from sea. This is the only material difference between the two systems.

When lateral marks are lighted, red marks have red lights and green marks have green lights. Cans and nuns in U.S. waters are rarely lighted, however; when a lighted buoy is called for, a **pillar buoy** (consisting of a lattice tower on a flat base and typically including a sound signal, as in a bell buoy or whistle buoy) is more likely to be used instead. Daymarks may or may not be lighted; when they are, they are considered **minor lights**. More powerful lights—visible from a greater distance and typically marking more dangerous hazards—are called simply **beacons**, and the most powerful of all are lighthouses.

U.S. AIDS TO NAVIGATION SYSTEM
on navigable waters except Western Rivers

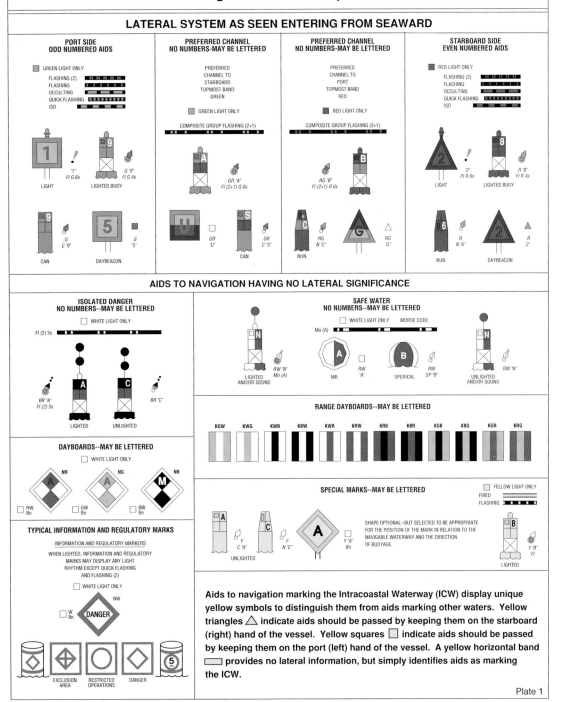

The aids to navigation used throughout North America (except the Mississippi River, its tributaries, and a few other rivers in the Western Rivers System). The lateral system quickly becomes familiar and predictable in practice. Your local navigation chart will clarify almost any possible point of confusion.

Here the lateral system navaids from the top of the previous illustration are shown as they might appear in a three-dimensional graphic representation by day and by night.

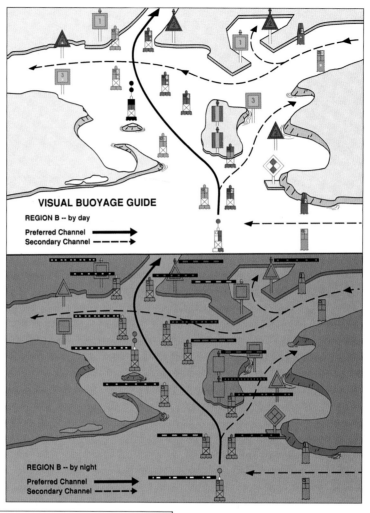

VISUAL BUOYAGE GUIDE

REGION B -- by day

Preferred Channel →
Secondary Channel ----→

REGION B -- by night

Preferred Channel →
Secondary Channel ----→

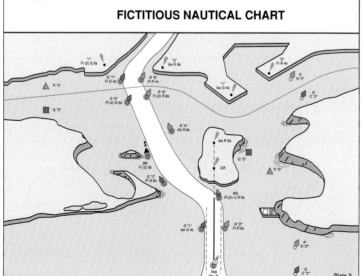

FICTITIOUS NAUTICAL CHART

Plate 3

A fictitious nautical chart corresponding to the idealized 3-D graphic representation in the previous illustration.

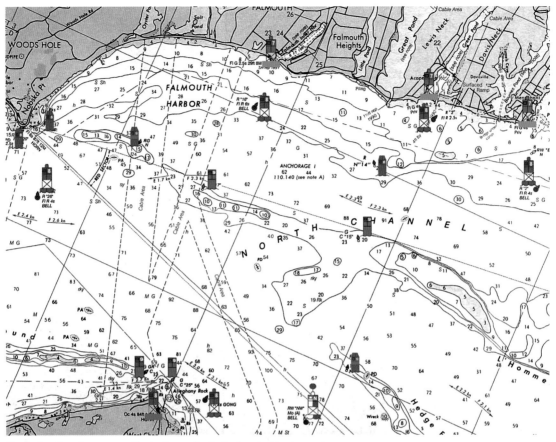

For instructional purposes, illustrations of selected navigation buoys have been superimposed on this chart segment next to their corresponding chart symbols.

Lateral marks are comforting and easy to follow once you're in a channel. But if you are approaching shore and come upon an isolated buoy, it's often difficult to tell where safe water is. It helps to know that "returning" is taken to mean heading generally inland from more open water. It's also nice to know that the U.S. Coast Guard construes "returning," when there's doubt, as heading clockwise around the United States—i.e., south along the Atlantic Coast, north along the west coast of Florida, west along the Gulf Coast, and north along the Pacific Coast. Still, there are channels and passages that defy all such categorization. In those waters the Coast Guard makes an arbitrary determination of which direction through the passage constitutes "home-ward," and you must consult a local nautical chart to orient yourself.

Aids to navigation take some getting used to, but you wouldn't want to leave home without them. The more you use them, the more you come to appreciate the quantity of vital information they convey in elegant shorthand.

A selection of navaids *on the Maine coast.* **1.** *Can buoy #1. Navaid numbering is strictly local; with each new channel or harbor approach, the numbering begins anew.* **2.** *Nun buoy #24 must lie along an extensively buoyed channel, because otherwise the numbering wouldn't get this high.* **3.** *Buoy "2A" marks the approach to a channel and needs to be detectable from a good distance regardless of visibility. Therefore a prominent pillar buoy is used instead of a nun, and the buoy has both a light and a sound signal—either a bell or a whistle. The even number and the red color tell you to leave this buoy to starboard when "inward" bound, but determining which way is "inward" on the convoluted Maine coast is often difficult. Let your chart—which should be at your elbow in printed or digital form—be the final arbiter of which side to pass the buoy.* **4.** *The color of this silhouetted daymark cannot be seen, but you know it is red because the shape is a triangle.* **5, 6.** *A daymark might be out of the water or in it, often depending on the stage of the tide. The latter one is topped by an osprey nest.* **7.** *A small buoy like this pillar usually marks the inner reaches of an approach or anchorage, with more prominent buoys to seaward.* **8.** *Goose Rocks Lighthouse in the Fox Islands Thorofare between North Haven and Vinalhaven islands, Penobscot Bay, Maine. The chart tells us that this light stands 51 feet above mean high water. Its light flashes red every 6 seconds and is visible from 11 miles, and it has a horn. Lighthouses like this one, known locally as The Sparkplug, are highly recognizable landmarks.*

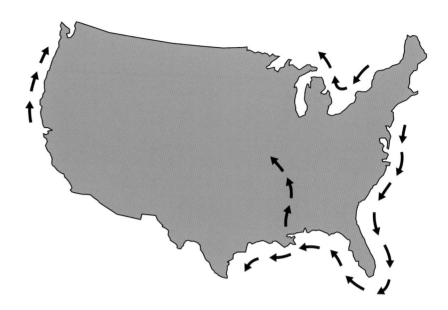

The "red, right, returning" convention.

Junction Buoys

In a system of red and green, what does it mean when both colors are on the same buoy? That makes the buoy in question a **preferred channel mark**, or **junction buoy**. A junction buoy may be either a can or a nun and is positioned at a fork between two channels or sometimes in front of a hazard that may be passed safely on either side. The markings are horizontal bands of red and green, with the upper band signaling the preferred channel. If green is the top color, leaving it to port will put you in the preferred channel.

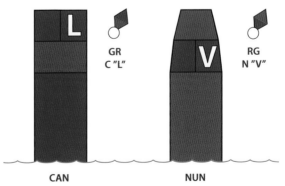

GR
C "L"

RG
N "V"

CAN

NUN

Buoys marking preferred channels and their chart symbols. Leaving the can to port or the nun to starboard (when returning from seaward) will put you in the preferred channel.

Other Marks

Isolated danger marks display red-and-black horizontal bands with black double-sphere topmarks. **Special-purpose marks** are solid yellow and may or may not be lettered or lighted; these denote everything from underwater cables and military firing ranges to recreation areas—in other words, waters that are quarantined due to use, not rocks or shoals. **Information** and **regulatory marks** are white buoys or dayboards with orange outlines or markings denoting zones of no wake, low speed, dredging, or other restrictions.

A regulatory mark warning boats away from a swimming area.

Fairway Markers

A buoy with red-and-white vertical stripes is in deep water and may be a traffic separation guide. Known as a **safe water mark**, it is in the middle of the **fairway** and can be passed on either side. Safe water marks are identified by letters but never by numbers. When lighted they display a white light, often in a Morse code letter A (• –) pattern. The buoy itself may be spherical or a pillar buoy with a spherical topmark.

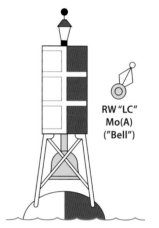

RW "LC"
Mo(A)
("Bell")

A midchannel bell buoy with its spherical topmark.

The Intracoastal Waterway

The Intracoastal Waterway (ICW) is a system of interconnected bays, sounds, and canals running south along the U.S. East Coast from New Jersey through Florida, then west along the Gulf Coast to Brownsville, Texas. The IALA-B buoyage system applies here as elsewhere in North America, but each navaid includes an additional small yellow symbol (a square for "green" aids, a triangle for "red" aids). An aid with a yellow square should be left to port, and one with a yellow triangle should be left to starboard when proceeding south or west along the ICW.

Cardinal Marks

In the IALA-A system used in Europe and elsewhere, isolated offshore hazards are sometimes marked with **cardinal marks**, which feature black-and-yellow horizontal bands in varying patterns to indicate on what side they can be safely passed—north, south, east, or west. Cardinal marks are rarely used in North America.

The black-over-yellow banding and two right-side-up cones identify this as a north cardinal mark, meaning that the hazard lies south of it and you should pass it on the north side. This mark is off the island of Tortola in the British Virgin Islands.

Using a Compass

Sailors have been using compasses for over a thousand years, and they remain as important in this age of GPS navigation as they ever were. Use yours for steering, to determine laylines, to track wind shifts, to fix your position, to measure leeway or current set, and to make sure your anchor is holding. Racing, cruising, or daysailing, you'll appreciate and rely on your compass.

A magnetized needle pointing steadfastly north is the heart of any compass, but don't fall into the "small boat, small compass" trap. Even on an open dinghy or daysailer a compass should be big enough to be read accurately and good enough to perform without lag as the boat turns. In a good **ship's compass** (also called the **steering compass**), a glass dome filled with a viscous oil or alcohol covers (and magnifies) the **compass card**, which pivots on a needle point and thus stays level as the boat heels and pitches. The liquid dampens the movements of the compass card, permitting a more stable reading. In a ship's compass it is the entire compass card that is magnetized to point north, not just a needle; thus, when the card appears to be swinging, it is because the boat itself is turning. A good compass has a jeweled pivot for the card and an internal bellows to accommodate pressure changes without introducing bubbles in the fluid.

On wheel-steered boats, the steering compass is often conveniently mounted on a binnacle in front of the wheel (see photo, page 37). Smaller boats, particularly those that are tiller steered, are more likely to have deck- or bulkhead-mounted compasses. A top-reading compass displays your course heading against a **lubber line** on the far edge of the compass card—i.e., the edge toward the front of the boat—a configuration that most sailors find more intuitive and less confusing to steer by and take bearings with than an aft-reading compass. No matter what your style of compass is, align its lubber line with your boat's centerline.

Steering a compass course is simple in theory—put the lubber line on the desired compass heading and keep it there. It may be simple, but it's not easy in practice. Your boat doesn't usually want to hold a steady course. Here are some pointers to stay on course:

- Don't try to peg the boat rigidly on course. It can't be done. Instead, allow her 5 or even 10 degrees of wandering either side of the desired course, trying to balance the right-hand wanderings with the left. Average your course, don't try to inhabit it.
- Look to the horizon more often than the compass. Changes in the big world ahead of the boat are easier to see, anticipate, and

LUBBER LINE

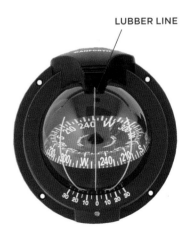

LUBBER LINE

Binnacle-mounted (top) and bulkhead-mounted (bottom) sailboat compasses.

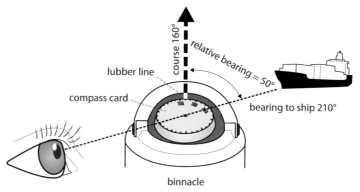

When you obtain the bearing of an approaching vessel, what you care most about is its relative bearing. If the approaching ship remains 50 degrees off your bow as its distance decreases, you need to alter course, speed, or both to keep clear.

respond to than changes in the compass's little globe.

- Find a reference out ahead in the real world. Use a star, cloud, landmark, or even a shadow on the deck as your course indicator. A slow-moving object in the distant sky will serve you well for minutes at a time. When the star you've chosen shifts significantly in the night sky, find a new one to hitch your wagon to.

Taking a bearing is simpler than steering. Sight across the compass card at your target (or use a hand bearing compass as discussed in Chapter 5). You may be sighting a charted buoy or landmark or another boat, but what you're determining is

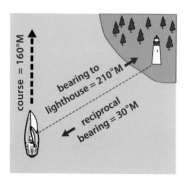

When you obtain the bearing to a charted navigation buoy or landmark, the absolute bearing is what matters. Draw the reciprocal bearing (the sighted bearing minus 180 degrees, which in this case is 30 degrees) from the object on the chart, and you know you are somewhere along that plotted line.

the direction of the target from you. Using the flat of your hand, trace the line from the compass pivot to the target. Where that line crosses the card perimeter is the bearing to the object in question. What you do with that bearing depends on your reason for obtaining it.

Suppose your compass course is 160 degrees and the bearing to an approaching ship is 210 degrees. That means the ship's relative bearing—i.e., its angle off your bow—is 50 degrees. If it was 50 degrees 5 minutes ago, too, and the ship is now a mile closer than it was then, what you're observing is the classic indicator of a **collision course**—a steady bearing with decreasing range. You should make a pronounced change in your course, speed, or both.

On the other hand, suppose the object at 210 degrees is a lighthouse and your reason for

obtaining the bearing is to get a handle on where you are. Find the lighthouse on your nautical chart and plot the bearing as described in Chapter 5. You are somewhere on that line.

Deviation

Deviation occurs when shipboard influences cause your steering compass to deviate from the earth's magnetic field. Any magnetic object close to the compass—the engine, electronic instruments, electrical wiring, a radio speaker—can cause deviation. Furthermore, because the relationship between the earth's field and the boat's field changes with every heading, the error is not constant—it disappears on some headings and is accentuated on others. The errors aboard sailboats tend to be small, often in the 2- to 3-degree range, at which point (since it is impossible to steer a course with more than 2- or 3-degree precision) they can be safely ignored. If the deviation on some courses is greater than this, you should address the problem either by compensating the compass or constructing a deviation table as described in Chapter 5.

Magnetic Variation

The earth's magnetic field holds your compass card steady while your boat turns. It's so simple that it seems magical, but there are one or two slight complications. Chief among these is that magnetic north is a distance removed from the geographical north pole and in fact wanders around through the high Canadian arctic. That sets up a difference between **true directions** (described relative to true, or geographic, north) and **compass directions**. That's why the **compass rose** on a chart displays an outer ring labeled in degrees true and an inner ring labeled in degrees magnetic that corresponds with the compass. The difference between true and magnetic is called **variation**, and it varies from place to place and from year to year. Though the change with time is gradual and predictable, it does eventually accumulate. If your chart is years out of date and you're in an area of large variation, you should multiply the local rate of change, which is printed on the chart, by the number of years since the chart was published, and add that change to the local variation.

Professional navigators trained on ships' bridges often prefer to do their chart plotting in degrees true. This insistence requires them to convert compass bearings to true bearings before plotting them, and to convert true plotted courses to compass courses before steering them. Most small-boat sailors avoid this extra work with its back-and-forth potential confusion by doing their plotting in degrees magnetic and using the inner ring of the compass rose.

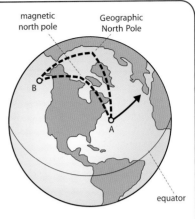

The relative positions of the true and magnetic north poles. From point A, magnetic north is west of true north. Said another way, the local variation at point A is westerly. If the difference is 12°, the local variation is 12° West. Suppose you want to plot a course from point A to Portugal, and a small-scale planning chart of the North Atlantic tells you that the course is 73° true. To find the course in degrees magnetic you add 12, obtaining 85° magnetic. From point B, on the other hand, magnetic north is east of true north, so the local variation is east. If the difference were 12°, a true course of 73° would equate to 61° magnetic. We'll return to the concept of variation as it affects compass courses in the navigation chapter.

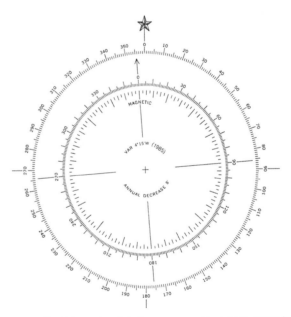

A compass rose like this one is printed on every nautical chart. Most charts carry multiple roses for your convenience. The outer circle shows degrees true and the inner circle degrees magnetic. The magnetic arrow and the label in the center of this rose both tell you that the local variation was just over 4° West when the chart was printed in 1985, and the label further tells you that the local variation is decreasing at an annual rate of 8 minutes. If you had been using this chart in 1995, you would have multiplied 8 (annual decrease in minutes) by 10 (number of years of change) to obtain 80 minutes, or 1° 20'. The corrected variation in 1995 would thus have been 4° 15' minus 1° 20', or 2° 55' West. In most places and for most purposes, there is no need to worry about such precision.

Discovering Charts

The depth of the water, the shape of the coastline, nearby landmarks, shipping lanes, the direction home, the nearest hazard, the names of points and islands, the locations and purposes of aids to navigation, the seabed composition . . . a **nautical chart** tells it all. Maybe your "chart" is the picture in your head of your home waters, but whenever you sail beyond the familiar, and often even close to home, you need charts.

We all need charts to keep us out of trouble. White areas on the chart denote deep water, but shades of blue indicate shallower water and should get our attention. A green hue indicates an area so shoal it uncovers at low tide. Soundings (which are referenced to mean lower low water, or MLLW, on U.S. charts) tell us how deep the water is. Soundings are usually given in feet on U.S. charts, but sometimes they're in **fathoms** (1 fathom = 6 feet), and increasingly they're in meters, so be sure you know what units are used.

Most of the things sailors fear are underwater, and rocks, wrecks, bars, and banks that we can't see are all pictured on the chart. Landmarks are positioned and identified.

Points of equal depth are connected with **contour lines**, or **depth curves**, which are in effect the mirror images of the altitude contours seen on topographic maps. Most U.S. charts have contour lines at 6, 12, 18, 30, and 60 feet, and sometimes at greater depths as well, and these are a great aid for staying in safe water as your boat travels across the chart.

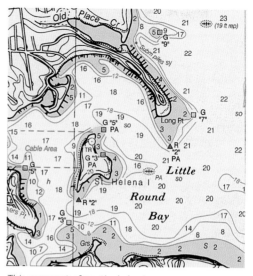

This segment of nautical chart number 12282 (scale = 1:25,000), showing the Severn and Magothy rivers in the Chesapeake Bay, introduces chart symbology and language. Vertical, roman type is used for beacons and land features; slanted, italic type is used for hydrographic features. Soundings on this chart are in feet, though often they are in meters and occasionally in fathoms (1 fathom = 6 feet). The chart's title block will tell you what units are used as well as the vertical datum, when the chart was published, and much other valuable information. The chart shows depth contours at 6, 12, and 18 feet; these numbers appear in a smaller, lighter font to distinguish them from spot soundings. Blue denotes shoal water—on this chart, less than 6 feet deep. Note the symbol for a dangerous wreck in the center. PA = position approximate and TR = tower.

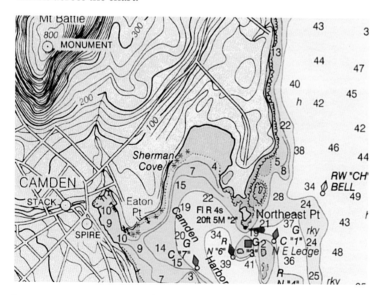

A section of chart number 13305 (scale = 1:40,000) of Penobscot Bay, Maine. Contour lines on land are every 20 feet, with every fifth one (100-foot intervals) bolder. Position dots tell us that the monument, stack, and spire are all accurately charted, and their capital-lettered labels tell us that these are prominent landmarks, useful for navigation. Buoy labels, unlike beacon labels, are italic. Intertidal areas are green.

Right: *Here's a portion of a larger-scale chart (1:20,000) of Camden Harbor than the one shown in the previous illustration, showing us more soundings and greater detail. If you had any interest in passing between the Inner and Outer Ledges, for example, you'd prefer this chart. Note the red-and-white fairway bell buoy "CH" marking the approach to Northeast Passage. The superimposed red arrows (#1 and #2) designate the locations from which the accompanying aerial photos were taken, and the superimposed blue arrow corresponds with the recommended harbor approach track superimposed on the photo below.* **Middle:** *This photo—on which buoy symbols are superimposed for visibility—offers a glimpse into the translation between chart language and the real world. Interpretations get more difficult at sea level because islands and peninsulas in the foreground blend into the landmasses behind. If you keep your eyes open and follow the navigation buoys, however, charts allow you to enter unfamiliar anchorages in safety.* **Bottom:** *In Camden's inner harbor you should have no trouble locating the charted church spire and factory stack.*

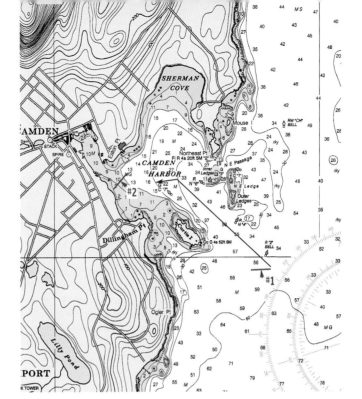

Chart Symbology

You can use a chart without understanding much more than which areas are land and which are water, but charts can tell you much, much more than that. The bulk of that information is encoded in symbols and abbreviations. Most are easy to learn as you go, but the National Ocean Service (NOS) of the National Oceanic and Atmospheric Administration (NOAA) in conjunction with the National Geospatial-Intelligence Agency (NGA) publishes a guide to chart symbols, abbreviations, and conventions that makes decoding simple. It's called Chart No. 1: Nautical Chart Symbols, Abbreviations, and Terms, and it's available from the U.S. Government Printing Office or by free download

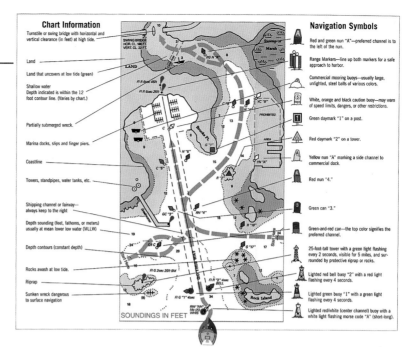

More of the symbol language used on charts.

from http://chartmaker.ncd. noaa.gov. Chart No. 1 is also printed by various commercial publishers, and their editions are distributed through bookstores and marine stores.

Mercator Projection

Most nautical charts are **Mercator projections**. Imagine a sheet of paper wrapped around a globe to make a cylinder that is in direct contact with the globe only at its equator. Now imagine that globe being lit from within so that its landmasses and other features are projected upon the paper cylinder. The result would be a Mercator chart of the world. In a Mercator projection, all parallels of latitude are horizontal and straight, and all meridians of longitude are vertical and straight. The parallels intersect the meridians at right angles. The result—and this is the great advantage of a Mercator projection—is that the navigator can measure and plot directions and distances directly on the chart and use them for navigation.

In the real world, of course, meridians aren't parallel. Thus, Mercator projections distort the shapes and relative sizes of landmasses and ocean basins. This distortion becomes exaggerated near the poles, but it's almost unnoticeable in nautical charts for low- and middle-latitude waters.

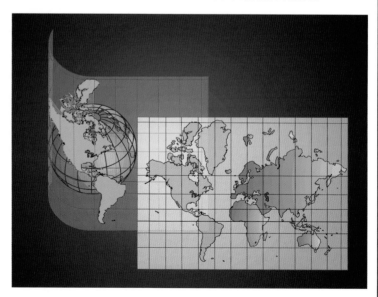

A Mercator projection shows lines of longitude as vertical parallel lines rather than converging at the poles. This allows compass courses to plot as straight lines.

Latitude and Longitude

Across the top and bottom margins of a chart run scales that measure longitude in degrees, minutes, and tenths of minutes. Lines of **longitude**, known as **meridians**, would run from pole to pole if inscribed on a spherical globe, converging at the poles, but on most charts they are depicted as straight parallel lines running north to south (i.e., top to bottom). Meridians are numbered from 0° at the **prime meridian** (which, for historical reasons, passes through Greenwich, England), increasing by degrees both west and east until, on the opposite side of the world, they meet one another again at 180°. Meridian lines are printed at regular intervals on your chart, with the interval depending on the scale of the chart. A **large-scale chart** covering a small geographic region might show meridians at 2-minute intervals, whereas a very **small-scale chart** covering a large region might show them at 30-minute intervals.

Latitude is measured from 0° at the equator to 90°N at the north pole or 90°S at the south pole. Lines of equal latitude are called **parallels**, since each one is parallel with the equator. The parallels form the horizontal grid lines on your chart. No matter where on the planet you may be, 1° of latitude is equal to 60 nautical miles and 1′ of latitude equals 1 nautical mile. This means that you can use the latitude scale on the chart's left-hand and right-hand margins for measuring distances. Note, however, that 1′ of longitude is equal to 1 nautical mile only at the equator, diminishing to nothing at the poles. Thus, the longitude scale cannot be used to measure distances.

By drawing lines parallel to the nearest meridian and the nearest line of latitude from any point on the chart to the degree scales on the edges you can find the latitude and longitude coordinates for that point. Each spot on the earth is uniquely identified by its latitude and longitude.

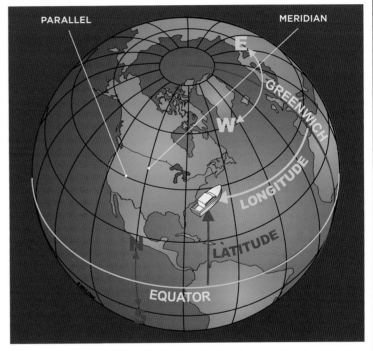

Each combination of a latitude and a longitude defines a unique location on the earth.

To figure out where you are in the world, take **bearings** on surrounding buoys or landmarks whose positions are charted, then plot two such bearings on the chart (we'll cover this in Chapter 5). Where the bearings cross on the chart is more or less where you are, with allowances for imprecision. You have obtained a **fix**. If a third bearing crosses the other two near their intersection, you have a triangulated fix and can treat it with a high degree of confidence.

Alternatively, read the number on a navigation buoy you're passing. Find it on the chart and you know where you are. Once you know that, you can read the **coordinates** (latitude and longitude) of your position from the chart margins, and then you can let someone else know where you are. The chart gives you lots of ways of finding your position.

To plot a course from where you are to where you want to go, draw a line on the chart between the two locations, then read the direction of that course from the compass rose. We'll see how in Chapter 5.

Nautical charts are amazing graphic distillations of huge quantities of data, and they help keep trouble at bay. Most people keep their charts belowdeck. If you're navigating while steering, though, you should have your chart with you on deck. Fold it so it shows where you are; fumbling to find the right spot on the chart has put more than one sailor in the wrong spot on the water. I like to orient the chart the way I'm sailing—if the land you can see is to starboard, put the land on the chart on your starboard hand. You can protect your chart by wrapping it in clear plastic or sliding it into a self-sealing, see-through vinyl pocket made for the purpose. Praise Poseidon for charts.

Obtaining Charts

In the United States, marine charts are prepared by the Office of Coast Survey (OCS) and published by the NOS, its sister agency within NOAA. The U.S. Coast Guard has the responsibility for siting and maintaining navigation aids and also publishes the Local Notices to Mariners, reflecting week-by-week changes in key navigation information. These changes are accumulated and annotated on charts for updated publications. The United Kingdom Hydrographic Office, within the British Admiralty, produces the high-quality British Admiralty Charts used in large parts of the world. Canada and Australia both have national hydrographic offices as well.

Ship chandleries and large nautical bookstores sell government charts, and what they don't have in stock can be ordered to your needs. Nautical charts are also available from NOAA, which offers print-on-demand versions of charts annotated with the most recent Local Notices to Mariners.

An ever-increasing percentage of nautical charts come from commercial suppliers. These companies usually start with the official masters from national hydrographic institutions, layer them with additional information, and present them in a variety of convenient formats. Paper charts are giving way to waterproof charts, which are more suitable for use in the wet cockpits and confined spaces of small boats. Such charts also come in books or are prefolded for ease of use and storage. Often their scales have been modified to create more convenient sizes.

A number of commercial suppliers offer digital charts that can be displayed and used on computers and in chartplotters. Digital charts and related navigation software are available from most marine stores, often—and conveniently—as a portfolio of digital charts covering a large region on a single CD-ROM or removable data chip. You can also download free electronic charts in raster format directly from the OCS website, http://chartmaker.ncd.noaa.gov.

Chart Scales

Charts come in a variety of scales, with the scale indicated as a ratio. For example, on a 1:40,000-scale chart, 1 inch or 1 centimeter on the chart equals 40,000 inches (approximately half a nautical mile) or 40,000 centimeters (400 meters) in the real world. A 1:20,000 chart is typical for local waters; a 1:10,000 scale may depict a specific harbor; and a 1:80,000 chart depicts a wider boating region. A 1:10,000 chart is considered **large scale**—ideal for navigation in narrow, rock-strewn waters. A 1:120,000 chart is considered **small scale**—excellent for "big-picture" cruise planning but insufficiently detailed for picking your way among ledges, buoys, and islands. Large-scale charts show more detail but cover smaller areas. Think of it as large scale = large detail.

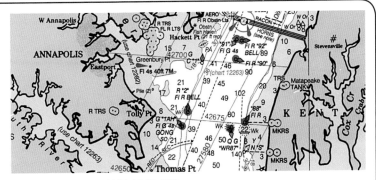

CHESAPEAKE BAY 12280 1:200,000

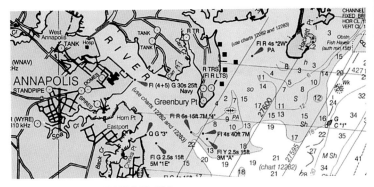

CHESAPEAKE BAY 12263 1:80,000

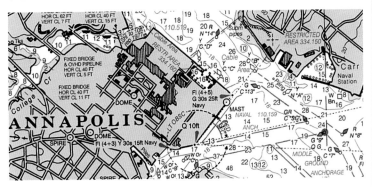

CHESAPEAKE BAY 12282 1:25,000

A series of chart extracts of the same area around Annapolis, Maryland, varying in scale from 1:200,000 to 1:10,000. The small-scale chart (top, 1:200,000) shows all inshore waters as "shoal" (blue) and provides no soundings. The larger the scale, the more detail and soundings, until finally even individual slips in the Santee Basin are shown.

CHESAPEAKE BAY 12283 1:10,000

Piloting by Eye

Nothing replaces a nautical chart, but with or without charts sailors for centuries have studied the waters around them for clues to safe piloting. You need charts, yes, but you also need to stay connected with what is around you. Develop your sensory awareness whenever you're on the water. It will serve you well.

How deep is the water? In the Bahamas, Caribbean, and South Pacific, where the water is clear, color is a reliable guide to depth. Dark blue indicates deep water, light blue is navigable, and turquoise to white is shallow. In the murkier waters of North America, the principle is the same, but the indicators are harder to read. Sunlight reflects off the bottom more noticeably the shallower the water. Even a grassy or muddy bottom will bounce back some light. In general, then, the darker the water, the deeper it is. Also, the clearer it is, the deeper. The closer the bottom is to the top, the more likely it is to get stirred up and make the shallow water murky.

We've all seen waves break on a sandbar. The shallower the water, the more agitated the water surface becomes. You can tell from the behavior of your wake when the water is getting shallower. As a wave encounters shallow water it begins to steepen and will eventually break. Even when the waves are small, you can observe this change in their form as they go from deep to shallow water. An agitated surface means shallow water.

Sometimes the surface of a current-riven channel may appear more agitated than the water over the flats on either side, but this jumbling together of an accelerated flow looks very different from the breakers that pile up on a sandbar. The water in midchannel is moving faster than the water over the shallows and has a distinct horizontal swirl, as opposed to the choppy vertical wavelets caused by a shoal.

When visibility is limited, a nearby shore may suggest its presence as an indistinct loom in the fog or an inky, featureless swath of blacker black against a dark night sky. If there is a rolling ground swell beneath your keel and it begins to steepen, you may be approaching a shoreline or shoal. If under power, stop your engine. Do you hear surf, or even the gentle wash of small waves on a shore? And while you're listening, what about other nearby boat engines? Your chart can't tell you where the other boats are—that's up to you!

When visibility is good, keep your gaze ahead of the boat. Intermittent breakers mark a subsurface rock. Sometimes only the larger waves will break—say, every 30 seconds or so. You have to be alert to see a subsurface rock.

The more closely you observe, the more help your eyes will provide.

> ## Build Your "Eyeball Library"
> Make your observations more useful by honing your estimating. By comparing your estimate of a distance, direction, or speed with accurate information, you'll become more accurate. For instance, if your GPS receiver says a buoy is a mile away, file that picture: "That's what a mile away looks like!" If you know the current flow in a channel is 2 knots, look at the markers and other indicators. "That's what 2 knots look like!"

The Trend of the Land

A most useful guide to water depth is the trend of the land around the water. In your mind's eye, continue the slope of any foreshore under the water as a rough indicator of what the offshore bottom will be like. A flat, low point will extend shallow water well offshore, while a beach with a steeper slope usually means that depths will increase gradually but steadily away from shore. A bluff headland that juts up from the sea is a pretty fair indicator of deep water close inshore. A rocky outcrop visible above the water quite likely has an invisible cousin under the water nearby.

The bold shoreline in the left fore-ground of the photo suggests deep water close in, and the chart extract confirms this. At the head of Owls Head Harbor, on the other hand, the gentle shelving of land into water hints at shallow water inshore, and the chart confirms this, too. But rocks can pop up anywhere along the coast of Maine, as both the chart and photo make clear.

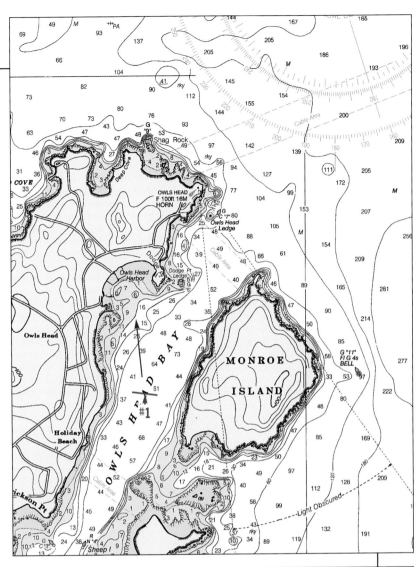

The current around this lobster pot buoy looks like a little less than 1 knot.

Reading the Current

Boats at anchor tend to point into the current, but they are also influenced by the wind. Powerboats with lots of windage above water and little depth of hull below the water will react more to the wind and less to the current than a deep, full-keeled sailboat. A shallow-hulled, fin-keeled sailboat will behave somewhat between these extremes. If all boats are pointing directly into the wind, either the wind and current are coming from the same direction or the current is negligible. Use the difference between the way a boat is riding and the true wind to extrapolate the direction and strength of the current. Channel buoys tilt with the current. If the flow is less than 1 knot, you can still get a picture of it from the size and character of the disturbed water downcurrent from a buoy. For this kind of guess-timation you can also use a stake, rock, or lobster pot buoy.

Improving Your Tacks

Tacking is such an essential and unavoidable maneuver that most sailors quickly acquire both tacking experience and a sense of what's involved. But there's more to coming about than giving the commands and putting the helm down. Because we do it so often, it pays to do it well, and what that takes is analysis and practice.

Imagine tacking your boat without a rudder. To steer her from one tack to the other using only the sails, you would ease the jib (to relieve pressure on the bow) and trim the main (to increase heel, increase the wind pressure aft of the boat's center of lateral resistance, and exert weather helm). To accelerate the turn you could shift your weight to leeward to heel the boat even more and, perhaps, move the mainsheet traveler to weather. If you were patient and lucky, you'd come about.

Steering with a rudder is a lot more efficient than steering with sails alone, but sails and heel angle can be adjusted along with the rudder for optimal control. Increasing the rudder angle produces steerage but also drag. The more you turn the rudder, the more you slow the boat. Use the elements at your command to tack with minimal rudder. Orchestrating all these components may not always be necessary, desirable, or even possible, but you should be aware that they are there to improve the efficiency, effectiveness, and grace of your tacks should you wish to deploy them.

You will find, too, that different sorts of turns suit differing conditions. As much as possible, use your tack as an occasion to glide directly upwind. This is most possible when your boat goes into the tack doing better than half her top speed, the breeze is moderate, and the water is flat. In conditions like these you'll have ample momentum to spare for the turn. Use that excess headway to coast directly upwind for as long as you can before rounding off onto your new tack.

In steep waves, or when the breeze is strong, or both, not only do you lose power when you tack, but your boat will be slowed dramatically as you cross through the no-go zone. Rather than prolong that passage, scoot through the eye of the wind as cleanly as you can. Minimize the flogging of the jib because that adds drag. If possible, a trimmer should get the sheet down to the minimum number of turns on the winch drum (big boat) or free of the jam cleat (small boat) and in his hand before the tack. Don't release the sheet until the jib backs, however, because its turning force will help spin the boat through the wind and speed the sail past the mast onto the new tack. (You can inadvertently stop the boat, however, if you leave the jib backed longer than it takes to accelerate the turn.) None of this works smoothly unless the jibsheet pays out smoothly when the sail is released.

Of course, "moderate breeze" and "flat water" are relative terms. A light sailing dinghy will stop in short order when head to wind in 14 knots of wind and a 1-foot chop, whereas a 30-foot keelboat in those same conditions can carve out a big chunk of windward progress with a slow, majestic turn.

Waves are a big consideration when you tack in heavy air. Climbing a wave as you pass

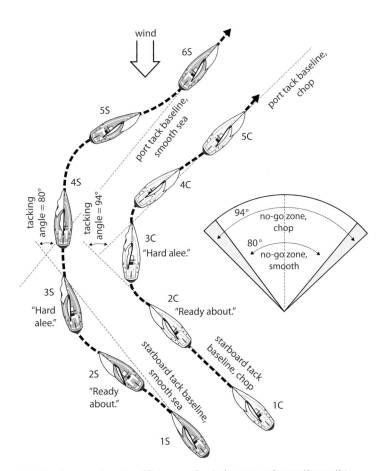

Tacking in smooth water. 1S. *In a moderate breeze and smooth sea, this close-winded sailboat is trimmed for maximum pointing ability, with its sails flat and close to the centerline. With the windward jib telltales lifting slightly and the main leech telltales stalling about half the time, the boat sails just 40 degrees off the wind.* **2S.** *In preparation for a tack, the helmsman bears off a few degrees, and the trimmers ease the main- and jibsheets slightly to put more fullness in the sails and power the boat to its best close-hauled speed.* **3S.** *The helmsman initiates a slow tack using minimum helm pressure. The main is trimmed back in but the jib is not, and this helps turn the boat into the wind. Shifting crew weight to leeward may also help.* **4S.** *With both sails luffing, the helmsman slows or even pauses the turn while the boat headreaches—i.e., carries its momentum—several boat lengths to windward.* **5S.** *The tack finishes slowly as well, giving the jib trimmer plenty of time to get the sail in. Initially the helmsman steers a few degrees below his new close-hauled baseline so that the boat can power up to speed with slightly eased sails.* **6S.** *As the boat speeds up, the helmsman gradually pinches up to his new close-hauled course while the trimmers flatten the sails.*

Tacking in a chop. 1C–5C. *If we add some short, steep waves to the equation, however, everything changes. The boat needs power to punch through this chop, so the sails have to be eased and deepened a bit, and the helmsman will have to bear down as appropriate to the conditions. In this example the boat can sail no closer than 47 degrees off the wind. Further, the tack must be executed faster or the chop will stop the boat in its tracks, so headreaching to windward isn't possible. With enough (but not too much) wind, the boat may sail faster on its close-hauled baseline than it would in a smooth sea with less wind, but it's also sailing lower. Which conditions would give it the fastest arrival at a windward destination is an open question, but the crew will have a more comfortable and elegant sail in the smooth sea. The very worst combination, it should be clear by now, is a sloppy, choppy, leftover sea with no wind.*

Tacking Angles

Most modern monohulls tack through 85 to 90 degrees in average conditions—possibly improving to 80 degrees in flat water and dropping to 95 in sloppy seas with little wind—whereas multihulls typically tack through 100 degrees. Get a feel for your boat's tacking angle in differing conditions and develop a sense of how much you should be changing course to assure a good tack.

Falling off too far on the new tack gives up some of that windward progress you worked so hard to get. It also makes life harder for your jib trimmer, who won't enjoy the reduced pull of a partially luffing jib while trimming the sheet. And in a strong breeze it may even leave your boat vulnerable to getting knocked down by a gust of wind. That's because the boat will be moving slowly as it comes out of the tack, and a slow-moving boat cannot develop the hydrodynamic lift around its keel or centerboard that helps it resist heeling.

through the eye of the wind can leave you starved for power and dead in your tracks. If you can manage to tack when you're accelerating down a wave, on the other hand, you'll enjoy a much shorter and surer trip from one tack to the other. If that doesn't seem possible, look for a patch of relatively small waves in which to tack.

Don't tack through too wide an angle or head lower than necessary on the new tack. Most boats tack through 75 to 100 degrees (as read from the compass) from close hauled on one tack to close hauled on the other. A boat that will tack through 75 degrees is extremely **close winded**, or **weatherly**, while one that tacks through 100 degrees is anything but.

Shifting your weight from side to side is a key element in any boat small enough to be sensitive to crew weight. Carry some heel into the tack, then transfer your weight fluidly across the boat in sync with (but opposite to) the boat's motion as she straightens, then heels to the new tack. In most small boats, the transfer of sides dictates a transfer of steering and sheeting hands, which takes some practice before it becomes effortless.

Honor Thy Trimmer

No part of sailing is work, but one thing that resembles work is trimming a big genoa jib. When you tack faster than conditions require, you don't just lose an opportunity to eat up a boat length or three to windward, you also make life more difficult for your poor jib trimmer. Consider the trimmer's plight. As the boat turns through the wind and the flogging genoa works its way ponderously across the foredeck—snatching at mast-mounted winches and cleats, deck-mounted ventilator cowls, shrouds, and anything else it encounters en route—he (or she) is poised to bring in the new working jibsheet with all possible speed. Yet if he begins trimming too soon, he will back the jib, slowing or even stopping the turn. So he must wait until the bow turns well past head to wind, still hoping to get the genoa trimmed most of the way in before it fills on the new tack and makes further trimming three times as hard. A smooth, deliberate tack will give him a fighting chance.

Sailing through a Tack

Sailing a boat through a tack involves careful trimming both before and after. Never tack unless the boat is going full speed. Trim the main and jib for maximum power before the tack, and **foot off** slightly (head down no more than a few degrees from close hauled) to build the velocity you need to make an efficient turn. Because the boat will be slower coming out of the tack than she was going in, her sails will need wider, fuller trim angles at first to help her accelerate. As you get up speed on the new tack, trim the sails flatter for maximum pointing ability.

Improving Your Jibes

The risks involved in jibing increase with the wind. No wise sailor treats a jibe in a fresh breeze lightly, but the more you understand about how to jibe—and the more you focus on and practice the steps and techniques involved—the more confident you can be when the time comes.

Stability isn't a problem when you're jibing in light to moderate air. Still, safety should remain your main concern because it doesn't take a lot of wind in the sail to fling the main boom across the cockpit with head-cracking speed. All hands need to anticipate the possibility of that swing, and that makes communication from the helm important. Almost as unsettling as an accidental jibe is a purposeful jibe executed before the crew is ready. "Ready to jibe?" is meant to be a question, not an announcement of an event in progress. You should wait for the appropriate acknowledgments before calling "Jibe ho" and steering into the maneuver.

Your next goal after safety is to jibe without losing any more speed than necessary. When jibing, as when tacking, rudder action slows the boat, and so does trimming the sails closer to the boat's centerline than their ideal setting.

Chapter 1 extolled the virtues of controlling your jibes by trimming the mainsail to the centerline while heading directly downwind, and this is true, but when the breeze is light to moderate you can afford to place a greater premium on getting from boom-out on one side to boom-out on the other as smoothly and fast as possible. Most boats of any size have at least one mainsheet block on the boom and another on the traveler, and the mainsheet forms several parts as it runs back and forth between these. You can pull the main boom to the centerline a lot faster in a gentle to moderate breeze by pulling hand over hand on all the parts of the mainsheet at once than you can by trimming in the normal fashion. When you do this, however, watch out for bights of loose sheet as the boom sweeps across.

Jibing gets tougher when it's breezy. Boats that are sailing downwind don't heel so much as bury their bows and roll from side to side, which is harder to counteract, and there is no way to depower the mainsail—you can let it all the way out, and it still won't luff. Losing speed only makes the apparent wind stronger while reducing your stability. Add the mainsail's capacity to create enough weather helm to overwhelm your rudder, and you have some stumbling blocks to overcome.

Trimming a mainsail while turning downwind is too hard and induces too much heel and weather helm when the wind is strong. Indeed, trimming the main may make it impossible to head the boat down. On relatively heavy, stable boats the best bet is to head downwind first, then trim the boom as tightly as possible, jibe, and let the sheet run out on the other side—all on virtually the same heading.

Jibing through a Course Change

When your jibe is part and parcel of a sharp course change—around a mark, around a point or island, or simply around the whim of the moment—consider decoupling the jibe from the rest of the turn. In other words, leave yourself room to make the jibe on a dead downwind heading and then complete the turn rather than trying to jibe around the corner. The stronger the wind, the more advisable this becomes.

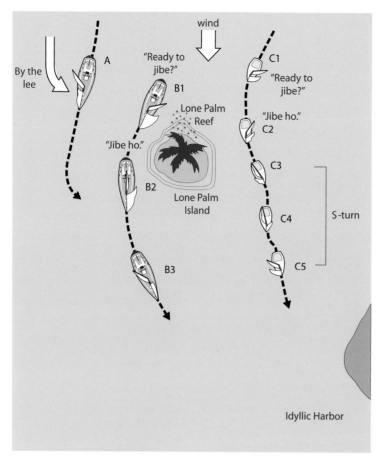

wind

By the lee

A

"Ready to jibe?"

B1

Lone Palm Reef

"Jibe ho."

B2

Lone Palm Island

B3

C1

"Ready to jibe?"

"Jibe ho."

C2

C3

C4

S-turn

C5

Idyllic Harbor

Three boats en route to Idyllic Harbor approach Lone Palm Island on a downwind course. Keelboat A, *the* Lazy Day, *is on port tack, mainsail to starboard, and wishes to avoid a jibe, which would only necessitate a second jibe to reach the harbor. Besides, the crew is enjoying lunch in the cockpit and doesn't want to be disturbed. The helmsman therefore alters course to starboard. He can tell by the masthead fly and by the uneasy, lifting main boom that he is sailing by the lee and wind is curling around to the backside of the leech.*

The boat slows down and the jib collapses listlessly in the shadow of the main, but no one has to put down their chicken salad sandwiches and lemonade and the helmsman is confident that he can avoid Lone Palm Island and an accidental jibe. If he's right—and let's hope he is—he can then return to his former course and reach the harbor without having had to jibe.

Keelboat B, *the* Right Way, *is on starboard tack, mainsail to port, and the helmsman hardens up a bit* **(B1)** *to avoid the island. She must then*

jibe to reach the harbor, however, so the crew rushes through their sandwiches. When all is ready, she bears off directly downwind and trims the main boom to the centerline. If the wind is light to moderate and the mainsheet configuration includes multiple parallel parts, she or a crewmember can grab all the parts at once and haul the boom to the centerline much more quickly than by hauling on the free end of the sheet; this also facilitates letting the mainsail out quickly on the new tack **(B3).** *The boat is now headed toward its destination on port tack, but the jib is still trimmed to port because the jib trimmer hasn't yet finished his sandwich (he should be on the* Lazy Day*!). That's no big deal on this downwind course—in a minute or two he'll move the jib to the starboard side or perhaps wing it out to port.*

Meanwhile **dinghy C,** *the* Tippy, *approaches the middle of the island on starboard tack* **(C1).** *Hardening up on starboard would take it well out of its way, so a jibe is in order. Fortunately the two crew have already finished lunch. At* **C2** *the jibe is in progress. Again, if the wind is not too strong, the helmsman can speed the jibe by grasping multiple parts of the mainsheet to haul the boom to the centerline. At* **C3** *the main begins to swing out to starboard, but the helmsman is afraid this is happening with enough force to broach or even capsize the boat. He therefore turns the bow back toward the mainsail* **(C4),** *thus dampening or even halting the boom's swing. Once the boom is under control, he resumes his turn to port* **(C5).**

What about the Jib?

The jib is for the most part a docile beast downwind. On most boats it has no boom, and downwind it dwells in the mainsail's shadow. Getting the main boom uneventfully across the boat is your primary concern. If you've been sailing downwind prior to the jibe, the jib may already have been wung out on the new leeward side, and all you'll have to do is adjust its trim when you settle on your new course. If you'll be sailing downwind after the jibe, on the other hand, you may choose to leave the jib where it is, so that it will be wung out on what will become the new windward side of the boat. Even if you'll be jibing the jib along with the main, your only real concern will be keeping excess slack out of the jibsheets so that the jib cannot wrap itself around the headstay.

Remember, you want to trim the main as much as possible before it swings in order to control its travel and dampen its power. The boat can turn faster than you can trim, so hold a course straight before the wind as long as it takes to get the boom close enough to the centerline for a safe jibe.

"Let it run" is easier said than done, but the handling of the mainsheet is the single most crucial element in a heavy-weather jibe. If you make sure the sheet runs free on the completion of the jibe, you vastly increase your likelihood of a calm, uneventful outcome. When the boom comes across you don't want it to fetch up against any-thing—even the sheet—until it is almost all the way out on the new tack. If you can let the sheet run freely, either through your hands or with a single loose wrap around a winch, you will dissipate the power of the swing so that nothing gets broken, and you will keep the sail from twisting the boat and broach-ing her with a shot of unwanted weather helm.

In dinghies and other boats without great inherent stability you might try an **S-turn** to soften the boom's swing across the boat. Steer the boat into the jibe as normal; then, when the wind catches the back of the main and begins to send it across the boat, steer momen-

> **Steering through a Jibe**
> When you are running dead downwind, the course change to put the stern through the eye of the wind and onto the other tack can be as little as 5 degrees. Heeling the boat to windward will make her head off, and sometimes you can jibe without moving the rudder at all. If you have raised your centerboard or daggerboard to reduce resistance while sailing downwind, lower it a quarter of the way to provide a definite pivot point and make your turn crisper.

tarily in the direction of the boom's swing—i.e., back toward the tack you're leaving. This should cause the boom to decel-erate as it approaches the cen-terline, at which point you re-verse course again and complete the jibe—softly, you hope.

Reading the Wind

There are numerous ways to read the wind. As discussed in Chapter 1, your masthead fly will give you the direction of the apparent wind, which is the same as the true wind when your boat isn't moving. A tell-tale on a windward shroud is another good apparent wind indicator. (A leeward shroud telltale, on the other hand, indi-cates only the jib's exhaust.) An electronic wind instrument can tell you not only the direction of the wind but also the angle it makes with your course; when connected with an anemome-ter it can give you apparent and true wind strengths, too. Big-boat racing sailors wouldn't be without such instrumentation.

But there are wind indicators off the boat, too, and some of these will tell you not only what the wind is doing now but also what it's likely to do in the next few seconds, minutes, or hours. Look around. Any flag on shore tells you the true wind direc-tion. Smoke, boats under sail, and birds all have their mes-sages to share. If that sailboat a half mile to windward is heeling more than you and sailing faster, the breeze may be building—or **filling in**, as sailors like to say.

WINDLESS BAND

VESSEL WAKE

Here's a welcome sight to a sailboat that has been becalmed all morning—a breeze filling in from seaward at midday. The wind ripples in the foreground suggest a wind of less than 5 knots. If you study the ripples closely you'll see that their crests are oriented left to right with their steep fronts—no more than an inch or so high—facing us, while their more gently sloped backs face seaward. This tells us that the breeze is blowing directly at the camera. The wave in the right foreground has nothing to do with the local wind; it's either a vessel wake or a leftover sea from a breeze now dead. In the middle distance is a band where no wind appears to be touching the water—bands like this are typical when a breeze, which is organized in cells, first descends from aloft to bear upon the water. This does not mean you would be becalmed in that band, however—there might be ample breeze above deck level. Beyond that band the ripples look darker than in the foreground. This might mean that the breeze is fresher out there—which would not be at all unusual for a sea breeze filling in—or it might just be an illusion of distance. You could try training your binoculars on those two sailboats on the horizon. Are they leaning to a fresher breeze than you've got? If so, be patient—it may very well reach you in a few minutes.

Wind Shear

The wind at the top of your mast is often stronger than the wind at deck level. That's because the wind along the water is slowed by friction, while the air above it glides on a low-friction air-to-air cushion. Thus, tall-masted boats tend to ghost along when smaller ones lie becalmed. Also, because boatspeed is slower relative to the stronger breeze aloft, the apparent wind aloft will blow from farther aft than the deck-level breeze. This has implications for sail trim in a light breeze, when the effect is most pronounced. To prevent the top of the sail from being overtrimmed when its bottom is trimmed correctly in these conditions, you'll want some twist in the sail, and the way to accomplish this is to ease the sheets more than you ordinarily would. If the breeze builds, trim the sheets in again.

STREAKS

The darker patch of water just to windward tells us that a puff is approaching. The wind velocity is usually 10 to 12 knots or more when you see embedded streaks like these. The ripples in the immediate foreground tell us that our camera is facing directly into the wind over the deck, but the orientation of the streaks as well as the moored boats to windward tells us that the puff is going to be a header if we're on starboard tack. If we're close hauled on starboard, we'll have to bear off.

Reading the Weather from the Wind

The wind provides a rough but reliable key to reading the weather. Using a technique developed centuries ago by a Dutchman named Buys Ballot, face the wind. Hold out your right hand, and if you're north of the equator, the nearest low-pressure system will be centered 15 to 30 degrees behind your outstretched hand. (In the Southern Hemisphere, the low will be 15 to 30 degrees behind your left hand.) Low-pressure systems are the source of most inclement and unsettled weather, and weather systems tend to track west to east. Thus, if the nearest low is to your west, you can expect the weather to deteriorate. If it's to your east, you have reason to hope that the weather will improve. This rule of thumb is no substitute for an official forecast, but it's useful nevertheless.

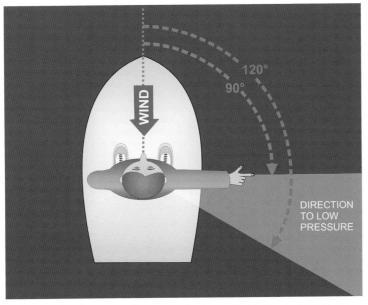

Estimating the direction to the center of a low in the Northern Hemisphere.

Sea Breeze

Along virtually any coastline it's possible for sunshine to raise the temperature of the land to the point that it heats the overlying air. That warm air then rises and creates a pressure differential, which causes cooler, denser air from over the water to flow—often powerfully—toward the shore. The strength of the sun, the temperature of the water, the local topography, and the strength of the **gradient wind** (i.e., the wind caused by large-scale weather systems, as opposed to local heating) are among the factors that determine what happens in each case, but some of the best breezes in many sailing areas are sea breezes. San Francisco Bay and the waters off Fremantle, Australia (where the afternoon sea breeze is called "the doctor" for the relief it brings from heat), are two of the more famous.

On the other hand, it could be enjoying a stationary wind band that you'll have to tack to find. And if it's burying its lee rail or putting in a reef, maybe you should reef before that stronger wind reaches you.

Harder to interpret but still useful are boats at anchor, trees, clouds, or reeds along the shore. But always look first at the wind on the water. Whether as inch-high ripples or 4-foot waves, the wind pushes the water downwind. When a strong wind blows the tops off waves it's easy to trace the trail of foam downwind, but even cat's paws on flat water are great indicators of which way the wind is blowing. The scalloped crests of the ripples will array themselves more or less at right angles to the wind's direction. Study the ripple pattern with that in mind, and you'll see where the breeze is coming from.

You'd like to know not only what the wind is doing now, but also what it's going to do. By looking at the water to windward you'll find clues. Puffs show up as dark spots on the water. Study the time it takes a puff to get to you. Estimate the strength of the puff and try to get a feel for what increased wind speed looks like on the water. When you're close hauled, try to gauge whether an approaching puff is going to head you farther away from your destination or lift you closer. Those approaching from off the bow are headers, and those coming in more from abeam are lifts. When you're sailing downwind, a puff from astern is a lift, while one from the quarter is a header.

When you're wallowing in a flat calm on a glassy sea, a patch of breeze ruffling the water is visible from a good distance. Watch it over time. Is it spreading and building—i.e., is it filling in? If it is you'll be able to tell, and you can position your boat to receive it as soon as possible.

Sailing the Groove

Sailing is a balancing act. A boat's forward motion is generated from the resolution of the wind's force—which acts more sideways than forward—with the water's resistance—which resists the boat's sideways motion much more than its forward motion. Water resistance slows us down, yet without it we'd go nowhere but sideways.

Trimming a sail is likewise a matter of balance. You trim a sail to prevent it from luffing, but if you trim it too far it will stall. Steering, too, involves an equilibrium—the rudder directs the boat, but rudder action also slows the boat. It takes time to recognize the forces at work behind a sailboat's seemingly haphazard tipping, sliding, and luffing, but the effort is well worthwhile.

As you develop a mental image of the forces at play, you begin to replace intellectual responses with instinctive ones. You get in sync with your boat. Sailors who have developed instinctive mastery aren't superhuman; they're just a few clicks farther down the nautical road than the rest of us. And the road is ridiculously simple: Identify the forces in play, read their relative strengths, and balance them. In other words, find the groove and sail it.

The Upwind Groove

Sailing upwind, sailing close hauled, sailing to windward, tacking to windward, beating to windward, sailing to weather—they all mean the same thing. No matter what you choose to call it, you accomplish it by trimming the sails as far in as they can come without stalling, then heading as close to the wind as you can sail without luffing or killing your speed.

When you're sailing close hauled, heading up is good because it points you closer to

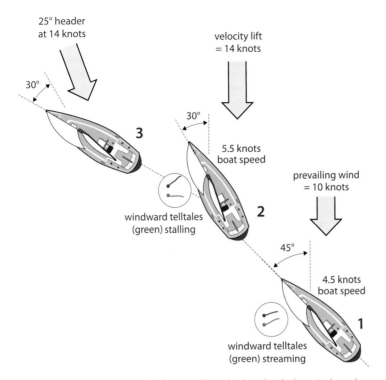

25° header
at 14 knots

30°

3

velocity lift
= 14 knots

30°

2

5.5 knots
boat speed

windward telltales
(green) stalling

prevailing wind
= 10 knots

45°

4.5 knots
boat speed

1

windward telltales
(green) streaming

Playing the puffs close hauled. 1. *A sailboat is close hauled on starboard tack, making 4.5 knots in a 10-knot breeze. With good trim and sail shape the helmsman is sailing 45 degrees off the wind, with the jib luff's windward tell-tales streaming aft but lifting slightly above the horizontal.* **2.** *Then a 14-knot puff rolls in. The true wind direction remains steady, but the higher wind ve-locity moves the apparent wind aft—a so-called velocity lift—and the boat is able to head up another 15 degrees. This causes the windward jib telltales to stall and even induces a luff in the forwardmost portions of the jib, but that's actually good because it reduces the boat's heeling angle. Despite the luffing the boat picks up speed and eats ground to windward.* **3.** *As boatspeed in-creases to 5.5 knots and the wind velocity drops back toward 10 knots, how-ever, the apparent wind moves forward again, forcing the helmsman to bear off a little, and he's more or less on his previous baseline course when a new puff comes in. Once again the wind velocity jumps to 14 knots, but this time it's a 25-degree header. The greater wind strength enables the helmsman to sail, at least momentarily, just 30 degrees off the wind, but even so he must bear off 10 degrees from his previous baseline course. This constant process of nibbling to windward in a puff or a lift and bearing off as necessary in a lull or a header is what staying in the groove when close hauled is all about.*

head down, the boat heels more and heads farther from your target, but it also speeds up. These interactions suggest the nature of the groove when sail-ing upwind, and it's really quite simple: **You can point higher in the puffs than in the lulls.**

The formula works because it neatly balances the forces involved. The power added by a puff compensates for the power lost by pinching. Thus, when you head up into a puff, the strength of the puff lets you maintain most of your speed, while the depowering effect of heading closer to the wind keeps you from heeling excessively or needing to spill wind from the sails. As the puff subsides, you can maintain your boat speed by heading down to widen the wind's angle of attack on your sails and thus increase its force. It's a rhythm that gets the most from the conditions.

Bear in mind, however, that the puff may be a header. If it is, pointing higher in the puff does not mean you can head up from your baseline course. You may in fact have to bear off—but not as much as you would if the wind headed you without in-creasing in velocity at the same time.

your target, but heading down is also good because it adds power and speed. So how do you bal-ance "up" and "down" when sailing to windward? Do you travel farther at a faster speed,

or a shorter distance at a slower speed? Which gets you to your destination sooner?

When you head up, the boat slows down and loses power. It also straightens up. When you

The Downwind Groove

Heading directly with the wind, while not a no-go proposition like heading directly into the wind, is slow. Whether you call it **running, sailing downwind,** or—like the old schooner-men—"chasing away before it," it also puts you on the edge of a jibe, requiring a constant watch for signs that the main boom might be about to swing across the boat. The considerations are similar to those you face when beating: should you go direct and slower or roundabout and faster? Even if your target is directly downwind, it's often faster (and safer) to take advantage of the extra boatspeed you'll gain by heading up from a run to a broad reach and **tacking downwind**—sailing first on one tack, then (after a controlled jibe) on the other. Even though you travel a longer distance, you can often get where you're going more quickly by tacking downwind.

Notice that the tables are turned when you're sailing downwind. Now it is heading up that makes you faster but forces you to sail farther, whereas heading down makes you slower but cuts distance. The formula here is opposite what it is for upwind sailing: **Head up in the lulls and down in the puffs.**

By heading up—by **heating up**—you move the apparent wind forward, and in so doing you increase its speed (which is the vector sum of the true wind speed and your boat's speed). A puff lets you head back down (closer to your target) because the force it adds moves the apparent wind forward.

If you're in a catamaran or planing monohull, the rule of thumb is to put the apparent wind on the beam and go. In other words, sail as "deep" toward your target as you can while keeping the apparent wind angle at 90 degrees. This puts the boat at its best, and the best performance of a catamaran or planing multihull can be

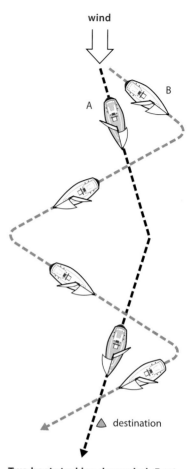

Two boats tacking downwind. *Boat A is deviating less than 20 degrees from a dead downwind course and has its jib wung out opposite the mainsail. In a monohull sailing at close to hull speed in a fresh breeze, this is probably close to the ideal angle for fastest arrival at the destination, but it's not hot enough for a light to moderate breeze. Boat B is sailing a much hotter angle, deviating 40 degrees from dead down-wind. This jibing angle might be justified if B is a multihull or a high-performance monohull capable of planing, or if the wind is extremely light, but otherwise B is likely to arrive at the destination after A, having sailed a greater distance to get there.*

Velocity Lifts

Another way of thinking about the upwind groove is that a puff increases the true wind's velocity relative to your boat's speed and therefore swings the apparent wind farther aft, enabling you to head up. Sailors call this a **velocity lift**, because the puff widens the apparent wind angle even if it doesn't change the true wind's direction. The conclusion remains the same: Head up in the puffs and off (i.e., down) in the lulls.

Cat's-Paw Puffs

When a puff of wind is descending in addition to blowing horizontally, it forms a **cat's paw**, the leading edge of which will be a header. The northwesterly breezes that herald the approach of a high-pressure cell over New England are typical. This northwesterly air is sinking, and as it moves from land over water it tumbles to the water surface in cat's-paw gusts. This is one time when an increase in wind velocity will not give you a lift—at least not right away. You'll be headed on the leading edge of the puff, but as the puff moves past you'll get a lift on its trailing edge. Sailing in these shifty conditions can be a challenge.

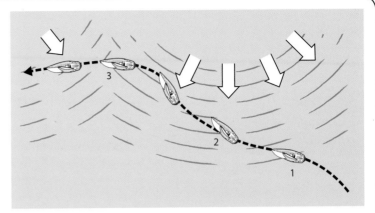

Sailing through a series of cat's-paw gusts like this one requires constant course adjustments. The leading edge is a header (1), but the trailing edge is a lift (2). That feels good for a few seconds, but when the next leading edge arrives (3), you might be pointing so high that your jib backs, forcing you into a tack you didn't intend to take. You have to be poised to react swiftly when sailing in these conditions.

Reaching

Heading up in the lulls and down in the puffs works well not just when running, but when sailing on a reach as well. Unlike when sailing downwind, however, you can maintain a good reaching speed while pointing more or less at your target, so you should steer the puffs in broad scallops rather than marked zigzags. If the wind is gradually dropping, sail a bit below your destination initially so that you can round up toward it and maintain a hotter angle at the end of the leg. In a building breeze, head a bit above your destination initially so as to maintain a hotter angle, then ride the apparent wind down as it moves forward.

In a very light breeze, when wringing power from any zephyr that chances along is your main concern, you'll find

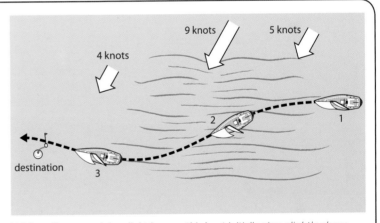

While sailing a reach in a light breeze, this boat initially aims slightly above the destination (1) so as to maintain as much apparent wind and boatspeed as possible, hoping for a header, a puff, or both on which to sail back down. When the boat gets its puff it rides the puff down (2), which keeps it in the stronger wind as long as possible and also carries it below the destination. This enables the boat to heat up near the end of the reach (3), thus preserving some apparent wind if the true wind drops.

it doubly advantageous to head down in the puffs and up in the lulls. The former will maximize a puff's duration, while the latter will add apparent wind when you need it most and will get you to the next puff that much faster.

three times its speed when sailing dead downwind.

In most monohulls, however, the speed gains of heating up are only a fraction of the boost that a high-performance catamaran gets. Thus, deviating any more than 20 to 30 degrees from a downwind course usually means adding more distance than your increased speed will justify. The stronger the breeze, the less speed a monohull gains by heating up. Reduce your downwind tacking angle accordingly, but maintain enough of an angle to keep your jib filled and drawing. If you head down too far the jib will be blanketed by the main.

Using Mainsail Controls

Despite the alluring array of mainsail controls you may have at your command, far and away the most significant factor in the sail's performance is how you trim it. A sail derives its power from the flow of air along it, and its angle to the wind—its so-called **angle of attack**— affects that flow more than any other single factor. Since you establish that angle with the mainsheet, it's safe to say that the sheet controls at least 90% of the sail's efficiency. What my father told me all those years ago remains true: "Let it out 'til it luffs, trim it in 'til it stops."

To wrest from the mainsail its remaining 10% of efficiency, however, you'll need those other controls. Use the halyard, downhaul, or cunningham (when available) to adjust luff tension; the outhaul to adjust foot tension; a boom vang (when available) to adjust leech tension; and the backstay (if adjustable) to flatten or deepen the sail. We introduced the more universal of these controls in Chapter 2. Now is a good time to look at them a bit more closely.

Mainsail Shape Upwind

Sailing close hauled, seek the optimal balance among power, close windedness, and weather helm. That balance will change with the conditions, and you are always dealing in trade-offs. The three aspects of sail shape you can control are its fullness, or depth; the fore-and-aft distribution of that depth; and the amount of twist in the leech.

Depth refers to a sail's degree of curve, or **camber**, as it would appear to you when sighting straight up from the boom. The deeper the sail, as we saw in Chapter 2, the greater is its maximum **draft**, measured as a percentage of the chord length from luff to leech. A mainsail carrying a draft of 10% is considered a flat sail, while one with a draft of 15% is full. A deeper shape is more powerful, while a flatter shape depowers the sail and enables your boat to stand up straighter and point higher.

Tighten the outhaul as the wind builds to flatten and depower the sail's lower portion. Loosen the outhaul to make the sail fuller and more powerful when the breeze is light or you need to power through a chop.

Bending the mast also flattens the main. In masthead rigs the headstay counterbalances the backstay, so the first thing you accomplish by tightening the backstay is to take slack out of the headstay, which flattens the jib or genoa. Further back-

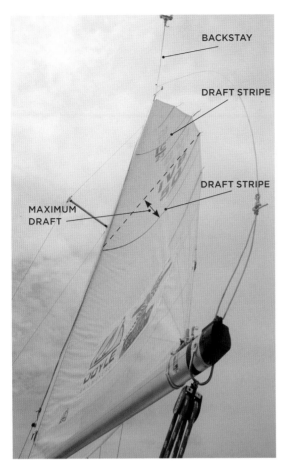

BACKSTAY

DRAFT STRIPE

MAXIMUM
DRAFT

DRAFT STRIPE

MAXIMUM
DRAFT

Mast bend is easily induced with backstay tension on the fractionally rigged IC-24. (See page 77 for a photo of the adjustable backstay on this boat.) At left we see close-hauled trim with moderate backstay tension. The draft stripes show generous camber and a powerful shape. At right the backstay tension has been increased, bending the mast, and the result is a flatter, less powerful sail.

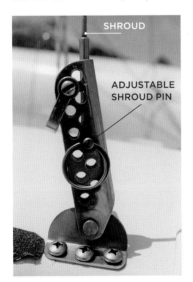
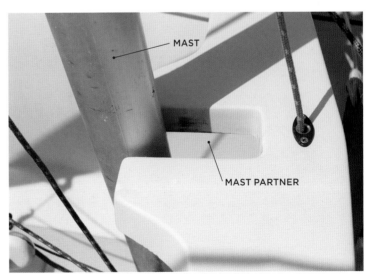

SHROUD

ADJUSTABLE
SHROUD PIN

MAST

MAST PARTNER

The 420 sailing dinghy has no backstay, but the spreaders are angled aft, making it possible to induce mast rake with the shrouds. To facilitate this, the shrouds are easily adjustable (left) and the mast is free to move aft in its partner (right). To rake the mast aft, reduce jib halyard tension and increase the shroud tension, then retighten the jib halyard as necessary. Mast rake is helpful in a fresh breeze, as is greater rig tension.

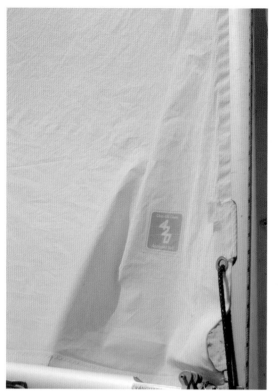
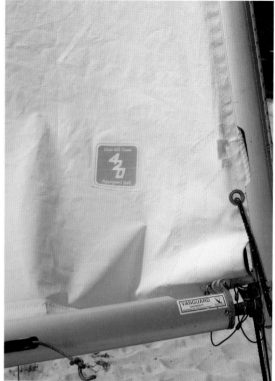

Light cunningham tension (left) and slightly greater tension (right) on a 420 mainsail. (The sail is luffing in both photos.)

MAINSHEET

TRAVELER CAR

TRAVELER

Moving the mainsheet lead to windward on this cruising sailboat brings the main boom close to the boat's centerline for maximum close-hauled pointing ability. Most racing sailboats mount the mainsheet traveler in the cockpit rather than on the cabintop, making it easier and more convenient to play the traveler in puffs and after each tack.

What about the Vang Upwind?

The primary purpose of the boom vang (assuming your boat has one) is to keep the leech tight when the mainsail is eased off the wind. When close hauled in a light breeze, loosen the vang (so that it doesn't close the leech and stall the sail) unless your boom is so limber that it bends upward. You can take the slack out of the vang to help limit leech twist in a moderate breeze, but on most keelboats you don't want much vang tension close hauled.

Vang tension upwind isn't often needed or desirable on a keelboat, but on a sailing dinghy like this 420 it's a useful way to induce mast bend and depower the sail. The wrinkles emanating from mast to clew in this sail indicate substantial vang tension, and you can see the resultant bow in the mast. If this is carried too far, however, it will cause the headstay to sag and the jib to become too full even as the main is flattened, and the result is an unbalanced rig.

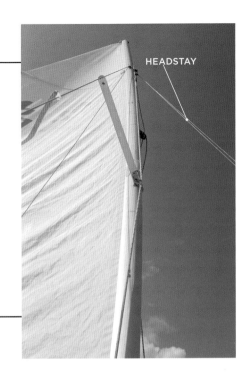

HEADSTAY

stay tension, however, bows the middle of the mast forward. On a fractionally rigged boat, mast bend is much easier to induce and more effective because the top of the mast is free to move. The mainsail, in any case, is flattened just aft of the mast as the mast bows forward.

Most mainsails are at their best upwind when their maximum draft is 40% to 45% of the chord length aft of the mast. Many mainsails have horizontal draft stripes running from luff to leech to make this estimation easy—the deepest part of the curve is where draft is greatest. As the wind increases, it forces the draft aft. If you want to keep your boat's performance optimal, you'll need to tighten the luff to counteract this—first with the halyard (until the sail is at full hoist) and then with the downhaul or cunningham. Pronounced vertical creases along the luff of the sail when full of wind are a sign of too much tension, but unless you see a few small wrinkles and get the feeling others are just bursting to appear, you've got room to crank some more. If you see vertical wrinkles when the sail is luffing that disappear when the sail is drawing, you've got it about right.

Leech twist is adjusted principally with the mainsheet (see the photos on page 100). As you trim the boom toward the centerline, you will reach a point from which further trimming will pull the

When Should You Depower the Main Upwind?

When your boat is staggering along and heeling excessively—when it's sailing "on its ear"—and when it's carrying excessive weather helm, it's time to depower the sails. You want slight weather helm, but excessive weather helm slows the boat. Bend the mast, tighten the outhaul, feather into the puffs, and ease the traveler car to leeward. If you're still overpowered, ease the mainsheet to add leech twist aloft and spill wind. If these changes (and analogous changes in the jib) don't fix the problem, it's time to reduce sail.

boom more down than in, tightening the leech and reducing twist aloft. Here, too, you must strike a balance. A tight leech is more powerful, but if it's too tight the flow of wind over the sail will stall. Also, more often than not, you'll need some twist in the sail because the stronger wind aloft will strike the top portions of the sail at a wider apparent wind angle. You have your trim about right on most boats when the sail's topmost batten is parallel with the boom and the leech telltales are streaming aft with just an occasional stall. Mast bend will also induce twist in the main's leech, but mast bend should be employed only when the wind is strong enough to make depowering the sail desirable.

With your sail properly shaped, you'll maximize your boat's pointing ability if you pull the mainsheet traveler car to windward until the main boom is nearly over the centerline. If the wind builds, you may need to ease the traveler to leeward to reduce power and relieve weather helm. Racing crews sometimes play the traveler rather than the mainsheet when sailing through puffs.

Mainsail Shape Off the Wind

You want the fullest, most deeply curved sail you can carry when you're reaching or running.

Loosen the cunningham or downhaul, and perhaps the halyard as well. Ease the outhaul and the backstay. What you are doing is allowing the main to assume the shape the sailmaker built into it. A fully curved sail bends the wind more than a flat one, developing more power. When you are sailing off the wind and let the sail out, it is pulling almost completely in the right direction, and you want it to pull as hard as it can. For reaching, then, give the sail its deepest possible draft.

The boom vang comes into its own off the wind. Easing the sheet lets the boom rise as well as go out, and that will cause the leech to twist and spill wind unless you counteract it. That's why you should add vang tension as the boom is eased, keeping a firm leech and a more powerful sail. You can ease the vang together with the mainsheet to depower the sail and reduce weather helm in puffs. If you're consistently overpowered, however, ease off the vang and let the mainsail leech twist.

Using Jib Controls

Because there are fewer controls for the jib than the main, there's more art in headsail shaping. On most boats you have just the sheets, the halyard, and the headstay to work with.

As with the mainsail, maximum draft, draft position, and leech twist are the three aspects of sail shape you can control. A jib or genoa should be a bit

fuller than the main—with a draft ranging from, say, 12% when flat to 20% when full—and should carry its draft a bit farther forward—say 30% to 40% of the chord length aft of the luff. Headsails aren't blocked by the mast or subject to interference from other sails. Get the most from yours.

Headsail Shape Upwind

Headstay sag makes a headsail fuller and adds power in light air, but a tighter headstay is de-

sirable when the wind builds in order to flatten the sail. Since headstay tension is controlled by the backstay, and since you'll want to tighten the backstay in order to flatten the mainsail as the wind builds, the jib should flatten at the same time.

You should also tension the halyard as the wind builds in order to keep the draft from being blown into the after sections of the sail. A few jibs are equipped with downhauls for further adjustment of luff tension, but this is rare.

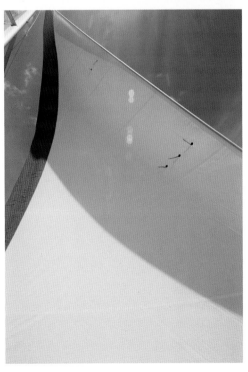

When the jibsheet lead block on this Oceanis 323 is all the way aft in a fresh breeze (above left), trimming to close hauled tightens the foot of the sail but not the leech. The leech spills open, and the upper part of the sail luffs well before the lower part (left). From another boat you can see how much leech twist there is and how poor the set of the jib is (above).

When the jibsheet block is moved all the way forward (above), close-hauled trim tightens the leech but leaves the foot deeply curved (above right and right). You cannot point well with this shape, and if you respond by overtrimming you will simply close the leech and stall the sail.

Here the block has been moved aft of center, and you can see how much this flattens the foot of the close-hauled jib. You might choose this setting to maximize pointing in a flat sea and light to moderate breeze, but you'll need to trim hard enough to keep the leech from spilling open. Or you might choose this setting in a fresh breeze (as here) to flatten and depower the jib, in which case you'll trim less closely so that the leech can open and spill excess wind. At other times, however, you will want a deeper, more powerful shape than this. You'll want the curve of the foot to more or less match the curve of the leech, which should in turn be in harmony with the curve of the mainsail leech.

On many boats the headsail sheet lead block rides on a length of track and can be moved forward or aft on the side deck. Sometimes there are two tracks on each side of the boat, one for the jib and one for a genoa. The jib may sheet inside the shrouds and the genoa outside. Whatever the configuration, moving the lead block forward or aft is the heart of good headsail trimming. Start so that the leech curve matches the mainsail curve and the sail luffs almost simultaneously along its entire leading edge when you pinch up above close hauled. (The upper inside telltales should luff just before the lower ones.) From there, moving the block forward will tighten the leech and loosen the foot, making the sail fuller with less twist—a

Leech Lines

Most jibs have leech lines (drawstring controls) running inside the sail from head to clew (see the photo on page 104). Use a leech line to control excessive leech flutter (which is called **motoring** when it really gets out of hand), but not to combat twist. A residual tremor along the leech is better than overtightening, which would cause the leech to cup and disturb the flow of air over the sail.

Self-Tacking Jibs

Some jibs have just one sheet. These headsails are called **self-tacking** because the sheet rides on a **traveler** (more traditionally called a **jib horse**) forward of the mast, swinging from tack to tack without trimming. The setup usually involves a **jibboom** (or **club**). **Self-vanging** booms like the one pioneered by sailboat designer and developer Garry Hoyt make boomed headsails more efficient, and the non-overlapping jibs on some sport boats are self-tackers, but the conventional headsail with its bridled sheets remains more versatile and controllable.

good shape for light air. Moving the block aft will tighten the foot, making the sail flatter, and will also loosen the leech, letting it spill more wind—a good shape for a fresh breeze.

Finally comes sheet tension. Trim the sail so that its shape matches the main (but with a bit more fullness). An overlapping headsail that trims outside the shrouds is trimmed too tightly when it rubs against a spreader tip aloft or a shroud at deck level. Some boats have their shroud chainplates well inboard, however, forcing you to find other clues to an overtrimmed headsail. When further trimming fails to improve your pointing ability, or when the jib is constantly backwinding the main, you're overtrimmed; ease the sheet a few inches to improve your speed without loss of pointing. Occasional signs of backwinding in the mainsail are probably fine. Ease the sheet further to induce leech twist in very light air (to keep air flowing over the sail and to account for the broader apparent wind angle aloft) or in heavy air (to open the leech and depower the sail).

Headsail Shape Off the Wind

Off the wind, the enemy is twist. Easing the jibsheet releases tension on the leech and allows the upper part of the sail to twist off to leeward. To stop this and keep the top of the sail working, move the jib lead forward when you crack off onto a reach. If your boat has provision to move the lead outboard (most don't), do that as well. The object is to chase the clew of the headsail with the sheet lead.

Headstay sag is desirable downwind, so easing the backstay tension is good for the jib as well as the mainsail off the wind. Halyard tension can also be loosened for light-air reaching, though it should remain tight enough in a fresh breeze to keep the draft forward.

Sailing Wing and Wing

When you are broad reaching or running, the wind hits the mainsail first, putting the jib in a blanket of dead air. Your choices are to lower or roll up the sail (and then perhaps to set a spinnaker), to head up until the jib fills again, or to sail **wing and wing**. The latter entails moving the sail to the windward side and trimming it via the windward sheet. You can either use a pole to hold it out to windward or sail (carefully) so the wind fills the jib on its own.

Sailing wing and wing with a crew-member serving as temporary whisker pole. The full battens show clearly in the backlit mainsail, as do the reinforcement panels at the head, tack, clew, and both reef positions.

Headsail Sheet Lead

It's hard to change the position of a headsail lead block while the sheet is under load, as this crewmember is doing. The easier approach by far is to observe the set of the jib or genoa on one tack and make the appropriate adjustment on the other side. If you notice while on port tack that the leech is too tight, move the port-side (lazy) lead block aft. Then, when you tack over to starboard, see if the set is now optimal. If it is, set the starboard-side lead block in the same position. If it isn't, move the starboard-side lead block slightly forward or aft to suit. Usually this incremental approach is all you need.

Since racing makes every sail trim adjustment more pressing, some race boats provide systems involving ball-bearing cars and high-powered tackles for moving leads under load. But there is, in addition, a handy low-tech alternative. Simply tie or clip to the clew of the headsail a short length of line that is at least as strong as the sheet. Take the line's other end aft to a convenient strongpoint, tension it, and make it fast. Now ease the "real sheet" to relieve the load. Make the change of lead position and retrim the jib. Release the temporary sheet after the change has been made.

Flying a Spinnaker

Like sailing in heavy air, flying a spinnaker is a challenge best saved until you are ready for it. The bigger the boat, the bigger the spinnaker, and the bigger the spinnaker, the more care it demands. Many sailors never fly one at all. It's a wonderful, versatile sail, however. It's hard to think of racing without one, and it can add miles and smiles to cruising. Simple in theory and demanding in practice, the "round sail" is a good sail.

Most spinnakers—which are often called chutes for their resemblance to a parachute—are constructed from ripstop nylon fabric, as opposed to the Dacron, Mylar, and Kevlar fabrics used for other sails. Nylon is marvelously light and strong, but it is also elastic, which is a disadvantage for other sails but not for spinnakers. Most spinnakers are symmetrical about a line bisecting the sail from head to mid-foot. (Asymetrical cruising spinnakers are discussed on page 236.)

A spinnaker is set **flying** (i.e., unattached to boom or stay), and that requires a lot of gear. The windward clew of the sail is held out to the wind by a spinnaker pole, the inboard end of

A J/42 sailing under a poleless cruising spinnaker on Narragansett Bay, Rhode Island, USA. See page 236 for more on poleless spinnakers.

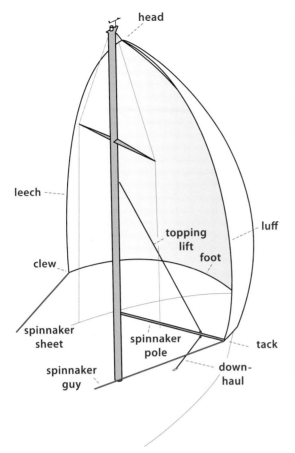

Spinnaker controls. This symmetrical sail has two clews and two luffs. To avoid confusion, however, it is customary to refer to the clew attached to the pole as the tack, and the luff opposite the pole as the leech.

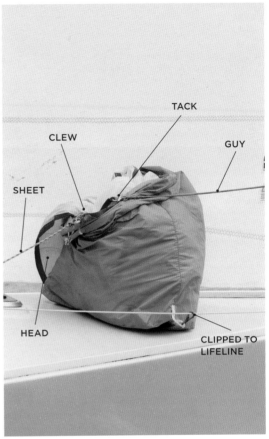

This spinnaker is packed and ready to hoist. The bag is clipped to a lifeline on the leeward side deck or foredeck, and the sheet and guy have been clipped to the clew and tack, respectively. Now it is time to clip the spinnaker halyard to the sail.

which attaches to the front of the mast. The pole is held up by a **pole lift** (also called a **topping lift**) and down with a **foreguy** (also called a **downhaul**). The chute usually has its own halyard so it can be set independently of the jib, and also because it's important that there be a working swivel at the top of the sail. Spinnaker sheets control the sail's clews, with the windward sheet being called the **afterguy** or simply the **guy**. You might also use a special launching bag, or **turtle**.

Hoisting

The mantra for flying a spinnaker is to keep it outside everything. It flies in front of and outside the mast and rigging, and the sheet and guy should be rigged outside the shrouds and quite possibly the

Hoisting the spinnaker on a 420 sailing dinghy. 1. *The crew leads the guy (i.e., the afterguy) through the spring-loaded jaw in the spinnaker pole's outboard end.* **2.** *Then he prepares to attach the pole's inboard jaw to the ring provided for it on the front face of the mast. If you look carefully you will see that it is the spinnaker sheet—not the guy—that runs around the headstay before being attached to the sail. This configuration requires the crew to raise the spinnaker to windward of the jib, where it is harder to control, though it does confer the advantage of not requiring the crew to lead the spinnaker halyard around the headstay and under the skirt of the jib before attaching it to the spinnaker. Windward hoists are popular for sailing dinghies, but larger boats typically choose a leeward hoist for greater control.* **3.** *The pole is deployed, and the crew is ready to hoist the chute. On this boat the spinnaker pole topping lift and downhaul (i.e., the foreguy) are a single length of line that clips to the pole at midlength.* **4.** *The crew hoists the spinnaker.* **5.** *Having hoisted to windward of the jib, the crew now struggles to sheet the spinnaker around the headstay and to leeward of the jib, a difficulty he could have avoided by running the guy instead of the sheet around the headstay before attaching it to the chute, then hoisting to leeward of the jib. The helmsman could help matters now by bearing off to a more nearly downwind course. Simply put, a windward set is difficult unless the boat is sailing almost directly downwind—and even then it's easier if you take the jib down first.* **6.** *Success! The spinnaker fills ahead of the forestay, and now it is time to focus on efficient trim.*

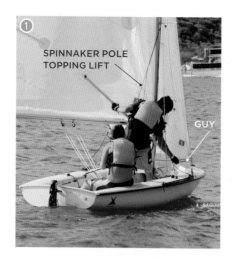

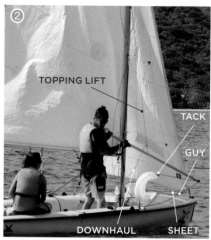

lifelines. I begin spinnaker lessons by setting the sail in a very light breeze (under 8 knots) at the dock or mooring, because it's easier to see how the sail works when you're not trying to go anywhere. Point your boat downwind and tie her by her stern. Pack the spinnaker as described on page 234, then place the bag or turtle on the leeward foredeck, forward of the leeward shrouds (your choice of "windward" and "leeward" sides is likely to be arbitrary in this instance). Tie the bag in place, as you won't have hands enough to hold it while you hoist the sail. Attach the halyard to the spinnaker's head. Lead the sheet from the cockpit outside the leeward shrouds, then attach it to one clew of the sail. Lead the guy from the cockpit outside the windward shrouds, in front of the headstay, then back along the leeward foredeck to attach to the sail's other clew. Set the pole on the windward side, secure the pole lift and foreguy, and drop the afterguy through the jaws in the end of the pole. You're ready to hoist.

You don't want the sail to fill with wind until it's hoisted, because that makes it hard to hoist, but neither do you want it to hang loose and wrap. The solution is to pull the bottom corners apart as the sail goes up, but not so far apart that the sail fills prematurely. It's an art acquired through a number of sets. Often, in practice, the chute is set behind the jib or mainsail, which makes it easier to set but harder to see.

Trimming

Once the halyard is at full hoist and cleated, it's time to pull in the guy until the windward clew fetches up on the pole. Assuming you hoisted to leeward (not to windward as in the accompanying photos—the more difficult approach), this will move the windward luff of the spinnaker around the headstay and to the boat's windward side, where it belongs. Keep trimming the guy until the pole is perpendicular to the apparent wind. If you find the guy hard to trim, it usually means that the sheet is too tight. Get some slack into the sheet, and the guy should come around easily enough. Once the pole is square to the wind, you can trim the sheet so as to fill the sail and then make it flatter and more stable. The sail will fill with impressive suddenness and energy in any kind of breeze and will then

SHEET

GUY

TOPPING LIFT

Hoisting the spinnaker on an IC-24 fractionally rigged keelboat. 1. *The fact that the bag is on the foredeck suggests that this will be a windward hoist. (A leeward hoist—the preferred method on a boat this size or larger—works better when the bag is farther aft, abreast the mast.) Therefore it is the sheet—not the guy— that is led around the headstay.* **2.** *The crew has led the guy through the spinnaker pole jaw, attached the pole to the mast, and is rigging the pole topping lift.* **3.** *The pole has been adjusted to horizontal using the topping lift and downhaul, and all is ready for the cockpit crew to start hoisting. Note that the guy runs outside the shrouds and lifeline, and the same is true of the sheet on the other side. If this were to be a leeward instead of a windward hoist, the spinnaker bag would be abreast the mast on the port side (for a starboard-tack hoist) rather than on the starboard foredeck, the sheet would lead aft outside the shroud and lifeline from spinnaker clew to cockpit, the pole would be exactly where it is now, and the guy (instead of the sheet) would be leading around the headstay and aft to attach to the chute.* **4.** *The hoist has begun.* **5.** *While hoisting continues, the trimmer tries to get the clew around the headstay by hauling on the sheet. But this is the drawback of a windward hoist, especially on a keelboat. Note the hourglass in the sail. This will probably come out—it's why you want a swivel between the head of the sail and the halyard—but it may not come out easily.* **6.** *Finally got it!* **7.** *It is customary on a keelboat to take the jib or genoa down when the spinnaker is flying. This simplifies spinnaker trim and handling—especially jibing—and when you're well off the wind the headsail is doing very little anyway.*

③

SPINNAKER
HALYARD

TOPPING
LIFT

DOWNHAUL

GUY

GUY   SPINNAKER HALYARD   SHEET

④

⑥

⑦

begin to pull like an elephant. Now it's time to trim for fine-tuning. Ease the sheet to put more belly and power into the chute, but trim it again when you see the windward shoulder begin to curl and collapse. Wait a few seconds, then ease again. Try to keep the hint of a curl in the shoulder, so you know the chute is as full and powerful as you can make it. Ease, then trim. Ease, then trim.

When cruising with a chute I like to cleat the guy and make adjustments to trim with the sheet and by changing course, but even in that case it's essential to keep the pole at least roughly perpendicular to the apparent wind. If the pole is too far aft, the windward edge of the sail loses all stability and will collapse. If the pole is too far forward, on the other hand, the sail will oscillate and swing out to weather, and will lose much of its pulling power besides. In shifty breezes, or in a boat that planes or accelerates fast enough to change the apparent wind rapidly, positioning the pole can be a full-time job.

The pole should be horizontal in order to push the sail as far out from the boat (and the dead wind behind the mainsail) as possible. Ideally, both clews should be the same height above the water.

Spinnaker trim on a 420. 1. *The mainsail position suggests this boat is sailing almost directly downwind, which means the spinnaker pole is too far forward. Trim the guy to move it aft until it's square to the wind, easing the sheet as necessary.* **2.** *The same spinnaker trim as seen from ahead of the boat. The spinnaker clews are too close together. Trimming the pole aft will move the tack to windward and open the foot of the sail.* **3.** *This looks better; the pole has been trimmed aft and the spinnaker clews are a bit more open as a result, for a more efficient shape. The pole should be raised a bit with the topping lift, however.* **4.** *Once the guy and pole are correctly trimmed, the crew eases the sheet until the spinnaker's windward shoulder begins to curl as shown by the arrow. Then he trims the sheet until the curl stabilizes. Constantly testing trim this way ensures the most efficient sail shape. The pole is still drooping.* **5.** *Spinnaker trim for a beam reach. This is about as close to the wind as a boat can carry a symmetrical spinnaker, and the pole is all the way forward (though the trimmer wants to keep it from bearing too heavily on the headstay). This looks like good trim—the pole is level and so, apparently, are the clews of the spinnaker. Apart from raising the halyard those last few inches, it's hard to see how this trim could be improved.* **6.** *Beam-reach trim seen from leeward. The clews are level and well separated, the shape full but not overly so.* **7.** *Now either the wind has swung more ahead or the helmsman has headed up. Since the pole is already all the way forward, the trimmer cannot stop the luff in the chute without oversheeting it into a poor shape that will backwind the jib and mainsail. Instead the helmsman will have to bear off the wind somewhat.*

Spinnaker trim on an IC-24 keelboat. 1. *The sheet and guy attach to the sail with a quick-release snapshackle.* **2.** *While the foredeck crew secures the just-lowered jib by lashing it to the lifelines, the spinnaker trimmer adjusts the sheet with his left hand and the guy with his right. He should cleat the guy as soon as the pole is properly positioned, because the guy pulls much harder than the sheet and can become too much to handle even with turns around the winch. Once the guy is cleated he can make ongoing trim adjustments with the sheet— letting it out until the luff begins to curl as previously described, then trimming in. Meanwhile the boat is flat, the pole is horizontal and looks square to the wind, and the spinnaker trim looks good except that the halyard is about 18 inches short of full hoist. (The halyard jammed when these photos were taken, and the crew was unable to get the sail all the way up.)*

Jibing

If you want to turn from a broad reach on one tack to a broad reach on the other with the spinnaker set, you will have to jibe the spinnaker. Though it might sound daunting, it needn't be difficult in practice. You have two big factors working in your favor: First, since the spinnaker's luffs are interchangeable, you don't have to jibe the sail itself. You only need to switch the pole from one clew to the other. The old sheet then becomes the new guy, and the old guy becomes the new sheet. And second, when the boat is heading directly downwind, a well-handled spinnaker will remain full even without the pole attached.

Here's how a jibe works: The helmsman turns directly downwind, and as he does the spinnaker guy is trimmed and the sheet is eased to keep the pole square to the wind. The helmsman then pauses before the wind while the mainsail is trimmed to the centerline, and while that's going on, the foredeck crew detaches the outboard end of the spinnaker pole from the guy, then detaches the inboard end from the mast. The pole is now hanging from the pole lift, while the

Jibing a 420 under spinnaker. 1. *The crew removes the inboard end of the pole from the mast ring.* **2.** *By pulling a lanyard attached to the spring-loaded piston on the outboard end of the pole, he takes the pole off the sail.* **3.** *Because the boat is sailing directly downwind, the spinnaker remains full even with no pole to support it.* **4.** *What was the inboard end of the pole on starboard tack will be the outboard end on port, and vice versa.* **5.** *Here the crew captures the new guy in the pole's new outboard end and clips the new inboard end to the mast ring.* **6.** *Now the helmsman turns to port, jibes the mainsail, and . . .* **7.** *the boat takes off on a port-tack broad reach. The jib has not yet been jibed, but that incidental can be completed when convenient. Note that the jib does not interfere with jibing the spinnaker because the crew can accomplish the entire operation from behind the mast.*

Sheets and Guys

As if spinnakers don't engender enough confusion, they also introduce a situation in which the same line can be called the **sheet** on one tack and the **guy** (more correctly the **afterguy**) on the other. A sheet is a line to a sail, while a guy is a guide for a boom or pole. The leeward clew of the spinnaker is controlled by the sheet, whereas the windward clew is attached to the afterguy that runs through the jaw on the end of the pole. To make it still more confusing, the **foreguy** is the separate line that holds the spinnaker pole down.

unsupported spinnaker remains full. Next the crew clips what was formerly the inboard end of the pole to what will be the new guy, then pushes the pole out to the new windward side until he can clip the new inboard end to the ring fitting on the front of the mast. When you have trouble with this part, it's almost always because there isn't enough slack in the old sheet/new guy. Get the trimmers to give you more slack, and you should have no trouble landing the pole on the mast. Meanwhile the helmsman is completing his jibe and the mainsail is swinging out on the new leeward side. When well choreographed, the entire maneuver is smooth and almost effortless.

Jibing a keelboat spinnaker. 1. *The foredeck crew takes the inboard end of the pole off the mast and . . .* **2.** *clips it to the port-side spinnaker sheet, which will become the guy once the jibe has been completed. Meanwhile the helmsman has turned directly downwind and has trimmed the mainsail to the centerline. Note that he is holding all the parts of the mainsheet in his fist—a faster and more convenient way to corral the mainsail than by simply hauling on the free end of the sheet.* **3.** *Once the foredeck clips the new inboard end of the pole to the mast . . .* **4.** *the helmsman turns to port and lets the mainsail out to starboard.* **5.** *All that remains is to trim for the new point of sail. Here the pole has been squared to the wind and the new sheet eased until the luff begins to curl. It's easy to imagine how much more difficult that foredeck work would have been if the jib had been flying.*

Dousing the spinnaker on a 420. 1. *Due to its small chute and manageable loads, dousing aboard a small center-boarder should be easy.* **2.** *The crew slacks off the halyard while retrieving the spinnaker beneath the main boom.* **3.** *Here the spinnaker is almost wholly retrieved, yet the crew has not yet eased the guy. Slacking the guy is the first thing to do when doing a leeward takedown on a keelboat. That enables the crew hauling on the spinnaker sheet to gather it in beneath the main boom as the halyard is lowered.*

Lowering

Dousing the chute should be easier than setting it. If you are racing, begin by setting the jib that you will use next. Even when cruising it makes sense to roll out some jib to help blanket the spinnaker. Release the guy and let it run free, taking the pull out of the sail. Now gather the sail in to leeward, from the sheet corner, bringing it aboard as the halyard is lowered. On most boats the gathering is done aft of the leeward shrouds, beneath the main boom.

Packing the Chute

To assure that the spinnaker comes out of the bag cleanly, you must pack it cleanly into the bag. Beginning at any one of its three corners, gather one edge of the sail (luff or foot) in pleats and accumulate the pleats in your hand. Go all the way around the sail in this fashion. You've now traced all three edges of the triangle and have all three edges in your hand, with the body hanging beneath, so nothing should be twisted. Next feed the body of the sail into the bag or turtle, keeping the corners uppermost. You can stow the packed sail like that, with the emergent corners ready to receive their lines. When it's time to set the spinnaker, attach sheet, guy, and halyard to their respective corners and pull!

Stops

You might wonder what sort of turtle was used on the classic, majestic J-class yachts and other monster racers to house their acre-large chutes. Many big spinnakers and most spinnakers set in heavy air are set in stops. The sail is stretched taut on deck or ashore, the clews are brought together, and the rest of the sail is rolled on itself to form a tight tube head to foot. The tube is then tied in place with fragile twine. This "rotten cotton" is made just strong enough to hold the tube in place until the sheets are attached. The crew would hoist the tube, bring it to the pole, and then pull on the sheets to break the twine and set the sail free.

Spinnaker Turtle

The name undoubtedly originated because a packed chute with head and legs poking out of one of these looks very much like a tortoise. The idea is the opposite, however— to be hare-like in the speed of your spinnaker sets thanks to this pre-organized bag. They come in many forms, but turtles generally take advantage of a particularly suitable place to rest (like on the bow pulpit or hung from the lee shrouds), and they make it simpler to tell which part of the sail goes where.

Spinnaker Shackles

In theory a well-packed spinnaker should go up cleanly, but hourglass wraps are common in practice. If and when your spinnaker wraps, the standard cure is to pull down on the two lower corners so as to force the twists up the sail. That cures the problem only if there is a swivel on the spinnaker halyard, and then only if that swivel actually turns. Most spinnaker head fittings have some sort of swivel. Couple this with a swivel shackle on the halyard, and you have good insurance that the sail will be free to spin out its twists and set properly.

A shackle that opens easily under load is a must for attaching sheet and guy to the spinnaker. That way, if the sail should ever overpower the boat and the guy or sheet can't be released in the cockpit, you can detach one or the other from the sail and allow it to fly free. Remember, a spinnaker won't pull unless all three corners are anchored, and that's the key to corralling a renegade sail. Lanyard releases have given way to trigger release shackles that can be activated by jamming a finger (or a fid) onto the trigger.

Cruising Spinnakers

A symmetrical spinnaker with its pole is a big, majestic offwind sail, but on a boat over 30 feet long it can also be a bit intimidating, especially for a shorthanded crew. That's why cruising sailboat crews often prefer an asymmetrical cruising spinnaker, which can be flown without a pole and is easier to handle. Unlike a conventional spinnaker, a cruising spinnaker has a definite luff and leech, the former being somewhat longer than the latter. Because a cruising spinnaker is intermediate in shape and size between a big genoa and a symmetrical spinnaker, one of its early brand names, Gennaker (now standard usage), is particularly apt.

The sail can be set with a spinnaker or genoa halyard. Its tack pendant should lead to a turning block on the foredeck at the base of the headstay, and from there aft to the cockpit. The sheet should run outside everything from the clew to a turning block aft, then forward to the cockpit. The easiest way to raise or douse the sail is to bear off nearly to a run, then hoist or lower in the lee of the mainsail. On boats over 30 feet long, a **sock** is a good idea. This is a fabric tube that you pull down over the sail by means of a control line to collapse it for dousing, and pull up to the top of the sail after hoisting to allow it to fill. When dousing, you may have to release the tack pendant to collapse the sail and slide the sock down over it.

Like a jib or genoa, the cruising spinnaker will have a lazy sheet, which should be led around (forward of) the headstay. To jibe, you ease the active sheet until the sail collapses, bear off directly downwind, trim the mainsail to the centerline, complete the mainsail jibe, then haul the cruising spinnaker's clew around the headstay with the new active (old lazy) sheet to fill it on the other jibe.

An asymmetrical spinnaker is effective as much as 155 degrees off the apparent wind and can be carried up to a beam reach or perhaps even a close reach if the breeze is light enough. On a close reach the tack should be hauled down close to the foredeck to straighten the luff, but on a broad reach the tack should be 2 to 5 feet above deck, depending on the length of the boat, and should certainly be above the bow pulpit.

TACK PENDANT

A cruising spinnaker on a Lagoon 38 catamaran sailing along Croatia's Dalmatian coast. A catamaran offers the option of tacking the spinnaker to the windward hull, making the sail more effective on a very broad reach.

Sailing in Tight Quarters

When maneuvering through an anchorage, sailing in a channel, or approaching a dock, you want full control. Even before you determine your boat's characteristic turning radius, glide distance, and handling traits, consider some general principles:

- **You can always head up, but you can't always head down.** This is due to weather helm. Almost all sailboats, left to their own devices, are designed to turn into the wind. That makes heading up an easy collaboration between you and your boat. To head down, however, you must overcome your boat's weather helm. You can do this by flattening the boat (because heeling increases weather helm) and by easing the sheet as you head down (because pressure on the tightly trimmed leech of the main likewise increases weather helm). Keep the jib tight, since wind in the headsail helps you head down.

  As you can see, heading down is much tougher than heading up. Objects to leeward can easily be avoided in tight quarters, but when you pass to leeward of a boat or put any obstruction to windward, remember that it's not so easy going down. Watch out that a sudden puff doesn't spin you to weather toward or into the obstacle despite your steering. Be cautious, anticipate puffs, and leave as much clearance as you can when you dip to leeward of an obstruction.

- **Keep the boat moving.** The only problem you may encounter by going to windward of an obstacle is straying into the eye of the wind. If you lose momentum, even with your sails full, you may lose steerageway—your ability to turn—and you could wind up sliding helplessly down on the obstruction instead of sailing past it. Don't pinch into the wind to try to sneak to windward of a mark or anchored boat.

  On the other hand, though you should keep the boat moving, there's no need to keep moving at full speed in tight quarters. Luff your sails partially and slow down—less than half your top speed or so should give you plenty of control and a lot more time to use it.

- **Visibility is critical.** If you can't see beneath the jib, who knows what's there? Most boats will handle well under mainsail alone, and unless your boat is one of the few that won't, it's best to

Rudder Stall

Steering power comes from water flowing over the rudder. When the boat is still, the water is still and you have no steerage. Even when you're moving you can lose steerage if the water flow separates from the rudder blade, as may happen when the rudder of a heeling boat is lifted into aerated water or out of the water altogether. Smooth, laminar, attached flow is what makes a rudder effective. A stalled rudder is a rudder that won't turn your boat. Turning the rudder too sharply can also induce a stall.

When the boat is still, you can steer by sculling—i.e., pumping the rudder to spin the stern—as we saw in Chapter 1. If you're simply sliding sideways, center the rudder. Provided the rudder is in the water, this should reattach water flow and restore your steerage. Then steer using a more gradual turn. Pinning the helm hard over will only cause the rudder to stall once again.

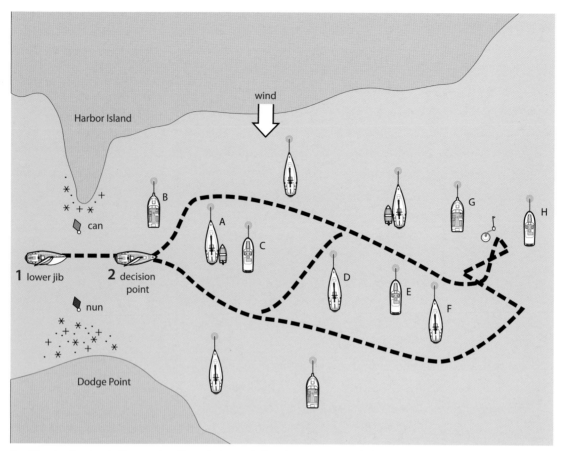

A sailboat returning to its mooring *through a crowded anchorage gets its jib down* **(1),** *then faces its first decision* **(2).** *If the skipper can squeeze to windward of boat A, the route to his mooring will be easy. But getting around boat A requires luffing upwind, and he must be sure he's carrying enough momentum to pull this off. Otherwise he might drift into boat A or B. If at all unsure he should instead sail astern of boats A and C, but he cannot skim immediately under their sterns, because a sudden puff of wind could round him up directly into boat C's transom. He must leave a wide berth to guard against this, but that in turn will make it harder to get to windward of boat D. If he can pick up enough speed and momentum while bearing off behind A's and C's sterns he may still be able to pull this off, but again, if in any doubt, he should sail astern of boats D, E, and F. At that point he will have to tack back upwind to reach his mooring, but that's far better than risking a collision. When he does finally reach the mooring, he must be careful not to overshoot it. If he does he could wind up in irons between boats G and H, which would put him at risk of bumping one or the other. As you can see, there are many inflection points in this game. When the boats are swinging at their moorings and other people in dinghies, powerboats, and sailboats are weaving through unpredictably, it can get downright interesting.*

Shooting a Mark

Sometimes on an upwind course to an obstacle you doubt you'll be able to **fetch**, or **make**, the mark (pass to windward of it). The worst thing to do is to pinch closer into the breeze. The boat slows, the **foils** (the rudder and keel or centerboard below the water, and the sails above) stall, and even though you're pointing to windward of the mark you're sliding to leeward. Instead, sail a slightly freed course (slightly below close hauled) with the sails **cracked** (eased slightly) and the boat footing. Even if your bow is pointed below the mark, you can shoot it at the last instant if you're close enough (say, within two boat lengths) and the boat is moving fast enough. Simply turn into the wind as you approach the mark and let the boat's momentum carry you to windward. When the mark is abeam, steer back off the wind to kick your stern around, and sail on. If you're more than two boat lengths to leeward of the mark, you'll have to tack around.

lower the jib before you sail in crowded waters. Not only does this give you better visibility; it also slows you down and clears the foredeck for mooring or docking maneuvers.

- **Anticipation is important.** Keep a running mental list of alternatives, escape routes, and fallbacks in case your maneuvers don't go quite as planned. Like a pilot, you're always looking for places to "set her down." Keep a sense of the space that you need to maneuver, and pay attention when anything closes in on it. Signal your intentions. Finally, keep in mind that shallow water (including long anchor rodes and underwater projections from docks and jetties) places decided limits on maneuvering space.

Braving Heavy Air

There is a distinction to be made between heavy air and heavy weather. In **heavy weather**, the mode of handling your boat is dictated to you rather than by you. **Heavy air**, on the other hand, can be not only manageable but enjoyable to sail in. Heavy weather conjures visions of storm clouds, driving rain, and towering seas, but heavy air suggests a whitecapped bay under a summer sun. Think of heavy air as a breeze that is somewhere between fresh and stiff. Heavy air is relative to the boat. In a dinghy that planes in 13 knots of wind, 15 knots will seem heavy. In a heavy cruising sailboat with a small sail plan, 25 knots may seem fresh but not heavy.

In most boats, however, there is a threshold somewhere in the 15- to 25-knot wind range that begins to feel exciting. Wind force increases with the square of wind velocity, and a jump from 14 to 18 knots means a 30% increase in force. Any breeze

Handling heavy air is enjoyable.

Onshore Wind

Wind blowing onto the land from the water will be relatively steady and pack more moisture than an offshore breeze. That makes fog a possibility. Waves are the big thing, though. Because they roll in across considerable distance with no intervening land to stop or disturb them, onshore waves are big. In deep water they should be regular and relatively smooth, with good distance between crests, but as the waves enter shallow water they pile one atop the other and increase in height and steepness.

Offshore Wind

Wind blowing over land onto water is likely to be shifty due to passing over varied terrain. The water closest to land is most protected and smoothest. High land will block wind close to the shore. Waves close inshore will be small for the given wind force, and even well offshore they will be limited in size by their limited fetch. Inshore valleys and high, smooth headlands, however, can generate **downdrafts**, or **williwaws**, that carry high-altitude air down to the water with force.

Steering Control

When a boat is moving fast or heeling a good deal, the water around the rudder may become aerated and cause the blade to begin to stall. The best way to reattach solid flow is to pump the rudder hard through about 45 degrees and then return it to the centerline.

that whips up whitecaps makes sailing more intense. It's smart to be wary.

The first decision when the breeze pipes up is whether to stay out—or to go out in the first place. Make sure you don't subject your boat or crew to strains they can't handle. Capsizing, breaking something, getting hurt—these are all possibilities, and you should weigh the odds. There are no guarantees, but sailing a well-prepared boat with an able crew in a stiff wind is not foolhardy. Sailboats come alive in heavy air, and putting them through their paces is a pleasure. On any summer Sunday on Buzzard's Bay or San Francisco Bay you'll see hundreds of boats at play in winds like these.

Make your boat as bulletproof as possible. Weak links—poorly fastened deck hardware, worn rudder fittings, etc.—tend to show up when the wind blows, and the pace of heavy-air sailing is slam-bang. A lapse that would be inconsequential in a moderate breeze might push a weak piece of gear past its redline. Look for ways to strengthen, streamline, and simplify for heavy air.

Stow gear securely, because anything that can move will move. And water will come aboard. The more watertight you are, the happier you'll be. Still, be prepared to bail. Protect yourself and your crew. You'll get wet, so dress accordingly with foul-weather gear and boots. You might even get caught out longer than you'd planned. It's not as grim as it sounds, but even those who handle heavy air routinely don't take it lightly.

Sailing upwind is work in a stiff breeze. Try to do it early and avoid a long thrash home when you're tired and wet. Sail in protected water. Looking for a **lee**—the relatively flat and sheltered water under a windward shore—is a constant in heavy weather. And stay clear of a lee shore; you want lots of safe water between you and the nearest ledge or shore in case you miss a tack, break a sheet or halyard, or suffer some other setback.

Flatten your sails to depower them as described earlier in this chapter. Trim the sheets or main traveler by hand to meet the puffs. Dump heeling pressure by easing. Trim to keep the boat moving and the sails from flogging.

Dead downwind is the most dangerous course because either an accidental jibe or a **death roll** capsize (see page 242) is possible.

Heaving-To

Exciting though it is, heavy air can tire you out. When you want a temporary respite from the hyper-alertness required for heavy-air sailing, try **heaving-to**. Tack from close hauled on one tack to close hauled on the other, but don't release the jibsheet as you tack. When the tack is complete your jib will be sheeted to windward, trying to force the bow off the wind, while the closely trimmed mainsail tries to force the bow into the wind. The result on most boats is a balance of forces that leaves your boat in a docile stasis, inching slowly ahead while nosing up and down in response to the main and jib. This tactic doesn't work well with an overlapping jib that bears on the windward shrouds and mast when backed—but then again, you shouldn't be flying an overlapping headsail in heavy air.

Try heaving-to. You'll be amazed how quiet things suddenly seem.

This IC-24 keelboat was amazingly docile while hove-to in a fresh breeze. Experiment with mainsail trim until the balance is just right.

Avoid running straight before a strong breeze. Sail on a reach broad enough to get you downwind but close enough to stabilize the boat with a bit of heeling force. Tack downwind to get to leeward, and if jibing from one tack to the other feels dangerous, tack instead to make each turn. Stabilize the main by vanging it down.

Reaching in a breeze is a blast. If you keep your boat flat, each puff will squirt her forward at top speed. Ease the boom vang to open the leech and keep the boat on her feet. Reach up toward the puffs as they approach, then ride them as long as you can.

When you're sailing upwind, feather up into the puffs just enough to defang them but not enough to kill your speed or put you in danger of backwinding the jib. The sails will luff a bit when you inch above close hauled, but that's desirable in this instance, because you're gaining ground to windward with excess power that otherwise would just be putting the boat on her ear. When you feel the puff easing up, head off again to repower. It's the best technique for sailing fast to windward in heavy air, but when waves get too big they make it hard to keep momentum going.

Negotiating the waves is important on any point of sail. Off the wind, surf them but don't bury your bow into the back of the one ahead. If your boat is small enough to respond to crew weight, move your weight aft to keep the bow up. Waves on the beam are the hardest to navigate; steer with one as it passes under

Longshore Wind

A wind blowing along the beach may have some of the characteristics of onshore or offshore winds, depending on its angle. The wave pattern is unique, however, because friction with the bottom makes the waves inshore move slower than those in deeper water. This creates jumbled beam seas that make approaching or leaving land problematic.

Lee Shore

An onshore breeze can drive sailboats onto the land. Many square-riggers were wrecked after being trapped between headlands by a rising wind, simply because they weren't close winded enough to sail clear of the bay on either tack. Modern sailboats sail well enough upwind to avoid being similarly "embayed," but even today a lee shore is a dangerous thing, leaving little margin for piloting error or gear breakage. A lee shore calls for all the sea room you can give it.

you, then round powerfully up into the next. Upwind you'd like to steer from one flat spot to another, but usually there's no direct route. Drive off to power over a big wave rather than letting it lift you and stop you.

If the breeze blows harder, think about reefing or dropping one of your sails, but until then, enjoy the heavy-air rodeo.

Becoming a Sailor

Being capable of sailing your boat away from the dock, back to the dock, and anywhere else is a major part of becoming a sailor. Knowing which sails to set and how to set them is important, too, as are finding your way and avoiding navigational hazards. But there's more.

Skipper comes from the Dutch schip, for "ship." A sailor is always prepared to be the skipper when called on, and as such you are the keeper of the ship and of all those who ship in her. That means the crew. Be as clear as you can about what you want and expect from your crew. They'll function best and be happiest if you mesh your expectations with their sailing backgrounds, strengths, and desires. A skipper's own inexperience may make it hard to foresee every eventuality, but if you make your crew a team from the outset—giving them the orientation, information, and practice they need—you'll weather whatever comes up.

You have no one to blame but yourself if your boat—even a rented or chartered boat—lacks equipment you and your crew need. See Appendix 4 for required and recommended safety gear, and before you leave the dock, check for a paddle, an anchor, a bucket, and a good, comfortable PFD for everyone aboard. All boats are required by the Coast Guard to carry a foghorn or whistle, and all sailboats with engines, cabins, or a length of 26 or more feet must carry visual distress signals (VDS). (Smaller, engineless sailboats must carry VDS only when operating after sunset.) If your boat has an engine or stove, you should carry a fire extinguisher, and if you're going to be out after sunset, you need navigation lights.

Safety is up to the skipper. Neither a VHF radio nor a GPS receiver is required equipment to have aboard, but both are desirable. The first is your best means of summoning help in an emergency, and the second is amazingly adept at telling you where you are and how to get where you want to go. There's a great case to be made for having both aboard. Lots of sailors want a depth sounder too, though some might choose wind instruments or a speedometer instead.

Calamities could happen under your command. You could lose a crewmember overboard (see Appendix 5) or suffer a dismasting, or a holing, or a fire. Skippers should think about these unthinkables. What to do in each case is important, but so is communication. How can you let everyone know what to do? What if you're the one who falls overboard? Give some thought to developing step-by-step responses to each emergency and putting them down in an "emergency procedures" notebook for all aboard to study and make use of.

If there were no rewards to balance the risks of sailing, who would sail? Risk itself is a kind of reward. Managing challenges and overcoming difficulties are at the heart of sailing. There are lots of easier ways to spend your weekend afternoons, but getting where you set out to go thanks to your ability to harness the wind and deal with the waves is a fundamental pleasure. What you accomplish out there can be traced back to your knowledge, your decisions, your skills, and your character. Sailing is pleasurable because it involves us so totally and because we express ourselves through it so completely.

The fantasy of sailing away for a year and a day has a lot to do with the sport's appeal. Once you've done some sailing, however, you might find yourself asking, "Away from where?" Yes, sailing is an escape from the digitized, mechanized realities of life in a new millennium, but "escape" means simply avoiding—running away. Sailing, whether around the buoys or over the horizon, is an escape *to* something. The law of the sea is a natural law. The elemental forces that have been squeezed out of shoreside life are still vital out there on the water. Sailing puts us in deeper touch with nature.

Tradition dictates that there be only one skipper. I can see why, but many of the best racing partnerships have blurred the lines of command. It's an open question how my wife, Carol, and I call the shots on our cruising boat. Being a skipper, in essence, means being a sailor, and the opportunity to become a sailor is available to all.

CHAPTER FIVE

Navigating

"Where are we?" "How do we get where we want to go?" Since time immemorial, these have been the two fundamental questions of navigation, and you have to answer the first before you can answer the second.

To those two questions sailors have lately added a third: "Where would we be without GPS?" It's a reasonable question. GPS, the global positioning system, has answered questions (and prayers) by the boatload since it arrived in the early 1990s, and today you can purchase for a mere hundred bucks or so a reliable handheld receiver that will "acquire" the necessary GPS satellites and triangulate your position with an accuracy closer than 100 feet. If you're sailing beyond your backyard, don't cast off without it.

Still, a true sailor has always had to be a navigator too, and a true navigator can answer the where-are-we question in any conditions with or without GPS. The answer is rarely as precise without GPS, of course, but one aspect of the art of navigating is building a sufficient margin of safety around that imprecision.

A navigator would be foolish not to use GPS whenever it's available, but it's equally foolish not to know and practice the fundamentals of chart, compass, and eyeball navigation. An anecdote will help illustrate the point.

A four-person crew begins a 21-mile race on Penobscot Bay, Maine, in thick fog. They have on board their fast 33-foot fin-keeled racer-cruiser a new handheld GPS receiver that tells them exactly where they are at all times. They do not have electronic charting software, however, so they must manually transfer their GPS latitude and longitude coordinates to a paper chart in order to locate their position relative to nearby shorelines, ledges, and buoys. This procedure takes 3 or 4 minutes with a pair of dividers and a pencil, by which time the boat is no longer precisely there, so the preoccupied navigator, who is also the headsail trimmer and tactician, tends to neglect this task.

At first that doesn't matter, because the coordinates of the first racing mark—a mid-channel bell buoy 2.6 miles to windward of the starting line—constitute one of a number of waypoints programmed into the receiver at the factory. When the navigator finds this waypoint in the receiver's memory and hits the GoTo button, the bearing and distance to the buoy are displayed. After three tacks, the boat stands out from shore on starboard tack until the bearing to the buoy nearly matches the boat's previous compass heading on port tack—which the navigator has made a point of remembering—at which point he calls for another tack. Once they are on port tack the GPS receiver indicates the buoy to be almost dead ahead, and sure enough, as the GPS range

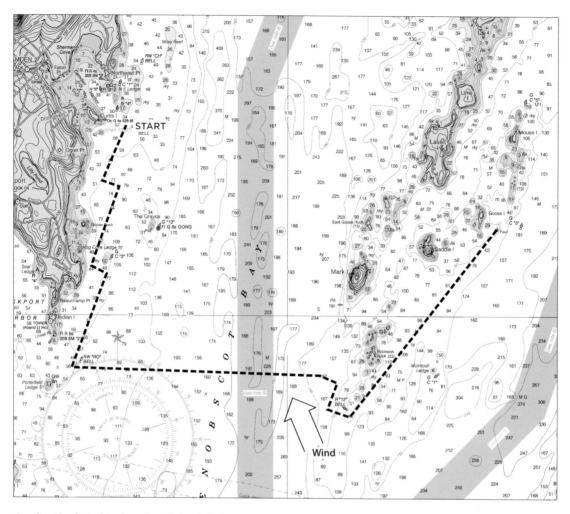

An after-the-fact plot of a sailboat's track during a race on Penobscot Bay, Maine. If the navigator had maintained this plot during the race, perhaps the last plotted leg wouldn't terminate on a ledge.

dwindles to 0.1 nautical mile, the buoy materializes from the fog ahead. The navigator is a momentary hero.

The next buoy, however, is 3.25 miles away, and it is not one of the waypoints programmed into the receiver. Using the compass rose on the paper chart (as covered in this chapter), the navigator reads the course to that buoy from the one they are now departing and gives that course—118 degrees magnetic—to the helmsman, who proceeds to steer 118 degrees by the compass. So far, so good. Now the navigator should use a pair of dividers to take the coordinates of the buoy from the chart (again, as covered in this chapter), then enter those coordinates as the next waypoint in the GPS receiver. The receiver will then give them a constantly updated bearing to the buoy so that they can make any necessary course adjustments en route.

At this point, however, a small problem surfaces. The navigator does not know how to enter waypoints into this new receiver, and the instructions have been left ashore. After several minutes of menu-surfing

The fog has closed in around this family in their small cruising sailboat. Ghosting along with barely a trace of wind, they can hear more than they can see—perhaps the throaty stop-and-go diesel of a lobster boat running from trap to trap; the deep, steady throb of a ferry engine; the regular foghorn signal of a lighthouse a few miles off; irregular air horn blasts from other sailboats like theirs, nearby in the fog; or even the gentle wash of waves on a beach not far away. In the fog your world contracts around you. Without visual references, you could steer in a circle and not know it. So this helmsman is steering a course by his bulkhead-mounted compass. He may also have a GPS receiver—either a handheld unit in the cockpit or a fixed unit in the cabin—and he should have a paper navigation chart close at hand for quick reference. If the crew hears or sees another boat closing with them, they should sound their own foghorn. And they should be sure their engine will start at a moment's notice in case they need to maneuver away from another boat or any other hazard.

and button-punching fail to solve the mystery, the navigator gives up and goes back to headsail trimming. Halfway to the mark he spots two competitors well to windward, at the limits of visibility in the fog. What do they know that he doesn't? Is the incoming tide taking his boat up the bay and thus to leeward of the mark? Without constantly updated bearing-to-mark information from the GPS receiver, the only way to be sure is to plot the boat's current latitude-longitude coordinates on the paper chart (once again, as covered in this chapter), but by the time he completes that task they will be almost to the mark. He asks the helmsman to harden up from a close reach to close hauled, but it is already too late. When the mark looms from the fog they are to leeward of it and must make an extra tack to get around it. This costs them a half-minute of time—significant but not decisive in a 21-mile race.

Rounding the mark, they begin the next and final leg of the race, a leg that is 15.5 miles long. The navigator plots a magnetic course of 60 degrees on the paper chart and gives this course to the helmsman to steer. This should take them east of a string of ledges that lie to the north. In fact, the course should take them to the can buoy that marks those ledges. The race instructions do not require the boats to leave this can to port, but doing so will keep them clear of the ledges. Still, this course leaves little margin for error. Under other circumstances the navigator would have shaped their course to a midchannel buoy farther to the east, but that would add nearly a mile of distance, and this is, after all, a race.

The can is 3.4 miles ahead, and the navigator wishes he could program it into the receiver as a waypoint, but again, he doesn't know how. The boat is on a broad reach now, and the crew debates whether to hoist the spinnaker. Will the additional boatspeed it confers be enough to justify the confusion of spinnaker work in the fog? Finally they rig and hoist the spinnaker, during which process the navigator is again too busy to plot their position on the chart, and the entire crew is too busy to maintain a bow watch.

Just as the chute fills they hit a rock that is barely awash—an eastward outlier of the ledges they were trying to skirt. They hit at 6.5 knots, damaging the hull and throwing the crew around on deck. Beyond a couple of cracked bones and a few cuts, no one is seriously hurt, but within a few hours the boat has been hauled for expensive repairs, and the crew is getting stitched up in a hospital emergency room—not where they were planning to be when the race began. Later they ascertain that the rock they hit was just west of the can buoy they were

aiming at, and which they never did see. After sailing almost 3.4 miles at 60 degrees magnetic they had wandered 0.20 mile west of their intended course. It wasn't a big error—about 5 degrees, within the accuracy limits of a steering compass—but it was enough. If the navigator could have programmed the can as a waypoint in the GPS receiver, the accident wouldn't have happened.

This story is a rich trove of lessons. Among them:

- When the navigation is tricky, the navigator should navigate, not trim headsails and spinnakers, make sandwiches, or anything else.
- The ideal crew size for racing a boat 30 to 35 feet long is at least five. If you only have four people on board, maybe you should leave the spinnaker in the bag. (While not directly affecting navigation, this factor had a big indirect effect.)
- If you're using GPS you should know how to use it—and that includes knowing how to program waypoints.
- GPS does not excuse us from traditional chart-and-compass work.

- When you're plotting courses in poor visibility, favor mid-channel buoys and buoys that make noise over buoys that brood silently over hidden hazards.
- When you're steering by the compass, remember that your course across the chart is approximate. Until you can fix your position by GPS or more traditional means (which we'll cover in this chapter), you won't know precisely where you are. Under those circumstances, a 3-mile course that takes you within ¼ mile of a submerged rock is asking for trouble. You might not find trouble, but that doesn't mean you didn't ask for it. Recognize when your position and course are imprecise, and take appropriate countermeasures to keep yourself in safe water.
- And finally, always maintain a lookout—especially in poor visibility.

What if our crew had had electronic charting capability—either from a laptop computer with digital charts and interfaced GPS or from a dedicated chartplotter? Would that have made a difference? Absolutely. Many of their competitors had electronic charting and were able to watch their progress along that line of ledges on a digital screen. This is a huge advantage, and when the system works correctly it reduces approximations to certainties, opacity to transparency. But what happens when the laptop batteries die, or the screen freezes up, or the chartplotter simply quits? Don't leave your paper charts, dividers, and parallel rules at home, and don't neglect to learn how to use them.

Many sailors feel pangs of nostalgia for the "old ways" of navigation, but frankly, the good old days of navigation weren't all that good. In the old sailing ship logs, "two days without a sight" was a terse way of describing a ship and a crew in trouble—and never more so than when they were close enough to shore to blunder into something hard and unforgiving. To read those logs and associated stories is to conjure some idea of how bad those days could be.

But the navigator remains more important than his or her instruments, and the most salient qualification of a navigator is the depth of his understanding. Your GPS receiver can give you positions and courses and can even calculate speed and leeway, but to be a good navigator you have to know more than it does. It doesn't, for example, know the difference between upwind and down, shallow and deep. It won't say if the buoy on the horizon is Waypoint 1 or the buoy just to the right of that one. It won't even say if the course home runs alongside the island or through it. Those calls are for you.

Redundancy is a cornerstone of seamanship. If you depend on something, have two of it. Carry a couple of GPS units for that reason, but also carry something besides the black box. Carry a clear understanding of navigation's basics and seamanship's cornerstones. By making yourself a better navigator, by learning how to make a move without consulting the satellites and how to function when the Lo Batt message flashes on your GPS display, you help assure that you'll know where you are, wherever you are.

Navigation versus Piloting

When the men of HMS *Bounty* took their ship from Captain William Bligh in 1789, the mutiny, as many moviegoers know, was led by acting lieutenant and second-in-command Fletcher Christian. But why were there so few mutinies in the navies of the world back then? Why didn't the shanghaied, maltreated, scurvy-prone, cat-lashed British sailors of yore revolt more often when they were far from Mother England and the long arm of the Admiralty?

One answer is that they couldn't navigate on the open sea, though many of them weren't bad at coastwise piloting. Mr. Christian was an officer, and he'd had tutelage and practice in the art of celestial navigation—of finding one's position at sea from the sun and stars. Able-bodied seamen, on the other hand, could hand, reef, and steer their ships but were more or less lost when they couldn't see land. The sextant, the hourglass, and the mathe-matical formulas needed to **reduce a sight**—to transform the time of a sextant sighting and the position of the celestial body sighted into a position at sea—were mysteries that officers kept on the afterdeck and took grave pains not to share with sailors. Knowing how to navigate gave an officer and a gentleman the upper hand over the tars sailing under him. Without Christian, the *Bounty* would have completed its humble breadfruit mission and sailed home rather than into infamy.

Navigation—the art of knowing where you are when there's no land in sight—still seems a bit like magic, cloaked as it is in the aura conferred on it by Captains Cook, Bowditch, Maury, and the other great navigators of the Age of Sail. **Piloting**, which consists of making sense of coastlines, landmarks, and charted aids to accomplish the same thing, might seem simple by comparison, but it's actually the trickier and more trying of the two. For one thing, piloting requires greater precision. An error in a sun line far at sea will show up eventually and will be corrected in time because the open ocean is, after

> ## When Is Navigation Piloting?
> Piloting comes before navigation, because you have to get from the dock to the open sea. It includes navigation, which is essentially piloting across big waters where the marks are harder to find. And it comes after navigation, because your sextant is the last thing you'll need to get you up the English Channel after you've crossed the Atlantic. To move on the water you need a pilot. Ships are accustomed to pick one up off the mouth of the channel or in the harbor approaches. Sailors take pride in being their own pilots.

In addition to a compass, the basic tools of traditional piloting include a chart, dividers, and parallel rules. Most cruising sailboats over 30 feet long have a navigator's station with a small chart table like this one on which to do your plotting. If you don't have a chart table, a dinette table, the top of the icebox, or any other flat surface will do.

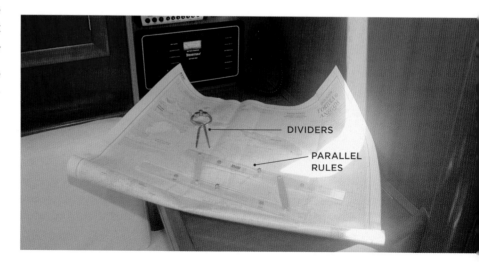

DIVIDERS

PARALLEL RULES

LANGUAGE OF NAVIGATION

Here are a few of the terms you'll encounter in this chapter.

Aids to navigation (ATONs): Also called navigation aids or navaids, these are the charted buoys, beacons, and lights that help you determine your position on the water and plot safe courses to your destinations. Navaids are discussed in Chapter 4.

Bearing: The direction from your boat to any charted feature—e.g., a navaid or landmark—or to another boat.

Course: The direction your boat is traveling. When you are unaffected by leeway and current, your course through the water and your course made good (also called the course over ground, or COG) will both be the same as your heading. When you are affected by leeway but not current, your courses both through the water and over the ground will differ from your heading. If you're sailing a heading of 90 degrees on port tack with 4 degrees of leeway, your course through the water and your course over the bottom are both 94 degrees. When you are affected by current but not leeway, your course through the water will be the same as your heading, but your course over ground will differ. If you're sailing at 5 knots on port tack toward a heading of 90 degrees while being set to starboard by a beam current of 1 knot, your course over ground will be 102 degrees.

Dead reckoning: Thought to derive from "deduced reckoning," dead reckoning (DR) entails plotting your boat's progress across a nautical chart using measured values or best estimates for boat speed, course or courses steered, and time on each course. A DR plot does not account for possible effects of leeway, current, steering error, or incorrect speed estimates, which is why a DR position should be regarded as a first-order estimate and should be confirmed by bearings, GPS, or other means whenever possible.

Fix: A known, accurate position for your boat. A fix can be obtained in various ways, as we'll see in this chapter, and when two or more independent methods yield the same result, your confidence in the fix can be very high.

Heading: The direction your boat is pointing when you sight along the fore-and-aft centerline directly over the bow.

Line of position (LOP): A line drawn on a chart such that it passes through your location. The line might be a bearing or a range, or it might be a circle of position (COP).

Navigation: The art of directing a boat from one place to another. The two fundamental components of navigation are determining where you are at any given time and knowing what course to steer to arrive at your next chosen destination.

Piloting: The art of directing a boat from one place to another by means of visible landmarks and navigation aids. Piloting is navigation done within sight of land.

Range: When two charted objects line up as viewed from your boat, you can draw a line through the objects on the chart and know with certainty that you're somewhere along the extension of that line over the water. Ranges are a fast and accurate means of locating yourself, and opportunities abound once you start looking for them. A charted water tower behind a point of land; a charted church spire behind a daybeacon; a lighthouse behind a half-tide rock—potential ranges are everywhere.

GPS and the Navigator

Today there's magic in a GPS receiver. Its powers aren't reserved for officers and gentlemen. It works on cloudy days and is as helpful in coastwise piloting as it is in open-ocean navigation. Still, though we may learn to trust what GPS tells us, we should always verify. Keep track of your position by the time-honored piloting techniques in this chapter as well as by GPS. Then, if the GPS receiver starts giving you aberrant readings, you'll notice right away, and if it stops working altogether you'll be able to carry your chart-and-compass navigation forward without interruption. A navigator who knows what he needs to know and how to get it remains the ultimate navigation tool.

all, open. Inshore, where rocks lurk and currents run harder and waves steepen and lee shores lie in wait, there is much less room for error. It may be easier to grossly approximate your position coastwise than offshore, but when you're near the coast a gross approximation is rarely good enough.

Much of the historical distinction between navigation and piloting resided in the tools they used. Navigation depended on a sextant, a timepiece, a nautical almanac, and trigonometry, whereas piloting depended on a chart, a compass, a pair of dividers, parallel rules, a tide table, and simple arithmetic.

But the distinction was always somewhat phony—a compass was invaluable at sea as well as along the coast, for example—and in this age of GPS—when the best tool for navigation and the best tool for piloting are the same—it has blurred almost to vanishing. You need to know where you are whether you're inshore or offshore. It's *all* navigation and it's *all* piloting. Any source of good information and safe courses is a good source.

Early Polynesians in open canoes transited hundreds of miles of the vast Pacific between the tiny atolls of Oceania. They navigated by the stars, by clouds, by wave patterns, by observing bird flights, and by sea lore, and they hit their targets time and again after days at sea. European sailors came along later and, using compasses, sextants, charts, and tables, were able to do pretty much the same thing. The two approaches, different as they were, demonstrate the same thing—a star, a needle, a swell, or a grain of sand is valuable if it tells you something. Masters of both traditions were distinguished by receptivity, alertness, and a capacity to learn from experience. Different though the tools of the two traditions were, the navigators they produced were a lot alike.

Where Are We?

Whether you call it navigation or piloting, this is its first and last question. If you don't know where you are, you don't know how to get where you want to go—or anywhere else, for that matter. If you don't know where you are, you are, quite literally, lost.

So where are you?

Your answer might be "a hundred yards off the dock," or "just upstream from the bend in the river," or "on the east side of Bartlett's Island." Those are all perfectly good answers.

Most of the time, when you're in familiar territory, you know where you are and can put that location into words.

Piloting is a way of giving yourself the same certainty in unfamiliar territory. Buoys, marks, lighthouses, and landmarks plus your compass and charts are the essentials. Use a depth sounder and radar if you have them, and by all means employ the magic of GPS. They're all part of answering the two-part question, "Where am I?" and "Where do I go from here?"

Finding a position starts with looking around. The shore is there, the rocks are astern, there are three buoys on the bow. From elements like these you can give yourself a rough posi-

tion on the chart. Often that's all you need to know. You can mark it on the chart—a #2 lead pencil is good for this—or file it in your head. Keep track of your approximate position. Update it. Refine it. Watch how it changes. Knowing approximately where you are is a fine and convenient thing. Practice it.

Where are we? That's easy. We're about 200 yards east of that stone monument, which you can be certain is charted. In clear weather along the coast there are always navaids or distinctive shoreline features in sight to help you guesstimate your position, and in clear weather a guesstimate is likely all you need.

Plotting a Line of Position

When you need to know more precisely where you are, you need a fix. Begin by establishing a line of position (LOP) using a charted landmark or navaid that you can see from the boat. Suppose you see a lighthouse on a nearby shore. You are somewhere along a line with you at one end and the lighthouse at the other. To assign a magnetic bearing to that line, bring the lighthouse into view directly over the card of your steering compass (as described in Chapter 4), then read the bearing to the lighthouse from the card. Alternatively—and more conveniently—use a hand bearing compass to read the bearing. Or, if you don't have a hand bearing compass and can't conveniently sight the lighthouse

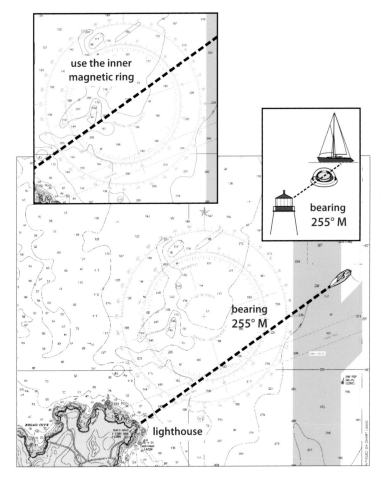

Sight the direction to the lighthouse (top right). Run that line over the compass. That gives you a bearing (255 degrees). Plot that bearing on the inner ring of the compass rose (top left). A line parallel to the line on the rose and crossing over the lighthouse gives you a line of position (above). You are somewhere along that line.

over your steering compass, point your boat's bow directly at the lighthouse and read your compass course. Let's say the bearing to the lighthouse is 255 degrees. Draw a line from the center of the compass rose on your chart through 255 degrees. (Remember to read the bearing from the inner ring of the rose, which gives directions in degrees magnetic.)

The Hand Bearing Compass

A **hand bearing compass** is a handheld magnetic compass with a built-in sight. Simply aim the sight at a landmark, navaid, or other boat and read its magnetic bearing. Hand bearing compasses cost as little as $25. Some marine binoculars contain an integral compass, which is displayed as you view a distant object, and most such units have crosshairs for accurate sighting. Like any magnetic compass, a hand bearing compass is subject to deviation caused by nearby iron-containing objects or onboard electromagnetic fields. For best results, therefore, find a location—preferably near the helm—from which your hand bearing compass gives you reliable readings in all directions, and make it a habit to use the compass from that spot. To quickly check the deviation of a hand bearing compass, point it at the bow and compare its reading with that of the steering compass.

If the two readings are close on headings in all quarters, you are in good shape. If they differ on some courses (and you know that your steering compass is accurate), try a different spot on the boat for taking bearings. If you can't find one that's free of deviation, you can build a deviation curve for the hand bearing compass as described later in this chapter for a steering compass, but this is rarely necessary. Deviations of less than 5 degrees can probably be ignored.

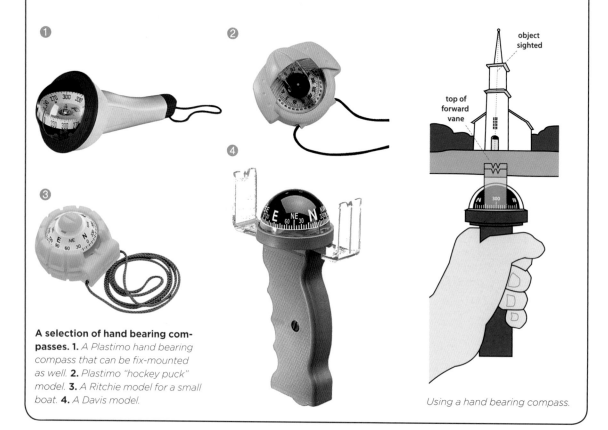

A selection of hand bearing compasses. **1.** A Plastimo hand bearing compass that can be fix-mounted as well. **2.** Plastimo "hockey puck" model. **3.** A Ritchie model for a small boat. **4.** A Davis model.

Using a hand bearing compass.

object sighted

top of forward vane

Drawing Parallel Lines on a Chart, Option 1

Perhaps the simplest tool for plotting is a set of **parallel rules**, comprising a pair of rulers joined together by two or more swinging hinges. The rules serve as straightedges for plotting courses, while the hinges allow you to "walk" the rules across a chart while keeping them exactly parallel to each other. This is an easy and accurate way to transfer a measured bearing from the printed compass rose across the chart for plotting (or a plotted course line across a chart to the compass rose for measurement, as described later in the chapter). The mechanics of the process are simple. You merely press down on one rule while swinging the other outward, then press down on the lead rule while you swing the trailing rule after it. Repeat as necessary until you get where you need to go.

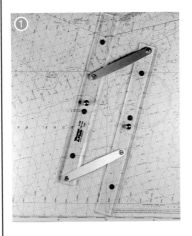 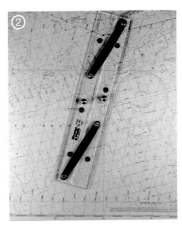 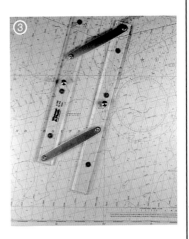

Using parallel rules to plot a bearing as a line of position. 1. *Align one of the rulers with the center of the compass rose and the magnetic bearing you sighted on deck. Anchor that rule with finger pressure and swing the other rule toward the charted object on which you just took a bearing.* **2.** *Now anchor the lead rule and swing the trailing rule up to it.* **3.** *Continue "walking" the rulers in this manner until the lead rule reaches the chart symbol for the sighted object. Draw a line of position from the symbol toward your location. You are somewhere along that line.*

Relative Bearings versus Lines of Position

Any bearing on a navaid or landmark becomes a line of position the moment you plot it on your chart. As described in Chapter 4, however, a bearing on a ship or another boat is not an LOP. All you care about is the other vessel's bearing relative to you. You might be tracking the other boat with a hand bearing compass, in which case you'll read its bearing in degrees magnetic just as you would an LOP. If you're steering 090 degrees, for example, and the other boat is 40 degrees on your bow, its bearing in degrees magnetic is 130 degrees.

But the 40-degree **relative bearing** is what matters. If the relative bearing in 5 minutes remains 40 degrees while your course has remained steady and the range to the other boat has shrunk from a mile to a couple of hundred yards, the two boats are on a collision course.

When the other boat is to starboard, you are the give-way vessel under the Rules of the Road and should slow down, alter course to starboard, or both—and your actions should be of such magnitude as to be obvious to the other boat. If you're to starboard of the other boat, the Rules designate you as stand-on boat, and you should maintain course and speed unless a collision seems likely— at which point you should take action to avoid it.

Now, using parallel rules, draw a line parallel to that one such that it passes through the lighthouse's charted location. Your boat is somewhere along that second line. You have just plotted a bearing to a charted object, which is one kind of LOP.

Drawing Parallel Lines on a Chart, Option 2

Alternatively, you can measure courses and plot bearings in degrees true using a **protractor plotting tool**. These tools are inexpensive and reliable. If you're in cramped quarters or on a small charting table, protractors can be less cumbersome than parallel rules. Plus, because a protractor scale is printed directly on the plotting tool, you won't need to access the compass rose for angles. This added flexibility is especially helpful when lack of space forces you to do your plotting on a folded chart. Murphy's Law being what it is, the nearest compass rose is always folded underneath and therefore inaccessible. The simple rectangular plotting tool shown here was designed by the United States Power Squadrons. Two protractor scales and parallel lines are printed on the template, with one for use with latitude lines and the other (printed in reverse order) for use with longitude lines.

To plot a bearing, find the sighted object (whether a navigation buoy or a landmark) on the chart, then align the plotter's edge with the object such that the plotter's bull's-eye is on a latitude or longitude line and the protractor replicates the angle of the sighted bearing. This device takes some practice to avoid reading or using the wrong scale, and it requires you to convert magnetic bearings to degrees true for plotting—all of which you can avoid by using parallel rules. Most navigators prefer parallel rules.

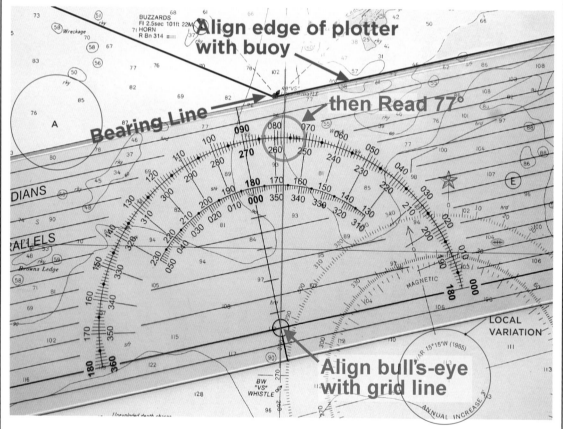

Using a protractor plotting tool to plot a bearing. *With your boat somewhere in circled region A, you take a bearing on a whistle buoy to your east. The bearing is 92 degrees magnetic. To convert that to degrees true, you must correct for the local variation, which you learn from the compass rose is about 15 degrees west. A westerly variation must be subtracted when going from magnetic to true, so your bearing is 77 degrees true. Place the protractor's bull's-eye over the nearest meridian, rotate the protractor until the appropriate scale registers 77 degrees, then slide the protractor up or down until the straightedge aligns with the whistle buoy as shown. Now you can plot a line from the buoy back to your location and know that you're somewhere on that line.*

Crossing Two or More LOPs to Get a Fix

A single line of position doesn't give you a fix, because you don't know exactly where you are along it. The simplest way to establish a fix is to cross another LOP with the first one. If your boat is on LOP #1 *and* on LOP #2, the only place it can be is where the two LOPs intersect.

There are various ways to get this second LOP. Do you have a navigation buoy, daybeacon, or other navaid in sight? If not, what about a charted structure such as a spire, water tower, or pier, or a feature of land such as the center of a hill, a bold headland, or the well-defined end of an island? Anything that's charted, stationary, and well defined will work. Take and plot a bearing on this second target just as you did the first one. Let's imagine that you take a bearing on red-and-white channel gong "PB." Draw the second line on the chart through the inside ring of the compass rose, then draw a line parallel to that one such that it runs through gong "PB." Parallel rules are a common way to do this, but there are several other methods. The point where the bearing to the light-

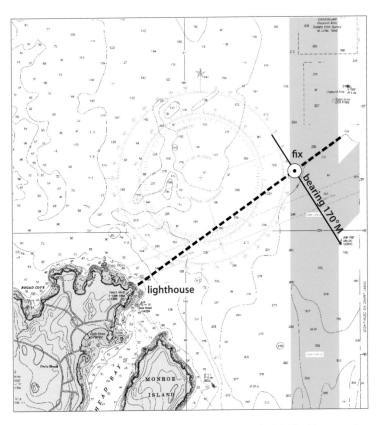

If you cross a second bearing with your first (here to the RW flashing gong), you can be reasonably confident that your location is at or near the intersection of the two bearings. You have obtained a fix, which is customarily denoted with a solid dot enclosed by a circle.

house crosses the bearing to the gong is where you are.

Not all LOPs are bearings. One of the most elegant ways of arriving at an LOP is to line up two objects that are identifiable on the chart so that they form a **range**, or **transit**. When you line up the landmarks (a charted church spire behind a daybeacon; a hilltop behind a nun buoy; the end of an island behind a half-tide rock; etc.) so that the more distant one is directly behind the nearer one, the pencil line drawn between them on the chart, if extended, will pass right through your boat. A range does not need to be plotted from the compass rose and makes a quick, convenient, and highly accurate LOP. Once you start looking for ranges, you'll see them everywhere. Cross a range with any other LOP to get a fix.

Lines that cross at close to 90 degrees yield the most accurate

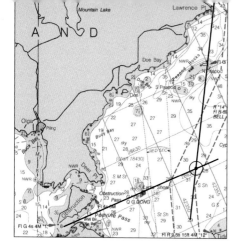

When gong "13" aligns with the south shore of Obstruction Pass and North Peapod Ledge aligns with the end of Lawrence Point on Orcas Island, Washington, you are here.

That daybeacon off to port is just about to pass in front of the bell buoy in the distance. Draw a line through their chart symbols, and when the two line up you'll be on the extension of that line.

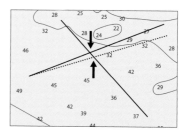

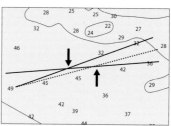

A fix is most solid when LOPs cross at right angles (top). Small angles between LOPs (above) make the position less precise.

fixes. When LOPs intersect at angles smaller than 30 degrees or larger than 150 degrees, a slight error in either one can yield a fairly significant error in the fix. Nearby targets yield more accurate readings than distant marks.

One common problem in piloting is finding on your chart the targets that you see across the water. Are you seeing *that* church spire or the one to the west of it? Is that nun "2" or nun "4"? Answering such questions often takes sleuthing, binoculars, contextualizing, and some luck. Take the trouble to be as certain as you can be.

To make a more reliable fix, add a third LOP. Triangulation diminishes the margin for error. Your boat is most likely inside the cocked-hat triangle formed when three LOPs cross. A small triangle is, safe to say, more certain than a big one. Three relatively equal angles at the corners (approaching 60 degrees) make a three-LOP fix still more trustworthy.

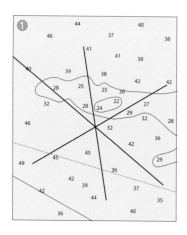

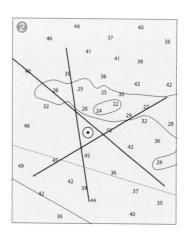

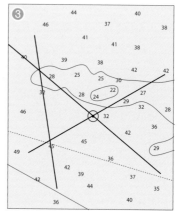

A three-line triangulation is far more certain than a simple two-line fix. *Rarely, if ever, will all three LOPs meet at the same precise point* **(1)**. *Usually they will form a cocked-hat triangle that encloses your probable position* **(2)**. *If the hat is too big* **(3)**, *take another bearing, choose another landmark, or, failing that, throw out the least reliable LOP.*

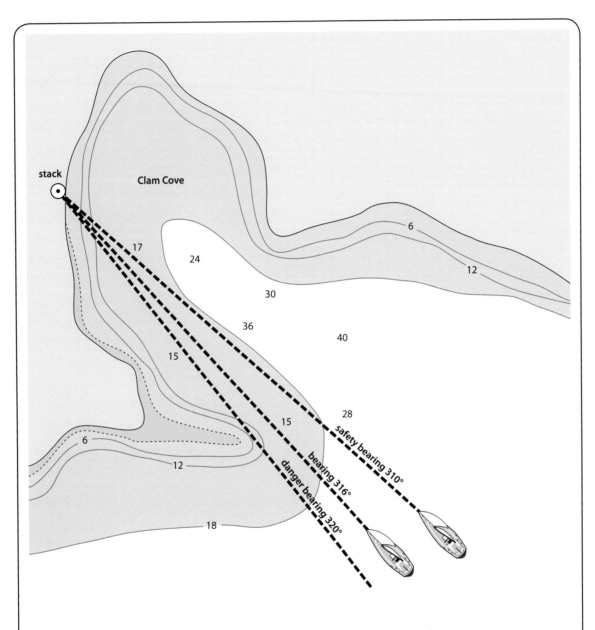

In this situation, any bearing less than 310 degrees means you're making a safe approach.

Danger and Safety Bearings

Suppose a long sandbar extends seaward from a harbor entrance. As you approach the harbor, how can you be sure you're safely clear of the bar? One way is to draw a line seaward from a landmark inside the harbor entrance such that it skirts the edge of the bar. Now "walk" that line to the compass rose with your parallel rules, and read the bearing. Suppose that bearing is 320 degrees, and you need to stay east of the bar. If the harbor entrance bears less than 310 degrees, you are clear of the bar. If the entrance bears 320 degrees or more, you are headed right for the bar, and if the entrance bears between 310 degrees and 320 degrees, you may be cutting it too close for comfort. Your **danger bearing** is 320 degrees, and your **safety bearing** is 310 degrees.

Obtaining a Fix from an LOP and a Distance Off

Another way of fixing your position is to locate your boat along a single LOP. You might do that by taking a bearing on a lighthouse as above, then locating yourself along that LOP by estimating your **distance off** the lighthouse. If your estimate is a rough one, consider the resultant fix equally rough. Distances over water almost always seem greater than they are. From a viewer height of 4 feet, the horizon is 2.3 miles away; thus, if you can see the surf at the foot of a lighthouse, it is probably closer than that. On the other hand, if you see only the top of the lighthouse, and you know the top is 50 feet above mean high water, it's a good bet the light is between 8 and 9 miles away. If you can see a 4- to 5-foot can or nun buoy at all, it is probably less than 1 mile away, and if you can distinguish a can from a nun either by color or shape, it is probably no farther away than a half mile. Train yourself to estimate distances on the water. You'll refine your ability quickly, and it's a highly useful skill.

The height of a lighthouse will be noted on the chart, as will the heights of bridges and some hills and towers. Such heights are usually referenced to mean high water (but check the chart you're using to be sure of its high-water datum), and at other stages of the tide you'll need to apply a tidal height correction (see Chapter 3). By measuring the angle between the top of the target and the water, you can solve for the base of the triangle, which is your distance off. The formula is Distance = Height ÷ Tangent of the observed angle, or you can enter the Distance Off tables in the *Nautical Almanac* (an annual publication listing the positions of stars, planets, and the moon and sun at specified times and dates) or use a programmable calculator. For a close-enough approximation, however, simply use Height ÷ (100 × observed angle). To measure the angle you can use—in descending order of accuracy—a sextant,

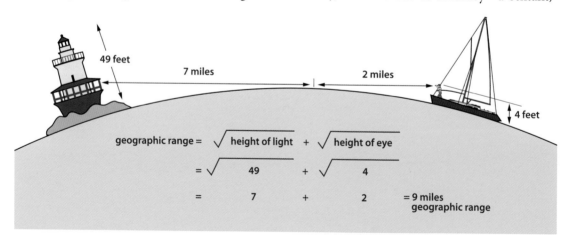

The distance to the horizon in nautical miles from any given height is approximately equal to the square root of the height in feet. If your height of eye is 4 feet and the lighthouse bobbing on the horizon has a charted height of 49 feet, the light is approximately 9 miles away. If you can make a hill, bridge, or lighthouse disappear by squatting or sitting, you know you're at the limit of its geographic range. Charted heights above water are referenced to mean high water. If the tide tables tell you that the tide is low and the range is about 5 feet, you should add 5 feet to the charted height.

Nasty reef
Fl 8 sec
120 ft 10M

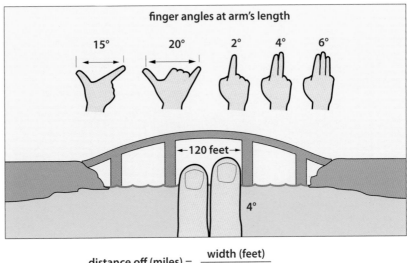

If you hold your hand outstretched in front of you, two finger widths subtend an angle of about 4 degrees. If the charted height of a lighthouse is 110 feet above mean high water and the present height of tide is 10 feet below MHW, the light's actual height is 120 feet. If its vertical angle is about 4 degrees, you are approximately 0.3 mile from it. The same technique works for horizontal distances that can be reliably measured on your nautical chart.

finger angles at arm's length

15°   20°   2°   4°   6°

←120 feet→

4°

$$\text{distance off (miles)} = \frac{\text{width (feet)}}{100 \times \text{angle}}$$

$$\frac{120 \text{ feet}}{100 \times 4°} = \frac{120}{400}$$

$$\text{distance off (miles)} = 0.3 \text{ mile}$$

a folded sheet of paper, or an outstretched finger or two. This technique requires an object of charted height, and you have to be close enough to it to make its vertical angle large enough to measure with reasonable accuracy.

Outstretched fingers can also be used to measure horizontal angles. Two fingers held together vertically at arm's length cover an arc of roughly 4 degrees. Four fingers cover roughly 8 degrees. Suppose a small is-

land measures 500 feet long on the chart and you can cover it almost exactly with three vertical fingers, or 6 degrees. Its distance off (in nautical miles) is 500 ÷ (100 × 6 degrees) = 500 ÷ 600 = 0.83 mile. Given the inaccuracies inherent in this system, you can guess that you're a little less than 1 mile from the island.

Or you can use radar to measure distance off. Indeed, radar can't be beat for deriving a fix from a single bearing and a distance off, and the advent of

digital radar displays has made the technique quick and simple. Simply move the cursor over the end of that bold headland on the display, and it will tell you not only what the bearing to the headland is but also its precise distance. Now you have all the information you need to plot an accurate fix on the chart—provided, of course, you identify the correct headland on the chart. We'll come back to radar later in the chapter.

Dividers

Dividers are used to measure distances and latitude and longitude coordinates on a chart. In its basic form, a pair of dividers comprises two arms ending in points, the distance between which can be adjusted by means of a friction pivot. To determine the latitude of a spot on the chart, you simply place one point of the dividers on the spot of interest, then adjust the arms to place the other point on the nearest line of latitude. Once this gap is set, move the dividers along the line of latitude to the latitude scale in either margin. Now one point lies on the latitude line and the other marks the latitude measurement for your desired location.

Measure longitude similarly by placing one point on the desired location and the other point on the nearest meridian line. You then transfer this setting to the scale in the top or bottom margin of the chart and read the longitude.

To measure distances on a chart, place one point of the dividers on each end of the distance to be measured. While maintaining that setting, move the dividers to the distance scale on the chart, put one point on zero, and read the distance to the second point.

Alternatively, you can use the latitude scale and count the number of minutes (nautical miles) and tenths of minutes between the dividers' points.

If the distance you wish to measure is greater than the dividers can span, draw a line between the two locations. Now you can use the distance scale or the latitude scale to preset the dividers to a convenient distance—for example, 5 nautical miles. Next, set one point of the dividers on one end of the line and walk the dividers along the line by advancing from point to point, counting the number of preset segments as you do so. Let's

(continued on page 264)

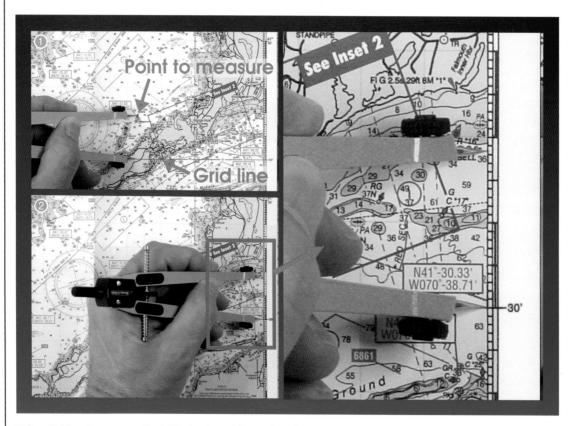

Using dividers to measure the latitude of an object or location. 1. *Place one point of the dividers on the object to be measured and the other point on the nearest latitude line.* **2, 3.** *Preserve that setting while you slide the dividers along the latitude line to the nearest chart margin, where you can read the latitude of the object in question—in this case 40° 31.84' north. Measure longitude in similar fashion using the nearest meridian line.*

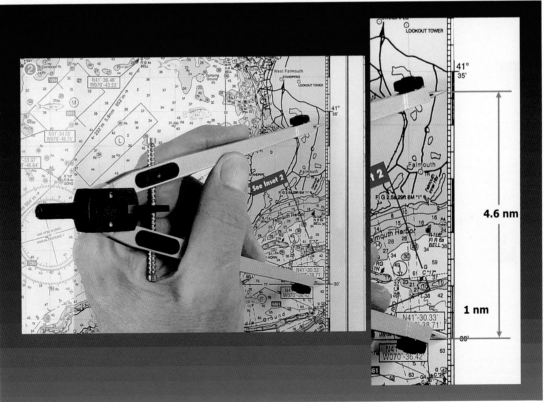

Using the latitude scale to measure distances. 1. *Place the divider points on either end of the span you want to measure—in this case the distance between two buoys.* **2.** *Without altering the setting, transfer the dividers to the nearest distance or latitude scale. One minute of latitude (but not longitude, except at the equator) equals 1 nautical mile.*

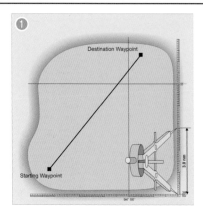

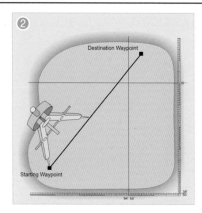

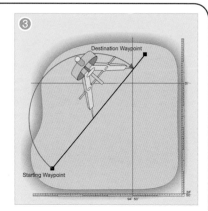

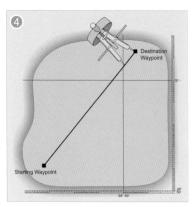

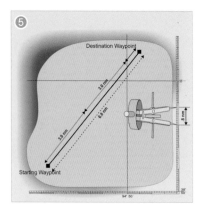

Here we set the dividers to 3 miles (1), swing them once along the span we wish to measure to obtain a total distance of 6 miles (2, 3), then readjust the setting to measure the remaining distance: 0.8 mile (4, 5). The total distance of interest is 6.8 miles.

say you've set the dividers to 4 miles and are measuring the distance between two buoys that are 10 miles apart. You count off two divider spans for 8 miles, then see that the remaining distance is less than the gap between the divider points. So you close the divider points until they precisely span the remaining distance, then read that distance on the chart scale: 2 miles. Add this distance to the sum of the fixed intervals you just counted, and you get the answer: 10.

Obtaining a Fix from an LOP and a Depth Contour or a DR Plot

If you have a depth sounder, you can even obtain an approximate fix by crossing an LOP with the depth contour you're following—though this is trustworthy only where the seabed is steeply sloped and even then only if you know what tidal height correc-

tion to apply to the charted sounding.

Finally (for now), you can cross an LOP with your DR plot—assuming you're maintaining a DR plot (see page 270)—or you can use two bearings taken to the same object at two different times to obtain a running fix. These techniques are discussed below. You can do a lot of slick things with LOPs.

see page 270

The Easiest Fix of All

When you're right next to a midchannel bell or on the safe side of a can or nun, you can point to the chart and say with certainty, "I am here!" Sometimes a buoy is off-station—so it pays, as always, to be cautious—but this is rare. Ninety-nine times out of a hundred, this is the easiest and most reliable fix available to a navigator. And since most of us run buoy-to-buoy course legs when the visibility is poor, this sort of fix is a lot more common than you might at first think.

NAVIGATING

Pinpoint Piloting

A navigation text once used at the U.S. Naval Academy in Annapolis, Maryland, tells us that "the secret of success in dead reckoning can be summed up in two words: 'practice' and 'neatness.'" The author, Commander Richard Hobbs, put together a manual filled with ingenious evolutions, arcane equipment, and challenging formulas. His book could hardly be a more far-reaching or authoritative guide to moving ships across the sea and around the land, yet the two words he chose to describe the secrets of piloting could hardly be more ordinary.

And the commander was no doubt right, at least in part. There is, after all, nothing about piloting that's beyond the grasp of any focused sailor. On the other hand, there's also nothing about piloting that a cold and tired sailor or a bored navigator couldn't screw up in a heartbeat. Routine, protocol, and practice are good defenses against error and against ourselves, and we probably *do* need practice and neatness to assure that things get done consistently well.

But the navy way is not the only way. It's wise to suit your standards of precision to the realities of a small boat without a large navigation table on which to spread charts and without a fulltime navigator who focuses on nothing else—a boat that pitches, rolls, heaves, yaws, and heels enough in a seaway or breeze to add yet another layer of challenge to piloting. What works in such conditions is not always what works on the bridge of a navy ship.

Develop your own checks and balances, your own routines for success. For instance, learning the symbols for an expanded fix and a celestial fix— once common components of the navigator's routine but now rarely used—would make more sense to me if I ever used them, but I don't. I know competent navigators who don't even use parallel rules or dividers—because they do their navigating in an open cockpit where traditional plotting techniques are impractical, or because they use GPS and electronic charts, or because they sail in their own

ford the leisure of doing all this below. When I'm sailing along a coast, however, despite doing what I can beforehand, I still need the local chart in hand as I survey the scene. A good way to take a chart on deck and have it last is to enclose it in a clear plastic bag. I often use chartbooks from commercial publishers rather than the individual charts issued by the government, and my books fit inside a jumbo zip-top bag. If the chart isn't shifting in the bag, you can use a grease pencil to lay down courses on the outside without letting moisture in or marking the charts themselves.

A Running Fix

It should be clear by now that there are a lot of position-finding tricks. One of the ones I like best is the running fix. You get

backyard and can eyeball their way through safe waters. (But every one of those navigators has dividers and parallel rules on board and knows how to use them should the need arise.) Whatever your style may be, pilot by the lights that steer you right.

As you learn piloting, pick out the conventions and procedures that serve you best. Practice them—and be neat about it!

Nav stations below are all well and good, but I do almost all my navigating in the cockpit. That puts a premium on preplanning. If courses are laid out, hazards identified, and options outlined before they're needed, things go more smoothly. Ocean passages af-

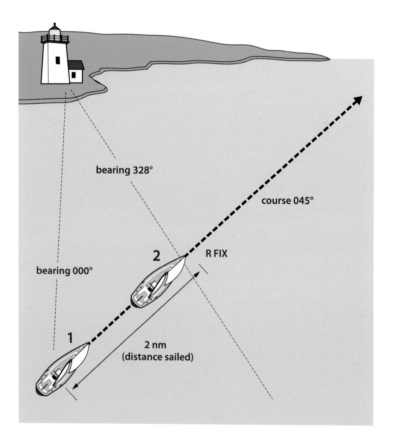

Sailing at 6 knots, you take a bearing (000 degrees) on a lighthouse. Twenty minutes later the lighthouse bears 328 degrees. The place at which a 2-mile segment of your course line intersects both bearing lines is your running fix position, commonly denoted with a solid dot and labeled R FIX.

Bow-and-Beam Bearing

A variation on the running fix is the **bow-and-beam bearing**. As you approach a charted landmark or navaid, note the time when it is 45 degrees off the bow. You are interested in its relative bearing—the angle between the object and your boat—*not* the magnetic bearing itself. For instance, if you are steering 090 degrees magnetic and the mark bears 120 degrees magnetic, the relative bearing between the centerline of your boat and the mark is 30 degrees. When the mark is 45 degrees off your bow it will bear 135 degrees magnetic, but the relative bearing of 45 degrees is all you need for a bow-and-beam bearing. Note the time, then continue on until the mark is abeam, with a relative bearing of 90 degrees. The distance you have run in the intervening time is also your distance off the mark. If it takes 15 minutes at an estimated speed of 4 knots to move the mark from 45 degrees to 90 degrees off your bow, you are 1 mile from the mark.

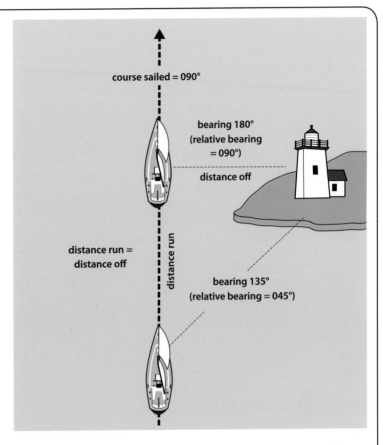

course sailed = 090°

bearing 180° (relative bearing = 090°)

distance off

distance run = distance off

distance run

bearing 135° (relative bearing = 045°)

The distance you cover while bringing a landmark from broad on your bow (relative bearing of 45 degrees) to abeam is the same as your distance from the mark when you are abeam of it.

Doubling the Angle on the Bow

Actually, doubling any relative bearing works the same way as a bow-and-beam bearing. The technique is called **doubling the angle on the bow**. Take a bearing on a mark when it is off your bow. If its compass bearing is 130 degrees and you are steering 090 degrees, it is 40 degrees off your starboard bow. Take bearings until the mark bears 170 degrees, and you will have doubled its relative bearing to 80 degrees. The distance you ran between bearings is your distance from the mark. This way you can find where you are without waiting to pass abeam of the mark, and that can be helpful. Remember that set and drift affect the outcome.

For a quick approximation of distance off use another bearing-on-the-bow trick. Take a bearing on a landmark off the bow. If you are powering or sailing at 6 knots, note the time it takes to change the bearing 6 degrees. (If your speed is 5 knots, make that 5 degrees, etc.) That time in minutes equals your distance from the mark in miles. If you are sailing at 6 knots and it takes 1 minute 30 seconds to alter the bearing to a landmark or navaid by 6 degrees, you are 1.5 miles from the mark. Given the steering and speed accuracies of a small boat, I wouldn't bet the farm on the accuracy of this drill, but it's one of the quickest ways I know to get information you can use to organize an approach or establish a fix.

it by taking a bearing on a landmark in the usual way. Proceed on your course for an interval that gives you a convenient distance run: 20 minutes at 6 knots = 2 nautical miles, for example. Take another bearing. Plot the two bearings on the chart. They form a V extending toward you from the landmark. Draw a line parallel to your course such that a 2-mile segment of it (the 2 miles you ran between bearings) fits precisely between the LOPs. Where the course line crosses LOP #2 is your position.

The accuracy of a running fix depends on the accuracy of your bearings, your distance run between bearings, and your course over ground between bearings. That's a lot of variables for a fix to depend on, and that's the principal knock against a running fix. A head current will slow you down—i.e., your speed over ground will be less than your speed through the water—and a running fix based on speed through the water will put you farther from the beach than you really are. Similarly, a crosswise current will cause your course over ground to vary from your compass course. The more accurate your dead reckoning (see below), the more valuable the technique. Many times, especially when you're closing with a strange coast, a single landmark is all that stands out. A running fix lets you make the most of it.

Setting Courses

"Where are we going?"

After you've answered the "where are we?" question, the next challenge is getting where you want to go. A course to steer can be as basic as "head for the lighthouse," but choosing a destination and the headings to get to it is as important as finding your position. The course might be as long as Newport to Bermuda or as short as a leg between buoys, but you need to know what direction to steer.

Survey the chart. Can you head straight from where you are to where you want to go? If no shoals or hazards intervene between you and there, draw a line on the chart from your position to your destination. When you draw a line parallel to that course line through the compass rose, the heading where the line intersects the destination side of the rose's inner ring is the heading to steer—assuming your compass has no deviation. It's salty and efficient to couch that number in three digits for the helmsman, even if you're talking to yourself: oh-eight-five! A persistent 5 degrees course error would put you a mile off course after 12 miles, so steer 085 degrees as best you can. Your course will wander some, but if you do your best to wander equally either side of the nominal course, showing no persistent bias to one side, you'll do fine. Steering within 3 degrees of the desired course is considered very good on a small boat, so don't overly sweat the accuracy of short legs, but do be aware that your courses mean something—they lead somewhere.

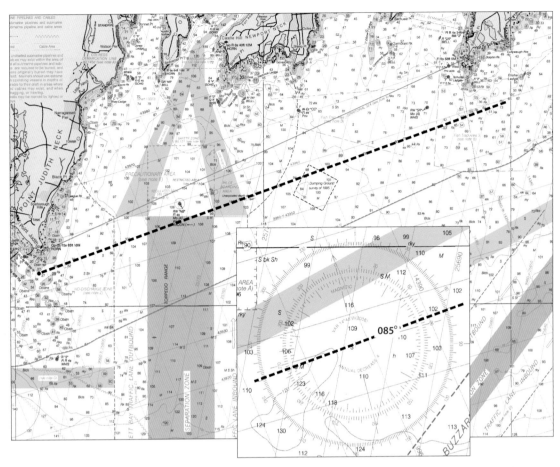

Rounding Point Judith (lower left) you want to sail across Rhode Island Sound, making sure to leave Elisha Ledge (upper right) well to port. Plot the course, then go to the compass rose with a parallel line. Read "085" on the inner ring. That's the course to steer assuming you do not need to correct for current or leeway.

Plotting a Route with Multiple Legs

Rarely will you find a broad, deep fairway leading right to your ultimate destination. The first thing to consider is the dangers that lie between you and your goal. The farther offshore you go, the fewer dangers you'll find, but inshore not all water is navigable. Survey your intended route for problems. (I like to circle all intervening hazards on the chart.) Now, rather than a single straight line, plot a series of shorter courses that will pick your way through that briar patch of danger zones, angling the courses so as to keep you a comfortable distance from the problems. Make this exercise part of your preplanning, because it's much easier to do this *before* you go rather than *as* you go.

As we saw in Chapter 4, large-scale charts cover small areas in profuse detail, whereas small-scale charts cover large areas with scant detail. Thus, small-scale charts are best for planning coastal passages or long cruises, whereas large-scale

Rhumb-Line versus Great-Circle Courses

When your GPS receiver offers you the choice of a rhumb-line or great-circle course, you have the right to wonder what the difference is and which you should be using. Imagine passing a geometric plane through the globe such that it cuts precisely through the center of the globe and intersects both Newport, Rhode Island, and Bermuda on the globe's surface. The line it scribes between Newport and Bermuda is the **great-circle course** between those locations. The great-circle course between two positions is always the shortest course, and this is its great advantage for long passages. It's why airplanes flying from New York to London travel near Nova Scotia and Greenland en route. On the other hand, a great-circle course will appear curved, not straight, on a Mercator chart and must be approximated by a series of short-segment compass courses in order to be steered.

A **rhumb-line course** is the compass course between two locations, and it plots as a straight line on a Mercator chart. Rhumb lines are much more convenient to plot and steer, so all piloting and even most offshore work is done with rhumb lines. The great-circle course from San Francisco to Yokohama is a lot shorter than the corresponding rhumb-line course, but over a 25-mile coastal passage the difference isn't noticeable.

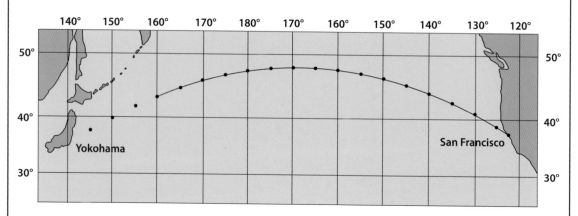

A straight line may not be the shortest path between two points, but a great circle always is. Every meridian is a portion of a great circle, which is why the shortest trip between any two points A and B that are separated by 180 degrees of longitude takes you "over the pole." More generally, that's also why a curved line makes for a shorter passage (between Yokohama and San Francisco, for example) than a rhumb-line or straight course. For passages shorter than 1,000 miles, though, rhumb lines are fine.

charts are best for navigation. If you should ever be caught on the water without the appropriate local chart, sail defensively. Pilot by eye. Follow the buoys as best you can, observe other boats and everything else that looks significant, and move always with the knowledge that you don't know all there is to know about where you are. It's much nicer to have the right chart.

Dead Reckoning

Having fixed your position and plotted the course for the next leg of your journey, now you're steering that course. How do you track your progress? Elec- tronics can make short work of this task, as we'll see later in the chapter, but if you're not depending on electronics you're probably depending on dead reckoning. **Dead reckoning** (which is short for "deduced reckoning") involves deducing where you are from the course, speed, and time you've

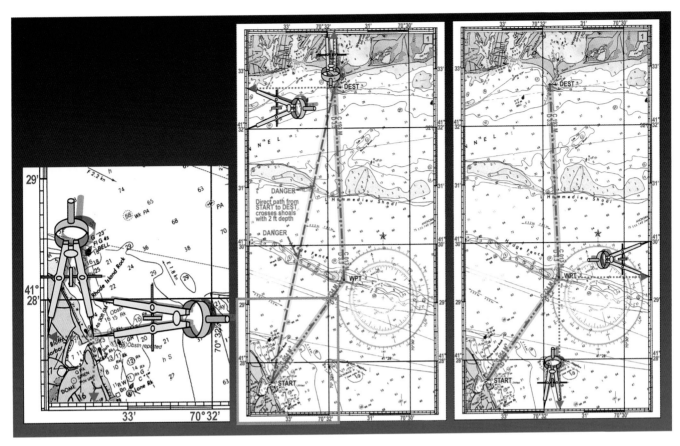

If a straight course from starting point (left) to destination (center) takes you into danger, as it does here, you'll need to plan at least one dogleg (right).

traveled since your last fix. A faithfully maintained dead-reckoning track forms a more or less continuous plot of your progress across the chart. The more taxing the navigation, the more faithfully you will want to maintain your DR plot. In clear weather and safe, familiar waters, a mental DR track is often all you need, but at night or in fog, when threading your way through coastal hazards, you'll want as precise a DR track as you can plot on your chart with a sharp pencil.

To see how this might work in practice, let's return to the story with which this chapter began. After a 2-mile beat to windward in thick fog, our four-person crew rounded a mid-channel bell and began a 3-mile close reach to the next mark, steering 118 degrees magnetic. When they rounded the bell they knew exactly where they were—the bell represented a highly reliable fix. Once the bell disappeared into the fog astern, however, the certainty of their position began to decrease.

Their speed was varying between 6.2 and 6.8 knots and seemed to be averaging about 6.5, and the next mark was 3 miles away, so the navigator figured they should see it in about 25 minutes and perhaps hear it 2 or 3 minutes earlier. There were no hazards along the leg, but there were rocks ¼ mile north of the gong buoy at which they were aiming, so the navigator knew that a miss on that side should be avoided at all costs. About 15 minutes into the leg the navigator spotted

Variation and Deviation

Variation and deviation are the twin demons of compass navigation. Confusing the two comes with the territory, but variation is universal, whereas deviation is peculiar to your boat. The concepts were introduced in Chapter 4. Depending on where you are on the globe, variation can be large or small, and it varies east or west. The variation in parts of the Pacific Northwest as of this writing is 20 degrees east, which means that a true course of 110 degrees will translate to a magnetic course of 090 degrees. In the Gulf of Maine the variation is roughly 20 degrees west, which means that a true course of 110 degrees will translate to a magnetic course of 130 degrees. Along the Gulf Coast the variation is small or nonexistent. Your local variation shows up as the difference between the inner-ring (magnetic) compass-rose reading and the outer-ring (true) reading on any heading, and as we saw in Chapter 4, at the center of any compass rose you'll see a printed note on the rate of change in local variation.

As long as you use the magnetic circle on your compass rose, variation will rarely be an issue. It pops up only when you need to convert bearings or courses to or from degrees true—and I can't remember the last time I needed to do that.

Deviation refers to inaccuracies in your compass resulting from shipboard disturbances. Any magnetic object—an electric motor,

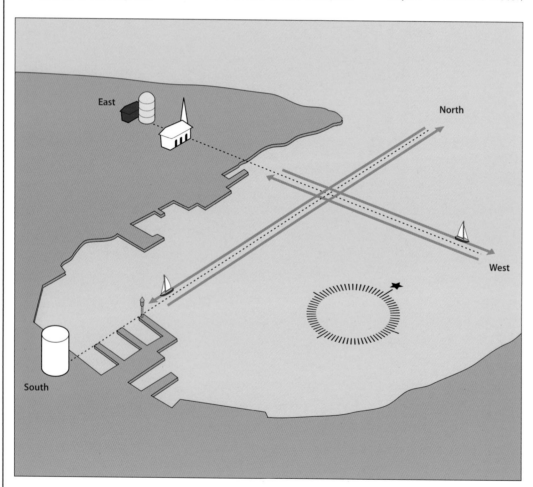

Run a known course such as the line defined by a range. If your compass reading is accurate (the same as the charted line), that's good. Otherwise note the difference. When you have run courses in all four quadrants, you have "swung ship." Use your observations of your compass to make a deviation table. It will allow you to correct for compass error through a full 360 degrees.

speaker, tool, sunglasses, current-carrying DC wiring—can affect the compass. Deviation must be checked for, then either corrected or accounted for.

Before you check your compass for deviation, make sure its lubber line is parallel with (though not necessarily on) the boat's centerline. Make sure the card pivots freely and won't bind or drag during a full rotation. Remove any sources of magnetism you can see, but when you test your compass for deviation, make sure the instruments you normally use are on.

Then, with your compass as free from interference as you can make it, see how well it works. To do this, identify ranges in each of the four cardinal directions. A charted church spire behind a daybeacon might make a range at 005 degrees magnetic, which is close enough to north for our purposes. A water tower behind the north end of a small, bold island might give us a range at 087 degrees—and so on for ranges to the south and west. Line up each of these ranges in turn, then compare your compass course with the magnetic bearing of the range as plotted on the chart. Any differences you see can usually be removed by means of compensating magnets built into the compass. You will find separate adjustment screws for E-W and N-S adjustments. Turn these a little at a time until

the chart and compass agree. Recheck all headings after an adjustment on any heading. If the range of adjustment isn't big enough to correct the problem, you should probably consult a professional. You can, in the interim, make up a rough deviation table. It might look like:

Heading	Deviation	Correction
000 N	0	0
045 NE	2W	−2
090 E	4W	−4
135 SE	2W	−2
180 S	0	0
225 SW	2E	+2
270 W	4E	+4
315 NW	2E	+2
360 N	0	0

Cumbersome and annoying to use, it will still give you the amount to add or subtract from your compass reading to make your headings in each quadrant relatively accurate. To adjust a bearing taken with the steering compass, use the correction factor for the direction the boat was heading when you took the bearing, *not* for the quadrant of the compass in which you took the bearing.

If you plot your bearings and courses in degrees true but steer them in degrees as read on a compass, you'll have to convert from one to the other. This is why so many small-boat navigators prefer to do their plotting in degrees magnetic. When you convert from true to magnetic, you need to add westerly variation—remember,

True ←E −E **V**ariation W→ −W

←W +W **M**agnetic E→ +E

Deviation

Compass

When converting a course or bearing from degrees true to degrees magnetic, add a westerly variation or subtract an easterly one. When converting from degrees magnetic to compass degrees, add a westerly deviation or subtract an easterly one. To go from compass to magnetic or magnetic to true, add easterly or subtract westerly. A handy mnemonic device is **T**ele-**V**isions **M**ake **D**ull **C**hildren, add **W**onder.

"West is best." By the same token, if your compass has residual deviation, to go from magnetic direction to what you would read on the compass, you will add westerly deviation. In other words, going down (T to M to C), you add west. Conversely going up (C to M to T) you add east. This diagram provides an easy way to remember this. On the "west" side of the diagram, you add west (either V or D). On the "east" side you add east. If your compass has negligible deviation and you plot courses and bearings in degrees magnetic, no conversions will be necessary, and I highly recommend this.

two other boats about a tenth of a mile to windward at the limit of visibility, and that started him worrying that the tide was setting them north of their intended course. A few minutes

later the crew reported hearing what they thought might be the gong off the starboard bow, and the navigator asked the helmsman to head up to close hauled.

It was the right move, but too late—they had indeed been set north by the incoming tide, and even close hauled they could no longer fetch the gong. They were forced to make a

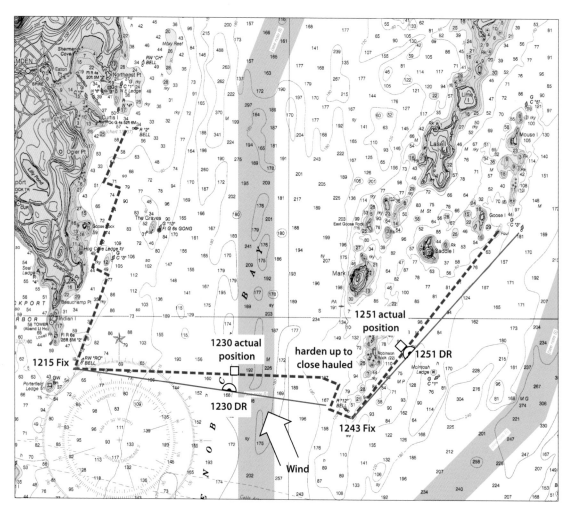

Another look at the Penobscot Bay chart image on page 246, this time with a DR plot (shown in blue) added to the second leg of the race. The boat's COG, as determined in retrospect, is shown in red. At 12:30 the boat's actual position was north of its DR position due to a north-setting incoming tide and perhaps also to leeway.

short, unplanned port tack in order to round the mark, but this was far from the worst that could have happened. Had they wandered even farther north, they might have strayed across the rocks north of the mark. (As it was, fate granted our crew another 25 minutes

of good sailing before placing a rock in their path!)

Rounding the gong at last, the crew once again knew exactly where they were. The uncertainties surrounding their DR track were replaced by the certainty of a solid fix, and the DR plot began anew

from that point on the chart.

That's the way dead reckoning works. If you've sailed 165 degrees at 5.5 knots for half an hour since your last fix, you plot a line from the fix in the direction of 165 degrees for a distance of 2.75 nautical miles. Your DR position is at the end of that line.

The longer you go between fixes, the less confidence you can have in your DR position. When the navigation is tricky, you'll want to update your DR plot with actual fixes every chance you get. But your DR plot is the line that connects the dots. At best it is a bridge between islands of certainty. At worst it may be the best position information you can get.

Suppose you depart mid-channel bell buoy "EG" (your last known position) steering a compass course of 245 degrees at a speed of 3 knots. To get a DR position after 30 minutes on

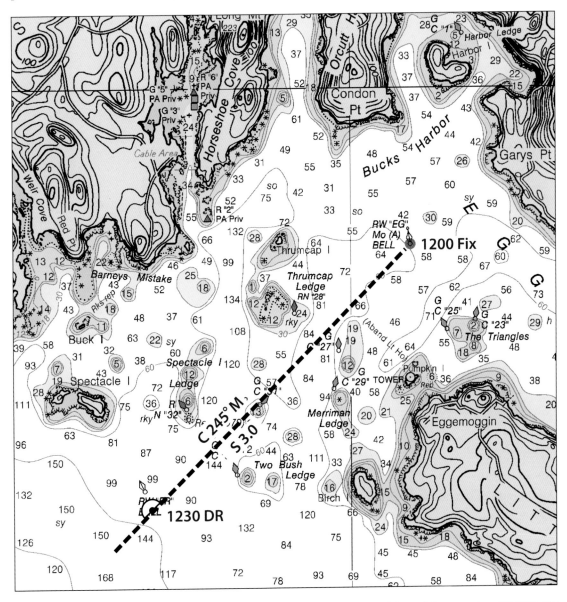

Dead reckoning involves "deducing" your position by means of your known speed, time, distance, and course. Here you depart bell "EG" steering 245 degrees magnetic at 3 knots. Half an hour later your dead reckoning places you just east of bell "ER," which which you should be able to see or (in fog) at least hear. Along the way you have passed several other navaids. Had you sighted any of these you could have confirmed your DR plot or corrected as necessary.

that course, plot a course on the chart from the bell buoy toward 245 degrees magnetic (from the inner circle of the compass rose) and measure 1.5 nautical miles along that line using the chart's distance scale. That's where you are if (1) your course and speed have been unaffected by current or leeway; (2) your compass has no significant deviation; (3) your steering has been accurate; (4) your timekeeping has been accurate; and (5) your estimate of boatspeed has been accurate. That's a lot of ifs.

Correcting for Current

It takes longer to sail or motor 5 miles upstream than to move 5 miles downstream. Current has no effect on your speed through the water, but it has a significant impact on your speed over ground. Point east and sail 1 hour at 6 knots, and you'll travel 6 nautical miles through the water. If you're bucking a west-setting current with a drift of 2 knots, however, your distance covered over ground will be only 4 miles. If you're riding an easterly 2-knot current, you'll have traveled 8 miles.

As we saw in Chapter 3, currents, unlike winds, are named for where they're going, not where they're from. **Set** and **drift** are fine old nautical terms for the direction and speed of a current, respectively. Calculations for any angle of current—on the bow, the beam, the quarter, or in between—are easy to make as long as you know the current's set and drift.

Nautical almanacs and government-prepared tidal current tables will give you times, velocities, and directions of maximum flood and ebb currents. In some waters these data are augmented by current charts (like the examples in Chapter 3) that show you graphically how the ebb and flood flows around islands or through passages, and where countereddies might be found. But these predictions are not nearly as precise as tidal height predictions (which are themselves subject to such variables as atmospheric pressure and onshore winds), and you might find a current flowing at as little as half or as much as half-again its predicted velocity.

As noted in earlier chapters, you can get a feel for the current by your own observations. Check out any lobster buoy or navigational marker that you pass close aboard. From the direction and length of the wake trailing downcurrent of the buoy, you can confirm the current's set and guesstimate its drift.

Another good yardstick—and the one sailors use more than any other—is the effect a current has on your boat. Sail a course for 20 minutes, then take a bearing back to where you started. How far has your course made good diverged from your course steered? If, after 20 minutes underway, you are ⅔ of a mile east of where you thought you'd be, the current is running east at 2 knots. (Wind causes leeway and helmsmen

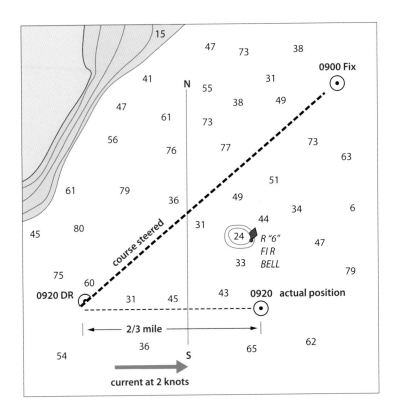

The chart shows depth soundings with the following labeled features: 0900 Fix, course steered, 0920 DR, 0920 actual position, 2/3 mile, current at 2 knots. The buoy is marked R "6", Fl R, BELL, with value 24.

How a current affects your course and position can help you determine its strength and direction. From a known position at 9:00 a.m. you sail southwest in thick fog at an estimated average speed of 3.75 knots. Twenty minutes later, however, a momentary hole in the fog-bank shows you bell buoy "6" to the north, and you confirm by radar that the buoy is 0.25 mile away. With this range and bearing you plot a 9:20 fix and find it to be ⅔ mile east of your DR position. That tells you that you are in an east-running current of about 2 knots and had better compensate by steering farther west.

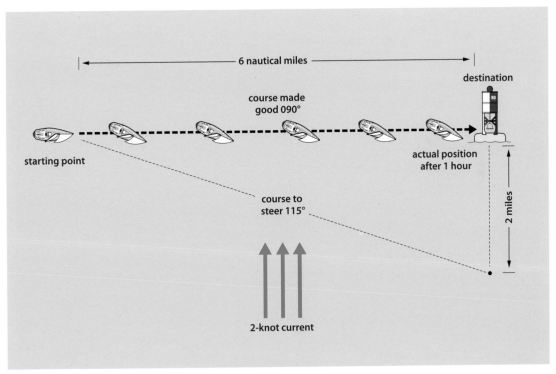

Labels: 6 nautical miles, destination, course made good 090°, course to steer 115°, starting point, actual position after 1 hour, 2 miles, 2-knot current.

Allow for the effect of a current by correcting your course upstream.

stray, but these factors are usually minor relative to current.) Apply an appropriate correction going forward in order to stay on your intended course.

Any GPS receiver includes a cross-track error feature that tells you graphically (and sometimes with an audible alarm) when your course made good is varying from your course steered or the bearing to the next waypoint. With a feature like this, the guesswork is mostly gone. GPS gives you a supremely clear picture of what the current is doing to you.

Current is a fact of sailing. If you know what it is, you can allow for it. If you can get a fix, you can deduce it. If you must, you can estimate it. The simplest way to do all these things is by applying approximate corrections to your courses steered. That's what most sailors do, and it works perfectly well in buoy-to-buoy navigation if you keep the course legs short and plan them to give a wide berth to any hazards. If you want more precise corrections, however, the way to do it—in the absence of electronics—is with vectors.

Say the course to your destination is 090 degrees (see art

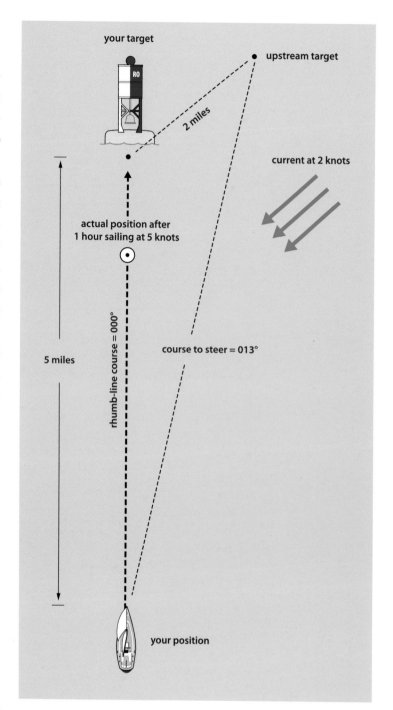

Steer a corrected course, not the rhumb-line course, to allow for current.

on page 277). Your target is 6 miles away, and there's a current running north at 2 knots. Lay out your course. At 6 knots it will take you an hour to get where you're going, but during that hour the water through which you're moving will have

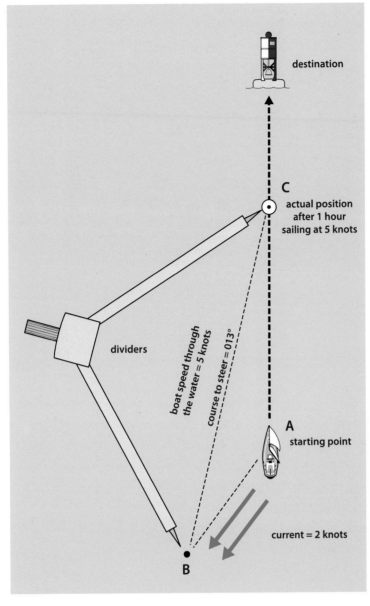

Here is a different approach to the current problem of the previous illustration. This time we plot the current vector from our starting point at **A**. Setting the dividers to 5 miles (our speed through the water), we put one point at **B** and swing the other to intersect our desired course made good at **C**. The line from B to C is our course to steer, and C represents our position after 1 hour.

will allow you to proceed crabwise to your destination.

Two caveats are in order. First, the current sets as given in tidal current tables are usually in degrees true, so if you do your plotting in degrees magnetic (which I recommend), you might want to apply the local variation so as to convert the sets to degrees magnetic. In our example, if the local variation were 15 degrees west, you would add this to the current's true set, 000 degrees, in order to get its set in degrees magnetic, 015 degrees. But given that predicting the effects of current is an approximate game to begin with, why bother with conversions? I just don't think that level of precision in one step of an estimating process is justified.

Second, we should note that although your destination is 6 miles away, you will have to sail more than 6 miles through the water on your corrected course to reach it. You will therefore not arrive in an hour, but at least you will still be on course and will reach your goal in a few more minutes.

The same geometry works no matter what the current's angle to your desired course. Assume a 1-hour sail at 5 knots

moved 2 nautical miles north. To compensate, plot a line from your intended destination running 2 miles south. Then draw a line from your starting point to this upstream endpoint, and transfer that course line to the compass rose to read its magnetic heading. That's the course that allows for the current and

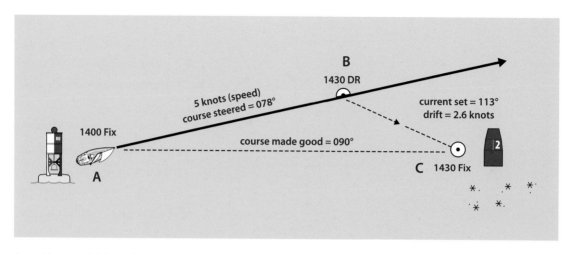

*Departing your 2:00 p.m. fix at **A**, you sail at 5 knots, steering a course of 078 degrees. At 2:30 you expect to be at **B**, but instead nun "2" emerges from the fog, and you know you are at **C**. You can see a strong tidal current sweeping past the nun, but what is its set and drift? Using this vector solution, you find that the current is setting 113 degrees with a drift of 2.6 knots, and you've been proceeding crabwise along a course made good of 090 degrees. Thank your lucky stars you weren't set the other side of nun "2" and factor the current into your course going forward.*

into a current approaching from 45 degrees on the starboard bow with a drift of 2 knots (see art on page 278). Lay out your uncorrected course to your destination, then plot 2 miles upstream from that point, at an angle of 45 degrees from your rhumb line. Steer for that upstream point, and remember that it's going to take you longer to reach your destination than it would without the current.

If the current is approaching from your stern quarter, the plotting is the same. This time, however, the corrected course line is shorter than the uncorrected line. That's telling you that the current is helping you along your course, and at the

end of an hour you will have covered more distance over the ground than through the water. If going farther than expected will cause you to hit anything, you'd better factor this in.

If you want to know how far you'll go in an hour, apply the current vector downstream from your starting point rather than upstream from your endpoint. Then, from the downstream end of the current vector, draw a line with its length proportional to your speed through the water and its far end intersecting your intended course line. The direction of that line is the course you should steer, and its point of intersection with your "intended course

made good" line represents approximately where you will be after one hour. If you're sailing at 4 knots with a boost from a quartering current, you will have covered more than 4 nautical miles.

Suppose the current catches you by surprise. You steer 078 degrees at 5 knots for 30 minutes between fixes, but at the end of that time you're not where your DR navigation predicted you would be. Then you notice a current sweeping past a nun buoy and realize you're being set—but how much, and in what direction? Time for another vector diagram. Quite simply, the vector from your DR position to your actual fix

Estimated Position (EP)

Strictly speaking, a DR plot is based solely on courses steered and speed through the water over the measured time since your last fix. But if you can estimate how the current is affecting you, you can do better than that. Applying a correction for current elevates your DR position to an **estimated position** (EP). An estimated position is your best educated guess of where you are, but until you can confirm it with a fix, it's still only a guess.

represents both the set and drift of the current. Assuming the current remains steady over the next interval of time, you can apply that same vector correction to your DR plot going forward, as already described.

You may never have to use a current vector diagram. Even if you find yourself doing DR navigation through current-riven waters in poor visibility without GPS or radar, the chances are good that you can lay short courses between buoys that mark safe water or announce themselves with a gong, bell, or whistle, then simply guesstimate a steering correction that will get you close enough to find your marks. Still, knowing how current diagrams work gives you a way of *thinking* about currents that will serve you well.

Leeway

Leeway is sideslipping caused by the wind. It means that the course you are making good is to leeward of the one you are steering through the water. You can always adjust, but if you know your leeway angle you can adjust accurately. Did you recently pass close aboard a navigation buoy or headland? Take a back bearing on this buoy or landmark astern. In the absence of any current, the difference between that bearing and the reciprocal (course in the opposite direction) of your heading is your leeway angle. Sometimes you can see the trail of disturbed and oxygenated water your boat leaves behind. If that wake is angling noticeably to windward astern, you are making leeway. If you have nothing to sight astern, you can stream a tin can on a length of twine. The twine should be as long as possible—preferably three or four boat lengths—with the boat end tied as near the boat's centerline as possible. Your sideslipping will drag the can to windward, and the angle the string makes with the reciprocal of your heading is your leeway angle. You only have to do this once or twice to get a fair idea what kind of leeway your boat makes in particular conditions.

You can correct for leeway by steering farther upwind to compensate, but leeway is a concern most often when you are already close hauled and cannot point much closer into the wind. The next best bet is to allow for leeway by advancing your DR along a course that is the proper number of degrees to leeward of your heading. As with current corrections, the object is to elevate your DR position to an EP. Leeway, however, is rarely a significant factor on a modern, well-sailed boat and can safely be ignored under most circumstances.

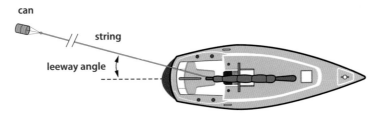

A tin can on twine streamed astern can tell you about your leeway. It tows straight, whereas the boat may slip to leeward. Your leeway angle is the angle between the string and the boat's fore-and-aft centerline.

Running in Fog

Running in the fog is vastly simplified when you can home in on a GPS waypoint. GPS gives you your speed and course over ground, the range and bearing of your next waypoint, and your estimated time of arrival (ETA) at that waypoint. It also includes a cross-track error feature that tells you when your course over ground is diverging from the bearing to the waypoint. Gone are your uncertainties about current set and drift. Simply adjust your course steered until your course over ground matches the bearing to the waypoint. *You* may not be able to see, but GPS makes you feel that *it* can.

But even if you know where you are and where you're going, you still have the critical responsibility to see and be seen, hear and be heard. Steer clear of other vessels. Give sound signals consistently. If your engine is running, the Rules of the Road advise you to give a 5-second blast on a foghorn every 2 minutes. If you're sailing, the prescribed signal is one 5-second blast followed by two 1-second blasts every 2 minutes. Often, it must be admitted, these rules are observed in the breach, but whenever you're in the fog you should have your horn close at hand. If you hear horns, engines, or even fluttering sails or grinding winches out there in the fog, grab your horn and make noise.

And listen for signals from others. Strongly recommended by the Coast Guard is the practice of shutting down your engines at periodic intervals to listen. I hoist sail in fog for that

Under sail in the fog, you can hear a lot more than when the engine is running.

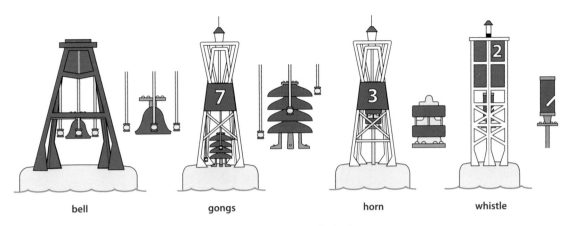

Many government marks have "auditory aids" to promote running in the fog.

reason. Sometimes it's blowing too hard to maintain a cautious pace—the rule of thumb is that you should be able to stop within half your radius of visibility—and sailing in a breeze can be noisy, but most of the time sailing gives you much better touch with what's going on around you than steaming ahead under power. Radar is superb in the fog because it not only helps you locate buoys and landmasses, but it also lets you "see" other boats. Whether or not you have radar, though, make sure to hoist a radar reflector in your rigging so that other boats with radar can see you.

When you plot courses in the fog, plot them whenever possible to navigation buoys that make noise. In addition to

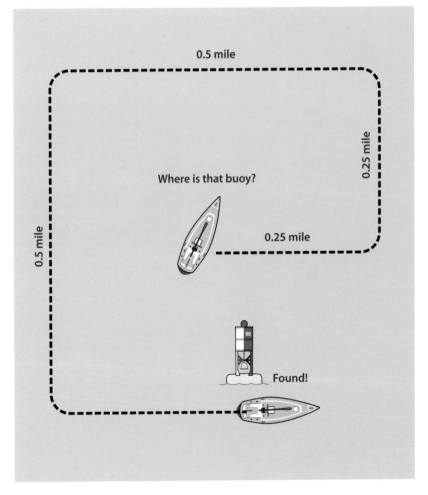

A square search is a good way to track down a buoy you can't find.

Rules of the Road in Restricted Visibility

The International and Inland Rules of the Road prescribe the same actions and sound signals in restricted visibility. A dash represents a 5-second blast, and a dot represents a 1-second blast.

Power vessel making way
Power vessel underway but stopped
Manned tow
Pilot vessel—optional signal
Not under command, restricted in ability to maneuver, constrained by draft, sailing, fishing, towing or pushing, fishing at anchor, or restricted at anchor
Anchored:
    <100 m—ring bell rapidly for 5 sec. once per min.
    ≥100 m—ring bell 5 sec. forward, then gong 5 sec. aft
Aground: 3 bell claps + rapid 5-sec. bell + 3 claps; repeat all 1/min.
    ≥100 m—add gong 5 sec. aft
    <12 m Inland option—horn, bell, or gong once per 2 min.

What to Do in Fog (*Rule 19*)

Fog Situation	What You Should Do
Regardless of traffic	Maintain safe speed; power-driven vessels sound one 5-sec. blast every 2 minutes. Most other vessels sound one 5-sec. and two 1-sec. blasts every 2 minutes.
Hear sound signal forward	Slow to bare steerageway or stop.
Radar target forward	Slow; do NOT turn to port unless you are overtaking the target vessel.
Radar target aft or abeam	Maintain speed; do NOT turn toward the target vessel.

Sound signals in restricted visibility (top) and safe actions in fog (bottom) are defined in the Rules of the Road.

Radar Reflector

Most small-boat radars transmit at an ultrahigh X-band frequency of 9 gigahertz (GHz), which is excellent for target resolution but not for penetrating rainstorms or differentiating wave clutter from true targets. S-band radar transmitting at 3 GHz does better locating large targets in rain and wave clutter but has lower resolution and is less adept at picking out small or closely spaced targets. Big ships typically carry both 3 GHz and 9 GHz radar, using the former offshore and the latter inshore. Consider, however, that the echo from a radar target has been degraded to as little as a fourth power of its transmitted magnitude by the time it returns to the radar. Even when a ship is using 9 GHz radar, a small fiberglass sailboat makes a poor target and is unlikely to emerge from

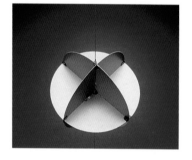

The traditional octahedral radar reflector (above) now gets competition from models like the EchoMax (right), in which a stacked array of trihedral cones is protected by a radar-transparent housing.

the background clutter on the ship's radar screen unless something is done to enhance its reflection characteristics. This is the role of a radar reflector, which is basically a concentrated configuration of highly reflective surfaces or lenses hoisted in a sailboat's

rigging. The most common design comprises three sheet-metal disks that intersect at right angles to create a sphere with octahedral reflecting surfaces. Other models encase the reflectors in a plastic housing that passes radar signals without interference.

bells (electromechanical and wave-activated), gongs, and whistles, there are guns, sirens, trumpets, and air, reed, electric, and mechanical foghorns. Virtually every coastal approach is guarded by buoys and beacons that make sounds, and each different sound is distinguishable from the others that may be nearby. When you hear a nav-aid through the fog, you can tell which one it is by the sound it is making. The chart will tell you what to listen for.

But sound through fog plays tricks. It might skip aloft and be muffled alow. The standard advice is not to trust your hearing to determine direction or distance in the fog. Nevertheless, make the most of the sounds you hear. Rotate your head until the sound is equally loud in both ears, so you can be as precise as possible about its bearing. Cup your ear to make your hearing more directional.

Without radar and GPS to take most of the anxiety out of it, fog running consists of:
- being as precise as possible with plotting, steering, and boatspeed
- running short, stepping-stone course legs

- watching the depth sounder, if you have one, for any signs of shoaling
- keeping a bow watch with eyes and ears open
- identifying hard-to-miss targets that, either by size or sound, would guide you to them
- avoiding targets that are close enough to hazards to penalize a slight plotting or steering error with a grounding
- watching and listening especially hard for other boats in the vicinity of a mark; any buoy that looks like an attractive target to you also looks attractive to other boats, so expect company
- paying particular attention to current set and drift and perhaps leeway
- running your time

The latter practice refers to calculating speed and distance so that you have an exact ETA for each mark. If that time arrives and you haven't found the mark, shut down. In still conditions—if the mark is a bell, gong, wave-activated horn, or whistle—you might try doing a few fast, tight circles under power. Then shut down again and listen in the hope that your

wake will "wake up" the buoy so you can hear it. Failing that, start a square search with legs of 30, then 45, then 60 seconds (see art page 283). Unless your navigation has gone drastically wrong, the buoy will show up.

Nathaniel Bowditch, whose *American Practical Navigator* has been the navigator's bible since 1802, advised that "in the absence of a known position, it is best to anchor and wait for the fog to lift." I disagree. Stumbling about lost can be dangerous, it's true, but so is anchoring in a fairway. Although I've failed on many occasions to raise my appointed mark, I've never stopped there and dropped the hook. My practice has always been to keep going for the next mark—albeit with an even higher level of caution—and the practice has never yet failed me.

Should you miss a mark, what's your best estimate of your position? Make a plan, then proceed. How deep is the water? Knowing that is a safeguard. Even if you continue on with your original DR, you are more likely than not to encounter a buoy or landmark or someone to yell to in the fog so you can get a fix. Know, too, that you can encounter shallow water, hazards, or dry land. Just sail defensively, cautiously, slowly, and with eyes and ears open. You know that you're within a reasonable distance of your planned track. That can make "finding yourself" easier than if you have a whole chart to stab at.

There are no automatic answers, but precision, calm, and common sense are good allies when you're running in fog.

Using GPS

Ever since the gods told Odysseus to keep the Great Bear (Big Dipper) on his left shoulder to point his ship homeward, sailors have looked to the sky for guidance, and thanks to GPS, we have better "stars" to steer by than ever before. Thirty satellites launched and positioned by the U.S. military now form a constellation of orbiting beacons that provide full-time, all-weather, around-the-globe positioning. A garden-variety handheld GPS receiver will give you a positional accuracy within 50 feet, and if you choose a differential GPS receiver and antenna you can reduce that to 15 feet.

The thirty medium-orbit satellites are distributed among six orbital planes such that at least six satellites are within line of sight at any time from almost any point on the earth's surface. Since only four satellites are required for a fix, your receiver should be able to give you a fix at all times. Just turn the receiver on, and it should require no more than a minute or two to lock onto the quartet of satellites that provides the best fix. When you ask "Where am I?" GPS answers.

If you've been navigating

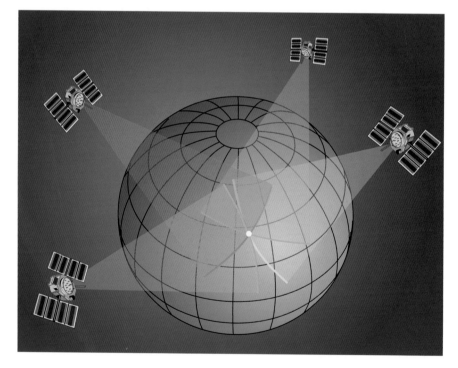

Your fixed or handheld GPS receiver triangulates the signals from four or more orbiting satellites to locate itself on earth.

for more than a decade or so, you'll remember the predecessors to GPS. The SatNav (satellite navigation) system could give you position fixes at sea, but with so few satellites you often had to wait minutes or hours between fixes—not good for coastal piloting. Loran (*long range aid to navigation*) depends on triangulating precisely timed radio signals from earth-based transmitters. The coverage is full-time where it exists at all, but loran is confusing to use and subject to signal error; when it's off, it can be way off. The U.S. Coast Guard still maintains its system of loran towers, and you still find navigation charts with loran time-difference curves overprinted on them. And you can still find devoted loran users. But GPS is easier to use, universal in coverage, and remarkably resistant to giving out bad position information.

With a GPS receiver at hand, your position is simply a beginning. The power and glory of the system is that the receiver is also a microcomputer that will take you where you want to go. Simply enter the latitude and longitude coordinates of

A handheld GPS receiver (left) can do everything a fixed console GPS (right) can. Both of these units have built-in digital charts, making them into chartplotters.

a waypoint—or select a previously entered waypoint from a menu—then press the GoTo button, and the receiver will give you the waypoint's bearing and range. Steer that bearing, and you'll hit the waypoint.

What if a current is pushing you off course? No problem. The receiver monitors your course over ground (COG), not your compass course, and if you match your COG to the waypoint's bearing, you will

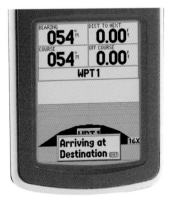

When you enter the GoTo command and then select a stored waypoint, your GPS receiver displays the course and distance to the waypoint (left). A screen message and perhaps an audible tone alert you when you arrive (right).

Meet Your GPS

All GPS recievers offer similar functions. The generic layout shown here is typical. Use your GPS manual to identify any differences in detail.

latitude and longitude of your current position and the precise time. (In this example, Satellite and Position appear on one screen; other models present them separately.) The Map Screen shows your current position with respect to other objects (waypoints) stored in your GPS, and the active course line. The Highway Screen shows a 3-D representation of your active course with your current position in the foreground and your next waypoint in the background. This is likely to be the most valuable screen to keep you on course.

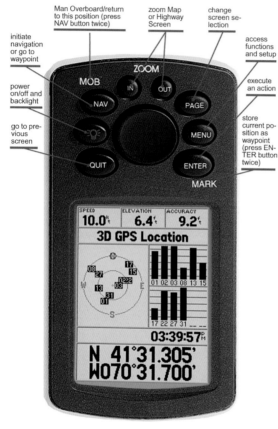

- Man Overboard/return to this position (press NAV button twice)
- zoom Map or Highway Screen
- change screen selection
- initiate navigation or go to waypoint
- access functions and setup
- power on/off and backlight
- execute an action
- go to previous screen
- store current position as waypoint (press ENTER button twice)

Satellite/Position Screen

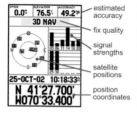

- estimated accuracy
- fix quality
- signal strengths
- satellite positions
- position coordinates

Map Screen

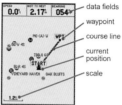

- data fields
- waypoint
- course line
- current position
- scale

Highway Screen

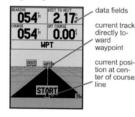

- data fields
- current track directly toward waypoint
- current position at center of course line

Map Screen with Map*

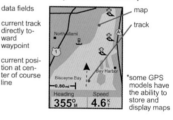

- map
- track
- *some GPS models have the ability to store and display maps

MENUS

Use menus to program the GPS, to initiate and control navigation, and to select display format. Most menus are accessed via the Main Menu using the MENU (or ENTER) button, or by paging to find the Main Menu Screen. In addition, most GPS sets offer screen-dependent menus that control how data are displayed on an individual screen. Access these from the current screen by pressing the MENU (or ENTER) button.

BUTTONS

The many GPS functions are controlled by a set of buttons, restricted in number by the space available. Most of the buttons control how the GPS processes and displays information. The button labeled NAV or GOTO controls navigation functions. Press the ENTER button to execute actions. Press the QUIT or ESC button to revert to a prior screen instead of executing an action. The labels may vary slightly by model, but the general approach is always the same.

Move cursor to highlight:

Points: Enter/edit waypoints; view list of programmed waypoints

Routes: List/create waypoint sequences, each called a "route"

Proximity Waypoints: List/enter programmed danger coordinates

Tracks: Control/review recorded paths taken by GPS

Trip Computer: Set/review recorded times, distances, average speed, etc.

SCREENS

You can select screens as needed. The Satellite Screen indicates the quality of the GPS position and tells you if part of the sky is blocked to the GPS antenna. The Position Screen indicates the

Programming GPS Waypoints

Programming a waypoint into a GPS receiver. 1. *Make sure the path from your starting point to the chosen waypoint is free of charted hazards.* **2, 3.** *Measure the latitude and longitude of the waypoint with dividers as described earlier in this chapter.* **4.** *Enter these coordinates in your GPS unit's New Waypoints screen (or equivalent), following the instructions that come with the device.*

Either by saving your current position or by entering latitude and longitude coordinates, you can establish a waypoint. Entering waypoints is a useful part of the preplanning for a cruise or even a daytrip. Pick from the chart the points along your route that you would like to use as waypoints. Use your dividers to measure the latitude and longitude of each such point, then enter those coordinates into your receiver.

Use good navigational sense in creating waypoints. You might choose a midchannel buoy as a waypoint, for example, but what about a can buoy that's just 100 yards from the ledge it marks? In that case you might make your waypoint ¼ mile on the safe side of the buoy—close enough to identify it but far enough off not to hit anything. This is part of the beauty of GPS—any arbitrary point in a featureless expanse of water makes a legitimate

waypoint. You might choose a point 0.5 mile north of a bold headland, where you want to turn from south to east. GPS lets you do that.

Once you have waypoints, you can select these in sequence to create routes. Most GPS units can store at least 99 waypoints and 20 routes in memory. Waypoints are the bread and butter of GPS, so look for a unit that lets you create, organize, and retrieve them easily.

Plotting GPS Coordinates on a Chart

A GPS receiver provides the latitude and longitude coordinates for your position, but until you plot this position on a chart, it doesn't mean much. To do this, locate your GPS latitude on the appropriate chart's latitude scale and place one point of the dividers on that spot. Then adjust the dividers so that the second point rests on the nearest latitude line. Now move the dividers along the latitude line to your approximate location (by visually approximating the longitude) and make a small horizontal pencil mark. Then do the same for the longitude. Your current position is at the intersection of the pencil marks.

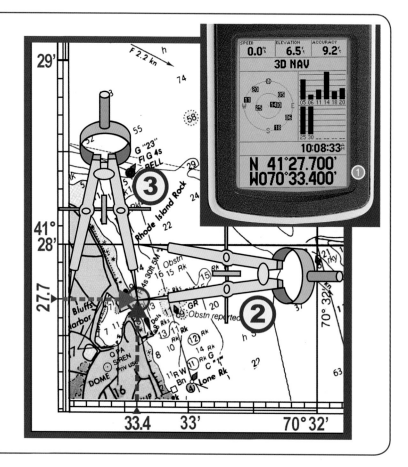

To plot GPS coordinates (1), use dividers to mark off the latitude (2) and longitude (3) on the chart.

Electronic Charting

The next step up in convenience (and complexity) from a GPS receiver is to send the signal from the receiver to a computer displaying digital charts. The computer can be a laptop PC with the GPS signal provided through a cable and serial port, or it can be a dedicated chartplotter that either has an integral GPS receiver or accepts the signal from an external receiver. A laptop is more versatile, whereas a chartplotter can be mounted in the cockpit, but either way this is the complete package. Your boat will appear as an icon on the chart, with your historical track showing as a dashed line. You can see at a glance if you're headed for trouble and how to avoid it. As long as your electronics function normally, all doubt is gone. But handheld GPS receivers consume batteries like candy, so bring plenty of spares, and when the laptop runs out of juice, know how to use the GPS receiver with your paper charts. And when the receiver itself dies, know the rudiments of traditional chart-and-compass dead reckoning.

A chartplotter displays your GPS position on a digital chart. The GPS receiver may be built-in or independent, and many chartplotters can also display depth sounder and radar information.

have automatically corrected for the current. Now compare your compass course with your COG to see how much the current is affecting you.

As you proceed toward the waypoint, the receiver also monitors your speed over ground (SOG) and your ETA. It updates your position at least once per second. In short, it gives you just about all the information you'll ever need.

What's missing, of course, is a sailor's eye. The course to the buoy may well be 090 degrees, but GPS can't tell you whether that course leads through safe water or shallows. Nor, if you are set off course by currents over the first half of a leg, can GPS tell you whether the corrected course you adopt to work yourself back on track will take you into danger. It makes obvious good sense, therefore, to compare the display with the chart, but as you get into a trip and GPS provides course changes and updates, it's easy to lose that caution in the shuffle. Be just as hard-nosed about checking courses in midtrip as you are at the outset.

And, of course, if you are using GPS without waypoints simply to monitor your position, the fix it gives you means nothing until you plot those coordinates on the chart. The story that began this chapter gives ample demonstration of that.

Handheld units are good enough to do it all. Console units have advantages, though, mostly in terms of data entry, display quality, and interfacing with other electronics. Display clarity (screen brightness and font characteristics) is always a concern, as is moisture-proofing. The alarm features that seem most useful include the arrival alarm (which tells you when you've reached a waypoint), the proximity alarm (which warns you that you're near a hazard you've designated), and the anchor alarm (which warns you that your anchor is dragging). The man-overboard function (hit a button to enter your position as soon as possible after the victim goes in) could be invaluable.

Using Radar

Nothing beats radar for seeing ships and other boats or getting ranges and bearings in the dark or the fog. Radar has limitations, but its combination of collision-avoidance and aid-to-navigation capabilities makes it—along with GPS—one of the two most useful electronic aids any sailor can have aboard. Though radar units were prohibitively expensive, cumbersome, and heavy for most small boats as recently as the 1980s, today they are more compact, durable, and affordable than ever, and the liquid crystal displays (LCDs) that have replaced the cathode ray tubes of yesteryear are easier to read (especially in daylight), more intuitive to work, and more capable. Radar is now feasible for most cruising sailboats.

The antenna is a key component. Circuitry for both transmitter and receiver are

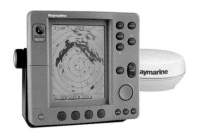

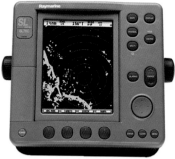

Marine radar includes two major components: the scanner/antenna (bottom) and the display unit, which can be mounted either belowdecks or on brackets in the cockpit.

fouling and damage, however, and simply won't fit on a small boat, so most sailboats use a 15- to 24-inch antenna enclosed in a circular fiberglass housing called a radome that is transparent to the radar transmissions. The radome is typically mounted on the forward side of a mast or atop a dedicated spar on the afterdeck. A 15-inch antenna produces a horizontal beam width on the order of 7 degrees—resulting in reduced but still highly useful bearing resolution—whereas a 24-inch antenna generates a narrower beam of 4 degrees.

built into it. The higher it is mounted, the better its range, since radar range is line of sight. It needs a nearly uninterrupted 360-degree sweep, though the small null sector introduced by a mast just aft of the antenna should do no harm. While its high-frequency microwave emissions have never been proven injurious to health, mounting it where its pulses won't be emitted directly at humans is a recommended caution.

In boats over 50 feet you might find a spot aloft for an *open-array* antenna bar. These antennas rotate in the open air and can weigh up to 50 pounds. A 4-foot-long open-array antenna transmits a beam

width of just 2 degrees, permitting precise bearing resolution on targets. These antennas are susceptible to

Looking aloft at a mast-mounted radome on a cruising catamaran.

The antenna emits super-high-frequency radio pulses through its 360-degree sweep, and whenever these pulses strike a target, they jump (within a millisecond) back to the antenna. The radar processor calculates range from the time lag between the transmission of a pulse and its "bounce-back," and bearings and ranges to targets are then displayed on the LCD screen. The resultant picture is refreshed with every sweep of the antenna.

If the beam is too wide, bounce-backs can come from several angles at once. That makes targets tough to resolve and identify. Phantom targets, too, are created when return pulses hit something else before the antenna and scatter or ricochet. Using a short antenna that's compact enough to suit your boat can thus mean sacrificing a bit of fine-tuning. Two boats in middle radar range—say, 5 miles—might show as a single target if they are fairly close together. But target definition at long range is not often critical. At close range, where it does become critical, it improves dramatically.

Most small-boat radar units offer a selection of five or six ranges, from a ⅛-mile circle out to the typical maximum range of 16 miles. If your an-

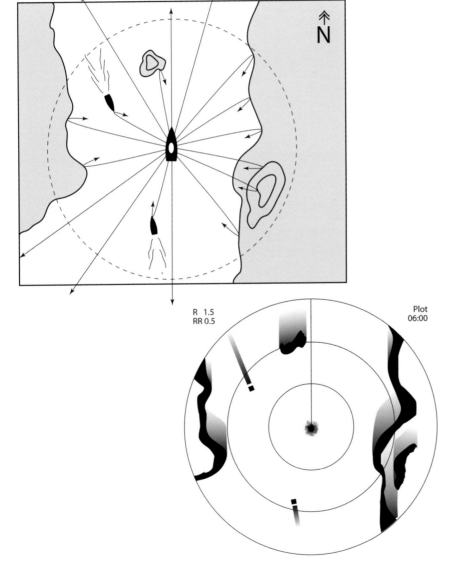

A boat's radar at work. The top view shows the rotating radar beam reflecting from various targets. The bottom view shows how these targets might appear on the radar screen. Your boat is always at the center of the display. The dark images are the targets; the gray trails mark target locations over the past 6 minutes using a plot option, which is available on most modern radar units. The beam rotates every 3 seconds or so and updates the radar screen on each rotation. This radar is set to look out to a maximum range (R) of 1.5 miles, and the range rings (RR) mark 0.5-mile increments. The heading line from the center of the screen marks the direction your vessel is headed.

tenna is mounted about 10 feet off the water, the horizon as seen by the radar is around 8 miles away, but you will "see" hills, bold headlands, big ships, and other such targets at longer range. Still, the 16-mile circle is all the effective range most sailors need. Some sets offer 36- and 48-mile ranges, but when you consider that a target 20 miles distant must be 170 feet high to be glimpsed over the horizon, the extra power is not very practical. Moving the radome higher up the mast

Three views of the world. The navigator's job is to coordinate what is seen on the radar, on the chart, and from the boat's deck. Each view tells us more about what the other views are showing.

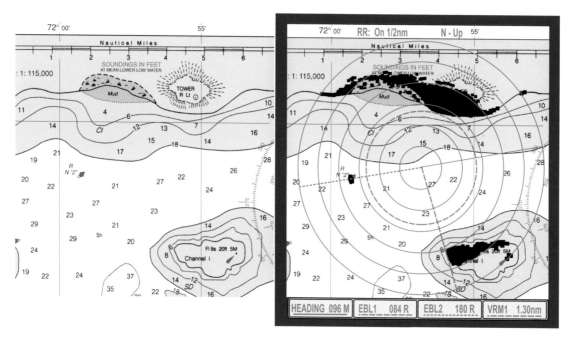

On the left is a training chart used by the United States Power Squadrons. On the right is a graphic representation of how the charted features might appear as targets on a radar screen that has been rotated clockwise to correspond with the chart's north-up orientation. Targets are shown in black. The buoy returns a discrete echo. The shoreline appears as a solid echo except where low-lying mud and swamp give patchy returns. Only the near side of the hill to the north can be seen—the tower on the hilltop is invisible—and similarly, only the near side of Channel Island is visible. The rest is screened from radar view by intervening topography.

will increase range, but hardly enough to justify the higher weight and windage aloft and the resulting decreased stability. The microprocessors in the set alter range at your command by altering the characteristics of the pulse sent out. Long pulses are for long range. As range decreases, pulses are sent (and received) faster. The closer in the target, the more rapidly the set bombards it with pulses and thus the clearer the image.

Vertical beam width for most units is 25 degrees. Thus, when you heel more than 12½ degrees, you start to send your signal into the water on one side and sweep the sky on the other. You can flatten the boat out or keep using the set with a smaller field of vision, or you might invest in a gimballed antenna mount.

The transmitting power ranges from 1.5 kilowatt (kW) for the smallest sets to 4 kW or 5 kW for the biggies. More powerful sets do a better job of resolving (and locating) targets, but lower-powered sets are kinder to the battery bank. Most modern units will "wake up" at an interval you determine (5, 10, or 20 minutes) to take a few sweeps and assure you that

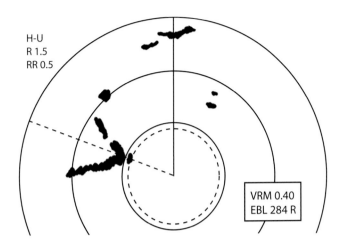

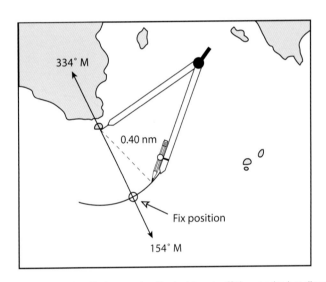

A range-and-bearing fix from radar. The bold rock off the nearby headland shows as a distinctive target on the radar display. When you adjust the variable range marker (VRM) until it passes through the target, the display tells you that the rock is 0.4 nautical mile away. (Note that the range rings are set to 0.5-mile increments.) Now rotate the electronic bearing line (EBL) until it too passes through the target, and you see that its bearing relative to your heading is 284 degrees. If you are steering 050 degrees magnetic, the magnetic bearing to the rock is 334 degrees, the reciprocal of which is 154 degrees. Plot this bearing on the chart as shown, then use dividers to measure 0.4 mile from the rock. That's where you are.

no one else is around. That conserves power. A useful feature is the ability to maintain an alarm while the display is shut down.

The antenna's high-voltage circuitry means that a radar set should be serviced at least every second year.

The Radar Display

Your boat is at the center of the radar display, with targets arrayed around it. The usual default setting is the **heading-up display**, which simply means that any target appearing at the top of the display is ahead of your boat, and any target at the bottom is astern. The best way to get used to a radar display is to use it in clear weather with chart at hand, comparing what you see on the screen with what you see on the chart and over the deck. Note how two closely spaced boats might merge into one target on the screen, and how a narrow inlet might disappear into the general shoreline trend. Note how navigation buoys appear on the screen, and observe how boats moving obliquely to yours travel across the screen. See what happens to nearby and more distant targets when you adjust the range setting. Turn on the range rings to get a quick visual reference to the ranges of targets, then turn them off (most units permit this) for a cleaner display. Play with the electronic cursor, which most radar units provide. Move it over any target and the corresponding data field will tell you the bearing and range to the target—a tremendously

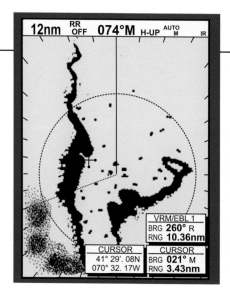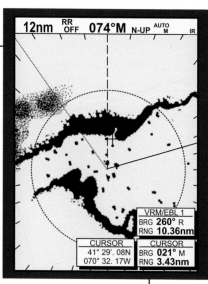

A heading-up (left) versus north-up (right) radar display. In both views your boat is at the center of the display. This radar is set to a maximum range of 12 miles, and in both views the variable range marker (VRM, the dotted circle) is set to 10.36 miles. The cursor, which you can move at will to get the range and bearing to any target of interest, is set 3.43 miles from the boat along a bearing of 021 degrees magnetic in both views. The heading line rotated 74 degrees clockwise to create the north-up view, and the electronic bearing line (EBL, the dotted line) also rotated 74 degrees to remain at 260 degrees relative to the boat's heading.

useful feature. Now change course 30 or 40 degrees and see what happens to the targets on the screen—in a heading-up display, they will shift clockwise when you turn to port and counterclockwise when you turn to starboard.

In a **north-up display**, your boat is still at the center, but the top of the display is always north, just as on a chart. Not all radar units offer north-up orientation, and use of this feature requires an interfaced electronic compass. It facilitates chart comparisons and prevents targets from rotating across the screen when you alter course, but most navigators prefer a heading-up display because it orients the screen with the boat.

LCDs are lighter, draw less power, and are more visible in direct sun than the CRT displays they have mostly displaced. They do not, however, necessarily permit the same degree of quantization.

Quantization is an onscreen system for displaying the nature of the target. When a radar return "paints" its picture on a CRT screen, different targets produce different echoes and thus different blips. Wood and fiberglass absorb energy, so their target signature is weaker and less defined than steel and aluminum. A granite cliff gives an even more solid return, whereas a mainsail lets the waves pass through it and is nearly invisible. A 1-foot-square radar reflector creates a blip bigger than an entire fiberglass sailboat.

On a CRT screen you can thus intuit something about the nature of the target you're

Electronic Bearing Line and Variable Range Marker

Most radar units offer an **electronic bearing line** (EBL) and a **variable range marker** (VRM) to help you track targets. The EBL is a line radiating from the center of the display (i.e., from your boat) that you can rotate around the screen until it falls on an approaching target. If the target remains on the EBL as it nears the center of the screen, you are on a collision course. This is equivalent to assessing risk of collision with visual bearings on deck, but quicker and more precise. The VRM is a circle of constant range and represents a convenient way to track the range to a target of interest or to establish the perimeter of a zone of particular interest to you. If you're particularly concerned about targets within ¼ mile, set the VRM to ¼-mile radius and pay closest attention to targets inside it.

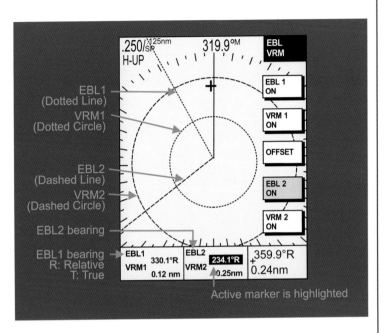

This radar permits setting two EBLs and two VRMs.

looking at—a capability that LCD displays don't inherently have. Via enhanced quantization, however, digitally based raster displays can still provide something of the old feel for the target.

Because of its relatively wide beam, radar yields fuzzy bearings. Tangent bearings on a headland or island shore may be off by as much as 10 degrees—not as exact as a good visual or GPS line. Still, radar bearings

are great as long as you recognize their limits. Ranges are extremely accurate. As mentioned earlier in the chapter, radar excels at providing a fix from the range and bearing to a single target.

Think of the radar signal as a light beam. There is a "shadow" behind a big target. There is a small but significant loss of energy to the atmosphere. Sometimes atmospheric conditions (such as temperature inver-

sions) will bend the beam. Targets close to one another or in line with one another can meld together. Overhead power cables can create confusing echoes. Intervening waves or rain will cause clutter, and occasionally you'll see ghosts—targets that aren't really there. Other radar transmissions create interference. The only limitation that matters, though, is your ability to interpret what you see.

Target Movements

What you see on a radar screen is relative motion, and that can take some getting used to. If your speed over ground is 6 knots, a stationary navigation buoy will head "downscreen" at 6 knots, while a boat with the same heading and speed as yours will appear motionless on the screen. A boat approaching you very slowly from ahead will appear to be moving much faster than it is, while a boat that you're overtaking will head slowly downscreen as you come up on its stern. If its speed is 5 knots and yours is 6, it will move downscreen at 1 knot. A boat approaching from your port beam will move to the right and down on the screen. All this can be confusing at first. Again, practice in clear weather, and remember, when a target remains on the EBL while its range decreases, there is risk of collision.

The motions of buoys and other boats relative to your own seem obvious and logical when viewed from the deck but can be baffling when viewed on a radar screen. Here your radar display is set to a range of 1.5 miles, and you have selected a display option that shows a 6-minute "wake trail" for each target. The five targets shown in this simplified example are either stationary or moving parallel with your boat. You know your speed over ground is 5 knots, which means that in 6 minutes you will travel

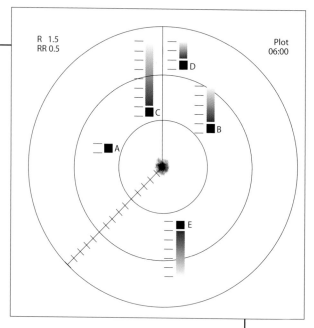

0.5 mile. Target A has not moved, so it must be another boat traveling at the same speed along the same course as you. Target B has moved 0.5 mile downscreen, which means it is stationary—perhaps a navigation buoy. Target C has a trail length of 0.8 nautical mile, corresponding to a relative speed of 8 knots, so it must be a boat traveling along a heading exactly opposite yours at a speed of 3 knots. Target D with a trail length of 0.3 mile appears to be moving toward you at 3 knots, so it is in fact moving at 2 knots in the same direction as you, and you are overtaking it. Target E is overtaking you with a trail length of 0.6 mile or a relative speed of 6 knots, so its actual speed is 11 knots.

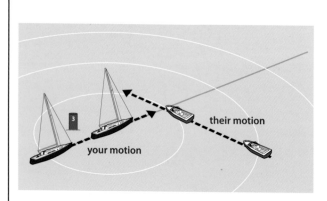

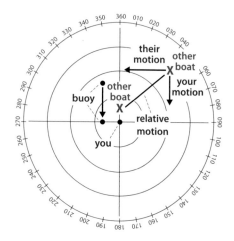

In this example (left) you're passing can "3" while a powerboat crosses your bow. On the radar screen (right) the buoy appears to be moving, though it is of course stationary, and the powerboat appears to be approaching you obliquely, though it is in fact crossing at right angles. Incidentally, because you are under power as well as sail and the power-boat is approaching from your starboard side, it is the stand-on vessel (see Chapter 3), and you probably should have turned to starboard to give it a wider berth. If you had been under sail only, with no engine power, you would have been the stand-on boat.

Radar and GPS

Most radar units can be linked with a chartplotter—so that you can see radar targets superimposed on an electronic chart that is also receiving GPS input—or with a GPS receiver, in which case you can display position, speed, track, cross-track error, and bearing and distance to an active waypoint on the radar screen.

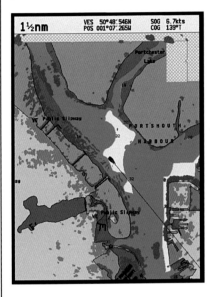

These two radar displays overlay targets on digital charts. Note the close correspondence between target and charted shoreline shapes. Many of the uncharted targets on the image at right are other boats, and the chart view makes it easier to distinguish these from buoys.

Celestial Navigation

Nathaniel Bowditch, the patron saint of sextant-wielders, once claimed, "I put down in the book nothing I can't teach the crew." The book he was speaking of is the *American Practical Navigator*, the 1938 edition of which included more than a hundred pages on celestial navigation. Sharing the same knowledge in a page or two would be impossible even were I so inclined and equipped.

I've shipped with some great, even legendary navigators. I remember Alf Loomis rolling a cigarette one-handed while he cradled his sextant in the other in a Gulf Stream norther. Chick "Chico" Larkin once navigated us close enough to Bishop's Rock to hear the fog cannon after nineteen days at sea—the last three socked in by cloud. I held the watch for Red Wright, and Eric Forsyth let me use his sextant. But learning celestial navigation is not a casual thing. Maybe I never knew quite where to grab onto it, but I sure didn't pick it up by osmosis.

Finally I took a course taught by Frances Wright at the Hayden Planetarium in Boston. She was the author of *Celestial Navigation* and co-developer at Harvard University of a celestial navigation tutorial system, and I don't think there's anything

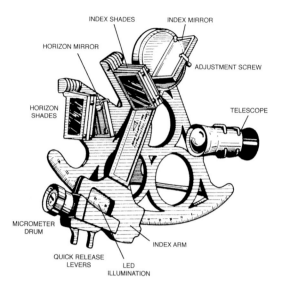

INDEX SHADES

INDEX MIRROR

HORIZON MIRROR

ADJUSTMENT SCREW

HORIZON
SHADES

TELESCOPE

MICROMETER
DRUM

INDEX ARM

QUICK RELEASE
LEVERS

LED
ILLUMINATION

Two views of a standard sextant.

about celestial that she didn't know. Unfortunately I had the bad habit of falling asleep every time the lights went out, and the so-called simple cookbook solutions to that great navigational triangle in the sky never did stop looking like hieroglyphic mysteries to me. To this day I have never shot the sun, moon, or stars when finding my way depended on it. Truth be told, celestial navigation has always reminded me of the Internal Revenue Service: endless tables, inscrutable allowances, and inexplicable errors with big penalties.

But there is envy bristling through my sarcasm. Celestial holds a special place in the history of seafaring, and its practitioners are special people. They can do what Captain Cook could do, and that makes them complete navigators in a way those of us who make our landfalls in more down-to-earth ways can only admire. Celestial navigation is a passport to the open sea, a connection with the explorers, and a nice thing to know. There is a special magic in finding your place on earth by reference to the heavens.

Still, though I laud the great navigators with whom I've sailed, I feel no keen desire to join their ranks. When I think about it carefully, I realize that what I admire most is that they were great sailors, great improvisers, and great pathfinders who could interpret the stars but, when the clouds closed off the sky, could find other ways into port. My ways have always gotten me where I aimed to go, and if I want a backup, why not buy another GPS receiver for $150?

And finally, let's be clear: Celestial navigation is a system for the open sea. It lacks the precision and accuracy for coastal piloting, even in the hands of a skilled practitioner. Those caveats behind us, here are the rudiments.

The sextant is an instrument for measuring the angle between two objects or, as is most commonly the case in navigation, the angle of a celestial body above the horizon.

Begin by realizing that every heavenly body possesses, at each instant, a spot on the earth from which it is directly overhead. That point on the earth's surface is called the **geographic position** (GP) of the body. Now imagine a flagpole in the middle of a field. Its tip is the sun (or star, moon, or planet), and its base is the sun's GP. Shooting with a sextant is like stretching a line taut from the top of the pole. It fixes the angle between the sun and your location on earth. If you walk all around the pole while keeping the line taut and its angle therefore constant, you will have created a circle of equal altitude. Everywhere on that circle the angle between the ground and the top of the pole is the same. Your position is somewhere on that circle.

To fix your position you might shoot another body, create another circle, and find where the two circles intersect. (They would, of course, intersect in two places, and it's the job of your DR plot to tell you which intercept point is your fix and which should be ignored.)

Also, because the altitude and bearing of any celestial body can be computed by tables, you could fix your position more closely using just a single body in the sky. If you enter the *Nautical Almanac* with the date and time of your sight, you can learn the bearing to the GP and its distance. That gives you a fix (with the aid of sight reduction tables or a calculator), but to plot it takes a bit more manipulating. Because the circle of equal altitude is too big to plot, the convention of using an assumed position and comparing it with the observed data has been adopted. From this the navigator gets an LOP.

From a light in the sky to a line on the plotting sheet. That's the idea, though there's a bit more to it than that. If it sounds interesting, by all means study it further. Knowledge of the night sky is its own reward.

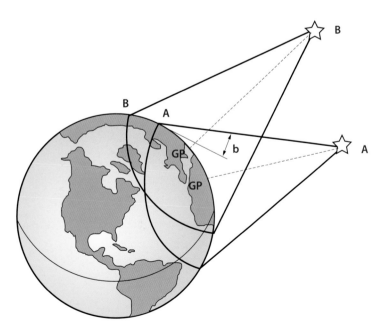

The basis of position finding through measuring the altitude of celestial bodies is the circle of equal altitude—the circle of locations on earth from which the body has the measured angle of elevation above the horizon. By sighting two bodies (stars A and B in this illustration) you can get a fix because two circles of equal altitude intersect in only two places. The one that's in the right part of the planet for you (i.e., closest to your assumed position) marks your position. GP is the body's geographic position. Angle b is the elevation in degrees of the star above the horizon (as measured with a sextant). What more do you need to know?

Making a Landfall

When you are where you think you are, a landfall after an ocean passage is pretty straightforward. GPS accuracy helps make that a realistic expectation, but even the best celestial navigation or DR plotting leaves room for doubt. The clouds, the current, a slip of the pencil, fog—things can conspire to make ocean navigation suspenseful. That's why a landfall is always anticipated with excitement and a tinge of nervousness. Begin by confirming your position. A solid fix is the first step of any approach to port. Don't carry your uncertainties forward, and don't compound your assumptions without testing them. Learn where you are!

I'd never navigated with a Russian chart before sailing to the port of Lethma. Not knowing how to read Cyrillic, I found a likely six-letter town on the chart and started in. Shortly before we hit the bricks, I could tell I was lost. What I thought was Lethma turned out to be the town of Gharda, and I had been following the right directions for the wrong town (or maybe vice versa). It sounds elementary, but don't just assume you're on the right side of the jetty, especially at night or in the fog. Challenge your assumptions and get proof that they're right, preferably from two independent means. Otherwise your assumptions might sink you.

A GPS position or other solid fix is nice, but you can't always count on one. You may be without electronics. You may not be able to identify any landmarks. You may not even be able to see any. But force yourself to focus on all clues. In the absence of something more tangible, bird flights, wave patterns, changes in water color, insects, or flotsam may advertise the proximity of land, especially around a low island.

High land breeds high clouds that can be seen from afar. In clear weather anything taller than 500 feet can probably be seen before you need to look for other signs of land. Like lights, however, peaks can be deceptive. You'd think that a 3,000-foot volcano (described in our piloting guide as "spewing red-hot lava down its slope") would be visible for quite a distance, but thanks to a haze so slight I hadn't noticed it through a night of searching, we were barely 3 miles from the island of Stromboli when I looked up to be surprised by the island's "fire in the sky." Even an active volcano proved not to be as spectacular a leading mark as I had hoped.

Charted ranges and sectors of major lights are helpful to navigators making a landfall, but seeing a light when and where it should appear is not exactly a clockwork phenomenon. The charted range is based solely on the light's candlepower, but frequently the earth's curvature will intervene at a lesser range. Suppose, for example, that a light with a height of 100 feet has a listed range of 18 miles. If your height of eye is 9 feet, the horizon is 3.4 miles from you, and the horizon distance from a height of 100 feet is 11.4 miles. Thus, your first glimpse of the light in unlimited visibility will come at a distance of 14.8 miles. Even a slight haze will reduce the range of visibility further. Be prepared to be confused by this at times.

On the other hand, the mountainous coast of Albania was so accurately profiled in the *Admiralty Pilot* that I could make a landfall on what was

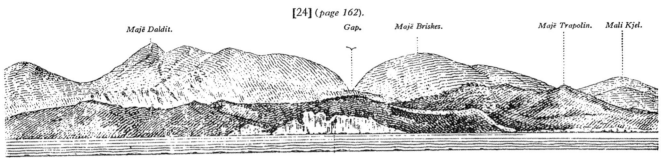

[24] *(page 162).*

Majë Daldit.   Gap.   Majë Briskes.   Majë Trapolin.   Mali Kjel.

Shkamb i Kavajës, in line with gap,
bearing 083°, leads southward of Talbot shoal.

Gji i Durrësit.

Illustrations like this (taken from the Admiralty Sailing Directions: Mediterranean Pilot, Volume 3) have been guiding sailors to landfalls for centuries. This one helped us make our first landfall in Yugoslavia without charts or electronics.

then Yugoslavia and be relatively sure I wasn't straying into the prohibited zone patrolled by the gunboats of (then) Communist Albania just 10 miles to the south. Be thankful for good visibility and piloting guides that pay attention to what you can see from a small boat.

Once you find land, even before you know what it is and that you have it on a chart, determine your distance off. The techniques for doubling the angle on the bow, discussed earlier in this chapter, work well for finding distance off in this instance. You don't need identifiable landmarks, just two or more bearings on the same object. No matter the doubts and questions, even if you don't have the proper chart and you're not where you wanted to be, good seamanship can get you in safely. Remember:

- **Pick your landfall target carefully.** Off-lying dangers should usually be avoided, but in thick weather you might want to use them as stepping-stones. It's simplest most of the time to approach a bold, shoal-free headland. Such a target is easier to find and identify than a chunk of low-lying coast. When you survey possible landfalls, look hard for prominent navaids and physical features.

- **Avoid a lee shore.** Problems begin when you are driven closer to a beach than you'd like, so leave a wide safety cushion when the wind is blowing onshore. Surf looks smoother from offshore than from the beach. If you need to enter an inlet or river mouth, especially when the tide is ebbing, stand off long enough to get a feel for the true height of the waves before you plunge into them. Better yet, ask yourself whether you really need to enter this inlet. Maybe there's a nearby anchorage with a safer approach.

- **Monitor the depth sounder as you approach.** Is the bottom shoaling sharply or gradually? Are the contours regular (indicative of a smooth bottom) or jagged (indicative of rocks)? The hazards will be different depending on the makeup of the seabed and shoreline you're approaching.

- **A direct approach is usually best,** but in limited visibility—and especially in fog—closing with the shore at an angle will let you follow bottom contours rather than cutting quickly across them, and slowing your approach will give you time to digest and respond to information from the depth sounder and other sources.

- **Observe everything!** That's the essence of piloting by eye. What does the trend of the land tell you about the inshore bottom? Are there any surface disturbances?

(It's not true that you can't hit what you can't see, but most shoals that are close enough to the surface to bother a small boat give some signs of themselves if there is any swell.) Why is that crab pot, speed-limit buoy, stake with a basket on it, or other object there? Signs for sailors do not come from the government alone. Where is that boat going and can I follow him? It's like asking directions on the street. Whom do you trust? I trust most anyone whose boat draws more than mine does.

You certainly don't want to be in the position of making an unplanned landfall on a coast where you have no chart or knowledge, but if you must, you can.

Assuming your landfall is planned, perhaps the worst scenario is being so lost when you arrive that you don't even know which way to turn. It's wise, sometimes, to avoid this by building a directional error into your approach. If the waters north of your intended landfall are safe, for example, aim deliberately to that side. Then, when you hit the beach—or better still, when you hit a preselected contour line—you'll know you need to turn south. But use your head and take wind and tide into account. You

---

Distance to Horizon

The range of a navigation light you see listed on a chart or in the *Light Lists* is its **nominal range**—the clear-weather range based solely on the power of the light. The **geographic range**—the maximum range at which you can see the light—may well be less if the curvature of the earth intervenes. The geographic range is the sum of the viewer's distance to horizon plus the light's distance to horizon, and in each case the formula for distance to horizon is 1.17 x square root of height (of eye or light) in feet.

If your height of eye is 9 feet, your horizon distance is $\sqrt{9}$ x 1.17 = 3.5 nautical miles. If the light you are searching for is 49 feet high, its horizon distance is $\sqrt{49}$ x 1.17 = 8.2 miles. Thus, its geographic range is 8.2 + 3.5 = 11.7 miles, even if its listed range is higher.

To ascertain how close you are to a light's geographic range, try lowering your height of eye. If crouching causes the light to drop beneath the horizon, you are at or close to its geographic range and can estimate your distance off with reasonable accuracy.

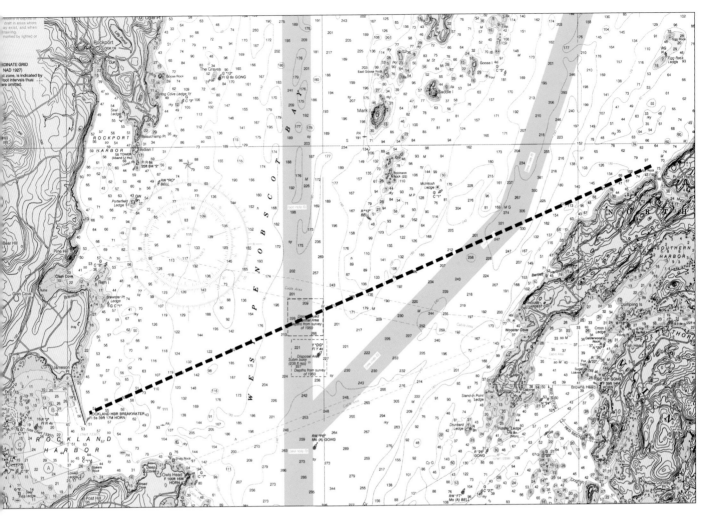

When you are making a landfall it's often useful to "stray" to one side (north in this case) so that when you close with land you'll know which way to turn to reach your destination. In this example a sailor making a passage in thick fog across Penobscot Bay, Maine, lays her course from Pulpit Harbor to the Rockland Harbor breakwater rather than the middle of the harbor entrance. There is deep water off the breakwater, and the fog signal at the lighthouse on the end of the breakwater will guide her in. Once in contact with the breakwater she can feel her way around it, sticking to the edge of the entrance and thus avoiding Rockland's ferries and fishing vessels.

don't want to put yourself downwind or downtide of your destination and have to slog back to it.

Try to arrive where you're going at a convenient time. Daylight is better than dark, and heaving-to offshore to wait for dawn almost always makes sense when you approach a strange coast. Flood current is better than ebb, though a strong current from astern can compromise your maneuvering and speed control. For piloting through coral you need the sun behind you. By working over the distance track and a realistic range of boat speeds, you'll be able not only to shoot for convenient arrival times but hit them.

Your progress in can be easier if you're aware of the progression of navaids. They'll go from ocean aids to coastal, to harbor. The buoys get smaller as you get closer in. Shoot for an ocean aid as your arrival mark. Its size, its relatively bright light, and perhaps its sound signal may make it easier to find than a little nun along the harbor channel. It can be worth your time, too, to line up alternative leading marks in case the ones you are counting

on don't appear or are hard to identify.

This is also where safety bearings (see earlier in this chapter) prove their worth. Whether you've laid them out beforehand or plot them as you go, bearings that will keep you clear of known hazards are highly useful.

You can make the approach easier, too, by identifying useful ranges on the chart. Plot and label the lines created when two landmarks line up. This will remind you that the range is available, help you find it, and provide you with an instant LOP once your course crosses any segment of a line you've laid down.

It's natural to relax your DR once you begin an approach, but resist this urge. Keep track of your position.

When approaching via GPS, you can set a waypoint a mile or two off the channel mouth. Once you arrive there, you can identify the important landmarks and verify the bearings and ranges you'll be using on your way in. Even GPS doesn't give you the whole story, though. It's important to build a mental picture of your destina-

Light Lists

A navigation chart will tell you the height, light pattern and nominal range, sound signal, and racon signal (if present) of a light. (A racon-equipped buoy or light paints a distinctive, unmistakable return image on your radar display, usually in the shape of a Morse code letter.) It won't, however, tell you the color and shape of a fixed light or what the sound signal pattern might be. The most reliable way to obtain that information in the United States is to consult the *Light Lists*, which are published in six volumes by the Coast Guard. The *Light Lists* are available online as free PDF files at www.navcen.uscg.gov/pubs/LightLists/LightLists.htm.

tion. Charts and pilots help create that image, but seeing the place on radar can be another useful step. The physical layout, the contours, and the relationships among landmarks are all more evident from a radar display than a chart. Comparing your DR plot with subsequent bearings is then a good way to get as accurate a picture of set and drift as possible. The GPS cross-track error feature works well, too, but I find its averaging makes readings suspect on short legs.

If, as part of your preplanning, you examine the negative possibilities, your planning becomes more valuable. What will you do if fog shuts in or if you can't find that light? What if your DR position doesn't agree with the depth sounder? What if your handheld GPS receiver stops working? Come up with contingencies before you need them. Landfalls are challenging, but you can't leave home without them.

CHAPTER SIX

Racing

Daysailing is one of life's purest pleasures, and some sailors never feel the urge to do anything else. Most, however, turn sooner or later to racing, cruising, or both. In my own sailing I've struck a roughly 50–50 balance between cruising and racing, and I wouldn't give up either.

Cruising lets you take a boat where you will and sail her how you will. It may be as close to complete freedom and complete self-reliance (for the two go hand in hand) as anyone can get. If you believe that racing is only for competitive types and prefer sailing at your own speed, you have plenty of company.

Lest you write off racing altogether, however, consider its benefits. There is, of course, the direct appeal to the competitive spirit. At least in the keelboat classes—which place a higher premium on sailing skill than athleticism—young and old compete on equal footing. The young have advantages in instincts and nimbleness—and maybe eyesight—but their elders have experience and judgment, and the results are usually up in the air. No other sport—indeed, perhaps no other activity except war—combines preparation, tactics, equipment, and physical effort to the same degree.

Less obvious, perhaps, is the degree to which racing enhances daysailing and cruising. The joy of sailing increases when you sail well, and nothing spotlights what it takes to sail well more effectively than racing. There have been two, maybe three times over the years when my cruising experience has helped me in a race, but every time I hoist sail to cruise, my racing experience is there to draw on.

Unless you win every race, competition will give you lots of teachers. Pay attention to the people in front of you. Imitation, in addition to being the sincerest form of flattery, is how sailors move from the back of the fleet to the front. Ask the leaders in your fleet how they rig their boats, play wind shifts, power up in a light breeze, or balance the rig in a heavy one. Most are happy to share what they know.

To broaden your experience, temper your skills, and pick up new ones, try racing. Even if the idea lacks immediate appeal, you may discover a latent competitive urge that blossoms as your results improve. It can become a magnificent obsession.

Most dinghy and some small-keelboat racing classes place a premium on agility (left), but there are plenty of one-design classes that don't (above left). In these—and when racing in a handicap fleet—skill and judgment rule the day.

The Elements of Racing

Sailboat racing comes in a variety of flavors. In **one-design racing**, all the boats are the same, and the first one over the finish line wins. In **handicap racing** the boats are different, and time allowances are assigned to make the racing fair. (You can't tell by watching a handicap race—or even sailing in one—who's winning.) And in **rating** or **development class racing** the boats are built to a formula but can vary significantly within the formula's confines. The boats race without handicap, and design innovations can play as large a role in the outcome as sailing skill.

Fleet racing is the norm, but there is also **match racing**, in which two boats race head-to-head. The America's Cup is a prominent example of match racing, while the Olympics include fleet one-design racing as well as boat-on-boat match racing.

One-design races are usually conducted around short closed courses, meaning that a race ends where it begins. In this **around-the-buoys racing**, the turning points might include navigation buoys surrounded by safe water, but one or more of the race markers are usually deployed by the race committee so as to provide upwind and downwind legs and perhaps reaching legs as well. There are, in addition, races around islands or from one harbor to another, and these frequently involve handicap fleets in which the owner of a boat used primarily for cruising can try his or her hand at racing. And there are races that involve ocean passages or even take participants around the world.

Some skippers revel in racing alone in a Laser, Sunfish, or other singlehanded one-design. Some even tackle long ocean races alone in specially adapted keelboats. Others race in two-person sailing dinghies or in keelboats with one to five crew, and a few sign up crews of dozens to choreograph the ballet of dueling 80-foot maxi racers. Big boat or little, protected waters or open, local or international, Tuesday evening recreational or Grand Prix, multihull or monohull, there is lots of racing going on.

All races are governed by rules issued—and updated every four years—by the International Sailing Federation (ISAF). Most are run by a race committee, which establishes the racecourse and issues course instructions and starting procedures that augment the ISAF rules. Boats, wind, water, some buoys, some rules, and a starting signal—there you have the components of a sailboat race.

Luck sometimes plays a big role in the outcome of a race. A new wind from the opposite direction can turn fleet positions upside down, thus giving concrete expression to the biblical admonition that the last shall be first. Over the long term, however—a five-race regatta, a season series, or a career—most of what happens on a racecourse is determined by tactics, boat handling, crew work, and boatspeed, and the greatest of these is boatspeed.

Boatspeed

Boatspeed refers to the combination of factors that make one sailboat faster than its competitors. Most races are won, not surprisingly, by the fastest boats. A fast boat can recover from a bad start or from getting on the wrong side of a wind shift. A slow boat will force you to split tacks with the rest of the fleet, hoping for a lucky wind shift, and nine times out of ten

Popular One-Designs

There's a one-design for any budget. Look for a boat that suits your age, crew size, and preferences and is actively raced close to home. How wet do you want to be? How much exercise do you care to get? How much leisurely sailing do you want to do between races?

Name	Sailplan	No. of Crew	Comments	Similar Boats
Sunfish	single sail	1	good training boat, good racing	El Toro, Sailfish, Optimist
Laser	single sail	1	higher performance, worldwide racing	Megabyte, Force 5, Contender, Europe
Coronado 15	sloop, no spinnaker	2 trapeze	popular husband-wife boat	Sweet 16, Holder 14, Buccaneer
JY 15	sloop, no spinnaker	2 no trapeze	tight one-design control	Vanguard 15, M 16, Lido 14, Snipe
505	sloop, spinnaker	2 trapeze	high-performance dinghy	470, 420, M 20, Fireball
Flying Scot	sloop, spinnaker	3	family oriented, large organization	Highlander, Ideal 18
Lightning	sloop, spinnaker	3	planing hull, strong racing class	Y-Flyer, Thistle
Scows	varies	varies	16–38 feet, strong class organization	E-scows, A-scows, MC-scows,
Star	sloop, no spinnaker	2	complex, Olympic class	
Soling	sloop, spinnaker	3	keelboat, former Olympic class	Etchells 22, Dragon, Yngling, Shields
J/24	sloop, spinnaker	4 or 5	keelboat, with cabin trunk	Ensign, Sonar, S-2 7.9, Cal 25
J/105	sloop, asymmetrical spinnaker	4–6	high-performance keelboat	Melges 24
Tartan Ten	sloop, spinnaker	5–7	larger keelboat	Mumm 30, One Design 35, Farr 40

(Reprinted with permission from *Getting Started in Sailboat Racing*, by Adam Cort and Richard Stearns)

you won't get lucky. Being faster gives you control; being slower gives you headaches.

Here are the principal boat-speed variables:

Steering. A deft touch on the tiller or wheel makes a big difference. Upwind this means staying in the groove, and it can also mean knowing when to pinch a bit to windward or drive a bit to leeward to work your way into clear air. It can also mean sensing and curing excessive weather helm before it slows the boat or causes the rudder to stall or be overpowered. Off the wind it can mean knowing when to head up for speed and when to bear off to decrease the distance sailed to the leeward mark. We've covered all these techniques in earlier chapters.

Weight and its distribution. Given equal sail area, the lighter boat is the faster boat except when the extra weight enhances stability, in which case weight is a plus. Move weight lower in a boat, and you make the boat more stable.

Weight placed high contributes to tipping. Stable is fast. Pitching, on the other hand, is slow. Weight in the ends of a boat increases its tendency to hobbyhorse in waves. Centering weight (crew weight, anchor gear, etc.) will reduce the pitching and make the boat more efficient.

Sails. Optimal sail trim greatly enhances boatspeed, but so does an optimal sail shape and a wrinkle-free surface that offers minimum friction and airflow deformation.

International Sailing Federation (ISAF) Classes

International Centerboard Boat Class Associations

14-foot dinghy	Laser
29er	Laser 4.7
420	Laser II
470	Laser Radial
49er	Lightning
505	Mirror
Cadet	Moth
Contender	OK Dinghy
Enterprise	Optimist
Europe	Snipe
Finn	Sunfish
Fireball	Topper
Flying Dutchman	Vaurien
Flying Junior	

International Keelboat Class Associations

11 meter	H-boat
12 meter	J/22
2.4 meter	J/24
5.5 meter	Melges 24
6 meter	Open 60 monohull
8 meter	Soling
Dragon	Star
Etchells	Tempest
Flying Fifteen	Yngling

International Multihull Class Associations

A-catamaran	Hobie 17
Dart 18	Hobie 18
Formula 18	Hobie Tiger
Hobie 14	Tornado
Hobie 16	

International Windsurfing Class Associations

Formula Windsurfing	Mistral Junior
Funboard	Raceboard
Mistral	

Recognized Class Associations

Open 60 multihull	Mumm 30
Aloha	Open 50 monohull
B14	Sonar
Byte	Splash
Farr 40	Tasar
J/80	X99
Maxi One Design	Zoom 8
Micro	

Classic Yacht Classes

GP14	Shark
IOD	

Olympic Classes

How better to give you a sense of the fun to be had sailing one-design racers than in these photos of the nine Olympic sailing classes? These boats are fast, wet, and exciting. This is athletic sailing!

470, a two-person dinghy

Finn, a one-person dinghy

Star, a two-person keelboat

49er, a two-person dinghy

Europe, a one-person dinghy

Laser, a one-person dinghy

Mistral, a sailboard

Tornado, a catamaran

Yngling, a three-person keelboat

Rig. Weight aloft is one enemy, and windage is another. A rig that reduces both while permitting fast sail-shape adjustments and making it easy to shift gears is fast.

Hull. A smooth, fair underbody is fast. Topsides contact the water when heeled and should also be smooth. A bottom fouled with weed or barnacles is slow. Hull stiffness is a variable in some classes, and hull weight may even be a factor. Lighter, fairer hulls are faster, all other things being equal, even if the advantage can only be measured in millimeters.

Controls. How well your boom vang, traveler, spinnaker pole lift, outhaul, and other controls work has a lot to do with how fast you go. They should work faultlessly and reliably while demanding the minimum crew effort and concentration. Organizing, engineering, designing, and building control systems that work well without distracting the crew is a fulltime quest.

Foils. Keels, centerboards, and rudders all work by means of hydrodynamic lift. Maximum lift with minimum drag is the ideal for a sailboat foil in almost all cases. Class rules and limitations most often govern foil size and shape, but all foils work better when they're smooth. Nicks and bumps on the leading edge of a foil are the biggest culprits for robbing efficiency. Surface protuberances are next, while hollows and scratches are less damaging, and the trailing edge is only about half as critical as the leading edge. The bottom line is that any blemish that interrupts a smooth flow of water over a foil will degrade its efficiency. The most efficient sectional shape for the majority of sailboat foils carries its maximum thickness forward of the fore-and-aft midpoint, with the leading edge somewhat more rounded or blunt than the finer, gradually tapered trailing edge.

Subtle variations in any of these areas will make one sailboat faster than its sisters. Testing your boatspeed against a competitor under nonrace conditions can be tremendously helpful. One boat is the yardstick and stays the same while the other makes a change in sail trim, sail shape, weight distribution, or rig tuning. Sail together with both boats in clear air, and see which boat is faster. Make

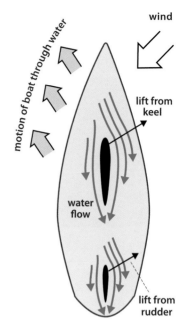

This fish's-eye view of a sailboat's keel (or centerboard) and rudder shows how these foils develop lift. Because the boat makes a small amount of leeway while sailing to windward, water hits the keel and rudder at an angle and therefore has to travel farther and faster around the foils' windward sides. This reduces pressure on the windward sides and generates lift to windward. Without this lift sailboats couldn't sail to windward, so the attached flow around foils is critical. Dings, humps, and hollows— especially near leading edges—will damage performance.

further changes and try again. This is a great way to find out what works and what doesn't.

Until you're able to match the speed of the boats around you, brilliant tactics, superior starting, a lawyerly grasp of the rules, or even a superbly prepared boat will fail to move you up through the fleet. If you are

A Few PHRF Boats and Their Ratings

PHRF (Performance Handicap Rating Fleet) racing is popular because it allows dissimilar racer-cruisers to compete against one another on a leveled playing field. The term **racer-cruiser** applies to almost any boat with a cabin, cruising accommodations, and a fair turn of speed. On a Santana 23 the accommodations are minimal, the boat being more racer than cruiser. The Hunter 25, though only 2 feet longer, is a heavier boat and more cruiser than racer. Yet the boats can compete against one another on reasonably fair terms by virtue of the Hunter's higher handicap. PHRF fleets enable cruising sailors to participate in the occasional race.

PHRF handicaps for boats or classes of boats are adjusted over time to reflect racecourse results. Thus, at least in theory, no boat retains an unfair handicap advantage for very long. The ratings are in units of seconds per mile. If a Colgate 26 finishes a 10-mile course in 2 hours 30 minutes or 150 minutes, its corrected time will be reduced by 168 × 10 or 1,680 seconds, which is 28 minutes. Its corrected time is thus 2 hours 2 minutes. If a J/30 finishes the same course in 2 hours 26 minutes, it has beaten the Colgate 26 by 4 minutes "boat-for-boat," but has it won on corrected time? The correction for the J/30 is 138 seconds per mile, or 1,380 seconds for the 10-mile course, or 23 minutes—and thus its corrected time is 2 hours 3 minutes. The Colgate 26 won on corrected time by 60 seconds. Put another way, the J/30 is "giving" 30 seconds per mile to the Colgate 26 and must thus beat the Colgate 26 around a 10-mile course by at least 300 seconds or 5 minutes in order to "save its time."

The ratings, however, are based on average results. In a ghosting breeze the light J/24 may actually beat the much heavier Tartan Ten around the course boat-for-boat, winning by a huge margin on corrected time. In a strong breeze, on the other hand, the Tartan Ten's sail-carrying power and longer waterline assert themselves, and it will easily save its time on the J/24 unless badly mishandled. To prevent such occasional inequities and keep the competition more interesting, large PHRF fleets are often subdivided into classes of similar ratings. A small handicap fleet doesn't provide this option, and competitors have to accept that on any given day the wind gods may not blow in their favor. On the other hand, the competitors in small, widely mixed fleets are likely to be out

In this weekday after-work PHRF race, a Tartan Ten rounds the leeward mark first, followed closely by an Etchells, with an Ensign bringing up the rear. Often in informal racing like this you're assigned a more favorable handicap if you forgo the use of a spinnaker, as most of these boats are doing.

there as much for socializing as for competition, and the inequities of weather are accepted in that spirit.

Boat Mfr. and Length (ft.)	PHRF Rating	Characteristics
Catalina 22	270	family cruising boat
Santana 23	172	smaller racing boat, light weight
Hunter 25	231	family cruising boat
Cal 25	223	family cruising boat
Colgate 26	168	daysailer/trainer
S2 9.1	135	performance cruiser/racer
Olson 30	105	narrow, light racing boat, fixed keel, also strong one-design
C&C 29	176	family cruising boat
Catalina 30	180	family cruising boat, occasional one-design racer
J/30	138	performance cruiser/one-design racer
C&C 99	102	performance cruiser/racer
Hobie 33	93	racer
Schock 35	72	racer
Beneteau First 36.7	75	performance cruiser/one-design racer
Farr 395	30	performance cruiser/one-design racer

(Reprinted with permission from *Getting Started in Sailboat Racing*, by Adam Cort and Richard Stearns)

open, observant, and flexible enough, the boats around you will provide good lessons in boatspeed. Concentrate on sailing fast. It's the best foundation to build on.

Boat Handling and Crew Work

Time in the boat is the currency of champions. Tacking and jibing are basic, but that doesn't mean they're easily mastered. There's always room for improvement in a spinnaker set, too, and if you ever hit it perfectly, how about practicing some spinnaker jibes?

Acceleration, deceleration, holding your spot, luffing, feinting, timing, and judging the line are all critical at the start—as we shall see—and should all be part of your boat-handling routine.

Unless you sail a one-person dinghy, sailing is a team sport, and you can't talk about boat handling without talking about crew work. Your tacks might be flawless and your spinnaker sets perfect one week, but the next week, with a substitute crew member, your tacks might be significantly slower and your spinnaker work a magnificent display of ineptitude that winds

Practice may not make perfect but it's the way to grow.

Doing it together is the key to doing it right.

up with the spinnaker deployed beneath the keel like a giant sea anchor. Getting, training, and keeping crew is hard, but the importance of a good crew to enjoyable sailboat racing is hard to overemphasize.

Crewmembers who don't have fun don't often return. Make racing fun. The crew you want are the ones who want to learn, so whenever possible, talk them through maneuvers ahead of time. Let everyone envision what will happen, in what order, and what their roles will be. Encourage crewmembers to trade jobs from week to week until everyone settles in to what they enjoy most: headsail trimmer, foredeck, tactician, main traveler handler, etc. The more responsibility you delegate, the saner and more effective you'll be and the more involved the crew will be. Accept responsibility for defeat. Share responsibility for victory. Between races or on the way home, talk about what went right and what went wrong. Take advantage of every learning opportunity. The more informed, observant, experienced, and supportive your crew is, the better racer you'll be.

Star boats sailing to windward on the first leg of a race. The fleet is tightly bunched after the start and you'll need boatspeed and good tactics, but don't lose sight of your strategic plan. As you tack upwind, if you think one side of the course is clearly favored now or will be in the next few minutes, that's the side you want to get to.

Strategy and Tactics

A successful race strategy answers such questions as these: Which side of a leg has the strongest wind? Which side is favored by the wind angle? How can you best exploit (or avoid) the current? Your strategy identifies the route you think would get you around the course fastest in the absence of competing boats. Once you identify that fast track, tactics are the moves and countermoves you use against other boats in order to execute the strategy. Tactics, in other words, are actions taken to get ahead of, block, avoid, or control your opponents.

Strategy is macro, tactics are micro. Strategy is big picture, tactics are small picture. Deciding to favor the right-hand side of the course on the windward leg because you expect the wind to shift clockwise as the afternoon wears on is a strategy. If you're on port tack on the windward leg and closing with a starboard-tack boat, dipping behind him (rather than tacking shy of him) so that you can continue toward the right side of the course is a tactic. Tactics are more likely than strategies to be developed on the fly.

The strategic and tactical choices you make probably have more to do with where you finish than any other factor. You may be saying, "Hold on! You just said boatspeed is the most important factor." Well, yes, I did say that, so let me clarify.

The two-part secret of success in sailboat racing is to go fast and make the right moves, and boatspeed provides the context for tactical decisions. If you know you're as fast as your competitors, you won't shy away from dueling them on the favored side of the course. If you know you're slower, you'll be a lot more likely to go your own way, even if it's not favored, hoping for an unexpected wind shift. Strategy and tactics give you control over a race, but lack of boatspeed can force you out of your chosen strategy. To repeat what I said, boatspeed gives you control, but lack of it gives you headaches.

The course, the conditions, and your competitors all pose problems and create situations. You sail a race making tactical decisions as you go, solving those problems and facing those situations. There may not be a clear right or wrong choice at every turn, but the nice thing about competition is that you get feedback. If you pay attention, you'll learn the right moves over time. Most tactical situations are predictable, and the number of moves to make is manageable. Every sailor can know good tactics and how best to use them. Distill principles from experience, apply them next time, and your chances of being right get better as you go.

Every phase of the race involves strategic and tactical decisions. Which end of the starting line is favored? Which side of the beat is favored? (The answer to this will inform your choice of where to start.) Should you jibe immediately around the reaching mark or hold on and jibe later? Should you sail high or low on the downwind leg?

At first your islands of certainty will be surrounded by oceans of confusion, but if you're honest, open-eyed, and humble about building it, your tactical knowledge will fill in fast. Experience is a superb teacher. Accelerate your learning by analyzing situations and keeping track of lessons learned—not only "What did I do wrong?" but "Why did I win?"

Rules

The rules for sailboat racing are designed to let boats duel at close quarters without actually touching. This is a difficult balance to achieve, and the rules are reviewed and refined as necessary every four years after the Olympics. Still, the rules as we know them were largely codified in the 1930s by America's Cup helmsman Harold Vanderbilt, then simplified in 1997 after a massive three-year effort by the ISAF with input from judges and competitors. The rule book contains ninety rules and a number of appendixes, but the rules you most need to know are the ones that spell out who has right of way when boats come together, and there are only ten of these plus a few associated definitions to learn. There really is no excuse not to know these ten, and frankly, if you do, you'll have a better working knowledge of the rules than at least half your competitors in a typical race.

To make things even more manageable, the ten rules can be mined for just five principles that apply in the vast majority of cases when racers come together. When the principles don't fit the situation, it's safest to presume that the other guy has the right of way. These are the five:

Starboard tack has right of way over port. Almost all situations where boats are on differing tacks come under this umbrella. The starboard-tack boat (wind coming over the starboard side—boom to port) has the right to sail her course. A port-tack boat must keep clear. A boat heading dead downwind is on starboard tack if its mainsail is to port.

A leeward boat has right of way over a windward one. When boats are overlapped (see page 323) on the same tack, the one closer to the wind must give room to the other. If the leeward boat established the overlap from clear astern, it must not sail above its proper course. It may do so if the overlap was established by the windward boat, however, provided only that it give the windward boat room to keep clear.

A boat that's clear ahead has right of way over one that's clear astern. A boat approaching from clear astern

Wind over your starboard side puts you on starboard tack. In any meeting with an opposite tack boat, you have the right of way.

must steer around a boat that's ahead of her.

A boat has a right to room to avoid obstructions. Any boat faced with the need to maneuver to clear an obstruction (other than a starting mark in navigable water) must be given the space to do so. This is commonly called **sea room.** When a boat hails for it, no matter what tack you're on or what position you're in, get out of

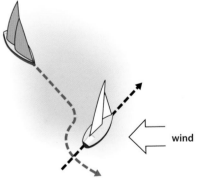

wind

The windward boat (right) must keep clear of the boat that is to leeward (downwind of her).

A boat overtaking another has the obligation to stand clear and avoid the boat in front of her.

Number 53 is clear ahead of number 89 and has leeward position on the boat on the right. Unless 53 established the overlap from astern, he has the right to luff above his proper course and force the windward boat to do the same.

When overlapped boats round a mark, the inside boat is entitled to room.

her way so that she can avoid the obstruction. Docks, shoals, moored boats, the beach—all are considered obstructions.

An inside boat must be given room to round a mark. Commonly called buoy room, this principle is similar to the sea-room provision. When an overlap exists, the boat closest to a mark of the racecourse deserves room to round it unless the inside boat established the overlap within two boat lengths of the mark. At a leeward mark,

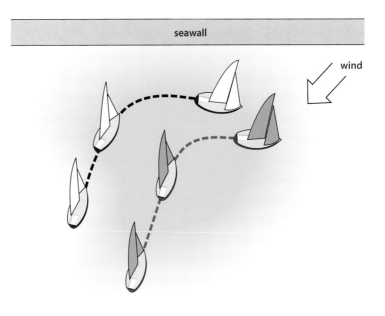

When a boat needs to maneuver to avoid an obstacle (such as a seawall), even though another boat might otherwise have the right of way she must give the obstructed vessel room to maneuver to safety.

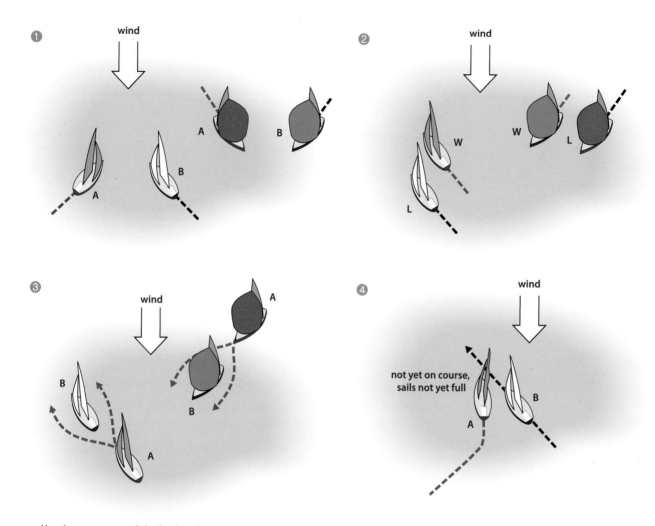

Here's a summary of the basic rules: 1. *Up- or downwind, port-tack boat (boat A) gives way to starboard-tack boat (B).* **2.** *Up- or downwind, the windward boat (W) stays clear of the leeward boat (L).* **3.** *Up- or downwind, the overtaking boat (A) stays clear of the overtaken boat (B).* **4.** *A boat in the act of tacking (A) must keep clear of a boat sailing its proper course (B).*

Luffing under the Racing Rules

The right of way conferred on the leeward boat when two boats are overlapped on the same tack is often called **luffing rights** by sailors. The leeward boat can alter course to windward, forcing the windward boat to do the same, and this defensive tactic is often employed to prevent a competitor from passing to windward on a downwind leg. There are two limitations: Under Rule 16, any course change of a right-of-way boat must be gradual enough to give the burdened boat time to keep clear. And if the leeward boat established the overlap from clear astern, according to Rule 17, she may not sail above her proper course as long as the overlap remains in effect.

COLREGS and the Racing Rules

As we saw in an earlier chapter, there is no such thing as "right of way" in the International Regulations for the Prevention of Collisions at Sea, or COLREGS. Rather, when two vessels meet, one is supposed to give way and the other to stand on, but neither has right of way. In contrast, whenever two competitors meet on the racecourse, one of the two has right of way. Racing rules thus take precedence over the COLREGS, though the former are designed to be compatible with the latter. For example, port tack gives way to starboard under both sets of rules.

Overlap

Under the rules, one boat is **clear astern** of another when her hull and equipment (including sails, spinnaker pole, etc.) in normal position are behind a line drawn abeam from another boat's hull and equipment in normal position. The other boat is **clear ahead**. When neither is clear ahead they are said to be **overlapped**. However, they also overlap when a boat between them overlaps both, as often happens at mark roundings. These terms do not apply to boats on opposite tacks except in certain situations—most notably a leeward mark rounding.

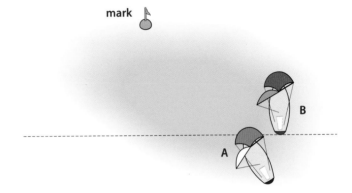

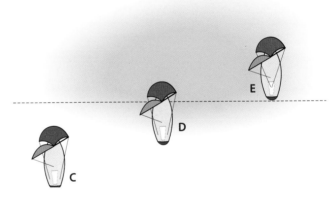

As these five boats approach a leeward mark, boats A and B are obviously clear ahead of boats C, D, and E. However, A has established an overlap on B because A's spinnaker in its normal position is ahead of a line drawn directly abeam from B's aftermost point. Unless the overlap was established when B was within two boat lengths of the mark, A is entitled to room for a proper rounding. (Note, however, that A cannot establish the overlap by easing its spinnaker halyard or sheets in order to fly the spinnaker forward of its normal position.) Meanwhile, although C is clear astern of a line drawn directly abeam from E's stern, the two boats are considered to be overlapped because intervening boat D overlaps both of them. Unless the overlap is broken before the mark, C is entitled to room for a proper rounding from both D and E.

Proper Course

A boat's proper course under the rules is the course it would sail in the absence of competitors in order to get around the course as fast as possible. Note that a proper course is defined by the shortest time, not the shortest distance. For example, a boat on a reach may harden up in lulls and bear off in puffs and still be following its proper course, because it's trying to reach the next mark as quickly as possible. No proper course exists before the starting signal.

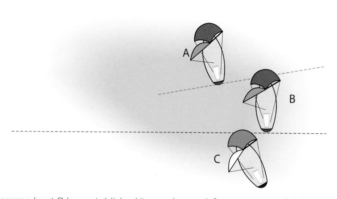

Assume boat B has established its overlap on A from astern, and C has established its overlap on B from astern. A and C are both leeward of B, and B must grant both room to round the mark. Boat A, however, has luffing rights on B, while C does not. Boat A may luff above its proper course in order to fend off B's attempt to pass to windward, while C, having established its overlap from astern, must not sail above its proper course.

Illegal Propulsion

According to ISAF Rule 42.1, a boat may be propelled only by using "the wind and water to increase, maintain, or decrease her speed." Her crew may not "move their bodies to propel their boat." Rule 42.2 specifically prohibits pumping the sails (waving them from side to side to generate a propulsive force), rocking the boat (moving crew weight repeatedly from side to side to roll the boat and generate force both from its sails and its underwater foils), **sculling** (whipping the tiller back and forth to generate a force from the rudder), and **ooching** (running toward the front of the boat, then stopping abruptly to transmit your momentum to the hull). Such unnatural ways of moving small boats are so effective in varying circumstances that this is one of the sorest points in sailing—which may be handy to remember next time you find yourself becalmed in a daysailer without paddle or engine.

the inside boat's right to room exists even if it is on port tack and the outside boat is on starboard.

If you sail by these principles and substitute politeness for aggression anytime you're not sure who has the right of way, you'll stay out of trouble while you hone your racing skills. The most enjoyable races are the ones in which the sailors know and show regard for the rules. Gamesmanship, angling for an edge, and bending the rules can happen anywhere. Kinetics, for example—the largely prohibited addition to speed by pumping, rocking, ooching, or sculling—is a recurring problem in some one-design fleets. Such instances diminish the sport for all involved. Practice good sportsmanship.

Preparing to Race

The right sails and number of crew are, of course, essential. Have the required safety or navigation equipment aboard. In most series, regattas, or events, the race committee will distribute written sailing instructions that include information on required equipment, course configurations, class assignments, starting schedules and signals, and other particulars. Lists of required equipment are intended to prevent sailors in search of a speed advantage from leaving paddles, horns, life jackets, anchor, and other necessities ashore. Make sure you're legal.

Some regattas are structured to give you a chance to dock between races. Others require you to be on the water virtually all day. For an ocean race you'll be gone longer. Take what you need—foul-weather gear, drinking water, sun protection, lunch, etc.

Take a compass and chart. Even in small one-designs you might need the chart, and in any racing boat a compass is invaluable for monitoring the wind and sailing the course.

The Course

It may be a few laps around the buoys, or it may be out to a mid-channel marker and back. It may be across the Gulf Stream to Bermuda from Newport, Rhode Island, or Marion, Massachusetts (the Newport Bermuda Race and the Marion-to-Bermuda Cruising Yacht Race, respectively), across the Pacific from San Pedro to Honolulu (the Transpac Race), or across Lake Michigan (the Chicago-Mackinac Race). But every race has a course, a prescribed route for the racers to run. The race committee chooses the course and either defines it in the sailing instructions (for long-distance races) or displays it on the committee boat (for around-the-buoys races). Protocols vary, but it's always the responsibility of the racers to learn the course—not the responsibility of the race committee to tell them. In a short-course series the course can change between races. Make sure of the course before every race. You need to know which marks to round in what order, and on which side to leave each one. Hint:

Imagine that you're leaving a string behind you as you sail the course. When pulled tight, the string should wrap around the buoys without doubling back on itself. Thus, if the race proceeds counterclockwise (as is commonly the case), the marks are left to port. In a clockwise race the marks are left to starboard.

Nearly all inshore races today take place on one of three course configurations: triangle, windward-leeward, or Olympic. In its simplest form a **triangle course** comprises an initial windward leg followed by two reaching legs. If the course is short, the race committee might tack on a final windward leg or send the boats around the triangle a second time. Reaching legs offer fewer strategic and tactical challenges and opportunities to pass competitors than windward or leeward legs, however, so triangle courses are no longer as common as they once were.

A **windward-leeward course** is just what the name implies. The course may comprise two legs (to windward and back), four legs (twice around), or five

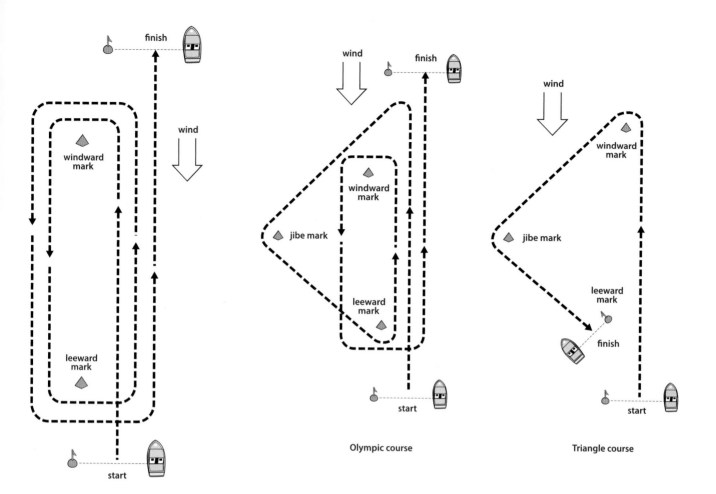

Windward-leeward course

Olympic course

Triangle course

Three common racecourse configurations.

(twice around plus a final windward leg). An **Olympic course** is a triangle followed by a windward-leeward-windward. A common variation of the Olympic course is the **Gold Cup course**, in which the start/finish line is located halfway between the leeward and windward marks. This configuration truncates the first and last windward legs but allows boats to start the next race where they finished the previous one, enabling more races to be run in a given time.

Even in one-design competitions in protected water, navigation can have a lot to do with the outcome. Find the marks before the start if you can. Even if you can't, visualize the shape of the course as best you can.

Other Signals

To communicate with the fleet, most committees use flags or hoists. Signals for a postponement (code flag "AP"), abandonment (code flag "N"), changed mark (code flag "C"), shortened course (code flag "S"), starting restrictions (code flag "I"), life jackets mandatory (code flag "Y"), general recall (first substitute pennant), and other adjustments all come from the committee boat. The sailing instructions should spell out the signals. Watch for them.

The red code flag "B" is the designated protest flag. Each boat carries one, and you should fly yours if you've been fouled.

When the blue-and-white "X" flag is displayed after the start, it means that one or more starters were early over the line. The race committee frequently hails the miscreants, but it does so as a courtesy, not as a requirement. "I didn't hear the recall" won't reinstate you. Recrossing the line and starting again undoes the damage, however. When restarting you must keep clear of all boats that are starting legally, and if code flag "I" is flying, you will have to sail around one end or the other of the line in order to restart.

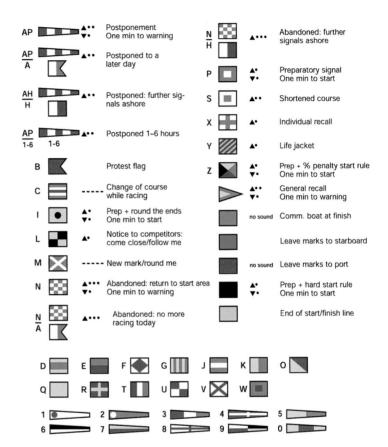

Race signals.

KEY
▲ means that a visual signal is displayed or ▼ removed
• means a sound and ----- means repetitive sounds

Before the Start

Getting a good start begins with getting to the starting area early. That lets you check out the wind on the course, evaluate the current, set your chute once or twice, and maybe get a fix on where the weather mark is. Arriving on time also lets you deal with various details of boatspeed—bailing the boat, checking for weed on the keel (back her down) and rudder, and setting the rig up right. You're going to need a lookout, at least one sail trimmer, and a timer, plus eyes enough to monitor the wind, the competition, and the lay of the line. If

When you get to the starting area, find the committee boat, which marks one end of the starting line. This is where the race committee will display letters and numbers specifying the course to be sailed, and it's also where flag and sound signals will count down to your start.

If the windward mark hasn't yet been placed, you might see a "crash boat" like this one heading off to windward to drop the mark.

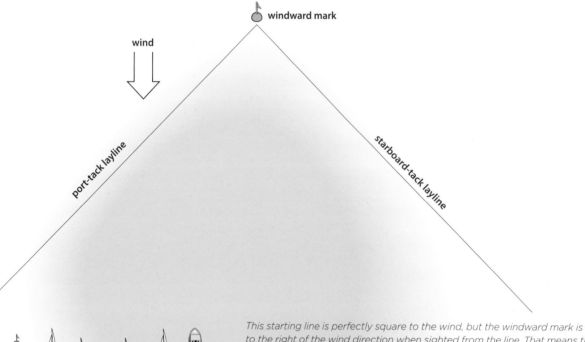

windward mark

wind

port-tack layline

starboard-tack layline

A

B

RC

This starting line is perfectly square to the wind, but the windward mark is to the right of the wind direction when sighted from the line. That means the port-tack layline (drawn here on the assumption that the boats tack through 90 degrees) passes closer to the starting area than the starboard-tack layline does. Think through the implications. Suppose boats A and B are both right on the line at the starting signal, sailing close-hauled on starboard tack at full speed. In other words, they both get great starts, with A at the pin end of the line and B at the committee-boat end. Neither is ahead of the other, but B is in a better tactical position, all other things being equal. Why? Because A doesn't have far to sail before he hits the port-tack layline, severely limiting his options. Rarely is it good to reach a layline early in a windward leg. Unless A knows something B doesn't, he should tack sooner rather than later, but he may be prevented from doing this by the boats on his windward quarter, or he may have to duck their sterns after tacking, which will cause him to lose ground. Boat B, on the other hand, is farther from the port-tack layline and can tack anytime he pleases without interference. He's in the catbird seat. Or maybe A is pursuing a winning strategy. Maybe he sailed a little way up the course before the start and knows that the wind is about to shift left, putting him in a favored position over the rest of the fleet. Or maybe he knows that a favorable current on the left side of the course will give him a major advantage. This is the kind of thinking you do before a start.

you're sailing alone, welcome to the world of multitasking, but if you're sailing with crew, these functions need to be assigned. If you haven't made assignments in advance, being early gives you time to divvy up the duties and figure out who will do what at the start. Arriving in the starting area late results in more bad starts than any other cause. Arriving early can't guarantee a good start, but it lets you do your homework and fuels the confident, organized attitude you need.

Where is the weather mark? It may not even be set when you arrive, but being early allows you to sail up the course and get a visual on the mark when it's dropped. Is it under a headland? Off a point? In a cove? To the left of the white mansion on the far shore? There are lots of possibilities, especially on closed courses in small bodies of water. Look for anything that could affect your approach to the mark and thus your strategy. If it is to the right, that puts the port-tack layline closer to the starting line than the starboard-tack layline. You should stay away from the laylines early in the windward leg, because once you hit a layline

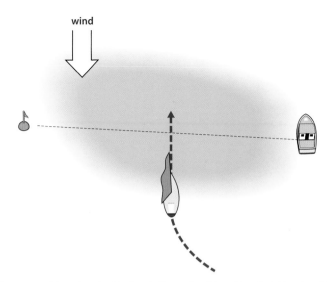

From a position close to the line, luff your boat head to wind. Your boat's fore-and-aft centerline will be perpendicular to the starting line if the latter is square to the wind. If your bow points closer to one end of the line than the other, that end is more to windward and therefore favored. All other things being equal, that's the end you want to start at.

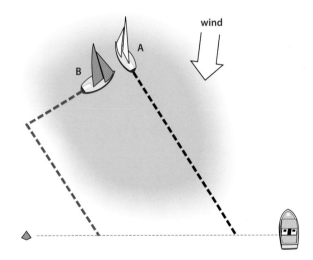

Even if a starting line is just 10 degrees out of square with the wind, it can make a big difference. Both of these boats have sailed the same distance, but A, which started near the favored end, is clearly ahead.

your tactical options become severely limited. In this situation, therefore, you must be careful not to go too far left.

Is the starting line square to the wind, or is one end upwind of the other? All other things being equal, the upwind end is the favored end. Starting there puts you a bit ahead of the boats at the other end. Turn head to wind in the middle of the line (it's best to do this with the jib down), with the mainsail luff-

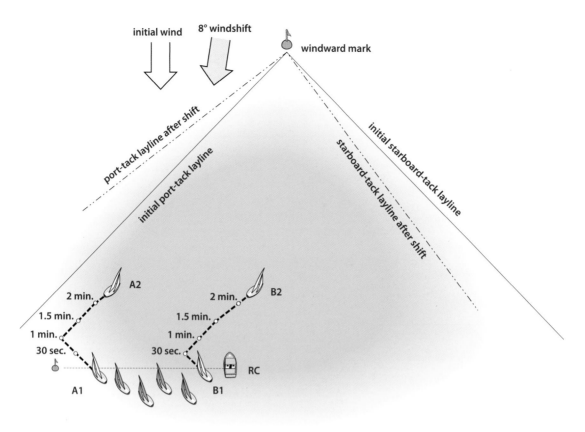

Expecting a clockwise wind shift, boat B tacks over to port 30 seconds after starting. Boat A, starting at the pin end, tacks 30 seconds after B. (We'll assume for this purpose that the intervening boats have also tacked, so that A is able to tack without running afoul of starboard tackers.) Boat B reaches the expected windshift 1 minute, 30 seconds after the start, and the shift reaches A 30 seconds later. Though the two boats were even at the start and have been sailing at the same speed, and though the shift is only 8 degrees—small enough to miss if you are not watching your compass headings or the shore ahead closely—it is clear after another 30 seconds that B is leading A. This is because the lee-ward boat is favored by a header, on top of which B also reached the header first and is more in phase with the wind than A. It helps to have a feel for this geometry when you decide where on the line you want to start.

ing and the main boom over the boat's centerline. If your bow points more toward one end of the line than the other, that is the favored end. It's help-ful, once you know which end is favored, to estimate how large that advantage is. An un-ambiguous number (in terms of degrees) tells you not only how much of a priority to make starting at the favored end but how much disadvantage you'll

incur by starting at other places along the line, where you might find more room and clearer air.

The breeze may be chang-ing, so don't saddle yourself with old information. Sight the line again within three minutes of your start, and be prepared to modify your plan if the wind has shifted. If you have time, sail one or two port and starboard tacks to windward of the line. You may discover a persistent

shift due to shoreline topogra-phy out there, and even if you don't, you can average the com-pass headings on your port and starboard tacks and gauge the line that way. If your compass headings are 140 degrees on starboard tack and 220 degrees on port, for example, the wind is coming from 180 degrees. Now sail the line between the committee boat and the **pin** (i.e., the mark on the opposite

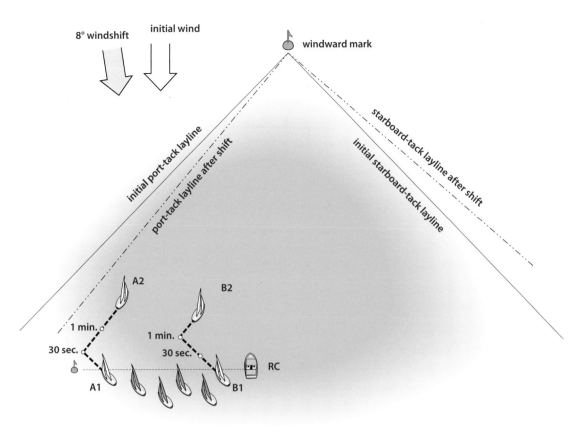

Expecting the wind to shift counterclockwise shortly after the start, boat A starts at the pin end. Thirty seconds later, when the expected shift reaches him, he immediately tacks over to port. After another 30 seconds boat B is also headed and tacks over to port. Boat A is now clearly ahead, though they were even at the start and have been sailing at the same speed. If the wind shifts any farther left, however, it will lift boat B to the layline and boat A past the layline, and A will lose his advantage.

end of the line from the committee boat). If your compass heading is 90 degrees, the line is square. If your heading is 100 degrees, the pin end is favored by 10 degrees. Race committees frequently orient the line so as to slightly favor the pin end in an attempt to reduce the crowd at the committee-boat end.

What is the wind doing? Just observing it for a while is often enough to tell you a lot. Either by recording your close-hauled headings or by luffing the boat head-to-wind every 5 to 10 minutes during the prestart, get a sense of what's happening. Is the direction steady, or are there shifts? Do they alternate left and right from the median, or are they trending one way? There are oscillations embedded in virtually any breeze. The most common wind pattern is an oscillation first to one side and then the other of a steady average direction.

If this is what you're seeing, time the periods between shifts. If you expect one to three oscillations during the time it takes to sail the weather leg, you'll want to be in phase with the wind right from the start. Boats to weather benefit when the fleet is lifted, whereas those to leeward gain from a header. If the wind is swinging clockwise at the start, and you expect that oscillation to last well into the windward leg, you'll want to start at the right-hand end of the line. On the other hand, if you expect the wind to shift counterclockwise shortly after the start, you may want to start at midline or near the left end and crack your sheets slightly to drive for the coming header. If you get there first, you'll be the lifted boat when you tack.

If you expect a progressive shift in one direction, your options narrow. If the breeze is going right, you must go right. Otherwise you'll sail to the most-distant layline on the outside of a lift and be forced to approach the mark on the headed tack, both of which are dead-slow. A persistent shift toward either side makes that side the only way to go. If the wind is shifting steadily clockwise, for example, you'll want to work your way to the right early in the windward leg. And if that's the case, you'll want to start at or near the right-hand end of the line, even if the other end is favored initially, because you won't want your competitors to prevent you from tacking over to port after the start so as to head to the right-hand side. In ways like this your judgment of what the wind is doing will inform your strategy for the start.

It's not unusual for closely spaced oscillations to the right and left to mask an underlying trend, over time, in a particular direction. Sea breezes in the Northern Hemisphere are like that. They oscillate right and left as they get stronger, but the underlying trend is toward the right, under the influence of the Coriolis effect. You can play the shifts as you would in a pure oscillating breeze, but if the beat is long enough for the average wind to move significantly to one side, favoring that side is the right move. Watch the wind long enough to determine its pattern.

As you think about where to start, consider these things:

- If current is a factor, which side of the course does it favor? You can gauge current flow by watching a sponge or some other object without much windage as it moves past a fixed point. An adverse current is a bigger consideration than a fair current because it prolongs the leg and therefore has a bigger effect on your speed.
- Which end of the line is favored, and by how much?
- Which side of the course will be favored immediately after the start and halfway into the windward leg?
- Might there be more wind on one side than the other? Once the rig is fully powered, a boat won't gain more speed from a further increase in wind velocity, and it might even slow down due to wave action and weather helm. That makes sailing the shortest course (spending the most time on the favored tack) at such times the number one priority. In lighter air, however, a puff can double the speed of a boat that catches it. In light and fluky winds, sailing where the wind pressure is greatest can be the fastest way up a beat, even if you have to sail farther to get that wind.

Other factors that might favor one side over the other include smoother water and less interference from ships (sailing in the lee of a container ship is not fast!), powerboat wakes, or wind-blocking shoreline structures or topography.

Rarely do all indicators point to the same decision. Current may be the determining factor, or it might be a nonfactor. After that, your priorities should probably be wind, favored end of the line, and position of the weather mark, weighted in that order.

Starting a Race

Successful racers are almost always successful starters. The start is critical. Before you worry about starting maneuvers, strategies, and techniques, however, let's run through the routine.

The starting sequence should be spelled out in the sailing instructions. For years the standard sequence began with a warning signal 10 minutes before the start, but ISAF rules now suggest a more compact sequence as in this table.

Signal	Flag and Sound	Minutes before Starting Signal
Warning	Class flag; 1 sound	5 *
Preparatory	"P" flag**; 1 sound	4
One-minute	"P" flag removed; 1 long sound	1
Start	Class flag removed; 1 sound	0

* Or as specified in the sailing instructions.
** "I," "Z," "Z" with "I," or black flag might be used instead if the race committee wishes to impose restrictions on the start.

Other sequences are sometimes used. With dinghies and small boats, the intervals might be as short as 1 minute each, with horn blasts (five at 50 seconds to go, four at 40 seconds, etc.) counting down to the start. Read the sailing instructions to learn the countdown for your starts. Under the rules a boat

A fleet of Lightnings drives toward the line in moderate conditions a few seconds before the start. Note the pin-end buoy in the foreground and the committee boat off in the distance. This is a good example of "midline sag," the tendency of boats at either end of the line to cross the line sooner than boats in the middle, where distance from the line is harder to judge.

begins racing at the time of her preparatory signal. From that time forward the racing rules apply.

Know where the starting line is. Yes, it's almost always between the committee boat and the mark at the other end of the line, which is also called the **pin**. But exactly what part of the committee boat—which might be 20 or even 40 feet long—does this mean? Usually it's a flag on the boat—often a rectangular orange flag—that marks the end of the line, but the flag might be at the bow, the stern, or somewhere between. This is a good thing to ask the race committee if it's not clear to you.

Visual shapes (usually flags) are the official signals. Even if the cannon fails to fire or no horn is heard, the race starts when the designated starting shape is hoisted.

A boat starts when, after the starting gun, any part of her hull or equipment crosses the starting line. If any part of the boat is on the course side of the line before the gun, she is a premature starter and must recross the line in order to start legitimately. (Some fleets make it illegal to be on the racecourse side of the line in the final min-

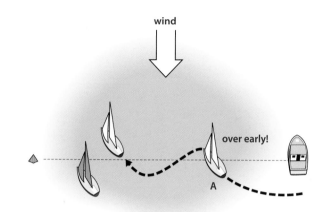

Boat A crosses the line early and must restart by returning to the proper side of the line, keeping clear of other boats as it does so.

ute before the start, but in most instances you are free to sail on either side so long as you are behind the line at the gun.) You have no rights while recrossing and must avoid everyone who is starting legally. If code flag "I" is flying, you must sail around an end of the line rather than doubling back across in order to restart.

The Elements of a Good Start

Starting on a short line with eighty or ninety highly competitive boats is one of the toughest challenges in this sport. World champions have trouble getting two good starts in a row in big-fleet competition. But most fleets are much smaller, and most starts are nowhere near that demanding.

Winning the start is actually much overrated. Yes, the start is important, but winning it isn't. Jumping out by a boat length or two at the beginning is nice, but it's only nice if it supplies you with clear air, allows you to pursue the strategy you've chosen, and keeps you clear of entanglements with other boats that can push you to the back of the pack. If you're in the back row at the start it's hard to recover, but the best way to avoid that pitfall is to be realistic and focus on getting a good start rather than staking it all on getting the best start. In order to get a good start:

Be on time. Being on the line at the starting signal is ideal, but judging speed and distance is tough. Especially in their early races, I've seen racers miss the gun by a minute or more. Don't get too far from the line. Make being close at the gun a priority.

Plan to start on starboard tack. Crossing the line at the pin end on port tack is too risky because you must avoid all the starboard-tackers. Once in a great while this tactic works—if the rest of the fleet is late to the starting line or if you're the only one to notice that the pin end is greatly favored—and when it works it's the talk of the fleet. When it fails to work, however, which is most of the time, you're buried.

Have clear air and good speed at the start. A single sailboat disturbs the air astern and to leeward. A fleet of boats truly disturbs the air. You want the wind to be blowing directly to you with no other boats contaminating it. You also want your boat to be moving well at the start; otherwise your competitors will shortly pass you to windward, burying you in bad

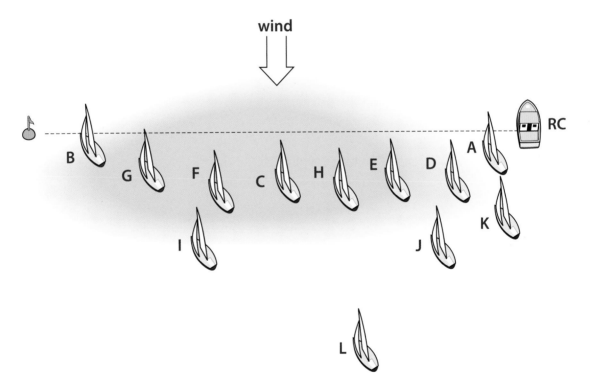

When the starting gun sounds, boats A and B are right at the line at the committee-boat and pin end, respectively. Since this line is square to the wind, the two boats are even, and only time will tell which has chosen the better end for starting. Boat C is farther from the line but has an excellent midline start. Assuming he is moving well, boats H and E pose no threat to blanket him to windward, and boat F is far enough off his lee bow not to be feeding him bad air. C has all his bets covered and will probably be able to go either left or right with minimum interference as the windward leg unfolds. Boats D, E, and F are a little more constricted by boats to windward and on their lee bows but can probably maintain clear air provided they are moving well at the start. If any of them is stuck in first gear at the start, he will be rolled to windward and cannot bear off without being gassed by a lee-bow boat. Boat G is getting bad air from boat B but has enough room on his windward quarter so that he might be able to luff up and away from B, freeing his wind. Boat H is in a tight spot and, if slowed enough by bad air from C, is in danger of being "rolled" by boats E and D. Boats I, J, and K have poor second-row starts and will have ground to make up, but at least they will be free to choose either side of the course without interference. They should focus on sailing fast and pursuing their strategy. Perhaps boat L was late to the starting area.

air. Thus, clear air and boat-speed at the start are closely related.

Start at the favored end if possible. Again, check the line to determine how the wind direction will affect the start. If the line is nearly square, you may want to avoid the left end (which is usually the pin end), because starting there means that you cannot tack without having to cross the entire fleet on port tack. In general, however, whichever end is favored is a good place to start. The trouble is that half the fleet tries starting at the favored end. Whenever boats crowd together, options close out fast.

Don't be afraid to start in the middle of the line if the favored end is crowded. In most fleets, midline crowding should be minimal. If you cross the middle of the line within a few beats of the starting signal, moving fast, you'll have a good chance of maintaining clear air. You may not win the start this way, but you don't have to. What you're doing is keeping your options open. If you're expecting the wind to shift left, you can crack the sheets slightly and drive for the shift. If you're expecting the wind to

shift right, you can tack to port, and you'll have to duck only a few transoms at most to get to the right side of the course. If you're lucky, most of the starboard-tackers on your windward quarter will flop over to port before you feel you have to—and you may not have to duck any transoms at all. The bottom line is that a midline start can be not only safe but advantageous.

Sailing in a big fleet (say, fifty or more boats) dictates a conservative mind-set. A handful of sailors will hit the line just right and get beautiful starts, while the rest must try to stay out of each other's way and find enough clear air to get going. If you can manage clear air and a spot in the front row on the favored third of the line in such conditions, you've made a great start.

Sailing in a smaller fleet (fewer than twenty boats), you can be more bold. It's going to be easy for just about everyone to find clear air, and if there are to be five or six beautiful starts, you want to have one of them. To get a jump on your competitors you've got to be in just the right spot. Go for it. Even if your plan implodes and you're slow

off the line, you've only got to pass half a dozen boats or so to get to the top half of the fleet. When you fall into a hole in a big fleet, the number of transoms between you and the top is a lot more discouraging.

In a middle-sized fleet, let your guides be your gut, the possible trade-offs, and the length of the line.

Some racers claim that if you're not over early at least once in every seven starts, you're not sailing aggressively enough. Certainly there's no better way to learn what being on or close to the line at the start looks and feels like than to be over it once or twice. Think of it as part of your racing education.

Just finding the line isn't as easy as you'd think. Sometimes other boats will block your view of one or both ends. Try sailing down the line well before the start to see if you can identify distant objects that perch on an imaginary extension of the line. When you're sailing down the line, do you see a water tower on the horizon directly behind the pin? Perfect. When you're approaching the line at the start, if boats are hiding the pin, use the water tower as your pin-end reference.

The Reaching Start

The first of the four starting tactics we'll discuss is the reaching start, the object of which is usually to put you at the committee-boat end of the line with good speed when the race begins. The boat end of the line (virtually always the weather end when you're on starboard tack) is popular because starting there on starboard tack guarantees an easy route out to the right if that's where you want to go. The approach is easy to judge, and you can tell with good accuracy where the line is. Sometimes you can even hear the race committee's countdown and use it as your own. You're also in excellent position to hear any recalls.

The reaching start is simple in outline. As you pass astern of the committee boat on a port-tack beam reach, you note how much time remains for the start. Let's say it's 1 minute 40 seconds. You continue your beam reach for 40 seconds, take 10 seconds to tack, and use the remaining 50 seconds to get back up to speed and back to the committee boat—in theory, just as the gun fires. A perfect start, right?

Well, maybe. The problem is that there's invariably a crowd at that end of the line, and most of them will be doing the same thing you are—reaching out and back. Remember, too, that leeward boats have the right of way, and boats to leeward of you who are approaching the line close-hauled on starboard tack have no obligation to give you room to squeeze under the stern of the committee boat. Indeed, before the starting signal, they can even luff above close-hauled to seal you off. In this situation you are **barging** and have no rights.

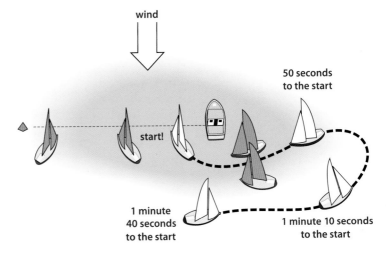

The elements of a reaching start. Adjust your time out and back to suit the boat, the wind, and what your competitors are doing.

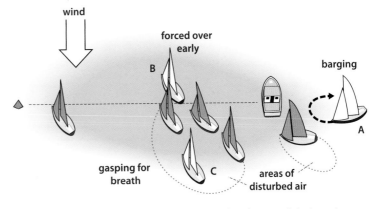

When you reach out and back intending to make a boat-end start, you're likely to have company. Here boat A is caught barging, B is forced over the line early by leeward boats, and C is wallowing in bad air from the boats to windward.

If the crowds and confusion at the committee-boat end are enough to scare you away—as they frequently do me—you can decide instead to arrive at the committee boat with good speed 10 seconds after the start. Sometimes this works well, giving you clear air and a clear path to the right-hand side of the course—assuming that's the way you want to go.

But what if you want to tack up the left side of the course? In that case you might want to reach back to the line early, before the crowd arrives, then reach down the line toward the pin end on starboard tack, hardening up to close hauled just as the race begins. Keep yourself a couple of boat lengths from the line if you can, so that you have room to yield to leeward boats if necessary. This tactic works well if the left end of the line is un-crowded but not unfavored.

The Vanderbilt Start

Sometimes, however, the potential rewards of a front-row start at the committee-boat end look big enough to justify the risks. When that's the case you need to gear up to win the start, not just contest it. You can do that by honing your approach.

If you sail the precise layline to the corner of the committee boat and time your arrival so you hit the line close-hauled at full speed at or just after the gun, you've got it. The boat is a fixed target (as opposed to the invisible line), and that can add precision to your timing. You'll probably have to fend off bargers, however, and you may also have to deal with "parkers" who block your way (see "The Dinghy Start" below). I've had the best success starting late at the weather end. When I arrive at the boat 5 to 10 seconds or so after the gun, I often find a hole between the boat and the pack. Sometimes the weathermost

front-line boats are still trying to get way on and are drifting down the line. After the starting signal is given, no one to leeward can legally luff above close-hauled to close the hole. It's a pleasure to claim it and blast through.

A Vanderbilt start works best in a small fleet. There's a real risk in a big fleet of finding too many boats to weather as you approach the line close-hauled. Yes, you have right of way and luffing rights over those boats, but with a virtual wall of sails between you and the wind, you may well find yourself "parked" and unable to assert your rights. Bear in mind, too,

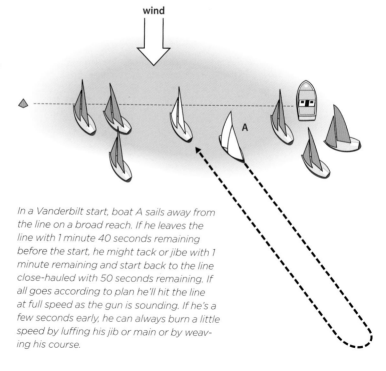

wind

A

In a Vanderbilt start, boat A sails away from the line on a broad reach. If he leaves the line with 1 minute 40 seconds remaining before the start, he might tack or jibe with 1 minute remaining and start back to the line close-hauled with 50 seconds remaining. If all goes according to plan he'll hit the line at full speed as the gun is sounding. If he's a few seconds early, he can always burn a little speed by luffing his jib or main or by weaving his course.

that the boat immediately to windward of you must be given time to keep clear, and so must the boat to windward of him and so on up the line. When several boats are stacked up to windward, the chances of getting them all to respond before you lose all boatspeed are slim.

Most committees give their starting lines a left-end advantage to try to thin out the crowd at the boat. That can make the pin a good place to be, especially if you think the left side of the course is the place to go, but if the pin end is heavily favored it will also be crowded. If the fleet is small enough you might try aggressively blocking and herding boats to weather, approaching the line at the bottom end of the parade of starboard-tackers, fighting for the leftmost spot, and sprinting to the pin with 15 seconds or so to go. If you can use the clear air at the end of the line to foot off into a developing header, or even if the breeze stays steady and you can use your safe leeward to advantage, you may find yourself in a spot to tack over to port and cross ahead of the fleet before too long. You need to be lucky and good to start that way, however,

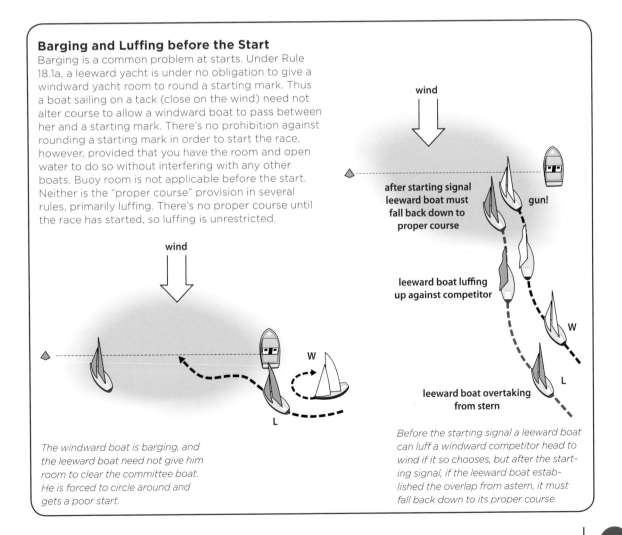

Barging and Luffing before the Start

Barging is a common problem at starts. Under Rule 18.1a, a leeward yacht is under no obligation to give a windward yacht room to round a starting mark. Thus a boat sailing on a tack (close on the wind) need not alter course to allow a windward boat to pass between her and a starting mark. There's no prohibition against rounding a starting mark in order to start the race, however, provided that you have the room and open water to do so without interfering with any other boats. Buoy room is not applicable before the start. Neither is the "proper course" provision in several rules, primarily luffing. There's no proper course until the race has started, so luffing is unrestricted.

wind

after starting signal leeward boat must fall back down to proper course

gun!

leeward boat luffing up against competitor

W

leeward boat overtaking from stern

L

wind

W

L

The windward boat is barging, and the leeward boat need not give him room to clear the committee boat. He is forced to circle around and gets a poor start.

Before the starting signal a leeward boat can luff a windward competitor head to wind if it so chooses, but after the starting signal, if the leeward boat established the overlap from astern, it must fall back down to its proper course.

and you need good boatspeed, too. If the boats to windward roll over you, you've lost your advantage and then some. And if the wind shifts clockwise instead of counterclockwise, you'll be trailing the fleet to the windward mark.

The Port-Tack Approach

The port-tack approach is another way of placing yourself in the front row. As with all the starts we're discussing, the concept of the port-tack approach is the soul of simplicity. With 2 or 3 minutes to go before the start (say, 2 minutes 30 seconds), you beam-reach away from the pin end of the line on starboard tack. Then, with, say, 1 minute 30 seconds remaining, you tack or jibe over to port and sail a course two or three boat lengths

to leeward of the pin. You pass the pin with 40 or 50 seconds remaining, then start looking for a space to tack into. The crowds at the boat and pin ends make this tactic better suited to starting in the middle of the line. Finding a hole may or may not be easy. Be flexible. Consider alternatives. Keep your sailing speed and maneuverability up.

When you've picked a space, tack into it, positioning yourself to leeward and just ahead of the weather boat and as far away from the nearest leeward boat as you can get. Ideally you'll glide into a controlling position, with your bow just ahead of the windward boat. Hold it. You have a hole to leeward. When the time is right, power into the hole and start with good speed on.

The great advantage of the port-tack start is that it keeps

your options open. You don't have to commit to your starboard-tack approach to the line until late in the prestart, and you have a good chance of finding a favorable gap in the parade of starboard-tackers to tack into. You also greatly reduce the chances of being forced over the line early. The disadvantages are that you have to keep clear of all starboard-tackers as long as you're on port, and you have to be able to accelerate quickly, with smooth crew work, once you tack to starboard.

Bear in mind that you must keep clear of the approaching starboard-tackers—even those to windward of you—until you are close-hauled on starboard tack. In other words, you don't acquire rights over boats to windward as soon as your boat passes head to wind.

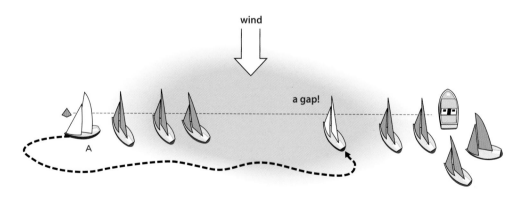

Approaching the line on port tack. In this instance boat A finds a big midline gap to fill. Once on starboard he can bear off slightly to pick up speed if he wants.

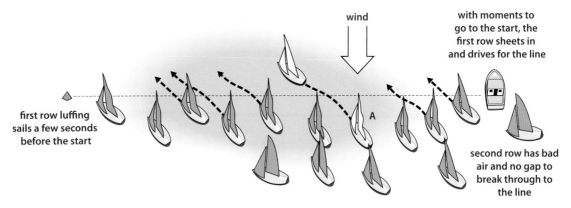

first row luffing
sails a few seconds
before the start

wind

with moments to
go to the start, the
first row sheets in
and drives for the line

A

second row has bad
air and no gap to
break through to
the line

In the dinghy start you get to the line a few seconds early, then luff your sails to "park" and wait for the gun. Here boat A is one of a number of boats starting in this fashion.

The Dinghy Start

Suppose you're competing in a big fleet of light, quick-to-accelerate dinghies or centerboard boats. With so many boats a front-row position is exceedingly difficult to obtain with a timed start. A surer way is to station yourself on the line and accelerate just before the gun. To do this, you need room to bear away momentarily to get up to speed—i.e., you need a "hole" just below you. A standard start that is competitive and relatively easy to pull off goes like this:

- Camp just behind the middle of the line with 30 seconds left before the start.
- To make a hole for yourself, luff into the wind—which you're entitled to do under the rules until the starting signal sounds (at which point you must resume your proper course, and you can't

Eleven boats in this one-design fleet hit the line in concert, with no midline sag. Boats in the second row, like the two in the background at far left, will struggle for clean air and boatspeed.

Penalties

The usual penalty for touching a starting mark is the same as that for touching any other mark of the course: you must get clear of other boats as soon as possible and make a complete 360-degree turn, including one tack and one jibe. If you fail to make the penalty turn, you can be disqualified.

The usual penalty for fouling another boat, either before the start or during the race, is to get clear of other boats as soon as possible after the incident and make two complete turns, including two tacks and two jibes. If your foul causes injury or serious damage, however, you can be disqualified and should voluntarily retire from the race.

luff above close-hauled unless the boat to windward established the overlap with you from behind). The object is to force the boats to windward to keep clear of you while the boats to leeward of you sail away. Protecting the space thus created requires precise boat handling and crew work, but if you're lucky it will still be there at 10 seconds to go. Now accelerate into your "hole" and toward the line—5, 4, 3, 2, 1, trim! You're off.

The better you handle your boat, know the rules, and work together as a team, the more aggressive you can be on the starting line. Design your starts to make the most of what you know and what you and your crew do best, and they'll be good starts. And remember that a good start is best defined not by your fleet position when you cross the line but by your position 1, 2, or 3 minutes later. If at that point you're sailing in clear air with good boatspeed, in the top half of the fleet, and on the side of the course you think is favored—then your start was at least good enough to keep you in contention.

The Windward Leg

Starting well is a tremendous advantage because it gives you clear air. Couple clear air with the fact that the first boat to the advantaged side of the course (if there is one) benefits the most, and you can see why the best strategy of all is to start first and sail fast. If you can do that, you can run away from infighting, go where the breeze is, and sail your own race. More often than not, though, a race is a struggle for position, and that struggle begins on the first windward leg.

Most races start to windward because that encourages boats to go off in different directions and spreads the fleet. Beating is also the traditional opening leg because it's the most difficult point of sail. Rather than pointing your boat at your destination, as you can on a reach or a run, you have to approach the mark by indirection, and that forces you into a chess match of position and placement, the overall objective of which is to be first at the windward mark. Here are some guidelines.

Avoid the Corners

Visualize the windward leg as a diamond, with the start at the bottom and the weather mark at the top. Halfway up the leg are the diamond's corners. If you were to sail close-hauled from the start directly to one of those corners, and the breeze were to stay rock-steady, you could then come about onto the other tack and head close-hauled on the layline to the mark. If the mark were directly to windward, you'd cover the same distance going to either corner.

In a rock-steady breeze and absent any current, obstacles, or other boats, **banging a corner** in this fashion would be your fastest course because it would minimize your tacks, and boats lose speed when they tack. You might choose the right corner rather than the left, because this would enable you to approach the windward mark on star-

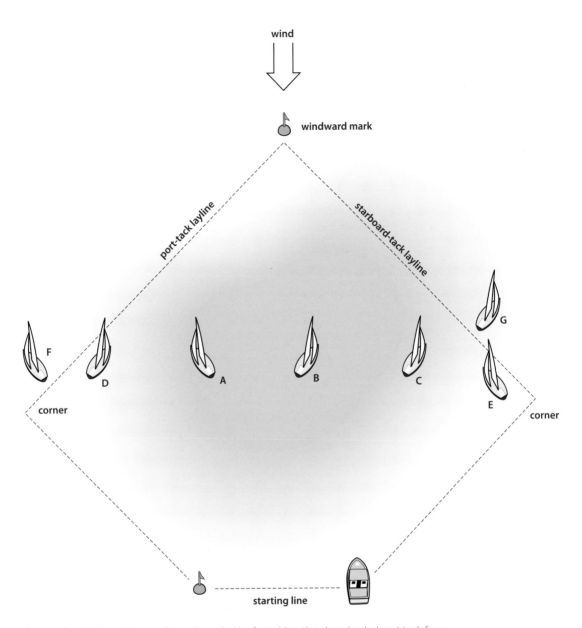

Picture the windward leg as a figure bounded by four sides: the close-hauled port tack from the committee-boat end of the line, the close-hauled starboard tack from the pin end, and the port-tack and starboard-tack laylines to the windward mark. As illustrated here, the starting line is square to the wind and the boats are able to tack through 90 degrees, so the left and right corners are square. Boat A is favoring the left side and will be helped by a counterclockwise wind shift. C is favoring the right side and will be helped by a clockwise wind shift. Uncertain which way the wind might shift, B is covering his bets by sailing up the middle of the course. D and E have banged the left and right corners, respectively, thus ensuring that any wind shift will hurt them. A counterclockwise shift will lift D above the windward mark, moving A in front of him, while it buries E to leeward of the fleet. A clockwise shift will lift E above the mark, favoring C, while it buries D to leeward of the fleet. Boat F has already overstood the mark. Trailing already, he must be hoping for a private blast of wind out there to help him catch up— but a flyer like that almost never works. Boat G has also overstood, but why is a mystery. He was leading the fleet a few minutes ago, but he's giving it all back now.

board tack, with right of way over any converging port-tackers. If the next leg involves flying a spinnaker, this would also give your crew plenty of time to set up the pole and lines, as you will not have to tack around the mark.

In practice, however, banging a corner is a bad idea because it puts you on the layline too soon, thus severely limiting your options. You can't count on the wind being steady—it almost never is. If the wind lifts you while you're sailing the layline to the windward mark, it will also lift the boats to leeward of you. Now the boats to leeward are on the new layline and can fetch the mark without tacking, while you are to windward of the new layline and have overstood. Boats under your lee bow will reach the mark before you because they will have sailed a shorter distance.

On the other hand, if the wind heads you on the layline, it means you're on the wrong side of the shift, and boats to leeward will gain on you when they flop over to the other tack. If the header forces you just below the windward mark, you'll have to make two quick tacks in rapid succession, which is slow and makes life difficult for the foredeck crew who are trying to prepare for a spinnaker set. And if other boats interfere with you or start to feed you bad air while you're on the layline, your options are either to hang on and suck their exhaust, or make two quick tacks to clear your air and wind up overstanding the mark.

Too many bad things can come from hitting a layline early. It almost never works in your favor and is only worth considering if you are so far behind that gambling is your only option.

Sail the Favored Tack

Ideally the windward mark is set directly to windward of the starting line. If it is, you can point equally close to it on either starboard or port tack. If the wind shifts, however, one tack will be favored—i.e., it will point you closer to the mark than the other. All other things being equal, you want to sail the **favored tack**.

Wind shifts may be frequent or sporadic. They may be regular or random. They may be as little as 6 to 8 degrees on the compass or as much as 30 degrees or more. Differing wind directions

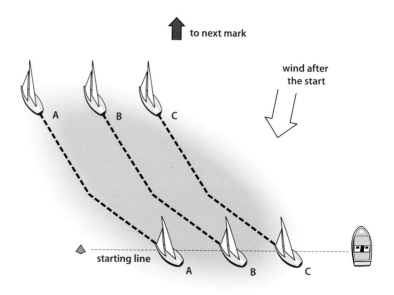

A wind shift that lets you head closer to the mark is a favorable shift or lift and ordinarily favors a windward boat—i.e., one on the "inside" of the shift—in this case boat C. But if boat A is lifted to the mark and boat C is lifted above it, boat A benefits by virtue of having sailed a shorter distance up the windward leg.

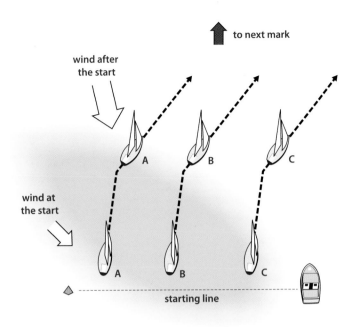

to next mark

wind after
the start

wind at
the start

A   B   C

A   B   C

starting line

A wind shift that forces your bow farther from the mark is a header or knock, but remember that a knock on one tack provides a lift on the other. A header favors the leeward boat, in this case boat C.

and atmospheric conditions produce differing shift patterns, but almost certainly there will be shifts. A wind shift that lets you head closer to the mark is a lift. Stay on that tack. A shift that heads you farther from the mark is a header or a **knock**. In most cases you should come about onto the opposite tack, because a header on one tack is a lift on the other.

If you were to sail the entire windward leg on the favored tack, tacking when the wind shifted to continue to point as close as possible to the mark, you'd sail a much shorter (and thus faster) leg than a boat that sailed much of the beat on the headed tack. It sounds simple enough, but sailing the favored tack is easier said than done in an oscillating breeze. The trick is to get **in phase** with the shifts.

Imagine, for example, that a race begins in an oscillating southwest breeze with the windward mark directly upwind, bearing 225 degrees. Before the race, you have recorded 10-degree oscillations about the average wind direction—i.e., the wind seems to back (shift counterclockwise) to about 220 degrees, then veer (shift clockwise) to 230 degrees—and these oscillations seem to be occurring every 5 to 10 minutes. At the start you find yourself sailing 177 degrees on starboard tack, which means (assuming your boat tacks through 90 degrees) that the wind is from 222 degrees, and therefore that port tack is slightly lifted relative to the average wind direction. Thus, shortly after the start you tack to port and are rewarded as the wind continues to back, lifting you from an initial heading of 267 degrees to as high as 265 degrees. Then, however, the wind begins to veer.

In another few minutes your course is 270 degrees, meaning that the wind has veered back to its average direction. Expecting it to veer another 5 degrees or so, you tack, and sure enough, over the next few minutes you are lifted from your initial starboard-tack course of 180 degrees to as high as 185 degrees. Even though these shifts are subtle, being on the right side of each one will save you several boat lengths of distance to the windward mark, and that can be a huge advantage.

Being so completely in phase with the wind as to sail the

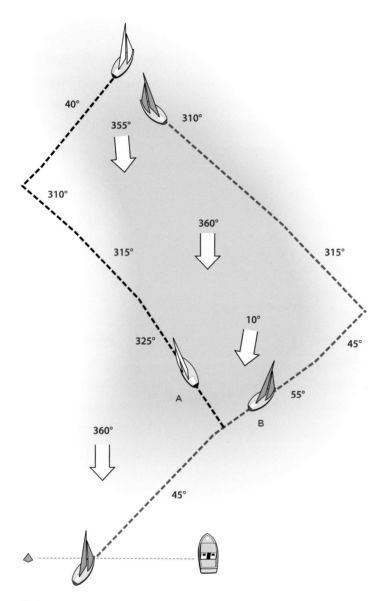

⬥ windward mark

40°
355° 310°

310°

360°

315° 315°

325°

10°
45°

A

55°

B

360°

45°

⬥

The boats on courses A and B are sailing at the same speed, but by tacking on 10 degrees headers so as to sail the lifted tack, boat A sails a shorter distance and finds itself closer to the windward mark.

Thermal mixing in an otherwise steady airflow produces a breeze that contains periodic shifts. A clear sky and maximum insolation foster this combination. The underlying flow may be gradient (a nor'wester on the New England coast, for example) or thermal (a sea breeze), but when pulses of colder air from aloft splatter through the surface wind onto the course, the result is puffs and lulls together with small (5- to 15-degree) oscillations. Velocity pulses are rhythmic, and the shifts are regular (trending to either side of the median wind) and rarely, if ever, more than 8 minutes apart.

Contrast this with a new wind springing up, a permanent shift in the old breeze, or a channeling of velocity down one side of the course. These happenings (plus current, traffic, wave conditions, and other less common circumstances) can serve up a beat in which the clear advantage is all on one side. Windward legs where it only pays to go one way are less common than the predictable shifts around a median wind direction. On a one-sided beat, you should get to the advantaged side as fast as you can, then stay there as long as possible.

Sail the Favored Side of the Course

If one side of the course is favored, your upwind strategy revolves around identifying and getting to that side. One side may be unambiguously favored due to current or a persistent and obvious wind shift,

entire leg on the favored tack is rare. Much of the time it's hard to tell what the shifts are doing. In that case, minimize your risk by sailing the lifted tack—i.e., the tack that points you closest to the windward mark.

but generally it's a tougher call than that. The oscillating breeze in the example above wasn't favoring either side of the course because its average direction was directly from the windward mark. But what if its oscillations were masking an underlying trend to the right? This, in fact, is common with the afternoon sea breeze along the northeast coast of the United States. The oscillation pattern might be 230–220 degrees, 233–223 degrees, 236–226 degrees, and so on as the underlying average veers from 225 degrees to, say, 240 degrees. If that veering will be significant over the time required to sail the windward leg, the right side of the course is favored, but you can see why such a trend can be difficult to spot in the heat of a race. Experience and local knowledge are helpful.

The breeze may appear stronger on one side of the course, but are you seeing a making breeze—a persistent jump in wind strength—or simply a transitory puff? The former is worth pursuing, at least in light air, but puffs are relatively short-lived compared with shifts. Stronger air may get you to the mark a boat length or

two ahead, while picking the right shift can shorten the course by fifty boat lengths or more.

Gradient winds arise out of pressure differences; they are the larger, systemic breezes that influence and accompany day-to-day weather. Thermal winds—like the afternoon sea breeze typical of many sailing locales—flow from local heat differences and are more short-lived. Local winds are created by the interplay between gradient and thermal winds and specific geographic features (mountains, forests, headlands, etc.). The winds we sail in are made from these three elements. The more you know about the wind's pedigree, the better you can judge whether to expect a persistent shift, or oscillations about a steady average direction, or oscillations superimposed on a persistent shift. You can also guess whether the wind will grow stronger, fade, or be replaced.

Calling the shifts is important. If you go right and the wind goes right, you can come about onto the favored tack and gain materially. If you go left and the wind decides to go right, you'll be sailing the long

way around on the outside or, worse yet, limited to sailing the headed tack. If the wind oscillates and you go "left-right-left" up the middle in phase with it, you'll beat the boats that either go to the corners or tack out of phase with the shifts. Hitting the shifts is the heart of upwind success.

If you think one side of the course is favored, cheat toward that side, but stay away from the corner. If you don't know which side is favored, stay near the middle and focus on staying in phase and sailing the shortest distance possible.

Keep Your Air Clean and Your Plan Intact

A sailboat disturbs the air that crosses its sails, and that turbulent air extends seven to as much as ten mast lengths downwind and astern from a close-hauled boat. That wind shadow consists of choppy and attenuated air, and when it blows into your sails, you lose power. Stay out of your opponent's wind shadow. Sail in clean air!

Whether or not your close-hauled opponent's dirty air extends to windward as well as to leeward in his wake is a bit more controversial. Some say

Rules of Thumb for the Windward Leg

When in doubt:

- Tack on headers and sail the lifted tack.
- In other words, sail the tack that points you closest to the mark.
- In other words, sail the shortest possible distance to the mark.
- On the other hand, recognize those rare instances when other factors (such as a dramatic current differential across the course, a persistently stronger wind on one side, or an expected persistent wind shift favoring one side) trump these rules.
- Avoid the corners. Once you hit a layline your options disappear, so avoid hitting either layline early in the beat.
- If a big wind shift turns a square windward leg into a dramatically skewed one, you'll be spending more time on one tack than the other. Sail the long tack first, or else you'll hit the layline too soon.
- Approach the windward mark on starboard tack if possible in order to come in with right of way and give your foredeck crew time (say, 2 minutes) to prepare for the spinnaker set.
- Slightly overstanding the windward mark is faster than having to take two quick tacks because you can't quite fetch it, and two quick tacks are usually faster than trying to pinch around a mark you really can't fetch.
- The time to work toward a favored side of the course is on the bottom half of the beat. Work toward the middle as you enter the top of the course.
- Be ready to break any of these rules when, in your judgment, circumstances warrant.

And remember:

- If you are expecting a persistent shift, sail toward the direction from which the new wind is expected. You will be progressively headed as the new wind fills in, but don't tack right away—instead, drive into the new wind until it either stops heading you or you are approaching the new layline to the mark.
- In other words, you want to sail the headed tack of a persistent shift early, so you won't have to sail a lot farther on the headed tack later on.
- If you have to duck a starboard-tacker's stern, do it smoothly—rather than sharply at the last second—in order to lose as little speed made good as possible.
- Don't try to tack on a starboard-tacker's lee bow unless you are confident you can get your boat up to speed before the other boat rolls over you to windward.
- When deciding whether to duck or tack shy of a starboard-tacker, be guided by which side of the course you want to be on.
- If you get pinned on the layline by a boat to windward or ahead and to leeward, it's often faster to make a short tack to clear your air—even if that means overstanding the mark—than to suffer dirty air all the way to the mark.
- Sail fast!

A fleet of Ensigns racing to windward. The leader is the only boat with clean air. The others should tack as soon as possible.

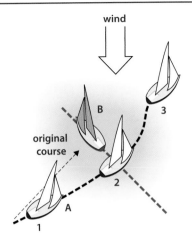

wind

B

original course

A

1

2

3

When you cross tacks with a starboard-tacker, fall off smoothly while there is still time and room to do so, easing sheets to pick up speed and reduce weather helm. As you pass his stern harden up while re-trimming the sails, and use the extra speed you've developed to pinch up and gain back some of the windward gauge you were forced to sacrifice. This maneuver is known as dipping the starboard-tacker's stern, and a well-executed dip will cost you very little—certainly much less than a frantic last-second swerve to leeward to avoid a collision.

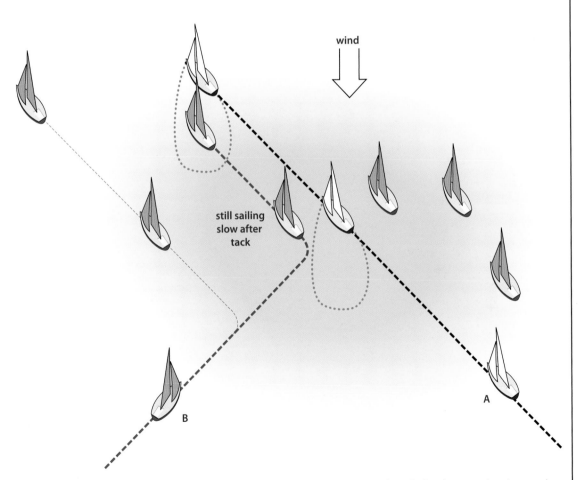

wind

still sailing slow after tack

A

B

Boat B attempts to tack into a controlling lee-bow position on boat A but misjudges. Before he can get up to speed on the new tack boat A rolls over him to windward, burying him in bad air (dashed outline). B will probably have to tack again to free his wind.

it does, and that this is what makes a safe-leeward position safe. Others say a safe-leeward boat's advantage comes not from the dirty air he feeds you, but from the lifted and enhanced wind that you feed him. According to this interpretation, when he's close aboard on your leeward bow, the wind approaching your sail plan is bent to leeward—lifting him—and then accelerates through the slot between his sail plan and yours, giving him more power. Regardless of which interpretation is correct, the result is the same—your opponent gains relative to you. Lee-bow your opponents when you can (and when doing so doesn't deter you from your favored course), and try to prevent them from lee-bowing you.

Control your opponents when the opportunity arises. As you drive off the starting line on starboard tack, the boats under your lee bow must either wait for you to tack or be prepared to duck your stern if they tack before you do. In this situation you can drive an opponent farther left than he wants to go. Why would you? Perhaps because you, in turn, have one or more starboard-tackers on

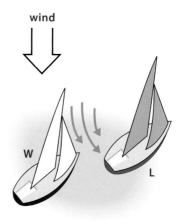

Left: The Laser on the right has established a safe-leeward position on his competitor. Right: The likely explanation for the lee-bow effect is that the windward boat's sails accelerate and bend the wind, giving the leeward boat a lift with more velocity.

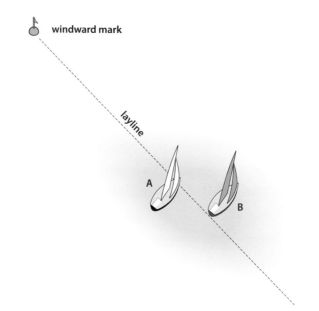

Boat B can't tack until A does. Boat A is free to carry his port tack past the layline, tacking only when he is sure he can lay the mark on starboard.

your own windward quarter. The windward leg is a big, constantly changing chessboard.

Or say you're on port tack and nearing the starboard-tack layline, and you're close enough to the windward mark to make the next starboard tack your last one. Under your lee bow is an opponent who won't be able to complete his tack to starboard without fouling you, so he's anxiously waiting for you to tack so that he can, too. Aware of this, you can force him to overstand the mark while at the same time protecting yourself from any chance of not being able to fetch it yourself. You're in a controlling position. Use it but don't abuse it; don't drive your opponent any farther across the layline than what is necessary to optimize your own approach to the mark. The line between tough, fair sailing and poor sportsmanship is a thin one.

Or say you start at the front of the fleet. In the absence of any compelling reason to do otherwise, staying between your nearest competitor and the windward mark will pretty much guarantee (assuming your boatspeed and tacking ability match his) that you'll get there first. Why? Because any wind shift that comes along will reach you before it reaches him. Use a loose cover—one that doesn't interfere with his wind—unless you're feeling super-aggressive, at which point you could try a **tight cover**, tacking when he does and endeavoring to park yourself on his weather bow so as to feed him bad air.

But unless he's one point ahead of you in the local season series, why be mean? This is supposed to be fun, after all. Don't make an enemy, and don't let an obsession with covering distract you from your race strategy or from the rest of the fleet. Unless you're match racing—which is rare—you have an entire fleet of competitors to worry about. For these reasons a tight cover is most properly an endgame—something to save for your approach to the windward mark or the last beat to the finish line—rather than a tool to deploy early on the first windward leg.

Sail Fast

In the chess match of position and placement that is upwind sailing, don't forget to sail fast! Sailing against the wind means the sails are at their least efficient. The skill of making the most out of that bad situation involves sail trim (as tight as possible while still maintaining a power-producing curve) and stability (as upright as possible except in very light air, when a bit of heel will help the sails maintain a more optimal shape).

From there, you must solve the puzzle of how close to sail into the wind. Is it better to sail "high" (closer to the mark) at a reduced speed or "low" (farther from the mark) at a faster pace? The objective is to maximize your **speed made good** toward the windward mark.

America's Cup boats use sophisticated instrument arrays for this, but you can do almost as well by feel and sight.

In addition to sailing with hawkish concentration along the edge of the breeze, you must be ready to **foot** (sail slightly lower and faster) toward a persistent header or out from under a boat to weather, or **pinch** (point slightly higher than the optimum) to work yourself into a lift or to climb away from a boat that is lee-bowing you. Shift gears to suit the situation.

Inside every breeze are small, scarcely noticeable oscillations. Responding with the right amount of "up" or "down" on the helm can keep you on that edge, locked into the optimum groove. There are likewise pulses in the wind's velocity, and these too require a response from the helm. If the true-wind velocity increases while its direction remains steady, the apparent wind will move slightly aft. Sailors call this a **velocity lift**, and the correct way to play it is to feather up into it so as to point closer to the windward mark while maintaining your speed. When the puff passes and the wind lightens, the apparent wind will move forward, and you'll have to respond by heading down. Staying locked into the groove requires complete concentration on the helm, and it can make a substantial difference in speed over the course of a windward leg.

Sometimes the puffs come in as headers. This is true of the puffs embedded in a northwesterly breeze off the U.S. East Coast, which fall from aloft as cat's-paws that you can see as darker ripples spreading on the water's surface. When the leading edge of a puff like this hits you, it will be a header, but as you near the trailing edge of the puff you are lifted. Fall off in a header grudgingly but in a timely fashion, and point up eagerly but not overly aggressively when you get lifted.

Think of your boat's bow as eating its way to windward. Your job at the helm is to nibble as much as you possibly can to windward while maintaining boatspeed. You know all this, of course, but now, in the presence of evenly matched competitors doing their best to go faster than you, you have a unique opportunity to see the effects of seemingly minor changes in sail trim. Fine-tune your trim whenever you're

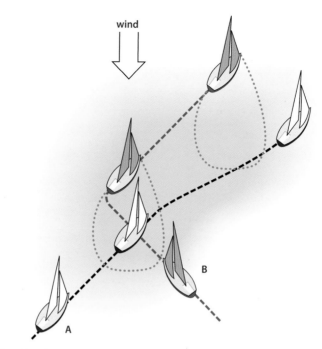

Boat B tacks on top of boat A so as to put A in his wind shadow (dashed outline). To escape, boat A foots off to leeward, easing his jib and mainsail for speed. Once clear he trims in again and resumes his optimum course. If you can't escape a weather-bow competitor this way, you'll have to tack.

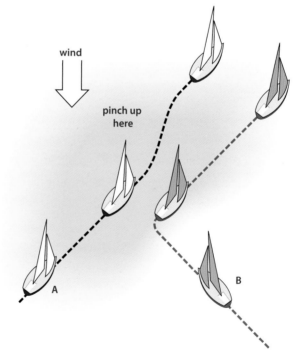

Boat B attempts to tack into a controlling lee-bow position on boat A, but A sees B coming, bears off a couple of degrees prior to B's tack, then pinches above his optimal course as B is tacking in order to open up some distance to leeward. If you can't escape a safe-leeward situation this way—i.e., if B is sailing faster and higher than you after both boats settle in—you'll have to tack.

sailing alongside a competitor. See what works.

Provided your jib is trimmed properly for the breeze, the jib telltales become your most reliable guide. When the windward and leeward telltales are both streaming straight aft, the flow over the jib is optimal and the sail is at its best. Unless you are sailing in significant waves, your object now is to drive to windward just enough to make the windward telltale flick above the horizontal, but not completely upright. That's your upwind limit. It stakes out how close you can steer into the wind—i.e., toward the windward mark. When the lee telltale droops, you're too far off the wind.

If your jib has two or three sets of telltales, adjust the sheet leads forward or aft (if your boat has track-mounted sheet lead blocks) until the telltales all break in unison—meaning that the jib luffs along its entire height at once. If anything, the upper telltale should break just before the lower ones. On some boats the lead-block car is rigged with a tackle so that it can be adjusted under tension. On other boats you have to adjust the lead on the lazy sheet, then wait for the next tack before adjusting the remaining sheet lead.

Nibble gently to find the upwind limit of your pointing. Drive off a bit to build speed, then nibble your way into the wind again. That's how you make sure you're on the edge of the breeze. That's how you make certain you're pointing as close to your target as you can. The harder it blows, the higher you can point. You'll recognize when you're pinching—the boat will flatten out and start to crab off to leeward while pressure on the helm decreases, and the jib telltales will confirm this. Test the edge of the wind constantly, nibbling to windward, then falling off just enough to keep the boat moving.

Tacking slows a boat, so minimize the number of tacks you make. Concentrate on making every tack a good one. Pick your spot—you want to head into the tack at top speed so you can come out of it with speed remaining. Tack in smooth water when possible, and do all in your power to avoid getting stuffed by a steep wave while the bow is swinging through the eye of the wind and the rig is depowered.

Use a roll tack in a dinghy: As you prepare to tack, shift crew weight inboard and to leeward to let the boat heel. This will cause it to round up into the wind without rudder pressure. Then turn the rudder just enough to carry your tack through the wind, moving crew weight toward the new leeward side as you do so. Minimizing rudder pressure in this way reduces rudder drag and maintains more speed through the tack. Finally, as the boat heels into the new tack, move crew weight to windward to level the boat quickly, which forces wind through the sails and builds speed faster.

In any boat your crew should wait until the jib is luffing substantially before casting off the old jibsheet, and they should get the new one in quickly and cleanly before the sail has a chance to billow and flog. You can help by keeping the bow high until the jib is in. Once the jibsheet is almost all the way in—but not before—foot off slightly below your proper course to let the boat build speed and power, then slowly come back up while the crew winches in the jibsheet that final 2 or 3 inches. Don't strap your sails tight before the boat gathers headway on the new tack.

Rounding the Windward Mark

There are three basic types of rounding. Rounding a windward mark (whether onto a reach or a run, whether setting a spinnaker or not) is different from rounding a reaching or jibe mark, which is different from rounding a leeward mark. In all cases the inside boat of an overlapped pair is entitled to room for the rounding, but the approaches and tactics involved in making the best turn are different in all three situations. For now we'll focus on the windward mark.

The first windward mark rounding is a time of truth. The fleet may have spread to both sides of the course on the windward leg, but now it converges again, and you'll see who is ahead and who is behind. The spread may not be large yet. If the fleet is bunched or clustered so that you approach the mark in company with several other boats, get ready for some close-quarters maneuvering. Keep your wits about you. You can go into a windward mark in ninth place and come out in fourth, or vice versa. Know the rules and apply them, but avoid melees if you can. Being in the right is little satisfaction when several

Seventy-year-old John Ulbrich and his 50-something crew winning a race at the Piana Cup. Ulbrich managed to pinch enough to fetch the weather mark and held on through two downwinds and another upwind to win the race over some of the best (and younger) Etchells drivers.

Things get interesting when the fleet is bunched at the mark.

other boats pass you during an altercation.

Port- or Starboard-Tack Approach?

Assuming the mark will be left to port, which is almost always the case, the standard wisdom is to approach it on starboard tack so that you will have the right of way going in. Conservative and defensive, this proposition makes sense. Joining the parade of boats on the starboard-tack layline will slow you down, however, feeding dirty air to your sails even as it limits your options (unless you happen to be leading the parade, of course!). Thus, this isn't always the fastest tactic.

The radical alternative is to approach the mark on port tack, find a hole in the line of starboard-tack boats, and tack in the hole to join the parade near the mark (see illustraton page 356). The rewards that come from sailing in clear air as long as possible or holding the favored tack until the end of the windward leg can be great, but this tactic is decidedly risky, especially in a large fleet. ISAF Rule 18.3a states that if you tack within two boat lengths of the mark, you cannot interfere with an approaching starboard-tacker, causing it either to sail above its close-hauled course or miss its rounding. This is true even if you complete the tack and are close-hauled on starboard when the interference occurs. (At all other times you can tack in front of a starboard-tacker provided your sails are close-hauled and drawing on starboard tack before he reaches you.) Slow your boat when looking for a hole, but don't bear off, because that sacrifices weather position and makes it hard to judge the gaps between starboard-tackers. This tactic is best used when there won't be a crowd at the mark and when you're feeling like a riverboat gambler.

The more moderate middle course—and the one many of your competitors will select—is to make your final port tack a minute or two shy of the port-tack layline so that you will have room to maneuver as you approach the starboard-tack layline. Attack the line where it's thinnest. Remember, though, that you must find an opening large enough to tack in, because none of the starboard-tackers are obligated to make room for you where none exists.

On those rare occasions when a windward mark is to be left to starboard, it sometimes pays to overstand the mark by a boat length or two in your port-tack approach. That creates enough room for approaching starboard-tackers to tack inside you, while you sail in clean air with good speed and room to round cleanly.

Buoy Room

Let's return now to the standard situation, in which the mark is to be left to port, and you're approaching on starboard tack in company with other starboard-tackers. As we said earlier in the chapter, the fundamental rule is that when two boats are overlapped, the inside boat (the one closest to the mark) is entitled to room for his rounding. This is what sailors call the buoy-room rule. (Note that when two overlapped boats approach the mark on port tack with the intention of tacking around it, the windward boat is the inside boat and entitled to room—but this confusing circumstance doesn't happen often.) Now for the nuances.

Imagine a circle with a radius of two boat lengths drawn around the mark. If you establish an overlap with the boat ahead of you before any part of his boat or equipment in its normal position encroaches on that circle (his boat, not yours), and you are the inside boat, he must give you room to round the mark. If you are the windward boat (i.e., the outside boat on a starboard-tack approach), you must not only give him room to round but must keep clear just as you would have to keep clear of an overtaken leeward boat anywhere else on the course.

If you establish an overlap to leeward inside the two-boat-length zone, the overlapped boat does not have to give you room. Obviously this is a situation that invites different interpretations from the boats involved. The ISAF knows this, and Rule 18.2e is clear: if there is reasonable doubt that a boat obtained or broke an overlap in time, it will be presumed that the boat did not. In other words, the burden is on you to prove in a postrace protest hearing that you established your overlap outside the two-boat-length circle.

Life on the Layline

The majority of windward legs will culminate with a final

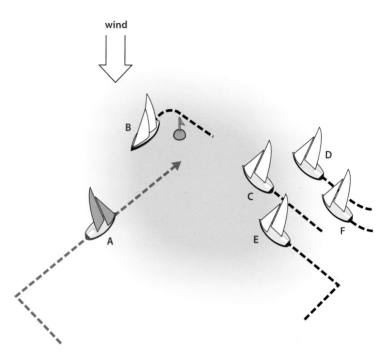

Approaching the windward mark on port tack is risky but can gain you several places. The key is finding a hole that's big enough to tack in. The hole that boat A is shooting for is closing fast, and if he can't squeeze in ahead of C he'll have to take the sterns of D, E, and F as well.

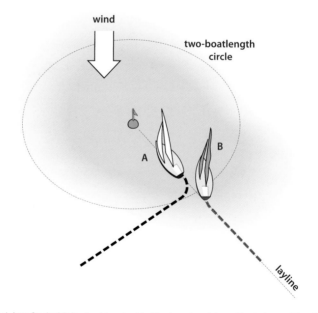

Boat A has fouled B by tacking inside the two-boat-length circle and forcing B to sail above close-hauled. Before continuing the race, A should get clear of other boats and make two full penalty turns.

approach to the mark on the starboard-tack layline. This is sometimes a confusing time and sometimes a stressful one. If you'll be setting the spinnaker on the next leg, your foredeck crew will be anxious to attach the spinnaker sheet, guy, and halyard and rig the pole. And if you're fetching the mark comfortably, an early start on these procedures makes sense.

Better be careful though. What if you're barely able to fetch the mark, and then an incoming port-tacker crosses your bow and tacks to windward and ahead of you? Now you're in his wind shadow, and if you were having trouble fetching before, your goose is cooked now. The best thing you can do at this point is swallow your medicine and take

another short port tack to clear your wind and ensure that you can fetch. This is never any fun, but it's a lot less fun when you have a spinnaker pole waving around above deck and spinnaker sheets interfering with the jibsheets.

This not-infrequent scenario illustrates why judging the layline correctly is an important part of the game. As

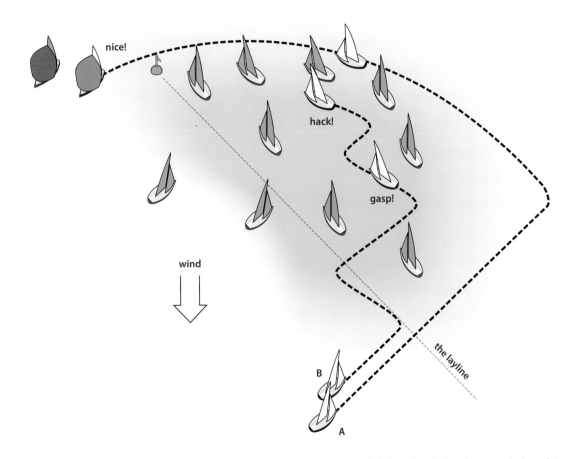

Boat B tacks on the layline but gets so much bad air from competitors that he's forced to tack twice more, losing a lot of ground in the process. Boat A carries his port tack well beyond the layline and is able to sail above the mess at the mark. He sails farther than B but comes out ahead.

you approach the starboard-tack layline on port tack, will you be passing astern of any starboard-tackers? If so, sight over their bows from directly astern to see how close they are to fetching. The optimal time to tack depends not only on your boat's tacking angle but also on its leeway and on ambient conditions. You can tack a lot sooner in smooth water with no current and no competitors interfering than you can with a steep chop and a 0.5-knot current knocking you to leeward while surrounding boats feed you bad air.

Practice judging the layline in nonrace conditions until you get a feel for what your boat can do; then adjust accordingly for conditions and circumstances. When there's a crowd at the mark, often it's wise to put a little extra in the bank before you make that final tack. Better to overstand in clean air with good boatspeed than to get buried at the mark.

The Rounding

You and your crew should all know before the mark whether you'll simply be bearing off to a reach on starboard tack or jibing onto a port-tack run or broad reach. You probably will set the spinnaker if you've got one. But preparations for the set must be balanced against the continuing need for speed. Multiple crewmembers jumping around on deck can knock the wind from your sails in a light breeze, and in a fresh breeze the premature removal of crew weight from the windward rail can cause your boat to heel excessively and develop weather helm. It could even prevent you from fetching the mark.

As you round the mark and bear off, make sure the mainsail is eased. This relieves weather helm and makes it easier to head down. If you fail to ease the mainsheet, you'll have to add more rudder pressure and slow the boat. Failure to ease a large mainsail could even prevent you from heading down altogether. The mainsail matters more than the jib at this point. In fact, keeping the jib relatively tight may even help your turn and will make it easier to set the spinnaker.

Where do you want to be a minute after you've rounded? Keep that goal in mind. Watch the boats ahead and behind, and maneuver to prevent your chosen avenue from being sealed off. The next leg will dictate whether you're bearing off to a reach with main and jib, bearing off to a reach or run with spinnaker, or jibing before setting a spinnaker. Whatever is coming, keep sailing fast.

Reaching Legs

If you're sailing a triangle or Olympic course, your next leg will be a reach. Sailing with the wind on or just abaft the beam offers fewer opportunities for passing people than either upwind or downwind sailing. That's one reason why windward-leeward courses have replaced the triangle in most regattas. Still, though it may seem like a parade, a reaching leg holds lots of potential for making gains.

Think of the reach as a way to gain distance. Even if you don't gain any places, if you can reduce the distance between

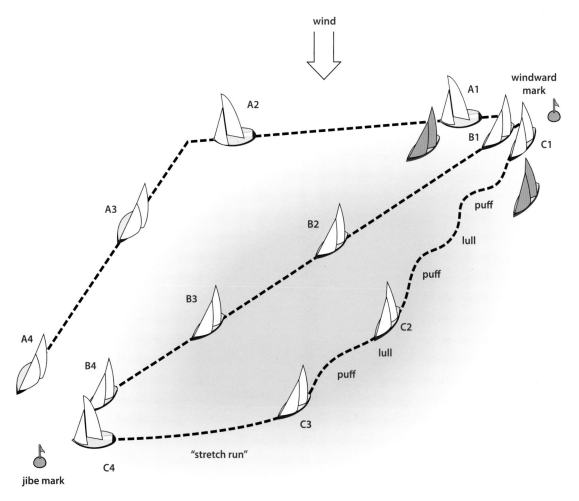

Three approaches to a reaching leg. Boat A holds high immediately after the windward mark (A1) in order to fend off the boat behind him, then decides to take the high road to the jibe mark. Boat B decides to sail the rhumb line to the jibe mark, while boat C elects to drive to leeward in the puffs and harden up for boatspeed in the lulls while continuously adjusting sail trim. Boat A is looking fast at time 2, having sailed a hot angle to that point, while C doesn't seem to have much to show for his work. By time 3, however, C's potential gain is becoming apparent, as is the hit A is taking from having to sail a low, slow angle into the mark. It all comes together for C at time 4, when his "stretch run" on a heated angle gives him inside position on B at the jibe mark. A, meanwhile, watches both competitors go by while feeling as if he's sailing through molasses. It doesn't always work out this way, of course. A might find a making breeze or a header to windward and ride it down in triumph to the mark ahead of B, C, and everyone else. Or C's strategy might be foiled by too many sails to windward feeding him too much bad air, and he could wind up losing several places. But that's life on the racecourse!

yourself and the boats ahead of you, you'll be in better shape to attack them on the upcoming leg. If you sail the leg well, you can bring yourself closer to the front even without passing any-one.

Straight Is Not Fast

Sailing the straight line between the windward mark and the turning mark is obviously the shortest course, but it's rarely the fastest. Sail in harmony with the wind. When the wind lightens, sharpen up slightly. This brings the wind more over your bow, increasing the apparent wind and boosting your speed. When you catch a puff, ride it down toward the mark. Pay attention, and you'll get the maximum boost from the gust by staying in it longer. "Up in the lulls, off in the puffs" is the way to sculpt a course along the rhumb line that is faster than dead straight.

Most sailors hold high on a reach. They do it in order to stake out a windward position and to discourage boats behind from trying to pass them to windward and steal their wind. They do it because a sharper angle makes them sail faster. When it's time to come down

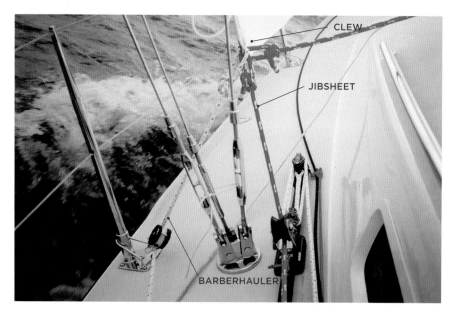

Easing out the jibsheet and taking in on a barberhauler will move the jib lead outboard, opening up the slot between jib and mainsail.

to the mark, however, boats above the rhumb line must adopt a low and slow sailing angle. The more nearly down-wind they are forced to sail, the more their boatspeed subtracts power from the breeze, and the slower they go. If the breeze picks up during the leg and they are able to ride a blast of heavier air down to the mark, boats that go high can prosper. Most of the time, however, sailing low pays off in the end.

The problem with sailing low is that it puts you downwind of the fleet. That means you can be blanketed, caught in the wind shadow of a boat that comes between you and the breeze. This is most catastrophic right at the windward mark, when boats

are close together and the wall of sails between you and the wind can be deadly. Hold high enough to maintain clear air at the beginning of the reach-ing leg, but as the boats around you reach ever higher, look for your spot. When you see a hole in the wall of sails that will let you carry clear air down with you, ease your way toward the rhumb line. The bonus of tak-ing the low road is that it puts you on the inside at the turning mark, and that gives you right of way and entitles you to buoy room.

Sail Fast

Reaching is a drag race. Sailing fast is always a good idea, but on a reach it's your major weapon.

Adjust the trim of the sail religiously to every variation in the wind. Let it out until it luffs, trim it in until it stops. Adjust the sail controls to give your boat its best sail shape. Reaching is about power. The deeper the curve in a sail, the more power it generates.

Loosen the mainsail controls—outhaul, backstay, and halyard, downhaul, or cunningham—to let more draft into the sail. As the main boom is eased beyond the outboard end of the traveler, take up on the vang to keep the leech from twisting. Whereas upwind you played the traveler in the puffs, now you'll play the mainsheet, easing it to relieve weather helm when the boat starts to heel excessively in a puff.

If you'll be sailing the reach with your headsail instead of a spinnaker, move the jibsheet lead forward as the jib is eased in order to prevent the leech from spilling open. The luff telltales become unreliable indicators at or below a beam reach, so look at the sail itself and let it out until it luffs; then pull it in until it stops. Off the wind your jib or genoa will tend to choke the slot between it and the mainsail. You can rig a **bar-berhauler** to reduce this tendency, but you can't eliminate it. Beware, therefore, of overtrimming the mainsail in an effort to remove the backwind bubble in its luff caused by the headsail. It's better to carry a slight luff in the headsail than to overtrim the main.

If you're in a dinghy, raise the centerboard or daggerboard partway to reduce drag (but leave enough down to keep you from skating sideways across the waves instead of driving ahead). Keep your rudder action to a minimum, because a rudder anywhere except amidships is like a brake. On many smaller boats, the skipper and crew steer more with body weight than with the rudder. Relieve persistent weather helm with weight to windward and by easing the mainsail.

Especially in a light breeze, you might want to induce a slight heel with crew weight in order to reduce wetted surface and to keep your sails in efficient foil shape.

Spinnaker Work

Before you hoist your spinnaker on a reaching leg, be sure you can carry it. Suppose the wind has clocked left during the windward leg so that the true wind is coming directly from abeam when you head toward the reaching mark. That means the apparent wind will be farther forward—say, from 80 degrees to as little as 70 degrees off your bow. In a light breeze the spinnaker will still help you, and you'd better get it up. But in a fresh breeze—anything more than, say, 14 to 18 knots, depending on the size of your boat—you'll have to ask yourself whether the spinnaker will speed up your boat or merely overpower it. When in doubt, prepare the gear as you approach the windward mark, but don't be in a hurry to set the chute as soon as you round. Let the boat settle down and see what the reach feels like. If boats around you set their chutes, see how they make out.

Let's assume the wind is either light or abaft the beam, and the spinnaker is needed. Getting the gear in place for a set is often your biggest stumbling block. Sending crew forward in the last couple of minutes of a frisky beat, removing crew weight from the windward rail, having someone on the leeward deck, distracting your crew from the task of round-

Judging by the eased mainsail, this boat is bearing down after rounding the windward mark. Getting the spinnaker tack out to the pole end like this will make the chute more likely to fill without wrapping around itself or the headstay. The lines dangling over the side and the fact that this hoist is a little tardy suggest that the boat ran into some excitement—perhaps an unscheduled last-second tack—in its mark rounding.

ing that mark—these are not things you want to be doing on a tightly contested beat, yet they must be done. Good crew work will minimize the distractions and the loss of boatspeed. Tasks should be clearly delineated for efficiency, and in a fresh breeze anyone who can be on the rail should be on the rail.

Be sure to double-check how things are led. In my experience more spinnaker sets are marred by bad leads than any other factor. Is the guy led outside all the stanchions? (It had better be!) Is the halyard wrapped around the headstay? (It had better not be!) Check and recheck, running it clear in your mind.

The second biggest problem is friction. Speed is important with a hoist. When the spinnaker fills before it's up, the game changes considerably. Check the parts of your system, especially the halyard system. Blocks, sheaves, fairleads—anything that can be done to take friction out should be done. In a four- or five-person crew, you may well want an extra hand at the mast to grab the halyard above the turning block and help with the hoist.

We'll assume you're leaving the windward mark to port and then simply bearing off and setting the chute—the **bear-away spinnaker set**. The procedure might go like this:

Preset the mast end of the pole at a height appropriate to wind speed and angle on your new course. The more air there is and the closer onto the wind you'll be, the higher the pole should be (though always remaining horizontal), because

The two boats on the right are hoisting their chutes after rounding the windward mark. The boat with the red spinnaker has rounded in first place and is taking the low road to the jibe mark, as is the boat on the far left. The others are all reaching higher to attack or defend.

this opens both the luff and the leech and flattens the top of the sail, enabling you to carry it higher. It's an excellent idea for a bear-away set to cock the pole up for the hoist so that it's perpendicular to the headstay. That opens the leading edge of the sail and lets it fill quickly.

Just before rounding the windward mark, trim the guy until the tack of the spinnaker is extended to the pole (which will be on or near the headstay). This pre-spreads the foot of the sail. It cannot be done too early, however, or else the sail might fill and drag the chute out of the turtle prematurely.

Pretrim the sheet to overhaul slack, but don't overtrim.

The boats at the top left have their chutes pulling. Behind them are several boats in the process of hoisting. The four trailing boats have their poles in position and are easing their mainsails to round the mark.

As you round the mark (assuming you're confident that you can carry the chute), hoist. The bigger the boat, the more critical it is to tail the halyard with a turn or two around a winch in case the sail fills before it's all the way up. Hoist all the way unless (perhaps) you're sailing a fractionally rigged boat on a tight reach, in which case you might (conceivably) stop a foot or so short of full hoist to open the slot between spinnaker and main.

Ease the mainsail during the rounding, but don't ease the jib more than a little, or it might interfere with the spinnaker hoist.

Trim the guy to square the pole to the apparent wind on the new course, easing the sheet as necessary. Be sure the crew doesn't overtrim the sheet before the pole is square; depending on how far aft the pole needs to come, you may in fact need the sheet to be eased.

Trim the sheet to fill the sail.

Drop and gather the jib, lashing it temporarily to the foredeck if necessary. On a tight reach the jib may be more help than hindrance, but it's unlikely.

Move the pole a little aft of square, playing the sheet as you do so, in order to make the sail as efficient as possible. Then adjust the pole height as necessary to make the spinnaker's tack level with its clew.

Play the sheet to maintain the intermittent curl on the spinnaker's luff. The curl should extend from midluff or just below midluff to a point high on the spinnaker's shoulder, but not all the way to the head. If the curl is too low, ease the pole forward. If too high, raise the pole somewhat to flatten the head of the sail.

Keep the sheet lead well aft on a beam or close reach in order to open the trailing leech and allow air to exit smoothly from the sail. In this mode the spinnaker is functioning almost like a full-cut genoa. On some boats you can widen the slot by leading the spinnaker sheet over the end of the main boom.

Needless to say, your spinnaker sets will go a lot more smoothly if you practice them in nonrace conditions.

If you find yourself overpowered on the reach, you may have to drop the pole some in order to tighten the luff, move the chute's center of effort forward, and reduce its heeling effect. Have someone on the vang and the mainsheet so that both can be eased in a puff as the boat heels and weather helm increases. Be prepared to steer lower in the puffs while the spinnaker trimmer eases the sheet as well. When you find yourself no longer able to fetch the next mark, it's time to get the chute down and the jib back up.

Luffing Matches

It is perfectly legal for a leeward boat to luff an overtaking boat that's trying to pass to windward. Under ISAF Rule 11 you can luff above your proper course, and you can luff sharply and decisively, provided only that you give the windward boat an opportunity to keep clear. It is rare, however, when luffing doesn't hurt both boats. Other competitors grin happily when two lead boats take themselves well to windward of the rhumb line in a protracted luffing match. Stay well clear of luffing matches if you can.

When a boat is overtaking you from astern, make eye contact early and let him know you know he's there. That might be enough to discourage him from trying to pass you closely to windward. He can either move two or three boat lengths to windward—hoping that will be enough to dissuade you from luffing him—or he can attempt to pass you to leeward (which is almost impossible in a one-design fleet but can work for a bigger boat in a handicap fleet). Or he can be content to ride your stern, then try for an inside overlap as you approach the next mark.

If he steers a course to leeward of you, Rule 17.2 prohibits you from bearing down below your proper course to try to block him. On the other hand, bearing down in a puff is a proper course in a reaching leg, and sometimes the race committee is left with the task of judging motive in a postrace protest hearing. If another boat establishes an overlap to leeward from astern, Rule 17.1 prevents him from exploiting that overlap to luff you.

Rounding a Reaching Mark

Holding low on a reach gives you an inside position on boats coming down to the reaching mark (which is often called the **jibe mark** or the **wing mark**), and this can make a difference of one, two, or even several places coming out of the rounding. Simply put, whatever you give up in order to get an inside position is better than what you lose by being on the outside.

Most often the wing mark of a triangle course takes you from a reach to a reach through a course change of roughly 90 degrees, sometimes more. If you are caught on the outside of that arc, you'll lose distance and position to any inside boat. The best bet is to be on the inside. Failing that, know how to round so as to minimize the damage.

A sailboat turns around her center of lateral resistance, which is usually near the midpoint of her keel or centerboard. If you come tight alongside the

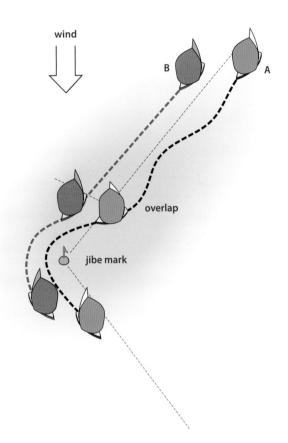

Passing another boat on a reaching leg is difficult, but you can gain one or several places by establishing an inside overlap at the jibe mark as boat A does here.

buoy and begin your turn when the bow is even with the mark, the bow will spin in the direction you want to go, but the center of the boat will continue on, describing a much wider arc. You'll be at least a boat length or two beyond and below the mark by the time you complete your turn. Instead, turn wide before you get to the buoy. Now, when you turn your bow right up against the mark, the boat (keel and all) will follow the line, and you'll cut straight and close onto your new course.

This rounding technique is especially advantageous when you have a competitor overlapped on your outside quarter. Typically you'll be approaching the mark on starboard tack and leaving it to port. If you're the inside boat you're also the leeward boat, and the rules allow you to harden up as you approach the mark in order to make the tactical rounding described above. Done correctly, this will prevent your competitor from taking your windward quarter in a controlling position as you exit the rounding.

Practice this turn when you are by yourself, and use it when racing, even if you have a boat on your outside. The rule allows you to take all the room you need for a proper rounding.

If you try for an inside overlap but fail to establish one before your competitor is inside the two-boat-length circle, slow down, drop astern, and make a tactical rounding—wide on the near side, tight on the far side. Don't follow the boats ahead too closely. You don't want to have to dive to leeward to avoid them should they slow down or mess up. You're still on the inside of the fast track, and you may be able to cross their wakes and assume a controlling position close astern and to windward on the next reach. Let yourself be overlapped from astern, though, and you'll be pushed to leeward and blanketed.

Jibing

It's not called the jibe mark for nothing. The tactical turn described above must be accompanied by a jibe. Especially if you're flying a spinnaker, poor crew work here can cost you several places.

How you jibe the chute depends on what gear you have onboard. End-for-ending the pole is most common on smaller boats with lighter poles. Dipping the pole happens more on larger boats with heavier gear. No matter how many hands you have aboard, though, chances are you'll need all of them to jibe the spinnaker.

The wider and more gradual the stern's arc through the wind, the easier it is to keep the spinnaker flying. Much as you'd like to hurry the process, rushing the crew through a jibe faster than they can handle it is a prescription for losing a lot by trying to save a little. This is another good reason to swing wide around the near side of the jibe mark.

Be patient. Meanwhile, so that you don't slow down the maneuver, move the main from one side to the other as fast as possible. Often that means trimming all the parts of the mainsheet at once and throwing the boom across to the new side. Trimming the main in heavier air can be harder, however. It may create weather helm and make steering difficult. The answer then is not to start trimming until the boat is heading almost dead downwind, then jibe the main fast. To lessen the force of the boom swing, you can steer momentarily back toward the side from which the boom is coming. This adds distance and complication to the turn, but the more boisterous the conditions, the more valuable the precaution becomes. After all, neither a broken boom nor a capsized boat is very fast. In any event, jibing the main shouldn't be an afterthought. Think it out before you tackle the chute.

As the wind increases, so does the difficulty of jibing the spinnaker. Magnified loads on sail and gear; a slippery, wet, and rolling platform; and the heightened consequences of any mistake add substantially to the challenge. Practice in light to moderate air until you get the evolution down. Do it until you've got both the big picture and a sense of the variables that make each jibe a unique adventure. The precision, timing, and teamwork necessary to jibe well in heavy air won't come without a lot of practice.

An **end-for-end jibe** begins by heading the boat off and squaring away toward a downwind course. That eases the load on the pole. The bowman should take the pole from the mast. Next he hooks the pole to the new guy (old sheet). It is still connected at this point to the old guy (new sheet). This technique makes it possible for the bowman to help "steer" the chute onto the new jibe.

While you jibe the main, the bowman unclips the pole from the new sheet. Pushing the new outboard end of the

An end-for-end jibe in process. The foredeck crew may have removed the pole from the port-side guy before the boat was dead down wind, and as a result the foot of the spinnaker has climbed out of view. This boat appears to have two pairs of spinnaker sheets rigged, with the stouter pair to be used if the wind gets any stronger.

pole forward toward the headstay (not outboard against the strain of the sail), the bowman attaches the new inboard end to the mast. This needs to happen quickly when you're rounding a jibe mark. Conscientious trimming through the whole process will make it much easier, and it's especially important to ease the new guy (old sheet) when the pole is being attached so that the bowman and trimmer aren't fighting each other. Keeping the chute flying and full not only keeps speed up; it also makes every part of the process simpler to see and easier to do.

A **dip-pole jibe** requires a sheet and guy for both corners of the spinnaker—four lines all told. The jibe begins by lifting the inboard end of the pole high enough on the mast that the outboard end, when dipped, can swing past the base of the headstay and be raised on the other side.

Square away and trip the pole. If you're lucky the sail will lift free, and the pole can be lowered. The sail is still connected to the old guy. Lower the pole topping lift so that the outboard end of the pole descends to the bowman on the point. The sail is still connected to the old sheet, but the bowman has taken the new guy (the other line of that pair), which has no strain on it, forward with him in a loose bight. As the pole comes to him he inserts the new guy in the pole jaws. The pole is then lifted on the new jibe, and tension is taken on the new guy until the sail is brought back to the pole. Keep tension on the new guy, ease the old sheet, and trim away.

A dip-pole jibe sounds more complicated than it is. It offers good security because the sail is trimmable throughout. It's more deliberate than an end-for-end jibe, but with either method you can set yourself up for a slam-bang turn by jibing the chute completely before you jibe the main. Having jibed the chute, you can make as sharp a turn as the rounding or tactics demand. After a jibe it's a good idea to sail above your eventual course for a bit to accelerate out of the turn.

The Downwind Leg

If you're sailing a windward-leeward or Olympic course, at least one leg will be more or less directly downwind. A downwind leg is tactically more challenging than a reaching leg. Indeed, a run is at least as challenging as a beat. One reason is that sailing directly before the wind puts you in the borderland between two different types of propulsion. On most points of sail a boat moves forward due to the lift generated by the wind flowing over the curved surface of her sails. You can visualize that force as a pull on the middle of the back (leeward) side of the sail. When you're heading straight before the wind, however, there is little or no flow of air around the sails. Instead the force you derive from the wind comes entirely from its push on the front (windward side) of the sail. Pulling works better than pushing, and lift is more effective than thrust. A boat going in the same direction as the wind subtracts its speed from the wind's force. Suffice it to say that "dead down" is "dead slow," at least until the wind starts to whistle and the waves begin to break.

3.5 knots of boatspeed

4.5 knots of boatspeed

10 knots true wind

6.5 knots apparent wind

8.5 knots apparent wind

A

B

Sailing dead before a 10-knot breeze, boat A can go no faster than 3.5 knots, at which point his apparent wind is only 6.5 knots. Identical boat B heats up to a broad reach, pulling his wind forward and developing lift from the sails, and sails a full knot faster while experiencing an apparent wind of 8.5 knots.

Tacking Downwind

Changing course as little as 10 degrees to windward from straight downhill brings the airflow around behind the sail, returning you to a more efficient mode of sailing. Also, as the apparent (relative) wind swings forward, it gains force from your boat's forward speed. On a downwind leg, therefore, you gain speed as you head closer to the wind. This is just the opposite of close-hauled sailing, when you can increase your speed through the water (though not necessarily your speed made good toward the windward mark) by footing off.

Tacking downwind is the process of zigzagging down the course as you jibe back and forth between a broad reach on one tack and a broad reach on the other. The object is to sail just high enough above the rhumb line to produce more in speed than you lose in added distance sailed. If you were to sail even higher you might go faster, but you'd arrive later at the leeward mark by virtue of sailing too much extra distance; if you were to sail lower you'd have a shorter distance to cover, but you'd be too slow. As always, what you're seeking to optimize is your velocity made good toward the mark.

The lighter the breeze (and the faster the boat you're sailing), the wider your jibing angle should be. In 8 knots or less of true wind, your optimum angle can be as much as 40 degrees from the rhumb line. In heavier air (generally above 15 knots or so), when you approach hull speed or are surfing or planing downwind, it's hard to go any faster, so you should sail the straightest course to the mark. Between those extremes, the best angle depends on your boat. Experience will tell you what it is.

In consequence, downwind tactics are in many ways the mirror image of upwind. You want to sail the lifted tack when you're beating. Try to sail the headed tack downwind. That's because when the apparent wind swings forward, it allows you to maintain your speed while heading closer to the mark. The racers' downwind gospel is to jibe on the lifts: when the apparent wind swings aft, jibe onto the other tack. The new wind should let you sail closer to the mark while still maintaining an angle that's "hot" enough for good speed. Maximize boatspeed by riding the puffs down and hardening up through the lulls.

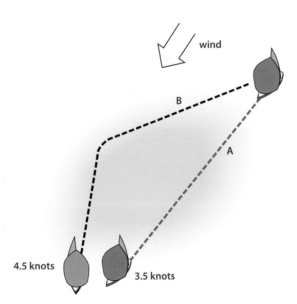

Tacking downwind (boat B) can often prove faster despite the longer distance sailed. Sailing on the favored (closer to the mark) jibe can make the tactic work even better.

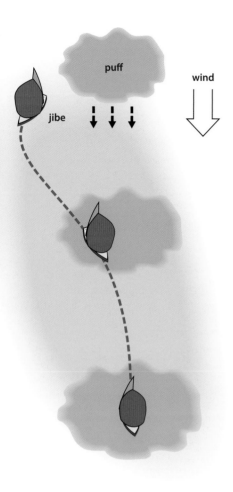

Steer for puffs—visible as darker patches of wind on the water—and stay in them as long as possible, riding them down toward the leeward mark.

Sail the Favored Jibe First

A true downwind leg gives you a choice of jibes, and you'll need to decide as you approach the windward mark which jibe to sail first. If the wind is coming over your right shoulder as you look down the course to your next mark, the starboard jibe

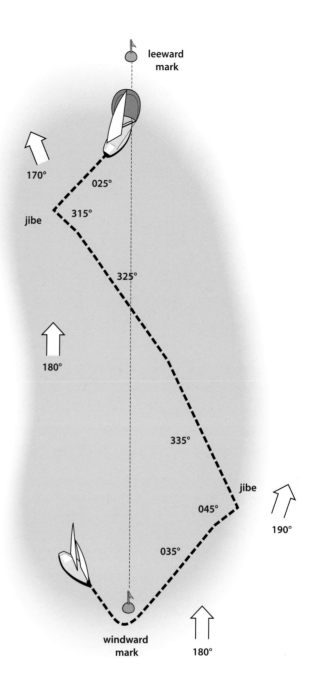

This boat is sailing a 35-degree jibe angle for maximum speed made good toward the leeward mark. At the top of the downwind leg neither jibe is favored, so he does a bear-away spinnaker set on starboard jibe. When the wind veers (swings clockwise) 10 degrees, however, it favors the port jibe, and after jibing he is on a compass course of 335 degrees, which is 20 degrees closer to the mark than he was before the jibe. When the wind oscillates back to 180° and then to 170 degrees he jibes back to starboard.

(mainsail to port) is favored. A wind over your left shoulder favors the port jibe. Unless there's a good reason not to (such as a strong opposing or favorable current on one side of the course), sail the favored jibe first. That shortens your distance, helps you stay near the center of the course, and puts you in position to profit if the wind shifts back eventually to favor the opposite jibe.

Suppose you've sailed a windward leg in an oscillating breeze, and you're lifted as you approach the windward mark along the starboard-tack layline. Since starboard tack is lifted, the port jibe will be headed, and thus favored, downwind. This suggests that you should jibe around the mark before setting the spinnaker, and your crew should set up for a jibe-set (see below) rather than a bear-away set. If a jibe-set seems too alien (it's really not difficult), or if your spinnaker gear is already set up for a starboard-tack hoist, you'll want to jibe over to port immediately after the hoist.

Recognizing the shifts is more difficult downwind because their effects are more subtle. A header does not cause your jib to luff, nor does a lift cause the leeward telltale to droop. Instead, unless you have electronic wind instruments, you must depend on your compass, the masthead fly, and the feel of the boat. Suppose, after a bear-away set, you start the downwind leg on starboard jibe on a compass course of 35 degrees with the wind from 180 degrees and the leeward mark bearing 360 degrees. If the wind then veers to 190 degrees, you'll have to turn to 45 degrees in order to maintain your tacking angle and apparent wind and therefore your boat speed, but 45 degrees heads you too far from the mark. On port jibe you'll be able to sail 335 degrees, which is closer to the mark, so it's clearly time to jibe—but it's only clear if you're paying attention to the masthead fly, your compass, the feel of your boat, and the relative bearing to the leeward mark.

Downwind Tactics

Much of the challenge of a run comes from wind shadows. Any boat behind you is between you and the breeze, and if you allow her to envelop you in her blanketed zone, she will slow you down. Here the masthead fly (wind indicator) is very helpful. If the fly points at a boat behind, she's lined up to be on your wind. If she is less than seven to ten mast lengths astern, she is on it already.

To clear your air, just sail outside the shadow. You might sharpen up or jibe away, but if you stay in the dead zone your air will be sapped and the boat astern—and perhaps others as well—will catch you. Unlike a tack, a well-executed jibe costs very little in terms of boatspeed. Don't hesitate to jibe to exploit a wind shift or to escape a wind shadow.

On the other hand, it's important to stay between your pursuers and the mark, because doing so forces your opponent to come to you and thus puts you in the optimal downwind covering position. This exposes you to possible blanketing by the boats behind, but it's nonetheless wise to be in the middle and be wary. Look for streaks (or better yet, "streets") of clear air and make the most of them. Cover serious competitors that seem to be going the right way or gaining. Let desperate gamblers go their own way.

Sometimes it takes nerves of steel to stay in the middle downwind. Any increase in

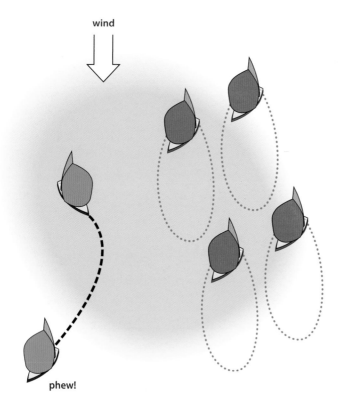

wind

phew!

Wind shadows (dashed outlines) can extend seven to ten mast lengths downwind in the direction indicated by your masthead fly. Jibe away from bad air when necessary.

wind velocity comes from astern, and those behind you will ride it down to you. This phenomenon—along with the tactical advantage the boats behind gain from their wind shadows—is what causes fleets to bunch up downwind. The result is more exciting racing, which is why windward-leeward courses have become popular. It's frustrating and scary to watch the gap behind you narrow, but don't panic.

Do what you must to keep your wind clean, but don't abandon your strategy. Keep looking for those shifts.

When you're attacking a boat in front of you, by all means aim your masthead fly at her and do your best to wrap her in your blanket. The offensive and defensive possibilities of blanketing are a big part of every run.

Make the most of your wind shadow. For instance, if you

aim your blanket zone at the boat ahead, she will harden up to clear. Where will her wind shadow be aimed when she does? Often you can slow the boats ahead by remote-control attacks mounted through an intermediary.

Even early in the leg, bear in mind the advantages that accrue from holding an inside position at the leeward mark. If the mark is to be left to port—and unless the right side of the course is greatly favored—the left side is worth thinking about. That creates both inside position at the mark and a starboard tack approach to it. You'll have right of way over any boat converging with you from starboard, whether it's on port tack or starboard; in the first instance you'll be the starboard-tacker, and in the second instance you'll be the leeward boat. Having the right of way outside as well as inside the two-boat-length circle is a big advantage. For one thing, it allows you to swing wide on your approach to the mark so that you can make an optimal rounding.

Boatspeed

There is little or no side force on the hull during a run, so you

There are good reasons to heel to windward while you're running—it reduces weather helm and wetted surface and adds to air speed and projected sail area.

can raise your centerboard to eliminate its drag. To minimize the braking effect of the rudder, heel the boat to windward. The boat may go straight on her own, with little or no rudder pressure.

Another small benefit of heeling the boat to windward is that it lifts the mainsail higher off the water and into a slightly fresher breeze. In an extremely light breeze, however, a slight leeward heel may help the sails maintain their shape and make the most out of what little air there is. In a fresh to moderate breeze, most boats go faster if you move your crew forward enough to lift the broad stern sections out of the water. In heavy air, on the other hand, it's often best to move crew weight aft to counteract the bow's tendency to bury as the puffs drive the rig forward.

It's normal off the wind to put more shape into your sails by loosening the backstay, outhaul, and halyard (or cunningham) on the main and moving jib leads forward and outboard. On a broad reach or run, however, shape is a lesser concern than area. You're being pushed by the wind, so provide the maximum surface for the wind to push against. Apply vang tension to keep the mainsail from twisting. Not only does vang tension help ensure you're presenting the maximum mainsail area to the wind, it also helps prevent the boat from rolling to windward in a strong breeze, a tendency that, if left unchecked, could lead to a windward broach.

Downwind Spinnaker Work

You can set a spinnaker anytime the wind is on or aft of the beam, but you'll definitely set one on a run if you've got one. If you're leaving the windward mark to port and simply bearing away and setting, proceed with the bear-away set as already described.

If port jibe is favored, on the other hand, you'll want to jibe around the mark before setting. The jibe-set isn't difficult if your crew runs the lines correctly— they'll need to move the spinnaker bag or turtle to starboard and run the guy around the headstay. You can help by giving them as much time as possible to make the adjustment, instead of announcing the maneuver 30 seconds before you reach the mark.

In a jibe-set—unlike a bear-away set—you can't raise the pole before rounding the mark, because doing so would prevent you from jibing the jib. You can attach the inboard end of the pole to the mast, but leave the outboard end resting on the port-side foredeck so that the jib can pass over it. (Note: The jibsheets must lead over—not under—the pole, or

A twing in use on a spinnaker sheet.

else the pole will foul the jib when you attempt to jibe.) Hoist the spinnaker as soon as you've jibed the main and jib. It isn't necessary to lift the outboard end of the pole prior to hoisting, because the chute will fly perfectly well without the pole on a broad reach or run. Concentrate on getting the chute up and drawing and the jib down before you add the pole.

The speed you get from your spinnaker depends on how you trim it. The goal when reaching was to maximize the flow of air across the sail, but the goal downwind is to get as much sail area in front of the wind as possible. Raise the halyard to full hoist, because the air gets better higher. Trim the sheet to the widest part of the boat. Square the pole to the apparent wind to begin, then try mov-ing it even farther aft. You want to spread the sail as much as you can while keeping the foot horizontal.

A curl in the leading edge of the sail means that the sail is as open as possible to the wind. An even curl from midluff (or just below) to the top of the shoulder is ideal. If you ease the sheet too far, the sail will break. Still, it's much better to ride the edge of a break (even if you lose the sail once or twice) than it is to overtrim into a solid but wind-starved sail. The leading edge is your guide, but the trailing edge (or leech) is just as critical. If it's too loose, it will spill more wind than you want. If it's too tight, the air from the spinnaker will exhaust into the mainsail and slow you down. Most of the time, with most spinnakers, you want the leech as open as you can make it. For that reason, especially as your jibe angle heats up, lead the spinnaker sheet as far aft as possible.

Running downwind in a fresh breeze and a seaway introduces rolling. When the spinnaker gyrates to one side it rolls the boat that way, and if the oscillations become synchronized with the waves, the result can be unnerving as well as slow. Lowering the pole (which hardens the upper part of the luff) may dampen the roll and allow you to go faster as well.

If that doesn't work, try strapping the sheet down with a **twing**, which is a small block attached to an adjustable pendant that's tied just aft of the stays on either side. Lead both sheets through their respective twings, and when the pole is to starboard, tighten the port twing. This holds the sheet down and firms the leech, which will help prevent the sail from swinging back and forth. When you jibe, let up on the port twing so that it rides loose along the sheet, and tighten the starboard one.

If the spinnaker is still difficult to control, ease the pole forward to hide some of the chute behind the mainsail. If that doesn't do it, it's probably time to douse.

Rounding the Leeward Mark

Boats behind have the edge downwind because their wind shadows extend ahead of them. The basis of your defense is to make sure you're inside at the mark. The object of your attack is to make sure you're inside at the mark. Not only is an inside rounding a faster rounding, but it also represents your best shot at retaining clean air, the freedom to choose where you want to go on the ensuing beat, and the freedom to tack when you wish. An inside position may not be paramount, but it sure is nice.

The ideal rounding is a lot like the one you should use at the jibe mark. You want to swing wide just before you reach the mark, shaping your turn to leave it close aboard as you depart. Your wide-approach, tight-departure turn should put you at the mark, trimmed for the beat as your bow passes inches from the buoy. From this position you may be able to sail over the boats ahead and pin them on port tack. If not, you can tack away to clear your air.

The tactics for the rounding are similar, too. If you're to leeward of an outside boat, or if you're on starboard tack versus his port tack, you have rights outside as well as inside the two-boat-length circle, and you can force him to give you room enough for the tactical rounding just described. If your rights accrue only inside the two-boat-length circle, however—i.e., if you have the inside position but not leeward-boat or starboard-tack rights—competitors aren't obligated to give you any more room than you need to make a tight rounding. When you're forced into a tight rounding, you must be on your guard against a competitor coming out of the rounding with a controlling position on your windward flank, or perhaps even rolling over you to windward as you leave the mark.

Conversely, if you're the outside boat in this situation, force the inside boat into a tight rounding, then swing wide yourself at the last moment of your approach to the mark. Try to hang far enough back to cross the inside boat's stern and sail into the space between him

A leeward-mark rounding. One of the boats approaching the mark is on starboard tack and will have rights outside the two-boat-length circle over converging port-tackers. He'll also have rights inside the circle by virtue of his inside position, but he'll have to jibe around the mark, and he appears to be sailing a slower approach angle than the port-tackers. The boat that's about to round the mark is swinging wide in his approach in order to leave the mark close aboard in his departure.

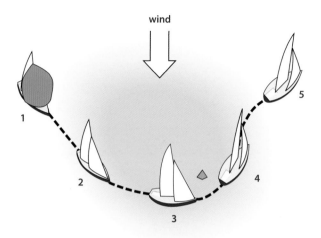

wind

When rounding a leeward mark *it's best to approach wide and depart tight.* **1.** *Prepare to raise the jib and douse the spinnaker (in that order).* **2.** *Get the jib up and the chute down.* **3.** *Trim the main to close-hauled as you round.* **4.** *Momentarily steer above your close-hauled course as you leave the mark. This will protect you from being attacked from behind, may give you a windward gauge on boats ahead, and will help the jib trimmer.* **5.** *Bear off for speed, then decide whether and when to tack.*

and the mark as he turns. In this way you may succeed in sneaking to windward of him. When, at the bottom of the downwind leg, you foresee this situation developing, you might want to get your spinnaker down a bit earlier than planned so that you're set up and ready for this close-quarters maneuvering.

Still, you don't want to be overlapped by an inside boat if you can help it. If a boat to weather of you on a run has inside position, luff hard to break the overlap. As you luff, the line drawn abeam from your tran-

---

Rights at the Leeward Mark

Boat B has just reached a point two boat lengths from the mark, which means he has now established his personal pecking order. Specifically, boat A needs to give B room, while B is obligated to give room to both C and the distant E. The fact that D has an overlap with C means nothing to B, since B is clear ahead of D. If D tries to stick his bow in, he will be breaking the rules.

Note that, although the situation has been established for B, the other boats have yet to sort things out, as none of them has reached the two-boat-length radius. For example, while it appears that C will have to give E room at the mark, that is not yet certain. If C were to surge ahead and break E's overlap before C reaches the two-boat-length radius, he will be able to cut the corner as closely as he wants. Then again, while A is clear ahead of E for now, that could change before A reaches the two-boat-length circle, in which case A will have to give E room to round. E may also be able to slip inside by default, since he has an overlap with B, who in turn has an overlap with A. Boat B must provide room for E whether A likes it or not!

(Reprinted with permission from *Getting Started in Sailboat Racing*, by Adam Cort and Richard Stearns)

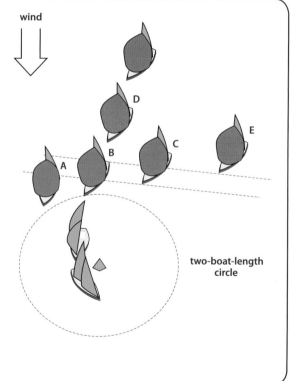

wind

two-boat-length circle

---

som swings aft, but as you fall off again, it swings forward. If you can swing it past his bow, you've broken the overlap.

Plan your attack on a boat ahead of you so as to get an inside overlap just before the two-boat-length circle, but beware of the limitations on this tactic. If you get overly aggressive you may be protested, and the onus will be on you to prove that your overlap was established in time.

If you do find yourself trapped on the outside, make a fast, wide, gradual turn while trimming for upwind speed. Foot off to leeward as you depart the mark. If you can get your bow ahead of your rival's, you have a shot at establishing a safe-leeward position and forcing him to tack away.

If there's a crowd at the leeward mark, as there often is, complexities multiply. An outside boat may not be able to grant you room due to the boats outside him, and in this situation the rules do not allow you to force your way in. Trying to pry open an inside position will at least make you unpopular and might get you disqualified. Instead, it is sometimes best to slow yourself down just before the mark so that you can round cleanly on the heels of the herd. Consider dousing your spinnaker a bit early, and get your rig set up for upwind sailing. Hold yourself back, swing wide, then slingshot yourself past the mark at full upwind speed; you may pick off several competitors in the dueling crowd.

Sail Handling at the Leeward Mark

As you approach the leeward mark, set up the rig for upwind sailing. Tighten the backstay, the main outhaul, and the main halyard or cunningham, and relieve the vang tension. You might as well move the main traveler car to its upwind position now, too, leaving one less thing to worry about during the rounding.

The next question is when to set the jib. If you delay so as to get the last second of performance out of the spinnaker, will you be able to douse and round well enough to be competitive on the next beat? If you set the jib in plenty of time, will the boat on your hip roll over you by virtue of last-minute spinnaker speed? These are common questions. My experience

A leeward mark rounding. The wind has swung left, forcing the boats to approach the mark on a tight reach. The boat at left is late getting his spinnaker down and may lose one or two places.

This leeward mark is left to starboard. All the boats are making a wide-approach, tight-departure turn to guard against attack from behind. When you have to jibe around the mark, the spinnaker has to come down a little sooner.

should keep his eyes open and adjust the speed of lowering to the circumstances.

The genoa of a larger boat should blanket the chute and make taking it in easier. With the jib set, hold the chute as long as you can. Luffing the spinnaker at the turn makes it possible to gather the foot. Then ease the guy. Unless you have to jibe around the mark, the foredeck crew can lower the pole as you depart close-hauled.

Every time you douse the spinnaker, it's important that the halyard reeve freely. Make sure it's free to run. Some racers flake it, bitter end first, into a bucket. Avoid carrying a half-up spinnaker away from the mark if you care about where you finish.

A windward takedown offers some advantages. The sail most often pulls you toward the mark rather than away, and any flailings or mistakes are restrained by the jib and so hurt your speed much less than a sail flogging to leeward. One of the keys in a windward takedown is to get the pole off and stowed early. Sometimes that means flying the sail by hand, but getting the pole off at the beginning of a takedown makes cleanup simpler.

has been that a sloppy douse and rounding cost much more than whatever I might gain by carrying the chute to the bitter end. Set the jib early, douse the chute early, but work on being able to hold on longer with confidence.

A leeward spinnaker takedown is the norm. Uncleat the halyard, release the guy, and lower the sail as it is gathered in under the main boom. The halyard handler wants to lower as fast as possible without dropping the sail in the water. He

Finishing

Sail the race right to the end. It's demoralizing to be nipped at the line. It's great to win a close finish. Don't get into counting boats and accepting your fate until you've crossed the line.

Most finishes occur upwind, but distance races, wind shifts, or committee preference can sometimes lead to downwind finishes. In either event, what made for good strategy through-out the race holds true at the finish: keep clear air, avoid the corners, and be ready to seize the opportunities that come up. At the finish, though, you should also think about covering.

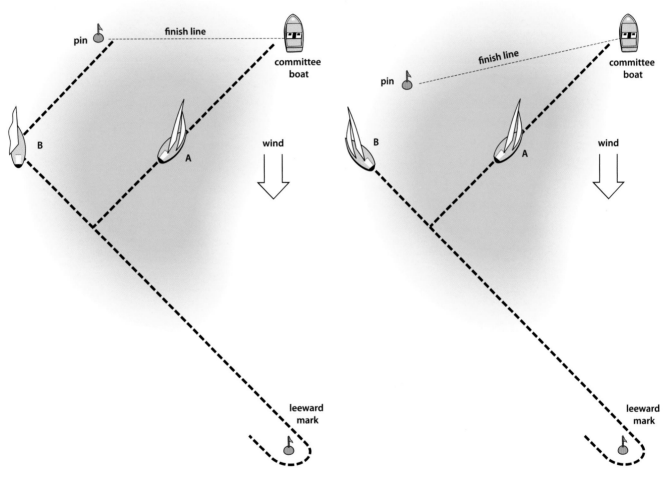

This finish line, though not directly upwind from the leeward mark, is perfectly square to the wind, and neither end is favored. Boats A and B both leave the leeward mark on starboard tack, but A tacks to port as soon as he can fetch the committee boat, while B is just now tacking for the pin end of the line. Yet both have the same distance to sail before finishing.

In this scenario the pin end of the line is favored, but A fails to see that and splits tacks with B as soon as he can fetch the committee boat. Within three or four boat lengths it is obvious that B has chosen the better course. A's best bet now is to tack again and hope to assert his starboard-tack rights over B to win a close finish, but A has already overstood the pin end of the line and will have made two tacks to B's one, so B is probably going to win this race.

Upwind and down, it's possible to protect your lead on the boats closest to you by staying between them and the mark. Downwind, try to do this without falling into your opponents' wind shadows. Upwind you have the added advantage of sending turbulent air to the boat(s) you are covering if you position yourself right. Protecting your lead on the boats behind you, however, limits your chances of passing boats close in front. At the start of the beat to the finish, decide whether to attack or defend. You might use the first half of the leg to try to pass people and the last to hold onto the gains you've made, but don't get hamstrung by a decision to the point that you accomplish neither.

When sailing to an upwind finish be aware of the backwind ("bad air" or "dirt") spiraling off the leech of your sail(s). Do your best to aim it at your pursuers to hold onto your lead until the finish.

To pass boats in front of you, try to move closer to the side of the course favored by wind direction or velocity. If you can be the first one to stronger air or the inside of a lift, you'll make up ground. Try tacking when another boat is crossing the boat ahead of you. That way, if he tacks to cover you, he buries himself behind the crossing boat. If he stands on, he lets you get farther out to your chosen side of the course. If you're most concerned with breaking through the boat in front of you, try a series of short tacks to break his cover. You might also try a fake tack to break clear, but these tactics slow you down relative to the rest of the fleet.

The classic dilemma when you're covering other boats is what to do when two boats right behind you go in opposite directions. The classic answer is to cover the one that's going the way you want to go.

You would like to finish at the favored end of the finish line—i.e., the end closest to you. If the line is square to the wind—even if it's not directly upwind from the leeward mark—neither end is closer. This may seem counterintuitive until you diagram it with a ruler and protractor, but it's true.

When the line is out of square, however—even by just a little—one end is favored. Just a one- or two-boat-length difference can earn you or cost you a place or

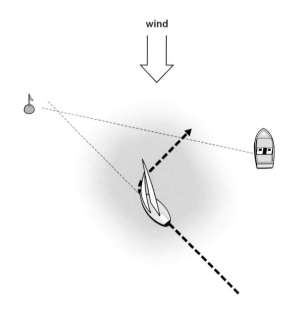

If you find yourself sailing more along the line than toward it, you're on the wrong tack. Tack immediately unless prevented by another boat.

A close finish.

two in a tightly contested finish. Often the line runs between a boat and a mark, and the boat, being bigger, looks closer, but look again. If the flag on the committee boat points toward the leeward mark, neither end of the line is favored. If it points, instead, more toward the pin end of the finish line, the pin end is favored, and if it points away from the pin, the committee boat is favored. Monitor the boats finishing ahead and take bearings. Before you get to the point where you have to pick one end or the other, have a pretty good idea which way to go. In an oscillating breeze, the last shift before you finish is the one that counts. Don't make a premature call.

Your fastest finish is as nearly square to the line as possible at the favored end. If you find yourself converging gradually with the line on your final approach, you are sailing away from the favored end and should tack immediately to cross the line more squarely. To get there even quicker, try **shooting the line**—luffing head to wind and pointing squarely across from your maximum gliding distance. Drop your jib, and you'll glide farther and faster. Congratulations!

On a downwind finish you can accomplish the same last-minute burst by bearing away and heading directly downwind rather than crossing the line at a broad-reach angle. On the other hand, you must keep your wind clear on a downwind finish. Don't hesitate to jibe even 50 yards or less from the line if that's what it takes to keep your wind clear. You want to sail, not drift, over the line, and nothing is more discouraging than losing a position or two at the last instant to boats you led all the way around the course.

As soon as any part of your boat crosses the line, you are finished. You must not recross the line onto the course without the committee's permission.

Going Cruising

The Cunard Line used to say that getting there is half the fun. Cruising is a lot better than that. Taking a vacation, having an adventure, getting away from it all—a cruise combines all these enticements. Cruising in your own sailboat, even a chartered bareboat, is a multi-layered and very special treat. An island outside time, a world to yourself, a deeper connection with the natural world and with your crew—all such clichés apply, but even they don't capture cruising at its best. At a sailboat's pace you truly *see* the world. You travel, but you're under your own roof, and you're free to make your cruise a cus-

tom adventure—from snorkeling to siestas, from museums to margaritas. But it's not a passive ride. You negotiate the passages, sail the boat, meet the challenges, and knit the crew together. Cruising in a sailboat is much better than Cunard-style cruising. It's *all* the fun.

My wife, Carol, and I stepped off the plane at Gatwick, England, in the summer of 1971, bent on serious cruising. Buying a British-built auxiliary sailboat (a 25-foot Westerly Tiger) for less than $10,000, we set out to explore Europe in the summers while teaching in the States during the winters. Five summers and two kids later we shipped the boat home, off-loading her in Port Newark, and we've been cruising the East Coast ever since.

We didn't sail our boat to Bora Bora, but we managed to get there in a chartered 40-footer. The Florida Keys, Virgin Islands, St. Lucia, St. John's River, the Thousand Islands, the Finnish archipelago, Tahiti, the Marquesas, the Greek Isles—chartering has taken us to all those places and more.

Cruising was part of my life from the beginning. I thank my parents for that and hope my

kids say the same. But you don't have to be born to cruising. If you've picked up the sailing basics from your walk down the dock and through this book, you already know much of what you need. You know how to handle your boat under sail and power, how to anchor and dock, how to navigate, how to negotiate boat and ship traffic, and how to read the wind, water, and tides.

But cruising is more than sailing, and there's always more to know. Learning how to live the cruising life and learning about the places it takes you are just two of them. Cruising also gives you the freedom to express, discover, and be yourself. Choosing a boat, for instance, has as much to do with your plans, expectations, and limi-

I thank my parents for my early start in cruising.

Cruising experiences range from solo adventures to group charters and quiet anchorages. Donna Lange (top), a singlehanded circumnavigator finished her trip in Narragansett Bay, Rhode Island, USA. New Zealand (bottom) is a popular cruising ground.

tations as it does with design, equipment, size, or construction. Cruising means living on your own—to what extent is up to you. Cruising means fending for yourself, being in or out of touch, exploring or avoiding the world.

Boat handling takes on a new dimension when your boat is your home, and it's an everyday cruising necessity. Small-boat handling is a fact of cruising, too. Your dinghy may trail astern, but loading, handling, stowing, beaching, securing, and docking it should not be afterthoughts. "Little boats, little problems" only applies after you've mastered balance, trim, and perhaps the dinghy's outboard.

If you pay attention to the weather only when you're on the water, you're shortchanging yourself. Watching the weather channel and the win-dow at the same time from your living room can add to your education. Monitoring NOAA weather when you're not "out there" helps you know what to make of it when you are. Theoretical and practical meteorology books help, too.

You don't have to have all the answers at the start. The experience itself holds the most important ones. You'll develop ways of cruising as you go. Chartering (you can take a paid skipper or do it yourself) is an excellent way to sample cruising. Work into it gradually. If the slap of waves against the hull keeps you awake and you can't sleep on a boat, it's better to find that out in Long Island Sound than three days into an Atlantic crossing.

It's safe to say that cruising can cost more than you might think. Chartering, on the other hand, is priced to compete with a shoreside room at most resorts. Bareboat or captained charter vacations compare favorably with what you'd pay to sit by the pool, yet they provide a good deal more. Stretching the budget to cover more miles or enjoy more days is an ancient and honorable cruising art. Find your own ways to find cruising value.

Seamanship is a cruising essential involving not just the boat-handling and navigation skills we've already covered but constant care for your boat and crew as well. Forehandedness, resourcefulness, and grace under pressure—cruising demands them all. But when you look across a cove or up at a star-filled sky and say, "This is great, and we didn't have to take a cruise ship or an airplane to get here," you won't regret a bit of it.

Cruising Boats

If it floats, you can cruise in it. Webb Chiles sailed an open 17-foot Drascombe lugger around the world—though not without incident. Arnaud de Rosnay made overnight inter-island cruises on a sailboard—though not in comfort. Fritz Fenger circumnavigated the Caribbean in 1901 in a 17-foot sailing canoe named *Yakaboo*. But what's the *right* cruising boat? Around anchorages and in countless books that ques-tion is addressed, dissected, analyzed, and even occasionally illuminated.

I like what Don Casey said in his book *Sensible Cruising: The Thoreau Approach*: "It's not the sea that keeps cruisers in

A Boat for Cruising

Throughout this chapter, by way of introducing the wonderful range and diversity of production cruising sailboats for every taste, use, and budget, I'm including a series of cruising boat vignettes taken with permission from Daniel Spurr's estimable book, Your First Sailboat: How to Find and Sail the Right Boat for You *(International Marine/McGraw-Hill, 2004). Here is the first.*

CATALINA 22

SAIL magazine's tenth-anniversary issue in 1980 listed the Catalina 22 as the boat that best represented the "breakthrough" in trailer cruising. As in other swing-keel trailer sailers, the centerboard is replaced with a ballasted keel, though it pivots on a pin

(through a fixed keel stub) in the same manner. This reduces draft for trailering yet provides stability for higher winds and bigger waves. Though there are many other similar designs, none has equaled the success of the Catalina 22. More than 15,000 have been sold since 1969. It's hard to figure, given the boat's shortcomings (wasted storage space, some dubious construction practices, uncomfortable bunks, need for a trailer tongue extension at some ramps, etc.). But it looks more shippy than some other boats, and the double lower shrouds suggest a certain readiness for sea. A fixed-keel version was offered but the percentage sold was very low. A few years ago, an updated MKII design was offered, and is still in production.

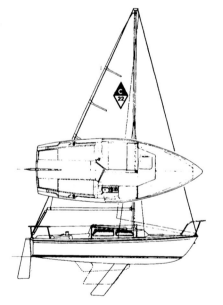

LOA	21'6"
LWL	19'4"
BEAM	7'8"
DRAFT	1'8" (KEEL UP)
DISPLACEMENT	1,850 LB.
BALLAST	550 LB.
SAIL AREA	212 SQ. FT.
DESIGNER	FRANK BUTLER
PRICE NEW	$14,326
PRICE USED	2,350 – $2,750 (1970 MODEL) $3,750 – 4,350 (1982 MODEL) $4,800 – $5,200 (1986 MODEL)
SIMILAR BOATS	O'DAY 22 CHRYSLER 22 RHODES 22 SOUTH COAST 22 KELLS 22 VENTURE 222 TANZER 22

[Reprinted with permission from *Your First Sailboat: How to Find and Sail the Right Boat for You*, by Daniel Spurr (International Marine/McGraw-Hill, 2004)]

port but their attitude that they somehow don't have the right boat." His advice is to get the most out of the boat you have rather than saving and searching for years for the boat you think you need. The idea of perfection in a cruising boat is ultimately a silly one.

We bought Shere Khan for $10,000, and she has repaid that investment many times over with decades of cruising adventure. There are good cruising sailboats for every budget.

Shere Khan's cockpit (shaded area on plan) has always seemed too small, but it's a seaworthy feature and it leaves room under the wide sidedecks for two comfortable quarterberths in the cabin below. All that cabin space in a 25-footer proved ideal for my family. Every aspect of sailboat design involves compromise, and you'll be happiest with a boat that shares your priorities.

A Boat for Cruising

TANZER 22

Johann Tanzer, designer and builder of the Tanzer line of sailboats, was born in Austria and later emigrated to Canada, where he founded his business. The Tanzer 22 flush deck is a bit unusual, though it provides additional space below. The flip side is that there's no cabin to brace against when going forward on deck. Note how much heavier it is than the Catalina 22. The advantage of this is that it is stiff, with a big boat feel. The disadvantage is that there is more weight to lug around on a trailer. And the 2-foot draft makes launching on some ramps difficult. The cabin is smallish, but the cockpit is large. Construction quality is above average. Interestingly, the keel versions are not that much slower than a J/24; PHRF (Performance Handicap Rating Fleet) ratings are between 92 and 98 (seconds per mile). Production started in 1970 and ended with 2,270 of them

being built, making it one of the more popular day sailers of that decade.

LOA	22'6"
LWL	19'9"
BEAM	7'10"
DRAFT	2' – 4' (CB UP, CB DOWN) 3'5" (FIXED KEEL)
DISPLACEMENT	3,100 LB. (CENTERBOARD WITH STUB KEEL)
BALLAST	1,500 LB.
SAIL AREA	227 SQ. FT.
DESIGNER	JOHANN TANZER
PRICE NEW	NOT IN PRODUCTION
PRICE USED	$2,650 – $3,250 (1970 MODEL) $3,950 – $4,800 (1981 MODEL) $5,450 – $6,600 (1986 MODEL)
SIMILAR BOATS	CATALINA 22 O'DAY 22 CHRYSLER 22 RHODES 22 SOUTH COAST 22 KELLS 22 VENTURE 222

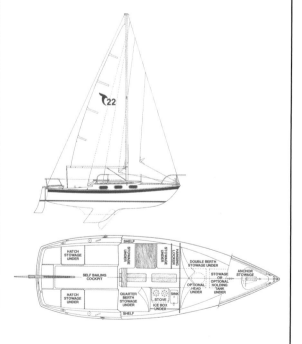

[Reprinted with permission from *Your First Sailboat: How to Find and Sail the Right Boat for You*, by Daniel Spurr (International Marine/McGraw-Hill, 2004)]

Yet it's true that some sailboats make better cruisers than others, and this is why the search for perfection is not as silly as the notion that you can attain it. The search will lay bare the features that detract from a good cruiser—at least for you. But how do you know which features those are?

First, use *your* standards. You're looking for a real boat to float the waters you sail, cruise the coasts you have in mind, and fit the life you're leading. Sure, we all think of a boat to *change* the life we're leading, but that leap is not necessarily the passport to a happy landing.

Lack of cruising experience is a problem. It not only makes you hesitant about your own judgments but also makes you dependent on the judgments of others. There are lots of things to learn about cruising boats and many ways to learn them, but what matters most to *you*? Sell-up-and-sail-away voyagers whose home is where their anchor lies and whose agenda is "on to the next adventure" constitute a distinct minority, but they're visible, intriguing, and credible. Their strong suit is that they're talking from deep experience. The problem, however,

is that the voyaging life and the realm of a weekend or vacation cruiser are worlds apart.

Some aspects of cruising are the same no matter where you sail or for how long, but voyagers tend to have lots of time and not much money, whereas cruisers are usually time-limited but have at least a vacation's worth of money. Storms in the open ocean are a real (though rare) possibility for voyagers, whereas you can cruise along the coast for a lifetime and never encounter a storm except in a safe anchorage or marina. Voyagers carry months' worth of supplies, while cruisers carry enough for days. And the distinctions go on. Applying someone else's standards is like chasing someone else's dream. Find out what matters to you, and use your own standards to chart your own course.

Safety, speed, economy, looks, comfort, value, and size are all good qualities in a boat, but which do you think is most important to your cruising happiness? The more cruising you've done, the less abstract these qualities become. One good thing is that they're *not* mutually exclusive—for example, a good-looking boat can

be fast and comfortable, too. Maybe you'll have to choose a boat by matching it up against your expectations, not your experience, but try hard to develop a clear picture of the cruising you want to do. That's the best way of coming up with a good boat to do it in.

I've always thought that the cockpit on *Shere Khan*, our 25-footer, was too small. It made sense to me that because I spend more than half of my waking time on deck, the "upstairs" should be expanded. Of course, I'd have to think twice about stealing room from the "downstairs," but the main argument I've heard in favor of small cockpits is that they're seaworthy. When a wave comes aboard and fills the cockpit, the volume of water weighs the boat down. That's dangerous. A smaller cockpit not only will hold less water but will drain quicker. In 29 years of cruising the way we cruise, a wave has never filled our cockpit. I'd rather have had 29 years in a bigger cockpit with big, well-maintained drains, but when Laurent Giles designed the cockpit his priority was safety over comfort. What's right?

Your views, of course, change with experience. If I'd delivered *Shere Khan* across the Atlantic from Greece on her own bottom instead of on a freighter, I might be telling you about the necessity and wonders of small cockpits. One point on which salts of all sorts agree, however, is construction. There are many legitimate ways to get more from your cruising dollars, but a poorly built boat isn't one of them. The operative philosophy in elite racing is that if it never breaks, it's too heavy. Cruisers, on the other hand, know that if it does break, they're in trouble. No one wants to carry dead weight to sea, but hulls and gear that are overbuilt aren't dead weight. Robust, durable, and failsafe may not be leading-edge concepts, but they're a cruiser's gospel. Whether by using a surveyor, buying from a builder you trust, or simply tapping and thumping your way from bow to stern until you're satisfied, make sure your cruiser has been built well. No aspect of a cruising boat is more important.

Size

Big boats are faster than small ones, and it's commonly believed (with some justification) that they're safer, too. They afford more elbow room and creature comforts. They can carry more stores, fuel, and water. They also cost more to buy and maintain, take more energy and expertise to handle, usually draw more water, and can seem less friendly, cozy, and inviting than small boats.

If you put pocket cruisers to one side and professionally crewed gold-platers on the other, there's still a big middle ground of boats that are reasonably sized for cruising. Affordability is a good starting place. It's a mistake, in my opinion, to stretch your finances to get the biggest possible boat. For one thing, when you buy a boat you'll need to put at least 25 percent of her purchase price into equipping and running her. Keep something in the bank! More berths, more room, and a longer waterline are all attractive, but size shouldn't be valued in and of itself. I suppose prestige can come with length, but that can be a trap. Determine size by what you can handle—financially, nautically, and by being flexible.

Size = speed. The clearest connection between size and speed is in waterline length. A longer length in the water gives a boat a higher top-end speed potential. A boat with a 25-foot waterline has a hull speed of 6.7 knots. A 36-foot waterline yields 8.0 knots, and that's a genuine difference. But we rarely sail at top speed, and you can't summarize overall sailing performance with a single number. Waterline length is good, but there's more than waterline length to consider when judging overall performance or even speed under sail.

Size = space. If you double the size of a boat (length, beam, and draft) you increase its volume by a factor of eight. Boats can gain a big amount of room from relatively small increases in overall length. But is room what you're really after? A vast expanse of teak sole may look attractive in a boat show, and oodles of elbow room may appear a plus, but at sea a space that's too wide to brace across or a spot too far from a handhold can be a hazard. Space is nice. I like enough over my head so that I don't walk around wincing. It's much easier to stow everything in its place if there's space enough to stow everything. Still, at some point more space may not be worth what it costs.

Size = safety. In open-ocean storms, the weight of a big boat is a better deterrent to being rolled by a wave than the limited heft of a small boat. In the storm that ripped through the Fastnet Race fleet in the Irish Sea in 1979, the majority of the casualties came in boats under 38 feet long. High freeboard is a comfort and a stability consideration. Big boats may have a steadier, slower motion in waves than little ones. Still, big does not always equal safe. Big boats are harder to handle, sail and equipment loads are greater, and in some conditions light, "corky" boats fare better than heavier ones.

Size = comfort. Big boats support more and bigger systems and amenities than small boats. Our 25-foot *Shere Khan* has no shower, and we wish mightily that she did. There are two sides to creature comfort, though. Taking all the conveniences of your condo to sea can prove frustrating, expensive, and even foolhardy. Cruising with a VCR sure beats cruising without one, but waiting at the marina for the blender repairman is never fun, and it can wind up preventing you from being "out there." The great yacht designer L. Francis Herreshoff said simply, "simplicity is the key." To read his *Compleat Cruiser* is to be plunked aboard with cruisers who are having nothing but fun, and part of that fun is getting away from the beeping, ringing, and buzzing

COST COMPARISON

	Trailer Sailer	Coastal Sailing	Cruiser
Purchase price	2003 Seaward 25—new $29,950	1979 Sabre 34 $34,000	1982 Tayana 37 $70,000
Loan interest	borrow $15,000 at 6% $4,983.60	borrow $24,050 $7,991.20	borrow $60,000 $19,951.60
Upgrades needed:			
sails	included	new mainsail $1,200	new mainsail $1,800
engine	$1,800 outboard	$3,000 rebuild	$10,000 new diesel
other		$2,000 refrigeration	———
Equipment needed:			
trailer	$2,500	———	———
safety (PFDs, horn, etc.)	$250	included	$4,000 life raft
ground tackle	$400	included	included
electronics	$1,200	$1,600 basic instruments	$3,500 radar
Total Cost to Buy	**$41,083.60**	**$49,791.20**	**$109,251.60**
Annual expenses:			
insurance	$400	$800	$1,600
yard work (e.g. bottom sanding)	do yourself	$400	$500
summer storage	trailer	$3,000	$3,000
winter storage	backyard	$650	$750
fuel and oil	$50	$120	$200
Total Cost to Operate	**$450**	**$4,970**	**$6,050**
Comments	small new boat: must buy all gear; save by trailering and storing in backyard	older boat with lots more room; needs electronics and engine rebuild	rugged world cruiser; needs reliable engine for world cruising, plus new sails and life raft

As this 2003 cost comparison between a new 25-foot trailer sailer, a 24-year-old 34-foot coastal cruiser, and a 21-year-old 37-foot world cruiser makes clear, the purchase price is only step one in the cost calculations when you buy a cruising sailboat. [Reprinted with permission from *Your First Sailboat: How to Find and Sail the Right Boat for You*, by Daniel Spurr (International Marine/McGraw-Hill, 2004)]

Boats for Cruising: A Pair of 28-Footers

These two boats are almost identical in length overall and on the waterline, but there are all resemblance ends. The Sabre 28 is a foot wider, almost twice as heavy, and a great deal more commodious for cruising. For good cruising with a family of four, choose the Sabre. For effortless daysailing in the classiest boat on the bay, with Spartan overnighting for a couple, it's hard to beat an Alerion Express.

ALERION EXPRESS 28

The original Alerion sloop was designed and built about 1912 by Nathanael Herreshoff, perhaps America's greatest yacht designer. Beginning in the 1970s, a number of spin-offs began to appear—one by grandson Halsey Herreshoff, and another by Alfred Sanford of Nantucket. In the late 1980s, Carl Schumacher was asked by Connecticut sailor Ralph Schacter to design a similar boat—traditional above the waterline and modern below. The result is the Alerion Express 28, first built by Holby Marine of Bristol, Rhode Island. Today it is built by Pearson Composites. If automobile analogies work for you, think of the Alerion as a gentleman's sports car—a Porsche or Jaguar. The emphasis is on speed, comfort, and simplicity. Although equipped with berths and a small galley for overnighting, its forte is the afternoon sail on the bay. It's quick to get under way, and with Garry Hoyt's patented Jib Boom, the entire rig (mainsail and jib) is self-tending (which means that you don't have to trim the sails when tacking). The boats are built by Pearson using balsa core sandwich and the SCRIMP process, in which the fiberglass cloths are laid up dry inside a plastic envelope in the mold; vacuum draws in the resin through a system of tiny hoses. It yields a higher glass-to-resin ratio and minimizes environmental hazards. The Alerion is a very classy (and pricey) small yacht. Many owners buy them on their way down in size, not up. There are very few similar boats.

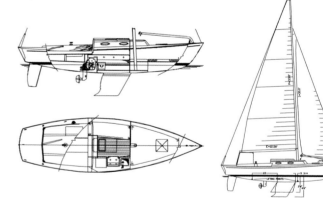

LOA	28'3"
LWL	22'10"
BEAM	8'2"
DRAFT	4'6"
DISPLACEMENT	5,700 LB.
BALLAST	2,200 LB.
SAIL AREA	352 SQ.FT.
DESIGNER	CARL SCHUMACHER
PRICE NEW	$95,995
PRICE USED	$46,800 – $51,400 (1997 MODEL) $72,700 – $79,800 (2002 MODEL)
SIMILAR BOATS	ANTRIM 27

of shoreside life. Big boats are better at isolating you from the marine environment, but do you truly want to be isolated?

Balance all of the above against the fact that most sailors, once they've owned a cruising boat for a while, buy a bigger one. Sometimes more is more, but as a rule we undersail our boats. Few are the cruisers who sail as often as they'd like. As she sits there plaintively on the mooring, I can look my boat in the eye when I'm shorebound and not feel too much guilt. After all, she's paid for. Were she sitting idle and costing me more than keeping the kids in college would, "use her or lose her" might become a refrain around our house. The bigger the investment, the bigger the commitment.

SABRE 28

Roger Hewson, designer of the Sabre 28 and founder of Sabre Yachts, was a Canadian building contractor who was fascinated with sailboats. This, his first creation, is a near classic. Production lasted from 1972 to 1986. From the outset, Hewson decided to aim at the high end of the market; that is, with above-average quality and above-average price. Today, Sabre and Tartan Yachts are arguably the two best builders of production sailboats in the United States. The 28 has good clean lines that aren't easily dated. It's a bit heavier than comparable boats, so it's solidly built, but not particularly fast. The interior is all wood, tabbed (fiberglass strips of mat) to the hull and deck. This is a much more expensive way to build interior furniture and cabinets than plopping in a molded fiberglass pan; plus it makes for a quieter, drier, and more easily modified interior.

LOA	28'5"
LWL	22'10"
BEAM	9'2"
DRAFT	4'8" OR 3'10"
DISPLACEMENT	7,900 LB.
BALLAST	3,100 LB.
SAIL AREA	403 SQ.FT.
DESIGNER	ROGER HEWSON
PRICE NEW	NOT IN PRODUCTION
PRICE USED	$12,700 – $14,600 (1970 MODEL)
	$25,100 – $27,800 (1981 MODEL)
	$33,600 – $37,400 (1986 MODEL)
SIMILAR BOATS	CAPE DORY 28
	COLUMBIA 8.7
	S2 8.5 METER
	YANKEE 28

[Reprinted with permission from *Your First Sailboat: How to Find and Sail the Right Boat for You*, by Daniel Spurr (International Marine/McGraw-Hill, 2004)]

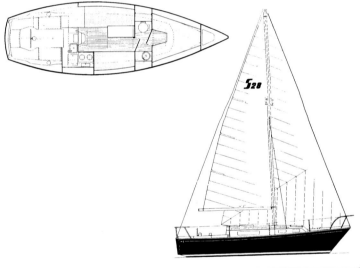

And finally, consider that a big boat is more likely to be undersailed than a smaller one. Once aboard, it takes my wife and me a mere few minutes to get our little boat away from the mooring and under sail. An afternoon sail is a spontaneous thing, whereas a sail on a 50-footer requiring a crew of three or four may have to be planned a week or two in advance, making spontaneous daysails a thing of the past. If you want your 50-footer for long passages, that's one thing, but if you intend to use her for weekending and daysailing and the occasional vacation cruise, remember what Fagan said in the musical *Oliver*: "I think I'd better think it out again."

Displacement

Displacement equals weight. Once you've put as much sail on a boat as she can handle, the best way to get her to go faster is to remove weight. One measure of a sailboat's performance potential is the ratio of its sail area to its displacement. The less weight per unit of power (i.e., sail area), the greater the sailboat's speed potential in light to moderate breezes. Displacement also equals volume (the volume of water that the hull displaces), which also translates into interior volume and payload. Gear and stores weighing 5,000 pounds may not overly burden a 20,000-pound boat, but they'd definitely tax a 10,000-pound boat. Light-displacement boats are racehorses. Heavy-displacement boats are packhorses. To my mind, neither makes a great cruising steed. Here, as so often in yacht design, moderation is best.

Ultralight-displacement boats move as much over the water as through it. Every ounce that weighs them down, slows them down. Their hulls tend to be dinghy-like, shallow and flat. Therefore (in addition to being cramped inside) they pound, and their motion in a seaway can be jerky and quick. And where cruising sailors most need strength (upwind in waves, for example), lightweights tend to fall down. Some cruisers love their ultralights, but I'd say these boats are better suited for racing and performance daysailing than cruising.

The heaviest of heavy-displacement yachts evolved from barges and fishing boats and have slack bilges, bluff bows, and boxy underbodies. They must shove aside a considerable volume of water to move at all, and that limits their speeds. They can provide stability and volume, but they are ponderous and are most often slow to respond to breeze or helm. Stout and sturdy, they make good homes, but to my mind they're not as good for cruising as boats that are more fun to sail.

In 1975, Seattle-based designer Bob Perry kicked off something of a revolution with his Valiant 40, a boat targeted for cruising and built to go anywhere (a number of them have circumnavigated the planet), yet designed with a performance underbody. With a fin keel, efficient hull, and skeg-hung separated rudder, Valiants sail fast and well. Called "performance cruisers," boats like these—and their lighter, sleeker descendants—now make up the majority of today's cruising sailboats. A big part of the performance-cruiser formula is moderate displacement. Light enough to step lively, substantial enough to be comfortable, boats from the middle ground make good cruisers.

Design displacements tell you what boats weigh (minus food, fuel, and crew). If boats are of different sizes, use the displacement/length (D/L) ratio to see which is chunkier. The D/L ratio is displacement in long tons [i.e., pounds divided by 2,240] $\div$ (.01 $\times$ waterline length [in feet])^3. The D/L ratio is dimensionless, but what it gives you is essentially the boat's displacement per unit of length. The lower the number, the lighter (in relative terms) the boat. When she was launched over 25 years ago, the Valiant 40's displacement of over 20,000 pounds was light for a cruiser. A typical 40-foot ocean racer of that period weighed between 15,000 and 18,000 pounds. The Valiant 40's D/L ratio is 264, whereas the more recently designed and slightly larger Oceanis 411 (a full-cruising auxiliary built by Beneteau) has a D/L ratio of just 147. Displacing just 15,000 pounds, she illustrates the fact that performance cruisers have gotten noticeably lighter. These newer boats represent genuine and worthwhile advances over older cruisers.

Many sailors suggest that you should buy a boat by the pound, not the foot, and in some ways that's true. Displacement promotes sail-carrying power, volume, load-carrying capacity, and a kinder, gentler motion. On the other hand, weight slows you down and loads up you and your sail-handling gear. Excess weight is the enemy.

Today most cruising boats represent an uneasy compromise between these two truths. Light and heavy both have their merits for cruising, and not all of the virtues of either side can be captured by cutting things down the middle like Solomon's baby. Today's boats, however, are definitely more weight-efficient than yesterday's. Developments in hull forms, the strength-to-weight gains permitted by modern construction materials and methods, miniaturized systems, and lighter engines have all taken out some of the weight. In the tug of war between "built

A Valiant 40 under sail.

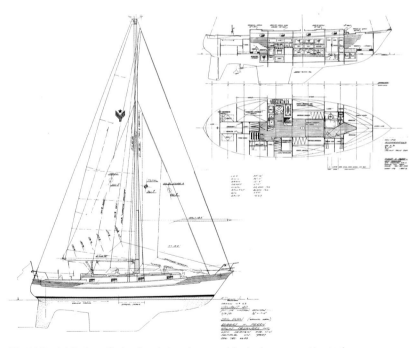

The Valiant 40's long fin keel and skeg-hung rudder look conservative today but were considered a radical alternative to the traditional full keel when the boat was introduced in 1975. Her accommodations plan shows how many more cruising amenities will fit into a 40-footer than a smaller boat. Though no longer in production, the boat can be purchased used for as little as $75,000 for the 1975 model or as much as $200,000 for the 1991 model.

The Beneteau 423 features a fin keel, spade rudder, wide stern sections for sail-carrying power and cockpit room, and a cutaway transom step for a swim platform and for boarding from a dinghy. With lots of room, lots of comfort, and good performance, these boats are a staple of charter fleets.

for speed" and "built for comfort," you can look for (and get) the best of both.

Keel

Most modern cruisers have some form of fin keel. Fins—when paired with a skeg-hung or balanced-spade rudder—provide better lift and create less resistance than full-length keels. A fin keel is faster upwind and down, yet some sailors still champion the long keel. The argument is clearly set out in Nigel Calder's essay on page 403.

Rig

Cruisers have traditionally favored a simple sloop rig for smaller boats and a divided rig (ketch, yawl, or schooner) for larger boats. The former provides optimal efficiency, while the latter breaks the sail area into units small enough to be handled easily by a shorthanded crew.

Modern developments such as roller furling (for mainsails as well as jibs), oversized and powered winches, simpler spars with less running rigging, autopilots, full-length battens, mainsail tamers (such as lazyjacks, StackPacks, and even solid hydraulic boom vangs that support a boom in place of a topping lift) have conspired to help cruisers handle bigger sails with

less sweat. Despite niceties that come with divided rigs (such as leaving the mizzen hoisted and sheeted flat at anchor to keep a yawl's bow pointing into the wind; or reducing sail on a ketch to a jib and mizzen combination; or the awesome off-wind wonders of a schooner's fisherman staysail or even its gollywobbler), the overwhelming majority of cruising boats today are sloops.

Not all sloops have the ability to set a small storm jib or a storm trysail, but many cruising boats that are heading offshore do. These sails are for "ultimate conditions," and they are rarely needed and seldom set. Still, they are the ticket for handling heavy weather. The trysail is heavy duty and boomless, and it goes in place of the mainsail (on its own track or into the main luff groove in the mast). It allows you to lash down your boom instead of dipping it in the waves and replaces the main with a durable, shapable, smaller sail suitable for Forces 6 and above. Many offshore cruisers forgo the trysail in favor of a triple-reefed mainsail. Either way, the storm jib should set close in front of the mast. Setting it out at the stem (where

A pretty yawl participating in the Eggemoggin Reach Regatta for wooden boats, sponsored by WoodenBoat magazine in Penobscot Bay, Maine. Sailing a bit higher than a beam reach in a light breeze, she is barely able to carry her spinnaker. Note how tightly the mizzen must be sheeted, even though the boat is not close-hauled. A small sail laboring in the mainsail's backwind, a yawl's mizzen provides very little push when the boat is sailing to windward and is often lowered in order to reduce weather helm. The mizzenmast has other uses, however, and here it proves a great place to mount a radar antenna. This traditional yawl has been retrofitted with a roller-furling genoa to boost her performance and ease of handling.

In this shot from a preliminary feeder race for the Eggemoggin Reach Regatta, a sloop on a reaching leg maintains a precarious lead over a schooner. The schooner's foresail and mainsail are both *gaff-rigged* (four-cornered sails with a yard called a *gaff* extending the top edge), though the mainsail is hidden behind the foresail in this view. A gaff rig does not sail well to windward (i.e., it is not *close-winded*), which is why it's rarely seen these days, but a gaff-rigged mainsail or foresail spreads a lot of surface area to the wind on a broad reach or run. This schooner may well overtake and pass the sloop on this point of sail.

With her jib and foresail furled, this lovely schooner is instead flying a big reaching jib and a huge gollywobbler with her Marconi-rigged mainsail, a combination that gives her maximum sail area.

The sail plan of the Lelanta, designed by John Alden in 1937, shows the amazing range of sails a schooner can set. Her working sail comprises the mainsail, foresail, and forestaysail (often called simply a staysail on a schooner), and she can carry that combination even in a fresh breeze. In a gale she can single- or double-reef her mainsail and keep going when other boats can't, and if the gale becomes powerful she can heave-to comfortably under foresail alone. In a light breeze she can increase her sail area by hoisting her main topsail, fore topsail, jib, and jib topsail in any combination, and if that's not enough while sailing a light-air reach or run, she can complete her *plain sail* complement by breaking out her main topmast staysail (blue outline), which is often called the fisherman staysail. And if she wants still more sail in a light breeze, she can set her huge *gollywobbler* (brown outline), which sheets to the main boom, and either a reaching jib (green outline) or spinnaker (yellow outline).

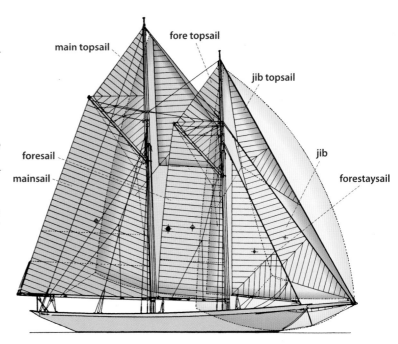

main topsail

fore topsail

jib topsail

foresail

mainsail

jib

forestaysail

Watching the New York Yacht Club fleet on its summer cruise is like watching people in a crowded airport terminal—endlessly fascinating. **Top left and right:** *Here the lovely yawl* Rugosa, *owned by yacht designer Halsey Herreshoff, shows another use of the mizzenmast: for flying a mizzen staysail on a reach. Note that the mizzen halyard has been cast off, possibly to relieve weather helm or to prevent the mizzen from interfering with the mizzen staysail, which sheets to the end of the mizzen boom.* **Above left:** *More racer than cruiser, this powerful sloop almost certainly has a deep, high-aspect fin keel with a keeltip ballast bulb to balance that tall rig.* **Above right:** *This J/133 with its high-tech Kevlar sails, purposeful lines, hydraulic vang, and hydraulic backstay is representative of the modern breed of high-performance cruiser. This is a comfortable boat, fast and close-winded yet easy to handle.*

a light-weather headsail tacks) would give it a long lever arm and thus create an unbalanced rig. You need an inner forestay.

Fixed roughly halfway between the mast and the headstay, it lets you hoist the storm jib where the waves won't savage it. A

storm jib can provide the drive you need to control your boat in trying conditions. It's a simple matter to make the forestay demountable so you can swing it out of the way and have a clear foredeck for normal sailing.

The "BOC alternative," developed by round-the-world racers but applicable to fast cruising, is two headsails set on roller furlers at the stem (see photo on page 426). One is cut full for off-wind sailing. The other has a flat cut (and is roller-reefable) for upwind work. Adding a demountable forestay would give you the ability to set a hanked-on stormsail to complement the everyday workings of both big jibs.

Full-length battens make added sail area possible and extend the life of a mainsail. Running backstays are a nightmare that no cruiser need endure.

Hull Form

Eric Hiscock begins his classic reference *Cruising Under Sail* by saying, "There is no real need for the newcomer to cruising to understand much about yacht designing . . . but he should acquire some knowledge of hull form, [especially] in relation to performance at sea." Though

I've already glossed size, weight, and underwater shape, other aspects of hull form are important, too.

Beam is critical in several ways. For one, it adds resistance. Water must travel farther to slide around a beamy boat than around a narrow one. That detracts from upwind performance in light air. On the other hand, beam adds initial stability and thus sail-carrying power, which can add to reaching speed in stronger air. All cruisers enjoy booming along on a reach, whereas we might avoid sailing upwind in the light stuff by turning on the engine or cracking off in another direction. This is a good example of the fact that performance plusses and minuses are largely determined by the sort of performance in which we're most interested.

Beam adds deck space and augments the waterplane. It also adds displacement and volume much more quickly than length. You can make a boat significantly bigger by making her just a little wider.

Increasing freeboard is apt to make a boat drier, and even though it raises her center of gravity somewhat, it will in-

An offshore racing yacht powering to windward under storm jib and trysail. The same arrangement works for offshore cruising boats in heavy weather.

crease her stability by making it harder to put the rail under. A higher freeboard adds interior volume, too. High sides can make a boat heavy, ugly, or even hard to climb aboard, but generous freeboard is usually a good thing.

Rocker is the variation in depth over the length of the hull body exclusive of appendages. Most hull bodies are deeper in the midsection than at the ends.

The dynamic lift necessary to plane or to surf on following seas comes from flat sections aft, but cruising boats are pushed in the opposite direction by their need to incorporate accommodations and stores. Boats with lots of rocker tend not to be rockets off the wind, but a barrel-chested shape is a good one for going upwind in waves.

Overhangs can make a boat prettier. They also afford deck

Rig Types
by Robert H. Perry

Sloop

This is a boat with one mast carrying a headsail (or headsails) and a mainsail. A sloop can have a jib and a staysail, but this does not make it a cutter. It's just a sloop with two headsails. A masthead sloop has the headstay going to the masthead. A fractional sloop has the headstay landing on the mast below the masthead. This is usually expressed as a fraction of the mast height, as in a *seven-eighths rig* or a *three-quarters rig*. Masthead or fractional, one headsail or three, a sloop is still a sloop based on the location of the mast, which is generally around station 3.2 to station 4 in a ten-station waterline scheme.

Cutter

A cutter has one mast, like a sloop, but the mast is farther aft, which is to say at or aft of station 4. This fine distinction is further blurred if the boat has a bowsprit, even to the point of becoming a matter of judgment in the eye of the beholder. I would consider a boat with its mast at station 3.75 and a five-foot bowsprit to be a cutter. In short, the real difference between a sloop and a

true cutter is in the relative sizes of their foretriangles—larger in the latter than in the former. A Valiant 42 is a good example of a true cutter. Again, although a double-headsail sloop is commonly called a cutter, I think this is misleading. I prefer to call it "a sloop rigged as a cutter" or just "a sloop with staysail option."

Ketch and Yawl

A ketch has two masts, the after of which is shorter and is called the mizzen. Ketches are often confused with yawls, and the old distinctions between the two no longer universally apply. We used to say that a yawl carries its mizzenmast aft of the helm or rudderpost, but boat shapes and helm locations have changed too much for these old rules to work reliably. The real difference between a ketch and a yawl is in the relative size of the mizzen sail, which is larger on a ketch. Any center-cockpit boat with a short mast located aft would be a yawl by the old rule, but if the mizzen is large, it's a ketch.

Yawls experienced their heyday during the 1950s and early '60s, when the Cruising Club of America (CCA) rating rule was in use. The CCA rule did not penalize any sail area for sails "set flying" from the mizzenmast off the wind. Thus, to remain competitive in off-the-

wind races, you had to be able to carry a complement of mizzen staysails and mizzen spinnakers. In those days where this sail area was free, unmeasured sail area, the yawl ruled.

Schooner

Schooners are lovely rigs, possibly the most picturesque of them all. A schooner can have as many as seven masts, with the shortest being the foremost, but most schooners have only two. Unfortunately, with its biggest sail well aft, a schooner can be a tricky boat to trim for helm balance. You can fly a fisherman's staysail between the masts, but this sail is not a very efficient shape (although it does add a lot of sail area up high, where the wind is more stable). If you replace the foresail of a schooner with a jiblike staysail, you have a staysail schooner.

The problem with a schooner—or any boat with multiple sails—is that the apparent wind is different for each sail. For instance, even if the jib or genoa is trimmed optimally, you may need to over-trim the aftmost sail to get good sail shape. This can aggravate helm balance and add heeling pressure. This is especially critical on a schooner, where the largest sail is all the way aft.

1. *This masthead-rigged sloop has a fairly short rig and a bowsprit to add foretriangle area. You could add a staysail on an inner forestay, but that would not make this sloop into a cutter because the mast is between stations 3 and 4.* **2.** *This fractional sloop has a higher-aspect rig but still has the mast between stations 3 and 4.* **3.** *With its mast aft of station 4, this is a true cutter. A yawl* **(4)** *has a smaller mizzen than a ketch* **(5)***. Of the two, the ketch is the more practical rig, conferring an advantage of divided sail area with no sail being overwhelmingly large.*

Catboat

Cat rigs have become popular today primarily through the Nonesuch and Freedom series of production boats. There is also a rich yachting history of the famous Cape Cod catboats. The cat rig certainly has its place, especially on smaller cruising boats in which simplicity is a primary goal, but cat rigs lack versatility. Tom Wylie's cats are special boats and deserve attention, but most of his cats offer spinnakers for off-the-wind performance. In my book that makes them something other than textbook catboats.

The cat rig has also been adapted to ketches. With two masts, the forward of which (the mainmast) is taller, with no headsails, you have a cat ketch. This type was popularized by the early Freedom models and remained mainstream for a while. I'm not sure why it died out. I sailed two different Freedom cat ketches. One sailed wonderfully and the other quite poorly. I attribute this difference in performance to overall design and not the cat ketch rig.

Catboats don't allow their skippers an easy way to "shift gears" and keep the rig effective through a wide range of wind speeds and directions. A study of PHRF ratings of various catboats can easily prove this out. For all their subjective faults, PHRF ratings remain the best way to compare boatspeeds and put a quick end to dockside arguments. Nevertheless, a nice, gaff-headed catboat like a Beetle Cat (see photo page 6) is one of my favorite boats to sail. Traditional Cape Cod catboats like the Beetle Cat are notorious for weather helm, but that's just part of the fun of sailing them. It is not unusual to see a short bowsprit mounted on a Cape Cod catboat with a tiny jib flown from the bowsprit. This can do wonders to help balance the catboat's big mainsail. A true Cape Cod catboat is one of my very favorite traditional models.

Each rig has its advantages, and I don't think we can point to any one of them as the "ultimate cruising rig." The benefits of each will depend largely upon the sailor's sailing style and experience, and where he or she sails. A laid-back approach to sailing might favor a catboat or schooner, while a performance-oriented approach might favor a sloop.

The sloop rig is generally considered the most weatherly (closest pointing) of the rigs. The ketch suffers upwind because the mizzen operates in the backwind of the mainsail and jib, and many ketch sailors lower the mizzen when on the wind. Note that some modern Whitbread-type racing ketches step the mizzen much farther aft than in the traditional ketch, which opens up the slot behind the main and allows the mizzen to get cleaner air.

Still, the chief advantage of a ketch is its ability to fly downwind and reaching staysails off the mizzenmast and to break the total sail area down into three smaller sails. Some ketch aficionados also like to sail under "jib and jigger" (i.e., jib and mizzen) in heavy air. This is a convenient and comfortable combination, especially on a beam reach, but not one that will allow a boat to sail optimally upwind. This is due to the lower apparent wind angle seen by the mizzen. Offshore in a big sea, however, you may find yourself falling off to ease the motion of the boat, and in this case, your optimal upwind apparent wind angle may be in excess of 40 degrees. At this angle of attack, the mizzen is less affected by the jib's backwind, and the jib-and-jigger combo will work admirably.

A cutter likewise suffers from backwind problems upwind when both jib and staysail are carried, but the cutter comes

into its own when reaching or when sailing in heavy air under reefed mainsail and staysail. In moderate to light air, if you are after an apparent wind angle of less than 34 degrees, you will find your cutter more close-winded without the staysail provided you have a reasonably low-clewed genoa.

A mainsail and a high-clewed Yankee headsail, while popular and traditional, do not make an efficient combination for beating. The two sails have to work in concert upwind, like one big foil. Think of the genoa as the leading edge of the foil and the mainsail as the trailing edge. That's partially what makes a sloop efficient. A cutter flying a high-clewed Yankee alone with its mainsail leaves a big hole where the staysail would normally be, with no sail to smooth and guide the flow of air into the mainsail.

Upwind efficiency is not simply about boatspeed. It's about velocity made good (VMG) toward an imaginary target dead to weather. If you hoist a mainsail, jib, and staysail, then chase a maximum boatspeed upwind, you will end up falling off to a close reach and watching your boatspeed climb while your VMG falls. Having raced Valiants on numerous occasions under all possible sail combinations and conditions, I can assure you that a good genoa-style headsail—i.e., one with a relatively low clew—and mainsail make the best combination for upwind work.

The only sort of cutter that might perform better upwind with both headsails is an older design with a full hull entry and a wide sheeting angle (the angle between the boat's centerline and a line drawn from the jib tack to the sheeting position). This hypothetical boat probably has a less-than-optimal keel—perhaps like a Westsail 32 with a full keel—so its weatherliness is reduced by hull form even before any rig considerations. If the

sheeting angle is in excess of 10 degrees, you might possibly be able to fly both jib and staysail effectively upwind, but you will not point high. The sheeting angle is affected both by the chainplate location and the location of the jib track, and this may be the determining factor in how far in you can sheet your jib. If the angle from the jib tack to the chainplate is in excess of 15 degrees, you might find it advantageous to fly both jib and staysail. Boats have personalities, and you must get to know what makes your boat come alive.

On the other hand—and here's a tough one—if you are having trouble determining the correct upwind trim for your main and jib, throwing a staysail into the mix is probably going to ensure failure. A good rule of thumb for most modern boats is to reserve the staysail for heavy air when the jib is down or for apparent wind angles in excess of 40 degrees.

The schooner is the least weatherly rig of all, and "schooner" and "upwind performance" seldom appear in the same sentence. The problem with a schooner, as discussed earlier, is that the biggest sail, the mainsail, operates in the backwind of the jib and foresail, and this decreases the apparent wind angle on the mainsail and forces the skipper to sheet it in hard, further exacerbating any weather helm. Schooner sailors like the aesthetics of the rig, and for good reason. They will rave about a schooner's off-wind performance, which is true, and they will extol its many possible sail combinations in response to changing wind conditions, which might be true. But the real reason they sail a schooner is because they like the way it looks.

[Reprinted with permission from *Yacht Design According to Perry: My Boats and What Shaped Them*, by Robert H. Perry (International Marine/ McGraw-Hill, 2008)]

space and add sailing length when the boat heels, and a bow overhang can contribute to dryness and facilitate anchor handling. In a long boat with a short waterline, however, a little shifting of weight can cause big alterations in flotation and trim. Then too, have you ever tried to sleep with waves slapping an overhanging counter? The traditionally balanced look of a boat with long ends is lovely, but hulls with ends that are more nearly plumb (and thus make better use of space and are better hydrodynamically) make better cruising boats.

Stability is the complex outcome of weight, form, and sail plan, but there's not much doubt that it makes cruising better. Initial stability is a boat's resistance to heeling when a puff hits. A hard turn to her bilge or a chine (corner) where hull side meets bottom strengthens that resistance. So does the inertia of her overall weight. I think of initial resistance as "stiffness." A stiff boat is a pleasure to sail, because working her is less akin to clinging to a cliff face than to reclining on a knoll.

Once a boat is heeled through the first 20 to 25 degrees, however, the effects of hull shape

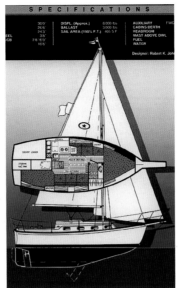

SPECIFICATIONS

30'0"	DISPL. (Approx.)	8,000 lbs	AUXILIARY FWD
26'6"	BALLAST	3,000 lbs	CABINS-BERTH
24'3"	SAIL AREA (100% F.T.)	465.5 F	HEADROOM
KEEL	3'8"		MAST ABOVE DWL
CB	2'6"/6'0"		FUEL
	10'6"		WATER

Designer: Robert K. Joh

From small (27-foot, top left, but no longer in production), to midsize (37-foot), to large (48-foot, bottom), Island Packet Yachts builds full-keeled cruisers.

and beam fade, and the amount and depth of ballast become the primary determinants of how much the boat resists further heeling and how quickly it "bounces back" from being heeled over. A boat with good initial stability *and* good recovery is a good cruising boat. These qualities can help performance in some ways, but you have to recognize that they come at a cost in all-around ability. Stability adds resistance and weight, and both are slow. When the going gets tough, however, I want a boat that gets tougher. For cruising I favor a forgiving, self-rescuing boat over one that I have to wrestle back from the brink. Good stability is more than a plus. In my mind it's an essential.

It should be clear by now why cruising sailboat design is an unending source of lively debate and disagreement. It's because there are no absolutes, and opposing viewpoints can be defended with equal plausibility. Before we go on, therefore, let's hear from two expert sailors their views on hull shape and performance and on how to compare cruising sailboats; and how to choose a boat for offshore voyaging.

A Boat for Cruising

SOUTHERN CROSS 31

Tom Gilmer, a professor of naval architecture at the U.S. Naval Academy in Annapolis, drew the Allied Seawind 30, the first fiberglass boat to circumnavigate. Later, he updated the design as the Seawind II. He didn't design many production sailboats, and the next was this Southern Cross 31, with a hull very similar to the original Seawind (except that the Southern Cross is a double-ender). Clark Ryder, of Bristol, Rhode Island, built about 130 of them between 1976 and 1987. A number were sold as bare hulls for owner completion. The hull is cored with Airex foam in the topsides only. The deck and coachroof are cored with balsa. The hull-to-deck joint is an outward-turning flange that is more vulnerable to damage than inward-turning flanges. Ballast is internal. Bulkheads are tabbed to the hull. Overall construction quality is above average and suitable for offshore sailing. The Southern Cross 31 is fairly heavy, which affects light-air performance, but she has made good passages and will be comfortable at sea, which is more important. The cockpit is small, which is a desirable characteristic offshore. A 1981 boat had a base price of $62,500. If you're considering buying one, be sure you know whether it was factory- or owner-completed.

Second Wind, a Southern Cross 31, crossing the Gulf of Maine.

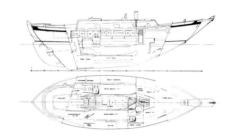

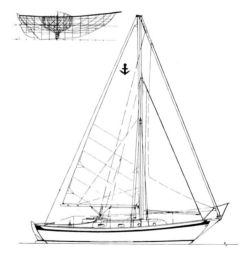

LOA	31'0"
LWL	25'0"
BEAM	9'6"
DRAFT	4'7"
DISPLACEMENT	13,600 LB.
BALLAST	4,400 LB.
SAIL AREA	447 SQ.FT.
DESIGNER	THOMAS S.GILMER
PRICE NEW	NOT IN PRODUCTION
PRICE USED	$40,400 – $44,900 (1982 MODEL) $51,700 – $56,800 (1986 MODEL)
SIMILAR BOATS	ALLIED SEAWIND II MARINER 31 DOWNEASTER 32 WESTSAIL 32

[Reprinted with permission from *Your First Sailboat: How to Find and Sail the Right Boat for You*, by Daniel Spurr (International Marine/McGraw-Hill, 2004)]

Hull Shape and Boat Performance

by Nigel Calder

Nigel Calder is the author of Nigel Calder's Cruising Handbook *and* Boatowner's Mechanical and Electrical Manual, *two of the most popular and most useful books for cruising sailors around the world. Here's what he has to say about cruising sailboat hull shape and performance.*

A generation ago, many boats, especially cruising boats, had long keels and attached rudders. The propeller was in an aperture in the rudder. The boat's cross section had a wineglass shape. There were long overhangs fore and aft. Such traditional full-keel designs were popular for many years.

During the 1970s, '80s, and '90s, the keel's forefoot was progressively cut away. A separate skeg supported the rudder, and the space between the keel and the skeg grew larger as they each grew smaller. The skeg was first reduced to a partial skeg and then was eliminated altogether to leave a freestanding (spade) rudder. During the process the boat's overhangs were trimmed and became quite short, if not eliminated altogether. The re-

sult of these changes is a "contemporary boat."

In its most extreme form, the contemporary boat has a deep, narrow, vertical fin keel and a spade rudder, both of which are suspended beneath a hull with an almost flat bottom and with a plumb (vertical) stem. The propeller is supported by a strut or incorporated in a saildrive leg. The contemporary boat is much lighter than its forebears and looks nothing like them, especially below the waterline.

For a given displacement, the evolution from a long keel and attached rudder to a fin keel and spade rudder has dramatically reduced the wetted surface area. Given that the wetted surface area creates the primary resistance that must be overcome in light winds (the predominant condition experienced by most sailors), any reduction results in an improvement in performance. The resulting reduction in lateral surface area, which creates resistance to turning, also improves responsiveness and maneuverability.

If you add a fine entry for upwind work and a flat bottom aft for off-the-wind speed, much of the time a contemporary boat will outperform a more tradi-

This racer shows all the attributes of a performance boat—narrow waterline beam, high flared topsides, minimal wetted surface, and a deep fin keel carrying most of its ballast in a bulb.

The opposite extreme. The Folkboat exemplifies traditional thinking in cruising boat design—pretty overhangs, low topsides, a full keel, and protected rudder.

tional boat on all points of sail. And yet slower underbodies are still popular with many sailors, especially those who go offshore. Is this simply nostalgia?

Theory versus Practice

A contemporary boat has a less comfortable motion than a traditional boat in many sea states. If its limited load-carrying ca-

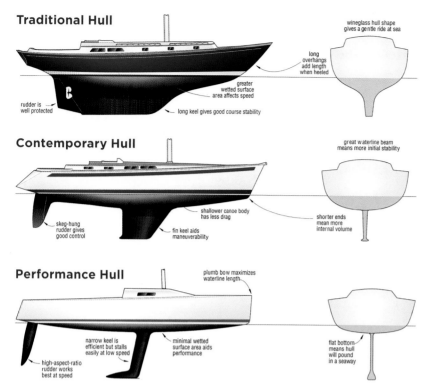

Traditional Hull

wineglass hull shape
gives a gentle ride at sea

long
overhangs
add length
when heeled

greater
wetted surface
area affects speed

rudder is
well protected

long keel gives good course stability

Contemporary Hull

great waterline beam
means more initial stability

shallower canoe body
has less drag

shorter ends
mean more
internal volume

skeg-hung
rudder gives
good control

fin keel aids
maneuverability

Performance Hull

plumb bow maximizes
waterline length

narrow keel is
efficient but stalls
easily at low speed

minimal wetted
surface area aids
performance

flat bottom
means hull
will pound
in a seaway

high-aspect-ratio
rudder works
best at speed

pability is exceeded, its performance suffers disproportionately. It generally has poorer directional stability than a traditional boat. This makes steering tiring, increases an autopilot's energy consumption, and may make using a wind vane difficult or impossible. The contemporary boat will likely not heave-to quietly in nasty weather and will need to be helmed continuously. With a shorthanded crew this can be a safety hazard. In survival conditions, the contemporary boat is inherently more likely to capsize than the traditional boat.

In declining order of suitability, the contemporary boat is best for racing, for sailing in relatively protected waters, for coastal cruising, and for offshore cruising. In some respects, the farther offshore a boat is intended to sail and the more shorthanded the crew, the stronger the argument for sacrificing performance in favor of comfort, directional stability, ease of handling, and security.

The longer the passage, the more unpleasant the conditions encountered, and the smaller the crew, the more likely it is that a sacrifice of nominal performance will not, in fact, result in any loss of actual performance: There are plenty of examples of traditional boats

making better passage times in heavy conditions than nominally faster, lighter boats when lightweight boats become too uncomfortable or too much work to sail to their full potential. The crew of the more traditional boat is also likely to arrive less bruised and better rested.

Gunkholing

Aside from comfort and security, several considerations related to draft and running aground may lead to a willingness to sacrifice performance. Performance to windward can always be enhanced by lowering the ballast and increasing the draft. However, my family enjoys exploring regions with relatively restricted depths. Some of our favorites include the northern waters of Belize and the Rio Dulce in Guatemala (both limited to 6-foot draft), parts of the Bahamas, and our home waters in Maine. Thus I prefer boats with a draft of 6 feet or less, regardless of the impact on performance.

Groundings

What about the keel shape? The most efficient shape for upwind work is a narrow, vertical, foil-shaped fin similar to an airplane wing. In terms of the way I use a

This cruising boat's full underbody indicates a moderate to heavy displacement, which gives it the ability to carry stores for extended voyaging. The hull shape will give a comfortable ride at sea.

Above left: *This rudder is protected by a full-depth skeg. Its lack of balance (area ahead of the rudder-stock) may mean the boat is heavy on the helm.* **Above right:** *Semi-balanced spade rudders like this one provide excellent control at speed but are vulnerable to damage.* **Left:** *A typical long-keeler's rudder— no balance, but well sheltered behind the keel. The prop is also protected from stray lines or nets.*

boat, this is a terrible design. The corollary to my desire to explore relatively thin waters is that I run aground a great deal. If you hit something hard with a vertical fin, you stop dead. People get thrown across the boat and may be hurt. Tremendous shock loads are transmitted to the keel root (the point at which it attaches to the hull) and its supporting structures within the boat. Damage is likely. Even if you don't run aground, if a fishing net or lobster-pot warp gets wrapped around a vertical fin, especially one with a torpedo-

type bulb at its base, disentangling it can be a devil of a job.

So I require that the leading edge of a keel must curve back from the underside of the hull in a way that will reduce the shock of a grounding and shed nets and lines. This results in a longer keel (good for directional stability) with a substantially larger root (which spreads shock loads over a larger area of the hull). If the keel stub is designed with a step or an angled face, shock loads will be transmitted to the hull rather than just the keelbolts.

At different times in boats with fuller keels we have run over floating telephone poles and hit rocks at up to 8 knots with nothing more than cosmetic damage. In a contemporary boat the same incidents would almost certainly cause damage requiring an immediate haulout.

I also like to have a longer keel designed so that, if necessary, we can lay the boat up against a dock at high tide and let it dry out without the risk of it toppling over on its ends.

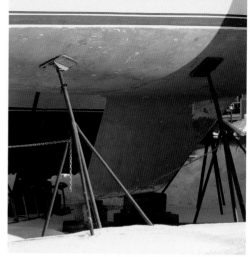

Above left: *Long-keeled boats are much less likely to be damaged in a grounding than fin-keeled boats.* **Left:** *Long, shallow-draft fins like this offer the advantages of a long keel without some of the disadvantages.* **Above:** *This keel design is fairly typical and offers good all-around performance.*

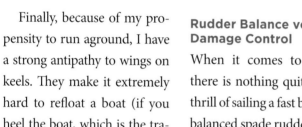

If a deep, narrow-rooted fin keel like this one hits bottom with any force, the stresses will be transmitted to the hull floor; major damage can result.

Finally, because of my propensity to run aground, I have a strong antipathy to wings on keels. They make it extremely hard to refloat a boat (if you heel the boat, which is the traditional way of reducing draft, the wings dig in).

Every one of my requirements for the keel has some negative impact on performance. Clearly, they are somewhat idiosyncratic, but my point is that there can be all kinds of good reasons for compromising performance. Each individual boatowner must determine his own priorities.

Rudder Balance versus Damage Control

When it comes to rudders, there is nothing quite like the thrill of sailing a fast boat with a balanced spade rudder that has fingertip response and control. I love it on other people's boats but have always done without it on my own.

Again, because I like to nose around in shallow water, my overriding concern is the difficulty of building a spade rudder strong enough to withstand a serious impact. This is because of the shock loading that occurs at the point where the rudder-

stock enters the hull. Any kind of a skeg, partial or full, introduces at least one and sometimes two more shock- and load-absorbing points of support.

With a full skeg, you get the most potential support for and protection of the rudder. Unfortunately, a full skeg requires all of the rudder to be located aft of its turning axis, resulting in an unbalanced rudder. Such a rudder is heavy on the helm when a boat is loaded up, or if it is prone to weather helm.

A partial skeg is a compromise that provides a second bearing for the rudder midway down its forward face and also allows the lower part of the rudder to project forward of its turning axis. This results in a semi-balanced rudder that is much lighter on the helm. Unfortunately, the lower bearing can attract fishing nets and pot warps (as can the gap between the forward edge of a spade rudder and the hull), which are then extremely difficult to disentangle. Ideally, this bearing will be protected by some kind of a line deflector. With a partial-skeg arrangement my preference is to make the lower part of the rudder sacrificial. In the event of serious impact, it will break away, leaving the remainder of the rudder functional.

The deeper the rudder, the more effective it tends to be. Once in a while you will see a boat whose rudder has a deeper draft than the keel. From my perspective, this is absurd. In a grounding, the rudder, the most vulnerable part of the underbody, will hit the bottom first.

Keeping Bilge Water in the Bilges

I am willing to make further compromises in terms of hull shape. One of the most significant of these is driven by the need to remove bilge water from the boat, a subject rarely considered by boatbuyers.

Sooner or later every boat gets water down below. Many a traditional boat with wineglass sections will retain water in its bilges even when heeled 30 degrees or more. In contrast, some contemporary boats won't do this at any heel angle (especially if, as is sometimes the case, there is no keel sump). On all contemporary flat-bottomed boats, whenever the boat heels more than a few degrees, even a small amount of bilge water has a tendency to run all over the boat, soaking goods in lockers and, in some cases, submerging equipment and wiring harnesses. Aside from the inconvenience and the damage that may be done, submerging of the wiring harness can lead to rampant stray-current corrosion.

Somewhere between a traditional hull and a contemporary hull is a happy medium. This will vary depending on the perspective of the owner. Given that most modern boats sail at their best heeled no more than 20 degrees and that once this angle is reached, the boat should be reefed down, on my boats I look for cross sections and a bilge sump that will retain bilge water at heel angles up to 20 degrees. The necessary curves result in a softer motion in unpleasant conditions, which agrees well with my other priorities for long-distance short-handed offshore cruising.

If a boat has a structural grid (as many do nowadays), it is important for the grid to have limber holes that allow bilge water to drain at all angles of heel. This is frequently not the case.

Compromise, Compromise

Just as there are excellent reasons for the popularity of fin keels, spade rudders, and flat-bottomed boats among racer/cruiser and coastal-cruising aficionados, so there are excellent reasons for the retention of longer keels, skegs, and more rounded sections on offshore boats. In terms of the design continuum, there are no right and wrong answers about where to draw the line. The decision is a complex one that can only be made on the basis of carefully articulated individual needs.

If these needs change, a different underbody is called for. Recently Lyman Morse, the builder of the relatively traditional Seguin 44, had a client whose focus had shifted more toward performance. They cut the full skeg off his boat and replaced the unbalanced skeg-mounted rudder with a balanced spade rudder. They also cut the lead keel off and remolded it with a more modern foil shape and a small endplate. The result is a dramatically lighter and more responsive helm and an improvement in performance, especially upwind—but at the price of a somewhat less protected rudder. With its relatively narrow beam and rounded sections, the boat remains an extremely comfortable sea boat that is now optimized more for performance.

At a boat show recently I met with a designer who is famous for his fast, relatively lightweight contemporary cruising boats. At one point in our conversation, he remarked, "You know, Nigel, if you want comfort offshore, you need weight." He has recently poured his heart and soul into a cruising design that looks nothing like most modern boats (or many of his other designs), demonstrating how there can be good reasons for breaking with the contemporary mold. These reasons have nothing to do with nostalgia. They are all about getting the boat best suited to individual sailing plans and dreams.

[Reprinted with permission from *BoatWorks: Sailboat Maintenance, Repair, and Improvement Advice You Can't Get Anywhere Else,* by the Editors of *SAIL* Magazine (International Marine/McGraw-Hill, 2008)]

Comparing Sailboats
by Robert H. Perry

More cruising sailboats have been built to Bob Perry designs than to those of any other designer. Perry coined the term "performance cruising" and initiated the trend toward fast voyaging sailboats with his world-famous Valiant 40, which has been in production longer than any other cruising boat in the United States.

The terms and ratios that help to characterize a design constitute a language of their own—the most efficient and descriptive one there is for conveying the particulars of a boat. The language is nearly universal throughout the yacht design world, but different designers use terms differently. I believe my method reflects mainstream usage. If you become a collector of design data, the important thing is to use the same definitions consistently so that you compare "apples to apples" over the years.

The ratios listed here provide a quick and fairly easy way to compare dissimilar boats over a range of sizes. The validity of the comparisons may not hold when one of the boats being compared is shorter than 25 feet or longer than 75 feet, but within that range, valid comparisons can be made. The ratios are nondimensional, which simply means that they have no units. The technical term for such comparisons is parametric analysis, but that makes it sound more complicated than it is.

Length-to-Beam Ratio (L/B)

This ratio is useful for determining whether a boat is beamy or narrow. You simply divide the boat's length overall (LOA; see below) by its maximum width. A narrow boat will have a L/B of

4.00 or more. A moderate-beam boat will have a L/B of around 3.30 to 3.65. A beamy boat will have a L/B of 3.00 or less. A 40-foot boat with a 10-foot beam is narrow, but couple that 10-foot beam to a 30-foot LOA and you've got yourself a fairly beamy boat.

Displacement-to-Length Ratio (D/L)

The D/L can ascertain how heavy a boat is relative to its waterline length. Divide the displacement of the boat in long tons (one long ton being 2,240 pounds) by the cube of 1 percent of the waterline length (in feet). Suppose, for example, that a boat has a waterline length of 32 feet and weighs 15,680 pounds, which is (conveniently!) 7 long tons. Then $32 \times 0.01 = 0.32$, and $0.32^3 = 0.032768$, and $7 \div 0.032768 = 214$.

Heavy boats will have a D/L greater than 300 and sometimes higher than 400. Most full-keel boats, by virtue of the volume in their keels, have D/Ls over 325. A moderate-displacement boat will have a D/L of around 220 to 280. I consider a D/L of 260 the "middle" of the overall displacement range. Light boats will have D/Ls from 200 down to 100. Boats with D/Ls less

than 100 should be considered ultralight-displacement boats, or ULDBs.

Sail Area–to-Displacement Ratio (SA/D)

The sail area–to-displacement ratio is a sailboat's version of horsepower to weight. The ratio is calculated as sail area in square feet or square meters divided by the displacement in cubic feet (pounds divided by 64) or cubic meters to the two-thirds power. The boat from the previous example has a displacement in cubic feet of $15,680 \div 64 = 245$, and 245 raised to the two-thirds power is approximately 39.1. If the boat has 704 square feet of sail area, its SA/D is 18.0.

It's important early in the design scheme to define just how powerful the rig will be. SA/D numbers range from a low of around 11.00 for motor-sailers to 40.00 for an extreme racing type. Clearly, one set of numbers needs to be used for racing designs and another for cruising designs.

To calculate the SA/D, you need the sail area of the boat as derived from its I, J, E, and P rig dimensions (see illustration on page 410). I do not include genoa overlap area or the addi-

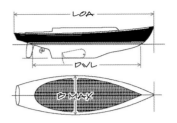

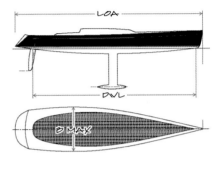

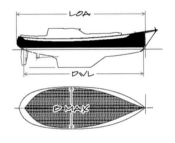

Profiles and plan views of three boats, showing length overall (LOA), which I consider equivalent to length on deck (LOD); designed waterline (DWL, also known as length waterline or LWL); and maximum beam (B max). **Top to bottom:** *A 48-foot keel-centerboard yawl showing the long overhangs encouraged in the 1960s by the Cruising Club of America (CCA) rating rule (L/B = 3.68; D/L = 275); a modern 66-foot cruising sled with reverse transom, high-aspect keel, and beam carried aft (L/B = 4.45; D/L = 68); and a 45-footer with canoe stern and low-aspect keel (L/B = 3.18; D/L = 230). Note: LOA includes a reverse transom but does not include a bowsprit, overhanging bow pulpit, or any other non-integral overhanging gear; and DWL in my lexicon does not include a surface-piercing rudder blade.*

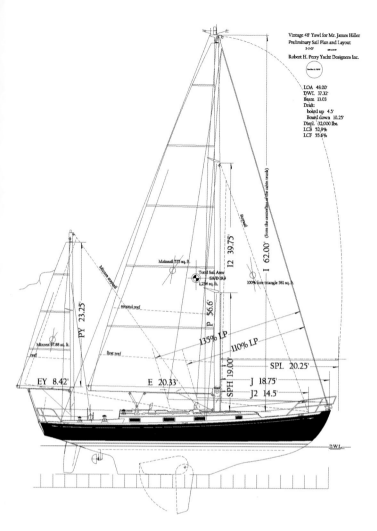

Vintage 48' Yawl for Mr. James Hiller
Preliminary Sail Plan and Layout
Robert H. Perry Yacht Designers Inc.

LOA 48.00'
DWL 37.32'
Beam 13.03
Draft:
board up 4.5'
board down 10.25'
Displ. 32,000 lbs.
LCB 52.9%
LCF 55.6%

Mainsail 725 sq. ft.

Total Sail Area
SA/D 19.9
1,254 sq. ft.

100% fore triangle 581 sq. ft.

Mizzen 97.88 sq. ft.

I 62.00' (from the centerline of the cabin trunk)

I2 39.75'

P 56.6'

PY 23.25'

135% LP

110% LP

SPH 19.00'

SPL 20.25'

EY 8.42'   E 20.33'   J 18.75'

J2 14.5'

D.W.L.

This sail plan for the classic yawl shown in the previous illustration gives the principal rig dimensions and lists design data from which to calculate comparative ratios. The principal rig dimensions are as follows:

J=*foretriangle base to headstay*

J2=*foretriangle base to inner forestay*

I=*foretriangle height (here taken from centerline of cabin trunk to masthead)*

I2=*inner foretriangle height*

P=*length of mainsail hoist*

PY=*length of mizzen hoist*

E=*length of mainsail foot*

EY=*length of mizzen foot*

SPH=*height of lower spreaders*

SPL=*length of spinnaker pole*

The boat's LOA is 48 feet and the maximum beam is 13.03 feet, so the L/B is a moderate 3.68. The displacement is 32,000 pounds or 14.28 long tons, and the waterline length is 37.32 feet, so the D/L is 275—which, again, is moderate. The total sail area (main + mizzen + 100 percent foretriangle) is 1,254 square feet; note that headsail overlap is not counted, and neither are such light-weather sails as a spinnaker or mizzen staysail. This makes the SA/D 19.9, which is a bit higher than you might expect for a traditionally inspired cruising sailboat, but the split rig makes a higher total area desirable as well as feasible. The mizzen doesn't generate a lot of drive, and when it's lowered the operative SA/D drops to 18.3.

tional area that a staysail might provide. Sometimes marketing hype will include anything and everything that can be called "sail area" in order to inflate this number, but I do not support this practice. I also do not include in the mainsail any area added by roach, which is modest in most modern cruising boats. You can make a strong case that the exaggerated roach of a multihull or high-performance monohull should be added to the (E ÷ 2) × P area,

although this is a judgment call. If I think that the roach area is a significant part of the mainsail area, I will add it, but I always note that in the review.

To get an accurate SA/D you also need an accurate displacement. This can be problematic, as displacements are frequently low-balled in order to make the SA/D and D/L ratios look more attractive. Whenever possible, the displacement you use should reflect the true weight of the boat in cruising trim.

A typical cruising boat today will have a SA/D of 17.5 to 18.5. This is enough power to drive the boat reasonably well in light air while not overpowering it too quickly when the breeze picks up. Of course, a boat with a powerful hull form and good stability characteristics can carry more sail, but hull shape aside, a SA/D of 18.00 will do nicely for most cruising sloops and cutters. A sailor looking for a benign and forgiving rig will want to stay closer to 17.5

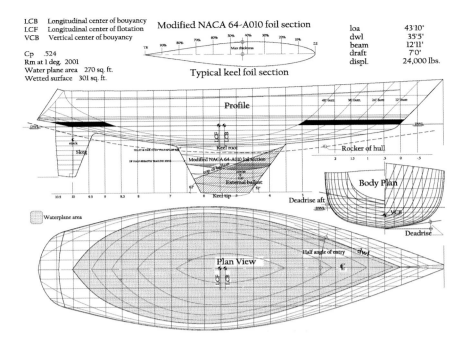

LCB Longitudinal center of bouyancy
LCF Longitudinal center of flotation
VCB Vertical center of bouyancy

Cp   .524
Rm at 1 deg. 2001
Water plane area   270 sq. ft.
Wetted surface   301 sq. ft.

Modified NACA 64-A010 foil section

Max thickness

Typical keel foil section

loa   43'10"
dwl   35'5"
beam   12'11"
draft   7'0"
displ.   24,000 lbs.

Profile

Keel root

Modified NACA 64-A010 foil Section

External ballast

Keel tip

Rocker of hull

Body Plan

Deadrise aft

Deadrise

VCB

Waterplane area

Plan View

Half angle of entry

Skeg

Interpreting a hull-lines drawing:

The lines plan is the heart and soul of a design. Anyone interested in hull shapes must be able to read a lines plan. The drawings include at least three views of the hull: the profile, the plan view, and the body plan. Each view is like a topographic map showing the contours of the hull in that view.

The buttock lines in the Nordic 44 hull lines are curved in the profile view, horizontal and parallel with the centerline in the plan view, and vertical and parallel with the centerline in the body plan or sectional view. The waterlines are curved in the plan view and horizontal in both the profile and sectional views. The sections are curved in the sectional view and vertical in both the profile and plan views. The sections aft and forward of the maximum beam are shown on the left and right sides, respectively, of the sectional view. The stations in the profile and plan views are numbered from 0 at the cutwater (the forward end of the waterplane, which is lightly shaded in the plan view) to 10 at the after end of the waterplane. Note the hull rocker in the profile view and the half-angle of entry in the plan view. In the sectional view you can see that there is more deadrise aft than amidships. The Nordic 44 has a L/B of 3.39, a D/L of 241, and (given its ballast of 9,356 pounds) a B/D of 39 percent, all indicative of a moderate hull. The waterlines in the plan view and the prismatic coefficient of 0.524 suggest a hull with fine ends that is easily driven in a light breeze but has a lower hull speed than a boat with the same waterline length but fuller ends. The moderate rocker, moderate deadrise, and fairly soft bilges further reinforce the overall impression of a hull that emphasizes comfort over top-end speed, as does the skeg-hung rudder. With the right sail plan, however, this hull will give you good performance.

or lower, while a sailor who might like to race his or her boat once in a while should look for a SA/D around 18.5 or more. Smaller cruising boats can get by with lower SA/Ds, while larger boats with more stability can use a higher SA/D.

High-performance racing boats and even boats that will see an active PHRF racing life should have a SA/D of at least 21.00. A boat with a lower SA/D will get a lower (slower) PHRF rating, but a slow boat isn't much fun to race no matter what its rating is. At the extreme end of today's high-performance boats, classes such as the Open 40 have SA/Ds around 40.00, but 25.00 to 30.00 is a more typical high-performance SA/D.

Several months after buying my current 26-foot boat, I calculated its SA/D and came up with 15.6. That number seemed too low to satisfy my need for speed, yet the boat sails well, so I did the calculation again, certain I had made a mistake. I had not. After years of pushing for SA/Ds in cruising boats of 17.5 or better, I ended up with a boat having a surprisingly low SA/D. While my boat was designed for the Baltic and is no light-air rocket, it is not a light-air pig either. This is just another indication that we should use these ratios as guides and starting points, not as absolutes.

Ballast-to-Displacement Ratio (B/D)

To get this ratio, divide the weight of ballast by the overall displacement, using the same units in both numerator and denominator. The calculation is simple if you have accurate numbers for both components, but using the ratio to assess a boat's potential performance is not so simple. It might be best when considering the B/D ratio to treat race boats and cruising boats separately.

Let us use as an initial example two racing boats with an LOA of 40 feet. One displaces, or weighs (the two words mean the same thing), 12,500 pounds, and the other displaces 9,500 pounds. If they both have B/Ds of 40 percent, the heavier boat will have 5,000 pounds of ballast, leaving 7,500 pounds for all other components of the boat's structure, machinery, gear, and rig. If these other components weigh more than 7,500 pounds, the boat will float below its designed waterline.

Our lighter boat, displacing 9,500 pounds, has 3,800 pounds of ballast, leaving just 5,700 pounds for essentially the same components of structure, machinery, gear, and rig. This tells us that the lighter boat must have a lighter structure, in this case 2,000 pounds lighter, which might be achieved with a carbon-fiber hull and deck.

The weight difference would typically be reflected through the other components as well, but the structure absorbs the greater part.

Does the B/D tell us anything about race-boat stability? It would if all the comparative components of the two boats were equal, but they will not be. Obviously a high B/D with the ballast low would indicate a stiffer boat than one with a low B/D and its ballast high, but there is not enough information in a simple B/D to make reliable judgments about a boat's stability. We need to know where that ballast is before we can make a stability judgment. If both boats draw 8.5 feet and carry their ballast in a bulb at the keel tip, the boat with the higher B/D should be stiffer provided both hull forms are reasonably normal.

When reviewing a racing boat design, I prefer to use B/D as an indication of relative structural weight rather than stability.

Cruising boats are different. Let's compare, for example, a long, light cruising boat—say 59 feet LOA, displacing 30,000 pounds—with a heavy 50-footer weighing 50,000 pounds. Both boats are set up for long-distance cruising, and both carry full complements of cruising gear and accessories. To simplify this, let's assume that the cruising gear and accessories are the same—and therefore weigh the same—for both boats. Both have gen sets, A/C, refrigeration, copious batteries, an inverter, big tanks, extra anchors, a dodger, solar panels, a wind generator, a dinghy or two, an all-chain anchor rode, and so on.

Our light 59-footer loaded down with all this cruising gear can carry 10,000 pounds of ballast and still hit its designed displacement target of 30,000 pounds—and therefore float on its designed waterline. That gives it a B/D of 33 percent. The heavy 50-footer carrying the same cruising gear is able to carry 20,000 pounds of ballast, for a B/D of 40 percent. Though 9 feet shorter than the lighter boat, its bigger hull displaces 20,000 pounds more water when it floats on its designed waterline, and 10,000 pounds of that is allocated to additional ballast. The other 10,000 pounds goes to heavier construction, bigger tanks, and most probably heavier machinery.

Generally speaking, if the

weight of all the cruising gear is more or less the same, some portion of the additional displacement of a heavier boat can be assigned to ballast for a higher B/D ratio. You simply cannot design a fully found, long, light cruising boat with a high B/D. This is why you see more radical fin and bulb keels on light cruising boats. The stability has to come from getting a relatively small amount of ballast as low as possible, whereas a heavy boat has the luxury of a high B/D and can carry that large amount of ballast in a relatively shoal keel and still hit its stability parameters.

All else being equal—displacement, rig size, keel configuration, draft, accommodations, and gear—the boat with the higher B/D would be the stiffer boat. But I have never seen an example like that.

A B/D less than 30 percent is low, whereas one higher than 40 percent is high. Typical grand prix racing yachts can have B/Ds approaching 50 percent, but a modern, medium-displacement cruising boat will have a B/D from 40 percent down to 35 percent. Generally speaking, the lower the D/L of a cruising boat, the lower its B/D.

Prismatic Coefficient (Cp)

You seldom see the prismatic coefficient (Cp) published. It's a little difficult to comprehend. This ratio measures the distribution of volume in a boat from its most voluminous immersed section toward the bow and the stern. In short, the prismatic coefficient tells us if the boat has full ends or fine ends.

Picture a boat in which the most voluminous immersed section (usually, though not always, the midship section) is carried without shrinking right to the forward and after ends of the designed waterline (DWL). In other words, this improbable-looking boat has no taper either forward or aft. Its ends are not pointed—they are not even pinched. This boat—*this barge*—would have a prismatic coefficient of 1.00.

In the real world, all boats have a prismatic coefficient less than 1. To get this ratio for a given design, you multiply the area in the greatest immersed section (in square feet or square meters) by the DWL (in feet or meters) and divide the product into the boat's displacement (in cubic feet or cubic meters; since a cubic foot of seawater weighs 64 pounds, a displacement of 25,000 pounds would be 390 cubic feet). You can use imperial or metric units provided you use the same units consistently in the numerator and denominator.

You will get a number for most sailing boats between 0.50 and 0.56. The textbook "medium" Cp is 0.54. The lower the Cp, the finer the ends of the boat. The higher the Cp, the fuller the boat's ends will be. A low prismatic will give you an easily driven hull, and a high prismatic will give you a hull that is harder to push through the water. The catch is that a low-Cp boat will have a lower hull speed (i.e., a lower speed-to-length ratio) than a high-Cp boat. If you wanted a boat that was fast in light air, you would want an easily driven hull with a low Cp. If you sailed in an area where the winds were consistently strong, you would want a boat with a higher Cp. I generally target a Cp for my cruising boats in the 0.54 to 0.55 range.

Vertical Center of Gravity (VCG)

The vertical center of gravity is the most important number there is for determining the stability of a boat. Combined with the hull shape and its contribution to form stability, the VCG will determine the length of the boat's righting arm— i.e., the distance between the VCG and the transverse center of buoyancy. The length of the righting arm at a given heel angle times the displacement of the boat will give you the righting moment at that heel angle.

In technical terms, the VCG is the centroid of the sum total of all the weights in the boat on a vertical axis. In a typical cruising boat with modest draft, the VCG will be just above the DWL, say four to six inches. In a modern light-displacement racing boat with a deep fin and bulb keel, the VCG can be as much as 12 inches below the DWL, or even lower in some cases. The lower the VCG, the greater the righting arm and the stiffer the boat. This reinforces the importance of draft.

Longitudinal Center of Buoyancy (LCB)

The longitudinal center of buoyancy (LCB) is a function of hull shape and the distribution of underwater volume. The typical location for a modern boat's LCB is at about station 5.4—that is, about 54 percent of the DWL

aft of the cutwater. I will accept up to 57 percent, but anything more than that makes me suspicious of the shape I am developing. The LCB must be vertically aligned with the boat's longitudinal center of gravity (LCG). If the LCB is aft of the LCG, the boat will trim bow-down. If the LCB is forward of the LCG, the boat will trim stern-down.

Longitudinal Center of Flotation (LCF)

The longitudinal center of flotation (LCF) is the center of a boat's flotation plane, otherwise known as its waterplane, which is simply the boat's footprint on the water surface. Imagine taking a horizontal slice through a hull right at the water's surface. That's the waterplane. LCF has nothing to do with immersed volume, and it is always aft of the LCB. I will generally place the LCF at about station 5.6 to 5.75 (that is, 56 to 57.5 percent of the waterline length aft of the cutwater). The boat will trim around the LCF, not the LCB.

If you multiply the waterplane area by 64 and divide that product by 12, you will get the "pounds-per-inch immersion." This number will tell you how many pounds of additional

weight would be required to sink your boat 1 inch—or, conversely, how much the boat will sink in the water for every pound of weight that is added. Of course, as the boat sinks, the waterplane will increase and the pounds per inch will also increase.

Length Overall (LOA)

This seemingly simple term causes all kinds of trouble, as most boats carry some type of gear or extension beyond the bow and stern. On any given boat a bowsprit, a stern pulpit, davits, or the main boom might overhang the bow or stern. I do not include any such items in a boat's LOA. LOA should be confined to the extent of the hull itself, from the tip of the bow to the aftermost projection of the transom (or the stern, in the case of a double-ender).

If the boat has a wooden caprail that extends beyond the hull, I measure the LOA from the joint between the caprail and the hull. If the boat is made of fiberglass, I measure its LOA between the forward and after extents of the molded fiberglass hull.

While I think of a boat's length as the length of the hull itself, a marina operator may include the bowsprit. It's hard to

COMPARATIVE DIMENSIONS FOR REPRESENTATIVE SAILBOATS

BOAT NAME	LOA	DWL	BEAM	DRAFT	DISPL. (LBS.)	D/L	SA/D	L/B
WESTSAIL 32	32′	27′6″	11′	5′	20,000	435	13.89	2.9
FRIENDSHIP 40	40′11″	29′7″	12′10″	10′3″/3′11″	22,500	388	17.24	3.18
ISLAND PACKET 370	37′10″	31′	13′1″	4′3″	21,000	315	17.1	2.89
CATALINA 387	39′10″	32′5″	12′4″	7′2″/4′10″	19,000	249	16.15	3.23
ISLAND PACKET 420	44′7″	37′4″	14′3″	4′4″/4′1″	28,400	244	18.9	3.16
MOODY 47	47′8″	39′4″	14′5″	6′9″/5′3″	32,890	241	14.25	3.22
VALIANT 42	40′	34′10″	12′4″	6′3″	24,500	240	16.5	3.24
HALLBERG-RASSY 40	40′	34′9″	12′6″	6′3″	22,000	234	16.44	3.23
SABRE 426	42′6″	36′	13′5″	6′10″/5′	24,000	230	17.7	3.22
ISLANDER 28	28′	23′	10′	5′3″	6,000	229	15.89	2.9
SOUTHERLY 110	36′	30′3″	11′10″	7′2″/2′4″	13,750	221	16.05	3.04
SABRE 386	38′7″	32′6″	12′8″	6′10″/4′10″	16,950	220	18.5	3.05
TARTAN 3700	37′	32′6″	12′7″	7′3″/4′5″	16,150	210	18.2	2.92
TARTAN 4400	45′	44′	14′1″	5′6″	24,000	203	18.13	3.19
FARR 50	50′	43′10″	15′5″	7′6″	37,400	198	18.27	3.25
HALLBERG-RASSY 37	37′2″	33′6″	11′8″	6′3″	16,500	196	18.07	3.19
OUTBOUND 44	44′11″	40′5″	13′4″	6′4″	28,000	189	18.44	3.37
SAGA 48	47′10″	43′7″	13′9″	6′	30,000	188	19.98	3.47
OYSTER 62	63′3″	55′1″	17′8″	8′6″/6′6″	70,550	188	17.28	3.49
BENETEAU FIRST 36.7	36′7″	30′4″	11′7″	7′2″/5′11″	11,552	185	20.6	3.1
BAVARIA 36	37′5″	30′10″	11′10″	6′5″/5′1″	12,100	184	18.6	3.04
HYLAS 66	66′5″	58′1″	18′0″	9′2″	76,060	173	18.21	3.69
C&C 99	32′6″	29′1″	10′10″	6′6″/5′3″	9,265	168	20.38	3.01
SWAN 75	75′	64′0″	19′0″	9′2″	83,800	165	22.1	3.9
J/109	35′3″	30′6″	11′6″	7′	10,900	165	21	3.06
J/46	46′	40′6″	13′10″	6′2″	24,400	164	19.4	3.33
BENETEAU 323	32′10″	29′2″	10′8″	5′11″/4′9″	8,448	152	18.93	3.08
SWAN 601	60′1″	52′11″	14′10″	11′10″	39,700	120	28.79	3.7
J/145	40′1″	42′6″	13′	8′11″/7′	19,000	110	29	3.7
FARR 52	52′	45′6″	14′7″	10′8″	20,277	96	34.19	3.17
ULTIMATE 24	24′	21′2″	8′6″	5′6″/2′11″	2,040	96	35.3	2.88
SANTA CRUZ 63	63′	54′	16′5″	9′1″	32,640	93	27.6	3.8
COLUMBIA 30	30′	26′6″	9′6″	7′/2′	3,400	82	30.6	3.18
SYNERGY 1000	32′10″	29′2″	9′9″	7′	4,400	79	33.96	3.36
OPEN 40	40′	40′	14′4″	11′10″	7,260	51	56.2	2.78

When two drafts are given, the shoaler of the two is with centerboard up or a shoal-keel option.

ignore a seven-foot-long, six-inch-diameter bowsprit with its whisker stays and bobstay when your income is based on linear dock footage rented. The same applies to a dinghy suspended by davits six feet aft of the stern. When a boat has a bowsprit or other protrusion from either end, the more descriptive term for its length might be length on deck (LOD).

When I measure LOD, I measure it as described above for LOA. Here, too, there can be complications. If the boat has a reverse transom, I do not measure the deck length per se; depending on the transom angle, the LOD I measure may be several feet more than the deck length. Here, as elsewhere, the key is consistency. However, a boat with a reverse transom probably would not have a bowsprit anyway, so, with reverse transoms, LOA is the more appropriate and descriptive number.

Designed Waterline (DWL)

The designed waterline is sometimes called the length at waterline (LWL), or occasionally the load waterline. All these terms are synonymous. The DWL is measured on the boat's flotation plane, from the cutwater forward to the aftermost end of the waterplane.

Even here there is room for interpretation. What do you do if the top portion of your rudder breaks the waterplane aft? This feature is common on modern designs. Maybe you have a transom-hung rudder or an outboard rudder like that on a Westsail 32 or on my own boat,

the Cirrus 5.8. I do not include a rudder in the DWL, but designers occasionally do so in order to make a DWL appear longer and the boat's hull speed (on paper at least) correspondingly higher.

There is no point in deceiving yourself that a rudder adds to the DWL. There is simply not enough volume in the rudder to make it an effective extension of sailing length. I can think of only one exception to this, and that would be a boat designed under the old meter-boat rule—America's Cup 12 meters, for example. These designs have short, stubby, thick rudders that are fully faired into the run of the boat. I could make a good argument, just for the sake of argument, why the chord of these rudders should be added to DWL. However, even the meter-boat rule does not count the rudder as an addition to the DWL.

If there is room for argument when measuring the DWL, it has to be in what flotation condition you measure the waterplane. A boat right out of the manufacturer's box will float light, and if the boat has an overhang in either or both ends, it will have a shorter DWL floating light than it would in a

loaded or even a half-loaded condition. If the counter aft has a long overhang, changing the load condition can add feet to the DWL measurement. On the other hand, if the boat has a plumb or near plumb bow and a truncated stern overhang, the load condition will have little effect on DWL.

Most racing handicap rules specify how a boat must be loaded when determining its waterplane and DWL. Consider also that measuring a boat with overhangs in fresh water will yield a longer DWL than you will get when measuring it in denser salt water, because the boat will float deeper in the fresh water.

Beam at the Waterline (BWL)

The BWL is measured roughly amidships, where the topsides cut the waterplane at its widest point. This dimension is not often listed in boat specs. Some designers use DWL and BWL to get L/B—and this is probably the more accurate method—but it's more common to use LOA and B max (maximum beam).

[Reprinted with permission from *Yacht Design According to Perry: My Boats and What Shaped Them,* by Robert H. Perry (International Marine/McGraw-Hill, 2008)]

A Seaworthy Offshore Boat

"Seaworthy" is a wonderful word, at once absolute and relative, precise and vague. Most boats are seaworthy if used in the way the designer and builder intended, but the majority of production cruising sailboats are designed and built for summer weather and light-duty coastal cruising simply because that's precisely how the majority of boats are used. To be seaworthy offshore, your boat needs to be a good sea boat. Boats from across the design spectrum have, in fact, fared well offshore—the key is that they were well prepared and well handled. Still, certain elements identify a good sea boat, and one such element is stability. We've already touched on stability; now it's time to examine the concept in greater depth (so to speak!).

Stability means comfort in normal weather and safety in heavy weather. It's the product of a number of variables, but you can get a rough reading on the resistance your boat offers to being rolled by subjecting her to the capsize screening formula developed by the Cruising Club of America in the wake of the 1979 Fastnet Race storm.

Divide the gross weight of your boat (displacement plus food, crew, and stores) by 64 to obtain its cubic feet of displacement in seawater. Then divide the cube root of that number into your maximum beam. A boat that yields a number less than 2 from these calculations can be considered stable enough to take offshore.

Shere Khan displaces about 6,000 pounds or 93.75 cubic feet. The cube root of 93.75 is 4.55. *Shere Khan*'s maximum beam is 8 feet, and 8 divided by 4.55 yields 1.75. Phew!

Certainly there's more to a good sea boat than a number. Hull form, construction, steering, rig balance, the speed with which the cockpit drains a boarding sea, and much more determine how boats behave in heavy weather. But *Shere Khan*'s ability to handle what she has handled tells me that the relationship between beam and displacement identified by the screening formula is significant.

When you're offshore, especially when the weather is rough or at night or when you're alone on deck, you should wear a safety harness. One with two tethers is preferable, so you can clip the lead one in before unclipping the trailing one as you move about on deck. In heavy weather you should clip your tether to a padeye in the cockpit (middle photo) before going on deck, and when you have to leave the cockpit you should clip into a jackline that you've rigged for the purpose.

Stability

by Robert H. Perry

Entire books have been written about stability. I'll touch on the basics here. The best way to understand stability is to think of it as a sum of parts, and those parts include the sail plan and rigging; the hull shape and displacement; the keel shape, draft, and ballast; and hull construction (i.e., heavy construction will reduce ballast weight and raise the vertical center of gravity). You must consider all these when you set out to balance the heeling force of the wind against the righting moment (RM) of the hull. Righting moment is influenced by the boat's vertical center of gravity, VCG, and the shape of the hull.

The heeling force is the easy part to grasp, at least in a simple, two-dimensional model of the rig. It is a vector resolution of the sail force vectors, which result from sail area, sail shape, the vertical center of effort (or pressure) of the sail plan, wind speed, and heel angle. For simplicity's sake, the center of pressure for the sail plan is generally taken as the sail plan's geometric two-dimensional center of areas.

There is no quick way to determine a boat's VCG. To get an accurate VCG from drawings, you need to do a weight estimate for each component and keep track of vertical weight distribution. At the same time, you'll need to track the fore-and-aft weight distribution in order to determine the boat's longitudinal center of gravity (LCG), which is used to determine ballast location and to control fore-and-aft flotation trim.

To calculate the vertical center of gravity, moments (distance times weight) of components will be taken

around the boat's waterline. The VCG for a typical cruising boat is generally right around or just above the designed waterline (DWL). For a 40-foot cruising boat with modest draft, for example, a VCG at 4 inches above the DWL is considered normal. A modern 50-foot racing yacht with a deep fin-and-bulb keel may have its VCG 2 feet below the DWL.

Consider that adding 20 pounds in the rig, 25 feet above the DWL, will result in a vertical moment of 500 foot-pounds. In order to maintain the boat's previous VCG, you will have to add 500 pounds 1 foot below the DWL or 250 pounds 2 feet below the DWL.

Stability is measured as righting moment. Again, a **moment** is a weight times a distance, and in this case, the weight is the displacement of the boat and the distance is the righting arm, which is the distance from the boat's VCG to the center of buoyancy of the immersed hull. The center of buoyancy of the immersed hull—and

thus the righting arm—will change for every heel angle as the shape of the immersed hull changes. Therefore, the righting moment is measured at various heel angles to generate a stability profile or curve for the boat.

A hull's center of buoyancy (CB) is a function of its sectional shape. Stability created by hull shape is called **form stability**. Hull shape rarely affects the VCG, although obviously a boat with very high freeboard will have a higher VCG than a boat with low freeboard, all else being equal.

When a hull is at rest and upright, its transverse center of buoyancy (TCB) is on centerline, which means there is no righting arm and thus no righting moment. When a boat begins to heel, the TCB moves to leeward with the immersed hull sections, creating a righting arm. This resistance to the first increments of heeling is called **initial stability** and is almost purely a function of hull shape and the moment of inertia of the waterplane. Nothing helps

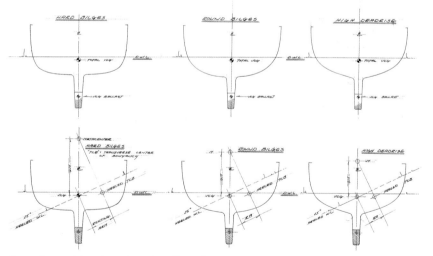

These three midsections show the effect of hull shape on initial stability. The boats have equal beam, draft, ballast VCG, and total VCG, yet the righting arm developed by the hard-bilged midsection on the left at 25 degrees of heel is significantly greater than that of the round-bilged midsection in the center, which is in turn greater than the high-deadrise midsection on the right.

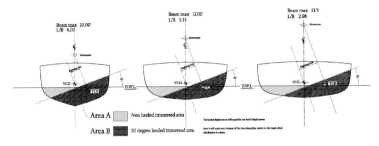

Beam max 10.00'
L/B 4.00

Beam max 12.00'
L/B 3.33

Beam max 13.5'
L/B 2.96

Area A — Non heeled immersed area

Area B — 20 degree heeled immersed area

The effect of beam on initial stability is evident in these midsections of three hypothetical 40-foot boats, each displacing 18,000 pounds. The boat on the left has 10 feet of beam (L/B of 4.00) with deep bilges, while the boat on the right has 13.5 feet of beam (L/B of 2.96) and shallow bilges. At 20 degrees of heel, the transverse center of buoyancy (TCB) of the boat on the right moves farther outboard, and the righting arm is substantially longer. In other words, the boat on the right has greater initial stability and is said to be stiff. Note that the immersed midsection area will remain more or less constant regardless of heel angle, since the boat's displacement doesn't change.

initial stability more than beam. All else being equal, a beamier boat will always have more initial stability.

As the boat heels beyond 5 degrees, the shape of the immersed hull comes more into play. The more hull you immerse, and the farther outboard of the centerline you immerse it, the farther your TCB will move to leeward. This will increase the length of the righting arm (i.e., the distance between the TCB and the boat's VCG, which is always on centerline unless you have water ballast, a canting keel, or movable crew weight). As the righting arm grows longer, the righting moment becomes larger.

Because a righting moment is weight times distance, all other things being equal, a heavier boat will have more RM. Stated differently, a heavy boat with a relatively high VCG can have the same righting moment as a light boat with a low VCG, because the heavy boat doesn't need as long a righting arm as the lighter boat. This is why today's light racing designs all have very deep keels with big lead bulbs

at their tips. They need a long righting arm, and you can create that righting arm with hull form, a low VCG, or both.

Over the years, I've learned that cruisers like stiff (i.e., initially stable) boats, but stiffness comes at a price. A boat with a lot of form stability can give a jerky, quick ride in waves. A boat with low initial stability (i.e., low form stability, like a Valiant 40) can be initially tender but gives a soft ride with a slower heeling motion, and this is the preferred motion for a boat intended to spend a long time at sea. The boat with high initial stability works hard to remain perpendicular to the wave surfaces at all times, and it is this that creates that quick, jerky motion.

Also, although it sounds counterintuitive, boats with low initial stability often have greater **ultimate stability**, which is the ability to resist rolling over in extreme conditions. Technically

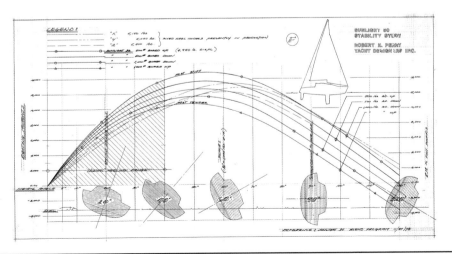

The results of a stability study I conducted in 1978 for the Sunlight 30. A prototype of this boat was built, but it never went into production. The sail plan sketch shows an IOR-influenced fractional rig with short, high main boom. The lighter curves are fixed-keel variations, and the darker curves show the effects of moving 500 or 1,000 pounds of ballast into a lifting keel, with keel-up and keel-down positions shown. In this graph of righting moments (RM) versus heel angles, the lifting-keel versions are stiffer through the normal sailing range (up to 40 degrees of heel), but the stability advantage begins to evaporate at higher heel angles. With a 1,000-pound lifting keel in the up position, the boat reaches its point of vanishing stability (where RM turns negative) at 106 degrees of heel, whereas the fixed-keel model still retains positive stability at 120 degrees of heel.

speaking, ultimate stability is the heel angle at which the righting moment becomes a negative number and the boat will no longer right itself. Once you reach this **point of vanishing stability**, the boat may continue over. This is the point where a knockdown turns into a true capsize.

However, caveats are required regarding ultimate stability. Rodney Johnstone of J-Boat fame did an exhaustive search of rollover case studies about ten years ago. His findings showed that the boats with the consistently best static stability numbers were more likely to roll over than some boats with poor static stability. I think that the key word here is *static*. It's one thing to assess the stability profile of a boat in the office with a three-dimensional model, and it's another to be confronted with a multidimensional storm sea and 80 knots of wind. A lot of variables, subjective and objective, could be identified in Rod's study, but the main thing I took from it is that numbers don't tell the whole stability story. Extensive tank-test studies in Australia recently came up with only one hard conclusion: the bigger the boat, the more it resists rolling over.

So how should a designer balance initial with ultimate stability? To most of us who spend our sea time racing around the bay or cruising near-shore waters on sunny afternoons, a boat with good initial stability is probably the higher priority. The bottom line is that most sailors prefer a stiff boat. Ultimate stability can be determined easily on the computer, and more is always better if it doesn't have to be bought at too high a price in the boat's proportions and performance.

I consider a limit of positive stability (LPS) of 120 to 130 degrees to be a safe and conservative range for a cruising boat. In other words, if the ultimate stability—the heel angle at which the righting moment turns negative—is 120 to 130 degrees, the boat will take anything likely to be encountered by a cruising sailor. Valiant 40s have been measured with LPSs of 112 to 128 degrees in incline experiments. This range can only be attributed to measurement errors and the way the trial boats were loaded. I'm inclined to think that the true LPS for most Valiants is around 124 degrees. History has proven the Valiant to be an able and safe offshore boat.

[Reprinted with permission from *Yacht Design According to Perry: My Boats and What Shaped Them*, by Robert H. Perry (International Marine/McGraw-Hill, 2008)]

Any boat, whether or not designed specifically for offshore use, can be made more fit for storm sailing and thus more seaworthy. You can mount a separate track on the mainmast for a storm trysail, and you can practice setting the trysail in pleasant weather so that when the heavy stuff comes along you'll be familiar with the procedure. You can install a demountable inner forestay on which to set a hanked storm jib. Short of these precautions, you can make sure your mainsail and smallest headsail are heavy and *flat* enough to use in a storm. Are all your fittings and stanchions backed and bedded to hold up in ultimate conditions? Are your scuppers and drains as big as you can make them? Do you have storm covers for oversized windows? Timber braces for hatches? Dodger-type covers for hatches so you can crack them for storm ventilation? How watertight are your ven-

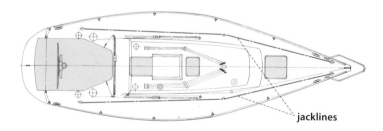

When you rig a jackline, it should run from bow to stern and end about 6 feet forward of the transom. You should be able to clip on before leaving the cockpit and reach the mast or foredeck without having to unclip. Jacklines of flat polyester webbing don't roll underfoot like rope does, but they stretch more.

tilators? How much air can you provide below when water is breaking on deck?

Most bilge pumps are undersized, awkward, and dependent on electric power. Hand pumps that can be worked from on deck and below—the bigger the better—are stormfighters par excellence. Steering systems are weak links. Check yours for slop, wear, and friction, and consider beefing it up by adding a reinforcing plate to the quadrant, a stronger cable, or more securely fastened sheaves and pulleys. Try your emergency steering before you need it.

"Shipshape" is another word that speaks volumes. Before a storm hits, you might run light-line messengers aloft in place of idle lifts and halyards. This removes windage and also cuts back on the infernal howl of a storm wind through the rigging, which many sailors report as being the most unnerving part of a storm. Rig jacklines so you can travel bow to stern with your safety harness fastened. Check that your safety harness fastens securely. Plug the hawsepipe; close the engine room vents. Deck gear, steering vanes, fuel jugs, and certainly a bimini top should go below.

Batteries, anchors, the dinghy, and other such potential missiles should be secured in bulletproof fashion. Look around on deck. Anything movable will move.

Look around below, securing bunk-top lockers, the navigation table, floorboards, etc. Most of the things that gravity normally keeps in place could be set free by heeling or pounding. Check lamps, the stove burners, the companionway ladder, and other such objects you don't normally think of. Lock the dropboards in the companionway. They're not totally watertight but are much more so than the hole they'd leave behind if they fell out.

Boats for Voyaging
by Beth Leonard

Since completing a three-year, 35,000-mile circumnavigation of the globe with her husband, Evans Starzinger, in 1995, Beth Leonard has lectured widely, written for leading sailing magazines, and outfitted a new 47-foot aluminum sloop aboard which she and Evans once again set sail in 1999. They have since logged an additional 55,000 nautical miles, many of these in the world's high latitudes. Their voyages have

Lin and Larry Pardey's traditional voyager Taleisin *has circled the globe and doubled the Horn.*

Scott and Kitty Kuhner's Valiant 40, Tamure, *has sailed more than 100,000 nautical miles, completing a circumnavigation and competing in numerous demanding offshore races.*

Jim and Sue Corenman completed a circumnavigation on their racer/cruiser, the Carl Schumacher–designed, custom Concordia 50, Heart of Gold.

Janet and Ken Slagle have cruised aboard their Santa Cruz 52, Aquila, for seven years and 30,000 miles.

taken them from the Arctic Circle to Cape Horn and include a 60-day, 9,000-mile nonstop passage through the Roaring Forties of the Southern Ocean.

Even a cursory look at the variety of "expert" opinions out there makes it clear that reasonable people can come to very different conclusions when picking a boat for offshore, long-distance cruising. One key to finding a boat *you* will be happy with, one you will trust and enjoy living aboard, is understanding how your needs match up against the strengths and weaknesses of the various types of cruising boats.

Offshore monohull design has produced four major cruising boat types as shown in the accompanying table. Each new type has incorporated proven innovations in design and materials from offshore racing yachts into offshore cruising boats. These types are not discrete—they lie along a continuum, and many boats straddle the borders between them. But they differ markedly along all the major design parameters and make very different trade-offs between comfort and speed.

Over the last half century,

production yachts have become lighter, more powerful, and more manageable. Boats at the cutting edge have always pushed the limits of durability and comfort, and sometimes of safety. Each stage of yacht design includes seaworthy, livable vessels that can make excellent long-term, bluewater voyagers as well as boats that lack the stability or durability to live up the sea's exacting standards.

Traditional voyagers can be characterized as slow but safe and comfortable. By modern standards, they displace a lot and don't carry much sail area for their displacement. They will rarely reach hull speed and will exceed it only if caught running downwind under full sail by a 40-knot squall. The large keel area and heavy displacement damp motion in a seaway, allowing the crew to move around safely and sleep comfortably.

Traditional voyagers take care of their crews and are comfortable even in a blow. They are easy to heave-to and to control when running off in anything but extreme breaking seas, and they can manage just about any conditions as long as they have sea room. But their shal-

low keels and low ballast ratios make for disappointing performance to windward. They are sluggish under power, difficult to maneuver in a marina, and all but impossible to back up in a straight line. They'll get even inexperienced crews safely to port, but they may take a few days longer to do it than more modern designs.

The vast majority of cruising boats sailing the world's oceans fall within the performance cruiser category. They run the gamut from the Island Packets with their cutaway full keels to middle-aged Swans with their fin keels and spade rudders. Although performance cruisers are still heavy enough to carry cruising loads without sacrificing performance, they are large enough, light enough, and have enough sail area to average an extra 10 to 15 miles per day on long passages. Their moderate keel areas and displacements keep motion comfortable even in large seas, while more efficient ballasting provides greater stability (and therefore sail-carrying ability) than many traditional designs. Depending on keel configuration, these boats range from easy to all but impossible to heave-to, but their

MONOHULL DESIGN TYPES

Traditional Voyagers	Performance Cruisers	Racer-Cruisers	Cruising Sleds
Examples:			
full keel	modified fin keel	fin keel, spader rudder, round sections	fin keel, spade rudder, flat sections
Bermuda 40, Bowman 36, Westsail 32, Mason 43, Nicholson 40, Trintella 45, etc.	Valiant 40, Swan 46, Oyster 43, Island Packet 38, Baltic 38, Norseman 447, etc.	X-402, Swan 45, J/160, Beneteau 50, etc.	Hunter HC50, Santa Cruz 52, etc.
Ratios:			
Displacement to length ratio (DLR)*			
> 300	200–300	100–200	< 100
Sail area to wetted surface area ratio (SA/WSA)*			
2.3–2.5	2.3–2.6	2.6–2.9	> 3.0
Sail area to displacement ratio (SA/D)*			
15–17	17–19	23–26	> 25
Length-to-beam ratio (L/B)*			
2.8–3	3–3.2	3.3–4.0	> 4
Ballast ratio**			
33%–35%	36%–39%	38%–42%	> 43%
Motion comfort ratio***			
35–45	25–35	20–25	< 25
Rated speed to theoretical hull speed*			
67%–72%	70%–74%	73%–78%	75%–80%
Profile of an "average" boat:			
Length overall (LOA) (ft.)			
40	40	44	54
IMS displacement (lb.)			
24,300	21,650	20,425	26,300
Length at waterline (LWL) (ft.)			
31	33.5	38.4	48
Beam (ft.)			
11.6	12.5	13	13.7
Draft (ft.)			
5.5	6.4	7.7	9.8
Wetted surface area (sq. ft.)			
350	350	380	533
Working sail area (sq. ft.)			
850	858	1,100	1,800
Estimate of average miles per day on passage			
120–125	130–135	140–145	175–180

* Calculated using data from USSA's *Performance Characteristics Profile of the North American IMS Fleet* (2004 edition) for comparability.
** Manufacturer's ballast/displacement in IMS (International Measurement System) trim.
*** Motion comfort ratio = D ÷ [0.65 x (0.7LWL ÷ 0.3LOA) x $B^{1.33}$]. A result of 20 or less is very uncomfortable; 50 is very comfortable.
[Reprinted with permission from *The Voyager's Handbook: The Essential Guide to Bluewater Cruising*, by Beth Leonard (International Marine/McGraw-Hill, 2007)]

greater stability means they need to heave-to infrequently if at all in trade wind conditions. Most run off very well, although those capable of surfing may require some active management (such as trailing a drogue) to remain in control. Performance cruisers sail much better to windward than traditional voyagers and are reasonably agile under power.

The performance cruisers also have more interior volume than traditional voyagers and are almost as comfortable and as hard to get into trouble with. In the most extreme conditions, however, they are slightly less forgiving and demand slightly more from their crew.

Like the boats at the performance end of the performance cruiser spectrum, racer-cruisers all have fin keels and spade rudders. But their keels and rudders tend to be deeper, and their hulls have flatter sections, have finer entries, and carry their beam farther aft. Keel and rudder foils have improved in both hydrodynamic efficiency and balance. Ballast is often concentrated in a bulb endplate attached to the bottom of the keel, which increases the righting moment created by a given weight of bal-

last. Their lighter displacements allow them to carry less sail area than a similarly sized traditional or performance cruiser design, easing sail handling for a short-handed crew. In IMS (International Measuring System) trim, these boats sail faster on every point of sail, point higher, and surf far more easily than performance cruisers.

However, the current racer-cruisers have some drawbacks as long-distance voyagers when compared with their heavier counterparts. Their flatter, fatter hull shapes surf well and create spacious accommodations, but their shallow bilges offer little in the way of stowage and don't keep bilge water confined to the sump. To maintain their performance edge, these boats need to be kept reasonably light, which means they can't carry the same payload as heavier boats. While modern sail handling techniques have made large sail plans manageable for a short-handed crew, racer-cruisers can be unforgiving if caught with too much sail up in a 40-knot squall. As a result, they take some skill and forethought to manage. The speeds these boats are capable of reaching can lead to pounding in big seas. Many

crews we've met on racer-cruisers slow the boats down in stronger winds to improve the motion, which reduces their performance advantage.

Running downwind in heavy weather and large waves, these boats will surf at exhilarating speeds even under bare poles. Although most remain under control if hand steered, some will not look after themselves under self-steering unless slowed down. The forces generated when a boat falls off a wave at 15 or 18 knots instead of 6 or 7 put huge shock loads on sails, rig, rudder, and hull; as a result these boats need to be significantly stronger than heavier boats, in large part because they sail faster. At the same time, some extra material here and there to add strength makes little difference in a heavy boat, but a light boat has to be engineered and built exceptionally well to stand up to more than a few years of offshore cruising. Boats marketed as offshore cruisers from their inception are more likely to stand up to the rigors of long-distance blue-water cruising than those originally designed and built for racing and chartering.

Racer-cruisers sail extremely

well on any point of sail, so they will be able to sail themselves out of just about any situation. They are agile and efficient under power and easy to maneuver in a marina. These boats need an experienced crew to keep them out of trouble, but they'll often be the first boats into port, and their crews will be relaxing on deck drinking margaritas when the rest of the fleet makes its way in.

In the last decade, materials and building techniques have improved to the point that the fastest monohulls in the world now have D/L ratios of less than 100 and SA/D ratios well over 30. Sometimes called ultralight-displacement boats (ULDBs), these include maxi racers such as *Skandia*, the 2004 winner of the Sydney-to-Hobart Race, and the Open 60s used in the Vendée Globe nonstop around-the-world race. It was only a matter of time before someone translated this thinking to production cruising boats, and today there are a few examples of what have been dubbed cruising sleds, most notably the Santa Cruz 52.

All the attributes of racer-cruisers apply even more so to cruising sleds. The boats can be very fast, and they do manage 200-mile days, but they must be kept very light. Hal Roth completed two BOC races in his Santa Cruz 50, *American Flag*, which proves that at least some of these boats can withstand Southern Ocean–style punishment. However, production cruising sleds are too new to have a proven cruising track record, so their long-term durability remains to be demonstrated.

Cruising Sails

On *Shere Khan* we cruise port-to-port. We've made our share of overnight passages and weathered squalls and 3-day blows, but ours is decidedly coastal cruising. Over 29 years we've had the same main, jib, and spinnaker that we bought with the boat (plus a #1 genoa that we replaced recently). We've patronized sailmakers in half a dozen countries, mostly for genoa repair, but we've spent more on cookies over the years than on sails. That is not, by any means, to say that sails aren't a critical part of cruising. We might have spent more on sails if we'd had it to spend. Ours are general-purpose sails, overbuilt from now-soft Dacron. We spent the minimum, but we've gotten maximum value and satisfaction.

Sailing is at the heart of sailboat cruising. Time under power can be endured, but time under sail is why we're out there. That's the story behind the demise of our first genoa. It wasn't high winds that did it in, but the light stuff. We would have had to motor if we hadn't had the genoa's power, so we set it, and set it, and set it. When the wind blew too hard for the hanked-on genoa, we would take it off the headstay and replace it with our hanked-on working jib. In 29 years we've never had to set the storm jib.

Headsails
The traditional cruising rig for single-masted boats under 40 feet used to be the cutter. The thinking was that placing the mast well aft opened up a big

Red Dragon, *a Dubois 52-meter, displaying twin roller-furling headsails at the stemhead, a configuration pioneered by BOC racers. This arrangement has excellent potential for cruisers.*

foretriangle and allowed cruisers to set either a single big sail in light air or a combination of smaller headsails (a jib and a staysail, then the staysail alone in the heavier stuff) as conditions changed. Our sloop rig (though we have an inner forestay) never provided that flexibility, but we also never needed it. An efficient jib-main combination—with the simple expedient of chang-

ing down to a smaller jib in a breeze—has given us enjoyable and manageable sailing in all the conditions we've met.

Roller furling, however, has changed everyone's approach to cruising sails. Sloop or cutter—or ketch, yawl, or schooner, for that matter—chances are that a cruising boat today has a single overlapping genoa on a roller. Some still advocate the "clutter"

rig (which adds a boomed stay-sail or self-tacking jib), but to my mind the combination lives up to its name—boomed jibs are clumsy, somewhat dangerous, and hard to set effectively upwind and down.

The original roller-furling sails were introduced in the early 1970s. The systems were superb for deploying and stowing sails, but "roller reefing" was another story. Rolling a genoa to make it smaller also made it baggier. The "reefed" head-sails that resulted were ineffective upwind and hardly durable enough to be used as storm sails. Newer systems include jibs fitted with foam luff panels that help the sail maintain its shape as it's rolled, and these are a big improvement. Today's off-shore shorthanded racers favor a setup of twin roller-furling headsails, one for upwind and the other (set from a twin head-stay) for off the wind, but such an arrangement costs more and is more complicated.

Changing and stowing head-sails used to be part and parcel of cruising seamanship. Now it seems that knowing how to keep your roller-furler rolling is what counts. Most cruisers, it seems, would rather shorten sail by winching in a furling line from the comfort of the cockpit than brave a tossing foredeck to change to a smaller sail, and you can hardly blame them. As popular as they are, however, headsails on rollers are not without problems. The hardware has been hardened and improved over the years, but bearings can still seize, halyards jam, or swivels bind. Overrides on furling drums are not uncommon; the art of maintaining even tension on the sail when you roll it in is not easy to master. And a ripped and jammed luff tape can make a sail hard to get down. It's frightening to think you might be stuck with a sail you can neither roll in nor let down, but it happens. If it happens to you, head downwind. With the sail blanketed and depowered, you should be able to capture it and roll it into a sausage along the stay. By swinging a halyard around this furl you can cinch the sail into a tube tight enough to let you maneuver the boat.

The fairlead for the furling line at the drum should be close to centerline and *level with* the drum to minimize overrides. Also, I've yet to see a roller-furled headsail that could be reefed by more than 30 percent

and still be effective. The sail on the roller can be your main cruising sail, but it shouldn't be your only one. Most jibs are relatively light, certainly not bulletproof enough to get you through a storm. A hanked-on heavy staysail on an inner forestay is an effective alternative when the jib is rolled in.

Mainsail

Taming the mainsail is another concern for cruising sailors. If you sail shorthanded, it may even be your biggest concern. Improved roller-furling gear has given us convenient and controllable headsails, but similarly practical, safe, and elegant solutions for mainsails haven't been so easy to come by.

In-mast mainsail furling began in the 1970s, and generations of in-mast furlers have followed. Less-elegant, cheaper, less-efficient "behind-the-mast" systems came along too, and eventually some production builders, including Beneteau and Hunter, began offering in-mast furling as a standard configuration. Mast-furling mainsails present more problems than headsail rollers, however. They add weight and windage aloft, and even if you make use

of your existing mast and retrofit a system, they're not cheap. They offer a relatively narrow margin for human or mechanical error, and when a sail jams it usually means a trip up the mast. Above all, the battenless, no-roach, high-aspect sails required for in-mast furling are smaller (over 10 percent smaller on average) and less effective than conventional mains. The resultant performance loss can be 20 percent or more.

Boom-furling systems seem a better alternative. ProFurl (an American company) and Leisure Furl (in New Zealand) have developed in-boom furlers that, while demanding some operating acumen, produce superior consistency, versatility, and, especially, performance. These furlers allow infinite adjustment so that the right mainsail shape and area can be matched to the wind, and the weight of the reefed mainsail does not remain aloft as it does in an in-mast furling system. They also work with fully roached, full-battened sails so that mainsail efficiency isn't compromised.

Most cruisers and voyagers on boats less than 50 feet long still elect to lower the mainsail the traditional, manual way and

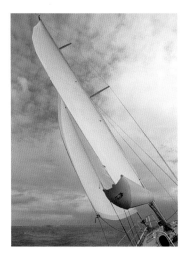

When fully furled the mainsail is tucked all the way into the boom on this in-boom furling system.

The mainsail on this Nonsuch catboat is furled using a StackPack furling system. StackPack is a fully battened mainsail with integral lazyjacks and a cover that opens automatically to accept the sail as it is lowered. The cover and lazyjack system neatly flakes and holds the sail as it is lowered or reefed.

to reef it with slab reefing as described and pictured on page 111. Various innovations make these operations less labor-intensive and more convenient. Full battens not only give the mainsail an optimum shape; they also tame it for reefing and lowering. A full-battened main

that is contained between lazyjacks will lower right onto the boom. When the lower ends of the lazyjacks support a canvas sail cover, as in the Stack-Pack system, the mainsail will lower into the sail cover, which can then be zipped over the top of the furl. Alternatively,

Shortening Sail
by Robert H. Perry

Racers reef to increase boat speed, but cruisers generally reef to improve helm balance, to prevent the boat from being overpowered by a rising wind, or just to smooth things out for the night watch. Keeping your boat on its feet and reducing sail area until the sails can be properly sheeted rather than carried half-flogging should both increase boatspeed and help preserve the comfort of the crew by reducing heel angle. (It also helps preserve the shape your sailmaker originally cut into your sails.) Think of reefing as a performance- and safety-enhancing technique.

Most boats begin to develop excessive weather helm when they are overly pressed. To combat this, the first sail reduction should be to put a reef in the main. Of course, this should be done after flattening (i.e., depowering) the main and genoa with increased halyard tension for both sails and for the mainsail more outhaul tension. Sheet leads for the genoa may also need to be moved as the wind picks up. Moving the leads aft will free the leech, allowing it to spill some wind. If you have the option you might also find it advisable to move your jib leads outboard, as high seas will prevent you from pointing high anyway.

The current trend in cruising sloops and cutters includes a roller-furled genoa with a luff perpendicular when fully unfurled of approximately 140 percent and a staysail that is usually hanked to a removable inner forestay. The typical cruiser will roll up all or part of the genoa first to reduce sail area quickly. The next step sees the genoa totally rolled up and the staysail hoisted. Simply furling the genoa and hoisting a staysail is like shifting from fifth gear down to first in one move. I would prefer to see the first step in sail shortening to be a reef in the mainsail in order to preserve helm balance and reduce heeling pressure.

In a masthead-rigged boat, the best way to preserve headsail efficiency through a wide range of wind speeds is to carry an inventory of hanked-on or luff-groove-extrusion headsails—say a 150 percent genoa, a 120 percent genoa, a 100 percent working jib, and a storm headsail. For pure cruising boats, hanked-on headsails offer some conveniences as they are always attached to the headstay by their hanks, while a luff-groove-style headsail will be only attached at head and tack when lowered. Changing these jibs is apparently too much work for today's average cruiser. Nowadays, roller furling is popular and, along with it, roller reefing. Having cruised both with furling gear and with an inventory of hanked-on jibs, I have to admit that the convenience of roller reefing is hard to resist, especially once a boat gets above 30 feet LOA.

One of the benefits of a fractional rig is that it reduces the need for a broad headsail inventory. The mainsail is the bigger sail in a fractional rig, so it's natural that your initial reefing reflex will be to reef the main. It's easier to control a boomed sail in a breeze than it is to corral a flailing genoa on a heaving foredeck. A tall, fractional rig can get by with one non-overlapping headsail. The caveat is that you will have to be more diligent about reefing the main, and you will need to learn how to depower and flatten the main to keep

the boat on its feet as the first move prior to tucking in a reef.

Years ago in Seattle, a dealer imported a fleet of fractionally rigged Scandinavian boats called Aphrodite 101s. These came with non-overlapping headsails. It was thought that the boats would need more horsepower in Seattle's light air, so a genoa was built for one boat and trials were set up against a boat with the standard jib to evaluate the genny's advantage. As it turned out, the genny conferred no speed advantages, and the fleet stayed with blade-type working jibs. The moral of the story might be that jib overlap on many boats can be seductive but misleading. In the old days of the CCA it was not uncommon to see genoa LPs of 160 percent or even greater, with the genoa essentially sheeting just short of the transom. Today I advise most cruisers to buy genoas with an LP not exceeding 135 percent.

You can rig a self-tacking traveler for a blade-type boomless jib, but it will need to be longer/wider than you might think. If it's too short, you will never achieve the sheeting angle required to correctly trim the sail in a variety of wind speeds. The only fully successful self-tacking jib system I have designed had the jib traveler spanning the entire beam of the boat at the mast. The sheeting angle for a self-tacking jib must be no less than 10 degrees or you will end up with a curl in the jib that will constantly pour backwind onto your mainsail. This poses a problem in heavy air, when the better sheeting angle would be outboard. This is slow and increases the heeling moment of the rig.

You also need a long traveler so that the jib lead can move outboard when the sheets are eased, at which point the lead should move forward as well. This is impossible with a self-tacking track system unless you have and take advantage of an aluminum clew board with three alternative sheet attachment points, but I have yet to see cruisers actually use these additional cringles. Face it, most of us are looking for the easiest way, and switching the jibsheet attachment each time you bear off is not the easiest way, even though it may be effective.

I'm from the old school. I believe that you need at least two headsails on any sloop or cutter in addition to the staysail. I have a two-headsail inventory on my own fractionally rigged boat, and I hank on my jibs the old-fashioned way, which makes jib changes easy. I realize that changing jibs in a breeze is no fun, but a full-hoist, 100 or 95 percent, blade-type jib with a clew no higher than the top lifeline is far more efficient than a partially rolled-up genoa.

I prefer low-clewed headsails, and my rule of thumb is that no clew should be higher than I can easily reach from the deck. The trick is to anticipate a headsail change so that it can be done in relative comfort and safety before the breeze really pipes up. In my latest designs, I have increased both the I dimension (from mast base to headstay attachment on mast) and the relative size of the mainsail in order to reduce the need for overlapping headsails. The days of 160 percent gennies are gone. The typical cruising boat of today should carry a genoa with an LP no greater than 135 percent. Keep in mind that the relative size of the genoa based on LP will be a function of the size of the J dimension. A 40-footer with an 18-foot J dimension (i.e., the base of the foretriangle) will carry a 140 percent genoa equal in size to a 157 percent genoa on a 40-footer with a J of 16 feet.

One way of adding a heavy-air staysail with a good aspect ratio is to pull the staysail stay as far forward on the deck as possible. This imitates a fractional rig and allows the center of effort of the staysail to stay well forward. This is commonly referred to as a Solent stay, and it's my preferred rig on any boat longer than 40 feet. I like this stay to be removable (although you often see it fixed), and you have to find a landing point on deck where you can support the stay adequately from below while avoiding conflicts with the windlass and other foredeck paraphernalia. A heavy-air sail flown from a Solent stay keeps sail area forward and makes for a better steering boat. Upwind, especially, this staysail may make the boat far easier to balance, as it reduces weather helm. Sailing with too much weather helm is like sailing with the parking brake on, not to mention the wear and tear it inflicts on the helmsman or autopilot.

A well-thought-out mainsail reefing system is essential. Conventional slab reefing can work fine if the leads are correct and you can get the appropriate lines to winches. I find it amazing that race boats are so frequently far better set up for easy reefing than cruising boats.

As a general rule, I'm not in favor of single-line slab reefing. There is generally too much friction in that single line for efficient reefing. Separate, properly led lines for the luff and leech, combined with a knowledge of the proper sequence of events to adjust them, is the key to easy reefing.

In-mast mainsail furling is popular these days, but not at my house. The typical mainsail designed for in-mast furling gives up as much as 20 percent of its area due to the lack of a headboard, the lack of roach, and the requisite hollow leech. This sort of mainsail is generally without battens, which means that you will inevitably end up with a tight leech that is hooked to weather—what we sarcastically call a "speed cup." This type of mainsail is also prone to a "catcher's mitt" shape, with the maximum draft pulled well aft despite your best efforts to move the draft forward. This does a lot more to increase heeling and weather helm than it does to increase drive. I know there are batten systems designed to work with in-mast furling, but I have yet to talk to a sailor who said they work.

In-mast furling systems also require large-dimensioned, heavy mast sections that increase the boat's windage and decrease its stability. This is slow. The vertical mast slot can also whistle and howl in a breeze at the dock if it is not fitted with a "whistle-stopper strip." I don't even want to talk about furling systems that roll up the main on a stay just aft of the mast. They may be convenient, but they certainly are not efficient, as the main luff inevitably falls away from

the mast and loses the benefit of the mast as a leading edge.

I recognize the appeal and necessity of mainsail roller-furling systems, especially on larger cruising boats, but if you want the convenience of rolling your mainsail up in increments as the wind pipes up, you should investigate an in-the-boom furling system such as the Leisure Furl system developed 10 years ago in New Zealand, or the Schaefer Marine system. These give you a normal main with full battens, generous roach, and controllable draft. In fact, when this mainsail is up, you can't distinguish it from a normal mainsail. This is the type of system I would want if I had a boat longer than 40 feet. The only fly in this ointment is the need to control the angle of the boom when you lower the mainsail so that the main rolls up neatly and squarely in the boom. This can be done several ways. You can use a boom gallows as a visual check (as in, "The boom needs to be 6 inches above the gallows before I roll up the main"). Or you can use a rigid vang that holds the boom at the prescribed angle. You could also use a preset and marked boom topping lift to get this required angle.

To give in-mast furling its due, it probably is the easier system to use, but to me the attendant loss of efficiency and stability are unacceptable. Once again, individual sailing style will play a big part in deciding exactly how you shorten sail.

[Reprinted with permission from *Yacht Design According to Perry: My Boats and What Shaped Them*, by Robert H. Perry (International Marine/McGraw-Hill, 2008)]

some sailors favor a flaking system such as the Dutchman, in which lanyards dangling from the topping lift are threaded back and forth through grommets in the sail before attaching to the boom. This system ensures that the mainsail, when lowered, drops onto the boom, though the friction it generates can make the sail harder to hoist and lower.

Slab reefing—also known as jiffy reefing—has been refined to a point of relative ease and can be carried out from the cockpit when properly rigged. Still, jib-style "now you see it, now you don't" stowage and safe, effective reefing have yet to arrive for mainsails.

Battens are something of an Achilles heel. Conventional leech-only battens need to be flexible enough to avoid hard spots (there's a wide range of bendability available). They can break or pop through flogging sails, but it's hard to get a leech to stand without them. Full-length battens are popular, and they simplify mainsail handling, but inboard-end friction remains a concern, as does chafe of the battens on shrouds when the main is eased. A battenless main detunes performance.

Offwind Sailing

Whether you use a spinnaker with it or not, a spinnaker pole is great for cruising. Pole a jib out to weather, and your offwind stability doubles while your speed climbs. Our pole is light enough to make a conventional spinnaker easy to set, and our happiest cruising miles have come under spinnaker, often with no main (but perhaps a boom awning). Cruising spinnakers are less versatile but less nerve-wracking.

A workable boom vang is good. A solid vang that holds up the boom on its own is great. Suit your boat for offwind sailing, or fair winds will be no fun!

Chafe, sunlight, and salt are three killers. Protect against chafe by padding spreader tips, shrouding stays in rollers, policing against sharp edges and cotter pins, and paying attention to the rub of lines, especially the topping lift, against sails. Cover sails or stow them in bags, even in midcruise, to keep them shaded. And sail in the rain every now and then to wash your sails clean.

Cruising Accommodations

No matter if you cruise far or near, you'd like your boat to provide shelter from the weather, places to sleep, something to eat and drink, and comfort and safety below. Some boats meet these needs better than others but, whether you go out overnight or for 6 months, whether your boat is 20 feet long or 70, these needs remain the same. So does the human form. The space that each of us needs for sleeping is the same regardless of the size of the boat. If you shrink an enclosed head compartment smaller than 24 by 36 inches, you probably won't be able to shoehorn yourself into it. An unenclosed toilet—or one sheltered by a sliding curtain—is better than a tiny enclosure. And you can only scale down a stove so far before it becomes a cigarette lighter.

I usually try to "accommodate" myself to the boat. That

The use of space on smaller cruising sailboats like the Sabre 28 is well considered and clever. A double V-berth fits snugly in the bow of this boat, visible beyond the bulkhead through the open door.

The view forward from the companionway of a 32-foot performance-cruising sailboat shows the efficient use of space in the main cabin, or saloon, of a small cruiser. The dropleaf dinette table is built around a compression post that transfers loads from the deck-stepped mast to the keel. The settees either side of the table are supposed to double as sleeping berths—let's hope you can slide the seats toward the centerline and fold down the backs to widen the berths when it's time for bed. The door in the bulkhead forward of the settees opens into a V-berth forward. Though advertised as a double berth, the V-berth isn't big enough for two adults, but it's a great place to tuck away the kids when the boat is in port. To the left of the viewer but out of the field of view is the boat's small galley, featuring a stove, icebox, and (just visible) peninsular sink. Installing the sink near the boat's centerline will keep it from dropping below the waterline and backfilling when the boat heels. Any outboard sink needs to have its seacock closed whenever you're under sail, and that's an easy thing to forget to do, at least until you've overflowed the sink once or twice. Aft of the galley is the door to a quarterberth cabin. To the right of the viewer and out of the field of view is a small navigation station, and aft of that is the head compartment.

resiliency can facilitate cruising adventures, but the joy of being on the water takes most of us only so far. Camping out in a boat gets old. How much comfort and convenience you expect or demand is up to you, but the more you know about cruising accommodations, the likelier you are to get what you're after.

Berths

Berths are important. At least when you're in port, you need a sleeping spot for everyone.

Berths are normally wider at the head than at the foot, but radical tapers (to less than 16 inches at the foot of a single or 22 inches in a double) make them uncomfortable if not unsleepable. Designers try for 6 feet 6 inches in length, but I've slept fine in a 6-foot 4-inch single. If the head is much narrower than 2 feet, though, it's too narrow. A double in your house is at least 54 inches wide, but two can sleep (companionably but well) in anything wider than 44 inches. Wide berths aren't good at sea because you're likely to get tossed around in them. But you can use pillows or duffels or a bunkboard to cushion or divide a wide berth to make it work at sea. A berth that's too narrow will always be too narrow.

Where should berths be? Double berths are best at the

The quarterberth in the 32-footer extends aft on the port side beneath the cockpit and is large enough to sleep two adults comfortably.

ends of the boat, where they enjoy some privacy. Bunks pressed outboard to gain floor space are hard to get into. It's best if berths run parallel to the boat's centerline. When they are angled to suit curving hull sides, your head and feet wind up at different levels when you heel. Sleeping in the forepeak is fine at anchor, but when you're sailing upwind in a chop, the exaggerated pitching and slamming in the forward part of the boat makes it a nightmare. An athwartships berth can be fine in port—better, in fact, than a fore-and-aft berth in a rolly anchorage—but it's no place to sleep when the boat is heeled.

Not all berths aboard need be good sea berths, but you should have enough to let half the crew sleep underway, and they should be accessible. Pilot berths set above the saloon settees can be comfortable, but climbing into one on the weather side can be precarious, as can tumbling out of it. A sea berth should be at or aft of amidships to minimize pitching, but it's nice if it's not in the middle of the saloon where meals, navigation, and conversation disturb sleep.

When the boat heels as much as 30 degrees, you should be reasonably sure that you'll stay in bed. Most seagoing bunks are fitted with canvas lee cloths or wooden bunkboards. These temporary siderails need to be at least 8 inches high (and sturdy) to keep you in. Lee cloths are softer than bunkboards. You learn pretty quickly to fold your mattress against a bunkboard rather than trying to sleep body-to-board. Quick-release lanyards to hold cloths up are nice, too.

The best sea berths are quarterberths, extending aft beneath the cockpit from the main cabin. Semi-enclosed and tight enough to be hard to fall out of, they're still right by the foot of the companionway. Though that may occasionally mean a refreshing splash for the sleeper, fresh air is also close—especially if you have an opening port in the topsides or the cockpit well—and you're close by if needed on deck but tucked well enough away to get sleep when you're not. Quarterberths can be a bit confining in port, but at sea they're the best nest to burrow into. On somewhat bigger boats, more elaborate quarter cabins on either side of the companionway are also good at sea.

Berths created by dropping a table, pulling out a platform, or reconfiguring furniture are fine examples of "two-way" space. Not often usable underway, they can stretch the in-port sleeping capacity of smaller boats to accommodate larger parties. Aside from their crankiness ("so easy that a child—and her brother, the engineer—can do it"), they invariably need to be reconverted before waking life can resume in the morning. And they often are less than ideal as sleeping places. One thing most bigger boats provide is bunks that can be left as beds fulltime.

Galley

The longer you cruise, the more you'll appreciate a good galley. It's used three times a day, minimum. No matter your cruising style, you never outsail your need to eat. On a passage the next meal can loom larger than your landfall. Anchor-down or in-port meals can turn into feasts to remember. A cup of hot soup at night can seem like ambrosia. But cooking on a boat isn't easy.

If the galley is located between the saloon and the companionway, serving food on

Looking to port from the companionway of the cabin shown in the previous photo, we see a seagoing two-burner propane stove with oven (note open oven door). The stove is mounted on a fore-and-aft rod, or gimbal, the forward end of which is just visible at right, enabling the cooking surface to remain horizontal when the boat heels. The stainless steel bar in the foreground separates the cook from burners and scalding liquids, and the stainless steel fence around the cooking surface keeps pots, pans, and kettles corralled.

LPG is the fuel of choice for cooking aboard, but propane and butane are both heavier than air, which means that leaking gas would pool in your bilge if you stored the fuel inboard—a potentially explosive situation. LPG bottles should therefore be stored outside the cabin, in a purpose-designed deck locker with a scupper that drains overboard. This propane locker (with lid removed) is recessed into the aft end of the cockpit.

deck or below can be equally practical. Rather than the floor space that you might think desirable in a shoreside kitchen, you want your galley to be a bit cramped. Counter and cupboard space should be generous, sinks should be deep, and stove and refrigerator should probably be as big as you can carry, but you'd like the sink, stove, and refrigerator to be conveniently close to one another. In a good galley you can manage everything you're preparing without having to move much.

You'd like the motion in the galley to be comfortable and its position central. Most galleys work well sited close by the companionway. In general, standing headroom can be overrated, but in the galley you want all the height you can get. Ventilation is an obvious priority. Cooking too close to a down-drafting companionway is frustrating, but most of the time the companionway exhausts air rather than bringing it below. Moisture, steam, odor, and smoke from the stove can thus escape. Opening ports are good, cross-ventilation is better, and, especially when you're cooking in warm weather, at sea, or in the rain, intake/exhaust fans are great. Here are a few other specifics:

On *Shere Khan* we have a two-burner, gimballed Campingaz (butane) stove. Though Carol discovered how to make pan bread and has learned to do a lot with a pressure cooker, we miss an oven. Otherwise, though, our choice of stove has a lot to recommend it.

A gimballed stove is a must for cooking underway. Athwartship gimballing keeps the stove level when the boat heels. (Fore-and-aft gimballing takes more room, is more complicated, and works less well.) You don't want to boil water or use a pressure cooker on a heeling stove. Even if you're just making sandwiches, the stove is an island of balance in the galley that lets you work without chasing the

The 32-footer has only a single sink, but it's a deep one and close to the boat's centerline. To the left of it, looking forward, is the icebox.

Because this 32-footer is in a Caribbean charter fleet, it has mechanical refrigeration—note the temperature control top left in the photo. Move the same boat to Puget or Long Island Sound, however, and you could cool this same compartment more simply and almost as effectively with blocks or containers of ice purchased at a marina or frozen in your freezer at home. A top-opening box keeps the cold air in when you open the lid. When the lid is closed, it becomes counter space.

Another view of the galley on the 32-footer. Note the fiddle along the counter edge and the lockers behind the stove and counter for cup and dish storage.

Well-placed reading and task lights over each berth improve the quality of life in an anchorage. These are easy to install on a boat that is missing them.

sliding mayonnaise jar or holding the bread between your knees.

Cooking with liquefied petroleum gas (LPG) is the way to go. I've used the alternatives. Alcohol has singed me, and sterno has scorched our overhead. A kerosene stove has arcane valves, mantles, and preheaters and still coats everything with soot. Compressed natural gas (CNG) is lighter than air and burns as well or better than LPG, but it's ridiculously hard to find and therefore not a good choice. All things considered, LPG is the best. It boils water before you've forgotten about coffee, operates simply and self-evidently, and makes cooking at sea as good as it can be. *Note: One exception to this might be a wick-fed alcohol stove (as opposed to pressurized alcohol) like the single-burner Origo model. This compact stove is reliable (though slow cooking) and makes a good choice for a small overnight cruising boat.*

The LPG fuels are propane and butane, both of which are heavier than air. That poses the threat of fumes sinking to the bilge and fueling an explosion. U.S. regulation requires that all tanks vent overboard. That means stowing them abovedecks (tough in a small sailboat, but premade mountable tank boxes sold now for the purpose are some help). Especially when fitted, as it should be, with a solenoid switch that allows remote shutoff at the tanks, an LPG stove is not only the most elegantly quick, simple, and satisfactory of systems, but it's also (when you weigh the very real fire hazard posed by other systems) the safest. Propane is the predominant LPG in the United States, Caribbean, Australia, New Zealand, and parts of Europe, while butane predominates in the United Kingdom, the Mediterranean, and throughout much of the tropics. An LPG stove will burn either fuel. A propane tank will hold butane safely, but not vice versa.

If we had an oven, it would certainly have a door lock to keep it from popping open underway and upsetting the balance of the stove. The door would be the "disappearing" variety that can slide beneath the stove when opened to maximize galley space.

A sturdy safety bar (stainless steel is best) should be erected between the stove and the cook so that it spans the near edge of the stove at a height slightly above the stovetop. You don't see guards like these on your ranges at home, but then your house doesn't lurch wildly enough to pitch you onto the burners. The clearance between stove and bar should be enough so passersby can grab the bar as a handhold without getting singed.

Waist-high pad eyes either side of the stove make it possible to rig a galley belt for the cook. The idea is for the cook to support his or her weight by leaning against the belt in rough weather, leaving both hands free for cooking. The

belt needs to be adjustable and workable on either tack. Tailor it, if you can, to provide motion enough to get the meal done. I've known some cooks who won't boil water if they're not belted up, while others feel confined and would rather brace themselves than buckle up. Another thing for the cook to wear is an apron. Bib-style foul-weather-gear pants may not be chic, but they can prevent burns and scaldings when the cooking is rough.

The only stove that I enjoy more than the gas range in the galley is the grill I use on the afterdeck. Taking the barbecue to sea has never been easier. I used to fill a four-legged hibachi with twigs and fan it on the fantail. Now, since Barbecue Bob teamed up with Barnacle Bill, we can choose from a shining line of domed grills (gas and charcoal) that clamp to the stern rail, clean up in a heartbeat, and make turning burgers to charcoal more scientific than it's ever been.

Sinks should be on the centerline. Ours isn't, and when *Shere Khan* dried out on her side in Maine we learned why that was bad. The sink was on the low side, and when the tide

came back in it came aboard through the drain. A centerline position aids drainage and inhibits back-siphoning. Sinks that are deep (10 inches or so, enough to accept plates on their side to soak) will stand you in good stead. Twin sinks work well, as any galley stander can attest.

Counters should be heat-resistant. Putting a hot pot down on raw fiberglass can be nasty. Fancy surfaces like butcher block or stainless are lovely. Formica has worked OK for us.

A nice element in a well-designed galley is "toe clearance," that 3-inch high by 3-inch deep indentation where counter meets floor that you never notice until you're in a galley without it. More and more galleys have these.

Corners on counters, and on virtually every other piece of furniture, should be rounded. If you can build a handhold into a large-radiused corner, so much the better. And inside the galley or out, the more (and more accessible) the handholds, the better. I dislike the gutter-style fingerholds that you see sometimes running along house sides. They invite you to hang on by a finger. Traditional grabrails look clunkier, I admit, but they are a whole lot more secure.

We cruised the Mediterranean for three summers without ice. Our marvel of an English icebox kept ice for 20 minutes or less, but we were never far from markets and shops. We provisioned day by day, stocked up for periods of self-sufficiency, and drank warm drinks. Today's iceboxes are five times more efficient than the one we endured. In a top-opening box I've seen an insulated lap joint used to make even the seam between the lid and box temperature-tight. Such a box will keep your perishables cold several days between ice purchases.

Mechanical refrigeration (as opposed to an icebox) has come a long way, but I still hesitate to recommend it. Powering a refrigerator can dictate as much as 2 hours of engine running time per day. Still, the vast majority of cruisers today, especially those in boats over 30 feet, find some way to have mechanical refrigeration aboard. I have nothing against frozen steaks and a cold O'Doul's, but for me the price of cruising with a cold plate is too high. The systems aren't complex or fragile, and solid-state refrigeration has

come into its own, but I decline to own a refrigerator because I'm scared it will come to own me—and that's not what I'm out there for.

There's more to a good galley than stove, sinks, and icebox. Retainers—known as **fiddles**—should run around the edges of flat surfaces like counters, tables, and shelves. From 1½ to 2 inches high (and often angled outboard to soften their "tripping" effect) these minirails, most always made of wood, are there to prevent pots, pans, and glasses from sliding off. What's underfoot is a consideration, too. Carpets get soggy at sea. Varnished flooring is breakneck slippery when wet. Unfinished natural boards absorb oil and dirt. Stained or flat-finished natural wood makes a good galley sole.

You'll find that big bins without internal compartments, while they may work for some kinds of stowage, are not what you want in the galley. Specialized stowage—spaces tailored to suit a particular item or purpose—is worth its weight in gold in the galley. Cutouts for wine bottles are one instance. Security, convenience, and safety are watchwords for good stowage;

add "quiet," too. If things can clink together, they will. Pad and jam and wedge and cram until you have a galley you can sleep with.

Cabin and reading lights are necessities. Galley lighting is just as critical. Fluorescent lights often work well over a sink or behind a counter. Newer LED lights might be even better.

Most trash bins are afterthoughts, and usually you'll find them jammed into an out-of-the-way corner. Planning a place for a bin that works into the working flow of your galley can pay big dividends.

Heads

Bathrooms on boats are called heads because the privvies on sailing ships used to be right forward—overhanging the sea and sluiced from time to time by the waves. Toilets in the forepeak were once common on yachts, too, and it was not unusual to have to lift up the forepeak bunk flat in order to gain access to the toilet beneath it—not a great arrangement if someone was sleeping there. If not in the forepeak, the "throne" would be crammed into a cubby or wherever it would fit. From a forepeak afterthought, the marine toilet has now evolved into a marine sanitation device (MSD), and on most boats over 25 feet long it warrants a full-fledged room (or at least compartment) of its own. Indeed, boats over 40 feet long are likely to have two head compartments—one for the owner and one for the guests— and heads generally incorporate showers these days, resembling more and more a bathroom at home.

Even on an airplane the toilets are less complicated than they are on boats. The need to bring flushing water in and pump dirty water out means that most marine toilets need to be "operated." It's always embarrassing to ask how the toilet works, but until you're clear about which lever is which and when to pump what, it can be more embarrassing to go ahead in the head without asking. Part of the system is a seawater intake, the through-hull opening for which should be protected with a screen and checked periodically to make sure flow isn't impeded by growth or debris. Most installations include an above-waterline hose loop with an antisiphon valve in the high point to keep water from coming aboard if the intake gets

The toilet is of course the centerpiece of the 32-footer's head compartment, but packed in with it are a vanity and standing and seated positions for showering with a handheld showerhead. The head compartment should have its own sump for collecting the graywater from the shower, and pumping that sump overboard through an above-water discharge is an advisable way to reduce your boat's number of below-the-waterline through-hulls. The toilet should discharge to a holding tank, but the outlet line is often fitted with a Y-valve so the discharge can be directed overboard when the boat is offshore.

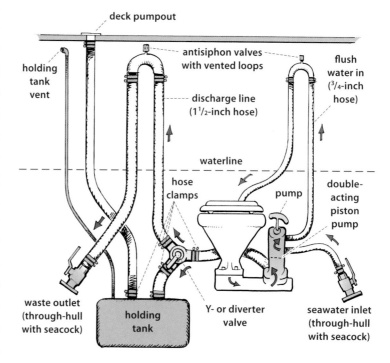

Typical marine toilet plumbing.

higher than the toilet (as it can when you heel), but closing the intake seacock whenever no one is using the head helps me rest easier.

Generally toilets mounted athwartships are easier to use than those mounted fore and aft. Offshore you'll find robust equipment invaluable. It's hard to forget the image of a friend rocketing out of the head during a hard beat. The toilet seat had come adrift and thrown him against the door, which sprang open to deposit him, still purposefully seated, among his startled watchmates. The head gets all manner of wear and tear when it's rough.

A related problem is your discharge system. U.S. Coast Guard regulations require that you be able to hold or treat sewage and that you not discharge it within 3 miles of land. I've found the most common arrangement on cruising boats to be a holding tank with a Y-valve downstream from it. That allows the tank to be either pumped at a marina pumpout station or discharged overboard, depending on how you throw the valve. Sailors have a big stake in water quality. The Coast Guard has demonstrated little interest in pursuing violations of the discharge laws, but the best friend the environment has is our sense of responsibility about how and where we pump our heads.

It's hard to keep the head from smelling bad. Men can certainly help by sitting or kneeling to pee in a seaway, but much of the problem isn't due to human use. It comes from the microorganisms in the seawater pumped into the head. If you're able to mix solid or liquid disinfectant with the seawater as you pump it into the bowl, much of the problem goes away. A final step is wrapping head hoses (which are permeable) with an impermeable covering to keep odor locked inside instead of letting it seep out through the hose.

At sea, you're the plumber. I keep a complete set of spares for everything except the bowl (on *American Eagle* we even broke one of those) and a manual aboard. I'm in favor of single heads in mid-sized cruisers, primarily because the space devoted to a second compartment can be put to better use—a bias that was reinforced in one of our chartering vacations. When our after head clogged, I buckled down to tear it apart, thankful at least that our center-cockpit 44-footer had another head forward. Then came a call of "Daddy!" Our two heads had become none. It's a shame I couldn't collect plumber's wages for the vacation day I spent upside down in the bilge unplugging both.

Stowage, Tankage, and Access

My father tells a story about his first cruise: Fresh from college he and two friends took bags and boxes of food and drink aboard for a Long Island Sound getaway. Sacks, duffels, parkas, a lantern or two, charts . . . it was a lot to cram aboard their chartered 28-footer. The breeze was right and adventure was calling. "Let's just put things below and go!"

That maiden sail was only an hour or two long, but by the time they'd gotten the anchor down the gear and stores below had been shaken and stirred into a soggy mess. It took them all night and most of the next day to rescue what they could and sort it out. I may be a bit paranoid, but through decades of cruising I've learned over and over again that whatever *can* shift or move around down below *will*. Secure stowage is the key to sanity and organization and to cruising enjoyably. Any cruising challenge—water below, a grounding, a gale, or merely fog—can be magnified beyond reason by a single can of corned beef hash rolling, rocketing, and banging around the cabin. That can indubitably turn a problem into a nightmare. Seamanlike stowage is the cornerstone of safety, sanity, and happiness.

Just putting aboard the necessities is a big task. You can figure on better than four pounds of food per person per day for cruising. As with most other stores, it makes sense to stow your food according to your needs. Staples (flour, sugar, etc.) should be handy. Nonperishables (onions, potatoes, etc.) plus canned goods usually go in deeper, harder-to-get-at lockers. Fresh fruits, snacks, drinks, etc., should be closest at hand.

Anything that can open will. Keeping drawers and lockers from popping open on their own is a problem. Positive catches—closures that don't depend on friction or gravity but that mechanically fasten a locker or drawer shut—are the answer. The evolution of the

clean, handsome, rugged push-button closures seen today on the best custom and production boats marks a small but significant milestone in cruising. Push once, the door pops free. Push again, you latch it tight. Cruder but just as effective are block latches you can fit to the outside of any closure. Wriggling breakable fingers through holes in locker fronts to fish for elusive catches is (hopefully) history!

Water for cruising (without provision for extended showers) amounts to something like 1½ gallons/day/person. To cruise for a week with four aboard you'll need at least 40 gallons. Whether that means refilling a 20-gallon tank in the middle of your cruise or carrying it all aboard, water shouldn't be an afterthought. The bigger your tanks the better, in many ways, but also the more space they take. It's common to put tanks beneath berths, but this prime stowage space is also an elegant and convenient place to fill with clothes, food, or gear. In choosing a boat, consider not only how much tankage she provides but at what price (in terms of stowage space hogged). Smaller tanks that can be isolated or

connected according to need offer versatility and make better use of space than a single monster. It's good, too, if you can inspect and clean tanks. Baffles are good to minimize noise and motion. Stainless steel tanks are top of the line and worth it.

Bilge water may seem far removed from stowage. When you heel, however, the distance decreases. In boats with shallow or non-existent sumps in the bilge (mostly U-shaped in hull form), or in any boat whose sump is half-full or better, water from the bilge can and will infiltrate lockers and slop over the cabin sole. The best protection is a bilge bailed religiously dry. I'm often prone to postpone that chore, but counting the number of sweaters soaked in diesel oil that I used to own helps me attend to the bilge before hoisting sail.

You need access to the equipment and systems that keep your boat going. Engine access is something that every boat-show-goer knows to ask about. If the oil fill, dipstick, and filters are accessible, and if you can inspect the belts easily, then even if your inboard is crammed into a seemingly

A Boat for Cruising

PACIFIC SEACRAFT 34

Pacific Seacraft was founded in 1976, changed hands several times, and (as of 2004) was managed by Don Kohlmann, former owner of Ericson Yachts. This explains why Pacific Seacraft used to produce several Ericson models in addition to its line of traditional cruising boats. The 37 was launched in 1980, and the 34 was launched in 1984. The two are similar in appearance with canoe sterns (round) and double headsail sloop rigs. Hulls are solid fiberglass, with outer layers using vinylester resin to help prevent osmotic blisters. The deck is cored with end-grain balsa. An interior pan runs the full length of the boat. The finishwork below is well done and attractive. Headroom is 6 feet 4 inches. The galleys are large, for living aboard. Sailing performance is about what you'd expect for a moderately heavy cruising boat. The best point of sail is reaching. Motion is comfortable. The cockpit is small, which is good for offshore work because it minimizes the amount of water that could flood it; on the other hand, it can quickly get cramped with too many people aboard, and the absence of an afterdeck or side

decks can make moving about the aft end of the boat a little tricky. All in all, an excellent couple's boat for bluewater cruising.

LOA	34'1"
LWL	26'2"
BEAM	10'0"
DRAFT	4'1" OR 4'11"
DISPLACEMENT	13,200 LB.
BALLAST	4,800 LB.
SAIL AREA	534 SQ.FT.
DESIGNER	WILLIAM CREALOCK
PRICE NEW	$190,000
PRICE USED	$59,900 – $66,200 (1984 MODEL) $119,500 – $131,000 (1992 MODEL) $232,000 – $255,000 (2000 MODEL)
SIMILAR BOATS	MASON 33 CABO RICO 34/36 CALIBER 35 LRC PACIFIC SEACRAFT 37

[Reprinted with permission from *Your First Sailboat: How to Find and Sail the Right Boat for You*, by Daniel Spurr (International Marine/McGraw-Hill, 2004)]

tight cavity you may have the access you need. If bigger jobs can be done by removing panels, that's good, too. But if obstructions are molded in place or if everyday contact is awkward, messy, or inconvenient, then engine access is indeed a problem. Apply the same sorts of tests to battery banks, generators, steering gear, tanks, and your electric panel.

Housekeeping

You already know most of what you need to know about keeping house afloat. Feeding people, organizing space, encouraging order—the needs at sea are the same as they are at home. Common sense is the best guide to adapting your land-learned priorities and routines to managing shipboard life. But experience is helpful, too. Carol and I have learned as we cruised, we've talked with others, and we've read books. Maybe some of what we've learned can help you better handle housekeeping afloat.

Attitude

When I step aboard a boat, I exchange my disinterested, couch-potato, shirker approach to housework for a concern with details. While disorder follows in my wake at home, it disturbs me afloat. Carol harps about picking up the house, but I'm the one who gets strung out about loose gear left around the boat. She cooks and shops and stows aboard, but I'm much more involved than I am at home.

This change, I think, is more than just a quirk of personality. Seamanship and "housekeeping" are really one and the same.

I might rather wear the gold braid than the galley apron, but either way it's my job to make sure things are shipshape. Due more to a resistance to *mal de mer* than to any natural aptitude or popular acclaim, I do the cooking when we're underway, but I think my major contribution to housekeeping is in recognizing how important it is. Our hull may be able to take pounding over big waves, but can our cabin do so without spewing forth its carefully stowed contents? We could press on after dark, but who wants to cook underway? How much stability, dryness, and order can we maintain under sail? That's the cruiser's true challenge; those are the things that make a boat a home. It's tempting to get underway immediately after breakfast, but setting sail before cleaning up the galley and doing the dishes makes those jobs five times as difficult and can sew the seeds of bigger problems. Cruising is a delicate balance between the nautical and the domestic. Too often I've come down from swashbuckling around on deck to a "downstairs" made unlivable by my heroics—and a crew no longer much interested in sharing it with me. A good cruising sailor remembers that his boat is also a house.

Galley Management

The foremost domestic concern for cruisers is food. Stowing, preparing, and serving food looms large in the cruising life. It's tempting and often fun to duplicate shoreside treats, but you can't cook consistently to shoreside standards. Even the best-equipped cruising galleys can't match the space and equipment of the average kitchen. And where can the cruising cook find the time to produce Cordon Bleu meals, never mind the ingredients? "Eating to cruise" comes before "cruising to eat" aboard *Shere Khan*, but that doesn't mean a steady diet of canned beans.

Simplicity is a virtue in cruising cuisine. Meals that demand precise timing and oven temperature and constant attention are tough to do on a boat, even at anchor or in a slip. Simplify from the outset. One-pot meals like stews and chowders tend themselves. Realistic planning will do a lot to ensure successful meals. Take into account that things taste better on a boat.

A Boat for Cruising

TAYANA 37

The popular Tayana 37 began life as the CT 37; it then had its name changed in 1979. The builder was Ta Yang of Kaosiung, Taiwan, which built 560 of these heavy-displacement double-enders. The Tayana 37 represents the better side of Taiwan boatbuilding during its heyday of the 1970s and 1980s. The interiors are all wood, with a great deal of solid teak and hand-carved detailing. It has a full keel with cutaway forefoot. Construction is strong, but the prospective buyer must be aware of certain areas, such as custom Taiwanese metalwork (which may be of low-quality alloys) and the inappropriate use of plywood (such as in cockpit seats). As with all boats, retain a competent surveyor before finalizing your purchase. Standard diesel engines have included Yanmar, Perkins, and Volvo. Spars may be wood or aluminum, with the latter much preferred. Perry himself recommends the cutter rig over the ketch. It has a reputation for being initially tender (it heels quickly and then stops, which some might object to, but this quality does take the snappiness out of the roll) and having some weather helm (which can be at least partly corrected with good sails and by raking the mast forward). This is a go-anywhere boat.

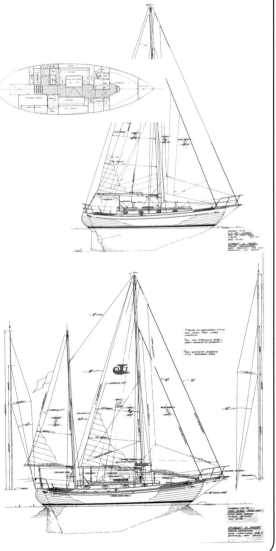

LOA	36'8"
LWL	31'10"
BEAM	11'6"
DRAFT	5'8"
DISPLACEMENT	24,000 LB.
BALLAST	7,340 LB.
SAIL AREA	864 SQ.FT. (SLOOP) 768 SQ.FT. (KETCH)
DESIGNER	ROBERT PERRY
PRICE NEW	NOT IN PRODUCTION
PRICE USED	$59,300 – $68,200 (1979 MODEL) $67,800 – $74,500 (1982 MODEL) $123,000 – $135,500 (1992 MODEL)
SIMILAR BOATS	HANS CHRISTIAN 34/36 MARINER 36 CT 37 AND 38 HANS CHRISTIAN 38

[Reprinted with permission from *Your First Sailboat: How to Find and Sail the Right Boat for You*, by Daniel Spurr (International Marine/McGraw-Hill, 2004)]

Shoot for ample, hot, and hearty before you worry about sophisticated or gourmet.

Then you can expand your horizons. Two of the best ways we have found to go beyond the basics are precooked meals and foraging. You don't have to be a Martha Stewart disciple to know that casseroles, lasagnas, and even baked goods like brownies or coffee cakes can be whipped up ashore, frozen, and enjoyed to the fullest days later onboard. When my sister goes cruising, she deep-freezes steaks, whole chickens, and even bladders full of her favorite boxed wines to take aboard. Even without a freezer they keep for days, and they add cold power to the icebox. For passagemaking, for the first meals of a cruise, or to build a cruising menu around, precooked meals are convenient, and what goes into them isn't limited by what you can do or carry in your galley.

Returning from a shoreside jaunt with something for the table is one of the joys of cruising. It could be a fudge factory on Mackinaw Island, a farm stand on Maryland's Eastern Shore, a bakery offering baguettes and chocolate croissants in Marigot, St. Martin, or a yogurt shop near the port at Piraeus, Greece, but the place where you're cruising most likely offers something edible that you couldn't (or wouldn't) have brought with you. Lobsters, swordfish, tuna, crabs, mussels, beach peas, blueberries, coconuts—chances are you're close to the source of a local delicacy. Markets are different from Ft. Lauderdale to Fiji, but they're not like the ones at home. Buying local food is a great way to get to know where you are.

It's something of an irony that we take off in our plastic boats to try to escape our plastic world. It's even more ironic to me that plastic, a dirty word ashore, is a lifesaver on a cruising boat. Ziploc bags solve a multitude of problems. Food, clothes, gear, and anything else that needs to be kept dry can be protected. We wonder how we went to sea without them.

Plastic jugs are fine for decanting anything that comes in a glass container. I've sailed with beer in bottles from time to time with only a few scars to show for it, but a good rule is to leave glass on the dock and take the beer and soda in cans. Glass can break, which means that sooner or later it will. Tup-perware seems made for a boat. From flour to matches, from canapés to a canister for flares, we keep house with party-marketed, tight-lidded plastic containers from stem to stern.

You never miss potable water until the tank runs dry. Fresh water is an obvious essential. Your tank capacity and setup have a lot to say about whether you should carry extra water, but for emergencies and replenishment, an extra 5-gallon jug is good to have along. Many boats today rely on watermakers (i.e., desalinators) and enjoy freedom from the dockside hose— but only at a price of complication. Whatever can break on a boat sooner or later will break, and watermakers are no exception. If you don't have one you won't have to repair it—but then again, I feel the same way about power windows on cars.

Water conservation makes good cruising sense. I always turn off the pressure water at night. It's quieter, and that way drips don't escalate into leaks. It's also sound practice to have a manual foot pump for fresh water in the galley. With a mechanical pump in place, you can still use the water in your tanks even if the electrically operated pressure system isn't working. It's also a way of limiting the water that goes down the drain due to washing hands or dishes. Steaming food rather than boiling it saves on water, too. So do shorter showers. On transatlantic trips I bathe in seawater using Joy or other dish detergent (which produces a passable saltwater lather).

It's hard to cruise without paper towels, and harder still without toilet paper. Carol and I overbuy when we can and stuff odd stowage nooks with paper goods sealed in Ziploc bags. Speaking of paper, trash can mount up quickly during a cruise. A lazarette or cockpit locker that accepts half a dozen full trash bags is an excellent design feature. We toss biodegradable garbage overboard when we're well offshore, but we've stepped over and swum through enough paper and plastic at beaches around the world to think it's worth the inconvenience to keep that sort of trash aboard until we can dispose of it ashore. If you're not convinced, consider this factoid, which I came across in a news magazine recently: the quantity of palletized plastic adrift in the world's oceans outweighs the biomass

of plankton by a factor of six. Apocryphal? I'm not betting on it. If sailors won't be bothered to take care of the oceans, it's hard to imagine who will.

Most of the world's islands and naturally beautiful cruising spots have their own difficulties with waste disposal, so sometimes the wait for the right dumpster is a long one. Discarding as much packing material as possible when we bring food aboard helps somewhat and is also a deterrent to roaches (who have been known to lay their eggs in cardboard). We don't have a trash compactor, but squashing cans and compressing whatever we can helps keep the trash from taking over the boat.

Since space is limited, galley items need to pull their own weight. We have pots that can stack like a double boiler to conserve space on our two-burner stove. In addition to these plus what pans we can fit in, we carry a good can opener, a sharpening stone, various knives (paring, carving, hacking), a flame-control toaster (for use atop our gas burners), a megapot for lobsters and pasta, a camping skillet with a folding handle, nonskid cups and plates (made

by coating their bottoms with a layer of contact cement), and a pressure cooker. Our boat is a 25-foot-long universe. While neither blender nor microwave have yet made their way aboard, many cruisers wouldn't cast off without them.

Comfort and Cleanliness

Sleeping bags are good on boats, but even lightweight ones are hot on a warm night. Crisp sheets are nice in the tropics or deep summer, but they're troublesome. Fleece bedrolls and blankets are versatile and lightweight yet warm. Your choice of onboard bedding is a personal one, but it involves stowage and maintenance as well as comfort. Avoid down-filled bags or quilts. They are nearly impossible to dry when they get wet— and get wet they will.

Thin cotton towels are much better than larger, thirstier beach towels, because they take up less space and dry in half the time.

I like to keep an all-purpose spray cleaner plus a heavy-duty grease-cutter aboard. My sister uses nontoxic, biodegradable Simple Green because it is kind to the environment. Hand soap and dish soap plus something to freshen up the head are also welcome in the cleaning locker. In addition to the normal rags, sponges, wipes, and chamois deck mop, we've found a battery-powered minivacuum cleaner very useful.

I learned the hard way to mount the galley fire extinguisher where I can get at it without reaching across the stove, which, after all, is the most likely source of a galley fire. Safety belowdecks is just as critical as it is topside. Sufficient, substantial, well-placed handholds, rounded corners, nonskid companionway treads, and a slip-proof sole in the galley go a long way to promote it. Your stove could do more harm than most hurricanes, so respect it well.

The trials of living on a boat are manageable, and the errors you make are unlikely to prove grave. The process, however, has taught us a lot. That's one of the biggest joys of cruising.

The companionway steps in the Oceanis 323 have a nonskid overlay, and each step is higher at its ends than in the middle, which makes the steps much easier to negotiate when the boat is heeled.

Engine Power

My experience, expertise, and philosophy when it comes to engines are summed up best in Sir Francis Chichester's admission: "The truth is that I hate motors on a sailing ship. I resent them and therefore I neglect them." And yet I've been cruising happily for decades. I therefore offer myself as living proof that you need not be a mechanic to cruise. You do, however, need to know how important "motors on ships" can be. You need to respect your engine—because if you respect it you will take at least minimal care of it—and respect starts with an idea of what can happen when you neglect it.

Shere Khan's engine when I bought the boat was a Volvo MD 1 diesel, which I later replaced with a BMW. Both of these single-cylinder 7 hp inboard diesels have taught me a lot. Both have given me whole seasons of downtime, seasons in which I came to identify and sympathize with Lin and Larry Pardey and other missionaries of the joys of engineless cruising. I assisted in not one but two rebuilds of my MD 1, losing friends and gaining mechanics along the way. You can't rebuild a flywheel, though, and when ours cracked I bought the shiny BMW. To fit it I had our prop repitched, but the old two-blade nevertheless proved too big for the lighter, higher-turning BMW. The more modern one-lunger eventually seized under that overload, turning itself into a precision-engineered mooring block. *Shere Khan* currently awaits her third engine.

The biggest lesson I learned in these escapades is that much as I might enjoy the uncertainties and heroics of engineless cruising, no one else, including my spouse, wants to cruise without auxiliary power. And what fun are heroics without witnesses?

Auxiliary power supplied via propeller simplifies things. If we had to sail everywhere, to wait for the wind to get where we're going, to dock and moor and anchor under sail alone, we might never go cruising. How many among us have the time, skills, ingenuity, and temperament to do it all under sail? And without the electricity that engines provide and maintain by recharging the battery bank, cruising would be, if not Stone Age, at least gaslit. The modern auxiliary makes a sailboat into an elegant cruising package: Take the wind where you find it. Go where it takes you. Then turn on the engine to get where you want to be.

We're probably safer because of our engines. It's true, as the Pardeys point out, that 20 of the 27 boats that were beached and wrecked at Cabo San Lucas, Mexico, when a hurricane swept the anchorage in late 1982 had engines. Because they were too

SECONDARY FUEL FILTER

ENGINE OIL DIPSTICK

OIL FILLER CAP

FRESHWATER EXPANSION TANK

BATTERY BANK

Removing the companionway steps on the Oceanis 323 provides access to the diesel engine. The "engine room" on a small cruising sailboat is almost always a cramped compartment like this, but at least here the most frequently serviced items are placed where they're easy to reach. It's best to check the engine oil and freshwater cooling system expansion tank levels before you start the engine, especially if you've been away from the boat for a-while. The battery bank is conveniently located, but the oil filter (out of sight at top left) will be harder to reach. Some engines include a small pump for getting old engine oil out of the crankcase when the time comes for an oil change. On others you have to suck the old oil out through the dipstick tube using a manual or electric pump.

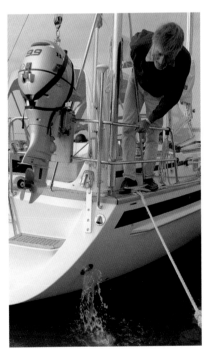

Make sure there is healthy cooling water flow in the exhaust each time you start an engine. If the flow is reduced or absent, shut down the engine and start looking for the cause. Is the raw-water seacock open? If not, you've found the cause. If it's open, close it and remove the raw-water strainer for inspection. If that's clean, the raw-water pump might have a broken impeller.

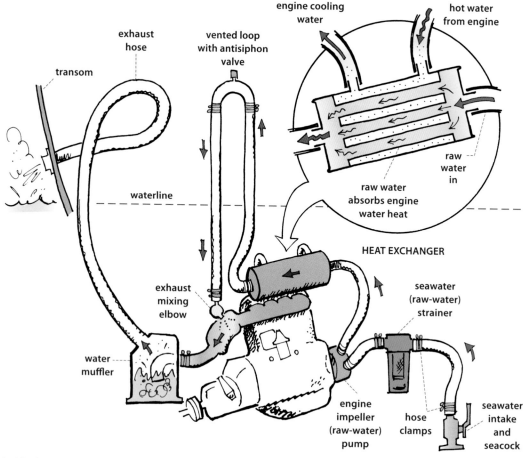

engine cooling water

hot water from engine

exhaust hose

vented loop with antisiphon valve

transom

raw water in

waterline

raw water absorbs engine water heat

HEAT EXCHANGER

exhaust mixing elbow

seawater (raw-water) strainer

water muffler

engine impeller (raw-water) pump

hose clamps

seawater intake and seacock

Typical freshwater cooling system for an inboard diesel engine.

small, or their cooling-water intakes clogged with sand, or they were immobilized by fouled props, those auxiliaries failed when called on to keep their boats out of terminal trouble. From that you might conclude that your engine can save you only if it works. The other point, however, is that an engine is no substitute for seamanship. Yours can't always get you out of situations you shouldn't have gotten yourself into. When my engine is running I'm constantly ask-

ing myself, "What if it quits?" I am mentally mapping escape routes, imagining alternatives, and looking for "places to set down." Make your engine as dependable as possible, but don't depend on it too much. If you find yourself skirting a dangerous lee shore, with surf crashing on rocks just a few hundred yards away and with too much or not enough wind to claw offshore should your engine quit, you are depending on it too much.

Driving a boat under power involves some basics. Reverse provides braking power, but don't depend on it the way you depend on the brakes in a car. Boats are heavy, engines can quit, props fold up or snag. Try not to test the stopping power of the engine any more than necessary.

Slow down to change gears.

Check for water flow through the exhaust at every startup and monitor engine temperature and oil pressure often. Make sure the transmission is in neutral before you start the engine. I prefer single-lever controls because they simplify maneuvering. And if you have to reach through the wheel to reach the throttle/gearshift lever, it becomes much harder than necessary to coordinate engine and rudder.

Diesel versus Gasoline Engines

The diesel engines of a generation ago were too heavy and bulky for sailboats, and gasoline inboard auxiliaries—most notably the Universal Atomic 4 —were truly universal. Today you can still find a Universal Atomic 4 on the occasional older boat—still running fine if faithfully maintained—but virtually all new boats and most older ones have diesel inboards these days. Diesels remain heavier and more expensive than their gas analogs, but the disparity is much less than it used to be. Modern diesels are smoother running, lighter, smaller, more reliable, less smelly, quieter, and in every way superior to their predecessors, and they retain the chief advantages of a diesel—they offer freedom from spark-and-coil ignition worries, and they're workhorses of prodigious capability and fabled endurance. Above all, they are safer.

Diesel fumes are noxious, but gas fumes are volatile and explosive. They are also heavier than air and prone to settle in the bilge, awaiting only a spark to ignite them. (The reason this is not a problem in a car is that a car's engine compartment is open underneath, with no bilge in which fumes can pool.) It's true that diesel fuel can cause an onboard fire—I know of one instance in particular in which a combination of atomized diesel from a loose injector and an electrical spark ignited a to-the-waterline incineration of a sailboat—but it's man-bites-dog news when that happens. Gasoline fires, on the other hand, happen all too often. Those of us who grew up with gasoline inboards know that you can live perfectly safely with these engines if you keep your fuel lines tight, wipe up all fuel spills, run the blower for at least 5 minutes after fueling or upon coming aboard, maintain switches and wires so as to eliminate sparks, and are generally careful. Diesel engines, on the other hand, require no such precautions.

This 6 hp single-cylinder long-shaft outboard engine is mounted on a bracket on the transom of a Tanzer 22. This is a four-stroke Nissan motor (model year 2003) yet weighs just 60 pounds and looks no larger than a 6 hp two-stroke, an indication of just how far outboard technology has progressed in recent years. Note that the long shaft for this engine model is 5 inches longer than the standard shaft.

Most sailors (and therefore most modern builders) prefer diesel. (See page 456 for more on diesels.)

Outboard versus Inboard Engines

A third option for auxiliary power is an outboard engine, which is almost always gas rather than diesel powered. Outboards are versatile and come big enough to push many good-sized cruising hulls. Their economy, light weight, and serviceability make outboards attractive for boats up to, say, 27 feet long. A 24-footer with a transom-hung outboard may have as much interior room for cruising accommodations as a 27-footer with an inboard engine. A transom-hung outboard makes a sailboat easier to dock under power, too, because you can steer with the engine in reverse, at which point the rudder is relatively ineffective. And an outboard gasoline engine poses little fire risk because, like a car engine, any fumes it generates escape to the big outdoors rather than pooling onboard.

Outboard engine technology has made huge leaps forward in response to antipollution regulations over the past decade. The two-cycle engines of yesteryear—like the two-stroke engine in a lawnmower—were notorious air polluters because the lubricating oil was mixed with the fuel and only partially burned in the combustion cycle. Unburned hydrocarbons and other pollutants in the exhaust found their way into the atmosphere in copious quantity. Newer two-cycle outboards trade the traditional carburetor for electronic fuel injection (EFI) or direct injection, making for much more efficient combustion and greatly reduced pollution. And the new wave of four-cycle outboards—with Yamahas and Hondas leading the way—use recirculating rather than mixed oil for lubrication, just as inboard engines do, and are thus even cleaner, albeit still somewhat heavier and more expensive.

Having your power hanging off the transom presents problems, though. Following seas are one concern. Loss of power due to pitching is another. Cavitation is a third. You can mount an outboard in an enclosed well, but it needs a lot of air to keep from starving. Also, chances are you still can't sink the prop into consistently undisturbed water flow or move it far enough forward to be effective when you're hobbyhorsing over head seas. Motorsailing with an outboard that's offset from the centerline can make course keeping problematic. So too may be tilting it clear of the water for sailing. Outboard brackets can be clever but are often cranky, and leaning over the transom is a poor way to spend your time afloat. In a monohull less than 25 feet long or a multihull less than 30 feet, an outboard engine may be the only option. Nevertheless, due to the drawbacks of outboards, I recommend an inboard if you have the choice.

How Much Power?

It's legitimate to wonder how big an engine you'll need. Matching the prop to the engine is, I wince to suggest, important, too. How much fuel should you carry? What size batteries are best? Do you need a generator for battery charging when the engine isn't running, and if so, how big?

An engine that's too small for its application can overwork itself into an early grave. One that's too big is saddling you with unnecessary weight and tankage and may also harm itself due to running under insufficient load. A properly sized engine is quieter, faster, and cheaper. Hull speed ($1.34 \times \sqrt{\text{waterline length}}$) is a realistic target speed. Beyond hull speed you'd need a lot more power to achieve just a little more speed, and most of that added power would be wasted, simply causing your boat to squat deeper in the stern and raise a bigger quarter wave. A realistic estimate for the power required to reach hull speed is 1 hp per 500 pounds of displacement. Then add 25 percent or so for survival situations, upwind passaging, or stemming big currents and head seas.

For example, *Shere Khan* weighs 5,800 pounds, and her hull speed is 6.14 knots. To get her there takes one horsepower for every 500 pounds of weight, or 11.6 horsepower total. Add a 25 percent safety margin, and you have a requirement of 14.5 hp. No wonder I burned up my 7-horse engines!

Hull forms vary. Narrow boats are easier to push through the water than beamy ones, so pounds per horsepower calculations are necessarily approximate. Using a benchmark, though, is much better than simply accepting someone else's choice of engine size on faith.

Propeller

Most of us use an engine selected by a builder or designer, but there's still no reason we can't match that power plant to a prop of optimal diameter and pitch. Chances are your inboard is fitted with a reduction gear that matches engine crankshaft speed (about 3,000 maximum rpm, on average) with the most efficient range of prop speeds (typically about 1,000 to 1,500 rpm). Thus, typical reduction-gear ratios are 2:1 and 3:1. Reducing shaft speed, however, means that you need a larger propeller to maintain comparable thrust. Prop choice might be simpler if we confined it to engine efficiency, but what does your propeller do to your sailing performance?

Big, three-bladed props are ideal for pushing boats like ours through the water, but they create enough drag to slow your sailing speed by as much as 40 percent. Reducing drag under sail means suffering some inefficiency under power. (Conversely, optimal powering means compromised sailing.) By chipping away at the problem for generations, however, sailors have developed some practical answers.

Two-bladed props have less drag than comparable three-bladed wheels, and the ability to immobilize them behind and aligned with the trailing edge of a skeg or keel when under sail streamlines them even more. But by reducing the number of blades you increase blade loading, and increased prop loads lead to cavitation (vibration due to uneven pressure over a prop's surface) and wasted engine power. The bigger you make your propeller, the bet-

UNDER POWER   UNDER SAIL

Typical powerboat three-blade

Typical sail three-blade

Fixed sail two-blade

Folding sail two-blade

Feathering Max-Prop two-blade

Feathering Max-Prop three-blade

Feathering Autoprop three-blade

Common propeller configurations as seen from astern when the boat is under sail and under power.

ter it deals with these problems, but—given a requisite hull/prop clearance of 15 percent of prop diameter and a low-drag priority—there are limits on size. Increased pitch adds thrust but slows blade speed. It's a complex proposition.

A feathering prop is an elegant solution. When the boat is under sail, water pressure rotates the propeller's geared blades into the straight fore-and-aft position, thus presenting minimum drag. When the engine is started and the shaft starts spinning, on the other hand, the resultant centrifugal force causes the blades to rotate to a preselected, optimally efficient pitch. Feathering blades lack the built-in helical twist of fixed blades and thus aren't as efficient in forward gear, but they're more efficient than fixed blades in reverse because their leading edges always pivot into the direction of rotation. Though more costly and complex than conventional props, feathering types have proven durable and efficient and are generally seen as the best combination of low drag under sail and good thrust under power.

Folding props originated on high-performance racing sailboats, where minimizing drag was the overriding objective. Like feathering props, folding props are closed by water pressure and opened by the torque of a spinning shaft. They have historically performed worse under power but much better under sail than the alternatives. Because you can "hide" large-diameter (and therefore powerful) blades by folding them, it's possible to mount an oversized folding prop that performs better under power yet provides the streamlining that minimizes drag under sail.

Keep in mind that nine times out of ten, or maybe even ninety-nine times in a hundred, the prop that comes with a sailboat provides suitable and satisfactory service to the cruiser. In cases where naval architects and engineers set about finding a suitable match between engine and prop for a particular boat, more often than not their choice is determined by experiment and observation as well as theoretical calculations and statistical predictions.

Finding the ideal prop remains, however, a worthwhile and realistic pursuit, especially if you repower your boat. Carrying a spare prop has always made me feel well prepared, and I've needed it, too.

The Electrical System

Boat batteries are discharged more deeply and charged less frequently than car batteries. Marine use therefore demands deep-cycle batteries. The possible exception might be a dedicated battery to crank the engine, but most cruisers prefer a more flexible battery-bank configuration in which any one of the batteries can serve as a house battery, operating onboard appliances, as well as start the engine.

Deep-cycle batteries have fewer, thicker lead plates and can tolerate repeated deep-discharge cycles much better than standard, thin-plate car batteries. The maximum ampere-hour rating for most deep-cycle batteries tends to be a bit less than that for comparably sized automotive batteries, but more of a deep-cell's capacity is actually available in use.

The familiar wet-cell construction, with the lead plates immersed in a liquid electrolyte, is still a good choice for all-around performance, but gel-celled batteries, while not as durable as an optimally maintained wet cell, are more forgiving and require no maintenance. The same is true of AGM (absorbed glass mat) batteries. Both gel-celled and AGM types come at a substantial price premium compared with wet-cell batteries, but unless you're the

TYPICAL POWER CONSUMPTION OF ELECTRICAL LOADS (12 VOLTS)

Equipment	Consumption
Anchor light	1.0 amp
Anchor windlass	40–300 amps
Autopilot	1/3–30 amps
Bilge blower	2.5 amps
Bilge pump	5.0 amps
Cabin fan	0.2–1.0 amp
Cabin light (incandescent)	1.5–3.5 amps
CD player/stereo	1.0 amp on up (depending on amplification)
Chartplotter	0.5–3.0 amps
Depth sounder	0.1–0.5 amp
Fluorescent light	0.7–1.8 amps
Freshwater pump	5.0 amps
GPS	0.5–1.0 amp
Knotmeter	0.1 amp
Laptop computer	5.0 amps
Masthead light	1.0–1.7 amps
Radar	4.0–8.0 amps
Refrigerator (typical)	5.0–7.0 amps
Running lights (port, starboard, and stern)	3.0 amps
Spotlight	10.0 amps
Spreader lights	8.0 amps
SSB (receive) (transmit)	1.5–2.0 amps / 25–35 amps
Strobe light	0.7 amp
VHF (receive) (transmit)	0.7–1.5 amps / 5.0–6.0 amps
Wind speed indicator	0.1 amp

[Reprinted with permission from *Boatowner's Mechanical and Electrical Manual: How to Maintain, Repair, and Improve Your Boat's Essential Systems*, 3rd ed., by Nigel Calder, (International Marine/McGraw-Hill, 2005)]

accept a charge a little faster and don't carry the price markup that usually accompanies marine items.

The capacity of your battery (or battery bank) is determined by your requirements. List all the electrical appliances aboard. Determine the amperage draw of each using ratings given on nameplates, in manuals, or in online catalogs. Multiply the amps for each item by the hours per day that you use it. Add the resulting amp-hours for all items, then try to at least double the total in your battery capacity. (Discharging a battery to more than 50 percent of capacity will wear it out fast.) Finally, build in a cushion of at least 25 percent. If your daily draw is 100 amp-hours, a 250 amp-hour battery is the minimum that will supply your needs with once-a-day recharging. A 400 amp-hour battery bank (two 200 amp-hour batteries connected in parallel) would cost twice as much and weigh a lot more, but it could prove a good investment if you've got room for it—providing an ample reserve, snappy recharging, and good battery life.

Heat reduces battery efficiency, and the hydrogen gases

type of sailor who will maintain your batteries faithfully, the no-maintenance feature justifies the higher price. Trojan, Rolls, and Surrette are leading wet-cell battery manufacturers. Deka and West Marine offer leading gel-cells, and Lifeline and Optima lead the AGM models.

Deep-discharge wet-cell golf-cart batteries are another viable option for cruising sailors. These do not have as high a cycle life as marine wet cells but

DAILY POWER REQUIREMENTS (12 VOLTS) OF A HYPOTHETICAL CRUISING BOAT ANCHORED OFF A BAHAMIAN BEACH

Equipment	Rating	Hours of Use (in 24 hours)	Total Load (in 24 hours)
6 lights	1.5 amps each	2 hours each = 12	18 amp-hours
1 refrigeration compressor	5 amps	10 hours	50 amp-hours
Masthead navigation lights	1.5 amps	8 hours	12 amp-hours
2 fans	1 amp each	5 hours each = 10	10 amp-hours
VHF radio, CD player, etc.	2 amps total	5 hours total	10 amp-hours
		TOTAL	100 amp-hours

Notes:

1. Power consumption will vary enormously according to the boat's intended cruising area. Refrigeration and fan usage in northern climates will be a fraction of that in the tropics.
2. Large items of occasional and short-term use, such as an electric anchor windlass, can in most instances be ignored, since they have little impact on the overall picture. On the rare occasions when sustained use is required, as when breaking out a deeply embedded anchor, the engine can be run during operation to provide a charging backup.
3. This example is for a boat with modest and simple electrical needs. It does not include inverter-based loads.

[Reprinted with permission from *Boatowner's Mechanical and Electrical Manual: How to Maintain, Repair, and Improve Your Boat's Essential Systems*, 3rd ed., by Nigel Calder, (International Marine/McGraw-Hill, 2005)]

generated in recharging need to be dissipated, so try to find a well-ventilated spot outside the engine room for the battery box. Batteries need to be restrained and strapped down securely on a sailboat—a dedicated battery box is best. Dirt on a battery case can form a mild short between the terminals that saps an idle battery, so keep batteries clean. I used to feel clever coating the cable-to-terminal connections with Vaseline to isolate and protect them until I read Dave Gerr's contrary advice in *The Propeller Handbook*: "High current means high temperature. This can liquefy grease so it trickles onto the battery top forming a dirty, salty path be-tween battery poles. Clean the battery top with a solution of baking soda and water to foam the grease away. Then wipe clean and reconnect. To protect your terminals just brush some polyurethane varnish over them once the connection has been securely made."

The advent of an American Boat and Yacht Council (ABYC, the standard-setting body for American boatbuilding) requirement that there be a reserved battery for all but hand-cranked engines means that most modern boats are set up that way. Cruising sailors can meet the requirement either with a dedicated cranking battery or with two deep-cycle house banks that are alternated in use, the reserve bank being always in a fully charged state. Let's look at the latter first.

Two deep-cycle house banks provide flexibility, but they must be charged in parallel—usually by means of a manual battery selector switch that can be turned to battery (or bank) #1, battery #2, or both. The batteries in both banks should be of similar type so as to have similar charge rates—otherwise one bank will be chronically under- or over-charged. *Note that if your boat is equipped with this type of switch, selecting the "OFF" position while the engine is running may destroy the alternator diodes. Consult your owner's manual.*

One disadvantage of two house banks is that each bank has only half the capacity of the single bank you could obtain by connecting all the batteries in parallel. A bank with only half the capacity will be discharged more deeply between charges and will thus have a shorter life. This brings us back to the first alternative above: a single big house bank augmented with a dedicated engine-cranking battery. An automotive battery is a good choice for the latter, because it will provide better, cheaper cranking power than a deep-discharge type. Charging a cranking battery in parallel with a deep-cycle battery bank is not a good idea, however. It is better to add a second alternator and create two isolated battery systems. There is a cost in money, complexity, and space for this arrangement, but the result could be well worth the effort on a bigger boat with more critical electrical needs.

Alternators vary in charging output, but charging time is generally controlled by a voltage regulator. To prevent overcharging, the final stages of charge generally are meted out very slowly. Belt your alternator so that it produces its maximum

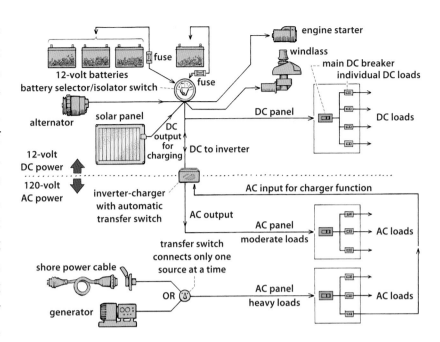

A schematic for a cruising boat with DC and AC electrical systems. AC power comes from shore (via a marina receptacle), from an on-board diesel generator, or from the battery bank via the inverter side of the inverter-charger. DC power comes from the battery bank, which is recharged by the engine (via the alternator), the solar panels, or by shore power or the generator via the charger side of the inverter-charger. Note that the largest DC power draws—the engine's starting motor and the anchor windlass—are wired directly to the battery bank, bypassing the DC electrical panel. The AC system isn't necessary on a cruising sailboat, though more and more boats have one.

output at engine speeds close to idle (for charging at anchor, etc.) and depend on the regulator to control the flow at higher speeds. Many cruisers prefer manually adjustable regulators that let them adjust the charge rate to suit their needs. Paying the premium for a high-output multistage alternator seems worth it to shorten charging times and stretch battery life.

Lots of cruising sailboats are big enough to carry genera-

tors. Once you settle on a type (gasoline versus diesel is only the beginning of the choices involved), noise and vibration seem the biggest concerns. Simple 12-volt systems are still the rule for cruising, but inverters, shore power, and AC generators can all pump 110/220 volts AC into your shipboard setup. Along with this convenience, however, comes the escalation from a relatively benign 12-volt system to high-voltage service that is unquestionably lethal if improperly handled. Oversized wire, well-placed circuit breakers, voltage and frequency meters, an isolation transformer, and waterproof receptacle covers are all part of a good, safe AC system.

Support Systems

Every inboard engine needs to be fueled, cooled, exhausted, and connected.

Fuel tanks should complement the engine they serve. Gas engines burn more fuel per hour than diesel in most cases, so you should carry more gas than you would diesel to feed the same-sized engine. Diesel engines for small to midsize cruising sailboats burn approximately $1/20$ of a gallon per horsepower per hour at cruising speed. When it was running, *Shere Khan's* 7 hp diesel consumed $7/20$ (about $4/10$) of a gallon per hour. That gave us, with our 10-gallon fuel tank, almost 24 hours of powering between fuel stops. That was great in our 25-footer. For passaging you might like more range, but by ballparking your diesel's consumption rate you can calculate the tankage needed to let you go where you want to.

Raw-water cooling, in which seawater is pumped directly through the engine's cooling passages, was once the standard cooling system. Now most sailboat engines include heat exchangers that allow for efficient transfer of heat from a closed-circuit freshwater cooling system to seawater (and usually provide hot water for shipboard use as well—see illustration page 448). In this configuration the heated seawater is injected into the exhaust through a mixing elbow after it leaves the heat exchanger. Since seawater doesn't circulate through the engine's cooling passages, internal corrosion is minimized. Also aimed at combating corrosion are the sacrificial zinc anodes (commonly called zincs) incorporated within most cooling systems. Inserted in a spot where it (rather than the block itself) will be preferentially consumed by galvanic action, a zinc should be secured so that it remains in complete contact with the block even as it deteriorates, and it should be replaced before it deteriorates completely.

A thermostat governs the cooling flow through your engine and will occasionally de-

Diesel Operator's Checklist

Long after I'd bled my first fuel line and splattered through a few dozen oil changes, I learned that the technical description for a diesel engine is a **compression-ignition engine**. Unlike gas engines, diesels have no spark plugs; rather, it's the compression of air in the cylinder that creates the temperature (over 1,000°F) that ignites the fuel when it is injected in an atomized burst. A diesel that has air, fuel, and adequate compression in its cylinders more or less has to operate. Troubleshooting a diesel can be as frustrating as diagnosing any dormant engine, but keeping those three essentials in mind is a good path to follow.

The compression-ignition process allows diesels to burn fuel that is less volatile than gasoline. It also explains why diesels are built so robustly (to withstand such pressure and explosive power) and why such a high degree of lubrication is required to keep them working. The importance of clean fuel seems clear as well. And, were there no air in the cylinder, combustion-ignition would be a bust.

That's certainly not all you need to know about diesels, but it's more than I knew when I bought my first one in 1971.

Air—I soaked the filter element in diesel, as the manual commanded, but it wasn't until later that I learned of using pressure air (available at your nearest gas station) to clean it out right. After viewing the innards of two diesels during rebuilds, I know that the precise tolerances of the moving parts make dirt a menace. Guard against it by energetically maintaining the filter that guards the air intake.

Fuel—I used to think "contaminated fuel" was a problem purely for those poor folks topping up their tanks in Pago Pago. I never bothered to test U.S. diesel fuel for contamination, any more than I'd fill my Toyota through a sock at the local Shell station. Fuel doesn't have to be very bad to be bad for a diesel, however. The diesel fuel pump, for instance, is not only one of the most precise and sensitive parts of your diesel—it's probably the most expensive. Giving the system consistently clean fuel to work with is a good idea. Just sitting in the tank, fuel without obvious grit or gunk can spawn fungi that can degrade or even halt engine performance.

Make sure your fuel system includes both primary and secondary fuel filters, as most do. Augmenting these with a filter-funnel with a medium to fine screen in it is a good first-line defense. Some fuel additives, particularly one to combat fungi and another to enhance lubricating properties, are worth the expense. So, too, is the nuisance of emptying any spare fuel cans into your main tank anytime you fill up. Keeping spare tanks clean is an obvious key to the health of the main reserve.

Water in the fuel lessens its lubricating abilities and thus threatens your precision workings. Your primary fuel filter should be the type that separates water from fuel. Mount it in the line between the tank and the lift pump that delivers fuel to the engine; that way it will have an unagitated, unaerated supply that lets it give better service than it would if you placed it upstream of the lift pump. Most filters let you just drain water from the bottom of the bowl. Keeping tanks as full as possible minimizes condensation, but you should avoid dry-gas additives, because the alcohol they contain can attack seals in the fuel system.

The factory-fitted secondary filter is geared to screen out finer particles, but it can clog easily and starve the system if you ignore it.

Oil—Diesels are hard on lubricating oil. The oil you use should be specially formulated for diesel service. The current API (American Petroleum Institute) designation is "C" (for compression-ignition). Designations like CC, CD, and CE denote differing additive mixtures, but if the first letter isn't "C," don't use it. I spent more time than I care to remember scouring the Mediterranean for the "DS" oils my manual said I needed. Bringing oil I knew would work from an English-speaking haven would have saved me lots of time and sign language.

Modern oils last better than they used to. The manufacturer's suggested intervals between oil changes may be as high as 100 hours or more. Considering the stakes, however, I like to play it safer—probably every 50 hours or less. I also try to level the boat every 20 minutes or so when I'm motorsailing. Heeling may not actually affect oil lubrication, but I'd rather set my mind at ease than

contribute another mooring block to the world.

It would be nice if more sailboat diesels were fitted with gauges instead of idiot alarm lights for temperature and pressure. Not knowing anything's wrong until a light goes on almost always means doing some damage. Monitor exhaust water; if you don't see cooling water coming out of your exhaust pipe, something is wrong. While you're peering over the transom, check the

exhaust smoke, too. If it's almost invisible, things are fine. If it's black, combustion is less than complete. If it's blue, you're burning oil. If it's white, compression isn't complete. Diesels are rugged. They don't need to be perfect to keep chugging, but by paying attention to their relatively simple signs (though the cures can be complex), you can greatly increase the chances that yours will provide power for as long as you need it.

	Seizure	High exhaust back pressure	Hunting	Rising oil level	Excessive oil consumption	Low oil pressure	Knocks	Misfiring	Loss of power	Poor idle	White smoke	Blue smoke	Black smoke	Overheating	Low compression	Lack of fuel	Cranks, but poor starting	Will not crank	Low cranking speed
Battery low/loose connections																		●	●
Engine overload/rope in propeller	●								●					●					
Auxiliary equipment engaged									●										●
Pre-heat device inoperative					●						●						●		
Plugged air filter					●				●				●				●		
Plugged exhaust/turbocharger/kink in exhaust hose	●				●				●				●				●		
Throttle closed/fuel shutoff solenoid faulty/tank empty																●	●		
Plugged fuel filters							●	●	●							●	●		
Air in fuel lines							●	●	●	●						●	●		
Dirty fuel							●	●	●	●			●				●		
Closed seacock/plugged raw-water filter or screen/plugged cooling system	●													●					
Defective water pump/defective pump valves/air-bound water lines	●													●					
Oil level low	●					●								●					
Wrong viscosity oil	●			●		●								●					●
Diesel dilution of oil	●			●		●								●					
Lift pump diaphragm holed									●							●	●		
Defective injector/poor-quality fuel							●	●	●	●			●				●		
Injection pump leaking								●	●	●						●	●		
Injection timing advanced or delayed							●		●	●				●	●		●		
Too much fuel injected													●						
Piston blowby					●				●	●	●	●	●		●		●		
Dry cylinder walls							●	●	●	●					●		●		
Valve blowby							●	●	●	●					●		●		
Worn valve stems				●									●						
Decompressor levers on/valve clearances wrong/valves sticking									●	●	●	●			●		●		
Dirt in oil pressure relief valve/defective pressure gauge						●													
Governor sticking/loose linkage			●							●									
Governor idle spring too slack										●									
Blown head gasket/cracked head	●			●							●			●	●		●		
Uneven load on cylinders	●													●					
Worn bearings							●		●					●	●				
Seized piston	●								●					●				●	
Water in the cylinders	●			●										●				●	

Diesel engine symptoms and their possible causes.

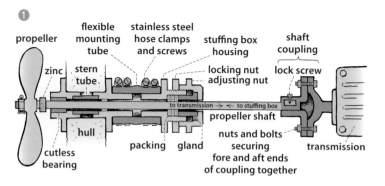

① propeller — flexible mounting tube — stainless steel hose clamps and screws — stuffing box housing — shaft coupling

zinc — stern tube — locking nut adjusting nut — lock screw

to transmission → ← to stuffing box

hull — propeller shaft — transmission

cutless bearing — packing — gland — nuts and bolts securing fore and aft ends of coupling together

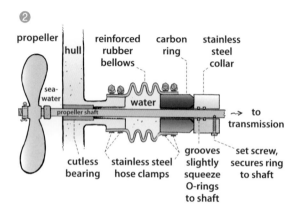

② propeller — hull — reinforced rubber bellows — carbon ring — stainless steel collar

sea-water — water

propeller shaft — → to transmission

cutless bearing — stainless steel hose clamps — grooves slightly squeeze O-rings to shaft — set screw, secures ring to shaft

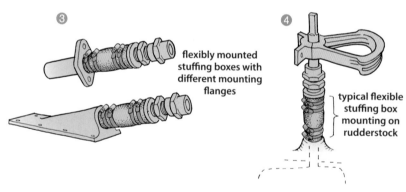

③ flexibly mounted stuffing boxes with different mounting flanges

④ typical flexible stuffing box mounting on rudderstock

1. *A traditional stuffing box, also known as a packing gland.* **2.** *A dripless alternative to a packing gland.* **3.** *Stuffing-box mounts are determined by hull shape. The bottom one is more typical of a sailboat.* **4.** *A through-hull rudderstock needs a stuffing box, too.*

mand attention. If yours malfunctions, remove it and test it in hot water before you replace it. Sometimes, if you have no spare, a frozen thermostat can be revived to let the engine run

cool enough to get you where you're going.

The cooling system's rawwater pump is a predictable Achilles heel in the system.

It's an excellent idea to carry a spare. That way you can replace the original and fix it (usually by replacing an impeller, a comparatively easy task) without any downtime for the engine. Then shelve the fixed pump as your new spare.

A water-lock loop in the exhaust line is essential to keep water from backfilling through the exhaust into the engine. This loop should be as high as possible and as close to the centerline as it can be. Some people fit the line with a positive shut-off to keep following seas from infiltrating the engine room while the boat is under sail. The danger of such an arrangement is that you might inadvertently leave this valve closed when you start the engine. Loops like these, even when they're not shut off, can partly clog with carbon and salt, which adds unwanted back pressure in the exhaust system. Check several times a season that your exhaust passage is clear.

It's nice if the exhaust comes out high up on the transom. That makes it easy to check for appropriate cooling-water flow by monitoring the exhaust, and it also makes it harder for following seas to enter the pipe.

The mixing elbow where gases and water mingle on their way out of the engine is prone to corrosion. It's wise to carry a spare. Use two hose clamps to secure any hose to a through-hull fitting, and make sure they're good-quality stainless steel. If in doubt, check with a magnet—the better grades of stainless steel are nonmagnetic.

So long as it remained strong and silent, I've been content to ignore my engine's gearbox, or transmission. Most transmission problems, says Nigel Calder in his encyclopedic *Boatowner's Mechanical and Electrical Manual*, stem more from the control cables that work them than from the units themselves. Letting your prop freewheel while you sail may induce less drag, but in addition to being noisy it accelerates transmission wear. Indeed, unless your transmission is lubricated even when the engine isn't running, you can burn out the transmission bearings by freewheeling. A shaft brake is the cleanest solution, but with a mechanical transmission you can leave the engine in gear while you're sailing to immobilize the prop. Keep transmission oil clean and topped up.

Stuffing boxes, also known as packing glands, are assemblies that seal the stern tube where the prop shaft exits the hull. Your stuffing box should ideally form a drip-free seal when the shaft is at rest but permit an inflow of a drop or two per minute (from water cooling the packing material in the gland) when the engine is running. I always felt that the worst thing I could do was to overtighten the gland and starve the seal, so I've tolerated the leak I could see to prevent the friction I feared. There are better ways. Drip-Free packing (a modern amalgam of Teflon and carbon that works along with the traditional flax packing) is touted as one. Mechanical seals similar to those on crankshafts are another, but keep in mind that an overflow at the stuffing box may signal that the shaft isn't properly aligned and is deforming the packing by "wobbling" when it turns. At any rate, if the hose that encases the entire Byzantine contraption ruptures or comes loose, the water that comes in will not be measured only in drops. Check the packing gland assembly every now and then.

Going Voyaging

When does a cruise become a voyage? Is it when you go out of sight of land or when you make an overnight passage? Does it take crossing an ocean? I don't know the technical definition, but I think maybe it's when going out and coming back turns into "onward." At any rate, people who cruise fulltime call themselves "voyagers." If you wanted to call voyaging "advanced cruising," you'd have a case, but cruising isn't competitive. I don't buy the idea that the fun I've had poking along the coast from harbor to harbor is somehow inferior to the sublime experiences enjoyed by passagemakers exploring the other side of the world. And yet, the other side of the world can be pretty appealing at times.

Sunrise over the Atlantic from the deck of Ripple, *a 51-foot Hinckley yawl en route to Bermuda from Newport, Rhode Island.*

With a place for everything, and everything in its place—including a solar panel—this boat is set up for voyaging.

Voyaging is obviously different from weekend or port-to-port cruising, but it's just as clearly connected to them. Voyaging is intense, committed, and virtually total, but it's still cruising. It seems to me the height of silliness to embark on a voyage without having gained some experience via coastwise cruising. Voyagers' experience, on the other hand, is a goldmine for coastwise sailors; even if you never leave San Francisco Bay or Long Island Sound, you can learn a lot from books written by voyagers. Their experiences spotlight virtually all the elements involved in successful cruising. Whether conducted on the open ocean or in your armchair via a good book, voyaging deepens your insights, sharpens your priorities, and suggests ingenious solutions to all manner of challenges.

Heavy weather is heavy whether you're on a cruise or a voyage. Even though the chilling thought of leaving port to find sea room has occurred to me once or twice, most of us would prefer to deal with storms at sea by being safe in port. Voyagers stand a better chance than cruisers of being caught at sea in a storm, though the severity and frequency of storms at sea are often overstated.

After a week of cruising for fun you can return to the comforts of home. While you are out there voyaging, though, the comforts of your boat are all the comforts you've got. I treat my boat like a "cabin in the woods" because she's my weekend getaway. When you're voyaging, there is no getaway. Your boat is not your escape, she's your *home* and should be treated as such.

Solutions and systems developed by voyagers trickle down to cruisers, and we sailors are all better off for it. The hope of voyaging someday strengthens my desire to learn what I have to learn to get there. I've crossed oceans on raceboats and crisscrossed the Mediterranean on *Shere Khan,* and those snippets of experience make me want more. If I want to take me and mine around the world, I need to know more about navigation, engine maintenance, weather, seamanship, and much more. Looking out at the horizon reminds me how far I need to go to get there. Just like that first walk down the dock, however, it's just a matter of steps.

A crusing anchorage in New Zealand.

A cruising catamaran approaches Bitter End Yacht Club on the north-eastern tip of Virgin Gorda, British Virgin Islands. The resort's cabins dot the hillside in the distance.

English Harbor, Antiqua.

Voyaging Gear

The gear you take cruising can be as simple or sophisticated as you want to make it. "Keep it simple" suits my needs and philosophies. On the other hand, I have to admit that comfortable cruising beats roughing it. Fulltime cruising makes major demands on gear, equipment, even philosophy. What works for voyagers can work for us all. It's true that passagemaking is different in important ways from weekending, but the lessons learned from the deep experience of the offshore cruisers, especially in terms of what's needed and what works, are good lessons whether you're "taking off" over night or around the globe.

Dinghies

The Howmar Hauler (built of fiberglass with encapsulated foam flotation) that we've had for the past 15 years has served us well. She's 7 feet 11 inches long, has a snappy sailing rig, takes a two-horse outboard, and rows moderately well for a beamy little box. She weighs just 70 pounds, so I can wrestle her onto roof racks or down the dock by myself. She's relatively stable and has a good payload, though stuffing the family of four into

her has always been precarious. And she's not so fancy that we worry much about leaving her unattended wherever we go ashore.

The big problem is that she doesn't stow easily, if at all, aboard *Shere Khan*. We've had to tow her everywhere. That's just barely acceptable for coastal cruising, but in the unlikely event that we were ever to take our 25-footer voyaging, we'd have to bring our dinghy aboard. At that point I'd invest in something like the Nest Egg, a clever combination of two 5-foot 11-inch halves that nest

I found the Nest Egg easy to paddle as well as ship. It makes a great 12-foot sailing dinghy or rowboat when you put the two halves together.

one inside the other on deck and bolt one against the other to make an 11-foot-plus tender.

I've used a number of inflatables. It's hard to argue with the

An inflatable dinghy with small outboard doing taxi service in the British Virgin Islands.

ability to deflate your dinghy for stowage, and modern pumps make the inflation process almost painless. And inflatable or rigid floorboards coupled with longer-than-manufacturer's-issue oars (7 feet is about the effective minimum) make them row almost, though not quite, adequately. An inflatable performs much better with a small outboard than under oars.

Voyagers spend almost 90 percent of their in-port time anchored out. That puts real pressure on the tender. Many long-distance cruisers carry both a rigid dinghy and an inflatable. Taking the beach and ground well becomes more important the more places you have to run your dink ashore, and hard-bottomed boats have proven more durable than even the newly toughened brands of inflatables when landed on rocky shores and rough beaches. I find mounting and dismounting the outboard a minor irritant, and I prefer the simplicity (quiet, exercise, and freedom from security worries) of rowing. For that reason I prefer a rigid dinghy. While there are sailing inflatables, I haven't seen one to set my heart pounding. A sailing dinghy (the Nest Egg is a superior little sailboat, and there are a host of rigid dinks that sail well) is a pure pleasure for exploring anchorages far and near.

Certainly on boats under 30 feet it's tough to find a good place to stow a rigid dinghy, but then it's hard to find a serviceable inflatable that doesn't cost twice the price of a good hard-bottomed dinghy. As with almost everything to do with sailing, there are a lot of variables in dinghy choice, experience offers conflicting directions, and the options are numerous.

Life Rafts

Even when you're not out of sight of land, it's comforting to have a rescue module nestled in its canister on your cabintop. I've often wondered about pulling the cord, but I've never had to do it. The primary purpose of a life raft design is to keep its occupants afloat and alive until they can be rescued. Choices range from canopy-less, unballasted flotation platforms for coastal waters to offshore rafts with durable construction, inflatable floors, closable canopies, and ballast systems. Stowage might be in a canister or valise. Sizes range from two-person up, and prices from

Life rafts come in many weights and sizes. Winslow's super-light (54 pounds, 4-person) extended offshore raft (top) is a survival module designed to keep you afloat until help arrives. This model includes a canopy, ballast system, and basic offshore survival equipment. Additional features including boarding platforms are visible (above) in Winslow's Offshore Plus model (42 pounds, 4-person). Winslow also includes a deck of waterproof playing cards.

less than $1,000 to more than $5,000.

Some sailors have gone so far as to label life rafts "death rafts." They say that having a life raft aboard encourages sailors to leave their boats, sometimes prematurely. Water in the boat doesn't necessarily mean it will sink, these sailors point out. A surprising number of abandoned sailboats survive, while the people who abandon them sometimes don't. "Stay with the boat" is a basic cornerstone of seamanship, and "Don't get in a life raft until you have to step up" has become something of a corollary.

Yet it remains true that there are sailors who owe their lives to their rafts. Some of these survivors suggest that the life raft as designed and sold today puts sailors in too passive a position, one in which waiting to be rescued is the only choice. On the less-traveled waters voyagers like to visit, that wait is likely to be a long one. The alternative is a "survival pod," an escape craft that can be sailed toward safety. You won't find rafts like these in the mainstream, but equipping your dinghy for survival (with positive flotation, a canopy, perhaps a propulsion kite, an EPIRB, and other standard survival gear) is a possible alternative. Steve Callahan, who survived 76 days in a raft and described the experience in the bestseller *Adrift*, suggests that combining a raft with a fixed or inflatable dinghy doubles survival potential. He wishes, too, that he'd had more mobility than his traditional raft afforded. "Ballast systems can keep you upright, but they keep you stationary, too," Callahan reports. The Tinker inflatable lifeboat is one of the few commercially available steps toward providing mobility in a raft.

One thing is certain: stuffing your raft in its canister and forgetting about it until you expect it to save you is like jumping overboard while holding the anchor. Sitting in the sun, touched by the waves, an on-deck canister rarely succeeds in keeping everything inside working perfectly. Every element in your survival system is potentially life saving. Steve Dashew checked his canister and found that flashlight batteries had exploded, knocking out the lights and damaging other essentials. Check that the survival gear you pack with the raft is well considered, that it survives its hibernation, and that the raft release mechanism (I prefer a lashing and a knife as opposed to the automatic hydrostatic release set to pop the canister free when it reaches a preset depth) is operative. Check the lashings every month or so. Most important, have the inflation system inspected and serviced yearly.

Through-Hull Fittings

Start by minimizing the number of holes in your hull. Generally a single raw-water intake can, if plumbed properly, provide the salt water you need. The outlet for the head might be the only other through-hull you'll have to have, but often it is best if the galley sink (with its predictable cargo of food particles) also drains directly overboard. Raise what drains (scuppers, cockpit, anchor well, etc.) you can above the waterline. Use a sump with an overboard pump for shower and head sink, and you'll have reduced the number of easy entrances for the ocean.

Guard those entrances with seacocks mounted on the through-hulls. These heavy-duty ball valves can be made of bronze or one of several newly developed plastics. It makes good sense to close off your through-hull fittings when you leave the boat. That prevents the boat from sinking should a hose let go. It also makes good sense to draw a map of your through-hulls so you don't have to stop and think where each one is should your boat start flooding one day.

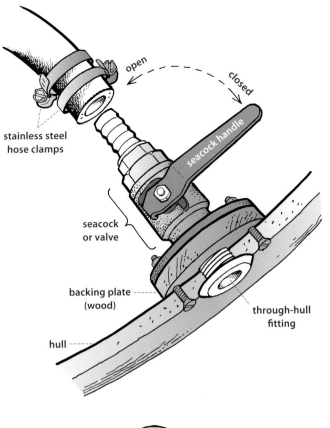

stainless steel hose clamps

open

closed

seacock handle

seacock or valve

backing plate (wood)

through-hull fitting

hull

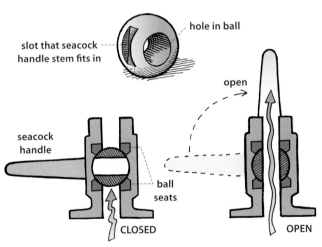

hole in ball

slot that seacock handle stem fits in

seacock handle

open

ball seats

CLOSED

OPEN

A through-hull fitting with seacock threaded onto it. When the seacock handle is perpendicular to the seacock barrel and exiting hose, the seacock is closed. The seacock nipple should be flanged the better to grip the hose, and you want two stainless steel hose clamps, not just one.

Recently I learned that through-hulls located close beneath the mast may become exit portals should lightning strike. The charge coming down the mast may find ground through the fittings and blow holes in your bottom. The farther your through-hulls are from the mast, the less likely this is to happen.

It doesn't take long for salt and corrosion to build up in seacocks and make them difficult to work. Just closing them periodically helps somewhat, but taking them out and lubricating them when you haul out helps even more.

Ground Tackle

Voyagers anchor more often than most of us. They cover enough ground to run into varied and challenging bottom conditions and a variety of holding situations. There's plenty of debate about what to carry, but here are some nuggets of anchoring wisdom that I've distilled:

Bigger is better. Given the ability of most boats to stow anchors securely and easily in rollers at the stemhead, grab for the added security of a bigger anchor. Especially if it comes at almost no handling cost, but even if you have to wrestle with it a bit, bigger is better. It's almost as easy to set and retrieve a 100-pound anchor as a 50-pounder, and the increased holding power of the bigger anchor (which in some cases might be more than doubled) provides safety, peace of mind, and relative freedom from the need to set two anchors or the hassle of setting yours more than once to get it to hold.

Chain is the way. I remember a midnight squall striking the boats we were rafted with in the Channel Islands. While fumbling about on deck making sure our anchor was holding, I heard from the British skipper in the next boat, "Is that *rope*? By God, Maude, the boat next door is anchored with *rope*." Up and down the U.S. East Coast I'd always anchored with nylon line, and when I bought *Shere Khan* in England I set her up the same way. But that was long ago. Stung by the Englishman's scorn, I retrieved from the bilge (where I'd stashed it) the 50 fathoms of chain that had come with the boat. I've been using chain ever since. It's heavy to carry, hard to stow, and awkward to work, but it sure helps an anchor hold. It won't chafe on the bottom, it works well with a chain gypsy on an electric windlass, and it can shorten your scope by a third.

Many cruisers prefer a chain-nylon hybrid rode to all-chain, and this is certainly a viable al-

A cruising sailboat at anchor.

ternative, as demonstrated in Chapter 3. Thirty to 50 feet of chain at the anchor end of the rode will resist chafing on rocks or coral while providing a favorable angle of pull to the anchor and encouraging it to dig in and hold. Meanwhile, the nylon line between the chain and the boat provides the superb shock-absorbing qualities for which nylon is noted. If you choose a hybrid rode you must be careful to match the nylon to the chain and the connecting shackles so that all components are of approximately equal strength, but a hybrid rode can prove an excellent compromise.

But ever since that midnight wake-up call in the Channel Islands, it's been all-chain for me—at least when I'm cruising

away from the sheltered waters of the U.S. East Coast. To overcome the chain's lack of elasticity, I attach one end of a length of nylon line to the foredeck and the other end about 25 or 30 feet down on the chain with a chain claw. Then I take up on this snubber (see Chapter 3) until it takes the strain at the boat end, leaving the top 25 or 30 feet of chain slack. The bitter end of the chain I tie to the bulkhead below with a length of line long enough to let the end of the chain come up through the hawsehole. That way I can cut it if we ever need to leave the chain behind in order to escape an untenable anchorage.

Three anchors isn't a crowd. Finding room for three anchors isn't easy on most small boats, and *Shere Khan* is no exception. Still, if you're going voyaging, or even if you're going to cruise extensively, three's the minimum number of anchors to take. If one doesn't hold well, set two. If you lose one (or if you need a stern anchor), you've got a third. The first two should be oversized. I'd make the third as big as it can be and still be handled in a dinghy or off the transom. This is your kedge anchor—the one you might row out in the dinghy to help you escape a grounding; the one you might deploy from the stern in a crowded, current-riven anchorage; the one you might use as a lunch hook for a picnic stop in light weather; the one you might deploy to windward to keep your boat from beating itself up on the windward face of a dock. When you cruise a lot, you'll find a lot of uses for anchors.

Variety is good. See Chapter 3 for a discussion of anchor types. Between them a plow anchor (e.g., the CQR) and a lightweight anchor (e.g., the Danforth) cover a lot of bases. On bottoms where the plow will bury I prefer it, because it swivels rather than tripping when the wind changes. Chances are the anchor won't break out. On

bottoms that are harder to dig into, the added fluke area and pointed attack of the Danforth provide better holding than a plow that skims. For a third anchor I like the Northill. Its collapsing crosspiece makes it easy to stow, and its grappling approach makes it better in rocks than the other two. But these anchors only scratch the surface, so to speak. Many sailors advocate the Delta (a fixed-shaft plow) over the hinged CQR. Others prefer the Bruce (which is a claw anchor), and still others have been won over by the new generation of roll-stable, lightweight plow types that include the Spade, the Rocna, and the Manson Supreme. The Fortress is an even lighter version of the lightweight Danforth, and it disassembles for stowage. All of these are pictured in Chapter 3.

Windlasses

It's easy to take anchor rollers for granted, but their design, durability, and efficiency are necessary ingredients for frequent anchoring of any boat longer than 27 to 30 feet, as is a good windlass. It can be deep out there. In places like Raiatea and Bora Bora or off the Dutch island of Saba in the Caribbean there's often no

place to drop the hook that isn't 80 or 90 feet deep. Your choices in a place like that are a windlass or an aching back.

And a windlass has other uses. You might need power to pull you off the ground if (when) you get stuck. And how does a wife crank her husband aloft? The answer is a windlass. When you anchor once or twice a weekend in friendly surroundings, a manual windlass might suffice. Suited to small boats, simple, and relatively failsafe, a hand-powered windlass doesn't take as much space on deck or under it as a powered unit. Geared hand-operated units can develop mechanical advantages as high as 40:1 and retrieve more than a foot of rode with each double-action stroke. When you set the hook hundreds of times a year, however, start to worry fulltime about your back, or operate most of the time with minimal crew, a powered windlass becomes a near-necessity.

Those built around electrically powered motors are lightest, cheapest, and most common. Hydraulically operated units are heavier, more rugged, more complex, and more expensive. Determining the pulling power you'll need

A Lofrans horizontal manual windlass.

A horizontal windlass with a chain-only gypsy and separate warping drum. The motor on a horizontal model is abovedecks—easier to maintain but more exposed to the elements and more in the way on the foredeck. The chain contacts the gypsy sprockets through a turn of no more than 90 to 100 degrees on a horizontal windlass, whereas on a vertical windlass the chain wraps more securely through a full 180 degrees before exiting the gypsy and falling through the hawse opening to the belowdecks chain locker.

A vertical electric windlass with a gypsy (around which the chain is wrapped) topped by a warping drum. A vertical windlass takes less deck space than a horizontal model and may be easier to align with the bow roller of a small boat. You need room belowdecks for the motor, however, and manual winching (assuming the windlass has a manual option, which is always a good idea) is awkward. The gypsy on this windlass has sprockets to capture the chain, but a V-shaped groove between paired sprockets will also self-tail a correctly sized nylon rode. A combined gypsy like this is ideal for recovering a chain-nylon hybrid rode. When recovering a hybrid rode with a windlass that has a chain-only gypsy, you have to transfer the loaded rode from the warping drum to the gypsy when you reach the chain portion of the rode. This tricky operation requires taking the load off the rode with a snubber while you make the transfer.

Chain stoppers.

is an issue that I resolve by getting the most muscle I can afford. That's largely because no available windlasses are designed to pull a boat up to its anchor against winds over 25 knots or to yank a dug-in hook out of the bottom. Instead, you should use your engine to come ahead along the rode while the windlass gathers the slack. Snub the rode tight and use the boat's motion to break out the anchor. Because these ideals aren't always easy to put into practice, though, and for that time when you'll want as much power as you can get to move your boat off the shoals or a reef, get as much pulling power as you can afford.

Even if your windlass is fitted with a mechanical brake, relieving the strain from the anchor (especially in waves or a surge or when breaking out a stuck anchor) is prudent. Many sailors use chain stoppers to do this. A snubbing line to provide shock-absorbing capacity works well, too. And make sure your windlass is fixed on deck by a backing plate substantial enough to handle the heavy loads that come with the job.

Many modern units come with a universal gypsy, the

gypsy being the attachment on the windlass drum that grabs the rode. A universal gypsy will accept both rope and chain and is self-tailing. The longer the fall from your gypsy to the bottom of your chain locker, the greater your freedom from jams. When you go to sea, don't forget to make the hawsehole opening watertight.

Because of the loads involved, you need circuit protection in the form of a high-amperage breaker or fuse as close to the battery bank as practicable. (This sort of protection won't, however, prevent overheating due to the motor running overlong or under heavy strain.) Many windlasses have solenoids, and it pays to carry a spare along with replacement brushes. Assuming short periods of use with the engine running, I think it simplest and best to power the windlass from the house batteries rather than inviting the charging and stowage complexities that come with a separate windlass battery.

Other Cruising and Voyaging Gear

The first electronic gear aboard *Shere Khan* was a VHF-FM marine radio my son Will pirated from a junkyard and installed. That was 18 years ago, and we had already been using the boat 18 years. I've yet to get a cell phone. Even the word processor that I'm using now is unfamiliar territory. I'm only peripherally involved in the electronic revolution, but I can nonetheless see that nothing has changed (and improved) the face of cruising more. We don't think twice about watching a live America's Cup race from New Zealand or getting an e-mail from Tanzania. If you can pay for it you don't have to think twice now about making a satellite phone call from the middle of the Indian Ocean (or any other ocean) to any telephone in the world. Communications are critical at sea. For centuries we had multicolored code flags, but now we've got satellites. Communications are no less vital—they're just worlds better.

VHF radio. Still the staple medium of ship-to-ship, coastwise, and ship-to-shore communications, VHF radio is so convenient and affordable that you find it everywhere. And you find everyone on it. Congestion has been eased a bit by separating the talking channels from Channel 16 (the hailing and distress channel), but if you're within 10 or 15 miles of someone or something, chances are you can raise them on VHF. All the newer radios are digital and have digital selective calling (DSC) capability, and within a few years these will be universal. Each DSC radio is assigned a unique Maritime Mobile Service Identity (MMSI) number, so that a boat making a distress call on a DSC radio can be instantly identified by search-and-rescue (SAR) personnel. Further, if the radio is interfaced with a GPS receiver, it will automatically broadcast the boat's location. The DSC distress channel is 70, while VHF Channel 16 is still reserved for analog distress calls.

SSB radio. VHF radio has line-of-sight range—which is roughly 5 miles for boat-to-boat communications with handheld VHF receivers at deck level, up to 15 or 20 miles for boat-to-boat communications between more powerful fixed VHF radios using masttop antennas, and roughly 25 or 30 miles for ship-to-shore calls. For radio communications from midocean, therefore, you may want a single-sideband (SSB) radio, the

PUSH TO TALK

GPS INTERFACE DISPLAY

CURRENT CHANNEL DISPLAY

SQUELCH

CHANNEL SELECT

PRESS FOR NOAA WEATHER

PRESS TO MONITOR CHANNELS 9 AND 16

DISTRESS ALL-STATION ALERT (DSC ONLY)

A fixed-mount VHF-FM radiotelephone with digital selective calling (DSC) capability. This radio is interfaced with a GPS receiver and thus displays the boat's latitude and longitude. If you initiate an automated distress call by pressing the DISTRESS button at lower left, your coordinates will be transmitted with the call.

A handheld VHF-FM radio provides a maximum ship-to-ship communications range of 3 to 5 miles.

range of which is often greater than 1,000 miles. SSB has been a standard way to communicate at sea for the past 20 years and, like VHF, is now making a transition to digital selective calling. It has, however, never been a perfect solution. The radio and antenna together may cost $3,000 to $5,000, and SSB transmissions are vulnerable to atmospheric interference. Even long-range cruisers

have embraced it only half-heartedly.

Ham radio. Amateur radio, also known as ham radio, has long been a popular alternative to SSB. For less money and with less red tape it provides better contact. Ham licenses take study, but once you've got one you have access to an array of pretuned marine band transceivers that are more powerful and versatile than SSB radios

and cost half as much. And there are hams all round the world to hook up with. Ham radio is only for personal communications, however—it is forbidden to conduct business transactions on ham frequencies.

Onboard computers, satellite phones, weather faxes, e-mail links between boats and the world, all of these have added to high-seas communication. It has never been easier to stay in touch at sea.

Self-Steering Gear

When you go from sailing along a coast or around a bay to making a passage across open water, one of the things that disappears is the joy of steering. It's fun for most of us to drive when there are things to do and places to see, but once land slips beneath the horizon, one wave gets to looking a lot like the next. Holding your boat on her course gets tedious, and the joy of the helm becomes the tyranny.

Getting your boat to sail herself is one answer. By locking the helm, balancing the sail plan, arranging a sheet-to-tiller setup, or balancing the helm (say by raising the centerboard or overtrimming the main), you can get most sailboats to average the desired heading pretty much on their own. Often, though, you have to reduce sail or detune performance to keep her pointed right. "Sailing herself" is a cheap, challenging, and educational solution to self-steering, but it's rarely fast, versatile, or trustworthy through changes in conditions. For most of us, self-steering entails mechanical or electronic help, the former coming from a wind vane and the latter from an autopilot.

Throughout their 50 years of development, wind vane self-steering mechanisms have steered by means of apparent wind angle. Various models differ in how they link the wind sensor with the steering mecha-

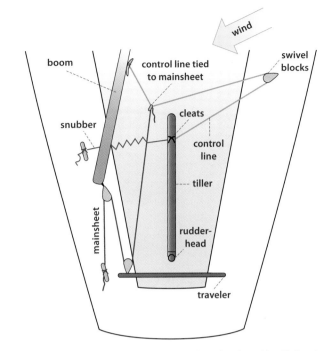

Conceived by voyager John Letcher and further developed by Al Gunther, the mainsheet-to-tiller arrangement shown here is a low-tech approach to self-steering.

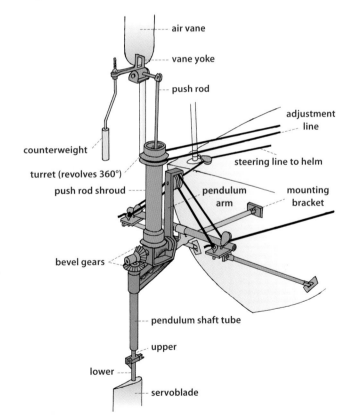

An overview of the Fleming Global 301. The majority of wind vane self-steerers employ a horizontal-vane servopendulum configuration like this one.

Under double-reefed sails, this boat makes easy work of beating to weather with the help of her Aries wind vane self-steerer.

nism and by what steering force they ultimately choose to steer the boat. They might be as trim as 30 pounds or weigh as much as 70, and they might be made of aluminum or stainless steel. You can get one for most cruising boats for between $2,000 and $3,000 dollars. There are three principal types:

Rudder steerers. Using the vane itself to move the rudder would seem the height of simplicity. Achieving a linkage that's sensitive yet durable and developing the power to overcome helm pressure and avoid broaching in big waves, however, re not that simple after all. You won't see many rudder steerers out there.

Servopendulum vanes. The key to this sort of vane is an oar-

blade counterbalance for the vane. Wind pressure bends the vane around a horizontal axis, and that motion is transmitted via a vertical linkage to a vertical oar blade. The blade pivots, which causes it to wing out to one side, which creates a pull (augmented by the force of the water past the hull) on controlling lines that are connected to the boat's rudder. The result is to magnify the torque of wind on vane through the system. Servopendulum vanes make the most of small vanes and relatively drag-free steering blades and are the most popular type of self-steerer. They can, however, have problems in light air or in rolly downwind conditions.

Trim-tab steerers. Another way of boosting the power of the

Top: *The autopilot on this 32-footer steers by means of the wheel-mounted ring.* **Above:** *The autopilot is ridiculously easy to engage and use with the pedestal-mounted control device. Currently it's on standby—i.e., disengaged. Once you've squared up on your approximate course, pressing the AUTO button will engage it, and you can thereafter turn port or starboard in 1- or 10-degree increments by pressing the appropriate button. Press STANDBY when you're ready to resume manual control.*

vane is to hook it to a diminutive trim tab, either on the trailing edge of the main rudder or on an auxiliary rudder. This magnifies the steering effect while minimizing steering effort, but when rudder pressure increases, such as when you're reaching in a breeze, a trim tab can find itself too small to do the job.

The beauty of a vane is that the wind is free. You don't have to create electricity to steer. You can adjust a vane or fix it yourself. Steering purely by the wind can be better than steering a compass course both upwind and down, especially in light and fluky conditions when wind angle can have a huge effect on speed.

But vanes are vulnerable back aft. They are also prone to drag, and their weight and windage don't help performance. New materials, especially bearings and bearing race systems, make modern vanes work better than their predecessors, but no one would mistake even the most up-to-date vane for a model of efficiency. Then too, large multihulls produce such rapid and pronounced changes in apparent wind direction that you can't steer them well with vanes.

These are all reasons to choose an autopilot over a wind vane, but for me the biggest advantage of an autopilot is that it will take the helm under power. A vane, on the other hand, is no help during those deadly hours under engine alone.

While vanes have improved and evolved in recent years, autopilots have been reinvented. You still need electricity to run them, and some of them are still too puny to handle every kind of steering, but their advantages are legion:

- They interface with GPS. Not only will they steer to a series of waypoints, but they have MOB (man overboard) functions. Hit the button, and the pilot will return you to the spot.
- They let you drive, with full dodging capability, from anywhere onboard.
- With the proper inputs they can steer by the wind, just like a vane.
- They "teach" themselves about the prevailing conditions and your boat.
- Their power consumption is low enough to be replaced in the battery by a trickle charge from a waterwheel, windmill generator, or alternator belted to a free-wheeling shaft.

Wheel and tiller pilots are prone to water damage and sometimes lack the power to do a consistent steering job. Belowdecks pilots (attached to the quadrant rather than the helm) provide much better service and reliability. They average over $5,000 but come very close to being the final answer when it comes to self-steering. Hydraulic, mechanical, or hybrid "drives" do the steering. The unit's power rating is important, but its rudder response time *under sailing loads* is a much better indicator of its ability to steer a given boat. Microprocessors with varying degrees of sophistication turn sailor input into straight-ahead performance. Steering algorithms embedded in the central processing units of most modern pilots let them assess the forces at work in any steering situation and learn to steer better. I was worried when I let the Robertson autopilot on a friend's cruising ketch steer us through a nighttime landfall in a line squall, but I needn't have been. From full rigged to jib and jigger to storm jib, from 15 to 60 knots and back down again—gusts, veers, waves, and rain—the pilot was sharper than I would have been and twice as reliable. I'm no techie, but when it comes to belowdecks autopilots, I'm a believer.

Multihulls

One of every three new sailboats built in the United States these days is a multihull. It's about time to give catamarans and trimarans the focus they deserve.

Almost everything written in this book about sailing, seamanship, handling, racing, and cruising applies equally well to boats with one, two, or three hulls. A sailboat is a sailboat is a sailboat. Still, multis are different—in concept, execution, use, performance, and aesthetics.

When European sailors discovered the multihulls of Polynesia in the seventeenth century they were impressed: "I do believe they sail the best of any boats in the world," William Dampier wrote in 1697. He went on to cite a primitive time trial, "better than 12 knots off the reel in less than thirty seconds by the glass," to back up his claim. Captain Cook, too, was delighted and humbled by the sailing outriggers he saw in Hawaii.

Multis and monos spring from very different histories and represent markedly different ways of doing things, but you can race or cruise as well in one as the other. Multihulls have earned increasing popularity because of design and construction advancements, stellar achievements in racing, and a solid track record in cruising. As more people sail both, the unfamiliarity that bred contempt for multihulls among tra-

---

A Boat for Cruising

CORSAIR F-27

The F-27 trimaran was designed by Ian Farrier around 1984. The patented folding mechanism collapses the two floats or amas in toward the main hull; beam then is a road-ready 8 feet 5 inches, making the boat legal for trailering. It is also possible now for this changeling to enter slips sized for monohulls. Construction is fiberglass cloth skins, Divinycell foam core, and vinylester resin, all vacuum-bagged. As one would expect, this is a very fast boat, with speeds in excess of 20 knots possible. Although it has made transoceanic passages across both the Atlantic and Pacific, a few have capsized, albeit while being raced and pushed hard. The interior is a bit tight, but serviceable. With the expansive trampolines and netting that constitute its "decks," this is a boat to enjoy topside. The boat was a success in southern California because it gave cruising sailors there (who h

so few islands or coves, other than Catalina) some mobility. The favored destination is Baja, but because most people don't have time to sail their boats south, trailering the F-27 at 55 mph made the Mexican adventure very doable. This boat is for people who value performance over sumptuous interiors.

LOA	27'1"
BEAM	19'1"/8'5" FOLDED
DRAFT	1'2" / 4'11" (CB UP, CB DOWN)
WEIGHT	2,600 LB.
SAIL AREA	446 SQ.FT.
DESIGNER	IAN FARRIER
PRICE NEW	NOT IN PRODUCTION
PRICE USED	$36,100 – $40,100 (1990 MODEL) $63,900 – $70,300 (1997 MODEL)
SIMILAR BOATS	F-28 TELSTAR 28

[Reprinted with permission from *Your First Sailboat: How to Find and Sail the Right Boat for You,* by Daniel Spurr (International Marine/McGraw-Hill, 2004)]

ditional sailors has more or less evaporated. At the same time, the "light makes right" pomposity that made some multihullers obnoxious has also eroded. Today most sailors seem ready to see and enjoy multihulls for what they are.

When a boat with a ballasted keel heels, its resistance to further heeling increases. Keelboats thus have a margin of safety built in, and most will right themselves if they do capsize. As a catamaran heels, however, it becomes less and less resistant to capsize, and it is even more stable upside down than it is right side up. Of all the differences, that's the major one. Multihulls make superior cruising boats, but there are still a good number of cruising sailors who prefer to have the odds on their side when it comes to heavy wind and seas offshore.

One circumnavigator kept tabs during a 3-year period in the 1980s. Of all the multihulls he and his wife encountered or heard about during that time, 8 percent were eventually lost at sea. There was, of course, no such survey for monohulls, but the safety issue, much as multihull designers cry foul, is a genuine one. I've been in squalls offshore in a trimaran in which failure to douse the main on time might have put us over. Vigilance and good seamanship can yield fast passages and a host of other multihull advantages, but I prefer to go to sea in a boat that takes care of me rather than one that demands error-free care from me. On the other hand:

Big cruising catamarans may become unstable when "flying a hull," but just try to make that happen! A Lagoon 38 in a beam wind of 25 knots heels not one iota—it's as "steady as a church," as sailors used to say. On such a boat I find myself worrying more about rigging tension (without the relief valve of heeling) than capsizing. Fortunately the rigging is sized to handle the loads, which are eased by the wide staying base of a catamaran. If you (or your family) don't like sailing on your ear, a multihull may be the answer.

Capsized multihulls don't right themselves, but neither do they sink as a ballasted monohull can do. Multihull voyagers recommend making prevoyage arrangements to let yourself climb back inside the boat when its bottom side is up.

Multihulls are fast—at least most of them are. Stability without ballast relieves them of dead weight and lets them carry large sail plans. The closer their foils are to vertical, the more efficient they are. The F-27, a trailerable cruising trimaran, will give you speeds greater than 20 knots—though you have to trade accommodation space to get that enhanced cruising range. Multihulls don't have hulls that plane; they get their slipperiness by being long and narrow—the greater the length per unit beam, the faster the boat.

Beating at 11 knots, more than twice what *Shere Khan* could muster on her best day, taught me what multihulls mean in terms of coastwise cruising. On the weekend that Carol and I chartered an F-27, we covered more of New England than we might have in a week aboard our 25-footer. And there was an added bonus. Drawing less than 2 feet, our tri took us to anchorages, beaches, nooks, and coves that we would never have seen otherwise. Groping in fog, we were confident enough to come close inshore to see where we were without much worry about hitting anything.

The cruising cat has been the backbone of much of the recent interest in multihulls. It seems

A Boat for Cruising

MAINE CAT 41

The Maine Cat 41 is a little masterpiece, built in Maine by craftsmen who have also produced the popular Maine Cat 30. The new 41-footer maintains the tradition of an open bridgedeck design, good sailing performance, and a practical and exceptionally well-finished interior. This daggerboard-equipped cat can easily be single-handed from a central wheel and navigation station located in the forward part of the cockpit. In inclement weather the entire bridge deck can be converted into an enclosure, via side curtains which quickly attach to the rigid bimini. The Maine Cat 41 has excellent seakeeping abilities, thanks to her high bridgedeck clearance, conservative sail plan and buoyant hulls. This catamaran is an outstanding choice for people looking for a spirited daysailer and safe passagemaker.

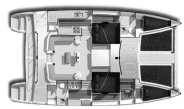

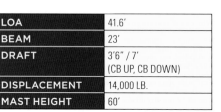  

LOA	41.6'
BEAM	23'
DRAFT	3'6" / 7' (CB UP, CB DOWN)
DISPLACEMENT	14,000 LB.
MAST HEIGHT	60'

[Reprinted with permission from *Catamarans: The Complete Guide for Cruising Sailors*, by Gregor Tarjan (International Marine/McGraw-Hill, 2007)]

an altogether different sort of boat from the flying machines that established multihulls at the forefront of the search for speed. These multi-stateroom tennis courts with sails seem almost square. Making them tip may no longer be an issue, but making them move seems an open question. When catamarans and tris are designed to carry cruising payloads, speed suffers. Not only does adding to the burden to be borne by each unit of sail area slow you down, but the resistance per unit length mounts as hulls sink deeper. To achieve the sort of speeds that multihulls are capable of, cruisers should be scrupulous about sticking to a displacement/length ratio of 60 or less. Cats and tris can get the most out of smallish sail plans. Overloading a cruising cat and then giving her a big sail plan in hopes of rescuing performance is a transparent trick, and dangerous, too.

Without doubt catamarans are the champions in the space-for-length race. Trimaran accommodations are limited to the main hull and tend to offer about half the living space of a similar monohull because they are so shallow and need to sacrifice space to a board of some sort. Cats, however, with deep hulls and a wide bridge deck, have natural units of space enough to make accommodations their strong point. A common problem, though, is that the bridge deck and deckhouse tend to isolate the cockpit aft.

A Boat for Cruising

OUTREMER 42

The Outremer line of catamarans belongs to one of the most proven and tested multihulls in the world. More than 160 of these performance-daggerboard cats have been constructed in a period of 25 years by the specialist builders from the south of France. Throughout virtually millions of ocean miles Outremers have demonstrated their seaworthiness and ability to safely sail through the worst weather. Centered weight, high bridgedeck clearance and efficient hulls provide excellent performance under sail or power. The new Outremer 42 is entirely infusion built and will out-rival equivalent length cats in handling and speed. Being able to order a custom interior greatly adds to the nature of these very special catamarans.

LOA	42.7'
BEAM	22.4'
DRAFT	1.9' / 7.9' (CB UP, CB DOWN)
DISPLACEMENT	14,800 LB.
MAST HEIGHT	59.9'

[Reprinted with permission from *Catamarans: The Complete Guide for Cruising Sailors,* by Gregor Tarjan (International Marine/McGraw-Hill, 2007)]

On the standard cruising cat it's hard to get much feel for the sails or see what's happening on the foredeck when docking or anchoring.

Trimarans have a slightly different motion from cats. More akin to a monohull at first, they heel until lift from the leeward hull (*ama*) counteracts the heeling force. From then on you'll be amazingly steady. Drinks don't slide, bracing is no chore—it's a different and very comfortable world. Carol simply found this motion strange on our chartered F-27, even though we were heeling and pitching less than we would have been on *Shere Khan*. Another time, on a Formula 40 ocean racer, I couldn't place the click-clack stop-start sort of motion. Then I realized that we were simply hitting wave tops at 22 knots, a lot faster than I was used to. I found the noise from the rudders intriguing, too. In a trimaran powering across the Gulf Stream in the Multihull Southern Circuit, I learned to steer by the whine of the twin rudders. When they were quiet I was in the groove, but a low-pitched groan told me I was too low and a high-pitched whine meant I was too high.

With most of the planet's distance and speed records to their credit, with circumnavigations by the score to point to, with charter boat success in the bag, and with a bright future in offshore cruising ahead, multihulls have earned the right to be taken seriously.

A Sailor's Weather

Your feel for the weather—like your feel for your boat—will go on developing as long as you go on sailing. It could hardly be otherwise, because the effects of changing weather are magnified aboard a small sailboat. This appendix provides a foundation and a context for the deck-level weather wisdom you will acquire with time. Learn the facts, watch the weather, and pay attention. Sooner or later all the pieces will fit.

It's hard to argue with the U.S. Coast Guard Auxiliary's #1 weather rule, which is to "know before you go." With good sources of weather information conveniently at hand, there really is no excuse not to stay on top of the regional weather synopsis and forecast. Some of those sources are listed below.

But regional forecasts developed from computer models do not always match what you experience on the water. A low-pressure system deviating slightly from its predicted track may cause unexpected changes in your local weather. A regional wind may be locally enhanced by uneven heating of air over land or by topographic effects—and while the difference between 15 and 25 knots of wind may not matter much on land, it matters a great deal to a sailor. Local effects can result in unpredicted, nonfrontal squalls and thunderstorms. And forecasts prepared for offshore waters, where there are few monitoring stations, may be several hours out of date by the time they reach you.

In sum, the local weather is always changing, forecasts are sometimes wrong, and even an accurate regional forecast may miss what is happening in the piece of water your boat is inhabiting. Know what the meteorologists are predicting, but keep your weather eye open.

For some of the information and images that follow I am indebted to *Onboard Weather Forecasting: A Captain's Quick Guide,* by Bob Sweet (International Marine/McGraw-Hill, 2004); *Boater's Bowditch,* by Richard K. Hubbard (International Marine/McGraw-Hill, 1998), and *Sailing Skills and Seamanship,* by the U.S. Coast Guard Auxiliary (International Marine/McGraw-Hill, 2007).

Weather Forecast Sources

Weather wisdom, a feel for the wind, local knowledge, and experience are all wonderful things. When it comes to forecasting the weather, though, they are not as wonderful as good information. Being "weatherwise" means knowing how important it is to get a forecast. It also means being able to assess the quality and accuracy of the information in the forecast to give yourself as clear an idea of what's coming down the weather road as you can.

The forecast in your morning newspaper is a good place to start. Radio and TV weather are easy to get, but they aren't often targeted to sailors. Even "marine weather reports" on commercial radio tend to sound like the same tape repeating itself or to focus overmuch on high and low tide at the nearest beach. Most TV weather shows, however, use synoptic charts of satellite time-lapse imagery that include Doppler radar displays of moisture content and deployment. These screen images tell you as much as you need to know—especially if you know what you're looking for.

Forecasts prepared by the U.S. National Weather Service (a branch of the National Oceanic and Atmospheric Administration) are available on the

Internet at www.nws.noaa.gov and provide coverage across the U.S. and much of the globe. The National Weather Service also operates NOAA Weather Radio, which broadcasts local marine forecasts from over 400 stations around the country on VHF frequencies from 162.400 to 162.580 MHz. Marine VHF radios enable you to quickly select one of these weather frequencies by choosing WX-1, WX-2, etc. Each station has a range approaching 40 miles, and the broadcasts are continuous with taped messages being repeated about every 6 minutes and updated every 3 to 6 hours. Almost anywhere in U.S. coastal waters, NOAA weather is a trusted resource. The Coast Guard also issues NWS weather reports as well as navigational warnings over VHF on Channel 22 (157.1 MHz).

Farther offshore, beyond VHF radio range, the principal source of weather information is MF (medium frequency) and HF (high frequency, i.e., shortwave) radio via voice or modem (for data or fax), and this is one of the principal reasons many offshore sailors equip their boats with single sideband (SSB) radio. The U.S. Coast Guard provides radio forecasts in both voice and text on HF and MF bands. These are more detailed and longer-range forecasts than the VHF broadcasts and can be received up to 150 miles offshore during the daytime. The USCG also supports NAVTEX, which is part of the GMDSS (Global Marine Distress and Safety System), providing MF text coastal forecasts to shipboard text receivers out to about 250 miles at sea. See www.navcen.uscg.gov for details.

NOAA's Ocean Prediction Center (OPC) provides forecasts for the high seas from 65° north to 15° south (except for the Indian Ocean) via radiofacsimile and shortwave radio broadcasts. A number of commercial global services are available via HF SSB marine radio for offshore mariners, mostly by subscription. Additionally, storm warnings are broadcast at eight minutes past the hour on U.S. (WWV—every minute on 2500, 5000, 10,000, 15,000, 20,000, and 25,000 kHz) and Canadian (CHU—continuous on 3330, 7335, and 14,670 kHz) time signal stations. Ham radio can bring you word on the weather, too.

Modern weatherfax (radiofacsimile) sets aren't cheap, but they're worth the investment. At less than $2,000 they add a new dimension to your forecasting by letting you receive weather synoptic and forecast charts on board. The language of weather charts is universal, as are the symbols. Weatherfaxing is practically worldwide. Most modern weatherfax machines receive a range of signals from 75 kHz to 25 MHz and include up to 500 pre-programmed channels as well as an assortment of programmable ones.

If you're on-line onboard the world widens. You can access National Weather Service analysis and forecasts at www.nws.noaa.gov or the Coast Guard homepage at www.navcen.uscg.gov, or the NOAA homepage at www.noaa.gov. Search the web for more weather (including a listing of weatherfax stations) if you need it.

At the exotic end of things, the Goddard Space Flight Center's Polar GOES satellite capture program lets you watch the world through satellite-mounted cameras. If you have the ability to access the Internet with an onboard PC, go to http://svs.gsfc.nasa.gov/search/Instrument/GOES.html. You can also receive weather buoy reports on a real-time basis via the Internet.

Environment Canada provides marine forecasts for Canadian waters at weatheroffice.ec.gc.ca/marine. The Met Office (www.metoffice.com) is the government source of marine forecasts for UK waters, and the British Broadcasting Corporation (BBC) provides another source at www.bbc.co.uk/weather. Weather forecasts around Australia are pro-

CHARACTERISTICS OF MIDLATITUDE HIGH- AND LOW-PRESSURE SYSTEMS

	High	Low
Weather	Generally fair	Stormy, precipitation
Temperature	Stable—long periods	Cool to warm changing to colder
Average motion (west to east)	Winter: 565 nm/day Summer: 390 nm/day	Winter: 660 nm/day Summer: 430 nm/day
Winds	Moderate, rising near edge	Strong and changing with possible high seas
Pressure (typical)	Rapid rise on approach, slow decline on retreat	Rapid fall on approach, slow rise on retreat
Clouds	Sparse, near periphery	Wide variety, all altitudes

vided by the Bureau of Meteorology at www.bom.gov.au. And commercial sources are easily located online with a web search.

For generations sailors have relied on a finger to the wind, an eye on the clouds, and a thought for the glass. We now have access to information that is light-years better, more current, and more meaningful than it has ever been. Making the best of that information, though, is still the essence of forecasting successfully.

Onboard Weather Forecasting

Middle-latitude weather—i.e., the weather between roughly 30° and 60° both north and south of the equator—is dominated by a west-to-east procession of high- and low-pressure systems. Highs are associated with fair and stable weather, and lows (or depressions) with foul and unstable weather. Cool, dry air subsides, or sinks, within a high, which is why barometric pressures are high there and the weather stable. High-pressure breezes can be strong, but high pressure generally means good weather. Warm, moist air rises within a low, or depression—which is why barometric pressures are lower—and the air cools as it rises. Cool air carries less moisture than warm air, so moisture condenses from the air as it rises, which explains why precipitation is routinely associated with lows. Rising

SIGNS OF STABLE AND CHANGING WEATHER

	Continuing Good Weather	Indicators of a Change
Skies	Clear, light to dark blue, bright moon, contrails dissipate	Hazy, halo (sun or moon), thick lingering jet contrails
Clouds	Few, puffy cumulus or high thin clouds, higher the better	Veil of clouds, clouds at multilayers and directions, cirrus
Winds Seas	Generally steady, little change over day; sea swells same direction	Strong winds in early AM, wind shift to S; seas confused, varying directions
Temperature	Stable; heavy dew or frost at night	Marked changes; increase in humidity
Dew point	Marked spread between dew point and temperature = no fog	Close spread: probable fog if temperature drops
Barometer	Steady, rising slowly	Falling slowly
Sunrise	Gray sky at dawn or sun rising from clear horizon	Red sky, sun rises above horizon due to cloud cover
Sunset	Red sky, sun "ball of fire" or sets on a clear horizon	Sun sets high above horizon, color purplish or pale yellow

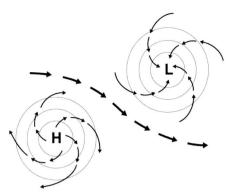

Air circulates clockwise around highs and counterclockwise around lows in the Northern Hemisphere. Where a high is close to a neighboring low, you may see strong winds between the two systems.

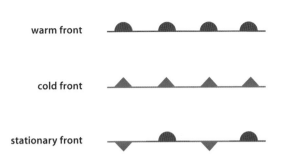

Graphic representations of fronts on weather maps. The symbols point in the direction the front is moving.

air is unstable air, which is why lows are often associated with strong winds.

Since lows are the weather-makers of the middle latitudes, it pays to know the direction of the nearest low. The wind blows counterclockwise around the center of a Northern Hemisphere low and clockwise around the center of a Southern Hemisphere low. In the Northern Hemisphere, therefore, face the wind and extend your arm to the right. According to Buys Ballot's Law (see page 207), the center of the nearest low will be slightly behind your outstretched arm—15 degrees behind it over water, up to 30 degrees behind (due to the greater friction encountered by the surface wind) over land. In the Southern Hemisphere, use your left arm instead.

If the low is west of you, the weather is likely to deteriorate over the next several hours. If the low is east, it has already passed you and the weather is likely to improve.

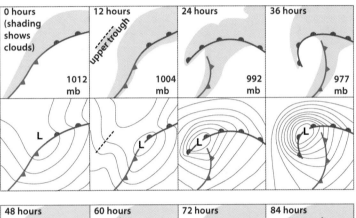

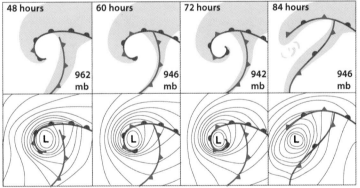

The typical life of a Northern Hemisphere low begins with a kink in the isobars (the curves of equal barometric pressure on a weather map) as cold air advances on warm. As more isobars close around the developing center, winds increase. Perhaps 84 hours and thousands of miles of downstream travel later, the low dissipates.

When a low spins into existence along the boundary between contrasting air masses, it entrains wedge-shaped pro-jections of the parent air masses that chase each other around the center of the low. Where warm air overtakes and over-

DECK-LEVEL FORECASTING (Northern Hemisphere)

Approaching Low

Clouds: high cirrus, gradually lowering and thickening to altostratus
Wind: backing to southeast and possibly increasing
Barometer: begins to fall (2 to 10 mb in 3 hours)
Offshore: swell increases, with decreasing period

What to Expect:

Rain: within 15 to 24 hours
If low is west to northwest and passing to your north, you will see fronts.
If low is west to southwest and passing to your south, you will not see distinct fronts, but
    wind will shift from southeast to east, northeast, then north to northwest.

Approaching Warm Front

Cirrus or cirrocumulus clouds: front is more than 24 hours away
Lowering, thickening clouds (cirrostratus to nimbostratus): front is less than 24 hours away
Rain: begins lightly, then becomes steady and persistent
Barometer: falls steadily; a faster fall indicates stronger winds
Wind: increases steadily, stays in the southeast
Visibility: deteriorates, especially in rain

Passing Warm Front

Sky: lightens toward western horizon
Rain: breaks
Wind: veers from south to southwest and may increase
Barometer: stops falling
Temperature: rises

Within Warm Sector

Wind: steady, typically from the southwest, will strengthen ahead of cold front
Barometer: steady—may drop shortly ahead of cold front
Precipitation: mist, possible drizzle
Clouds: variety of cumulus clouds

Approaching Cold Front

Wind: southwesterly, increasing; line squalls possible up to 100 miles ahead of front
Barometer: begins brief fall, could be rapid
Clouds: cumulonimbus build to the west
Temperature: steady
Rain: begins and intensifies, but duration is short (1 to 2 hours typical)

Passing Cold Front

Wind: veers rapidly to west or northwest, gusty behind front
Barometer: begins to rise, often quickly
Clouds: cumulonimbus, then nimbostratus, then clearing
Temperature: drops suddenly, then slow decline
Rain: ends, gives way to rapidly clearing skies, possibly with leftover altocumulus or
    stratocumulus

front is marked by characteristic changes in clouds, wind, and barometric readings, and these comprise the elements of deck-level forecasting as summarized in the accompanying tables.

Messages from Clouds

Clouds form when water vapor condenses in cooling air. Since temperatures fall with altitude (roughly 1° Fahrenheit per 150 feet of altitude on average), rising air will cool, and some of its water vapor will condense into water droplets, forming a cloud. If the air continues to rise, the clouds will develop vertically (a shape called **cumuloform**). If the air stops rising, the clouds will flatten into a **stratiform** shape. How high and how fast the air rises depends upon what is pushing it aloft, and thus cloud shapes are a direct indicator of atmospheric stability. The more vertically developed the clouds, the more unstable the atmosphere.

As you practice reading clouds, remember that the particular clouds you see are only part of the story. The sequence and speed with which the skyscape changes is just as important. As with a barometer reading, the rate of change is as important as the direction of change.

rides cold air a warm front forms. Where cold air overtakes and wedges beneath warm air, a cold front forms. Where neither air mass is overtaking the other, the front is stationary. The low typically matures, deepens, and dies over a 3- to 4-day cycle, during which time it may travel thousands of miles eastward ("downstream" in the overhead jet streams) from its point of origin, dragging its fronts along with it. The approach of each

Cloud Types

Clouds are categorized by altitude: high, middle, or low. Cumulus clouds can be found in all three "decks" of the sky, but they are always a clear sign of convection, of the up-and-down energy derived from a significant temperature differential. Cumuli signal instability no matter where you find them.

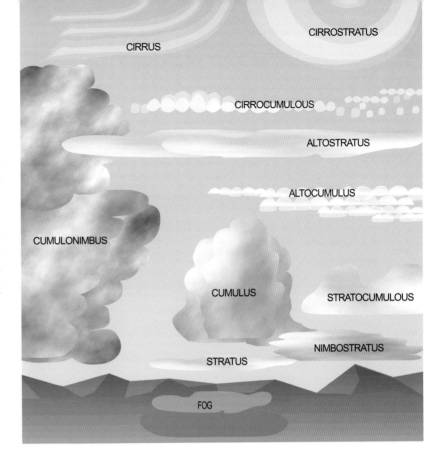

CIRRUS

CIRROSTRATUS

CIRROCUMULOUS

ALTOSTRATUS

ALTOCUMULUS

CUMULONIMBUS

CUMULUS

STRATOCUMULOUS

NIMBOSTRATUS

STRATUS

FOG

High Clouds (Cirro)

These clouds form above 20,000 feet, at which altitude water condenses as ice crystals rather than water droplets. As a consequence, high clouds are wispy and insubstantial.

Cirrocumulus clouds, often called a mackerel sky, are thin and bumpy. These clouds are lower than cirrostratus. Usually seen in winter, they suggest continued fair but cold weather.

Cirrus is Latin for "wisp," which describes these clouds perfectly. Sometimes called mares' tails, they are especially thin and often precede a warm front. The weather may remain fair for up to 24 hours, but the approaching front will bring a change after that.

Cirrostratus are flat, like a mild veil across the sky, and suggest that the coming warm front is 12 to 24 hours away.

Middle-Altitude Clouds (Alto)

These clouds form between 6,500 to 20,000 feet up and consist of water droplets. They are denser than high clouds and are often associated with precipitation. Mid-level clouds are hard to read, but you can establish a feel for rate of change just by observing periodically.

Altostratus clouds, near the upper end of the middle-altitude range, are flat and blue-gray and suggest the approach of long-lasting precipitation when they thicken. Regardless of their altitude, stratiform clouds denote an atmosphere in which air can't rise far without encountering colder air. This suggests that air is arriving in the upper troposphere on "ramps" of gentle updraft rather than "elevators" of convection.

Altocumulus clouds are fluffy and bumpy and often appear in "puff-ball" rows that signify moisture and approaching warm front. When the lines blur and blend and the clouds start to look like layer clouds, more moisture has arrived. It will rain soon. Altocumuli appearing late in the day often produce brilliant red sunsets, but when observed late in the morning they suggest strong convection and the possibility of late afternoon thunderstorms, especially when they puff up into castles or turrets (castellanus). If you're going to chart the clouds, the cumulus/stratus distinction is an excellent one to learn.

Low Clouds

Forming below 6,500 feet, these clouds likewise comprise water droplets. Denser even than midlevel clouds, low clouds often bring heavy or steady rain.

Clouds at ground level are fog.

Nimbostratus clouds, thick and dark gray, usually bring sustained precipitation.

Stratus clouds are the lowest of the low clouds. A uniform gray, they bring steady but often light rain and drizzle.

Stratoculmulus clouds are low, lumpy, gray, and thick and often foretell rain preceding a front.

Vertically Developed Clouds

As mentioned, some cumulus clouds develop vertically to such a degree that they defy categorization by altitude. Such clouds usually form from convectively rising, extremely warm, moist air or from warm air forced aloft by a cold front. Vertical lifting of air due to temperature differences is a volatile situation. Rain, lightning, thunder, micro-bursts, and tornadoes need those conditions, and those conditions are signaled by cumuli.

Cumulus clouds (cumulus being Latin for "heap") often have significant vertical development (up to 16,000 feet) but are widely spaced and associated with fair weather. They are sometimes left over from cumulonimbus clouds that have dissipated.

Cumulonimbus clouds are often associated with thunderstorms and squalls. These clouds can extend from low altitudes to the upper edge of the troposphere (from the Greek word "to mix," designating the lower layer of the atmosphere wherein all weather occurs) at 45,000 feet. This great vertical development is a sure sign of atmospheric instability.

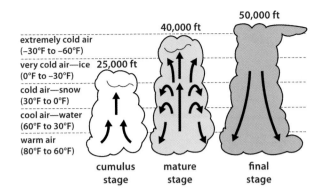

extremely cold air (–30°F to –60°F)	
very cold air—ice (0°F to –30°F)	25,000 ft
cold air—snow (30°F to 0°F)	
cool air—water (60°F to 30°F)	
warm air (80°F to 60°F)	

40,000 ft   50,000 ft

cumulus stage   mature stage   final stage

WEATHER CLUES FROM CLOUDS

Clouds	Precipitation
Cumulonimbus— vertical, developed cumulus	Rain, possible thundershowers, possible hail, tornadoes
Cirrus—thin, high level	None
Stratus—flat, often layered	Possible light drizzle
Cumulus—white, puffy	None (but may be windy)
Altocumulus— puffy, middle level	None
Altostratus—flat, middle level	Light rain or snow possible
Nimbostratus— flat, low level	Heavy, steady rain
Nimbus—lowest of clouds	Rain is falling

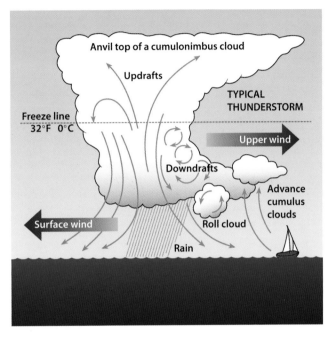

Top: *The stages of a thunderstorm.* **Above:** *A maturing storm.*

Thunderstorms

According to some estimates there are, at any moment of any day, 1,800 thunderstorms in progress across the planet. They are ten times more prevalent over land than water, but they are certainly no strangers to the midocean sailor. Thunderstorms are formed by convection. Hot air rising is the spark that sets them off. Cold air descending is what gives them their punch. The airflow in a thunderstorm is "up and down."

Two-thirds of all thunderstorms are associated with fronts and move with them at 15 to 30 knots, as the front provides the convection that feeds the storm. Warm-front thunderstorms travel from southwest to northeast in the Northern Hemisphere; cold-front storms move from northwest to southeast.

The remaining one-third of thunderstorms are freestanding and spring to life almost anywhere heat and moisture come together. Solo thunderstorms are harder to predict than frontal storms. Because they pop up on their own, the steering forces for them may be any local or gradient wind.

Whether along a front or on its own, a thunderstorm needs heat, atmospheric instability, and moisture to develop. There must be enough hot air to create updrafts, and those updrafts must not be quashed by ceilings of stability. When moist surface air rises in a column 15,000 to 25,000 feet high, you have the necessary convection for thunderstorm development. The rising air may cool as much as 80° Fahrenheit or more yet still remain warmer than the surrounding air. As it cools, its moisture condenses, releasing huge amounts of heat, and this is the power behind the developing storm. As the storm matures, clouds can reach heights of 40,000 to 80,000 feet—the higher the vertical development, the more severe the storm. As this convection spurred by hot air rising "grows" the storm, cold air sinking (in reverse circulation) brings storm winds to the surface. As air rushes aloft within the column, air descends in gusts with rain or hail around the column's perimeter.

A layered overhead filled with thick, flat, stratus clouds keeps storms from "getting off the ground." Thunderstorms are more prevalent in lower latitudes because tropical air is hotter and thus less stable than polar air. Early in the morning or late in the afternoon are their favorite times. Relative humidity exceeding 75 percent is a key. The higher the temperature, of course, the more moisture that figure represents, but there must be moisture. Dry air lacks the condensate to wet-nurse a storm to life. And there must be lifting.

Perched on pillars of convection, low-lying cumulus clouds will grow taller as they are swollen by increased updrafting. The height of a storm cloud tells you its power. Towering

Clouds like these indicate the approach of a squall line and are often associated with a thunderstorm embedded in or preceding a cold front. Expect rapid wind shifts and strong gusts.

banks of cloud mean powerful downdrafts. Surface winds affected by the storm will tend to blow toward it as the convection sucks them in. So long as the updraft is going up it takes moisture with it. In gusts and lulls similar to the puffs of a surface breeze, the updraft builds a storm cloud. Moisture condenses on the way as the cloud billows upward. The cloud may assume the classic anvil shape that distinguishes many mature thunderstorms (cumulonimbus) if its updraft bumps into a ceiling of air too cold to let it climb farther. Then the updraft flattens out, the moisture stops rising, and the cloud is given its signature flat-top.

Condensation has three results. Latent heat of vaporization is released and adds power to the climb. Rising condensate is elevated along the climbing column until it is cooled further (due to higher altitude) and freezes. Before long it is too heavy to climb or stay put. It starts to fall. In conjunction with this atomization, elevation, and refrigeration of the moisture in it, the cloud becomes electrically polarized. The distance between positive (going up) and negative (statically down) is increased until a spark jumps the gap between the top and bottom of the cloud. The flash creates both light and the sonic boom that gives these storms their name. The same exchange can occur between positively charged clouds and negative ions from the ground.

The downdraft is the reverse of a lifting process that accelerates particles from 2 miles per hour when they're picked up at the surface to over 60 mph when they near the top of the column. Cold, wet wind flows out of the cloud and strikes the surface with a force to be reckoned with. Depending on the size and maturity of the storm, this downdraft will sooner or later choke the updraft that started things. That marks the end of the storm. Remember, though, that the conditions that gave rise to it aren't rare; others may be on the way.

Frontal thunderstorms will certainly gang up on you.

Ranged at times over the whole 500- to 1,000-mile length of a front, or, especially with cold fronts, stretching 100 to 200 miles ahead of the front line, frontal squalls gain strength from their numbers. Updrafts and downdrafts rarely conflict, so the systems are longer-lived than stand-alone storms. They also benefit from the churning instability of fronts and travel at their accelerated speeds.

In the process of overtaking cold air, the warmer air behind a warm front rises. It rises enough to produce thunderstorms, but because the climb and the temperature differential are gradual, the power of these cells is usually limited. A cold front, however, can boil up the moist air in front of it and send it skyward in a hurry. Often that process creates a line of towering thunderheads that extend above and ahead of the front line. The wind from these storms will still strike the surface at the front line as long as the updraft is behind the front. It may veer up to 180 degrees, and the gusts may be in the 60-knot range.

When the cold air slips completely over the top of the warm mass it's chasing, however, it can extend well in advance of the front to set up a "ceiling." That lid keeps the churned-up warm air from rising and forces it, too, to run out well in advance of the border. These squalls may

A microburst.

have limited power and appear within 10 to 30 miles of the front, or they may be pushed well in advance and rise higher to form a formidable pre-frontal line that precedes the front by over 200 miles. Close to the front and low they rarely pack extraordinary wallop, but driven deep into the warm, moist air mass ahead, they tend to be very strong.

Both cold-front storms and isolated systems have been known to produce **downbursts**. Thankfully rare, these destructive vertical blasts from above must be avoided. Their winds can exceed 100 knots and they are the known or suspected culprits in sinking fully found vessels. The best index to whether a downburst is possible is the state of convective activity. It takes the maximum to generate a downburst. Sometimes though, particularly around areas of surface mixing like the Gulf Stream, that happens. Radar is a help in identifying energy cells in the upper atmosphere. Sometimes filled with

THE STABILITY INDEX

Factor	Least Stable	Neutral	Most Stable
Convergence or subsidence	Low dominant	Straight isobars	High dominant
Boundary layer thickness	Gradient wind	Sea breeze	Funneling wind
Surface heating	Air colder than surface	No difference	Air warmer than surface

rain, **microbursts** (localized downbursts) over water seem to grow from a particularly wet environment that forces the storm to suck in additional dry air to enable condensation.

Weather Clues

Twice meteorologist for the British Olympic sailing team, author of eight weather books, and a forecaster for almost 50 years, meteorologist Alan Watts has developed **crossed-wind rules** to help identify an approaching system. The difference between the winds on the surface and the winds on high is significant. Face the surface wind. If the upper wind (indicated by the movement of cirrus) is coming from your right in the Northern Hemisphere, the weather that's on its way is **cyclonic** (born out of low pressure). If the upper wind is on your left hand, a high approaches. These rules also work "Down Under" if you reverse them. If the upper wind and surface wind are the same, or if they are blowing in opposite directions, the potential for weather development

is "neutral," and there will be no change for a while.

When lower-level clouds obscure high-altitude cirrus, you can learn from them, too. A sharp edge (like the anvil top of a thunderhead) is indicative of a sharp difference in temperature. Therefore, sharp edges mean sharp breezes. "Castles" swelling upward or pouches bulging downward mean that updrafts or downdrafts are in the making. The cloud gives you the picture of its intentions.

Watts also suggests the following:

- Establish the type of airstream. Is it developing or deteriorating? Is it stable or unstable?
- Consider "the range of the possible." For example, sea breezes of over 15 knots generally rule out fog, so you can cross fog off the list of possibilities.
- "Long foretold, long hold." Weather that takes a while developing will have equal staying power. The opposite premise, "Sharp blast, soon past," is equally true.
- What goes up—speaking particularly of moisture—comes down.

- Wind won't start without a reason.

"Calling the shifts" can be valuable to a racing sailor. The ability, like other types of forecasting, is a product of information, knowledge, and experience leavened with a generous "seat-of-the-pants" factor. Frank Bethwaite, Australian Olympian, glider pilot, skiff designer, and student of the wind, helped popularize a matrix system that assembles the variables sailors should use in reading the wind. He calls it the "stability index," and it's a guide to how stable a given breeze will be.

A breeze is viewed as stable when there is regularity displayed in its changes. The more random its fluctuations, the more unstable it is. There are wind shifts that are random and unpredictable, but when the wind shifts in ordered, stable response to the factors outlined in the table, it *is* predictable and the advantage goes to he who calls the shift. The weather in general is much like the wind. It cannot always be anticipated, but the more you work at your forecasting, the more of what it does will come clear.

Wind and Wave

The Inuit have thirty words describing snow, and sailors have at least that many describing wind. A breeze may be **fluky**, **shifty**, or **gusty**, and a shift can be a **lift** or a **header** or **knock**. The wind can **breeze on** or **breeze up**, or it can **take off** or **drop out**. A wind blowing you where you want to go is a **fair wind** or a **leading breeze**. The schoonermen called it a **good chance along**. When the wind is blowing from where you want to go, on the other hand, it is **on the nose**.

A strong wind might be a **blow** or a **hard blow**. One sailor's **fresh breeze** or **reefing breeze** is **half a gale** or simply a **gale** to another—depending on his experience, his preparations, his crew, and the size and seaworthiness of his boat. But when it comes to communicating wind strengths and the seas that accompany them, something more objective and uniform is needed. Accordingly, in 1805, Admiral Sir Francis Beaufort devised a table that classified winds into groups called forces, and the system is still in use today with some modifications. Originally the forces were chosen for their effects on square-rigged sailing ships, but later they were associated with sea states instead. The Beaufort Wind Scale with associated sea state photos appears on page 62.

The force of the wind increases with the cube of its velocity, so a small increase in speed has a big effect on force. The time to reef is when you first think of it. Don't delay.

Because waves are more dangerous to sailboats than wind, there is value in developing an even more precise correspondence between wind and sea than that afforded by the Beaufort table. The accompanying tables of sea conditions do just that. The wave heights used in these tables are significant wave heights, which means the average of the highest one-third of the waves (trough to crest). Heights are further based on an assumption of **fully developed seas**, which means that wave height is unlimited by the **duration** of the wind or the distance **(fetch)** over which it blows. You can see that a Force 9 wind would need

> **"The wind and the waves are always on the side of the ablest navigators."**
>
> —Edward Gibbon,
> *Decline and Fall of the Roman Empire*

A freak storm struck the 1998 Sydney–Hobart Race fleet with winds of more than 80 knots, piling seas as high as 80 feet or more against the currents of the Bass Strait. In this photo taken from a helicopter, the twelve crewmembers of the 41-foot Stand Aside, *already rolled and dismasted, await rescue. This breaking sea, which looks between 60 and 80 feet high, almost rolled the boat again.*

Fetch in n. miles	Force 4 (11-16 knots)			Force 5 (17-21)			Force 6 (22-27)			Force 7 (28-33)		
	time in hours	height in feet	period in seconds	time	height	period	time	height	period	time	height	period
10	3.7	2.6	2.4	2.2	3.5	2.8	2.7	5.0	3.1	2.5	6.0	3.4
20	6.2	3.2	2.9	5.4	4.9	3.3	4.7	7.0	3.8	4.2	8.6	4.3
30	8.3	3.8	3.3	7.2	5.8	3.7	6.2	8.0	4.2	5.8	10.0	4.6
40	10.3	3.9	3.6	8.9	6.2	4.1	7.8	9.0	4.6	7.1	11.2	4.9
50	12.4	4.0	3.8	11.0	6.5	4.4	9.1	9.8	4.8	8.4	12.2	5.2
60	14.0	4.0	4.0	12.0	6.8	4.6	10.2	10.3	5.1	9.6	13.2	5.5
70	15.8	4.0	4.1	13.5	7.0	4.8	11.9	10.8	5.4	10.5	13.9	5.7
80	17.0	4.0	4.2	15.0	7.2	4.9	13.0	11.0	5.6	12.0	14.5	6.0
90	18.8	4.0	4.3	16.5	7.3	5.1	14.1	11.2	5.8	13.0	15.0	6.3
100	20.0	4.0	4.4	17.5	7.3	5.3	15.1	11.4	6.0	14.0	15.5	6.5
120	22.4	4.1	4.7	20.0	7.8	5.4	17.0	11.7	6.2	15.9	16.0	6.7
140	25.8	4.2	4.9	22.5	7.9	5.8	19.1	11.9	6.4	17.6	16.2	7.0
160	28.4	4.2	5.2	24.3	7.9	6.0	21.1	12.0	6.6	19.5	16.5	7.3
180	30.9	4.3	5.4	27.0	8.0	6.2	23.1	12.1	6.8	21.3	17.0	7.5
200	33.5	4.3	5.6	29.0	8.0	6.4	25.4	12.2	7.1	23.1	17.5	7.7
220	36.5	4.4	5.8	31.1	8.0	6.6	27.2	12.3	7.2	25.0	17.9	8.0
240	39.2	4.4	5.9	33.1	8.0	6.8	29.0	12.4	7.3	26.8	17.9	8.2
260	41.9	4.4	6.0	34.9	8.0	6.9	30.5	12.6	7.5	28.0	18.0	8.4
280	44.5	4.4	6.2	36.8	8.0	7.0	32.4	12.9	7.8	29.5	18.0	8.5
300	47.0	4.4	6.3	38.5	8.0	7.1	34.1	13.1	8.0	31.5	18.0	8.7
320				40.5	8.0	7.2	36.0	13.3	8.2	33.0	18.0	8.9
340				42.4	8.0	7.3	37.6	13.4	8.3	34.2	18.0	9.0
360				44.2	8.0	7.4	38.8	13.4	8.4	35.7	18.1	9.1
380				46.1	8.0	7.5	40.2	13.5	8.5	37.1	18.2	9.3
400				48.0	8.0	7.7	42.2	13.5	8.6	38.8	18.4	9.5
420				50.0	8.0	7.8	43.5	13.6	8.7	40.0	18.7	9.6
440				52.0	8.0	7.9	44.7	13.7	8.8	41.3	18.8	9.7
460				54.0	8.0	8.0	46.2	13.7	8.9	42.8	19.0	9.8
480				56.0	8.0	8.1	47.8	13.7	9.0	44.0	19.0	9.9
500				58.0	8.0	8.2	49.2	13.8	9.1	45.5	19.1	10.1
550							53.0	13.8	9.3	48.5	19.5	10.3
600							56.3	13.8	9.5	51.8	19.7	10.5
650										55.0	19.8	10.7
700										58.5	19.8	11.0
750												
800												
850												
900												
950												
1000												

Sea Conditions: Force 4 to Force 11

to blow at least 49 hours across at least 700 nautical miles of open water to raise a significant wave height of 40 feet. A Force 8 wind would need to blow at least 38 hours across 440 nautical miles to raise a sea of 27 feet. In practice, the seas you would experience in these wind ranges would almost always be less than this and closer to the seas predicted by the Beaufort scale.

A hard wind blowing over a great fetch for a long time is the formula for big seas, but big seas are not necessarily dangerous ones. To be dangerous a wave needs to be steep, and the steeper it becomes, the more dangerous it is. Waves steepen in shallow water, and when the wind opposes a tidal or ocean current, and when two waves from different directions or traveling at

Fetch in n. miles	Force 8 (34-40 knots)			Force 9 (41-47)			Force 10 (48-55)			Force 11 (56-63)		
	time in hours	height in feet	period in seconds	time	height	period	time	height	period	time	height	period
10	2.3	7.3	3.9	2.0	8.0	4.1	1.9	10.0	4.2	1.8	10.0	5.0
20	3.9	10.0	4.4	3.5	12.0	5.0	3.2	14.0	5.2	3.0	15.0	5.9
30	5.2	12,1	5.0	4.7	15.8	5.5	4.4	18.0	6.0	4.1	19.8	6.3
40	6.5	14.0	5.4	5.8	17.7	5.9	5.4	21.0	6.3	5.1	22.5	6.7
50	7.7	15.7	5.6	6.9	19.8	6.3	6.4	23.0	6.7	6.1	25.0	7.1
60	8.7	17.0	6.0	8.0	21.0	6.5	7.4	25.0	7.0	7.0	27.5	7.5
70	9.9	18.0	6.4	9.0	22.5	6.8	8.3	26.5	7.3	7.8	29.5	7.7
80	11.0	18.9	6.6	10.0	24.0	7.1	9.3	28.0	7.7	8.6	31.5	7.9
90	12.0	20.0	6.7	11.0	25.0	7.2	10.2	30.0	7.9	9.5	34.0	8.2
100	12.8	20.5	6.9	11.9	26.5	7.6	11.0	32.0	8.1	10.3	35.0	8.5
120	14.5	21.5	7.3	13.1	27.5	7.9	12.3	33.5	8.4	11.5	37.5	8.8
140	16.0	22.0	7.6	14.8	29.0	8.3	13.9	35.5	8.8	13.0	40.0	9.2
160	18.0	23.0	8.0	16.4	30.5	8.7	15.1	37.0	9.1	14.5	42.5	9.6
180	19.9	23.3	8.3	18.0	31.5	9.0	16.5	38.5	9.5	16.0	45.5	10.0
200	21.5	23.5	8.5	19.3	32.5	9.2	18.1	40.0	9.8	17.1	46.0	10.3
220	22.9	24.0	8.8	20.9	34.0	9.6	19.1	41.5	10.1	18.2	47.5	10.6
240	24.4	24.5	9.0	22.0	34.5	9.8	20.5	43.0	10.3	19.5	49.0	10.8
260	26.0	25.0	9.2	23.5	34.5	10.0	21.8	44.0	10.6	20.9	50.5	11.1
280	27.7	25.0	9.4	25.0	35.0	10.2	23.0	45.0	10.9	22.0	51.5	11.3
300	29.0	25.0	9.5	26.3	35.0	10.4	24.3	45.0	11.1	23.2	53.0	11.6
320	30.2	25.0	9.6	27.6	35.5	10.6	25.5	45.5	11.2	24.5	54.0	11.8
340	31.6	25.0	9.8	29.0	36.0	10.8	26.7	46.0	11.4	25.5	55.0	12.0
360	33.0	25.0	9.9	30.0	36.5	10.9	27.7	46.5	11.6	26.6	55.0	12.2
380	34.2	25.5	10.0	31.3	37.0	11.1	29.1	47.0	11.8	27.7	55.5	12.4
400	35.6	26.0	10.2	32.5	37.0	11.2	30.2	47.5	12.0	28.9	56.0	12.6
420	36.9	26.5	10.3	33.7	37.5	11.4	31.5	47.5	12.2	29.6	56.5	12.7
440	38.1	27.0	10.4	34.8	37.5	11.5	32.5	48.0	12.3	30.9	57.0	12.9
460	39.5	27.5	10.6	36.0	37.5	11.7	33.5	48.5	12.5	31.8	57.5	13.1
480	41.0	27.5	10.8	37.0	37.5	11.8	34.5	49.0	12.6	32.7	57.5	13.2
500	42.1	27.5	10.9	38.3	38.0	11.9	35.5	49.0	12.7	33.9	58.0	13.4
550	44.9	27.5	11.1	41.0	38.5	12.2	38.2	50.0	13.0	36.5	58.0	13.7
600	47.7	27.5	11.3	43.6	39.0	12.5	40.3	50.0	13.3	38.7	60.0	14.0
650	50.3	27.5	11.6	46.4	39.5	12.8	43.0	50.0	13.7	41.0	60	14.2
700	50.3	27.5	11.8	49.0	40.0	13.1	45.4	50.5	14.4	43.5	60.5	14.5
750	56.2	27.5	12.1	51.0	40.0	13.3	48.0	51.0	14.2	45.8	61.0	14.8
800	59.2	27.5	12.3	53.8	40.0	13.5	50.6	51.5	14.5	47.8	61.5	15.0
850				56.2	40.0	13.8	52.5	52.0	14.6	50.0	62.0	15.2
900				58.2	40.0	14.0	54.6	52.0	14.9	52.0	62.5	15.5
950							57.2	52.0	15.1	54.0	63.0	15.7
1000							59.3	52.0	15.3	56.3	63.0	16.0

different speeds reinforce each other. If the wave steepens to the point that its height is more than one-seventh of its length, it becomes unstable and breaks. A breaking storm wave can hurl tons of white water from its collapsing crest at speeds up to 40 knots, and a sailboat in the path of such a calamity is in for trouble. There are excellent books on heavy-weather tactics and strategies at sea, and notable among them are *Heavy Weather Sailing*, by K. Adlard Coles (revised by Peter Bruce); *Handling Storms at Sea*, by Hal Roth; and *Rough Weather Seamanship for Sail and Power*, by Roger Marshall.

This appendix closes with a lexicon of wave terminology taken with permission from *Rough Weather Seamanship for Sail and Power*.

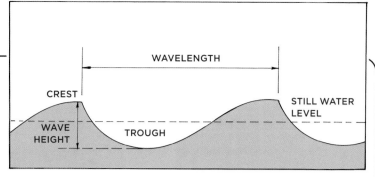

The anatomy of a wave.

Wave Terminology

Breaker—a coastal breaking wave. As a wave approaches shore, quite often at speeds of 15 or 20 miles per hour, water depth decreases until, at a depth roughly equal to 1.3 times the wave's height (or to put it another way, when the wave's height is about 80 percent of the water depth), the particles of water within the wave can no longer complete their oscillations. At that point the wave breaks, its crest falling forward into the trough ahead, and the kinetic energy of the oscillating wave is released in a rushing mass of surf. When the water shoals gradually the wave will also break gradually, and the result is a **spilling breaker**. When the water shoals abruptly the break is more abrupt and violent, and the result is called a **plunging breaker**.

Breaking wave—a wave at sea that becomes so steep that wind, an intersection with another wave, an encounter with a tidal or ocean current, or some combination of these factors causes it to lose stability. At that point the crest moves more rapidly than the water beneath it and it collapses forward, dissipating much of the wave's energy in a headlong rush and fall of foaming water. Breaking waves represent the single biggest danger to boats caught in storms.

Deepwater waves—waves inhabit a depth of more than half their own wavelength.

Fetch—the distance of open water—unimpeded by landmass—over which the wind blows.

Frequency (F)—the number of waves per second that pass a fixed point. A wave with a period (see below) of 10 seconds has a frequency of 0.1.

Fully developed seas—when wind-driven waves are as large as they can be for the given strength of wind—that is, when the wind has blown over a sufficient time and fetch to build the waves to the maximum extent of its capability—the seas are said to be fully developed.

Height (H)—the vertical distance from a wave's trough to its crest.

Length (L)—the distance from one wave crest to the next, which in an ideal deepwater wave is related to its period by the formula: L (in feet) = 5.12 P^2, with P measured in seconds.

Period (P)—the time in seconds taken for one wave (crest to crest) to pass a fixed point. In an ideal deepwater wave, period is related to wavelength by the formula: $P = 0.443 \times \sqrt{L}$, where L is the wavelength in feet.

Rogue wave—a transitory wave much higher than surrounding waves and much higher than the significant wave height. Though a rogue wave seems to come from nowhere, it is in fact the superimposition of two or more wave crests. For example, two 20-foot waves could, in theory, combine to produce a 40-footer of brief duration, which will break if the combined height makes the wave unstable. Rogue waves are sometimes called **freak waves**.

Sea state—prevailing wave conditions for the locale in question, often expressed in terms of direction of wave train or trains and significant wave height.

Shallow-water wave—a wave that exists in water that is less than $\frac{1}{20}$ of its wavelength.

Significant wave height—the average height of the highest one-third of the waves in a system. (The highest waves may be twice as high as this average.) Sea state forecasts are often expressed in terms of significant wave height.

Steepness—the ratio of wave height to wavelength. Any ratio higher than 1:7 (stated another way, any **crest angle** less than 120 degrees) makes the wave unstable and causes it to break.

Swell—a wave that has moved well beyond the gale or storm from which it originated. For example, a hurricane north of Bermuda may generate a swell on the coast of New England.

Transitional waves—waves that are neither deep- nor shallow-water waves.

Velocity (C)—the speed at which waves move past a fixed point. A deepwater wave's velocity (in knots) can be estimated by multiplying its period (in seconds) by 3. When the wave moves into shallow water and begins to "feel" the bottom, it slows down because of friction from the seabed, and in very shallow water (relative to wavelength) its speed in knots becomes $3.1 \times \sqrt{depth}$ (in feet).

Marlinspike Seamanship

The knots covered elsewhere in this book may be all you'll ever need, but there are a few others that, if not quite as versatile, are highly useful for certain tasks. The more you use the knots shown here, the more uses you'll find for them. (Visit internationalmarine.com for videos of selected knots.)

Likewise, whipping and splicing are handy skills to know. Whipping a line end keeps it from unraveling and is a more elegant and longer-lasting solution than burning or taping it. And splicing enables you to join two lines or make a loop in a line while retaining most of the rope's strength—whereas the strength of a knotted line is reduced by half. The instructions below for whippings and splices are reprinted with permission from *Knots, Splices, and Line Handling: A Captain's Quick Guide*, by Charlie Wing.

A Few More Knots

Sheet Bend

A **bend** is any knot that will join two lines together, and the most basic of bends is the sheet bend. This is a handy knot for joining two lines of approximately equal diameter. Make a bight in one end **(1)**. Pass the end of the other line around the bight and under its own standing part **(2)**, then over its standing part and through the bight **(3)**. Cinch tight **(4)**.

If you pass the end of the second line twice around the bight in step 2 before tucking it through the bight, you create a **double sheet bend**, which is more secure and less prone to slipping than the sheet bend. Especially when joining two lines of dissimilar diameter, use a double sheet bend (or two interlocking bowlines!).

When a sheet bend or double sheet bend is made through an eye rather than a temporary bight, it's called a **becket bend** or **double becket bend**.

Bowline in a Bight

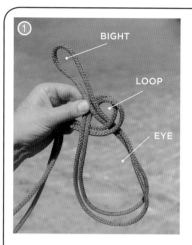

No knot is more versatile than a bowline, and you can make a bowline in the middle of a line, without access to an end, by tying a bowline in a bight. Make a loop in the midline bight, then pass the end of the bight up through the loop **(1)**, creating an eye just as you would for a bowline (see page 167). Now drop the bight over the eye **(2)**, pull the eye through the bight **(3)**, and tighten **(4)**. The finished knot **(5)** affords all the uses of a bowline, or the two loops can be separated to make a bridle or even an emergency (though uncomfortable) bosun's chair.

Round Turn and Two Half Hitches

Make a round turn around the ring, post, or other object (here a cleat base) you're making fast to **(1)**. Make the first half hitch as shown **(2)**, then the second half hitch **(3)**, and cinch tight. Two half hitches will temporarily secure a line that will not be subject to great strain or much shaking. You can tie the half hitches after a simple 180° turn, but the 540° round turn distributes the load over two turns, reducing chafe and also reducing strain, which makes the half hitches easier to tie and to adjust.

Anchor Bend

Also known as the **fisherman's bend,** this is similar to the round turn and two half hitches except that the first of the two half hitches is made through the round turn **(1)**, and the second through the standing part **(2**, **3)**. Except for an eye splice around a thimble (see below), this is probably the most secure way to fasten an anchor rode to an anchor. Adding a third half hitch and/or seizing the end to the standing part with twine will increase the knot's security still further.

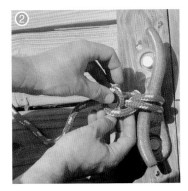

Trucker's Hitch

Nothing more than an overhand knot in a bight **(1)**, this hitch creates a midline loop. To know it is to love it. When lashing a dinghy to a deck (or a kayak to the roof of your car), fasten one end of the line, throw the line over the upside-down boat, insert a trucker's hitch, pass the line end around or through a strong point, then bring it back to and through the trucker's loop. Now cinch (as in **2**). You can put a lot of tension in a line this way. When you have enough, secure with two half hitches.

Whipping

Left alone, line ends fray and unravel. Melting or taping an end will postpone unraveling, but to prevent it you need to whip a melted end with cord or twine (also called small stuff).

Plain Whipping

This whipping is simple to produce but temporary. Start by forming a loop of twine with its apex ½ inch from the end of the rope. Wrap the running end of the cord around the loop 8 to 10 times, working toward the apex. Pass the cord's running end through the loop, then pull on the bitter end until the loop disappears under the turns. Clip the cord ends.

Sailmaker's Whipping

This version is more permanent yet doesn't require use of a sailmaker's needle. Start by unlaying the end of a 3-strand rope about 1 inch and pass a loop of twine around one of the strands, then relay the strands. Whip the rope 8 to 10 times toward its bitter end with the long end of the cord. Place the original loop back over its strand and pull tight using the cord's short end. Lay the long end back along the strands and tie the cord ends with a reef knot, and clip.

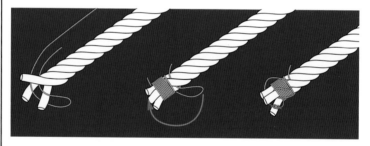

Sewn Whipping

This version can be used on braided as well as 3-strand rope. Start with two stitches through the rope. Tightly whip the rope 8 to 10 times toward its bitter end. Keeping the whipping taut, pass the needle through ⅓ (120°) of the rope and pull the cord taut. Now pass the needle through the rope at the other end of the whipping and tighten. Repeat until you have three double stitches spaced at 120° around the whipping. Take one final stitch and clip cord ends.

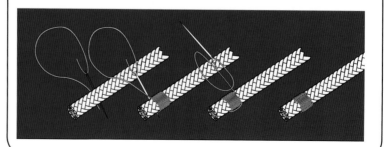

Splices

3-Strand Splices

Long Splice: This splice will join two ropes without increasing the line diameter—which is what you want for running the spliced line through blocks—but it's weaker than the short splice.

① Unlay all 6 strands 1" for each 1/16" of rope diameter and tape ends. Marry the ropes by interleaving alternate strands.

② Make an overhand knot in the first pair of strands. Then unlay one of the remaining strands in each rope 4–6 turns.

③ Seize the ropes at the overhand knot, then lay into each empty furrow the corresponding strand from the opposite rope. Tie overhand knots in the matching strands at each end.

④ Tuck each strand over the adjacent and under the next strand. Remove half of the fiber in each strand and repeat tucking operation.

Short Splice: Retains the rope's full strength but increases its diameter by 40 percent.

① Unlay all 6 strands 1" for each 1/16" of rope diameter and tape ends. Tape ropes to prevent further unlaying, and marry the ropes

② Remove one of the rope tapes. Cross a strand end over its adjacent and under the next.

③ Continue tucking strand over and under for a total of 4 tucks (6 for nylon).

④ Repeat Steps 2 and 3 for second strand.

⑤ Repeat for third strand against the lay.

⑥ Remove remaining tape and pull on loose strands to snug splice. Repeat Steps 2–5 going in opposite direction.

Eye Splice: This most useful splice retains 90 percent of the rope's strength, compared with 50 percent for most knots.

① Unlay rope 5" for each 1/4" of diameter. Tape both rope and strand ends to prevent further unlaying. Form the eye and seize rope to mark entry point.

② Raise the strand closest to the seizing (use a fid if necessary) and tuck the closest unlaid strand through. Proceeding in the direction of twist, raise the next strand and tuck the corresponding strand through.

③ Raise the third strand and finish the first series of tucks with the remaining unlaid strand. Remove the seizing and tug on the strand ends to tighten throat.

④ Following the same order, tuck each strand over and under for a total of 4 tucks (6 for nylon). For a neater appearance, taper the last tuck by removing half of the fibers in each strand.

Back Splice: An alternative to whipping a 3-strand rope end, a back splice increases rope diameter by 40 percent and provides a handle.

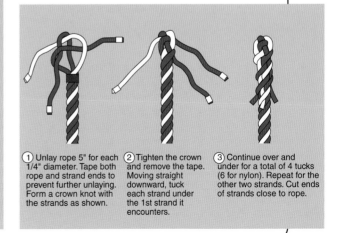

① Unlay rope 5" for each 1/4" diameter. Tape both rope and strand ends to prevent further unlaying. Form a crown knot with the strands as shown.

② Tighten the crown and remove the tape. Moving straight downward, tuck each strand under the 1st strand it encounters.

③ Continue over and under for a total of 4 tucks (6 for nylon). Repeat for the other two strands. Cut ends of strands close to rope.

Double-Braid Eye Splice

An eye splice in double-braid rope is complicated and time consuming, but the end result is strong, permanent, and attractive. This splice can be made around a thimble for a mooring pendant or anchor rode.

This is a splice that cannot be achieved without a tubular fid—a hollow tube having a pointed end and interior barbs for catching inserted line. The size of the fid must be proportional to the size of the line being spliced (see table).

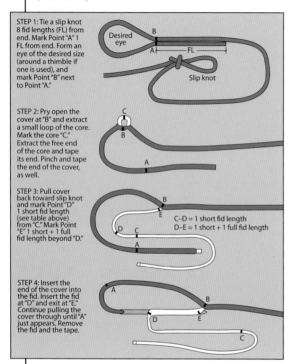

STEP 1: Tie a slip knot 8 fid lengths (FL) from end. Mark Point "A" 1 FL from end. Form an eye of the desired size (around a thimble if one is used), and mark Point "B" next to Point "A."

STEP 2: Pry open the cover at "B" and extract a small loop of the core. Mark the core "C." Extract the free end of the core and tape its end. Pinch and tape the end of the cover, as well.

STEP 3: Pull cover back toward slip knot and mark Point "D" 1 short fid length (see table above) from "C." Mark Point "E" 1 short + 1 full fid length beyond "D."

C–D = 1 short fid length
D–E = 1 short + 1 full fid length

STEP 4: Insert the end of the cover into the fid. Insert the fid at "D" and exit at "E." Continue pulling the cover through until "A" just appears. Remove the fid and the tape.

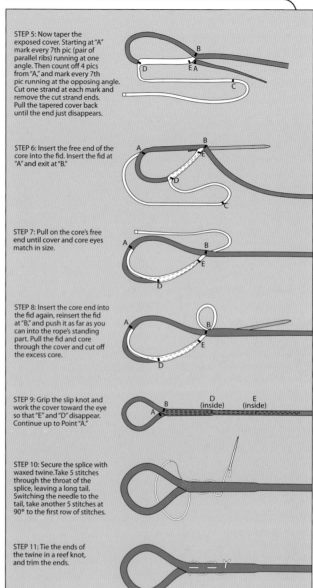

STEP 5: Now taper the exposed cover. Starting at "A" mark every 7th pic (pair of parallel ribs) running at one angle. Then count off 4 pics from "A," and mark every 7th pic running at the opposing angle. Cut one strand at each mark and remove the cut strand ends. Pull the tapered cover back until the end just disappears.

STEP 6: Insert the free end of the core into the fid. Insert the fid at "A" and exit at "B."

STEP 7: Pull on the core's free end until cover and core eyes match in size.

STEP 8: Insert the core end into the fid again, reinsert the fid at "B," and push it as far as you can into the rope's standing part. Pull the fid and core through the cover and cut off the excess core.

STEP 9: Grip the slip knot and work the cover toward the eye so that "E" and "D" disappear. Continue up to Point "A."

STEP 10: Secure the splice with waxed twine. Take 5 stitches through the throat of the splice, leaving a long tail. Switching the needle to the tail, take another 5 stitches at 90° to the first row of stitches.

STEP 11: Tie the ends of the twine in a reef knot, and trim the ends.

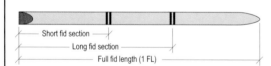

LENGTHS OF TUBULAR FID SECTIONS

Rope Diameter in. (mm)	Short Section in. (mm)	Long Section in. (mm)	Full Length in. (mm)
1/4 (6)	2 (51)	3 1/2 (89)	5 1/2 (140)
5/16 (8)	2 1/2 (64)	4 1/4 (108)	6 3/4 (171)
3/8 (9)	3 (76)	4 3/4 (120)	7 3/4 (197)
7/16 (11)	3 1/2 (89)	6 (152)	9 1/2 (241)
1/2 (12)	4 (101)	7 (178)	11 (279)
9/16 (14)	4 1/2 (114)	8 (203)	12 1/4 (311)
5/8 (16)	5 (127)	9 1/2 (241)	14 (356)
3/4 (19)	5 1/2 (146)	11 (279)	16 (406)

Safety Gear On Board

Putting safety equipment on board does not guarantee safety. Staying safe depends more on attitude and judgment informed by understanding—which is to say it depends on good seamanship. Still, a few basic accoutrements comprise the necessary prerequisite for safety. This appendix looks at some gear that is required by boating regulators including the U.S. Coast Guard, as well as a few items that are recommended even if not required.

The required items are summarized in the accompanying table. Registration and documentation have little to do with safety, so suffice it to say that if your sailboat has an inboard or outboard engine, it will need to be either federally documented or, much more commonly, registered in the state of principal use. If your sailboat is engineless, you will not need to register it unless you live in one of the U.S. states that requires registration for *all* boats.

Fire Extinguishers

If your boat has an inboard engine, a closed compartment under a thwart or hatch where a portable fuel tank can be stored, an enclosed cabin, enclosed storage compartments where combustible or flammable materials are kept, or a length of 26 feet or more, you must carry at least one fire extinguisher on board. Thus a 24-foot sailboat with an outboard engine need not carry a fire extinguisher *if* it has no cabin or stored combustibles and the portable gasoline tank is carried in the open cockpit. If it has a cabin or if the fuel tank is stowed in a cockpit locker, a fire extinguisher is required. And a boat of 26 or more feet requires two extinguishers.

Fires are categorized by their causes. Class A fires are fueled by ordinary combustibles such as paper or wood. Class B fires involve gasoline, oil, or grease, and Class C fires are electri-

COAST GUARD EQUIPMENT REQUIREMENTS: QUICK REFERENCE CHART

Vessel Length (in feet)				Equipment	Requirement
<16	16<26	26<40	40<65		
X	X	X	X	Certificate of Number (State Registration)	All undocumented vessels equipped with propulsion machinery must be state registered. Certificate of Number must be on board when vessel is in use. Note: some states require all vessels to be registered.
X	X	X	X	State Numbering	(a) Plain block letters/numbers not less than 3 inches in height must be affixed on each side of the forward half of the vessel (contrasting color to boat exterior). (b) State validation sticker must be affixed within six inches of the registration number.
	X	X	X	Certificate of Documentation	Applies only to "Documented" vessels: (a) Original and current certificate must be on board. (b) Vessel name/hailing port marked on exterior part of hull—letters not less than 4 inches in height. (c) Official number permanently affixed on interior structure—numbers not less than 3 inches in height.
X	X	X	X	Life Jackets (PFDs)	(a) One Type I, II, III, or V wearable PFD for each person on board (must be USCG approved).
	X	X	X		(b) In addition to paragraph (a), must carry one Type IV (throwable) PFD.

continues

COAST GUARD EQUIPMENT REQUIREMENTS: QUICK REFERENCE CHART (CONT.)

Vessel Length (in feet)				Equipment	Requirement
<16	**16<26**	**26<40**	**40<65**		
X				Visual Distress Signal (VDS)	(a) One electric distress light or three combination (day/night) red flares. Note: only required to be carried on board when operating between sunset and sunrise.
	X	X	X		(b) One orange distress flag or one electric distress light—or—three handheld or floating orange smoke signals and one electric distress light—or—three combination (day/night) red flares: handheld, meteor or parachute type.
X	X			Fire Extinguishers	(a) One B-I (when enclosed compartment)
		X			(b) One B-II or two B-I. Note: fixed system equals one B-I
			X		(c) One B-II and one B-I or three B-I. Note: fixed system equals one B-I or two B-II
X	X	X	X	Ventilation	(a) All vessels built after 25 April 1940 that use gasoline as their fuel with enclosed engine and/or fuel tank compartments must have natural ventilation (at least two ducts fitted with cowls). (b) In addition to paragraph (a), a vessel built after 31 July 1980 must have rated power exhaust blower.
X	X	X		Sound Producing Devices	(a) A vessel of less than 39.4 ft. must, at a minimum, have some means of making an efficient sound signal (i.e. handheld air horn, athletic whistle—human voice/sound not acceptable).
		X	X		(b) A vessel 39.4 ft. (12 meters) or greater, must have a sound signaling appliance capable of producing an efficient sound signal, audible for ½ mile with a 4 to 6 seconds duration. In addition, must carry a bell with a clapper (bell size not less than 7.9"—based on the diameter of the mouth).
	X	X	X	Backfire Flame Arrester	Required on gasoline engines installed after 25 April 1940, except outboard motors.
	X	X	X	Navigational Lights	Required to be displayed from sunset to sunrise and in or near areas of reduced visibility.
		X	X	Oil Pollution Placard	(a) Placard must be at least 5 by 8 inches, made of durable material. (b) Placard must be posted in the machinery space or at the bilge station.
		X	X	Garbage Placard	(a) Placard must be at least 4 by 9 inches, made of durable material. (b) Displayed in a conspicuous place notifying all on board the discharge restrictions.
	X	X	X	Marine Sanitation Device	If installed toilet: vessel must have an operable MSD Type I, II, or III.
		X	X	Navigation Rules (Inland Only)	The operator of a vessel 39.4 ft (12 meters) or greater must have on board a copy of these rules.

REQUIRED FIRE EXTINGUISHERS

Minimum number of hand-portable fire extinguishers on a boat with and without a fixed extinguishing system

Length of Vessel	No Fixed System in Machinery Space	Fixed System in Machinery Space
Less than 26 ft.	1 B-I	none
26 ft. to under 40 ft.	2 B-Is or 1 B-II	1 B-I
40 ft. to 65 ft.	3 B-Is or 1 B-I and 1 B-II	2 B-Is or 1 B-II

CLASS B FIRE EXTINGUISHERS

Coast Guard Classification (type-size)	Underwriters Laboratories Listing	Aqueous Foam (gals.)	Carbon Dioxide (lbs.)	Dry Chemical (lbs.)	FE-241 (lbs.)
B-I	5B	1.25	4	2	5
B-II	10B	2.5	15	10	10

cal. Class B fires are the chief danger on board, and thus the Coast Guard requires Class B extinguishers. These may discharge an aqueous foam, carbon dioxide, a dry chemical, or the gas FE-241, any one of which will extinguish Class A or C fires as well as Class B. Dry chemical extinguishers (many of which use sodium bicarbonate, or baking soda) are by far the most popular, however, because they are convenient to use, affordable, and free of various limitations that afflict the other types.

Personal Flotation Devices (PFDs)

Once upon a time these were called life preservers or life jackets and came in just one variety—bulky, ungainly international orange things that no one wanted to wear. Stuffed with kapok and fitted by means of canvas straps and quick-to-rust buckles, their fate was to mildew in lockers where, if needed, they were probably inaccessible.

Then they became PFDs and their varieties proliferated. Now, like sneakers, they're more stylish but also more complicated and expensive to shop for. Here's the rundown:

- **Type I PFDs.** Also known as **offshore life jackets**, these are designed to turn an unconscious wearer face-up in the water and keep a swimmer afloat for extended periods. The foam-filled **inherently buoyant** models are more comfortable and stylish than the life jackets of yesteryear (though bulkier than Types II and III), and adults who place a premium on comfort and appearance can wear an inflatable Type I. (Inflatable PFDs are not made in child sizes.)
- **Type II PFDs** are **nearshore buoyant vests**. The inherently buoyant models are less bulky but also less buoyant than their Type I counterparts, while the inflatable models are on a par with Type I inflatables.
- **Type III PFDs** are known as **flotation aids**. The inherently buoyant Type III vests are as buoyant as their Type II counterparts, but both the inherently buoyant and inflatable varieties lack the ability to turn an unconscious wearer face up. Thus these vests are most appropriate for inland waters.
- **Type IV PFDs** are throwable, and you should have at least one on board to throw to someone who falls overboard while not wearing a PFD.
- **Type V PFDs** are specialized according to activity and include work vests and immersion suits.

You need at least one approved wearable PFD (Type I, II, III, or V) for each person on board, plus at least one Type IV throwable PFD. If you're sailing offshore you should probably carry Type I's, but for coastal cruising you might choose Type II's instead, and Type III's may suffice for daysailing. Inflatable PFDs are more likely to be worn because they're more comfortable and stylish, but a non-swimmer should wear an inherently buoyant PFD.

Sound-Producing Devices

All boats must carry some means of making a loud noise. Acceptable devices include a bell, a compressed-air horn, a power horn, and a whistle (though the latter is not acceptable on a boat of 39 feet or longer). A boat of 39 feet (12 meters) or longer must carry both a horn and a bell under the U.S. Inland Rules.

Visual Distress Signals

If your boat is less than 16 feet long—or if it's open, engineless, and less than 26 feet long—and you're not sailing on coastal waters between sunset and

RED FLARE (HANDHELD, DAY AND NIGHT)

PARACHUTE FLARE (DAY AND NIGHT)

ORANGE SMOKE SIGNAL (HANDHELD, DAY ONLY)

FLOATING ORANGE SMOKE SIGNAL (DAY ONLY)

RED METEOR (DAY AND NIGHT)

Pyrotechnic distress signals.

ORANGE FLAG (DAY ONLY)

ELECTRIC DISTRESS SIGNAL (NIGHT ONLY)

DYE IN WATER

RED RIBBON IN WATER

Nonpyrotechnic distress signals.

sunrise, you are not required to carry visual distress signals. Otherwise on coastal waters and the Great Lakes you are, and the quick-reference table will tell you which combinations of the pictured VSDs will meet the requirement.

VISUAL DISTRESS SIGNALS

Pyrotechnic Visual Distress Signals		
CG Approval Number	Description	Use
160.021	Handheld flare	Day only
160.022	Floating orange smoke	Day/night
160.024	Pistol parachute red flare	Day/night
160.036	Handheld parachute red flare	Day only
160.037	Handheld orange smoke	Day only
160.057	Floating orange smoke	Day/night
160.066	Red aerial pyrotechnic flare	Day/night
Nonpyrotechnic Visual Distress Signals		
160.072	Orange flag	Day only
161.013	Electric distress light	Night only

Ventilation

Unless your sailboat has an inboard gasoline engine or permanently installed gasoline fuel tanks, the ventilation requirements in the quick-reference table do not apply to you. Still, if you carry a portable gas tank or use propane stove fuel on board, you're wise to ensure that your boat is well ventilated at all times. Gasoline fumes are heavier than air and will pool in the bilge of a boat, where they represent an explosive danger.

Other Recommendations

Though not required, the list of recommended equipment to carry aboard should certainly include the following:

- At least one bilge pump, manual or automatic, and at least one bucket
- A first-aid kit
- Anchors (see Chapters 3 and 7)
- VHF-FM radio (see Appendix 6)

- A judicious selection of tools and spare parts
- If you're headed offshore, an emergency position-indicating radiobeacon (EPIRB)
- And if you're headed offshore or sailing at night, a safety harness and tether for each person on deck (see Chapter 7).

An EPIRB is a small battery-powered transmitter that is activated by immersion or by a manual switch. Recreational boats are not required to carry EPIRBs, though commercial and fishing vessels must do so beyond the 3-mile limit. If you carry an EPIRB (a new one costs $600 or more), you want one that transmits on 406 MHz. This signal can be received worldwide by satellites and will summon search-and-rescue help when you're in need. In the U.S. you must register your EPIRB with NOAA (see www.beaconregistration.noaa.gov for details). Newer units are uniquely encoded to convey your boat's characteristics and to reduce false alarms.

Crew Overboard

You're at the helm and the boat is heeling to a fresh breeze when something attracts your attention to the leeward deck. What you see there makes your heart stop. A crewmember has lost his balance and is on the verge of falling overboard, his arms pinwheeling helplessly in the air, the backs of his knees pressed against the leeward lifeline, a look of disbelief on his face. The seas are boisterous, the visibility is poor, and the water is cold. This is serious. Should you round up sharply into the wind, or will that only ensure that he goes overboard? If he falls, how will you get back to him? Is he wearing a PFD? Do you have a Type IV PFD close at hand to throw to him? What if you can't find him? What if you can't round up and stop next to him? What if you can't hoist him back aboard? Where is the GPS receiver and why, oh why didn't you read the instructions and practice activating the man-overboard (MOB) button?

There isn't time to answer all these questions. You need to know the answers already, and that's why you should practice a crew-overboard recovery drill ahead of time. Use a fender or PFD for the person. Toss it overboard, and practice until you can return to it quickly, reliably, and under control.

Here's the drill:

- Whoever sees the person go overboard should shout the alarm until it is clear that the skipper has heard. Ideally, one crew should do nothing but keep the COB (crew overboard) constantly in sight and point constantly toward the COB.
- Throw cushions, a life ring or other Type IV PFD (preferably with an attached line; see Appendix 4), or a Lifesling toward the COB. A Lifesling comprises a buoyant yolk tethered to the boat via a long line, and circling the COB with the yolk deployed will bring it into his grasp. The COB then slips the yolk over his torso and can be dragged to the boat for rescue.
- If a GPS receiver is at hand, press the MOB (man overboard) button to record the exact coordinates of the accident, thus ensuring you can return to it.
- But above all, stay close to the COB, keep him in sight, and get back to him quickly by any expedient means. The

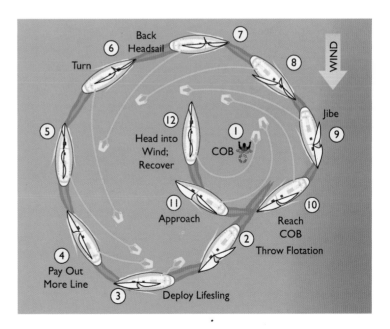

A quick-stop recovery under sail.

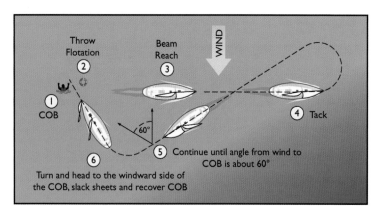

A figure-eight (reach-and-reach) recovery.

illustrations show two methods. Usually you can recover the COB over either side of the boat, but if the boat is drifting rapidly downwind it might be best to make the retrieval over the windward side.

- Once the COB has hold of a Lifesling or line, stop the boat immediately by taking the engine out of gear or luff-ing and lowering sails. Pull the COB to the boat.

- Get the COB back aboard by any means possible. Strong crew might be able to hoist him directly over the side or walk him back to a transom step or swim ladder. If the COB is wearing a Lifesling yolk you might be able to hook this to the main halyard and winch him back aboard. The operation doesn't have to be pretty—it just has to get the job done. Do not let other crew jump in to help unless the COB is unconscious or in grave trouble, and even then only if the rescuer is wearing a PFD and is tethered to the boat.

VHF Radio Call Procedures

> "Sea language would be a very terse and economical speech if the Old Man didn't lose the advantage by padding it with unnecessary expletives."
>
> —Robert Cushman Murphy, *Logbook for Grace*

When You Make a Call

Select: Usually you will initiate a call on CH16 (or CH9 when CH16 is crowded). Set the POWER to LO unless the call is urgent or must reach some distance. If another channel has been prearranged, use it or the listed channel of a shore station.

Listen: You may not interrupt or "step on" other communications. Wait for a brief period of silence. (Set the volume and squelch, then listen.)

Press: After pressing the MIC PTT (push-to-talk) button, wait a second before speaking to ensure that your transmitter is operating and will not cut off the first part of your message.

Speak: Hold the MIC a few inches from your mouth and slightly to the side. Speak normally, but clearly and distinctly. In less than 30 seconds, say "'Boat A' (up to three times, followed by MMSI or call sign if applicable) calling 'Boat B' (three times), Over."

Listen: Release MIC PTT button. If no answer, repeat in 2 minutes, then again in another 2 minutes. If still no answer, try again after no less than 15 minutes.

Exchange Messages: If you get an answer, listen for " 'Boat B' calling 'Boat A.' " Assuming you and your caller are not using DSC-capable radios, your caller should direct you to a working channel such as "six-ate" (not sixty-eight), then say, "Over." (DSC radios automatically retune from CH70 [the DSC digital call channel] to an analog working channel for the follow-on voice communications.) Tune to the working channel within 1 minute, press MIC, and say, " 'Boat A' calling 'Boat B,' " then provide your message, followed by "Over."

End: After the last message, either party says, "'Boat Name,' Out."

Marine frequencies are crowded. Take the time to pre-plan your call and message and write your station ID information in the blanks below so you have it handy:

Your Boat Name phonetically _____

Your MMSI (if DSC equipped)* _____

Your Call Sign (if you have a license)** _____

*Note: The Maritime Mobile Service Identity, or MMSI, is the nine-digit number that is assigned to a DSC marine radio and identifies its operator just as your telephone number identifies you at home. Only the new, digital radios have MMSIs. If your radio and the one you're calling are both DSC-capable, you can direct your call selectively to the station you want. And in case you're wondering, digital and analog radios can talk to each other just fine.

**Note: If you have an FCC radio license, use the call sign after the name of the boat at the beginning and end of the session.

Emergency Calls

There are three types of calls (DISTRESS, URGENCY, and SAFETY). These are transmitted on VHF CH16 or SSB 2182 KHz. The procedures are slightly different for each, as follows:

DISTRESS: is reserved for situations involving risk of life and/or grave and immediate danger. It calls for immediate assistance. It has priority over all other forms of traffic. (If you are using a DSC-equipped radio, initiate your Mayday call by pressing the Distress button.)

Distress Signal: MAYDAY

Provide the following message:

MAYDAY, MAYDAY, MAYDAY . . .
This is:
Boat Name _____ (repeat three times)
Call Sign (if you have a license)
_____ (once)
MAYDAY,
Boat Name _____
Position is:
Lat _____ Lon _____ , or
_____ nm _____
(N,S,E,W) of _____
Nature of Distress _____
Assistance Required _____
Boat description _____
No. of persons on board _____
Other _____
OVER

URGENCY: is reserved for situations involving the safety of the ship or some person on board that is serious but has not yet reached the level of immediate peril (loss of steering, medical difficulty, etc.). It calls for assistance.

Urgency Signal: PAN-PAN (pronounced PAHN-PAHN). Provide the following message:

PAN-PAN, PAN-PAN, PAN-PAN . . .

ALL STATIONS (or particular coast guard station) (once)
This is:
Boat Name _____ (once)
Call Sign (if you have a license)
_____ (once)
Urgency message (assistance required):
_____
Position is:
Lat _____ Lon _____ , or
_____ nm _____
(N,S,E,W) of _____
This is: Boat Name _____ (once)
OVER

SAFETY: is reserved for information regarding navigation safety. The coast guard encourages all mariners to transmit safety messages when they spot a hazard to navigation (buoy off-station, floating log, etc.).

Safety Signal: SECURITE
(pronounced SAY-CUR-I-TAY)

Provide the following message:

SECURITE, SECURITE, SECURITE . . .
ALL STATIONS (once)
This is:
Boat Name _____ (once)
Channel # for message: _____
OUT (go to channel, repeat above, and provide message)

Using DSC-Equipped VHF Radios

DSC (Digital Selective Calling) helps to free up crowded channels and vastly speeds rescue operations. On VHF, channel 70 is dedicated to DSC. (On SSB, the DSC frequency is 2187.5 KHz to call the U.S. Coast Guard.)

DSC transmits a digital signal that includes the MMSI number (Maritime Mobile Service Identity) unique to your boat, as well as your position (if your VHF transceiver is connected to a GPS receiver). It also transmits data about the type of call and the intended recipients. DSC calls can be placed to all users for distress or selectively to a single ship or group for routine message traffic. When not transmitting, your DSC-equipped VHF transceiver monitors channel 70 (SSB monitors 2187.5 KHz), sounds a tone corresponding to the type of incoming call, and automatically tunes to the appropriate frequency for the subsequent incoming message.

MMSI: You must register your DSC radio. You will provide key information about your identity and boat that will be essential in the event of a distress. To make individual or group calls, you will need the MMSIs of the radios you wish to call. The U.S. Coast Guard group MMSI is 003669999. In addition, local USCG and Canadian Coast Guard stations have individual MMSIs. Contact local authorities for these numbers.

(Note: SSB DSC frequencies include 2187.5, 4207.5, 6312, 8414.5, 12577, and 16804.5 KHz. Ships equipped for GMDSS [Global Maritime Distress Safety System] will monitor these frequencies in addition to VHF CH70.)

(Reprinted with permission from *Using VHF and SSB Radio: A Captain's Quick Guide*, by Bob Sweet.)

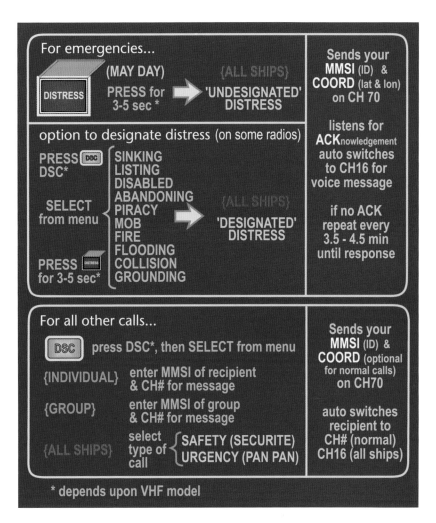

PUBLISHER'S ACKNOWLEDGMENTS

Heartfelt thanks go to the Bitter End Yacht Club, our host for a four-day on-the-water photo shoot. The entire BEYC staff pitched in to make our stay on Virgin Gorda comfortable and the shoot successful. In particular, public relations manager Elizabeth Berglund arranged the shoot; yacht club manager Erik Stacy provided the subject boats, the chase boats, and the sailors; Ashley Denise McGowan and George Pearce Hopkins IV drove the chase boats; waterfront director Eustace Joseph got us underway each morning; assistant merchandizing manager Jesse Barnes smoothed the way with a hundred kindnesses; and each evening Erik and Jesse helped us plan the following day's shoot.

BEYC sailing instructors Wampe van der Poel and Sam Talbot put numerous sailboats through hundreds of tacks, jibes, sail changes, and maneuvers. They never once complained, and their good-natured patience, helpful suggestions, obvious love of sailing, and even one or two emergency repairs contributed to this book in ways great and small. They were a pleasure to work with.

Photographers Erik Skallerup and Domenic Mosqueira, of YachtShots, stuck with us through four demanding days and stayed up late each night cataloging and archiving the day's work. For their high standards of professionalism, and for hundreds of the photos in this book, we are indebted.

Perched on the northeastern tip of Virgin Gorda in the British Virgin Islands, the Bitter End Yacht Club (www.beyc.com) is in part a resort with a sailing/diving/watersports focus and in part a provider of dock space, facilities, and a sheltered anchorage to visiting yachts. Sailors and resort guests mingle along its busy waterfront and in its comfortable restaurant. The food is delicious, and the air-conditioned duplex cottages that dot the hillside above the waterfront offer panoramic views of North Sound and the setting sun. Thanks, BEYC.

Thanks also to Helly Hansen for the gloves, footwear, and apparel worn in many of the photos. The company's participation was arranged through the good auspices of Kate Goodwin, of Hayter Communications. And thanks to Smith Sunglasses, who—through Drew Simmons, of Pale Morning Media—provided the glasses worn in the photo shoot.

Our aim from the beginning has been that this book be more than a launch-it-and-drive-it gloss on sailing. We wanted beauty that is more than skin deep. We wanted to replicate in these pages—good for a hundred reads—the most nuanced and revelatory instruction it is possible to receive on the water from a gifted sailor and teacher. We wanted to capture not just the how's of sailing, fascinating though these are, but also the multiform textures, moods, and experiences of sailing. For that we needed an authentic sailing voice. We needed a writer who could strip advice to bare essentials in one paragraph and impart universal seamanship wisdom through a well-chosen anecdote in the next. We needed someone who writes as if he is there in the boat with you. We needed Robby Robinson.

Our deepest thanks, therefore, go to Robby, who gave this book its keel, its drive, its personality, and its finest lines, then waited with inexhaustible patience while we fleshed his taut framework into the most visually complex book we have ever published. The task—his and ours—has taken years. Now you, dear reader, will judge how well we have succeeded. But whatever the verdict, Robby, you did your part magnificently.

Though Robby was the skipper, many expert hands helped sail this ship into port. A full list of photo/illustration credits is on page 510, but we'd like here to acknowledge International Marine books whose authors generously provided information, images, and excerpts:

The Weekend Navigator: Simple Boat Navigation with GPS and Electronics, by Bob Sweet (2005). Starting from the premise that all navigators these days use GPS, Bob shows how to use it right and how to backup and verify what it tells you with traditional chart-and-compass piloting. His marvelously intuitive illustrations and photos inform the discussions of tides and tidal currents in Chapter 3; navigation aids, chart symbology, and chart use in Chapter 4; and the use of parallel rules, dividers, a protractor plotting tool, and GPS in Chapter 5.

Your First Sailboat: How to Find and Sail the Right Boat for You, by Daniel Spurr (2004). This is a book for those who start sailing in adulthood, diving into the complexities of boat ownership and the complexities of sailing at the same time. Dan's clear, concise descriptions of the Widgeon, Snipe, Opti, Sunfish, Laser, and other racing and daysailing one-design classes grace Chapters 1 and 6, and a selection of his spot-on cruising-sailboat portraits provide great guidance in Chapter 7, as does his comparison of new-boat versus used-boat costs. Finally, his inspired sketch of how various sailboats react to increasing wind speeds was the basis for the illustration on page 108.

How Boat Things Work: An Illustrated Guide, by Charlie Wing (2004). Charlie is a master of explaining with pictures, and the illustrations on pages 22, 76, 77, 451, and 458 are derived from his popular book.

A Visual Cruising Guide to the Maine Coast, by James L. Bildner (2006). Jim is a helicopter pilot as well as a sailor, and his simple, powerful idea was to pair aerial photos of tricky channels and harbor entrances with corresponding segments of nautical charts. It's a highly effective approach to pilotage, as you can see from his photos on pages 147 and 193.

Yacht Design According to Perry: My Boats and What Shaped Them, by Robert H. Perry (2008). Bob is the godfather of "performance cruising" (a term he coined), and more cruising sailboats have been built to his designs than to those of any other designer. He is also an articulate commentator on

The view east toward the Bitter End Yacht Club resort on Virgin Gorda island, with the open Atlantic beyond.

sailboat design, and his essays on rigs, sailboat comparisons, shortening sail, and sailboat stability add depth and insights to Chapter 7.

BoatWorks: Sailboat Maintenance, Repair, and Improvement Advice You Can't Get Anywhere Else, by the Editors of *SAIL* Magazine (2008). Homeowners can choose from any number of full-color projects books when the time comes to hang a door or wire a room, but this is the only such book for boatowners. Gathered from the pages of *SAIL*'s late, lamented spin-off magazine *BoatWorks*, this book provides a great service to weekend warriors. From it comes Nigel Calder's insightful essay on hull shape and boat performance in Chapter 7.

The Voyager's Handbook: The Essential Guide to Bluewater Cruising, Second Edition, by Beth Leonard (2007). Among the many fine writers in the ranks of long-distance cruisers, Beth is one of the best. She and her husband, Evans, have logged 85,000 bluewater miles in boats they outfitted themselves, and *The Voyager's Handbook* is comprehensive, compulsively readable, and justly popular. Beth's essay on boats for voyaging and the photos on page 421, add another highly informed viewpoint to Chapter 7.

Radar for Mariners, by David Burch (2005). Founder of the Starpath School of Navigation, David is one of the world's foremost navigation writers. The radar screen illustrations in Chapter 5 come from this fine book, which we recommend for anyone wishing to learn more about radar.

Getting Started in Sailboat Racing, by Adam Cort and Richard Stearns (2005). Adam is a journalist, Richard is a sailmaker, and they're both avid racers. Together they wrote what we think is the clearest, most helpful book there is on sailboat racing. The tables of one-design and PHRF sailboats and guidance for a number of the illustrations in Chapter 6 came from this book.

The Complete Anchoring Handbook: Stay Put on Any Bottom in Any Weather, by Alain Poiraud, Achim Ginsberg-Klemmt, and Erika Ginsberg-Klemmt (2008). Alain is the inventor of the Spade anchor and Achim and Erika are liveaboard sailors and writers. They are advocates of a chain-and-nylon hybrid rode, whereas Robby Robinson prefers an all-chain rode with a nylon snubber. This is one of those ongoing debates that keeps sailing talk lively. Alain, Achim, and Erika's photos of windlass configurations (page 468) are a great addition to Chapter 7, and their table of holding power as a function of scope is a useful complement to

Robby's anchoring discussion in Chapter 3.

Catamarans: The Complete Guide for Cruising Sailors, by Gregor Tarjan (2006, 2008). Gregor compiled this glorious full-color book to announce to the sailing world that the modern cruising catamaran has arrived—and we think he's right. Two of his intriguing reviews of cruising catamarans appear on pages 466 and 467.

Boatowner's Mechanical and Electrical Manual: How to Maintain, Repair, and Improve Your Boat's Essential Systems, Third Edition, by Nigel Calder (2005). Nigel is arguably the world's foremost explainer of how boats work, and *SAIL* said of this book that it "should come as standard equipment with every boat." The tables of typical electrical loads (page 453) and daily power requirements (page 454) of a cruising sailboat come from this book.

The Captain's Quick Guides, International Marine's series of laminated, foldout, waterproof on-deck references for seamanship topics, feature a compact, highly visual approach to instruction that lends itself well to *The International Marine Book of Sailing*. The following Quick Guide authors have contributed to this book:

From *Knots, Splices, and Line Handling: A Captain's Quick Guide*

(Charlie Wing, 2004) come the line selection guides on page 92 and the splicing instructions in Appendix 3. *Rules of the Road and Running Light Patterns: A Captain's Quick Guide* (Charlie Wing, 2004) is the source of the Rules of the Road illustrations on page 162, the running light patterns on page 164, and the fog-signal advice in Chapter 5. *Anchoring: A Captain's Quick Guide* (Peter Nielsen, 2007) is the source for several of the tables, illustrations, and photos on pages 131 through 143. *Onboard Weather Forecasting: A Captain's Quick Guide* (Bob Sweet, 2005) contributed the Buys Ballot's Law illustration in Chapter 4 and some of Appendix 1. The illustrations in Appendix 5 were adapted from *Emergencies on Board: A Captain's Quick Guide* (John Rousmaniere, 2005), and the photos on page 417 come from *Heavy Weather Sailing: A Captain's Quick Guide* (John Rousmaniere, 2005). The photo at the bottom of page 447 and the table on page 457 are from *Diesel Engine Care and Repair: A Captain's Quick Guide* (Nigel Calder, 2007). And the VHF radio call procedures in Appendix 6 are adapted from *Using VHF and SSB Radio: A Captain's Quick Guide* (Bob Sweet, 2004).

Finally we wish to acknowledge *A Cruising Guide to Puget Sound and the San Juan Islands, Second Edition* (Migael Scherer, 2005) for the tidal current charts reproduced in Chapter 3; *Rough Weather Seamanship Under Sail and Power* (Roger Marshall, 2006) for the photos on page 120, line art on page 420, and the lexicon of wave terminology in Appendix 2; *Know Your Boat: The Guide to Everything That Makes Your Boat Work* (David Kroenke, 2002) for the illustrations of boat systems we colorized for inclusion in Chapter 7; *Seaworthy: Essential Lessons from BoatU.S.'s 20-Year Case File of Things Gone Wrong* (Robert A. Adriance, 2006) for the collision-course photos on page 166; *How to Read a Nautical Chart* (Nigel Calder, 2003) for the chart-scale com-

parisons on page 197; *Handling Storms at Sea* (Hal Roth, forthcoming), for the wave height tables in Appendix 2; *Boater's Bowditch: The Small-Craft American Practical Navigator* (Richard K. Hubbard, 1998, 2000) for the illustrations of a low-pressure-system life cycle and thunderstorm anatomy we adapted for Appendix 1; *The Windvane Self-Steering Handbook* (Bill Morris, 2004) for the illustrations we adapted for page 471; and *The Complete Sailor: Mastering the Art of Sailing* (David Seidman, 1994) and *Sailing Skills and Seamanship* (United States Coast Guard Auxiliary, 2008) for guidance and inspiration.

Credits

The following individuals and manufacturers contributed their resources on the pages indicated. All photographs not credited here were shot by the skillful and professional team of Erik Skallerup and Domenic Mosquiera of YachtShots, BVI Photography. All line art not credited here created by Joseph Comeau.

Robert Adriance 166; Richard Bennett 489; James Bildner 147, 193 (middle and bottom), 199 (bottom); Billy Black 8, 222, 244, 320 (middle), 328, 381, 382 (top), 390 (via Pearson), 421 (via Beth Leonard), 461 (bottom); Jane Boudrot 402; David Burch 293, 294 (top), 295, 298; Nigel Calder 171, 197, 447 (bottom), 457; Jenifer Clark, 157 (bottom); Walter Cooper 316 (bottom), 317, 328, 333, 354 (bottom), 362, 374, 375; Kim Downing 404; Jonathan Eaton 17(left), 61 (bottom right), 130 (bottom), 236, 292 (bottom); Daniel Forster 308 (bottom), 312–313; Uffa Fox 395; Kerry Gross 6 (top); Stephen Gross 12 (left), 14 (left), 19 (bottom left and right), 127 (#1–7), 315, 396; Pip Hurn 140 (bottom), 141 (bottom), 143; Steve Killing 104 (bottom); Alison Langley 70, 180;

Beth Leonard 421; Roger Marshall 120, 420; Bill Morris 471; Molly Mulhern 9 (middle, bottom), 14 (middle and right), 23, 24 (bottom), 44 (top), 50, 51 (right, middle), 75 (middle), 127 (#8), 159, 186, 200, 206, 247, 253 (top), 258 (middle), 373, 386 (middle), 395 (top), 449, 462 (bottom); Peter Nielsen 136, 403, 405, 406; Gary John Norman 460 (right); John Payne 321, 354 (top), 363, 377; Robert H. Perry 393, 398–399, 409, 410, 411, 418, 419, 443; Alain Poiraud et al., 133, 134, 140 (top), 466, 468; Robby Robinson 383, 386, 462; John Rousmaniere 417; Fritz Seegers 423; Andrew Sims 118; Jim Sollers 440, 448, 455, 465; Dan Spurr 402 (line), 443, 474; Richard Stearns 360, 374; Bob Sweet 149, 150, 152, 153, 160 (with Joseph Comeau), 161, 185, 194 (bottom), 195, 207, 254, 255, 256, 262–264, 271, 286, 287 (bottom), 288, 289, 290 (top), 294 (bottom), 296, 297, 507; Gregor Tarjan 476–477; Onne van der Wal 2, 124, 131, 239, 282, 308 (top), 316 (top), 319, 320 (top, bottom), 341, 348, 363, 378, 382 (bottom), 461 (top); Charlie Wing 92 (left), 162 (bottom left), 164, 284 (top), 451, Appendix 3 line art.

Aries Denmark 472; Aurora Pictures/Michael Eudenbach 460; Beetle, Inc. 6 (middle); Beneteau Yachts 394; Davis Instruments 254 (#4), 284 (left); Doyle Sailmakers/Mike Hunter 426, 428; Catalina Yachts 7 (bottom left); Colgate Sailing School 8 (right); Echomax 284 (right); Ensign Spars 9 (middle column, top); Environment Canada 62; Garmin 287 (top), 290 (bottom), 292 (middle); Island Packet Yachts 401; Manson Anchors 133 (#5); Maptech 194 (top), 299 (right); New England Ropes 91; NOAA 146, 151, 154, 155, 156, 163, 191 (bottom), 192, 304; Pacific Seacraft 441; Pearson Composites 390; PPL Picture Library 397; Profurl 428; Raymarine 292 (top); *Reeds Nautical Almanac* 157 (top); Ritchie Navigation 189, 254 (#3); Rocna Anchors 133 (#4); Sabre Yachts 391, 432 (top left); Sonar Class Association/Rick Doerr 7 (bottom right); Standard Horizon 470; Vanguard 6 (bottom left); Valiant Yachts 393; Weems and Plath 300; Winslow 463.